WARHAMMER ONLINE

AGE OF RECKONING

PRIMA Official Game Guide
Mike Searle

Product Manager: Jason Wigle
Associate Product Manager: Rebecca Chastain
Copyeditor: Asha Johnson
Design & Layout: Calibre Grafix
Map Design: In Color Design
Manufacturing: Suzanne Goodwin

Special Thanks:
Julie Asbury, Andrew Littell, Andy Rolleri, Veronika Monell, Sean Scheuble, Lex Scheuble, John Browning, Paul Giacomotto

ISBN: 978-0-7615-5927-6
Library of Congress Catalog Card Number: 2008921540
Printed in the United States of America
08 09 10 11 GG 10 9 8 7 6 5 4 3 2 1

Mike Searle

Mike Searle remembers playing the simple yet addictive *Missile Command,* and the days of Atari *Adventure,* where your square hero could end up in a hollow dragon stomach. His desire to play computer games into the wee hours of the morning really took hold when his parents made him play outside, instead of on the console, so the first chance he got, he bought a PC to play the *Ultima* series, *Doom,* and countless others. Mike started working with Prima Games in 2002 and has written more than 30 strategy guides, including *Lord of the Rings Online: Shadows of Angmar, Jurassic Park: Operation Genesis, Dark Messiah: Might and Magic, Pirates of the Burning Sea,* and several guides in the Tom Clancy's *Ghost Recon* and *Splinter Cell* series. He can't wait for thought technology, so game controls can catch up with his brain and stop all that needless in-game dying. At least, that's what he keeps telling himself about his FPS kill ratio.

We want to hear from you! E-mail comments and feedback to msearle@primagames.com.

Prima Games
An Imprint of Random House, Inc.
3000 Lava Ridge Court, Suite 100
Roseville, CA 95661
www.primagames.com

Prima would like to thank the following people at Mythic for their contributions:

Juli Cummins, Chrissy Zeeman, Gary Astleford, Brian Wheeler, Destin Bales, Christian Bales, Mike Donatelli, Gabe Amatangelo, George Smith, Chris Lynch, Martin Smith, Kate Flack, Jeff Skalski, Mike Stone, Craig Nelson, Adam Gershowitz, Greg Grimsby, Brian Audette, Mike Wyatt, Jason Mohr, DJ Larkin, Mike Finnigan, Mike Barr, Mark James, Ahmad Zabarah, Jerry Spencer, Michelle Mulrooney, Matt Witter, Sean Bosshardt, Tom Lipschultz, Tom Schwarzenhorn, Chris Behrens, and Ellisa Barr.

The Syndicate writers are:
Sean Stalzer, President/CEO, Byron-James Alcid (Team Lead), Chris & Brandi Massey, Christina & Gary Morrow, Glenn White (Team Lead), Greg Bowling, Hunter Hoyt (Team Lead), Ian Longley, James Gray, Jennifer Bayne, Jeremy Dvorak, Jerry Davis, Jon Fortner, Matt Wetzel, Michael & Stephanie Bowling, Michelle Miller, Randall Lekan, Ron Wild (Team Lead), Scott D. Wampler, Terry Julian, Thomas McGarry

Visit The Syndicate® at www.LLTS.org.

CONTENTS

WARHAMMER ONLINE
AGE OF RECKONING

INTRODUCTION

THE ART OF WAR

Yesterday you woke up to the fields and the chickens and a home-cooked dinner. Today, Mayhem. A plague chokes the land, and rumors say the old Thornland Estate atop the mountain has "dead men that will not die." Even Mayor Hallenstern hasn't received a courier since the emperor's proclamation that war has erupted in Karak Eight Peaks. What can one man do with a pick axe and shovel?

When you enter the world of *Warhammer Online*, you truly are in an "Age of Reckoning," with the realms of Order on the brink of annihilation. It's a massive confrontation of Dwarfs vs. greenskins (Orcs and Goblins), High Elves vs. Dark Elves, and Empire vs. Chaos in exciting battles with monsters or Realm vs. Realm™ combat that pits player against player. Whether this is your first MMO (massively multiplayer online) game or you're a seasoned veteran of virtual worlds, you haven't seen it all—until you've experienced *WAR*.

WHAT MAKES THIS GAME GREAT

You choose to join one of six races, and those "realms" go head to head in global battles called Realm vs. Realm (RvR) combat. Dwarfs, High Elves, and the Empire are on the side of Order, while greenskins, Dark Elves, and Chaos ally as the forces of Destruction. Everything that you do—completing quests, winning scenarios, conquering keeps, and battlefield objectives—contributes victory points toward controlling the game's various zones, with the ultimate goal to enter the enemy's capital city and defeat its king. Only when the king's head is on a pike displayed for all your kin to see will you feel the ultimate satisfaction of a champion.

WAR has hundreds of exciting quests throughout the world, though none so unique as the public quests. When you enter a location where a public quest occurs, you automatically join the quest, fighting side by side with any allied players in the area. These cooperative quests unfold over several stages and give solo players the opportunity to experience the thrill of party adventuring and tremendous treasure rewards.

With so much going on in the game, it's fortunate that you have a Tome of Knowledge that tracks your every action. The Tome unlocks lore, monster information, new abilities, and story revelations as it records the achievements of your life. Whenever you want to review a past accomplishment, just read through the Tome.

The best part of all this? You don't have to journey alone; guilds thrive in the game and allow like-minded players to work together to capture keeps and accomplish other goals. The game's advanced guild features give unprecedented options for leaders and members. You can create unique heraldry, carry standards out onto the battlefield to gain special abilities, and earn Guild Tactics that grow in power along with the guild enrollment.

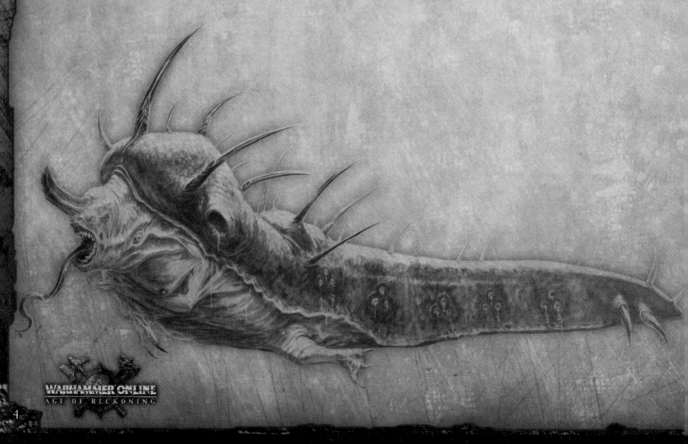

ENTER THE FRAY!

Flip through the following pages for everything you need to know on the much anticipated release of *Warhammer Online: Age of Reckoning*. From maximizing healing and damage with the High Elf Archmage to deploying the perfect pet as the greenskin Squig Herder, you can master the strategies of any of 20 careers in record time. Plus, we've jammed the guide full of detailed maps for every zone, RvR tips for besting the most ruthless scenarios and battlefields, tables of loot rewards, and more!

It may take decades to decipher every keep and castle, trainer and traitor...if you didn't have this handy game guide to reveal the infinite secrets of *WAR*!

THIS ISN'T YOUR MOTHER'S MMO GUIDE

Creating a guide for an MMO is no easy task. Not only are these some of the deepest and most complex games ever created, but from the moment they're conceived, they're being balanced and changed. So how do you write about a game that is constantly changing? What do you say about a skill that's forever being balanced? At first this was a monumental challenge, but then we began to look at it objectively. Most players are going to procure ever-changing loot tables, skill lists, item stats, etc. from a place that has up-to-the-minute accuracy: the internet. So how do we compete with the internet when we have to write, design, print, and ship to stores, while they can just log on and make a change? The answer is: We don't. We let the internet do what it does best, and we focus on what we do best: *writing expert strategy*.

When we met with Mythic in the fall of '07, we told them our approach to the book. To say they were excited would be an understatement. They had noticed, just as we had, the discrepancies between print and internet content and had their own concerns, which this approach addressed. They began to drop tome after tome of *Warhammer* lore in front of us, bizarre books filled with nothing but background lore and fantastic art. "We aren't interested in a book filled with tables," they said to us. "We want an artifact! We don't care about stats and stuff for this book. We want this book to be cool and weird and for players to pick it up and feel like they have a piece of the game in their hands."

This is the approach that we have taken with both the guide and the atlas for *Warhammer Online: Age of Reckoning*. Inside you will find few stats but tons of strategy and lore, few hard numbers but tons of flavor and insight. Be kind though, dear reader. Although we have endeavored to fight, farm, quest, and dive into the depths of this game, it is an ever-evolving, constantly changing world. Things are going to morph and change, and we are going to have inaccuracies; this is unavoidable.

To address these issues, we have put in place a team of authors who will continue to modify and correct the guide as the content evolves. These errata and updates will be posted on our site, and we will endeavor to do so as close to patch date as we can. To receive these guide updates, visit our site at *www.primagames.com* (we'll even e-mail you when new content is posted).

All abilities and morale in Warhammer scale to your level + gear. For the purposes of our abilities and morale charts we have scaled all effects to a base level 40 value.

ENGINEER

Wench! Bring me ale, fer tomorrow I march on Karag Dron, an' then we'll reclaim Karak Eight Peaks! Aye, I was there when those stinking Orcs an' Goblins came right through th' bleedin' wall an' broke into th' fortress. I'd have plugged that hole meself if High King Thorgrim Grudgebearer had not commanded me ta escort th' young'ns ta safety.

AH...there's me ale! Now ye see, I was down in th' armory working on a new thrower, when Renkel Stronghammer came in an' he says, "Let's go lads. There's a job ta be done, an' we have th' honor of doin' it." Never one ta look ill at a job what needs doin', I figgered it was important enough fer them ta send Renkel hisself, so's I said I'd do it. Besides, he said we had our weight in gold coming if we succeeded.

So I set aside th' new thrower an' went ta do me duty fer me king an' country. What...? Yes, I think that thrower was good enough ta save th' day. But ye see, when yer king calls, ye stop drinking an' do th' task set fer ye. Aye? So we gathered up all th' lads an' lasses that were millin' 'round th' back gate an' led 'em out ta safety.

Ye think yer wantin' ta be an Engineer, do ye? Well, ye must have a steady hand an' a keen eye. It's not all th' gold, beer, an' feasting ye may have heard about. Although plenty of it is, o'course.

By Bri

We must make sure th' world remembers Dwarfs when th' battle is over an' peace reigns again. An' th' only way we be about gettin' that done is wit' th' proper application of explosives. Our Ancestors be cryin' fer vengeance, an' it's up ta us ta deliver it with a very loud message. Ye know what I always say? "Ain't nothin' that can't be solved with a proper, large application of high explosives!"

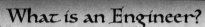

What is an Engineer?

The Engineers of the Dwarfs are skilled at delivering vast quantities of damage to their foes from a distant, protected, or even hidden position. Despite their bluster, these Dwarfs do not excel in hand-to-hand combat. If pressed into fisticuffs, they rely on little more than a trusty spanner to fend off the forces of Destruction. But they shine brilliantly when permitted to stand far away from an opponent and fire their vast array of ingenious weaponry at the target while it struggles across a trap-strewn killing field. Why stand in harm's way when you might simply strike enemies dead from a distance through the clever harnessing of explosives?

An Engineer is most effective when operating behind a "tank"—an armored ally capable of absorbing a great deal of damage while locking an enemy in melee a distance from the Engineer—and a healer who can undo a great deal of damage in case "Plan Tank" fails or the enemy can strike from range as well. Accompanied by such allies, the keen eye and deadly aim of an Engineer can lay down a field of fire that will wither all but the most resilient foes.

Additionally, Engineers can dictate enemy movement through the precise placement of trip wires, explosives, incendiary devices, and the like, all of which gives them greater opportunity to engage their enemies from a distance.

Engineers do not know how to heal themselves in battle without the use of potions or similar magical items. Their delicate work is possible only in light armor, so they take damage fairly easily. However, they are very effective in the proper use of explosives, which is often the skill that matters most.

—Aleister Schreiber, Scholar Emeritus, University of Nuln

STARTIN' AS A DWARF

Mordrin's Anvil is where ye head after leavin' th' homeland. If ye be fated ta grow a full beard, it be here ye will heed th' calling of Tharik Redaxe. He'll set ye on yer way ta bein' a thick-bearded, ale-swillin', greenskin-killin' Dwarf!

Yer first task as a beardling'll be ta clear th' Anvil of Squigs. Squigs be th' only thing that smells worse than a Goblin. They're foul, fungus-filled pests that found their way into th' Anvil. If ye lose yer way while fumblin' about, then looks ta yer map fer a red circle. That's where ye should be marchin' ta complete th' task before ye.

Use th' map ta find important folks with tasks fer ye. They're th' wee green circles with gold borders. Traders an' more important non-player characters (NPCs) just be silver dots. Make sure ye be takin' time ta talk ta all th' NPCs as ye travel. Hidden bits o' lore, treasure, an' experience can be found in th' most unusual places. They be falling outta packs or left behind whenever a piece o' history is lost or hidden from th' world.

Be sure ye completed all th' tasks before venturin' outside th' tunnel. If ye be list'nin', ye'll be ready ta leave Tharik an' seek fame as a hero in yer own right. Fer yer brothers an' sisters be waiting fer ye across th' bridge, where th' Battle of Bitterstone be thunderin' against th' Anvil like Mordrin's own hammer. Here ye earn influence an' glory! Finish all th' quest with yer brothers an' sisters, an' make sure yer name is ne'er forgot in song nor story.

Now that ye've completed yer training an' can tell th' splodin' end o' a handgun from th' other, get makin' yer way through th' mountain. When ye reach Redhammer Station, I'll be waitin' with a cool mug of stout fer ye.

ENGINEER'S GEAR

When ye arrives at Tharik Redaxe, ye have Me Ancestors' Ol' Spanner. This'll be useful fer getting through th' first few levels as ye clear Mordrin's Anvil of riffraff. But yer likely ta find a better hammer on th' greenies ye clunk over th' head.

Remember, though, yer always best standin' aways from combat. When ye need ta be gettin' their attention, try usin' Me Ancestor's Ol' Handgun. This belonged ta yer dad's dad's dad during th' days when they were cuttin' Mordrin's Anvil from th' great mountain. But don't ye be gettin' sentimental! As ye go along, keep yer eye out fer a better boomstick.

Th' greasy work clothes ye had on yer back when th' Squigs broke in an' th' bloody greenies swarmed over th' mountains, this be all ye have ta get started. Keep yer eyes open, though. With a little luck an' skill, ye'll be findin' a right fine suit of clothes fer travelin' th' world. Just don't go looking fer heavy armor: an Engineer needs ta travel quickly, so yer armor is classed as light. Look fer protection labeled Career: Engineer an' Skill: Light Armor.

Use a turret ta draw attention while ye shoot yer foe from farther away.

Land Mines! It brings a tear of joy ta me eye ta watch a Dark Elf fly though th' air after steppin' on me Land Mine.

Strengths

- Drop turrets fer greater damage an' ta help control foes' attacks.
- Damage targets outside melee range.
- Reduce enemies' effectiveness through debuffs.
- Explosives! What problem can ye not solve with large amounts o' explosives?
- Call in Artillery Strikes!

Ye already spent many a moonspan perfectin' turrets. These li'l marvels operate off just a li'l steam an' attract yer enemy's focus whiles ye shoot 'em in th' head. Turrets have minds o' their owns, though, so be careful where ye put 'em. Ye practiced so much already that now ye can build turrets in th' blink of an eye...even after one's destroyed.

Th' bigger th' boom, th' better—'ats th' Engineer's credo. Ye learn ta make grenades that throw shrapnel an' others that throw acid—ah, a fine mistin' o' acid melts th' armor right offa them greenies! When ye becomes a master, then ye can make a cannon. Once ye done that, yer ready ta have it fire on a spot of yer choosin'.

Weaknesses

- No self-healing.
- Limited melee abilities—opponents need to be kept at range.
- Lack of composite body armor. Leather doesn't stop razor-sharp blades very well.
- Performs best as part of a party.

Always remember that ye fights best from far off. Yer armor not be tough, an' ye cannot heal yerself well at all. An', when Destruction draws close, ye don' have near as many tricks as ye does from far away. If ye can find someone ta travel wit', someone as may be willin' ta stand 'tween yer enemies an' yerself, ye will travel faster then ye can alone.

When one kind of turret doesn't seem ta be workin' very well, change it out fer other types of damage.

SKILLS AND ABILITIES

Abilities

Yer basic melee ability be Spanner Swipe, an' th' only other one ye get later on be Friction Burn. That be it. Now, ye can toss grenades in melee, but inside o' five feet, guns don't work. That's when ye drop a turret ta' pull aggro, then move off a few feet an' blast holes in th' greenie's hide.

Ye'll be usin' Gun Blast from th' first time ye pull a trigger till yer a fully bearded Dwarf. It can usually be used twice when pullin' an enemy. Set yer turret so ye can control th' aggressiveness if ye don't expect ta be gettin' lots o' extra aggro. Use th' turrets right, an' ye can half kill a target before it ever takes a sniff of ye.

Abilities

Name	Level	Path	Cost	Range (in feet)	Type	Build	Duration	Reuse	Description
Gun Blast	Level 1	Rifleman	40	5 to 100	Ranged Attack	2s	0s	0s	Deals (300+DPS)*1.33 damage.
Spanner Swipe	Level 1	Core	35	Melee	Melee Attack - Hex	0s	0s	0s	Deals (187+DPS) damage. If target is Hexxed, Snare (40%) for 10s.
Fire Bomb	Level 2	Grenadier	25	5 to 100	Grenade	1s	0s	0s	Deals 225 damage. Deals Corporeal damage.
Gun Turret	Level 3	Rifleman	55	Self	Summon	3s	3 min	5s	Summons an immobile turret.
Field Repair	Level 3	Core	15/S	20	Turret Heal	0s	3s	0s	Heals your turret for 135/s for 3s.
Friction Burn	Level 4	Tinkerer	30	Melee	Melee Attack - Hex	0s	9s	10s	Deals (262+DPS)*1.33 over 9s. Deals Corporeal damage. Arc: 180, radius: 30ft.
Acid Bomb	Level 5	Grenadier	25	65	Grenade - Hex	0s	20s	0s	Deals 449 damage over 20s and lowers the Corporeal resist of everyone in the radius by 9.45/level for 20s. Radius: 20ft. Deals Corporeal damage.
Flame Turret	Level 6	Tinkerer	55	Self	Summon	3s	3 min	5s	Summons an immobile turret.
Blunderbuss Blast	Level 6	Tinkerer	35	CAE	CAE Ranged Attack	0s	0s	0s	Deals (112+DPS) damage to targets in radius. Arc: 120, radius: 40ft.
Addling Shot	Level 7	Core	20	100	Detaunt	0s	15s	15s	Detaunts (50%) target for 15s.
Bombardment Turret	Level 8	Grenadier	55	Self	Summon	3s	3 min	5s	Summons an immobile turret.
Incendiary Rounds	Level 9	Rifleman	40	5 to 100	Magical Ranged Attack - Hex	0s	10s	0s	Deals 798 Corporeal damage over 15s.
Barbed Wire	Level 10	Core	30	PBAE	CC - Hex	0s	5s	20s	PBAE Root for 5s. Radius: 30ft.
Flak Jacket	Level 11	Core	35	Self	Buff - Enchantment	2s	60 min	0s	Increases Armor by 22/Level. After taking damage 20 times, buff fades. Setback override: 100%. Stacking rule: Stacks with other buffs and Tactics (is NOT stack largest).
Hip Shot	Level 12	Rifleman	35	100	Ranged Attack	0s	0s	10s	Deals (225+DPS) damage. (Note: No min. range.)
Flashbang Grenade	Level 14	Grenadier	35	65	Grenade	1s	0s	10s	Deals 337 damage to target. Interrupts all enemies 20ft around target. Corporeal damage.
Fragmentation Grenade	Level 16	Grenadier	40	65	TAE - Hex	1s	15s	5s	Deals 748 damage over 15s to all targets in 20ft radius. Deals Corporeal damage.
Land Mine	Level 18	Tinkerer	50	GTAE 65	Create Bomb	1s	60s	15s	Creates mine on ground. When activated, deals 299 damage to all targets within 30ft radius and knocks down targets for 2s.
Concussion Grenade	Level 20	Grenadier	30	65	Grenade Attack	1s	0s	10s	Deals 337 damage and a short knock back to the enemy. Deals Corporeal damage.
Redeploy	Level 22	Core	30	Self	Turret Redeploy	0s	0s	20s	Destroy current turret. Resummon turret at feet with health % equal to previous turret.
Self Destruct	Level 25	Core	35	Self	CC	0s	0s	60s	Destroys current turret. Knocks down enemies around turret for 5s. Radius: 30ft.
Burn Salve	Level 28	Tinkerer	55	Group	Buff - Enchantment	0s	60 min	0s	Increases group's Elemental resist by 6.3 per level for 60 minutes.
Signal Flare	Level 30	Rifleman	25	100	DoT - Hex	0s	15s	20s	Deals 848 Physical damage over 21s and reduces target's Block/Dodge chance by 5% for 21 seconds.
Static Discharge	Level 35	Tinkerer	35	PBAE	PBAE Attack	0s	0s	5s	Deals 187 damage to all targets in radius. Corporeal damage. Radius: 20ft.

Firin' from behind cover makes it harder fer a foe ta find ye an' close ta melee distance.

Use yer turret ta increase yer armor by usin' Soft Cover.

Abilities

Name	Level	Path	Cost	Range (in feet)	Type	Build	Duration	Reuse	Description
Focused Fire	Level 40	Rifleman	25/S	5 to 100	Ranged Channeled Attack	0s	3s	8s	Deals (225+DPS) damage every 1s for 3s. Being hit while channeling removes 0.5s from the duration of the ability.
Specialization									
Crack Shot	Rifleman x5	Rifleman	35	5 to 100	Ranged Attack	2s	0s	30s	Deals (337+DPS)*1.33 and disarms target for 5s.
Snipe	Rifleman x9	Rifleman	30	5 to 150	Ranged Attack	3s	0s	10s	Deals (300+DPS)*2 damage. Undefendable.
Phosphorous Shells	Rifleman x13	Rifleman	40	80	Ranged Attack - Hex	1s	6s	20s	Deals (75+DPS) damage and 499 damage in 20ft radius over 15s. Deals Corporeal damage.
Sticky Bomb	Grenadier x5	Grenadier	40	65	Grenade Attack - Hex	0s	9s	10s	Deals 499 damage over 15s and then explodes for 249 damage in a 20ft radius. Deals Corporeal damage.
Napalm Grenade	Grenadier x9	Grenadier	35	GTAE 65	Grenade Attack	0s	30s	30s	GTAE. Pulses 100 damage per 2s for 10s. Then pulses 200 damage per 2s for 10s. Then pulses 399 damage per 2s for 10s. Total duration: 30s. Deals Corporeal damage. Radius: 20ft.
Vector Strafing Run	Grenadier x13	Grenadier	50	LAE	Grenade Attack	0s	0s	30s	Deals 412 damage and short knockback (sideways). Arc: 360, radius: 65ft. Effect delays 1s after build is complete. Physical damage.
Lightning Rod	Tinkerer x5	Tinkerer	45	Self	Deployable	1s	9s	20s	Deploys a Lightning Rod at your feet. Pulses 199 Corporeal damage every 3s for 9s. Radius: 30ft.
Bugman's Best	Tinkerer x9	Tinkerer	35	PBAE	Deployable	2s	15s	10s	Creates keg on ground at feet. Keg pulses a 120 heal every 3s for 15 seconds, healing all allies in 30ft radius.
Electromagnet	Tinkerer x13	Tinkerer	30	PBAE	Deployable	0s	4s	20s	PBAOE. Pulls players within 65ft in toward the center and then causes a 40% Snare for 4s, 1s later (20ft effect).
Turret Abilities									
Penetrating Round	Level 7 - Gun	Rifleman	Free	100	Turret Attack - Hex	2s	15s	10s	Deals 100 damage and reduces target's Armor by 24.75/level for 20s.
Machine Gun	Level 18 - Gun	Rifleman	Free	100	Turret Attack	0s	3s	5s	Channel. Deals 37 damage every 0.5s for 3s. 100% Armor penetration. No Setback override.
High Explosive Grenade	Level 13 - Bomb	Grenadier	Free	65	Turret Attack	2s	0s	4s	Deals 100 Corporeal damage. Radius: 20ft.
Shock Grenade	Level 23 - Bomb	Grenadier	Free	65	Turret Attack	1s	6s	8s	Deals 150 Corporeal damage.
Flamethrower	Level 11 - Flame	Tinkerer	Free	CAE	Turret Attack	2s	0s	5s	Deals 150 damage. Arc: 120, radius: 40ft.
Steam Vent	Level 21 - Flame	Tinkerer	Free	PBAE	Turret Attack	0s	3s	8s	PBAE around turret. Deals 75 damage every 1s for 3s. Deals Corporeal damage. Setback override: 0 (Not setbackable). Radius: 30ft.

Morale

As ye practices yer skills an' ye get th' bloodlust goin', ye can do extraordinary things by nothin' more 'an yer own force o' will. Ye gains yer first Morale ability at Rank 8, an' just like Tactics, ye can change 'em 'round when ye need ta.

Morale builds up in ye as ye fight an' win. See, there be four ranks ta Morale abilities, an' each rank builds on th' one before it. So ta cast a Rank 3 Morale ability, ye have ta first build up enough Morale ta be able ta use th' Rank 1 an' 2 abilities. If ye use a Morale ability, it uses all th' Morale ye built up ta cast it, an' then ye start buildin' up Morale all over again from nothin'.

Watch fer th' right time ta be usin' these Morale abilities, because they'll only be ready after ye been fightin' fer a few minutes. Use one too soon, an' ye might be wishin' ye had it later.

Ye have a few options fer castin' Morale abilities: Ye can dance around enemies fer 17 seconds, dodgin' attacks, or go fer th' kill with massive damage. Th' skill ye loaded in th' slot determines what ye can do. Try 'em. An' if ye don't like th' results, just change 'em an' try somethin' different.

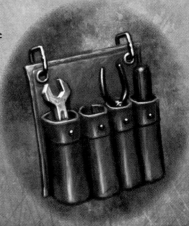

WARHAMMER ONLINE
AGE OF RECKONING

Morale

Name	Level	Rank	Range (in feet)	Duration	Description
Point-Blank	Level 8	Rank 1	65	0s	Attack that deals 600 damage and performs a long knockback on the target.
Unshakable Focus	Level 12	Rank 2	Self	10s	Self buff. For 7s, increase damage dealt by 100%.
Concealment	Level 16	Rank 1	Self	10s	Increase chance to disrupt and evade attacks by 100% for 7s.
Focused Mind	Level 20	Rank 2	Self	7s	For 10s, build times are reduced by 50%. Character purges and is immune to Silence, Disarm, Root, Snare, and Setback.
Explosive Shots	Level 24	Rank 3	Self	10s	Self buff. For 10s, ranged attacks explode in a AE around the target for an additional 300 damage. Radius: 30ft. Can only activate 1 per second.
Autoloader	Level 28	Rank 1	Self	10s	Increase AP regeneration by 30%.
Armored Plating	Level 32	Rand 2	Group	20s	Group Buff. Decreases damage taken by group members by 20%.
Cannon Smash	Level 36	Rank 3	100	5/30s	Deals 1,800 damage. Knocks down target for 5s. Reduce Armor by 35/level for 30s.
Hail of Doom	Level 40	Rank 4	100	5s	Channeled TAE. Deal 300 damage to all targets in the area every 0.5s. Max duration: 5s.
Scattershot	Rifleman x15	Rank 4	CAE	4s	Channeled. Deals 600/s for 4s. Cannot be interrupted. Arc: 120, radius: 65ft.
Artillery Barrage	Grenadier x15	Rank 4	100	4s	GTAE. Channeled. Deals 600/s for 4s. Cannot be interrupted. Radius: 30ft.
Fling Explosives	Tinkerer x15	Rank 4	PBAE	4s	Channeled. Deals 600/s for 4s. Cannot be interrupted. Radius: 30ft.

Tactics

Tactics be what sets one Dwarf apart from another. Th' best thing about Tactics, ye see, is that they be changeable at will. Ye earns Stoutness of Stone, yer first Tactic ability, at Rank 11. It's good fer an 11-point increase in Toughness.

There be six Tactic slots available, if ye survive ta see 'em all. Some ye earn fer livin', some ye earn fer doin', some ye earn fer havin' friends ta drink ale wit' while tellin' stories of gold an' adventure. Th' Tactics skills unlock as ye gain experience. At Rank 21, ye have six Tactics abilities ta choose from an' only two slots ta put 'em in. This be where ye can be changin' yerself round dependin' on yer environment an' peculiar strategies.

Be choosin' Tactics what can modify "career" abilities when ye be needin' ta modify yer role. Tactics what would cause ye ta do things ye wouldn't normally be doin' makes assignin' roles easier in a group. Ye see, ya might be taking on a "tank" role an' may be usin' Rune of Forging ta absorb more damage. An' that makes th' Rune Priest happy, cause th' Priest don't have ta heal ye so fast.

When ye be travelin' all by yerself, then ye be wantin' ta use Stoutness of Stone an' Well-Oiled Machine. These'll let ye take more damage an' deal more ta yer enemies by droppin' turrets instantly. Ye might e'en consider usin' Reinforced Casing an' Well-Oiled Machine in combination. These together be allowin' ye ta instantly drop stronger turrets an' keep th' damage levels high fer longer.

Tactics

Name	Level	Description
Stoutness of Stone	Level 11	Reduces the duration of Knockdown/Stun effects on you by 50%.
Expert Skirmisher	Level 13	Increases damage by +25% when under 45ft and decreases damage by -20% when over 45ft.
Reinforced Casing	Level 15	Turret gains 4/level Wounds.
Stubbornness	Level 17	Increases Corporeal resist by +6.3 per level of the character.
Steady Aim	Level 19	Increases Ballistic Skill by +4 per level of the character.
Hand-Crafted Scope	Level 21	Increases auto attack speed of gun attacks by 50%.
Ancestral Inheritance	Level 23	Increases Armor by +16.5 per level of the character.
Clever Recovery	Level 25	When the character's attacks are Dodged, regain 75 AP.
Concussive Mine	Level 27	Land Mine now disorients targets for 10s (Hex).
Pierce Defenses	Level 29	When the character is defended, he reduces the target's Block, Parry, and Evade chances by 15% for 10s.
Steady Hand	Level 31	Reduces chance to be set back when taking damage by 50%
Rune of Forging	Level 33	When you deploy a turret, it starts with an ablative that absorbs up to 825 for 180s.
Proximity Alarm	Level 35	Engineer and his groupmates get a 50% bonus to Stealth detect while within 20ft of turret.
Tangling Wire	Level 37	When Barbed Wire breaks, you snare the victims by 40% for 5s and deal 249 over 5s.
Coordinated Fire	Level 39	Signal Flare will also cause the victim to take 15% more damage from all sources.
Stopping Power	Rifleman x3	Hip Shot gains a (short) knockback.
Hollow-points	Rifleman x7	Snipe and Gun Blast deal additional DoT (399 over 5s, non-stacking, non-refreshing).
Quick Reloader	Rifleman x11	Gun attacks cost 35% less AP.
Extra Powder	Grenadier x3	Increases radii of Acid Bomb and Fragmentation Grenade to 35ft.
Throwing Arm	Grenadier x7	Grenades have a 50% increased range.
Bandolier	Grenadier x11	Grenade abilities cost 35% less AP.
Well-Oiled Machine	Tinkerer x3	Constructing a Turret has no build-up time.
Runes of Warding	Tinkerer x7	Increases Engineers's group's Disrupt chance by 10% within 40ft of your turret.
Tracer Rounds	Tinkerer x11	Increases Engineer's crit chance by 15% while within 20ft of your turret.

Yes, I know yer travelin' with friends a lot. Then ye can be usin' Steady Aim an' Well-Oiled Machine. Them together be th' best fer th' group: increasing yer damage an' helping ta keep th' Priest alive by pullin' aggro ta yer turret. If'n ye be in a group an' clearin' a public quest, switch over ta Steady Aim, an' Clever Recovery. Because yer turret be drawing any unwanted aggro, this configuration'll be th' most effective in a group, increasing yer damage an' keepin' yer action points up.

There be no certain classes or schools or ancestors when it comes ta Tactics. It be up ta you ta decide on th' best combination fer th' situation an' load those abilities. Ye can even preload 'em an' have 'em ready. Tactics abilities be passive, an' they help form th' baseline fer ye an' define how successful ye will be. As me Mammy used ta say, "If greenies had any brains, they would remember who their mothers were"—thar be no way ta talk bout all th' possibilities ye might find yerself in. So try different ones an' find what makes ye happy.

Mastery

By th' time ye hit Rank 40, ye will have earned a total of 25 Mastery points. Each skill tree takes 15 points ta obtain th' maximum ability in that tree. Yet each ability in th' tree ye decide ta take will cost ye more points ta activate. So th' initial ability will cost ye three Mastery points ta activate it an' one more fer a total of four points ta use that ability. Activation of each following ability will cost ye a total o' three more

> ### Avoid melee combat if ye can.

Turrets Syndrome

Definition: A neurological disorder whereby the afflicted verbally and physically abuses a nearby mechanical geegaw with uncontrollable rage, meanwhile ignoring the sentient being that caused the nuisance in the first place. Often this allows said nuisance the opportunity to shoot the afflicted in the face. Last year, Turrets Syndrome was a contributing factor in 75% of all cases of premature greenskin fatality, and is the fourth-leading unnatural cause of death among Squigs.

Common Causes of Turrets Syndrome: Dwarfs, massive alcohol consumption by non-Dwarfs, and PvP server lag.

Prognosis: If left untreated, Turrets Syndrome symptoms abate once the offending machine has been reduced to smithereens. However, lingering harmful side effects may include pain, embarrassment, and mild cases of death.

points. So if'n ye want ta max out one path, ye canna activate any other skills. If ye choose not ta reach th' top rank of a specific path, then ye can spread yer Mastery abilities across th' trees. However ye choose ta put 'em all together, ye only can spend a maximum of 25 points. So what ancestor will ye be followin' ta learn yer Mastery skills? Ye have three paths ta choose from.

- Path of the Tinkerer: If turrets are yer favorite way ta kill greenskins, then choose th' Path of the Tinkerer. Th' turrets are useful in layin' out damage that ye don't have ta worry about firin'. If ye follow this path, ye will be able ta play yer turrets an' create an ode ta death fer those smelly greenies ta appreciate.

- Path of the Grenadier: Or maybe yer idea of a good time be usin' explosives? Then th' Path of the Grenadier's likely ta be where ye want ta be spend Mastery points. Here ye refine yer talents fer usin' grenades an' bombs, increasin' th' effects of those li'l wonders, an' makin' greenies pay even more dear fer walkin' th' face o' our world.

> Use Barbed Wire ta stop Destruction from reachin' th' healers.

- Path of the Rifleman: But if'n ye prefer th' old-school meaning of "BANG! Yer'n dead!," then maybe ye were made fer followin' th' Path of the Rifleman. Next ta yerself, snipers'll seem like squint-eyed layabouts who na could hit th' broadside of a barn! But yer still an Engineer, so th' rounds ye use are beyond comprehension fer th' normal soldier. Ye can lay waste ta all what stand before ye with a couple pulls a th' trigger.

Ye need ta be deciding early on what yer specialty area will be. Th' downside ta Mastery abilities is that ye cannot reset them on th' fly. It requires talkin' ta a Trainer an' havin' 'em reset, an' that costs coin that ye could spend on ale!

Renown

There be three levels ta Renown abilities, an' ye must spend 20 points in each level ta access th' next. There be a total o' 60 points awarded, an' ye gotta decide how ta distribute 'em throughout th' different choices.

If ye spends some time killin' greenies an' their Chaos allies, ye should eventually get ta Rank 11 in yer abilities an' a Renown rank of at least 5. How many points ye have ta work with all depends on how much time ye spend in RvR instead of doin' tasks. At Renown Rank 5, ye

have five points ta spend. A wise course might be spendin' four points in Marksman an' one point in Fortitude. This assumes ye spend most of yer time shootin' things from a distance, an' don't get hit much. If ye get hit more frequently, or likes ta solo a lot, ye might consider puttin' a few more points in'a Fortitude.

As ye continue ta gain ranks, th' points just keep rollin' in. At Rank 21, ye have six Mastery points ta spend in yer chosen tree. At Renown Rank 10, ye have 10 points ta spend with yer Renown Trainer. Ye might consider spendin' points so as ta continue buildin' up Marksmen an' Fortitude, then start gainin' Blade Master fer added melee damage.

Once ye reach Rank 31, ye've gained most o' yer regular abilities an' ye now have 16 points o' Mastery an' 18 points o' Renown. If ye sniped enough Destruction, ye might e'en have reached Rank 20. Increase Blade Master an' take Fortitude ta Level III as ye continue ta move up th' ranks.

Play until ye reach Rank 40. When ye do an' have 30 Renown ranks, ye will have 25 Mastery an' 30 Renown points ta spend in character development. By this time, ye should have picked yer Mastery path, so now ye can respecialize an' start over as ye gain points. Ye should have Marksmen IV an' Fortitude IV, so take Sharp Shooter II. Then stick th' leftover points back in Blade Master, or yer might pick up some resistances fer Renown abilities.

Now ye have reached th' max rank fer abilities, but ye will continue ta gain Renown points until ye reach Rank 60. When ye have reached this exalted state—an' ta be sure, a good many songs'll let th' rest o' us know ye done it—ye will be viewed as an ancestral god among Dwarfs of lesser ranks. Yer Renown abilities might well be Resolve IV, Fortitude IV, Blade Master I, Vigor I, Sharp Shooter IV, Sure Shot, an' Greenskin Bane.

Solo Play (PvE)

Ye first finds yerself standin' in th' reclaimed mine in Ekrund. Th' mine is still in a precarious state, an' might be lost again at any moment if yerself an' yer fellow beardlings don't make a stout stand. Ye need ta be finishin' all th' tasks, startin' with clearing th' Anvil o' them nasty Squigs, just as ye promised ol' King Grudgebearer. When ye have done these tasks, yer led outside ta th' first public quest area. Ye should be Rank 6 an' travelin' ta th' inn at Red Hammer Station, which will be yer next home when yer ready ta start questing. Th' Mount Bloodhorn RvR area will be yer first chance ta show th' greenies that death is short an' stout an' drinks real beer.

Yer ability ta draw aggro wit' turrets'll be a major benefit in ranking up by yerself. It lets ye progress faster with little reliance on potions or downtime between fights—if ye let it draw aggro first. This be a skill that needs spatial awareness. Ye have ta know how far ta place 'em from th' foe so ye only pull one at a time and set yer turrets on defensive. Then ye wants ta use Gun Blast ta pull th' monster ta ye, an' another Gun Blast while it heads yer way. Just as it reaches ye, hit a Spanner Swipe. Once ye get a Gun Turret at Rank 3, be usin' it ta help cause damage as well. As ye gain abilities, ye get ta add Acid Bombs or Fragmentation Grenades ta this tactical sack o' tricks.

As ye grow in ranks, it be reflected in th' output on yer abilities, not in yer selection. Yer Gun Blast just gains power as ye gain ranks an' become more experienced at usin' it. Ye will be usin' most o' th' same abilities at Rank 20 that ye did at Rank 4 or that ye might at Rank 40.

Zone lines have a big red arrow on th' map pointin' ta th' next zone. After rescuin' Bugman's Best from th' train wreck, head fer th' Marshes of Madness an' Barak Varr, where th' greenies'll be hidin' like th' little princesses they are. It be here that ye find old foes an' new treasures. There're a bunch o' public quests available in th' area as well—it be easy ta gain influence, but also ta pick up experience an' roll fer PQ loot so as ye might get some new gear. Ye gets ta cause lots of damage in PQs so long as ye don't get suckered inta melee combat, which helps with a rollin' bonus fer PQ loot.

Make sure ye pick yer craftin' skills while in this zone so ye can start ta gain ability. If ye don't keep up on it as ye go along, ye'll find yerself unable ta use 'em in higher-tier zones. Keep an eye on yer opponent before ye attack, an' mind ye will find champions here fer th' first time. Whiles they may say "easy," they still be tough opponents.

BREAKING MONSTER HEADS AND GAINING GOLD

Don't drop a turret where it can pull more'n one bad guy unless yer party is ready.

Th' Marshes be where ye find th' first RvR area, wit' one-way doors ta both th' Dwarf zone an' th' greenskin zone. Start earnin' Renown points here an' usin' 'em ta adjust abilities an' be findin' th' path what makes ye happy playin'. Renown points be earnable only in an RvR settin', an' ye can earn 'em best by droppin' turrets an' usin' explosives in th' fight 'gainst Destruction.

Once ye have driven Destruction from th' Marshes, climb th' mountains ta Black Fire Pass. This area holds more than one scenario, so be makin' sure ye join th' one where ye wants ta fight.

As ye leave th' Badlands an' continue on yer journey ta reach Eight Peaks an' join yer fellow Oathbearers, stop by th' Shrine of Grimnir in Kadrin Valley ta clear th' area of ungors an' reclaim th' altar. Wieldin' a Doomstriker longgun as ye stand at th' pinnacle o' Black Fire Pass will be a story ye tell over many a mug of ale. If ye tire of th' Dwarf lands, travel ta th' High Elves, fer ye knows they'll need help. Or remember th' Oath yer ancestors gave ta th' manlings in Praag and stand against th' forces of Destruction there.

Group Play

If ye be travelin' with friends, yer role be ta provide damage from far enough away that ye can use yer firearm. This be where th' ability ta change Tactics is th' most useful at later ranks. When ye be helpin' a quest, yer best bet be ta cause damage. Drop a turret an' be throwin' grenades ta debuff th' mobs. Yer also good fer pullin' a foe from a distance so's th' main tank can grab aggro while ye shed hate usin' Addling Shot.

Now, if yer in a PQ, th' startin' stage be much like normal questin'. Yer enemies're not that strong an' ye be findin' turrets very useful fer drawin' th' foes ta somethin' other than a character, so set their aggression high. Most PQs seem ta have a fast respawn rate, but when th' PQ tips an' goes ta th' second or final stage, things change fast. Make sure th' main tank grabs aggro, then set yer turret ta defensive an' tell it ta shoot yer target. Then start shootin' yer target yerself while tossin' grenades an' bombs. Stay close by yer healers an' shoot til yer barrel is white-hot. If ye need ta, douse it with beer an' shoot some more. Course, I prefer ta pour beer down me gullet than on me trusty shooter, but ye gotta do what ye gotta do.

When in a scenario, ye be most effective when yer shootin' yer rifle an' throwin' explosives at th' enemy. Destruction forces can be stout foes, an' yer party will need yer strength ta stand victorious. Explosive Shots will cause damage ta multiple foes, helpin' ye build Renown points. Like's I told ye before, RvR is th' only way ta build Renown points. Th' more foes what falls ta yer sharp shootin', th' more ye earn. So both yerself an' yer warband are best served by th' smart deployment o' explosive devices.

Use Slow and Steady ta increase yer damage when there's no place or reason ta run.

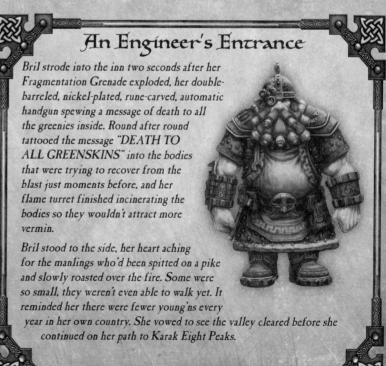

An Engineer's Entrance

Bril strode into the inn two seconds after her Fragmentation Grenade exploded, her double-barreled, nickel-plated, rune-carved, automatic handgun spewing a message of death to all the greenies inside. Round after round tattooed the message "DEATH TO ALL GREENSKINS" into the bodies that were trying to recover from the blast just moments before, and her flame turret finished incinerating the bodies so they wouldn't attract more vermin.

Bril stood to the side, her heart aching for the manlings who'd been spitted on a pike and slowly roasted over the fire. Some were so small, they weren't even able to walk yet. It reminded her there were fewer young'ns every year in her own country. She vowed to see the valley cleared before she continued on her path to Karak Eight Peaks.

BREAKING PLAYER HEADS AND GAINING RENOWN (PVP)

PvP fights is where ye really gets ta rock-n-roll. Ye need ta shield th' healers while th' tanks shield ye in turn, so stand behind th' tanks an' use Barbed Wire ta stop Destruction from movin'. Once ye got 'em all locked down, throw yer Acid Bombs followed by Fragmentation Grenades while yer turret lights them up. Place a Land Mine at yer feet ta protect ye in case a Dark Elf be able ta sneak 'round yer tank.

Me namesake ancestor was there when Grimnir helped th' High Elves defeat Chaos at th' northern Chaos Gates. It be rumored that Grimnir hisself called out, "Bril! I have a target 400 feet behind that gate." Suddenly, th' Marauder fell over with a bullet 'tween 'is beady eyes. This is how ye be needin' ta PvP. When ye come upon a target of opportunity, never let 'em gets close ta ye. Set up yer turret, then stand off ta th' side an' use Gun Blast ta make holes in yer enemies. Follow that wit' Incendiary Rounds fer more damage. Try an' keep yer foes at a distance. If they get close, use Spanner Swipe an' Friction Burn ta keep breathin'.

FER ME ANCESTORS

By Grimnir! Ye added too much saltpeter! Ye know how much gold that be costin' me?! If ye wants ta be an Engineer, ye can't be dreamin' about th' lost Gold o' Eight Peaks whiles yer mixin' th' powder! Now concentrate an' don't be foulin' me powder like some bloody greenskin punter. When I gets back from th' Red Station Inn, I expects ye ta have th' mixture right so's I can makes me way ta th' Bitterstone Gorge. I hears that them Dark Elves are usin' greenies ta carry gold outta th' Gorge, an' I swear on me ancestors that I shall deliver that gold ta th' High King...less a li'l bit fer me...fer th' effort, eh?

Climb onta Roof Tops when ye can ta make it harder fer Destruction ta hit ye.

Just before yer turret gets destroyed, cause it ta Self Destruct an' inflict that last bit o' damage.

IRONBREAKER

By Baalim

Hello thar lad! What's yer name? What be it? Cat got yer tongue? Ha ha, we'll get ye over that soon enough. Name's Baalim, and I 'ave been tasked by High King Throgrim Grudgebearer ta train ye new Ironbreakers properly so as we can get rid o' this green menace once and fer all. Ye know lad, I was there in th' bloody thick of it when this all began....

Them blasted greenskins blew a hole right through th' walls of Karak Eight Peaks. I fought and killed so many, but they just kept comin' through. They took me captive and forced me ta watch 'em tear down our glorious statues and destroy things me ancestors worked hard ta build. For th' luck o' me ancestors, I broke free while my guards was asleep, and managed ta escape back here ta Ekrund. I've killed more greenskins than most Dwarfs have seen in ages, and that throng was at least 10 times greater'n all them put together. Those greenies got th' best of me at Karak Eight Peaks. It'll not be happenin' again. We'll get our revenge on 'em....

Blast! Where was I? Oh right, yer trainin'. Let's see what ye've got ta start with, and we'll go from there. Yep, I said trainin'! Ye think ye have what it takes ta look a Black Orc in th' eye and call him names now? Just because ye be a Dwarf, it don't mean yer ready fer nuthin' like that yet. Ye got some trainin' ta get through first. Go get into yer armor, beardling!

Ye'll be stayin' near Mordrin's Anvil while ye learn th' basics of bein' an Ironbreaker. First, bein' an Ironbreaker means yer a nose-ta-greenie melee fighter. We don't play with no fancy magic or any o' that nonsense. Brute force be our game, an' we do it well. An Ironbreaker relies on 'is strength and 'is defenses ta survive th' foes' attacks. Then, when th' timin' be right, he beats 'em down with his axe. Th' only weakness ye need ta fear be ranged fighters. Ye see, all that armor be heavy, and ye'll have ta close th' distance with 'em ta attack. It's a good thing that once ye hit 'em a few times, they start tryin' ta escape. An Ironbreaker's specialty be his ability ta survive, and ta keep his friends alive while doin' so. When facin' monsters, yer role be ta take th' beatin' while yer friends do th' damage.

An Ironbreaker's most important possessions be his armor. Yer goin' ta be right up there with them greenies, beatin' 'em down with yer axe. Without good armor, they can do some damage ta ye. Startin' with th' family heirlooms be good, but you'll be wantin' ta upgrade 'em pretty quick.

When travelin', use Flee ta get 'round faster. Just be careful not ta Flee inta a group of critters... ye might find yerself low on action points with no way ta run away!

What is an Ironbreaker?

The resolute Ironbreakers, being durable melee-combat experts, most often serve a role in their war parties commonly referred to as "the tank." Among the Dwarfs, it is the Ironbreakers who stand in harm's way, holding the ground between their allies and those who would try to do them harm. Most Ironbreakers are well equipped for this dangerous role with the knowledge to don and fight in heavy armor, an adept's grasp of defensive stratagems and their proper deployment, and the stamina to heft a stout shield. While Ironbreakers are well versed in the use of axes and other offensive weapons, it is their ability to selflessly withstand the brunt of the enemy assault so their friends might accomplish their goals that makes Ironbreakers the backbone of Dwarf warfare.

A lone Ironbreaker can tackle daring adventures without aid. By simply exchanging their typical pairing of axe and shield for a two-handed greataxe, Ironbreakers become far more effective at actually dispatching enemies. That being said, you will still most likely find Ironbreakers at the vanguard of a group of adventurers, accomplishing the tasks for which they were born: leading a group of brave souls, and absorbing the brunt of the damage.

Being an Ironbreaker requires patience and skill. These stout myrmidons perform best when grouped with other classes of adventurer, as their defensive abilities, desire to protect allies, and natural leadership qualities can make such a group far more effective. Ironbreakers will find exceptional synergy with companions who are versed in the healing arts, and such a pairing unleashes almost unstoppable interactions.

It takes a relatively long time for an Ironbreaker to hone his martial skills to the pinnacle of their potential. Be assured that time will not be wasted, as their bravery and companionship are valued by all who fight on the side of Order.

—Aleister Schreiber, Scholar Emeritus, University of Nuln

BEIN' A DWARF

We once 'ad a glorious empire, with great cities like Karak Eight Peaks and Altdorf. We been in a battle with th' greenskins long as th' grayest o' beards can remember, and now are driven from our glorious cities and walls back into Ekrund and beyond. Nowadays, we're a proud race, recallin' th' great battles and victories of our ancestors. Th' world we knew 'as changed, thanks ta th' failures of th' Humans and th' pointy-eared High Elves. Now, looks like they be needin' us ta save their hides again.

We may not be in all our ol' cities, but that don' mean th' glory days're over. We be plenty proud of bein' th' best ale drinkers in th' land. No one can put away more ale than a Dwarf. And in case you were wonderin', th' only thing we likes better than an ale, if you can imagine such a thing, be gold. As a matter of fact, gold be one of th' few things that can draw a Dwarf from his seat in th' local tavern.

We now find ourselves in allegiance with them point-eared High Elves, and with th' Humans o' th' Empire, an' we may well have ta do their job fer 'em if anything is ta be done right. At th' same time, our king, High King Throgrim Grudgebearer, be plannin' ta take back th' land that belongs ta us, all th' way back ta Karak Eight Peaks.

Ye'll start yer adventures in Ekrund, at Mordrin's Anvil. This be an area in th' Bitterstone Mine that th' Dwarfs have taken back from th' greenskins. There you'll find friendly Dwarfs, a furnace, a mineshaft, a local tavern, hordes o' greenies ta smash—everything a Dwarf needs fer a relaxing holiday! You'll begin your adventures by doin' some work fer Tharik Redaxe. He'll assign you your first task: killin' Squigs in th' mineshaft. Check your map fer th' location marked and head there. Don't forget ta talk ta th' other Dwarfs on th' way, as they can give ye hidden lore, more quests, an' even train ye as yer gainin' ranks. Do all th' quests around th' Anvil before you head out ta th' bridge.

On t'other side of th' bridge, ye'll find more Dwarfs with quests fer ye and yer first public quest: th' Battle of Bitterstone. This probably be yer first chance ta be a tank fer a group. Ta tackle a public quest, every group needs a good tank fer th' champions and fer th' boss. Th' tank probably be th' most important person in th' group, because he keeps th' hard-hittin' enemies from hittin' 'is friends. Matter of fact, this is true even in normal questin' groups, as keepin' yer friends alive will always be good fer ye. In th' public quest, ye can earn influence and get ye some nice rewards. Join a group there if ye can find one, and help th' Dwarfs take back Bitterstone Mine once and fer all. Once you finish all th' quests, head ta Redhammer Station ta cool off with some ale and see what avails ye there.

IRONBREAKER GEAR

Ironbreakers wear heavy armor and generally wield an axe and a shield. However, it be possible ta wield a greataxe in place of these. Yer gear choices will depend on yer preferences. If ye be th' type that enjoys leadin' a group of friends into battle and takin' them greenskins' attacks fer yerself, then focus on armor with good stats in Wounds, Armor, Block Rating, and Toughness. Wounds will increase yer health, which allows ye ta' take more beatin' before ye needs ta be healed. Armor reduces th' damage of each hit ye take, Block Rating increases yer chance ta block incomin' attacks (with yer shield), and Toughness also decreases th' damage ye take by increasing yer Armor. Ye can get resistances ta th' different types o' magic damage, too, so don't ignore those. But ye should focus more on th' primary stats so ye can draw, and keep, th' most attention.

On th' other hand, if ye be th' type who wants ta dish out th' damage, then Strength and Weapon Skill should be yer primary focus stats, along with th' damage of yer weapon. Strength causes yer attacks ta do more damage, and Weapon Skill reduces yer chance ta miss or be blocked or parried when ye attack.

That be th' kind of gear choices a tank should be makin'. Either way, yer armor usually be more important than yer weapon, though upgradin' weapons will be necessary along th' way. Be choosin' gear that gives ye th' biggest upgrades.

Strengths

- Heavy armor fer better defense.
- Defensive skills.
- Debuffs ta slow down th' enemy.
- Yer always welcome in a party.

Ironbreakers are generally good fer gettin' in th' way o' th' enemy. They can't cut ye down, can't blow you away with fancy magics, and can't use lots'er fancy abilities ta get 'round ye. Ye can absorb lots o' damage, especially with a shield, which makes ye much harder ta kill than th' sissier classes. Ye also have abilities that makes ye (and even yer friends) tough, and ways ta debuff enemies that slow 'em, reduce their attack damage, or even immobilize 'em fer a little while.

Bein' th' one willin' ta stand in front an' get pounded earns a Dwarf lots o' friends, too. Ain't no one can do that an' survive better 'n an Ironbreaker, so yer'll be always welcome in a party. Plus, Ironbreakin' ain't clock science. Yer stuff be generally straightforward in how it works. T'ain't no fancy tricks or sneakin' around an enemy.

Weaknesses

- Limited ranged attacks.
- Vulnerable ta incoming ranged attacks.
- Low ta medium damage.
- Slow ta rank up.

If th' enemy can't be reached by yer axe an' a lil' running, then ye have ta call that target some other fella's problem. Ironbreakers can be picked off easily by ranged enemies, so fightin' 'em means runnin' fast as yer legs'll carry ye—either out of range o' that 'fraidy cat, or right up inta its face so's ye can pound on 'im.

Ironbreakers aren't gen'rally built ta deal lots'a damage compared ta other classes, either, which makes it take longer ta kill an enemy. This can be a problem when ye be adventurin' solo. Due ta th' lower amount of damage, th' rate at which you kill enemies is slower too, so it generally takes more time fer one ta' gain ranks. So, yeah, yer allies'll steal some o' th' experience while ye do th' hard work an' keep their robes from getting' too dirty. But without 'em, yer'll end up one big, steel pincushion in some greenie cave.

Most of th' public quests are soloable through th' first stage, makin' it fairly easy ta upgrade yer armor with influence rewards by grindin' out influence.

STRENGTHS AND WEAKNESSES

WARHAMMER ONLINE
AGE OF RECKONING

SKILLS AND ABILITIES

Abilities

Ye can divide th' Ironbreaker's abilities into three groups: defensive abilities, damagin' abilities, and buffs/debuffs. As an Ironbreaker, ye'll learn ta concentrate yer defensive abilities up front and keep your buffs up, as well as your Oath Friend's. Ye pick one party member as yer Oath Friend, and many of yer abilities'll grant buffs ta that Oath Friend as well. Ye'll also bear a Grudge against those who dealt damage ta yer Oath Friend, and a Dwarf Grudge is sumpthin' ta be feared.

Join groups for public quests and any other questin' ye can find in yer area.

Th' primary abilities ye use are Grudging Blow (a quick attack that makes enemies hate ye e'en more), Vengeful Strike (uses Grudges and gives ye a Toughness buff), Guarded Attack (increases yer armor), and Heavy Blow (which deals more damage than th' others). Ye'll use these in most every fight, especially Vengeful Strike and Guarded Attack, as those keep yer defens buffed fer most of th' fight.

Abilities

Name	Level	Path	Cost	Range (in feet)	Type	Build	Duration	Reuse	Description
Axe Toss	Level 1	Core	20	10 to 65	Ranged Attack	1s	0s	0s	Deals 75 damage.
Oath Friend	Level 1	Core	Free	166	Buff	0s	Unlimited	15s	Select a groupmate as Oath Friend. Does not trigger the GCD. May only have one Oath Friend at a time.
Grudging Blow	Level 1	Stone	30	Melee	Melee Attack	0s	0s	0s	Deals (112+DPS) damage. Generates double hate.
Vengeful Strike	Level 2	Stone	10 Grudge	Melee	Melee Attack	0s	10s	0s	Deals (112+DPS) damage and increases Ironbreaker's and Oath Friend's Toughness by 3 for 10s.
Guarded Attack	Level 3	Brotherhood	30	Melee	Melee Attack	0s	10s	0s	Deals (112+DPS) damage. Increases armor by 24.75 for 10s on self and Oath Friend (only if Oath Friend is within 40ft).
Binding Grudge	Level 4	Vengeance	20	Melee	Melee Attack - CC	0s	10s	5s	Deals (187+DPS)*1.33 damage over 10s. Snares by 40% for 10s. Damage is increased to (300+DPS)*1.33 / (412+DPS)*1.33 / (525+DPS)*1.33 / (637+DPS)*1.33 based on threshold.
Heavy Blow	Level 5	Vengeance	35	Melee	Melee Attack	0s	0s	0s	Deals (150+DPS) damage. Attack deals (75 / 112.5 / 150 / 187.5)*1.33 over 3s based on threshold.
Grudge Unleashed	Level 5	Core	40 Grudge	Self	Buff	0s	0s	20s	Gives 75 AP. Does not cause GCD.
Shield of Reprisal	Level 6	Stone	35	Melee	Reactive Melee Attack	0s	0s	10s	Deals (225+DPS) damage. Requires shield. Requires Block/Parry. Adds 30 Grudge.
Taunt	Level 7	Core	20	65	Debuff	0s	15s	15s	Interrupts target. For 15s, the tank deals 30% more damage against target. Monsters turn to attack tank until Taunt expires. After 3 ability activations and/or auto attacks from target hit tank, Taunt fades. Tank generates 2,250 in hate.
Shield Sweep	Level 8	Stone	30 Grudge	Melee	Melee Attack	0s	0s	0s	Deals 187 damage and hits up to 2 extra targets for 187, gains 10 Grudge for each additional target hit. Radius: 20ft. Requires Shield.
Inspiring Attack	Level 9	Brotherhood	35	Melee	Melee Attack	0s	10s	10s	Deals (150+DPS) damage and increases Strength by 3 for 10s and increases Willpower by 3 / 6 / 9 / 12 (based on threshold) per level for 10s on self and Oath Friend (Only if Oath Friend is within 40ft, both Strength and Willpower).
Guard	Level 10	Core	Free	42	Buff	0s	Stance	60s	Buff on friendly player that splits the damage between the target and the tank. Buffed player takes 50% of the incoming damage. Tank takes 50% of the incoming damage directed at the buffed target. Hate is split between player and tank.
Hold the Line	Level 10	Core	20/S	PBAE	Buff	0s	10s	0s	Toggled buff. Each second the toggle is active, bestows a buff that increases Evade and Disrupt chances by 45% to the tank and 15% to all friendlies in the radius that lasts 1 second. If the tank uses another ability, the ability ends. Buffs on friendlies stack up to 3. Arc: 180 (pointed to the rear), radius: 40ft.

Always bind ta th' Rally Master when yer advancin' ta a new chapter so ye can return ta camp quickly if'n ye find trouble.

Abilities

Name	Level	Path	Cost	Range (in feet)	Type	Build	Duration	Reuse	Description
Kneecapper	Level 12	Vengeance	30	Melee	Melee Attack	0s	5s	5s	Deals (112+DPS) damage. Reduces enemy's critical chance by 5 / 10 / 15 / 20% for 10s based on threshold.
Away with Ye	Level 14	Stone	45 Grudge	Melee	Melee Attack	0s	0s	0s	Deals (300+DPS) damage and a far knockback to enemy.
Stone Breaker	Level 16	Vengeance	30	Melee	Melee Attack	0s	5s	5s	Deals (150+DPS) damage. Decreases armor by 10% / 15% / 20% / 25% / 30% based on threshold.
Stubborn as Stone	Level 18	Brotherhood	5 Grudge	Self	Buff	0s	10s	0s	Buffs Corporeal resist by 9.45 for both you and your Oath Friend for 10s. Each time you (or your Oath Friend) is hit with an enemy spell, whomever was hit gains +50% auto attack speed for 10 sec.
Juggernaut	Level 18	Core	45	Self	Buff	0s	0s	60s	Removes Snare, Root, Disarm, and Silence effects from the tank.
Challenge	Level 20	Core	30	CAE	Debuff	0s	15s	30s	For 15s, the challenged target deals 30% less damage to everyone but the caster. Monsters turn to attack tank until Challenge expires or 5s. After 3 ability activations and/or auto attacks from target hit tank, Challenge fades. Also generates 22 50 hate. Arc: 90, radius: 65ft.
Sever Blessing	Level 22	Core	25	Melee	Melee Attack	0s	0s	5s	Removes a blessing from target. Deals (75+DPS) damage if successful.
Watch an' Learn	Level 25	Brotherhood	30 Grudge	Self	Buff	0s	10s	0s	Self buff increases Weapon Speed by 3 for 10s. For the next 10 sec, each time you hit an enemy your Oath Friend gains 25 AP if within 40ft.
Grip of Stone	Level 30	Core	30	PBAE	Crowd Control	0s	5s	1 min	Roots up to 4 targets within 30ft for 5s.
Rune-Etched Axe	Level 35	Vengeance	30	PBAE	PBAE Melee Attack	0s	0s	10s	Deals (112+DPS) to all targets in the radius. Ignores 25 / 50 / 75 / 100% Armor based on threshold. Radius: 20ft.
Punishing Blow	Level 40	Brotherhood	35	Melee	Debuff - Cripple	0	10s	20s	Deals (75+DPS) damage and applies a Movement Barb. Target takes 56 when it moves. (Should check every 0.5s.)
Ancestor's Fury	Vengeance x5	Vengeance	15 Grudge	Self	Buff	0s	10s	0s	Buff Strength by 3 and increase critical chance by 10% for 10s for both you and your Oath Friend. (Only if Oath Friend is within 40ft.)
Cave-in	Vengeance x9	Vengeance	20	Melee	Melee Attack - CC	0s	5s	60s	Knocks target down for 5s. Deals 187 / 375 / 562 / 750 over 5s based on threshold. Requires Great Weapon.
Grudge Born Fury	Vengeance x13	Vengeance	20/s	Melee	Channeled Melee Attack	0s	3s	8s	Deals (187+DPS)*0.6 damage to target every 0.6s for 3s. Increases chance to critical hit for duration of channel by 5 / 10 / 15 / 20% based on thresholds. Requires Great Weapon.
Oathbound	Stone x5	Stone	30 Grudge	Self	Buff	0s	10s	0s	Buff Initiative by 2 and increase Parry by 25% for 10s for both you and Oath Friend. (Only if Oath Friend is within 40ft.)
Avenging the Debt	Stone x9	Stone	20 Grudge	Melee	Melee Attack	0s	0s	0s	Deals (187+DPS) damage. If the enemy dies within 5s, then also heals self and Oath Friend for (375)*0.6 (only if Oath Friend is within 40ft.)
Oathstone	Stone x13	Stone	45	Self	Buff	0s	10s	60s	Requires shield. 100% Block rate, 10s or 4 charges, and deals 75 damage back for each block. At 25 / 50 / 75 / 100 Grudge, damage increased by 75 each step.
Runic Shield	Brotherhood x5	Brotherhood	30 Grudge	Self	Buff	0s	10s	0s	Buff damage absorb vs. magic damage for self and Oath Friend for 10s, max absorb is 375. Each time you are hit by a spell, you gain 15 Grudge.
Earthshatter	Brotherhood x9	Brotherhood	35	PBAE	CC	0s	6s	20s	PBAE Snare. 40% for 10s. Deals 187 / 375 / 562 / 750 based on threshold. Radius 30ft.
Grumble an' Mutter	Brotherhood x13	Brotherhood	Free	Self	Toggle Buff	0s	30s	60s	Toggle. Every 3s for 30s, gain 180 HP and lose 20 Grudge. Effect ends if you run out of Grudge.

Morale

As ye earn ranks, ye'll begin ta be able ta train additional abilities known as Morale abilities—special abilities ye can use once ye have th' Morale ta do so. Ye build Morale as you fight, either by winning or by defending against attacks, but it begins ta decay when ye ain't fightin'. Once ye use a Morale ability, ye use all th' Morale ye have built up, and must start from scratch. Ye cannot change Morale abilities while in combat, so be sure ye have th' right ones available fer th' situation you're in.

Fer example, when takin' on a damage-dealing role, ye might use Demolishing Strike, Raze, Distracting Bellow, and Axe Slam. Fer a defensive role, ye might choose Grapple, Shield Wall, Gromril Plating, and Strength in Numbers. Ye can find these abilities in yer abilities list, an' swap them out anytime yer not in combat. However, Morale abilities have ranks, an' ye can only put a Morale ability in th' proper slot fer it. Ye can't put a Rank 2 Morale ability in th' Rank 4 slot, fer example.

Ye'll start learning Morale abilities from yer class trainer at Rank 8. And ye can learn special Morale abilities through Mastery points.

Top 5 Things Ironbreakers Don't Like Breakin'

1. Eggs. Dwarfs not be blasted cooks.
2. Plague Zombie Skulls. 'Ave you not smelt them?
3. Flagons. Rather spill their blood than be wastin' ale.
4. Inn Tables and Chairs. Ye risk a bar fight, an' that could mean spillin' ale.
5. His Sworn Oath. If'n a Dwarf speaks it, he keeps it.

Morale

Name	Level	Rank	Range (in feet)	Duration	Description
Demolishing Strike	Level 8	Rank 1	Melee	0s	Deal 900 damage over 15s and lower armor by -26.4/level for 15s.
Shield Wall	Level 12	Rank 2	Self	10s	Self buff: Increase chance to block by 100% for 10s.
Grapple	Level 16	Rank 1	Melee	10s	Unbreakable Root on target and tank (both Roots break simulaneously).
Raze	Level 20	Rank 2	CAE	3s	Channeled Physical CAE attack that deals 1,200 damage to targets over 3s. Arc: 90, radius: 66ft.
Distracting Bellow	Level 24	Rank 3	100	10s	Target and all enemies around deal 50% less damage for 10s. Radius: 30ft.
Rock Clutch	Level 28	Rank 1	Melee	7s	Deals 600 damage and Roots target for 7s.
Skin of Iron	Level 32	Rank 2	Self	5s	Damage done to the Ironbreaker is reduced by 100% for 5s.
Gromril Plating	Level 36	Rank 3	Group	20s	Each member of the group absorbs the next 2,400 damage for the next 20s
Immaculate Defense	Level 40	Rank 4	Group	10s	Group members who stay within 65ft of the tank take 75% less damage for 10s.
Strength in Numbers	Vengeance x15	Rank 4	Group	10s	Increases Ironbreaker's Block chance by 100% for 10s. Increases group's Dodge, Parry, and Disrupt chances by 25% for 10s.
Axe Slam	Stone x15	Rank 4	CAE	0s	Deals 2,400 damage. Arc: 180, radius: 17ft.
Earthen Renewal	Brotherhood x15	Rank 4	Group	9s	Heals the Ironbreaker's group for 720 over 9s and restores 250 AP over 9s.

Tactics

Ye'll also learn Tactics as ye gain ranks. Ye can equip Tactics ta raise yer stats, damage, or defenses. As ye gain more ranks, ye can equip more Tactics at once and have different sets that are quickly changeable—though not while yer in combat.

Fer example, ye can equip Stoutness of Stone and Stubbornness as defensive Tactics, while swappin' over ta Focused Offense and Rising Anger fer a more damage-oriented set o' Tactics when called fer. There be really no "best" set ta use, so th' sky be th' limit on how you can combine yer Tactics.

Ye learn yer first Tactic by rank 10, and ye'll find th' Tactics ye have learned in yer abilities list. Ye can define six different sets of Tactics, an' as ye gain ranks, ye'll be unlockin' more slots. Drop th' Tactics in an empty slot ta put it in that set, and pick th' set from th' Tactics bar that ye want ta use at th' time. This makes it fast an' easy ta switch Tactics between fights.

Use yer map ta find th' quests that can be done together. Do all of 'em ye can before returnin' ta turn 'em in. This'll save yer legs.

Tactics

Name	Level	Description
Stoutness of Stone	Level 11	Reduces the duration of Knockdown/Stun effects on you by 50%.
Focused Offense	Level 13	Increase damage dealt by 25%. Increase damage taken by 20%. Decrease threat generation by 25%.
Rising Anger	Level 15	Gain +5 Grudge when you hit an enemy. Can not occur more than once per second.
Stubbornness	Level 17	Increases Corporeal Resist by +6.3 per level of the character.
Rugged	Level 19	Increases Toughness by +4 / level.
Long-Held Grudge	Level 21	All attacks generate 112 / 150 / 187 / 225 additional threat based on threshold.
Ancestral Inheritance	Level 23	Increases Armor by +16.5 per level of the character.
Menace	Level 25	Increases threat by 100% on all attacks.
Sweet Revenge	Level 27	Gain +15% crit chance while over 50 Grudge.
Unstoppable Juggernaut	Level 29	Juggernaut's reuse timer is lowered to 20s.
Seasoned Veteran	Level 31	On Block: Gain 15% reduced damage taken for 5s.
Seen It All Before	Level 33	Reduce total damage taken when critted by 15% and reduces duration of snares by 50%.
Dwarfen Riposte	Level 35	On Parry: Gain 30 grudge.
Relentless Training	Level 37	Reduces AP costs for Grudging Blow and Heavy Blow by 15.
Long Reach	Level 39	Increases radii of Shield Sweep and Rune-Etched Axe by 10ft.
Overprotective	Vengeance x3	Oath Friend gains a reactive proc: 25% chance to deal 187 damage to attacker.
Powered Etchings	Vengeance x7	Rune-Etched Axe's cooldown is lowered to 10s and also does medium knockback to targets.
Greataxe Mastery	Vengeance x11	Increases chance to Parry by 5% and all damage done by 10% when using a Great Weapon.
Furious Reprisal	Stone x3	Shield of Reprisal will also increase target's cooldowns by 5s for 10s.
Oath of Vengeance	Stone x7	Also buffs the toughness of your Oath Friend and all allies within 20ft of him by 3/level for 10s.
Shield Mastery	Stone x11	Increase chance to block by 10% and reduces all damage taken by 5% when using a shield.
Avalanche	Brotherhood x3	On Disrupt: Tank gains 30% run speed for 5s and self-heals for 135.
Punishing Knock	Brotherhood x7	Knock Ye Silly knocks target down for 3s.
Told You So!	Brotherhood x11	When you crit, your group gains 20 AP.

Mastery

An Ironbreaker chooses th' path he walks by how he views his role in battle. Some of us prefer ta be th' focus of an enemy's attack—th' tank. Those walk th' Path of Stone. Others will choose ta deal more damage, and walk th' Path of Vengeance. And still others will choose ta use their abilities ta increase their friends' abilities, th' Path of Brotherhood.

While an Ironbreaker be a good tank no matter his chosen path, each has its strengths and weaknesses. All th' paths will provide new abilities, Tactics, and Morale abilities, an' increase th' effect of a set of abilities related ta that path. Ye'll earn a total of 25 Mastery points by Rank 40. Each ability costs th' required points up th' tree ta unlock it, then one point ta train. You can also spread yer points across multiple trees, but doin' so'll cost ye th' ability ta master all th' abilities in any one tree. Ta reset yer Mastery points, talk ta th' class trainer.

Th' Path of Stone grants ye more damage-reducin' abilities. It be focused on defensive abilities and Tactics, and is good if yer th' one what wants ta keep a hero or champion busy while everyone else be killin' 'em.

Th' Path of Vengeance be more focused on dealin' damage. Some of th' abilities require a greataxe, meanin' ye'll be havin' ta put away yer shield. This be a good path if ye be wantin' ta deal more damage, especially if one o' yer friends has already volunteered ta be th' hittin' bag...er, tank.

Th' Path of Brotherhood be focusin' on buffs fer yer group, especially on yer Oath Friend. This be a good path if there be two Ironbreakers, or another tank class, in yer normal group, and yer role be that of a second tank.

Renown

As ye earn Renown ranks, ye be receivin' points fer yer Renown abilities. Ye can spend these at th' Renown Trainer, who ye'll be findin' in captured keeps throughout th' world.

There be three levels that ye be spendin' yer Renown points in. Once ye spend 20 points in th' first level, ye can start spendin' points in th' second. Once ye get 20 in th' second level, ye can put th' rest in th' third. Dependin' on yer path of choice, ye'll be wantin' ta put 'em in abilities that increase yer defenses or yer damage dealin'. Ye might e'en pick a combination o' these.

Ye should be puttin' yer first 20 Renown in Fortitude fer more health, or Might ta do more damage. Ye can get ta Rank 3 in each of these, or Rank 4 in one of 'em. Th' next 20 points should go inta either Vigor fer more health or Assault fer more damage again. Again, you can put 'em all in one, or spread th' points between th' two. Now, ye be spendin' yer last 20 points in Reflexes, Defender, or Opportunist. Reflexes be increasin' yer chance ta parry, while Defender be increasin' yer chance ta' block. Opportunist be th' damage option, increasin' yer critical hit chance. As with t'other options, ye can either be puttin' all th' points inta one, or spread 'em out between two or three of 'em.

Solo Play

Solo play ain't an Ironbreaker's strong point, but ye'll have ta be spendin' a bit o' time adventurin' on yer own. Soloin' quests and grindin' experience by killin' monsters and Destruction forces be a good way ta earn yer ranks. Ye'll start out with four abilities besides Auto Attack: Grudging Blow, Axe Toss, Oath Friend, and Flee. Oath Friend be only usable on a groupmate, so we'll cover that in a bit.

BREAKING MONSTER HEADS AND GAININ' GOLD (PVE)

Rank 1–10

Ye wants ta begin a solo fight by standin' off at some distance from th' enemy ye plan on whompin'. Then, go ahead an' use Axe Toss ta pull tha monster ta you—and away from his friends! Be followin' that up with a few Grudging Blows, and it'll be dead soon enough. As ye learn Vengeful Strike and Guarded Attack, use 'em first ta get th' buffs from 'em—both'll be increasin' yer defensive stats fer a time afta ye use 'em—then use 'em as needed ta refresh that buff. Binding Grudge be good fer keepin' monsters from gettin' away from ye. At Rank 5, ye'll learn Heavy Blow, which should be replacin' Grudging Blow in solo play due ta its increased damage. At Rank 9, start mixin' in Knock Ye Silly ta increase ta th' damage ye deal ta yer enemies. Use th' attacks that give ye buffs ta refresh th' buffs, and otherwise use Heavy Blow. So, by Rank 9, yer attack chain should be lookin' somethin' like: Grudging Blow, Heavy Blow, Vengeful Strike, Knock Ye Silly, Heavy Blow, Binding Grudge, Grudging Blow, Vengeful Strike, Heavy Blow.

Rank 11–20

Use th' same attacks ye's been usin', but start mixin' in a Kneecapper and a Rune Etched Axe (especially when facin' multiple monsters). Always keep yer defensive buffs from Grudging Blow and Vengeful Strike refreshed. When you learn Away With Ye, keep it handy ta temporarily keep a monster from damagin' ye. Also be usin' Stubborn as Stone when facin' magic ta reduce th' damage ye be takin from them pesky casters so ye can kill them easier. Be usin' Juggernaut when snared ta break free and close th' gap with 'em. Startin' at Rank 10, ye'll be earnin' Mastery points. Use th' abilities ye learn with those when ye needs ta improve yer damage or defenses.

Ranks 21–40

Ye'll still be usin' roughly th' same abilities fer solo play. Use Stonebreaker ta reduce enemies' armor, 'specially on Chosen and Black Orcs. Deliver a Punishing Blow ta damage them that be tryin ta run away. Mix these abilities, as well as other Mastery abilities, where they be needed, but focus on keepin' yourself alive first.

Be nice ta yer healers... or invest in lots of healin' potions.

The Sack o' Karak Eight Peaks

Th' smoke was thick as th' head on a mug o' Bugman's Best. I knew them blasted greenskins were comin', an I was sure there was gonna be quite th' battle. But I ne'er woulda thought them greenies would had enough sense, let alone th' ability, ta blow a hole through th' blasted wall. I grabbed me axe an' shield an' headed down ta' help th' guards, many of 'em me close friends, fight th' green mob back. I fought and killed what seemed like hundreds, maybe more, an' it went on forever. Finally, I thought I saw th' end of th' horde o' greenies, but it was only th' beginnin'. A big brute Orc came through th' blasted hole, an' while I was lookin' on him, one o' them little Squig Herders hit me from behind. Dropped me like an empty flask.

Th' next thing I knew, I was tied ta a pole watchin' that green menace destroy me beloved city of Karak Eight Peaks. They defaced th' glorious statues, tore down th' walls, and made off with th' best of brews. It was all dis longbeard could bear ta watch.

Later, at night, I caught me guards a sleepin' on tha job an' broke free o' me bonds. I decided it be best ta make haste ta High King Throgrim Grudge-bearer an' tell 'im what those greenies had done ta our great city. He tasked me with trainin' new recruits in th' effort ta take her back. I vowed ta honor me ancestors by helping with th' trainin', and eventually fightin' by their sides ta take back Karak Eight Peaks.

Group Play

An Ironbreaker always be most effective in a group, 'specially when that group be havin' at least one person ta heal and one more ta deal some damage. When ye be in a group, always be selectin' a group member as yer Oath Friend. Many o' yer abilities also trigger buffs fer your Oath Friend, increasing their defenses, healin', and damagin' abilities. But its share and share alike' as any damage they take'll be returnin' ta ye as Grudges. Ye can place yer Oath Friend on any player in yer group. Placin' it on a healer usually helps th' group more, especially when they be castin' group heals. Monsters build a lot of hate toward persons what keep healin' their dinner, so yer ability buffs that also affect yer Oath Friend will increase his defensive abilities, and sometimes his ability ta heal in general. However, yer healer be most likely ta avoid dealin' damage many times, as he be busy healin' people, so ye'll not be granting many damage bonuses if yer Oath Friend be a healer. Now, if ye be havin' a damage dealer that th' monsters seem ta hate more than yer healer, ye can cast Oath Friend on them. They still be getting th' same buffs ta their defenses, without th' healin' buffs of course, however they also be getting buffs that will increase th' damage they be doin'. Generally, its best ta cast Oath Friend on th' friend that is gonna bring more hate, because when a monster hits 'em, ye be getting Grudges.

A really good use fer Oath Friend is ta cast it on another tank in th' group, because ye'll most likely both be takin' some hits, and th' buffs will work well—especially if two Ironbreakers use it on each other. You'll also be wantin' ta use yer shield normally when ye be in a group.

Ranks 1–10

Start out with a few Grudging Blows ta build some hate from th' monster yer group be killin'. Follow that up with a Guarded Attack and a Vengeful Strike ta get yer defensive buffs goin'. Keep them two buffs up, and use Grudging Blow liberally ta keep th' monster on ye. Once ye have learned th' ability, keep Taunt applied ta th' monster ta reduce its damage output on yer friends and increase his hate fer ye. Be mixin' in Shield of Reprisal and Shield Sweep ta generate more Grudges when ye can.

Ranks 11–20

Be mixin' in Kneecapper and Stubborn as Stone where possible. Ye can also use Guard ta reduce th' damage ta one of yer friends if th' monster decides ta turn ta 'em. Away With Ye an' Rune Etched Axe be well used ta knock monsters away/down ta defend yer friends. Hold the Line works well fer yer friends with ranged attacks, but if yer friends are melee fighters, it not be affectin' 'em as they have ta stay behind ye.

If ye find th' next chapter too tough, head ta th' High Elf or Human zones and try some o' their quests of yer rank ta gain experience. They be needin' Dwarfs ta save their hides.

Ranks 21–40

Yer standard abilities stay pretty much th' same, just as they do in solo PvE. Use Watch an' Learn ta increase yer damagin' an' help regenerate some AP fer yer Oath Friend. Grip of Stone be a good way ta get monsters away from yer healer, at least temporarily. Finally, when ye learn Punishing Blow, mix it into th' attacks whenever possible.

As yer likely figurin' out, it be impossible ta use all th' Ironbreaker's abilities in one battle. What makes a good Ironbreaker great be learnin' which abilities ta use an' when ta help yer group win th' fight. Your job in group play be not ta kill th' monsters, but rather, ta defend your groupmates so theys can kill th' monsters. Fer example, if ye be fightin a single monster, use Taunt, Grudging Blow, Guarded Attack, Vengeful Strike, an' Heavy Blow liberally. However, if ye be fightin a group of monsters, use Challenge 'stead of Taunt, Rune Etched Axe 'stead of Heavy Blow, Shield Sweep often, and use any other ability ye have that damages multiple targets. If ye be tankin' two hard-ta-kill monsters, use th' multi-target abilities, but switch between th' targets fairly often ta make sure ye be gettin' hate fer both of 'em.

LEVELIN' UP

Ye'll be trainin' at Mordrin's Anvil. Find Tharik Redaxe an' talk

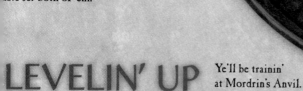

ta him ta get started on yer first adventure, killin' Squigs. Pick up all th' quests available ta ye, and get 'em done in any order that strikes yer fancy. Ye'll also want ta find th' class trainer, over by th' collapsed mine shafts, so that ye can train new abilities, and th' merchant, so ye can sell unwanted stuff ye pick up from th' monsters ye be killin'. Ye'll find these people shown as dots on your mini-map.

At Rank 1, Grudging Blow and Auto Attack will be yer primary means o' killin' monsters fer now. So get goin' shortbeard! Go kill th' blasted Squigs! Ye'll also pick up a couple more quests on th' way that ye can be doin' at th' same time. Before ye know it, ye'll be earnin' a new rank. Often, when ye earn a new rank, a new ability becomes available from yer trainer, so check with 'em when you rank up and train whatever be available. As ye gain ranks, start usin' Vengeful Strikes and Guarded Attacks ta keep th' buffs from 'em up, so ye be takin' less damage while killin' monsters. When ye learn Heavy Blow at Rank 5, use it in place of Grudgin' Blow while soloin', as it does more damage. Pick up a decent greataxe ta increase yer damage output. Just be sure ta keep yer axe an' shield at th' ready in case you see yer gonna need 'em. As ye finish out th' quests around th' Anvil, move ta th' Battle of Bitterstone and start workin' on th' public quest and th' other quests there. Ye should be 'round Rank 4 or 5 by th' time ye move on ta Chapter 2, Redhammer's Brewery.

In Chapter 2, ye'll find yer first RvR fights, th' Gates of Ekrund scenario and Grudgekeg's Guard warcamp. Don't be afraid ta participate in 'em, as ye will gain experience and Renown by doin' so. Use th' Renown ye earn ta buy armor upgrades from th' Hoardmasters there. Run th' public quests ta get yer influence rewards and a chance at a decent upgrade from th' quest chests.

At around Rank 6, ye be ready ta head off ta Chapter 3, Kron-Komar Gap. Around this time, ye'll learn Binding Grudge and Kneecapper. Start mixin' these in with yer normal attacks ta keep yer enemies debuffed. Again, meet th' Rally Master here and bind ta this camp. Start doin' quests and participatin' in th' PQs as usual. Ye'll also still have access ta th' Gates of Ekrund and a new warcamp, Roarhammer's Stand.

Now that ye have th' basics under yer beard, ye'll be learnin' advanced abilities fer th' rest of yer ranks. Yer basic abilities will still be th' most important ones you have, but don't forget th' newly trained ones either. They all be havin' a place and a purpose.

Continue ta work through all th' chapters, doin' all th' quests and participatin' in th' RvR and scenarios when ye see 'em available. Remember ta always bind yerself ta th' nearest Rally Master so ye can return ta camp quickly, and talk ta everyone ta find hidden lore and secrets. Try ta join parties where ye can and be friendly—it will take ye a long way into th' WAR. Ref...

Solo

Th' Ironbreaker be not th' best at soloin' in PvP. It will happen from time ta time, and ye best be prepared fer when it does, but ye'll fare best in group PvP. Whether it be a skirmish, a battlefield, a scenario, or a campaign, yer strategy should be about th' same.

Ranks 1–10

Work on keepin' 'em close ta ye. Most Destruction cowards are gonna run away when ye get a hold on 'em, so start off with a Binding Grudge ta slow 'em down. Keep yer Grudging Blow buff up and Vengeful Strike if you can. Use Knock Ye Silly ta get a damage increase, and then use Heavy Blow ta deal yer damage.

Ranks 11–20

Ye'll learn Away With Ye, which works well ta incapacitate an enemy. Just be careful with it, 'cause its gonna knock 'em a good distance away. Use Stubborn as Stone against casters ta reduce th' damage they do ta ye, and Juggernaut ta get free if ye be gettin' rooted down.

Ranks 21–40

Use th' same abilities and mix in th' new ones ye've learned as available. Watch An' Learn be a good self buff ta use ta increase yer damage. Keep Binding Grudge on yer target whenever possible, and use th' new abilities ta help immobilize 'im. Ye can use Grip of Stone ta root yer target in place and Punishing Blow ta do more damage if they try ta run. Ye'll also learn Stonebreaker, which be well used on other heavy armor wearers ta increase th' damage yer doin' ta 'em. Jus' keep whatever ye be killin close enough that ye can hit it.

Group Play

While th' Ironbreaker ain't th' best at solo PvP, ye can be very effective in a PvP group. Th' ideal version of a good group be consistin' of at least one healin' person and several damage-dealin' allies. Ranged damagers'll be doin' more 'cause th' Destruction forces'll be too busy bein' scared o' th' Dwarf standin' in their face ta notice where th' arrows and spells be comin' from. Because th' Ironbreaker does better in groups, it's best ta be joinin' a group as soon as possible, whether it be a skirmish, battlefield, scenario, or campaign. At lower ranks, keep yer enemies slowed with Binding Grudges and use Grudging Blow often. As ye gain ranks, ye can Taunt 'em so they do less damage ta your group, and ye have more defensive abilities ta survive their attacks. Always put Oath Friend on yer healer, as he's gonna be their first target if they have any sense. Be ready ta Guard 'im, or use Away With Ye ta knock a Destruction player away from 'im.

When ye be on th' attack, keep Binding Grudge up ta keep 'em slowed an' use Heavy Blow fer yer damage dealin'. Ye'll gain other abilities ye can throw in eventually, but those two are a must. Use th' same abilities ye would in solo PvP fer offensive attacks—Binding Grudge, Grip of Stone, Punishing Blow, and Away With Ye—ta keep yer target slowed or rooted in place. If a Destruction member be gettin' healed, either switch ta his healer or use Away With Ye ta knock him outta range temporarily. Ye can also use Away With Ye ta knock yer target into a group of yer friends, an' let 'em kill him before he can get away, as well as Rune Etched Axe ta knock away a group of enemies when they all start pilin' on.

Yer best role in campaigns and battlefields, due ta yer defensive strengths, be ta defend th' objectives. If it takes several Destruction members ta kill ye, chances are ye'll have friends around droppin' them while they be tryin ta get ta th' objective. In this situation, ye'll be wantin' ta switch back ta yer defensive tactics and fight ta survive. A well-balanced RvR battle be a sight ta' see, even if ye ain't th' one doin' all th' killin'.

SHORTBEARD SENDOFF

What!? Ye be done already? Har! Yer pretty good with that axe, lad! You remind me of meself when I was a shortbeard. Why, I remember back when me' gran'pappy showed me how ta' use an axe. Nay, it weren't fer choppin' no trees either. We used ta go out killin' Squigs back home fer fun! Anyway, I reckon ye did yer share out there today. Th' war 'as long way ta go, but we be makin' a difference every day in it. Come on, let's go have us a round of ale so we can talk about what ye be doin' tomorrow.

Use yer Axe Toss ability ta pull monsters away from groups, makin' 'em easier ta solo.

RUNE PRIEST

Aye, there be power in th' land. O', I'm not speakin' of that magical froufrou power ye often hear those pointy-eared Elf-clowns speakin' about—but real power! When ye can see that power, ye can lay a rune upon th' very earth from which it comes an' bring it forth ta focus, make it do things fer ye. It be this very power that'll see us victorious over them damn bloody greenies. They have no sense o' beauty, nor do they care fer th' land. They be just a bunch o' punters, an' they scar th' land wherever they walk, makin' it unfit fer minin' or livin'. Ye see, once th' darkness has settled in th' land, it stinks ferever.

By Deorer

Once yer able ta focus that earth power, then ye can make a difference on th' field of battle! Ye can cause yer enemies ta rue th' day they was born, or heal a fallen drinkin' mate...which I find ta be a most useful skill. I hate ta drink alone, ye know.

Let's see if ye have any ability here. First, concentrate upon that rock right there. Good! Ye feel th' strength of th' rock? Ye feel it flow through ye? Excellent! Now, see th' structure of th' power? Draw th' structure of that power. Then creates yer rune, just like I showed ye. Now focus, an' bring th' power into your rune an' bind it there...just like that!

Now th' tricky part. Make sure that ye be concentratin' on th' wounds that be in front o' ye an' see th' flesh as if it were whole an' not rent in twain. Slowly release th' power from out yer rune an' into th' flesh.

What is Rune Priest?

The fabled Dwarf Rune Priests harness secret power locked in the very veins of the ground they walk upon to buoy their companions up in battle. Rune Priests perform miraculous feats of healing that damage their enemies, even while they undo the injuries those beasts have wrought. They are faithful, even fanatical, servants of the Dwarf King Thorgrim Grudgebearer.

Dwarfs who prefer to stand in front of their opponents in open combat, an admittedly pervasive predilection among Dwarfs, do not attempt the path of Oath Runes and earth power. But they all realize that no one lasts long in mortal combat without the aid of great healers. The Rune Priests' primary obligation is to keep the brave war parties of the Dwarfs on the front lines of their conflict with the forces of Destruction by offsetting the damage to which they are ceaselessly exposed, resurrecting the honorable fallen, and invoking runes of earth power to bolster these allies in their dangerous struggles.

Recruits into the ranks of Rune Priest know that they will be nothing short of the very heart of any party in which they appear. They must be able to monitor multiple targets, both offensive and defensive, and they must do so from the thick of the fray. That is not to say that these priests are front-line berserkers like their Ironbreaker cousins, but in all cases, they must be close enough to the danger for their considerable powers to benefit fellow party members. As the Rune Priests themselves so colorfully say, their runes don't dissipate just because the priest who wrote them fell on a sword and died.

—Aleister Schreiber, Scholar Emeritus, University of Nuln

Well done! Very well done, indeed! Now, there be many more wounds ta care fer, an' practice ye must before I can try ta teach yer more. Use what I showed ye ta heal these brave lads so they can once more stand before th' breaches in th' walls. So they can let th' very earth know that we Dwarfs stand upon her still, an' that we be holdin' very dear account 'gainst those who stand 'gainst us!

Remember well what I say ta ye. Illusions an' parlor tricks are fer them what lack th' ability ta harness th' right powe o' th' earth!

Enough! Be off with ye! It be more than time fer me ta find some ale ta bolster me spirit, an' then I be off ta Battle Creek. I hear that them pesky greenies be tryin' ta move back in!

BEIN' A DWARF

Mordrin's Anvil is where ye'll first get yer chance ta invoke th' rune power. If ye be fated ta grow a full beard, ye will have ta survive th' tasks set before ye by Tharik Redaxe. We 'ave reliberated th' Bitterstone Mine from th' offal-swillin' greenies, an' it's ya job ta secure th' area. He'll firs' be wanting ye ta clear a bunch o' foul Goblin pets they call Squigs outta th' mine shaft. If ye be losin' yer way, look fer a red circle on yer map ta see where ye should go ta complete th' quest.

Now ye'll be using th' map ta find important folks with a task fer yer. They appear as small green circles wit' a gold border. Vendors an' other important NPCs just be a silver dot. Make sure ye be takin' th' time ta talk ta all th' non-player characters as ye travel th' world: they might have their share o' hidden tidbits or lore. Treasure an' experience can oft be found in th' most unusual places.

If ye be listenin' an' complete all th' tasks ye can in Bitterstone, ye'll be experienced enough ta set out on yer own. Seek yer fame with yer brothers an' sisters waitin' across th' bridge at th' Battle of Bitterstone.

Th' Battle of Bitterstone is yer first public area, where ye'll get th' chance ta join a group an' take on public quests. Here ye earn Influence, so be sure an' complete all th' quests with yer brothers an' sisters. An' do it right so th' ancestors'll be proud. Rune Priests are meant ta be primarily healers. Sure, ye're more than capable of doing th' damage, but yer skills are such that ye needs ta focus on keepin' yer fellow adventurers on their feet ta kill more o' them defilin' greenskins.

Now that ye've completed yer initial trainin' an' ye can tell end one of yer staff from th' other, be makin' your way through th' mountain. When ye reach th' Redhammer Station, I'll be waitin' wit' a nice cool mug of stout fer ye.

RUNE PRIEST GEAR

Rune Priests be startin' out wearin' cloth robes an' wieldin' Me Ancestors' Staff. Be sure ye keep yer eyes open fer gold an' treasure as ye travel th' world, not only fer yer personal hoard, but so ye can upgrade items an' purchase consumables like potions. Pick up gear as ye advance an' complete quests. Dressed in rune-inscribed robes, ye will be very regal lookin'. Yer power from being one wit' th' land will be evident in yer swagger, or even in yer drunken stagger. Only that gear what is marked fer th' Career: Rune Priest an' usin' th' Skill: Robe will be fittin' th' delicate work of callin' forth th' strength o' th' earth.

Ye not be needin' a hammer or axe like an uncouth Ironbreaker, nor any dimwitted manling's sword. Swingin' yer Ancestor's Staff like ye was minin' fer gold will do plenty ta cause yer opponent ta feel yer wrath, an' critical hits always make ye feel good. If ye be within melee range, take th' opportunity ta swing while ye prepare another spell. This is th' best way ta ensure maximum DPS an' earn yer share o' th' experience, so ye be needin' ta stay close while ye fight.

Build up Morale an' keep those abilities on th' cuff fer if'n things go bad.

When soloin', 'member that group healin' can still be used ta heal ye.

The Lost Oath Runes

1. Ye might 'ave guessed that th' Oath Runes that be useful ta adventurer's be not th' sum total of all Dwarf Runic knowledge. Matter o' fact, creative Priests be comin' up with new uses fer Oath power all th' time, often tailored ta what be annoyin' 'em most at th' time.

Goblin Wolf Rider

Oath Rune of Free Ale Refills
Good fer a night out wit' th' Ironbreakers.

Oath Rune of Sudden Sobriety
Good th' morn affa th' night out wit' th' Ironbreakers!

Miss Manners' Oath Rune of Proper Table Etiquette
Commissioned by a mighty-peeved barmaid affa th' mornin' affa yer night out wit' th' somewhat "uncouth" Ironbreakers.

Oath Rune of Honey Bunches
Part of a balanced breakfast.

Oath Rune of Dance Parties
Good fer when th' High Elves stop by.

Oath Rune of Pretty, Smooth, Silky Skin
Elves are thunk ta' 'ave had a hand in this one, too.

Oath Rune of Elf Repellin'
See both th' rune above.

Oath Rune of Yer Motha'!
More Elf repellent fer desperate, hazardously dance-prone occasions.

Oath Rune of th' Seven Dwarfs
Requires one sleepin' princess of inherently open mind 'bout her livin' arrangements.

Oath Rune of Puttin' th' Darned Seat Down!
Courtesy of said princess.

Oath Rune of Slim-Fast
Least used rune in th' long an' noble history of th' "stout" Dwarfs.

Look everywhere an' talk ta everyone fer hidden lore an' treasure.

STRENGTHS AN' WEAKNESSES

Strengths

- Th' ability ta heal.
- Drawin' upon th' power of th' land ta cause damage an' bestow buffs.
- Party buffs allow additional damage capability.
- Group heals (critical in most PQs at th' higher levels).
- Heal over time, which ye can stack on a target fer maximum healin'.

So ye be wonderin' what causes me ta be so tough? While Bugman's Best be part of it—ne'r a day go by I don't be sniffin' th' bung; it keeps me right as rain—but th' real reason I be this tough is cause th' earth is tough, an' I be drawin' her power ta heal me an' me mates. I be inscribin' th' runes ye see on th' armor an' bindin' th' power ta them. I have so many friends because, when th' gates be overrun, I heal all those who stand beside me. I can e'en cause yer wounds ta be disappearin' as they happen, while I go steal a sip of proper Dwarf brew! (Not that manling substitute fer good beer.)

Weaknesses

- Lack of real armor.
- Ye needs ta stand still fer most o' yer spells.
- Not a damage class.
- Slower melee weapon.
- Yer stats don' focus on Toughness, so ye'll have lower Health than other classes.

I be needin' these strengths as I enjoy th' feel of soft robes instead of chafin' hides or rustin' metal. I don't be jumpin' 'round like some prissy Elf; I needs ta keep me feet on th' solid earth. Aye, me staff not be as fast as an axe, an' I don't be claimin' ta be as tough as those who stress th' arms an' ignore th' brains, but I do be claimin' ta be th' one what keeps 'em all from dyin'!

When yer fightin' an' ye need a li'l help, pull th' mob back toward th' guards. They may help. Or they may watch ye die. It's worth th' effort to find out if yer 'bout ta toast wit' yer ancestors anyway.

SKILLS AN' ABILITIES

Abilities

Th' basic abilities ye be usin' are pretty consistent as ye grow in experience from Rank 1 ta Rank 40. Ye be usin' single-target heals fer yer defensive target, group heals fer keepin' th' group on their feet, an' offensive abilities ta cause yer enemies grief in between.

Ye still be usin' Rune of Striking when ye gets ta be like me, a fully bearded dwarf. Evens though ye be gettin' it at Rank 1, be expectin' ta use it at Rank 40—it just be more powerful. Valaya, Grimnir, an' Grungni will be grantin' abilities like Rune of Immolation ta stand against th' forces of Destruction as ye be travelin' th' world. They even be showin' ye Rune of Might an' Rune of Cleaving so that ye can attack e'en wit' no target an' cause damage all around ye.

Yer healing spells will be Grungni's Gift an' Rune of Restoration fer targeted heals. Rune of Valaya an' Rune of Serenity is how th' party is able ta offset damage. Th' first Oath Rune ye be learnin' is Oath Rune of Power, followed by Oath Rune of Warding, an' then Oath Rune of Iron. Oath Runes buff yer party an' allow 'em ta activate a spell without havin' ta use Morale or action points, but only one Oath Rune can be active at a time.

Name	Level	Path	Cost	Range (in feet)	Type	Build	Duration	Reuse	Description
Rune of Striking	Level 1	Grungni	25	100	Magic Attack	2s	0s	0s	Deals 299 damage.
Grungni's Gift	Level 1	Grungni	30	150	Heal	0s	0s	0s	Heals 202 to defensive target.
Rune of Immolation	Level 2	Valaya	30	100	Magic Attack - Curse	0s	15s	0s	Deals a DoT to target that does 499 over 15s.
Rune of Regeneration	Level 3	Core	30	150	HoT - Bless	0s	15s	0s	Heals for 1,496 over 15s.
Oath Rune of Power	Level 4	Grungni	25	Buff	Mark Buff - Bless	0s	60 min	0s	Increases target group member's Strength and Intelligence by 2 for 1 hour.
Power	=Sub Ability=	Grungni	Free	100	Magic Attack	0s	0s	60s	Deals 262 damage.
Rune of Fire	Level 5	Grungni	35	100	Magic Attack	0s	0s	5s	Deals 225 damage.
Grimnir's Shield	Level 5	Core	45	Self	Buff	0s	10s	60s	Damage taken is reduced by 50%, and reduces AP costs by 25%. Can not be set back and no threat is generated while this ability is active.
Rune of Shielding	Level 6	Valaya	35	100	Magic - Bless	0s	10s	20s	Target absorbs the next 562 damage. When the effect fades, the target is healed for 180 damage.
Rune of Might	Level 7	Grimnir	40	PBAE	Magic Attack	2s	0s	0s	Deals 249 damage to all targets in radius. Radius: 30ft.
Rune of Preservation	Level 7	Core	20	100	Debuff	0s	15s	15s	Detaunts target (15s duration, 50% redux).
Rune of Restoration	Level 8	Grungni	45	150	Heal	3s	0s	0s	Heals 1,125 damage. Setback override: 100% chance, 2s value.
Oath Rune of Warding	Level 9	Grimnir	25	Buff	Mark Buff - Bless	0s	60 min	0s	Increases target group member's Corporeal resists by 6.3 for 1 hour.
Grungni's Curse	=Sub Ability=	Grimnir	Free	PBAE	Crowd Control	0s	9s	60s	Deals 349 damage over 9s to all targets in the radius. Radius: 30ft.
Rune of Life	Level 10	Core	20	100	Resurrection	3s	0s	6s	Resurrect targeted friendly dead player.
Rune of Mending	Level 10	Valaya	55	150	Heal - Bless	1s	9s	0s	Heals 247 damage, then heals 658 damage over 9s.
Oath Rune of Iron	Level 12	Valaya	25	Buff	Mark Buff - Bless	0s	60 min	0s	Increase target group member's Initiative and Willpower by 2 per level for 1 hour.
Iron	=Sub Ability=	Valaya	Free	100	Magic Attack	0s	0s	60s	Deals 648 damage over 9s.

In yer group encounters with a buncha mobs, use th' ability Blessing of Valaya wit' Rune of Serenity fer maximum group healin'.

When soloin', 'member that group healin' can still be used ta heal ye.

Abilities

Name	Level	Path	Cost	Range (in feet)	Type	Build	Duration	Reuse	Description
Rune of Serenity	Level 14	Grimnir	40	150	Heal - Bless	1s	9s	10s	Heals target for 389 over 9s. Effect will also hit 1 ally within 360 units from the original target, and 1 ally within 360 units from that target, healing up to 6 allies total. Effect will not hit the same target more than once.
Rune of Cleansing	Level 16	Core	25	150	Magic Attack	0s	0s	5s	Removes a Curse or Ailment from target.
Rune of Cleaving	Level 18	Grimnir	30	CAE	Magic Attack	0s	9s	10s	Deals 349 damage over 9s. Arc: 120, radius: 65ft.
Blessing of Valaya	Level 20	Grimnir	60	150	Group Heal	3s	0s	0s	Heals 540 damage to all group members.
Rune of Sundering	Level 25	Core	40	PBAE	Crowd Control - Curse	0s	0s	60s	PBAE Knockback targets. Radius: 30ft.
Protection of the Ancestors	Level 30	Grungni	35	100	Buff - Bless	0s	60s	3 min	Increases target group member's Wounds by 4 for 1 minute. Heals target for value of HP increase. Wounds buffs stack largest.
Spellbinding Rune	Level 35	Valaya	30	100	Magic - Curse	1s	5s	30s	Deals 399 damage over 5s and silences target for 5s.
Oath Rune of Sanctuary	Level 40	Core	25	100	Rune Buff	0s	10 min	10 min	Increases target group member's Toughness by 2 for 1 hour.
	=Sub Ability=	Core	Free	Self	Resurrection	0s	0s	0s	Self resurrect.
Master Rune of Fury	Grungni x5	Grungni	25	960	Deployable	2s	30s	30s	GTAE deployable. Group members in the radius have a 20% chance on attack to proc a 50 point AP heal. Radius: 65ft.
Rune of Fortune	Grungni x9	Grungni	30	100	Magic Attack	2s	0s	0s	Deals 299 and heals defensive target for damage dealt.
Rune of Binding	Grungni x13	Grungni	35	100	Magic Attack	0s	3s	20s	Deals 337 damage over 3s. Stuns target for 3s.
Master Rune of Speed	Valaya x5	Valaya	30	960	Deployable	0s	30s	30s	GTAE deployable. Groupmates within the radius have their buildup times reduced by 0.25s. Radius: 65ft.
Rune of Burning	Valaya x9	Valaya	20/2s	100	Magic Attack	0s	3s	11s	Channeled. Deals 299 damage every 2s for 6s. Setback chance: 100%. (-1 step penalty).
Rune of Fate	Valaya x13	Valaya	30	100	Magic Attack	0s	24s	20s	Deals 948 damage over 24s and heals your defensive target for the amount of damage dealt.
Master Rune of Adamant	Grimnir x5	Grimnir	30	960	Deployable	2s	30s	30s	GTAE deployable. Heals groupmates in the radius by 150 every 3s for 60s. Radius: 65ft.
Rune of Battle	Grimnir x9	Grimnir	45	150	Buff - Magic Attack	2s	15s	60s	Buff a ally. That ally deals 249 to enemies in the radius every 3s for 15s. Radius: 20ft.
Grimnir's Fury	Grimnir x13	Grimnir	35	PBAE	Resurrection	5s	10s	3 min	Resurrects group members within radius. Heals them to 50% health. Increases damage of resurrected friendlies by 20% for 10s.

Morale

Yeah I know ye see others castin' runes an' not be payin' fer them. When ye have practiced yer skills enough, then ye be learnin' ta use Morale abilities. As ye be learnin' more of 'em, ye can swap 'em around by pressin' Shift an' right click ta remove th' old one, an' then click an' drag a new Morale ability of th' proper rank ta th' empty slot.

What be Morale? Morale be built up as ye fight an' win. See, there be four ranks ta Morale abilities, an' each rank be buildin' on th' previous rank. So ta cast a Rank 3 Morale ability, ye must 'ave built up enough Morale ta be turnin' on th' activation fer Ranks 1 an' 2 before it builds up enough fer th' Rank 3 ability ta be activated. If'n ye use a Morale ability, it uses up all th' Morale ye built up. Then ye Morale pool be startin' all over agai

Ye watch fer th' correct time ta be usin' these abilities, because they only be ready after ye been fightin' fer a few minutes. Be usin' it too soon, an' ye might be wishin' ye had it later. There be Morale abilities ta damage opponents while healin' yer group, or big single-target heals. It all be dependin' on what ye loaded in th' slot.

Don' use th' same Oath Rune on each party member.

WARHAMMER ONLINE
AGE OF RECKONING

Use natural terrain ta attack
Destruction unseen.

Morale

Name	Level	Rank	Range	Duration (in feet)	Description
Divine Favor	Level 8	Rank 1	150	0s	Heals target for 1,800.
Rampaging Siphon	Level 12	Rank 2	PBAE	0s	PBAE that deals 600 and heals the group for 100% of the value.
Steal Life	Level 16	Rank 1	100	9s	Magic attack that deals 900 over 9s. Self heals 50% of the damage dealt.
Focused Mind	Level 20	Rank 2	Self	10s	For 10s, build times are reduced by 50%. Character purges and is immune to Silence, Disarm, Root, Snare, and Setback.
Divine Protection	Level 24	Rank 3	Group	10s	Group buffs each group member with an ablative that absorbs the next 1,500 of melee damage, with a maximum duration of 10s.
Rune of Insanity	Level 28	Rank 1	100	0s	Deal 600 damage to target. Lower target's AP by 200.
Mountain Spirit	Level 32	Rank 2	Group	30s	Increase the group's armor by +33/level and resists by +12.6/level for 30s.
Rune of Rebirth	Level 36	Rank 3	Group	10s	Self heal for 1,200 and 2,400 over 9s.
Alter Fate	Level 40	Rank 4	PBAE	9s	PBAE resurrection for group members. Resurrected targets also get a HoT that heals 1,200 over 9s.
Rune of Ending	Grungni x15	Rank 4	Group	0s	Deals 1,200 damage to all enemies in 30ft radius and heals group members for damage dealt.
Valaya's Shield	Valaya x15	Rank 4	Group	15s	Heals group members 2,400 over 15s and gives 25 AP/s for 15s.
Rune of Skewering	Grimnir x15	Rank 4	Group	0s	Deals 2,400 damage to all targets in radius. Arc: 120, radius: 65ft.

Tactics

Name:	Level:	Description:
Swift Runes	Level 15	Cooldowns on Oath Rune click abilities are reduced by 30s
Cleansing Vitality	Level 21	Rune Of Cleansing will now heal your defensive target for (HH*1.5)*0.6 over 9s if an effect was successfully removed
Regenerative Shielding	Level 27	Each tick of Rune Of Regeneration has 25% chance to increase target's armor by 26.4/level for 10 sec and reduces incoming armor penetration by 100% (No penetration applied)
Blessings of Grungi	Level 31	Critical heals also place a buff on target that increases values of heals targeted at him by 25% for 10 seconds.
Potent Runes	Level 33	Rune of Striking and Rune of Immolation are undefendable.
On Your Feet!	Level 35	Rune Of Life, Rune Of Sanctuary, and Grimnir's Fury will heal the target (HH*1.3)*1.33*0.6 over 5s and grant 70 AP when the target is ressed.
Sundered Motion	Level 37	Rune of Sundering also applies a 40% snare for 10s and has its reuse lowered to 20s.
Thick-Skulled	Level 39	Removes setback chance when casting Grungi's Gift, Rune of Mending, and Rune of Serenity.
Runic Blasting	Grungi x3	Increases crit chance of Rune Of Fire, Grungni's Gift, and Rune Of Striking by 15%.
Ancestor's Blessing	Grungi x7	Healing abilities have a 25% chance to also increase the target's AP by 50 (can't give AP to yourself).
Rune of Nullification	Grungi x11	Critical attacks reduce healing in target by 100% for 5s.
Immolating Grasp	Valata x3	Each tick of Rune of Immolation has a 25% chance to snare target by 40% for 5s and drain 30 AP.
Earth's Shielding	Valata x7	Each attack against a Rune of Shielding debuffs a random stat of the attacker by 3/level for 10s.
Efficient Runecarving	Valata x11	Each tick of Rune of Mending has 20% chance to make next Rune of Immolation free AP and each tic of Rune of Immolation has a 20% to make the next Rune of Mending Insta-cast.
Extended Battle	Grimnir x3	Increases radii of Rune Of Cleaving and Rune Of Might by 50%.
Concussive Runes	Grimnir x7	Attacks in the path of Grimnir have a 25% chance to detaunt targets hit (50%, 15s).
Ancestor's Echo	Grimnir x11	Heals have a 25% chance to give the target (HH*1.3) absorb.
Stoutness Of Stone	Level 11	Reduces the duration of Knockdown/Stun effects on you by 50%
Stubbornness	Level 17	Increases Coporeal Resist by +6.3 per level of the character.
Ancestral Inheritance	Level 23	Increases Armor by +16.5 per level of the character.

Tactics

Th' best thing 'bout Tactics be they be changeable wit' only a click of th' mouse. Ye earn Stoutness of Stone, th' first Tactic ability, at Rank 11. It'll be providin' 11 points o' Toughness. Six Tactic slots be available eventually. Some ye earn fer livin'. Some ye earn fer doin'. Some ye earn fer havin' friends ta drink ale wit' an' tell gold stories. They unlock as ye gain experience, so at Rank 21, ye'll be havin' six Tactics abilities an' two slots ta put 'em in. This be where ye be settin' yerself apart: changin' yerself 'round dependin' on yer environment.

Tactics can modify "career" abilities when ye be wantin' or need ta modify yer role, e'en causin' ye ta do things ye wouldn't normally be doing, which can make assigning roles easier in a group. Ya might see a tank be usin' Focused Offense because it be causin' more damage, but it reduces defense an' agro generation, so it pull 'im away from's normal guardian role.

When ye be travelin' all by yerself, then ye be wantin' ta use Divine Fury an' Stoutness of Stone. These let ye take an' deal more damage ta yer enemies. What if ye are travelin' with ye friends an' ye be deep in th' earth? Then start usin' Regenerative Shielding an' Blessing of Grungni. This configuration be th' best fer th' group, increasin' their armor an' help'n yer heals work better. Ye needn't be goin' back ta town or havin' ta get help fer anyone because ye be makin' th' change as ye go along.

So as me great-pappy used ta say, "If worms had machine guns, birds wouldn't eat 'em." There's just no way ta talk 'bout all th' possibilities ye might find yerself in, so try different Tactics an' find what makes ye happy.

Mastery

Which ancestor'll ye be followin' ta learn yer Mastery skills? Fer a Rune Priest, there are three paths ta choose: th' Path of Grungni, th' Path of Valaya, an' th' Path of Grimnir. There be no path that be all healin', nor any that be turnin' ye inta a small cannon ta be killin' everything instead o' healin'.

Th' Mastery abilities be like yer regular abilities, an' be balanced in what they can do. Th' key ta 'em is that some fall into th' class o' Tactics, some others be usin' action points ta activate off th' spell bar, an' some e'en be requirin' a Rank 4 Morale activation.

Th' Path of Grungni be allowin' ye ta focus massive power in either healin' allies or crushin' foes. However, Grungni tends ta focus on single cast abilities that are not time related. Thus, 'is path allows a character ta bring massive healin' or massive damage ta yer targets, but not over time. This path will be useful if ye be targetin' a main tank, an' there be backup healers fer th' party.

Th' Path of Valaya be fer them who be seekin' Mastery, an' is more of a traditionalist path fer those what have th' patience of th' stone beneath their feet. Ye slowly builds up yer allies until they can stand as unbreakable pillars against th' tides of Destruction, or, as surely as th' rain wears at th' mountain, crush th' enemies o' yer ancestors who be foolish enough ta stand against ye.

Th' Path of Grimnir be fer those who enjoy area-effecting abilities an' hittin' more than one greenskin at a time. If ye take this path, ye can cause an entire party ta stand back up after a bad fight an' return ta crushin' the foes with renewed vigor. Or mayhaps crush an opposin' force all by yerself.

So ye'll be earnin' a total of 25 Mastery points after hittin' Rank 40. Each skill tree requires a total of 15 points fer maximum ability in that tree. Yet, each ability in that tree ye decide ta take will be costin' one point ta activate plus th' cost ta reveal that ability. So th' initial ability will cost ye three Mastery points ta activate an' one more ta learn it, fer a total of four points ta use that ability. Activation of each subsequent ability costs three more points. So it is possible ta max out one path, but ye will not be able ta activate any other skills. If ye choose not ta activate some, or not ta reach th' top rank, then ye can spread yer Mastery abilities across th' trees. However ye can put together an' spend a maximum of 25 points is what ye be havin' ta work wit.

Remember, Mastery abilities ye cannot be changin' on th' fly. Fer that ye'll have ta find a trainer so he can reset ye.

Renown

As ye prob'ly know by now, there be three levels of Renown abilities, an' ye must spend 20 points in each ta access th' rest. It's up ta ye ta decide th' best way ta spend 'em.

If ye spends some time killin' greenies an' their Chaos friends, ye should be Rank 11 in yer abilities an' have Renown of at least Rank 5, dependin' on how much time ye spend in RvR instead of takin' on tasks. At Renown Rank 5, ye will have five points ta spend. If most of yer time be spent healing instead o' hurtin', pay four points inta Resolve an' one point inta Fortitude. Ye might wanna reverse that an' increase yer Toughness wit' Fortitude if ye need ta get hurt less when ye get hit.

At Rank 21, ye'll have six Mastery points ta spend in your chosen tree an' probably Renown Rank 10, meanin' ye also gets 10 points ta spend with th' Renown Trainer. Consider spendin' these points ta continue buildin' up Resolve an' Fortitude, then start gainin' Acumen.

As ye be reachin' Rank 31, ye've gained most of yer regular abilities an' now be havin' a total of 16 points in Mastery an' 18 worth of Renown—if ye've slain enough Destruction ninnies ta have reached Rank 20, that is. If'n that be so, increase Acumen ta II an' be raisin' Resolve ta III.

Finally, when ye have reached Rank 40 an' have 30 Renown ranks, ye will have 25 Mastery an' 30 Renown points ta spend in character development. Fer a Rune Priest, this means ye should have picked yer Mastery path an' be well on yer way ta Mastery with Resolve IV, Fortitude III, Acumen II, an' Sage II fer your Renown abilities.

Now ye be at max rank fer abilities, but ye need ta fight on th' warfront ta gain Renown points until ye reach Rank 60. When ye have reached this exalted state, th' ancestors will be beamin' down at ye an' th' earth will purr at yer every boot fall. There, yer Renown abilities might look like Resolve IV, Fortitude III, Acumen III, Sage II, Spiritual Refinement I, Focused Power I, Vigor I, Reinforcement I.

Keep th' main tank as th' defensive target fer big heals.

Solo Play

As a Rune Priest, ye'll be more than capable o' adventuring on yer own, though ye'll always 'ave an important role ta play in healing a group of adventurers. Because of yer limitation ta wearin' relatively light armor, ye'll take a fair bit of damage while adventurin' alone. But in spite of that, yer healin' abilities let ye bring th' fight ta th' enemy while ye remain fairly free from injury...or at least keep ye from bein' injured fer long!

When ye first starts out, th' reclaimed mine in Ekrund is still in a precarious position an' may be lost at any moment if yerself an' yer fellow beardlings don't turn th' tide. Clear th' Anvil o' them nasty Squigs and complete th' other tasks as ye promised Ol' King Grudgebearer. Then ye'll be led outside ta th' first public quest area. Once that mess is cleaned up, ye should be Rank 6 an' travelin' ta th' inn at th' Redhammer Station, yer next home while ye quest in th' Mount Bloodhorn RvR area.

Yer ability ta heal durin' a fight is a major benefit in gainin' rank in solo play. Because ye be healin' yerself, ye be progressin' faster, with no or little reliance on potions or downtime between fights. Use yer Rune of Immolation when ye reach Rank 2 ta pull th' monster ta ye, then be castin' Rune of Striking. Just as it reaches ye, swing yer staff an' follow up with another Rune of Immolation. Once ye get Oath Rune of Power at Rank 4, use it as a buff an' a way ta cause additional damage ta your opponent.

As ye gain abilities, ye can incorporate a Rune of Fire or Rune of Cleaving into th' mix fer yet another way ta cause damage ta Destruction. As ye grow in ranks, it is reflected in th' output of these abilities—th' Rune of Striking just gains power as ye gain ranks an' become more experienced at castin' it. Ye will be usin' most of th' same abilities at Rank 20 that ye do at Rank 4 or that ye might at Rank 40.

Rescue Bugman's Best from th' train wreck an' get ready ta unearth new treasure an' old enemies as ye head fer th' Marshes of Madness an' Barak Varr. There be numerous public quests in th' area, makin' it easy ta fill in th' Influence bar. It's also a great way ta pick up experience an' roll fer PQ loot ta help get new gear.

Like th' rest o' th' Dwarfs, ye should pick yer craftin' skills in this zone so ye can start ta gain ability. If ye don't keep up on it, ye'll find yourself unable ta use them in higher zones. Keep an eye on yer opponent before ye attack, an' mind ye will find champions here. Easy my steel-toed foot! They be very tough opponents fer a beardling like ye.

Here ye enter yer first RvR area, accessible by us an' our lovely greenskin neighbors—make me an' yer ancestors proud! Start earnin' Renown points here an' usin' 'em ta adjust abilities an' find th' path that makes ye happy. Renown points be earnable only in an RvR settin', an' ye can earn 'em best by healin' th' party in th' fight against Destruction.

Beyond th' Marshes of Madness, ye'll climb th' mountains ta Black Fire Pass. This area contains more than one scenario, so be makin' sure when ye join that ye be joinin' th' one ye want ta fight in.

Use Oath Rune of Power fer melee an' magic characters.

Find a party. It's a lot more fun ta die with friends.

When goin' inta a dungeon, 'ave a well-balanced group an' multiple healers.

There be all kinds of hidden lore an' treasure in th' world, so take th' time ta look. Ye might find a new hammer under a rock, or an ability written on a scroll hidden under a bed. It be said that th' Blue Face Orcs have th' secret War Paint hidden inside th' hut.

As ye leave th' Badlands an' continue on yer journey ta reach th' Eight Peaks an' join yer fellow Oathbearers, make sure ta stop off at th' Shrine of Grimnir in Kadrin Valley ta clear th' area of Ungors an' reclaim th' altar. Wieldin' a Doomstriker Staff while ye bring forth th' power that lies just below th' surface of Thunder Mountain will be worth th' visit, I assure ye. Ye can also travel ta th' High Elves an' carry word of how th' Dwarfs fare in their struggle, or help th' manlings in Praag stand against th' forces of Destruction.

Group Play

Ye have th' ability ta channel th' power o' th' earth ta provide oft-needed healin' ta fellow adventurers. Some o' that ability may be channeled as "heals over time" ta help offset minor damage. Save yer group heals fer when more than one party member is under duress. When things get really hectic, use th' single-target heals; they be capable o' bringin' a friend from 'is ancestors' doorstep all th' way back ta full fighting strength!

With all that healing ability, ye also has th' power ta call upon th' earth an' place runes that channel that power into fellow adventurers, increasing their abilities an' making them more formidable in combat.

A Rune Priest don't have ta be in th' front ranks ta do 'is job. It's best fer ye ta stand off ta th' side an' play a role in th' battle as both attacker an' medic. Th' best Rune Priests will help slay their enemies while keeping their friends in good shape. A sense of timin' also be critical, because ye be havin' multiple abilities ta draw upon. Knowin' when ta use th' Morale ability an' keepin' th' right Tactics active will be th' measure of yer effectiveness, fer good or ill.

When ye be part of a party of fellow adventures, yer role depends on what type of event ye be participatin' in. This is where th' ability ta change yer Tactics is perhaps most useful at later ranks. When participatin' in a quest group, ye'll want ta be causin' damage an' might need ta cast a targeted heal on th' tank. If your group is forgin' ahead with just a lot of DPS characters, use th' Rune of Valaya. When ye travel across th' land as part of a party, there shouldn't be a lot of healin' goin' on.

Now if ye be in a PQ, th' initial stage be much like normal questin'. Th' enemies be not too strong, an', unless someone pulls more 'n than they should, it'll be more useful ta cast damagin' spells than healin'. When th' PQ tips an' goes ta th' second or final stage, things be changin'. Here ye'll want ta make sure ye have th' main tank as yer defensive target fer big targeted heals if needed; use group heals ta keep everyone else on their feet.

If ye be in a scenario, then ye be wantin' ta cast group heals an' use abilities that heals th' scenario party fer th' amount of damage that th' spell causes. Destruction forces can be stalwart foes, an' yer party will need yer strength ta stand victorious. Rampaging Siphon be a nice way ta kill Destruction an' heal yer party. Ye can watch th' Renown points rack up when castin' Rune of Serenity an' Blessing of Valaya. Be usin' th' Tab key ta keep an offensive target up for when ye can attack. An' don't be forgettin' ta buff yer party before th' timer clicks ta zero. And then do so again periodically throughout th' event, because they'll most likely die an' need ta be rebuffed.

A Survivor's Burden

Deoren stood at the edge of insanity as she watched her comrades become casualties. The Battle of Bitterstone had taken a toll on her fellow beardlings. Dwarfs never forget, and she knew that although she might find new travelers as she journeyed to Black Fire Pass, it would be these memories that would drive her to rid the world of those damn greenskins. She turned with a heavy heart and clouded disposition to make her way to Red Mountain Inn. There she would find a nice ale with which to toast those who fell and remember her ancestors before leaving for the Marshes of Madness.

She only hoped that her new abilities granted by Valaya and Grimnir would be enough to stop more friends from falling to steel and the daemonic magic used against them. She had heard stories of lost treasure, but didn't want to lose more companions in search of it. She had to seek out new masters and learn the ancient lore to be steadfast enough to bolster her companions.

Whether she were to travel alone or with other adventurers, Deoren would need to be resolute in her Oath to earn a Doomstriker and gain entrance to Karak Eight Peaks. She drank the last of her ale and uttered an oath to her ancestors. For outside the door Destruction waited, and one or the other would be speaking to their ancestors in person tonight!

BREAKING PLAYER HEADS AN' GAININ' RENOWN (PVP)

When ye be PvPing, ye might as well be holdin' a sign that say's "Hit me, I'm th' fraggin' healer!" Priests be targets early an' often. So if ye choose ta play a Rune Priest, don' be th' first one ta run out an' present a target. Let th' tanks run out first while ye use cover ta block th' enemy from seein' ye. If that means ye hide in th' bushes or under an overturned cart like some yella-bellied High Elf, so be it.

Fer a player ta participate in PvP in a non-RvR portion of th' world, one party or th' other must have RvR activated. So ye can run up ta an enemy camp an' they can't attack ye—unless ye turn on RvR or attack someone with RvR turned on. If ye see someone runnin' through a zone an' they look ta be all alone, but they 'ave RvR on, make triple sure it's not a trap. Once ye attack them, ye become RvR an' th' hidden Marauder an' Zealot gets ta play nine pins with yer skull.

When ye're first startin' out in PvP, ye needs ta keep a balance 'tween offense an' defense. Start by castin' a Rune of Immolation an' then nuke 'em with Rune of Striking. Repeat as necessary until they fall down. If ye be under attack, healin' duties should fall ta Grungni's Gift. Before combat stats, be sure ta use Oath of Power on e'eryone who be in yer group. As ye gain ranks an' abilities, yer selection will grow, an' ye can add a Spellbinding Rune ta silence spellcasters, or Rune of Sundering ta throw melee opponents away.

When ye go into a scenario, ye'll be given th' opportunity ta join a scenario party. This is th' best way ta gain RP fer a Rune Priest, because ye'll be usin' a lot o' group healin'. If th' parties are formed correctly, they'll be balanced, so set yer defensive target ta th' main tank in yer party. Make sure ta stack Rune of Regeneration with Rune of Serenity. This will give th' main tank a huge healin' over time. Then cast Protection of th' Ancestors ta increase their health an', if ye took th' Path of Grimnir, ye can scribe a Master Rune of Adamant fer added health every three seconds ta all party members.

Yer capable o' healin' as well as attackin' multiple targets at once. So while yer tank be yer main responsibility, ye can support th' rest o' th' party by castin' Rune of Cleaving, Rune of Skewering, an' Rune of Might without even havin' an offensive target. Just keep yer defensive target alive an' watch Destruction fall.

FULLY BEARDED DWARFS

Ah! Good ta see ye again! I see ye 'ave been practicin' since I last saw ye. Glad ye learned th' lessons well, fer ye saved me life an' brought me back from th' brink o' death itself. Now if only I had a sip of Bugman's Best ta stand me on my feet an' make me feel whole. Did ye know that one whiff of that heavenly brew will cause a fully bearded dwarf ta express their undyin' love fer ye? But don't be believin' that. They have no care fer yer heart, only yer drink, an' ye be sharin' that only with those who stand beside ye in battle.

Now if ye don't mind, I think I'll find me pack an' drink a little ale as I find me way back ta th' warfront. Ye did a right nice job mendin' me an' sortin' me out. Yes, I'm needin' ta watch me back better when travelin' through th' Badlands, fer there be foes at every turn in th' road. But all I ask is that when I finally leave this earth, it remembers Deoren stood in her defense an' gave a right fine accountin' ta her foes. Then when I stand before me ancestors, I can hold me head high while they recount me victories.

Ye 'ave ta fight ta win. There's no future in hidin' in th' back o' th' group castin' complete heal every 45 seconds.

Put potions in yer spell bar fer easy access.

BRIGHT WIZARD

By Ewe

Everyone! Get back to the camp! The barbarians are fleeing Grimmenhagen Village—no need to stay here any longer.

You, there! Yes, you! Come here, peasant. I wish to have a word with you. I saw what you did in that last battle. Yes, I know it was you who started the last house on fire. Oh, do not worry. I will not judge you for this. Quite the opposite, I can tell you why you did it. You do not fully understand what you did, or even how, so I will explain to you exactly what happened.

For a small second, Aqshy, the Red Wind of Magic, flowed through your body. When you struck at that barbarian, the fiery nature of Aqshy passed through you, into that house. Granted, you only succeeded in starting it ablaze, but still, you showed an ounce of what it is to be a Bright Wizard.

Yes, peasant, you heard me correctly. I think I should very well know a novice Bright Wizard when I see one—I am one myself. Who do you think was raining all that destruction down upon our enemies while the lot of you were trying to drive off a barbarian horde with pitchforks? I assure you, it wasn't your "heroic" and wholly ill-advised stand with farming implements that caused them to flee. In fact, I'm positive you would have all been lying in pools of your own blood had I not arrived in this dreary little burg when I did.

Ahh, I see you have questions. Yes, of course. They always have questions but are never happy with the answers I provide. Right now, you have but a hint of fire in those bleak, dull, peasant eyes of yours. Nurture that fire and it can become a blazing inferno of untapped power. Or it will kill you.

No! Don't waste your breath and my time with your questions. I already know what you're going to ask. Oh, very well. I know that look well; you seek power. Trust me, there is all the power you can handle as a Bright Wizard. Power, however, always—*always*—comes with a price. Are you ready for the backlashes of power? Do you have what it takes to continually push and push your magic till you've given so much that your very next spell may kill you as well as your enemy?

Oh, you may think so. They all think so. They all think so until they're left a burning corpse in the middle of some unknown and forgotten battlefield.

What is a Bright Wizard?

The appeal of wielding one of the most destructive forces in the Empire is a powerful craving that draws all who have the touch of Aqshy to the ranks of the Bright Wizards—or at least the ranks of their novices, for graduation rates are slim and self-inflicted mortality alarmingly high. Those who survive inevitably enjoy war. Carnage infuses the very fiber of their beings, and they are good at it.

Bright Wizards find little comfort in others. They do not learn to heal, and often have to be knocked unconscious and drug behind a line of soldiers, "minions" in their eyes. They uncover a few other tricks while adventuring, but Bright Wizards are tasked to do but one thing in battles: To purge through purifying flame, bring forth the Red Wind of Fire, and rain destruction upon any force that dares stand in the Emperor's path.

Bright Wizards must be wary, though, because their power is the most dangerous to wield. As they battle, they build up excess stores of "Combustion." Combustion knows no friend. Should a Wizard's Combustion rise too high; the destructive forces so precariously unleashed upon our enemies will turn to strike at their master. Bright Wizards who survive learn a fine balance that is the difference between killing the enemy and killing themselves. The second reason it is perilous to destroy one's foes in brilliant pyrotechnics is that survivors cannot help but take notice. From mindless undead to the most cunning forces of Destruction, anyone who stands against a Bright Wizard will recognize the imminent danger and do everything in its power to slay him. The matter is worsened by the Wizards' choice of raiment, which fails to provide any but the lightest of protection, but instead augments their already keen powers. "Indeed, each Bright Wizard is disciple, Templar, and inquisitor of the philosophy that the strongest defense is a ferocious offense."

—Aleister Schreiber, Scholar Emeritus, University of Nuln

STARTING AS A BRIGHT WIZARD

All Bright Wizards are granted the same starting equipment. Of course, it's nothing special—after all, we aren't completely sure you won't blow yourself up casting your first Fireball—but it does keep you from running around nude. Considering the number of robes and staves we lose to self-inflicted immolation, you're lucky we provide anything at all. If you're willing to work, you'll have no problem replacing all of it quickly enough. Quests and monsters are all around us, and everyone will be fighting for your help. Bright Wizards are the most eligible quest mates in the Empire!

As you can see, you're pretty bare as far as a soldier of the Empire stands—or a little schoolgirl of the Empire, for that matter. The main way to raise these stats is through gaining Ranks. The more things you set on fire, the more fantastic you'll become! You'll also improve your stats with new equipment. Each method comes easily at first, but as you progress, expect greater tests of your abilities, which also grow as you gain Ranks.

Grimmenhagen Village, or what's left of it, is where your journey begins. Oh yes, I have not forgotten that little conflagration you started there earlier. It's still burning, actually, as well as the rest of them. So we've sent Lanric to ask for assistance from other adventurers and townsfolk. He tells us there are villagers still trapped inside the houses, and the Northmen are still marauding, so you'll want to see him as soon as we're done.

You've been given a map of your local area. People who wish your assistance have a lit journal floating over their heads; it's hard to miss. Tasks you've accepted will be marked, so you can locate them without wandering around too lost. If for some reason you forget what to do, simply open your journal and read the passage that explains exactly what you should be looking for.

Another notable person in town is Viktor Riese from the Order of the Griffon. He welcomes newly drafted soldiers, and he will direct you to where your help is needed most. Seek out Elsa Schmidt once you've gained a rank or two, and she'll train you in even more advanced abilities.

The Grey Lady Coaching Inn has quite a few people of interest, surprisingly many for such a dismal place. Be sure to see if our local Dwarf Orgni Stouthammer has any work for you. You'll never have to wonder where he is. Dwarfs are always either smashing greenskins, drinking, or some combination of the two. Ruth Winslow is our local bartender. She keeps Orgni as deep as she can in the drink. I'd also heard a rumor that there was a local magician in there doing magic tricks—Barnabus, I believe his name was. He has no real magical talent, but the villagers seem to be impressed by his illusions and tricks, so we tolerate his presence.

A village on fire is a good beginning for any Bright Wizard, I would say! Do as many tasks as you can in this area, and you should easily attain Rank 4. In addition to those tasks, to the northeast, the Ravenhill Vanguard has a small detachment pillaging the countryside and kidnapping local farmers. You would be wise to assist in that public quest and gain the rewards that come with helping out.

After all your tasks have been completed, you'll be given leave to continue your journey to the north. Meet the Griffon Sergeant and participate in the Guns of Nordenwatch scenario along the way. It's an excellent chance to test your mettle against the forces of Destruction.

Use your surroundings. In every zone and scenario, there will be high spots, nooks, and crannies for you to hide in.

Getting the drop on the enemy is as important in PvP as it is in PvE. If you can fire four or five abilities before they even reach you, chances are good you'll win the fight.

That is some ratty garb we've given you, isn't it? Well, don't worry too much about your outerwear for now. Armor is important, do not misunderstand me. However, a Bright Wizard does

BRIGHT WIZARD GEAR

not use such meager foils to protect his body, but instead to increase the destructive powers of the fire within! You cannot wear anything but cloth armor anyway, which means that your defensive abilities will be, at best, paper thin. Likewise, you will never wield a mighty great sword in battle, but instead a staff much like mine. Oh, yours will not be as grand as mine—yet—but in due time, novice, in due time.

Look for weapons and armor that increase your Intelligence, which increases the magical damage of your spells and abilities. That should be your number-one priority, which you'd know if you've been listening at all! Additionally, Intelligence reduces the chance that enemies will interrupt your spells, which is also very important.

Increasing your Wounds will grant you more hit points for those rare occasions you find yourself face to face with an adversary—in other words, when you have made a very big mistake. Willpower also increases your chance to interrupt enemy casters, most importantly their healers. Being able to interrupt their spells while destroying them with fire is a nice synergy, I would say. Lastly, increasing your Initiative decreases your chance to be critically hit in general, which is good because you lack other defenses.

Next to those skills, I choose to raise my resistances to the other magics one can find in the world. You will face many enemies in your travels. Some choose to wield axes and swords, and others strike with the forces around them. Having resistances to those other paths of magic will give

Strengths

· Ignite lots of damage in a short period of time.

· Inflict that damage from long range, up to 100 feet away.

· Bright Wizards have abilities that disperse, eradicate, or otherwise control crowds.

· Group enhancements increase everyone's damage even more.

· You can shed monster attacks with Smoke Screen.

Being in our ranks will have its benefits, novice. You'll be one of the most destructive forces any enemy can come across—and usually the last force they come across. You'll be granted many abilities that inflict a massive amount of damage from very long range. Because of the obvious threat you pose, many enemies will rush your location simply because they fear that, if given time, you'll finish them all. Silence their casters with Choking Smoke or heat the very metal of the enemy's weapons with Burning Iron—which disarms them. Either power renders your foe impotent.

Weaknesses

· Low hit points.

· Cloth armor, if clothing can indeed be called "armor."

· Very low melee damage.

· Potential for power to backlash.

· No healing ability.

Being all-powerful, what on earth could a Bright Wizard fear? Trifles, really, but potentially damaging nonetheless. Bright Wizards will never have the fortitude of a warrior. What little armor you're granted is used for its stats and increasing your own damage—not protecting you. You wield a staff, yes, but it's merely another tool to enhance the fire you rain upon your foes' heads. And of course, you must take care with those powers lest they backfire and rain on you instead. That brings me to the last handicap Bright Wizards must learn to overcome: the complete lack of any healing ability. Your fire can cauterize a wound, but not undo the damage. Keep your healers close and your enemies on the far side of a Fireball.

Interact with everything you can touch. There are lots of secrets in the world, and you would be wise to find as many as you can.

SKILLS AND ABILITIES

Abilities

These abilities you've discovered by accident are dangerous powers, novice, and you should use them wisely—or, in your case, sparingly. We will train you to harness two to begin.

Fireball is a direct damage spell from the Incineration path. You conjure a fiery missile that streaks toward your opponent. It deals Elemental damage to your target on impact and additional damage over five seconds. Ignite is a damage-over-time hex from the Immolation path that causes your target to burst into flames, dealing Elemental damage to that being over nine seconds.

Fireball and Ignite are the bread and butter of any Bright Wizard. We all use them, no matter how powerful we become. Both have a range of 100 feet—always use that to your benefit. Also learn their timing. Ignite is instantly cast the second you wish it to be. Fireball takes three seconds to develop. In combat, you usually open with Fireball and follow up with Ignite the very second that the Fireball hits. This is the way of the Bright Wizard: Surprise your enemy with both attacks in the same instant to inflict as much damage as possible in as little time possible. Incinerate continues to burn long enough to build another Fireball for your second volley.

The abilities you learn as you gain ranks are almost all designed for damage and destruction. Which ones you use will mostly depend on the situations you get yourself into. Abilities such as Choking Smoke, which renders the very air your foe is breathing damaging and makes it impossible for them to cast spells for a few seconds, are powerful for their ability to control specific situations. Time, my young novice, will always be your ally if you use these abilities properly. Give yourself time, and you will go far as a Bright Wizard. Rush into battle firing the wrong ability, and you might find yourself under some ugly Orc's boot...again.

One of your most useful abilities is, of course, Fireball. It's a good way to get the energy flowing for your symphony of rage. What about that dirty Goblin closing fast with an axe? Use Burning Iron to remove the very weapon he so dearly depends upon. Then immobilize the green brute with Fire Cage so you have a few moments to back off and summon more of our arcane carnage. Lacking defensive abilities, as we do, you need to use offensive spells creatively to make yourself a dangerous target.

Abilities

Name	Level	Path	Cost	Range (in feet)	Type	Build	Duration	Reuse	Description
Meltdown	Level 1	Core	Free	Nuke	Magic Attack	1s	0s	5s	Undefendable nuke; applies flat damage based on Combustion thresholds as follows. Drains all Combustion. 1-10: deals 41, 11-30: deals 82, 31-70: deals 165, 71-90: deals 330, 91-375: deals 412.
Ignite	Level 1	Immolation	35	Nuke	DoT - Elem - Hex	0s	9s	0s	Deals 549 burning DoT over 9 seconds. Delays damage until first tick. Builds 5 Combustion.
Fireball	Level 1	Incineration	30	100	Magic Attack - Elem	3s	0s	0s	Deals 600 damage. Builds 10 Combustion.
Sear	Level 2	Incineration	40	100	Magic Attack - Elem	1s	0s	5s	Deals 337. Builds 25 Combustion.
Shield of Aqsy	Level 3	Core	20	Self	Buff - Enchant	0s	10s	30s	Self only. Increases Armor by 24.75/level and decreases chance to be set back by 50% for 10s.
Smoke Screen	Level 4	Core	20	100	Magic Debuff	0s	15s	15s	Deals no damage. Detaunts target (50%, 15s).
Scorched Earth	Level 5	Conflagration	35	PBAE	Magic - Corp	0s	0s	0s	Deals 150 damage. Builds 20 Combustion. Radius: 30ft.
Flames of Rhuin	Level 6	Incineration	30	100	Buff - Elem - Enchant	0s	60 min	0s	Group buff. Adds a 25% chance to deal an additional 150 damage after hitting with any attack.

Mastery, Tactic, and Renown abilities can be easily changed, so experiment with each to find your mix. Don't copy anyone else's just because they say it's the best.

Abilities

Name	Level	Path	Cost	Range (in feet)	Type	Build	Duration	Reuse	Description
Boiling Blood	Level 7	Immolation	25	100	DoT - Corp - Hex	0s	15s	10s	Deals 648 damage over 15s and lowers target's Elemental resist by 9.45/level for 15s. Delays damage until first tick. Builds 5 Combustion.
Fiery Blast	Level 8	Conflagration	35	80	Magic - Elem	3s	0s	0s	Deals 375 damage. Radius: 20ft. Builds 20 Combustion.
Cauterize	Level 9	Core	25	Heal	Dispel	0s	0s	5s	Removes 1 injury from friendly target.
Fire Cage	Level 10	Core	30	PBAE	CC - Hex	0s	5s	20s	Root target for 5s. Radius: 30ft.
Pyroclastic Surge	Level 12	Incineration	30	Nuke	Magic - Corp - Hex	2s	0s	0s	Deals 349 damage. If target is Hexed, disorient by 1s for 3s. Builds 10 Combustion.
Detonate	Level 14	Immolation	40	80	Magic - Elem - Hex	0s	9s	10s	Requires target Hexed. Deal 187 damage to target and 249 damage over 9s to targets within 20ft. Builds 25 Combustion.
Flame Breath	Level 16	Conflagration	40	CAE	Magic - Elem	0s	9s	10s	Deals 598 damage over 9s. Arc: 90, radius: 40ft. Builds 20 Combustion. Deals damage initially.
Flame Shield	Level 18	Immolation	30	100	Buff - Elem - Enchant	0s	60 min	0s	Group buff. Adds a 25% chance to deal 75 damage back to the attacker when hit with a melee attack.
Burning Iron	Level 20	Incineration	35	Nuke	Magic - Corp - Hex	1s	0s	20s	Deals 187 damage and removes 50 AP. Builds 10 Combustion.
Rain of Fire	Level 25	Conflagration	25/2s	80	Magic - Elem	1s	10s	20s	GTAE channel. Deals 299 damage every 2s for 10s. Radius: 20ft. Setback override: 100%. Builds 15 Combustion.
Burnout	Level 30	Core	Free	Self	Self Buff	0s	0s	0s	Deals 262 damage to self. Gain 110 AP.
Slow Boil	Level 35	Immolation	30	Nuke	Magic - Corp - Hex	0s	10s	20s	Increases cooldowns of target's abilities by 5s. At the end of the effect, target takes 449 damage. Builds 5 Combustion.
Choking Smoke	Level 40	Conflagration	25	80	Magic - Corp - Hex	2s	3s	30s	Deals 249 damage and Silences the target and those around him for 5s. Builds 20 Combustion. Radius 20ft.
Funnel Power	Incineration x5	Incineration	Toggle	Self	Magic - Corp	0s	0s	60s	Toggle. While active, every magical attack deals an extra 112 damage and the Wizard takes 75.
Nova	Incineration x9	Incineration	40	Nuke	Magic - Elem	0s	0s	10s	Deals 412 damage. Builds 40 Combustion.
Fireball Barrage	Incineration x13	Incineration	30/1.5s	80	Magic - Corp	0s	3s	13s	Channeled. Deals 450 damage every 1.5s for 3s to initial target, deals 150 damage to all targets in radius. Radius: 20ft. Setback override: 100% chance. Builds 15 Combustion.
Playing with Fire	Immolation x5	Immolation	30	Nuke	Magic - Elem - Hex	0s	10s	30s	Reduces healing on target by 50%. When target is healed, he takes 187 damage instead.
Withering Heat	Immolation x9	Immolation	25/2s	Nuke	Magic - Corp	0s	6s	11s	Channeled. Deals 399 damage every 2s for 6s. Snares target by 40%. Setback override: 100%. Builds 15 Combustion.
Stop, Drop, and Roll	Immolation x13	Immolation	30	Nuke	Magic - Elem	0s	5s	20s	Requires target to be Ignited. Deals 262 damage. Knocks down target for 5s. Removes Ignite. Builds 10 Combustion.
Annihilate	Conflagration x5	Conflagration	25/s	PBAE	Magic - Corp	0s	3s	8s	Channeled. Deals 225 damage each 1s for 3s. Radius 30ft. Caster loses 75 health. Builds 15 Combustion.
Spreading Flames	Conflagration x9	Conflagration	30	80	Magic - Elem - Hex	0s	15s	20s	Requires target to be Hexed. Deals 499 damage over 15s to target. Each tick outputs second DoT as an AE that deals 150 over 3s. Radius: 20ft. Builds 10 Combustion.
Favorable Winds	Conflagration x13	Conflagration	25	LAE	Magic Attack - Corp	0s	10s	20s	Deals 648 damage over 15s and does a medium knockback.

Always be ready to use Smoke Screen, especially in public quests. Many monsters can kill you quickly, and you do a great deal of damage, so it's easy to draw their attention.

Morale

To cultivate our merciless streak, all Bright Wizards have abilities fueled by Morale, which builds as you unleash your beautiful fires upon our enemies. Morale is separated into four categories, with Rank 4 being the most powerful. Each rank requires more Morale to cast, though, and each casting entirely depletes your Morale. So you have to choose between casting a Rank 1 Morale ability fairly often, or wait for your meter to be full and launch the big Rank 4 abilities. If you're impatient, or the battle is about to end, go ahead and use whichever ability is available. If the battle is still raging, think before you act.

Which Morale ability you use could very well turn the tide of the battle. Some are designed to help you survive a little longer. Others are more damaging effects to add to your arsenal. Once you've gained enough ranks, you'll have a selection of Morale abilities to choose from. Choose those that you believe will be the most useful. I choose to increase my damage potential and keep enemies at bay a little longer, but you should choose ones that are best suited to you.

Morale

Name	Level	Rank	Range (in feet)	Duration	Description
Mage Bolt	Level 8	Rank 1	100	0s	Magic attack that deals 1,200 damage.
Siphon Power	Level 12	Rank 2	100	30s	Drain 200 AP from target and give to character. Decrease target's Intelligence by 4/level for 30s.
Misdirection	Level 16	Rank 1	Self	10s	Self buff. For 10s, magical attacks return 50% of the damage back to the caster (resulting in 50% less damage to the target).
Focused Mind	Level 20	Rank 2	Self	10s	For 10s, build times are reduced by 50%. Character purges and is immune to Silence, Disarm, Root, Snare, and setback.
Scintillating Energy	Level 24	Rank 3	100	7s	Target takes 1,200 + Stun for 7s.
Magic Dart	Level 28	Rank 1	100	0s	Magic attack that deals 600 damage and does a long knockback.
Ruin and Destruction	Level 32	Rank 2	PBAE	10s	PBAE. Deals 600 and Stun for 5s.
Heart of Fire	Level 36	Rank 3	Self	15s	Remove all Curses and Hexes, HoT for 2,400 over 15s.
Unleash the Winds	Level 40	Rank 4	PBAE	0s	PBAE that deals 1,800 and knocks back enemies.
The Burning Head	Incineration x15	Rank 4	100	0s	Deals 2,400 damage to target and 1,800 to enemies within 30ft of target. Reduces Morale of anyone hit by 600.
Wall of Fire	Immolation x15	Rank 4	CAE	8s	LAE. Deals 300/s to anyone touching it. Arc: 360ft, radius: 67ft.
Conflagration of Doom	Conflagration x15	Rank 4	100	8s	Deals 300/s to targets in the GTAE.

Tactics

Name	Level	Description
Emperor's Ward	Level 11	25% chance when attacked to absorb 262 damage for 10s.
Devour Energy	Level 13	25% of the time, spells cast also gain the character back 30 AP/3s. (Non-stacking, non-refreshing.)
Lingering Fires	Level 15	Pyroclastic Surge and Scorched Earth cause additional DoT (187.5 over 5s). Elemental damage.
Unwavering Faith	Level 17	Increases Spirit resist by 6.3/level of the character.
Endless Knowledge	Level 19	Increases Intelligence by 4/level of the character.
Fueled from Within	Level 21	Flames of Rhuin damage is increased to 225 and Flame Shield's damage is increased to 150.
Sigmar's Favor	Level 23	25% chance when healed to be healed for an additional 135.
Sleight of Hand	Level 25	Decreases threat by 50% on all attacks.
Power from the Ashes	Level 27	Vent returns 1:1 AP for Combustion lost.
Close Quarters	Level 29	Increases magic damage by 25% when under 45ft and decreases magic damage by 20% when over 45ft.
Flashfire	Level 31	When you are disrupted, your next non-instant spell is cast instantly.
Fan the Flames	Level 33	Increases radii of Rain of Fire and Detonate by 50%.
Distracting Fire	Level 35	Smoke Screen and Fire Cage have their reuse lowered by 7s.
Embrace the Flames	Level 37	Burnout deals 112 damage to self instead.
Crown of Fire	Level 39	Any time you are hit by a melee attack, 25% chance to Stun the attacker for 1s (no immunity).

Tactics

Tactics are what differentiate you from every other Bright Wizard in battle—after all, if we wished to be indistinguishable, we'd have gone with a less colorful class name. I choose only those that increase my destructive power. However, I also see other good choices and have multiple sets from which I can choose that evening's payload. For example, if I'm fighting the forces of Destruction alone, I'll equip Tactics that allow me to hit quickly and hard! For heroes who are as wise as we Bright Wizards are, being able to choose which abilities we think will be best for a certain situation not only helps you, but also helps the groups you're in.

I prefer inflicting damage to ensuring my own safety. After all, few carbonized beings are a threat to one's safety. However, some Bright Wizards are more cautious, and so choose Tactics that increase their own abilities with less risk. For example, the Concentrated Power Tactic allows me to do 10% more damage, but from a 10% shorter range. Therefore, I do more damage, but put myself closer to harm's way to do so.

I almost never change my Tactics because I've chosen the ones I believe to be the most useful to the way I fight, and it's my choice and only my choice. You will eventually need to make those choices as well, novice, but don't hesitate to try out different combinations.

Mastery

Mastery abilities are granted to high-ranking members of our order and allow you to specialize in a type of magic. No single path is the best choice. Each offers distinct advantages to the promising pyromancer, enabling a wide variety of direct abilities that require action points or Morale to use, or passive Tactics. You have three to choose from.

The Path of Immolation is for those who relish inflicting a lingering, painful death. Down that path you will find skills and abilities that help your magic last longer and deal more damage. Followers of this path tend to prefer casting a number of quick spells at several targets, one at a time, like a painter who flicks many dots onto the canvas to make a whole work of art. Because most of these abilities inflict damage over time, it's easy to apply a few damage-over-time spells to multiple targets and watch as they all slowly burn.

Tactics		
Name	Level	Description
Searing Vitality	Incineration x3	Sear heals self for 67% of the damage done.
Draining Burn	Incineration x7	Burning Iron deals 225 damage and gives 50 AP to the BW.
Burn Through	Incineration x11	Fireball and Pyroclastic Surge become undefendable.
Fuel to the Fire	Immolation x3	Increases durations of Ignite, Detonate, and Boiling Blood by 3s.
Ignition	Immolation x7	Each tick of Ignite gains 33% chance to reduce target's Elemental, Spirit, and Corporeal resist by 9.45/level for 5s and Armor by 24.75/level for 5s.
Smoldering Embers	Immolation x11	Immolation abilities have a 25% chance to reapply themselves when their duration ends or they are dispelled (maximum of 3 reapplications).
Explosive Force	Conflagration x3	Miscasts deals 50% of explosion damage in a PBAE of 30ft around you.
Fiery Reserves	Conflagration x7	Reduces cooldown on Flame Breath and Rain of Fire by 10s (to 0 and 10 respectively).
Wildfire	Conflagration x11	Fiery Blast, Scorched Earth, and Flamebreath gain a 25% chance to cause 112 pulsing damage every 1s for 5s to enemies in 30ft (but not the holder). Can only be affected by 1 pulse per second.

The Path of Incineration focuses on single targets and unleashing as much power upon them as possible. To that end it increases your Fireball, a core ability to any Bright Wizard, and makes your entire arsenal of single-target abilities do more damage and critically hit more often. This path is for Wizards with the nature of an assassin, those who want to burn down a single foe as efficiently and reliably as possible without thought of any others. It takes a keen mind to be able to focus only on one target while others scurry like ants about your line of fire, but the explosions are well worth it.

The Path of Conflagration is for those who wish to rain destructive power on a wide area of forces. (As I did to repel those greenskins and save your village....Oh, but that's right, it's still on fire. What a misfortune. Thank the gods I am not a peasant!) Not only does it increase your current barrage of area-effect abilities, but it grants even more powers and abilities of awesome destructiveness. Although it's not as damaging to any single target, there is something very satisfying about Raining Fire upon a group of enemies before they can even react. In this path, you find the most damaging of all our powers and abilities. However, using them also carries the greatest chance for backlash. Conflagration does not appeal to everyone. It grants many benefits, but is not for the faint of heart.

A character can earn only 25 Mastery points by Rank 40, so that leaves you with a few choices to specialize and adapt yourself toward the arsenal you feel is your ultimate path. Remember that no Bright Wizard may fully specialize in all three paths. Most are forced to specialize fully in one, or split between two. To fully specialize in one path means spending all but three of your total points, leaving you without any abilities or skills from the other two paths.

Sadly, you cannot reset Mastery abilities on the fly as if you were changing garments, or wenches. Once you choose, you have them until you return to a trainer, who can reset your specialization points and allow you to begin anew.

Renown

The last way you may further yourself, novice, is through gaining Renown. Renown is bestowed as you perform tasks for the forces of Order, or as you kill the forces of Destruction. The abilities it unlocks are a means to raising your own stats and powers directly.

Renown also has ranks, three in this case, and you must spend 20 Renown points in each rank to unlock the next one. Investing your Rank 1 points should be an easy decision: Intelligence, again, will be your first priority, or Fortitude if you find yourself dying a lot. So spending points on Acumen and Fortitude are good choices.

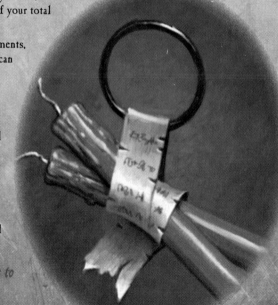

Lay down the damage! You are there to unleash hell, so get to it!

As you gain more Renown and open the second rank of abilities, you'll have more choices. Some Renown abilities even grant increased Renown points while tackling scenarios or taking keeps. If you've focused on gaining ranks while forgoing PvP combat, you may need to invest in this until you gain enough for Sage and the other important skills. No ability or skill is set in stone; choosing to respecialize is always an option once you've gotten more experience. Trial and error is a good way to decide which Renown abilities you would be most comfortable with come endgame sieges.

There are a couple notable abilities in the last rank of Renown, one of which is Focused Power, which increases your spell critical chance. Any Bright Wizard worth his hot sauce depends on massive damage, so increasing that even more is just a logical progression. As our Combustion level increases, our critical hit chance also increases, so this ability pushes your innate power even further – just less risk. Chaos Bane grants you more damage toward our invading neighbors, which is always a good choice if you plan on taking their cities and capitals lastly. King Slayer could be chosen as well, which does exactaly what you would think – increases damage done to enemy Kings. Your choice should be personalized toward your style of play. Once you've reached this rank, you should have more than enough experience in war and know exactly what you will want.

CRUSHING MONSTERS AND POCKETING TREASURE (PVE)

Solo

When I release you into the world, novice, you will most likely set upon the varying tasks of the locals in Grimmenhagen. You are, after all, only a peasant. Mostly, these "missions" can be accomplished without the aid of a party, so don't worry about being exposed as the incompetent peasant I suspect you to be. But never fear: As long as you remember my brilliant advice and use your abilities wisely, you can complete almost any task without too much trouble and can kill most anything before it gets to you—it is fun to watch an enemy creature expire just as it gets to your feet!

Take breaks in between the battles if you need to, but killing is our business and doing it will seem easy at first. Remember to open with your Fireball and time your next spell, Ignite, so it hits at the same time to maximize damage. As soon as one of them hits, that monster is going to charge you as if its life depends on it, which indeed it does. If your Ignite lands too early, those few seconds of wasted damage-over-time could be what the foe needed to succeed at cleaving your skull in twain. If your target does happen to get close, encase it in a Fire Cage. Then you'll have ample opportunity to fall back or finish the foe quickly by using Scorched Earth to burn the very ground at its feet. Always remember that range is your friend. Don't hesitate to back off and keep your distance, for those insignificant minions you are damaging would like nothing better than to return the favor.

Nothing will be too hard, even as you gain in ranks, and the strategies you use to succeed in these missions will mostly remain the same. Send maximum destructive power toward them before they can react. Use area-of-effect spells from the Path of Conflagration to clear the field if you get in a bind with multiple mobs, or even just to have a little fun in lower-level zones. I find it very appealing to visit the Ravenhill Marauders, cast Rain of Fire on their unsuspecting heads, and watch them all die at once! It's the simple pleasures in life that keep me going.

Dossier: Bright Wizard Ewe

Likes: Fire, mirrors, stuff that burns.

Dislikes: Stuff that doesn't burn, water, Dwarfs (subject claims "Most Dwarfs are very disturbing").

Scholastic Achievements: Named most likely to burn down the school.

Graduated? N/A: All four of Ewe's secondary schools were destroyed in mysterious fires before he was recruited into the Bright Wizard program.

Military Career

Battle of East Meadow

Objective: Repel Dark Elves invading the village.

Outcome: Dark Elves repelled. Village of East Meadow burned to the ground.

Battle of Riven Rock

Objective: Clear out greenskin warrens.

Outcome: Greenskins eradicated. Nearby village of Arabahn burned to the ground.

Battle of Cedar Towne

Objective: Exterminate termite infestation.

Outcome: Termite colony eradicated; species now extinct. Cedar Towne burned to the ground.

Psychological evaluation pending.

Grimmenhagen is just the beginning. It will prepare you for life as a Bright Wizard, but every new town requires new beginnings. From Grimmenhagen to Altdorf, the path to defending our realm will take you past many of the people of the Empire, Dwarfs, and possibly even Elves. Adventuring by oneself has its benefits—not sharing the loot, progressing only when you are ready, and also progressing in the direction you wish to progress. However the drawbacks are also plentiful, because you lack any real protection if you get in a bind, or if you wish to do public quests or instances.

As you gain ranks, more areas and quests become available, and more of the world will be at your fingertips. Move to the next area only after you complete all the tasks or quests available in your current area. You never know which one will grant you a nice shiny new staff, so do them all!

Group

By yourself, you cannot complete even the very first public quest. So when my little peasant is ready to take on the Ravenhost Vanguard, you need to enlist the help of others running around Grimmenhagen. It's the same regardless of which zone you're in, so to participate, find some strangers or make some new allies. A Bright Wizard need depend on nothing but himself, but fighting alongside a group has its own benefits.

The Skeleton Hunter

I remember years ago when I was just a kindling wanting to make my mark on the world here in Grimmenhagen Village. I visited the Crypts not far from here, hoping to burn the taint off the place with my mighty magic. I gained a little humility that day as I fought off the undead fiends inside.

I was overrun and backed into a corner when I finally managed to slay the last of the undead. When I recovered, I noticed the corner held a small gravestone marked Eoldred's Coffin. Being overly curious, I of course started to examine it when a strange voice cried out, "The nightbane curse be upon you." Then before I could even think, Eoldred Nightbane leaped out and assaulted me. This was a mighty foe for one so young.

I was no match for his long-dead spirit, and even though I tried to fight, I knew I wouldn't last long. When all hope was fading from my mind, a lone Bright Wizard entered the cavern and launched a massive Fireball toward the spirit, and eliminated it instantly. The power I saw in that Bright Wizard I have only dreamed about since. On that day I earned the title "The Skeleton Hunter," and I've kept it ever since as a lesson learned on that fateful day.

Being able to take on more enemies and do more damage than you could alone is the most notable benefit. That Rank 2 Champion mob is quite daunting to the lone Wizard, but to a whole group, it's but a small challenge. Your job remains the same, but in a group, make sure not to get too out of hand with your blasting. Taking a foe's attention off of whichever dumb warrior it's beating on is always a poor idea unless you can dispatch it quickly. Those warriors are there to take that beating, not you, so use them wisely. If you do make a mistake, hide in your Smoke Screen, or you might find yourself with a face full of Ogre. You'll always be welcome in a group for your ability to do a lot of damage, but no one has any use for a dead Bright, or at least not one of which I care to learn.

In addition to our own attractive offensive abilities, you'll receive Flames of Rhuin and Flame Shield to support your fellow adventurers and group mates. These spells increase everyone's chance to do fire damage, so always have them active in a group.

Solo

Dealing out pain is especially fun when used against the forces of Destruction, so scenarios and PvP zones are a great way to test yourself against

CRUSHING PLAYERS AND GATHERING RENOWN (PvP)

enemies of the Empire. As a Bright Wizard in PvP, your core concern is still to do as much damage as you can and survive long enough to destroy the enemy before he destroys you.

If you choose to attempt that solo, don't rush into any battle just because everyone else does. With no support, you'll be easy pickings for any group of Destruction players. Every map contains tactically advantageous positions from which to rain devastation down upon your enemy. Find a high wall or similar spot and sit and wait for them to come to you. No need to go to Destruction, because you have great range and should hit from as far away as possible. If enemies are getting too close, you have multiple ways of controlling them or sending them flying. Help allied players if you wish, or use them as distractions to get a better angle on your enemy.

If you choose to fight solo, however, you do so at your own risk. War is upon us and it is up to everyone to help out. One Bright Wizard will not make much of a difference alone. A brigade of 200 Bright Wizards can take down even the biggest army they could send at us.

Know your limits. Charging into battle against five enemies of your rank or greater is reckless and foolish.

Group

Fighting alongside allies is what war is all about. Competing against the forces of Destruction as part of a group gives you a few more advantages. Ideally you will have a healer, in case you are foolish and become wounded in battle. Also, you'll have a warrior to take beatings on your behalf. Having the enemy busy trying to kill someone else gives you time to attack from maximum range and blast them with direct damage and hexes. If your group is facing multiple enemies, choose whether you wish to attack them all at once with your area-effect spells, or pick and choose one at a time. Area-effect spells are an excellent way to destroy a horde of foes all at once. However, no one's going to doubt where that holocaust came from. If the rest of your group can't keep those irate enemies off you long enough for Aqshy's magic to burn them down, the survivors will be breathing down your neck quickly.

As mentioned above, you'll learn two buffs that increase every group member's potential damage as well. Be sure to use those and keep them active at all times. Being a lazy Bright Wizard is a good way to find yourself adventuring alone.

Focusing your destructive powers on the enemy healers is usually a good idea, because they are keeping those axe-wielding Orcs and Northmen alive and swinging. Kill them, silence them fast, and you won't have to waste a bunch of time reburning foes who should already be cinders. And help your healers, because if you are targeting their healers, chances are good they will be targeting yours. Standing near the healers allows you to quickly Fire Cage any enemy that dares get too close. It also means you'll get healed more quickly because you'll always be in range.

Be wary, for many times I have been the focus on the enemy's initial charge, and in those situations your main goal is to survive and keep your distance at all costs. Shield of Aqshy combined with the abilities and tactics that both heal you and keep the enemy further away are your survival tactics in those situations.

Surviving and doing damage: those are your primary goals when you meet the forces of Destruction. If you fail at the first, you may die with honor in a burning rage to take as many of the enemy with you as you can. Coincidentally, this also helps your group in the long run. Take that as you will.

Find a good rotation of spells and learn it well. The quicker you can unleash hell, the more efficient a destroyer you will become.

DEATH FROM ABOVE

We've come a long way in our conversation, haven't we? I've explained a lot of what makes me phenomenal at this profession, and I've tried to instill upon you the knowledge that I've gained over the years. For your sake, I hope you were listening. At least try to carry yourself with the honor and dignity of a true Bright Wizard. War is all around you, and war is what we excel at.

I plan to travel to Praag next. I hear there is a struggle going on there as we speak, and I wish to be a part of it. My friends will meet me there. Mostly, I prefer having friends at my side when I go to battle, although occasionally I wander off alone if I feel I can get the drop on the enemy. I will find a sweet spot in the city to sit and wait for those forces of Destruction to try to pass. Then they will get to know my fire more personally than any mortal wants to.

Before I leave you, novice, I want to reassure you: Don't worry too much about the damage you cause along the way—we are Bright Wizards, and we wield a force too unstable and destructive to care about every little house we accidentally burn to the ground.

WARRIOR PRIEST

By Sigmar's grace we have lived to see another sunrise. Aha, I see we have been sent another new recruit. Fear and confusion consume your eyes, young recruit, but do not dread the coming battle, for Sigmar blesses those who learn to rely on their own power in battle.

I am Erasmus, son of Ealhelm, Order of the Griffon. For many moons now I have fought under the banner of the Empire to defend Nordland from the relentless bile that spews forth from Norsca. My father, and his father, and his father before him devoted their lives to the glory of Sigmar and the Empire. From a young age I could feel the call of Sigmar drawing me to the battlefield. As soon as I was of age, I tirelessly poured myself into my training, and my devotion to Sigmar and the Empire was rewarded with victories on the field of battle.

Today, young recruit, Sigmar's divine guidance will illuminate your path if you are truly faithful. Through skirmishes and campaigns, Sigmar will grant you the strength to strike down your enemies and the righteous fury to raise fallen allies. By our hammer and by our blood, the justice of the Empire will pour out across our great land and vanquish all those who oppose us. We are the chosen defenders of the Empire! Let wretched Chaos come! Let them come and feel the wrath of Sigmar!

By Erasmus

What is a Warrior Priest?

The wise call the Warrior Priest one of the Empire's most devoted healers. Wielding a Hammer of Justice with lethality, and imparting Sigmar's blessings to regenerate health and raise fallen defenders, the Warrior Priest embodies both desired ally and formidable foe.

They heed the call of Righteous Fury. Forge too far onto the battlefield and they find themselves at the mercies of their enemies, but stray too far from the fray and they quickly discover their fury waning. In the heat of battle, Warrior Priests can summon forth the blessings of Sigmar onto themselves and their allies, oftentimes increasing the damage dealt to foes or providing a shield of protection for those who stand with them in battle. A Warrior Priest must always be acutely aware of the conflict and strike a balance between melee and magic to survive.

The role of a healer is not for the faint of heart. Citizens and combatants depend on the Warrior Priest's decisiveness to carry them through to victory. One fortuitous heal can change the course of fate and strengthen the Empire; one fatal miscast can doom us all.

—Aleister Schreiber, Scholar Emeritus, University of Nuln

If you are lost, confused, or need direction, check your Tome of Knowledge. You will be amazed at the information it contains.

STARTING AS A WARRIOR PRIEST

It's apparent that Sigmar has ordained that you become a Warrior Priest. With this blessing come innate abilities that set you apart from your fellow citizens.

As your rank increases with your experience, your innate abilities increase as well. You also gain armor and weapons befitting your station as you complete quests and slay the vile creatures who seek to destroy the Empire. The ability to choose armor and weapons that increase certain attributes will hasten your rise to greatness.

You should be aware though, young one, that not all attributes are worth your attention. Seek to maximize those that are most beneficial to you. Focus on Strength, Toughness, Willpower, and Weapon Skill.

Strength is required to increase the damage you deal to the enemy. Without Strength, your blows will be nothing more than a nuisance to your foes. Your blessed attacks will also benefit from increased Strength. The harder you hit someone or something, the more healing you will provide to your defensive target.

You want to not only crush your enemy with your hammer, you want to be able to withstand their hateful strikes. Increase your Toughness to decrease the amount of damage an enemy can inflict upon you. This allows more time to heal your allies instead of constantly healing yourself.

Healing is a necessary task in all battles. To become a more efficient healer, increase your Willpower; this aids your healing and allows you to heal your allies for more of their health.

You alone have been chosen to wield the mighty Warhammer of Sigmar. Increasing your Weapon Skill increases your ability to parry enemy blows and penetrate enemy armor. This is not a skill to be taken lightly. As a warrior of the Empire, you should constantly increase your Weapon Skill.

Grimmenhagen, nestled against the southern mountains of Nordland, is where you first put these skills to the test. Cannon blasts shake the foundations of the buildings, and the sound of clashing swords fills the streets. The forces of Destruction have descended and laid siege to the town and surrounding countryside. The citizens of Grimmenhagen and members of the Order of the Griffon need your help to stop the onslaught.

Upon entering town, seek out Viktor Riese. Victor can be found in the center of town illuminated by a large green book. He will ask for your assistance in defending the town from the invading Marauders. These Marauders are burning homes along the road south of the town. Follow Viktor's directions, complete his task, and he will reward you handsomely. As you gain experience and word of your skills travels, other defenders of the Empire will seek your services. Your training has just begun, young recruit, and as you become more experienced and gain new ranks, seek out Elsa Schmidt. She is a veteran fighter who can aid you in your training.

You have been given meager equipment to get you started. Your Torn Holy Shirt and Dull Holy Hammer will do little to protect you from the evil that is trying to destroy you. Do

WARRIOR PRIEST GEAR

not fret, though, for Sigmar blesses those who learn to rely on his or her own power in battle. As you prove yourself, you will find armor and weapons on the corpses of those you have slain, or be given armor and weapons as rewards for your aid.

Once you have proven yourself worthy, you can wear medium armor. This armor offers some protection from enemy blows, but is flexible enough to allow you to move freely through the battle to aid your allies. With the strength of your armor and the aid of your heals, you will prove to be a formidable foe. As we discussed earlier, always seek out armor that increases attributes most beneficial to your melee and healing abilities. Strength, Toughness, Willpower, and Weapon Skill will bolster your abilities and increase your victories.

Your weapon of choice is the mighty warhammer. All Warrior Priests carry the great hammer to pay homage to Sigmar. It is up to you whether you carry a hammer alone or a hammer and a tome. Wield a two-handed hammer if you choose to focus more on your melee abilities. If you choose to focus mainly on healing, a one-handed hammer and a tome will be most beneficial.

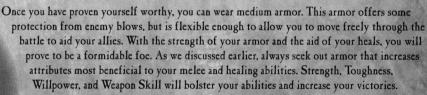

Always make sure you have a defensive target set when entering ba...

When the situation arises, group with others. Your trip will be much more enjoyable.

STRENGTHS AND WEAKNESSES

Strengths

- Call on the powers of Sigmar to heal oneself and one's allies.
- Bless your allies, granting them protection and the ability to deal increased damage.
- Resurrect fallen allies.
- Cripple enemies with vicious blows.
- As a healer, you will always be needed by others.

A Warrior Priest's versatility gives you a distinct advantage over other damage classes. Not only are you protected from an attacking foe by your relatively strong armor, you can heal yourself through fights others would not survive. Couple this with your prayers, which bolster your health, armor, and damage, and others will fear you in combat.

Your ability to heal and to resurrect fallen allies ensures that other citizens of the Empire will seek out your aid. You can empower your allies against the vile forces of Destruction, help them survive the battle, or restore the breath of life to them when they fall. Fellow citizens of the Empire will turn to you in many different situations, because you can turn the tide of battle.

Weaknesses

- You must inflict damage on a target to gain Righteous Fury and be able to heal.
- Your damage will never be equal to a true melee class.
- You must stay still to cast healing spells.
- Solo fights take longer to complete than if you were a true melee class.
- Destruction players will seek to kill you first because you are a healer.

Mastering the balance of melee and magical skills is a monumental task one must overcome to truly become a great Warrior Priest. You must charge into the thickest of fights, allowing the enemy to feel the wrath of your hammer to gain the Righteous Fury needed to keep your allies alive. Knowing when to enter the battle and where to position yourself will determine whether you and your allies will survive. You must get close enough to the enemy to strike them with your hammer, but far enough away that you can cast your spells without constant interruptions. Take cover behind the tank and the front line of melee fighters. This makes you harder to target and keeps you away from the worst of the enemy blows. You still can strike the enemy with your melee attacks, ensuring that your Righteous Fury will not dissipate. This can prove challenging, especially because the forces of Destruction will seek to silence you.

Your ability to inflict melee damage and heal yourself throughout the fight is both a blessing and a curse. You can survive fights others would not, but most fights will take you much longer and require more strategy. Your damage will be more than enough to bring an enemy to his knees, but you will never be seen as the champion of fighters because your melee training will not match that of a pure melee warrior.

It's important to increase your influence with all the factions you encounter. Participating in the local public quests will allow you to gain influence quickly and receive rewards for your endeavors.

Abilities

Though you are not a true melee fighter, you will still learn many deadly melee abilities. As you gain experience and rank, your Career Trainer will provide you will the opportunity to train several different types of abilities. Core training grants your basic combat and healing skills. At almost each new rank you achieve, you learn a new Core ability. I have compiled a list of all the skills you will gain as you grow in rank. Study each one and understand how it will benefit you in battle.

The second part of your training will provide you with specializations that set you apart from other Warrior Priests. Your Career Trainer will offer you Mastery abilities once you have achieved Rank 11. You gain one Mastery point upon reaching Rank 11 and gain additional Mastery points as your rank increases. By the time you have reached Rank 40, you will have received 25 Mastery points. There are three paths you may choose from to enhance specific abilities: Path of Salvation, Path of Grace, and Path of Wrath.

The Path of Salvation focuses on healing. If you choose this path, you become a master healer. Your Prayer of Absolution, Divine Assault, and Touch of the Divine skills greatly benefit from training in this path. Along with increasing the potency of several of your base skills, training in the Path of Salvation also grants you new skills and Tactics. All the skills and Tactics in this path increase your ability to heal yourself and your allies. This path is especially useful if you fight frequently alongside many allies. Most allies you group with will expect you to be able to heal them through the battles. Placing Mastery points in this path will greatly increase your ability to keep your group alive.

The Path of Grace allows one to inflict devastating blows on the enemy while bolstering the attributes of oneself and one's allies. Training in the Path of Grace increases your Divine Strike, Sigmar's Fist, Prayer of Devotion, Sigmar's Radiance, and Vow of Silence. You also receive new skills and Tactics that increase the attributes and damage dealt by yourself and your allies. While groups most often seek healing, this path can also be useful. The additional power your blessings and melee abilities gain from this path will help your group to quickly dispose of anything that opposes you.

The Path of Wrath increases the damage done by your melee abilities and the weakening effects caused by your punishing blows. Training in the Path of Wrath bolsters your Castigation, Weight of Guilt, Smite, and Prayer of Righteousness: Damaging abilities. By training in the Path of Wrath, one's melee and crippling abilities are also increased. You can strike your foes with more force. If you find yourself constantly battling the forces of Destruction, then consider placing most of your Mastery points in this path. This path bolsters those abilities that allow you to cripple and snare the enemy. This makes it much harder for your opponent to flee, and easier for you and your allies to defeat them.

Each path can increase your greatness, and if you focus on one path, you will be very strong in that area of expertise. I will caution you, though, young one. While you will greatly bolster those abilities tied to the path you have chosen, you will weaken your other abilities. If you find yourself primarily using abilities provided by one of the Mastery paths, then it may be wise for you to focus only in that area. If you use a variety of abilities during battle, you may choose to spread your Mastery points between two or more Mastery paths. This allows you to increase the strength of many different abilities. This can be both beneficial and a hindrance because none of your abilities will gain the full strength available to those who specialize in only one path. I cannot tell you how to best use these Mastery points because each Warrior Priest has a personal style of battle. Evaluate for yourself which abilities you use most often.

10 Things That May Occur If You Befriend A Dwarf

1. You know the exact location of all taverns within two-day's travel.

2. You wake up in the morning wondering what day it is and where all of your gold went.

3. You notice after a few weeks your belly now hangs over your pants.

4. When asked what you will be having for dinner, you quickly reply with your three favorite ales.

5. You use your Tome of Knowledge to balance your bar stool.

6. You realize that Dwarfs do not shave because they do not have a steady hand after a full night of drinking.

7. Shiny metal objects become a huge distraction.

8. You notice that most things are not designed for the vertically challenged.

9. When questioned about the accuracy of your information, you proceed to rant for the next 20 minutes about your lineage and the person's audacity in questioning your knowledge.

Name	Level	Path	Cost	Range (in feet)	Type	Build	Duration	Reuse	Description
Supplication	Starter Ability	Core	30 AP/s	Self	Other	0s	5s	10s	Channel: Gives 30 RF/s; when player runs out of AP, channel stops.
Divine Aid	Starter Ability	Salvation	55 RF	Heal	Heal	0.5s	9s	0s	Heals 247 damage, then heals 658 damage over 9s.
Judgement	Starter Ability	Salvation	15 (Builds 15 RF)	65	Magic Attack	1s	0s	0s	Deals 75 magic damage.
Bludgeon	Starter Ability	Wrath	30 (Builds 30 RF)	Melee	Melee Attack - Cripple	0s	0s	0s	Deals (150+DPS) damage.
Sigmar's Fist	Level 2	Grace	25 (Builds 25 RF)	Melee	Melee Attack - Bless	0s	10s	5s	Deals (112+DPS). Increases defensive target's Strength by 3/level for 10s.
Healing Hand	Level 3	Core	30 RF	150	Heal	0s	15s	0s	Heal target player for 658 over 15s.
Prayer of Absolution	Level 4	Salvation	Free	Group	Prayer	0s	0s	10s	Aura: Group members gain a 16.5 Armor buff while the prayer is active. Does not trigger the layer timer. Toggled.
Castigation	Level 5	Wrath	20 (Builds 20 RF)	Melee	Melee	0s	10s	5s	Deals (187+DPS)*1.33 damage over 10s, lower target's Initiative by 2/level.
Divine Strike	Level 6	Grace	30 (Builds 30 RF)	Melee	Melee Attack	0s	0s	0s	Deals (75+DPS). Defensive target and those within 10ft of him are healed for 100% of the amount of damage done.
Repent	Level 7	Core	20	100	Debuff	0s	15s	15s	Detaunts target (15s duration, 50% redux).
Divine Assault	Level 8	Salvation	25 RF/S	Melee	Melee Attack/ Lifetap	0s	3s	8s	Channel. Spirit damage. Deals (75+DPS) damage to target. Heals defensive target for 250% of damage dealt. 100% setback chance, sets back for 1.5s.
Weight of Guilt	Level 9	Wrath	30 (Builds 30 RF)	Melee	Melee Attack - Cripple	0s	5s	10s	Deals (187+DPS) damage. If target is Crippled, Snare by 40% for 5s.
Breath of Sigmar	Level 10	Core	20 RF	100	Resurrection	6s	0s	3s	Resurrect targeted friendly dead player.
Smite	Level 12	Wrath	45 (Builds 45 RF)	CAE	Melee Attack	1s	0s	5s	Deals (112+DPS) damage to everyone in the AE. WP gains 25% additional RF for each target hit. Arc: 180, radius 40ft.
Prayer of Devotion	Level 14	Grace	Free	Group	Prayer	0s	0s	10s	Aura: Group members have a 20% chance to heal themselves for 112 when they hit an enemy. Does not trigger the layer timer. Toggled. Does not get Willpower Bonus, does not crit. Maximum proc rate of 1 per 2s.
Purify	Level 16	Core	25 RF	150	Magic Attack	0s	0s	5s	Removes a Curse or Hex from target.
Prayer of Righteousness	Level 18	Wrath	Free	Group	Prayer	0s	0s	10s	Aura: Group members have a 20% chance to proc 187 damage. Does not trigger the layer timer. Toggled.
Touch of the Divine	Level 20	Salvation	60 RF	150	Group Heal	1s	0s	2s	Heals 540 damage to all group members.
Purge	Level 25	Core	25 (Builds 25 RF)	Melee	Melee Attack	0s	0s	5s	Deal (75+DPS). Dispel one enchant from target.
Sigmar's Radiance	Level 30	Grace	35 (Builds 35 RF)	Melee	Melee Attack, Heal	0s	0s	5s	Deals (150+DPS). Heals group members within the radius for 50% of damage done; does not affect self. Radius: 30ft.
Vow of Silence	Level 35	Grace	25 (Builds 25 RF)	Melee	Melee Attack, Ailment	0s	5s	30s	Deals (150+DPS) damage and Silences the target for 5s.
Divine Shock	Level 40	Core	40 (Builds 40 RF)	CAE	Escape, Crowd Control	0s	0s	60s	Enemies in the AE are knocked back (medium). Arc: 180, radius 30ft.
Divine Light	Salvation x5	Salvation	40 RF	Group	Group Damage Absorb	0s	10s	60s	Group absorb buff for 787.
Pious Restoration	Salvation x9	Salvation	40 RF	Group	Heal - Bless	0s	15s	10s	Group heal over time, heals 607 over 15s (Bless).

Name	Level	Path	Cost	Range (in feet)	Type	Build	Duration	Reuse	Description
Martyr's Blessing	Salvation x13	Salvation	20 RF/S	PBAE	Channeled Heal	0s	3s	13s	Channeled heal. Heals around him for 202 every second for 3s. 100% setback chance. Radius: 30ft.
Sigmar's Vision	Grace x5	Grace	30 (Builds 30 RF)	Melee	Melee Attack - Bless	0s	10s	5s	Deals (187+DPS), defensive target's Parry is increased by 10% for 10s. Builds RF.
Sigmar's Shield	Grace x9	Grace	25 (Builds 25 RF)	Melee	Melee Attack - Bless	0s	20s	20s	Deals (187+DPS) damage. Defensive target gains a buff for up to 20 seconds. Each time they are hit, they become healed for 150 and the WP loses 112 RF. Effect ends if RF is depleted.
Sigmar's Grace	Grace x13	Grace	35	100	Buff - Bless	2s	60 min	60s	Buff the group's Wounds by 2. Wound buffs stack largest.
Soulfire	Wrath x5	Wrath	35 (Builds 35 RF)	PBAE	Magic Attack - Cripple	2s	9s	0s	Deals 449 Spirit damage to targets in the radius over 9s. Radius: 30ft. Builds RF.
Absence of Faith	Wrath x9	Wrath	25 (Builds 25 RF)	Melee	Debuff - Cripple	0s	10s	20s	Reduces healing on target by 25% for 10s.
Hammer of Sigmar	Wrath x13	Wrath	30 (Builds 30 RF)	Melee	Melee Attack	0s	0s	10s	Deal (112+DPS). If target has less than 50% health, deal (337+DPS).

Morale

Morale abilities are another weapon in your great arsenal. These special abilities can heal, shield, increase damage, and allow you to resurrect your fallen group mates. You begin to gain Morale abilities upon reaching Rank 8 and receive most of these abilities when you train your Core abilities. You gain three additional Morale abilities by training in your Mastery paths.

Morale abilities are ranked based on how potent they are. The higher the rank, the more helpful or destructive the ability will be. Rank 1 Morale abilities will be helpful, but not as useful as your Rank 4 abilities. You will have one Morale ability for each rank available once you reach Rank 40. As you and your allies battle the forces of Destruction, your Morale will grow. Once you have gained enough Morale, your Rank 1 ability will be ready to use. You may choose to use this ability or allow your Morale to continue to grow to Rank 2, Rank 3, or Rank 4. Once the time is right, you may use any of the abilities. Once you use a Morale ability, all your Morale is lost and you must start building your Morale back.

Choose wisely when deciding which Morale abilities to use. Not all Morale abilities are useful in all situations. Before you engage in battle, take a moment to carefully consider which Morale abilities will be most useful to you and your allies for that fight.

Morale					
Name	Level	Rank	Range (in feet)	Duration	Description
Divine Favor	Level 8	Rank 1	150	0s	Heals target for 1,800.
Rampaging Siphon	Level 12	Rank 2	PBAE	0	PBAE that deals 600 and heals the group for 100% of the value.
Steal Life	Level 16	Rank 1	100	9s	Magic attack that deals 900 over 9s. Self heals 50% of the damage dealt.
Focused Mind	Level 20	Rank 2	Self	10s	For 10s, build times are reduced by 50%. Character purges and is immune to Silence, Disarm, Root, Snare, and setback.
Divine Protection	Level 24	Rank 3	Group	10s	Group buffs each group member with an ablative that absorbs the next 1,500 of melee damage, with a maximum duration of 10s.
Divine Aegis	Level 28	Rank 1	Self	7s	Self buff. Increase armor by +33/level of character and HoT for 360 over 7s.
Divine Replenishment	Level 32	Rank 2	Group	10s	Group buff. Melee attacks also regenerate 50 AP for 10s.
Penance	Level 36	Rank 3	Melee	3s	Channeled melee attack that deals 1,200 and heals self for 720 over 3s.
Alter Fate	Level 40	Rank 4	PBAE	9s	PBAE Resurrection for group members. Resurrected targets also get a HoT that heals 1,200 over 9s.
Gift of Life	Salvation x15	Rank 4	Group	9s	Heal all members of the group by 1,440 over 9s.
Avatar of Sigmar	Grace x15	Rank 4	Group	30s	Group buff. Increases all stats by 2/level for 30s.
Divine Amazement	Wrath x15	Rank 4	PBAE	10s	Silences and disarms all targets in cone for 10s. Arc: 180, radius: 30ft.

Tactics

Other weapons you possess are your Tactical abilities. These are special abilities you gain from your Career Trainer. Tactical abilities can bolster your melee and healing abilities. Certain Tactics are more useful than others, depending on your situation. You receive Tactics as you train in your Core and Mastery abilities. Most of your Tactics are part of your Core abilities, but nine Tactics are spread between the three Mastery paths. You will begin learning Tactics when you reach Rank 11.

You can create up to five sets of Tactics to be used in different situations. Craft each set of Tactics to aid you in specific situations. At Rank 11 you have only one Tactics slot to fill. As you increase in rank, you will gain additional Tactics slots and can use more than one Tactic at a time. At Rank 40 you have four Tactic slots.

If you often take the role of a healer, create a set of Tactics that aid your healing. This set of Tactics may include Persistent, which increases your Willpower. This set may also include Desperation, which causes your heals to become more effective on targets who are critically wounded. If you are helping your allies by blessing them and inflicting melee damage to the enemy, you may choose to use such Tactics as Strength of Conviction, which increases your Weapon Skill, or Overwhelming Faith, which causes all of your prayers to increase your group's Strength and Weapon Skill.

Renown

As you seek out and destroy the enemy, you gain Renown points. These points are a reward for your defense of the Empire and can increase your attributes and abilities. As you gain Renown points, seek out a Renown Trainer in your closest warcamp. You can train in three tiers of abilities. You must train 20 points in the first tier to be able to train abilities in the second tier. You then must train another 20 points in the first and second tier abilities to open the third tier.

Focus on those abilities that increase the attributes and skills most useful to you. From the first tier of abilities you may choose to train in Resolve, which increases your Willpower and, in turn, the effectiveness of your healing. Might and Toughness are also well worth training in because Might increases your Strength and Toughness reduces the amount of damage you take.

Once you have gained enough Renown points to open the second and third tier of abilities, continue focusing on specific abilities that are advantageous to your Mastery path. I myself have trained in Assault, Vigor, Reinforcement, Spiritual Refinement, and Opportunist to aid my Strength, Wounds, Armor, critical healing, and melee critical strike. As with all major decisions, take time to reflect upon how you use the powers of the Warrior Priest and select those skills that best benefit your style of adventuring.

Warrior Priest Joke

A Warrior Priest, a Disciple, and a Zealot walk into a tavern. The barkeep looks up and says, "Is this some kind of joke?"

Tactics		
Name	Level	Description
Emperor's Ward	Level 11	25% chance when attacked to absorb 262 damage for 10s.
Divine Fury	Level 13	Increase damage dealt by 25%, reduce healing values by 20%.
Hastened Divinity	Level 15	Whenever you critically hit a target, your auto attack speed is increased by 100% for 10s.
Unwavering Faith	Level 17	Increases Spirit resist by 6.3/level of the character.
Discipline	Level 19	Increases Willpower by 4/level of the character.
Charged Fury	Level 21	Abilities build up 10 extra RF when used.
Sigmar's Favor	Level 23	25% chance when healed to be healed for an additional 135.
Subtlety	Level 25	Decreases threat by 50% on all heals.
Shield of Faith	Level 27	Increase chance to Disrupt 10%.
Restorative Burst	Level 29	Critical heals return 40 AP over 3s to the caster. (Non-stacking, non-refreshing.)
Divine Reward	Level 31	Divine Aid and Healing Hand have a 25% chance to make the next attack cost no AP.
Exalted Defenses	Level 33	On defense (Parry/Evade/Block): Outgoing healing is increased by 20% for 10s.
Intimidating Repent	Level 35	Repent turns into a PBAE with a 30ft.
Fueled Fury	Level 37	On being hit: 25% chance to gain 40 RF.
Divine Petitioning	Level 39	Reduce Supplications over time cost to 75/s.
Cleansing Power	Salvation x3	Divine Aid, Touch of the Divine, Pious Restoration, and Martyr's Blessing dispel one Curse effect from target.
Refreshing Radiance	Salvation x7	Heals have a 25% chance to give the target 50 AP. (Cannot give self AP.)
Divine Warding	Salvation x11	Divine Assault is set back only 50% of the time when struck while channelling.
Greave of Sigmar	Grace x3	Sigmar's Fist also increases defensive target's Toughness and lowers offensive target's Strength and Toughness by 3/level for 10s.
Leading the Prayer	Grace x7	Prayer of Devotion also heals the Warrior Priest when a group member procs it.
Grace of Sigmar	Grace x11	Increases the percentage of damage healed by Divine Strike to 150% and Sigmar's Radiance to 100%.
Endless Guilt	Wrath x3	Weight of Guilt's Snare lasts 10s, and Weight of Guilt hits all targets within 20ft of the Warrior Priest.
Fanaticism	Wrath x7	15% increased chance to critical hit with damage abilities.
Guilty Soul	Wrath x11	Critical hits of abilities in Wrath deal an additional 299 over 9 seconds (Cripple) to target and heal the defensive target for 180 over 9s (Bless).

Solo Play

As a defender of the Empire, a Warrior Priest's place is on the battlefield. There will be time between battles, though, and you will be expected to help your fellow citizens. During these times you can find people in need of aid in all of the camps and towns within the Empire.

Rank 1~10

You begin your journey as a Warrior Priest in Grimmenhagen, Nordland. Here, you find the forces of Destruction desperately trying to overrun the town. If anyone in the Empire needs your aid, it is the citizens of Grimmenhagen. Viktor Riese will explain how you can help drive back the forces of Destruction. Prove your worth to him, and he will not only reward you, but will spread word of your good deeds to those in town. As your fame grows, you will be given more quests to help further the cause of the Empire.

As your journey places you in the path of danger, you must learn to rely on your abilities to bring you through the fights. You are young, and your skills are not yet shaped by countless brushes with death. Your abilities are limited to Judgement, Bludgeon, Divine Aid, and Supplication. While your abilities are few, they will serve you well. Judgement allows you to pull individual creatures to a safer area to fight, while Bludgeon is your main melee ability and does more damage than your regular swing. Divine Aid restores your health when you cast the spell and continues to heal you over the next few seconds. These heals over time allow you to regain health throughout the fight and move on to your next target without having to stop and wait for your health to regenerate. Use Supplication only when your Righteous Fury is waning and you need to heal. This ability regenerates your Righteous Fury at the cost of your action points, but only if you concentrate and are not interrupted.

In your quests to aid the people of Grimmenhagen, you gain valuable experience and quickly increase in rank. You can gain large amounts of experience and influence if you are willing to aid in the public quest. Find this battle raging just north of town. You and your allies must stop the forces of Destruction from enslaving the local farmers to do their evil bidding. This is not an easy task, so don't try it until you have gained Rank 4. As you participate in this public quest, you gain influence with Grimmenhagen. This influence is rewarded by Eldred Krebs. The more influence you gain, the greater your reward will be. If you are willing to help all those who require assistance in Grimmenhagen, you should be able to achieve Rank 5.

With each new gain in rank, seek out Elsa Schmidt in Grimmenhagen. She teaches you new skills befitting of your rank. Upon reaching Rank 2, you learn to use Sigmar's Fist. This blessed attack does large amounts of damage to your target and increases the Strength of your defensive target. If you are soloing, your Strength will be increased when you strike an enemy with this attack. If you are in a group, however, have your tank as your defensive target so that he may gain the additional Strength.

At Rank 5, Elsa teaches you your third melee ability, Castigation, which should be used with Bludgeon. Castigation is a crippling strike that deals damage over time and reduces your target's initiative. If you strike your target with Castigation and then with Bludgeon, you deal additional damage to the enemy. Rank 3 allows you to gain Healing Hands, which heals you or an ally over time. When you have reached Rank 4, Elsa Schmidt teaches you Prayer of Absolution, which increases the armor of all allies in your group. This is the first of many prayers you learn to help bolster yourself and you allies.

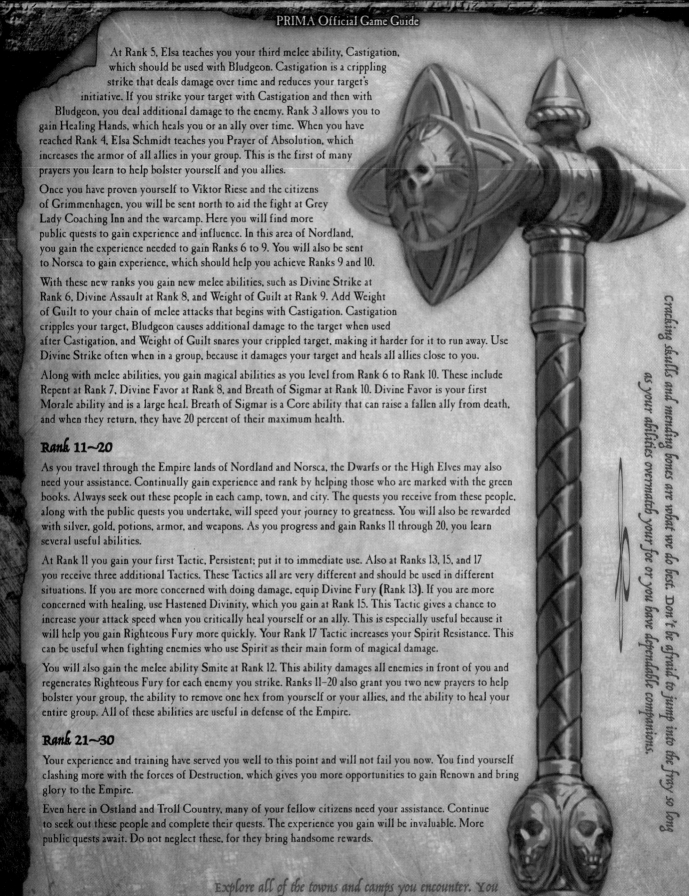

Once you have proven yourself to Viktor Riese and the citizens of Grimmenhagen, you will be sent north to aid the fight at Grey Lady Coaching Inn and the warcamp. Here you will find more public quests to gain experience and influence. In this area of Nordland, you gain the experience needed to gain Ranks 6 to 9. You will also be sent to Norsca to gain experience, which should help you achieve Ranks 9 and 10.

With these new ranks you gain new melee abilities, such as Divine Strike at Rank 6, Divine Assault at Rank 8, and Weight of Guilt at Rank 9. Add Weight of Guilt to your chain of melee attacks that begins with Castigation. Castigation cripples your target, Bludgeon causes additional damage to the target when used after Castigation, and Weight of Guilt snares your crippled target, making it harder for it to run away. Use Divine Strike often when in a group, because it damages your target and heals all allies close to you.

Along with melee abilities, you gain magical abilities as you level from Rank 6 to Rank 10. These include Repent at Rank 7, Divine Favor at Rank 8, and Breath of Sigmar at Rank 10. Divine Favor is your first Morale ability and is a large heal. Breath of Sigmar is a Core ability that can raise a fallen ally from death, and when they return, they have 20 percent of their maximum health.

Rank 11~20

As you travel through the Empire lands of Nordland and Norsca, the Dwarfs or the High Elves may also need your assistance. Continually gain experience and rank by helping those who are marked with the green books. Always seek out these people in each camp, town, and city. The quests you receive from these people, along with the public quests you undertake, will speed your journey to greatness. You will also be rewarded with silver, gold, potions, armor, and weapons. As you progress and gain Ranks 11 through 20, you learn several useful abilities.

At Rank 11 you gain your first Tactic, Persistent; put it to immediate use. Also at Ranks 13, 15, and 17 you receive three additional Tactics. These Tactics all are very different and should be used in different situations. If you are more concerned with doing damage, equip Divine Fury (Rank 13). If you are more concerned with healing, use Hastened Divinity, which you gain at Rank 15. This Tactic gives a chance to increase your attack speed when you critically heal yourself or an ally. This is especially useful because it will help you gain Righteous Fury more quickly. Your Rank 17 Tactic increases your Spirit Resistance. This can be useful when fighting enemies who use Spirit as their main form of magical damage.

You will also gain the melee ability Smite at Rank 12. This ability damages all enemies in front of you and regenerates Righteous Fury for each enemy you strike. Ranks 11–20 also grant you two new prayers to help bolster your group, the ability to remove one hex from yourself or your allies, and the ability to heal your entire group. All of these abilities are useful in defense of the Empire.

Rank 21~30

Your experience and training have served you well to this point and will not fail you now. You find yourself clashing more with the forces of Destruction, which gives you more opportunities to gain Renown and bring glory to the Empire.

Even here in Ostland and Troll Country, many of your fellow citizens need your assistance. Continue to seek out these people and complete their quests. The experience you gain will be invaluable. More public quests await. Do not neglect these, for they bring handsome rewards.

cracking skulls and mending bones are what we do best. Don't be afraid to jump into the fray so long as your abilities overmatch your foe or you have dependable companions.

Explore all of the towns and camps you encounter. You will find many people and items that will add history and lore to your Tome of Knowledge.

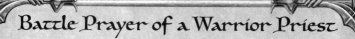

Do not be afraid to stray off the given path. You never know what you might find if you are a little adventurous.

Battle Prayer of a Warrior Priest

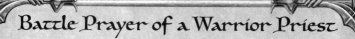

Bless me O Sigmar!

For today I will be faced with the vile stench of Destruction.

Pour out your blessing upon my hammer so that I

may strike down the heretics

who seek to destroy your kingdom.

Deliver into my hands the head of the enemy

so that I might forever silence the lies and deceit that spew forth from its mouth.

You, O Great One, created all that is good and righteous.

Use me this day, in battle, to dispel the stench of evil from your lands.

Also, do not neglect your training. You learn many more abilities as you rise through the ranks. You can add an additional Tactic. Strength of Conviction proves useful if you have chosen to master the Path of Grace or the Path of Wrath. You also receive the Morale ability Divine Protection, which shields your group from the enemy's wrath. While you must build up more Morale to use this ability, it is worth the wait when your whole group is losing health.

Rank 31~40

Your journey is quickly coming to an end and is only beginning at the same time. You have wisely heeded my advice and it has brought you far. Do not abandon the skills and abilities that have brought you to this point, for they continue to grow in potency along with your rank.

Now, more than ever, be mindful of the situation. You receive many new Tactics that increase the attributes of your allies. Learn to recognize when to bolster your group's Initiative and Willpower with Fervent Prayers versus when to increase their Strength and Weapon Skill with Overwhelming Faith. When your group faces the forces of Destruction, it's more useful to use Shielding Faith or Beacon of Truth. Shielding Faith increases your allies' ability to evade attacks and reduces their chance to be critically hit, while Beacon of Truth increases their Toughness. Also take into consideration the makeup of your group. Beacon of Truth may be more useful if you're grouped with many casters who have lower health. If your group contains sturdy melee fighters, use Overwhelming Faith to increase your group's damage. All this is added to your constant struggle to balance your melee and healing abilities while opportunistically using your Morale abilities. You have proven yourself a true master of balance and opportunity, and I have faith that you will quickly learn which Tactic to use in various situations.

Continue to seek out those who rely on your skills to aid in the war against Destruction. These quests give you the experience you need to obtain the greatness you strive for. You are constantly at war with the forces of Destruction. Use these opportunities to hone your skills and gain Renown. Both these things will only strengthen you and bring more honor and glory to Sigmar and the Empire.

Group Play

You have worked tirelessly to hone your skills and become a master of both melee and healing abilities. Your hard work will be rewarded when you find yourself grouped with fellow fighters against the forces of Destruction. Here you can put into action the skills you have so diligently tried to perfect. In many situations, you will be called upon to use your healing skills, especially if you have chosen the Path of Salvation as your Mastery path. The key to being a great healer is to make sure you have a defensive target set at all times. In a group situation, your defensive target should be your tank. This allows you to quickly heal the person taking the brunt of the damage without having to continually search for your target. Along with having your defensive target set, equip the correct Morale abilities and Tactics. These should be abilities that aid your healing such as Divine Favor, Hastened Divinity, Steal Life, Focused Mind, Emperor's Ward, Divine Protection, Subtlety, Desperation, and Alter Fate. Along with Tactics and Morale abilities, consider which prayer to place upon the group. If the whole group will be taking damage, bless your group with Prayer of Absolution or Prayer of Devotion. If your tank will be receiving most of the damage, bless your group with your Prayer of Righteousness to increase the group's total damage.

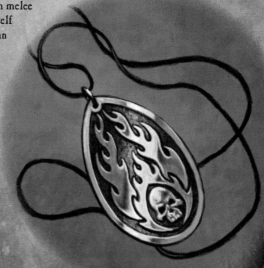

If you have chosen either the Path of Grace or the Path of Wrath, you will focus on dealing damage, blessing your group, weakening the enemy, and aiding the healer with your combat heals. Frequently use melee abilities that heal yourself and your allies, such as Divine Strike, Divine Assault, Sigmar's Radiance, and Penance. Use your melee abilities to cripple your target and enhance your allies' attributes.

Even when you're not in a primary healing role, you must bless your group with the appropriate prayer. Also be aware of which Tactics and Morale abilities you have active. Abilities that increase your groups' attributes and skills should be your first priority. Persistent, Divine Fury, Strength of Conviction, Faith Reward, Divine Aegis, Fervent Prayers, Overwhelming Faith, Shielding Faith, and Beacon of Truth are several appropriate Morale abilities and Tactics you should choose from.

CRUSHING PLAYERS AND GATHERING RENOWN (PVP)

Joining in the fight against the forces of Destruction is as imperative to the war effort as completing quests. Devote much of your time to this cause. Clashes with members of the forces of Destruction become more frequent as you gain rank. You must be prepared at all times, young one, to face your darkest fears and defend the Empire. While experience is the best teacher, allow me to impart to you the knowledge I have gained from many seasons of battles.

When you face a vile creature from the north, and you have no allies, you must call down the wrath of Sigmar and destroy the evil that has invaded our land. As in all situations, be mindful of your Morale abilities and Tactics. Bless yourself with a prayer before you enter battle, because success or failure is dictated by even the slightest advantage. Keep Divine Aid and Healing Hand upon yourself throughout the fight; this will help negate the damage intended for you and keep you from having to stop and cast your larger heal.

Always strike your enemy with Castigation followed by Weight of Guilt. This snares your enemy, allowing you to continue your onslaught of attacks. If your target is allowed to gain distance, you won't have adequate Righteous Fury and will be at the mercy of your enemy's attack. Set yourself as your defensive target so your melee abilities heal yourself.

You should feel right at home in the middle of a battlefield or scenario. This is where your abilities will stand out. Find a group or warband so your blessed prayers, group healing, and shielding abilities can be best exploited.

Just as when you face an enemy in a skirmish, make sure you have your correct Morale abilities and Tactics in place. Be aware of the allies around you. Keeping them alive can help change the tide of battle and ensure a victory for the Empire. Use a combination of spell and combat healing abilities to keep yourself and your allies' health up at all times. If you run out of Righteous Fury and cannot find an enemy within arm's reach, use Supplication.

Rely on Castigation and Weight of Guilt to keep your enemy from fleeing. When these effects wear off, renew them until your target dies or moves out of range. After applying Castigation and Weight of Guilt to your foe, use your melee heal abilities to make you and your allies harder to kill and to drain the enemies' resources.

In the midst of a campaign, your basic responsibilities are the same as if you were on a battlefield or in a scenario. Seek out a warband, bless your group with the most appropriate prayer, and equip the correct Tactics and Morale abilities.

Remember to include melee abilities that heal your defensive target in your hit rotation, while these may not do large amounts of damage, they help keep your allies alive.

WARHAMMER ONLINE
AGE OF RECKONING

In a campaign, you are most useful as a healer. The enemy will be beyond your reach and only those in the thickest armor can withstand the damage on the front lines. Supplication will be crucial, because it's hard to build your Righteous Fury. If your casters and ranged melee fighters can keep the enemy locked down behind the walls, you may be able to join the front lines and use your melee abilities on the keep. Once you break down the enemy walls, quickly enter the battle so you can strike down the enemy with your hammer and regenerate your Righteous Fury.

Always have your defensive target set in any battle. During a campaign you may have the ballista or ram operator as your target to keep them and their equipment alive. You can also bless all siege equipment (other than rams) to increase their damage. This is extremely helpful in all campaigns.

In any situation, you must always master the balance between your melee and magical abilities. This is never more evident than on the field of battle. No matter what rank you have achieved or how many battles you have fought, you will find new ways to use your abilities to better serve yourself and your allies. Approach each encounter with the enemy as a chance to learn something new about yourself and your abilities. No matter what lies ahead for you, always send your prayers up to Sigmar, embrace the lethality of your hammer, and draw upon your Righteous Fury to bring you victoriously through battle.

FEEL THE CALL OF SIGMAR

Your destiny now awaits you, young recruit. I have imparted to you my years of wisdom in hopes that you, too, will feel the call of Sigmar within your soul. You have shown great aptitude, and I can see in your eyes that you are ready to put your knowledge to use. This is good, for the enemy has started their advance, and the battle is upon us. Take heed of my words, lift up your prayers to Sigmar, and the strength needed to destroy the warriors of Chaos will fill you. Hold firm to your convictions and allow your instincts to guide your way.

Today we stand shoulder to shoulder in battle, driving the evil from our land. Sigmar has given us this chance to prove our devotion and worth. Let us send up our prayers, raise our hammers, and destroy the tide of Chaos with the full fury of the Empire. For Sigmar and the Empire!

Apply Healing Hand to your allies at the beginning of, and throughout, the battle. This helps reduce the initial damage taken and allows you more time to cast your larger heals.

WITCH HUNTER

By Heironymous

I do not know who will read this, so I will be as clear as possible. I do not have much time, so I will be brief.

I, Heironymous of Grimmenhagen, have traveled from one end of this wretched continent to the other. I am pursuing an unusually organized group of Chaos Marauders, and have been now for several weeks. The spread of their taint and corruption fouls the very path they walk, and a wide swath of corpses and burning villages makes them easy to track.

Although figuring out which way the foul creatures have traveled is not hard, the actual following of the path has been difficult. Along the way, I've lost many of my traveling companions, been gravely wounded twice, and have purged exactly 11 villages of the foul taint of corruption.

While I have been successful in rooting out the witchery in these towns, I fear it may swiftly return after my departure. I worry because I cannot stay in each of these towns, cannot ensure that they remain clean. I must trust that those who follow will deal with whatever recidivism occurs.

I know, however, that upon my departure, there is not the faintest hint of Chaos present. Of that I am sure.

The foul blood of Orcs, the disgusting black ichor that serves as blood in a follower of Chaos, the thin blood of those accursed darker brethren of the Elves—all of it stains my cloak, my hands, and my boots. No amount of scrubbing or washing can rid myself of these accursed reminders of my duty. I could say that I wear these badges proudly. In truth, I question whether my hands will ever be as clean as my conscience.

I do not ever question the importance of the duty that lies before me, before all of us. The spread of corruption, once but an insidious seepage, is now a raging torrent of Chaos and witchery. Never before has corruption been so firmly embedded within the Empire.

Never before have we been so important. To that end, I leave this diary so that others may know of these trials, and perhaps become more vigilant.

What is a Witch Hunter?

The histories tell of a highly devoted group of individuals whose sole purpose is to root out dark magic and Chaos, wherever it may lie. Initially comprising but a handful of men and women, Witch Hunters have become ever more important to the Empire with the spread of Chaos across our lands. With that increase in importance, so increases their numbers. Well known for their uncompromising methods, Witch Hunters would rather see the death of a hundred innocents than see a single follower of Chaos go free.

Witches have been with us longer than the Empire has been. Many, many years ago, Witch Masters dealt with witches, those who would truck with Daemons to learn the secrets of dark magic. In the many years since, we have discovered that many would trade their very souls for the easy path to wealth and power. It is an unfortunate truth that none are completely immune to the lure and seduction of these Daemons. A Witch Hunter exacts the true cost of that power, often at the end of a gun barrel.

As their reputation suggests, Witch Hunters rely upon cunning and surprise to engage the fallen. The idea of chivalry, or fighting fair, is a childish notion for their breed. They are far more effective leaping from the shadows to judge a single unsuspecting target.

Witch Hunters travel far and wide to stop the spread of Chaos, thus they travel light, and their armor and equipment are light. Consequently, a Witch Hunter is not much for standing toe-to-toe with the followers of Chaos. Additionally, their magic is limited to the relics they have been granted by their order. A Witch Hunter deals as much damage as possible, as fast as possible, through the use of sword and pistol.

Overall, their undeniable effectiveness is due to speed, surprise, and single-mindedness. When taken by surprise, few opponents can withstand the sheer force of righteousness that a Witch Hunter can bring to bear.

—Aleister Schreiber, Scholar Emeritus, University of Nuln

The prospective Witch Hunter may wish to consider the following primary stats while planning this career. Strength increases melee damage, and also makes it less likely that an opponent will block or parry attacks. At first glance, this seems like an obvious choice for consideration of training when the opportunity arises, and, truthfully, given what a Witch Hunter does, one could do worse than being highly regarded in Strength.

Toughness, on the other hand, minimizes the damage taken from melee attacks. Again, given that Witch Hunters spend their lives dispatching corrupted souls, the ability to shrug off some of that inevitable damage would seem useful.

Wounds stat represents how much damage you can take before you succumb to death. I shouldn't need to emphasize the importance of that characteristic. The higher the Wounds ability, the more damage a Witch Hunter can take. It isn't a measure of how badly hurt a Witch Hunter is, but rather, how badly hurt a Witch Hunter can be before dying.

Initiative measures how well one evades attacks. It also decreases the chance that an opponent will score a critical strike. Because a Witch Hunter stands in harm's way, the ability to sidestep some attacks can only be beneficial.

Weapon Skill increases the chance of parrying in incoming attack, but also gives the ability to bypass some of an opponents' armor. Any skill that allows a Witch Hunter to avoid some damage from an enemy while increasing his ability to harm that opponent is excellent.

Ballistic Skill increases the amount of damage done on ranged attacks, and also makes it more difficult for opponents to block or evade those attacks. While Witch Hunters do not do most of their damage at range, nor do they have any ability to automatically attack with a ranged weapon, almost all of their Executions are ranged in nature! Because a significant portion of the damage a Witch Hunter does to an opponent is based on Executions, it is important that enemies aren't ducking those shots! While I'll explain how Accusations and Executions work later on, suffice it to say that Ballistic Skill is an important part of a Witch Hunter's ability to purge this land of corruption.

Intelligence increases magical damage, but no Witch Hunter would ever use magical abilities. And although a Witch Hunter has a few channeled abilities, they aren't enough to justify concerning oneself with this stat. Similarly, Willpower increases one's healing ability, but a Witch Hunter has very little ability in healing.

So, how should a Witch Hunter focus their attention on their stats? Whatever aspect of the career a Witch Hunter plans to employ, the primary focus is on Weapon Skill and Ballistic Skill. Without strong capability in those stats, a Witch Hunter's ability to do damage is compromised. And the more damage Witch Hunters can do, the better chance they have of successfully executing their duties.

Now, if the Witch Hunter plans on confronting the forces of Destruction head on, or plans to travel with companions who are focused on damage output and healing, rather than damage reduction and armor, the Witch Hunter might want to consider Toughness, Wounds, Initiative, and Strength, in that order. By focusing in that direction, Witch Hunters can reduce damage they're taking, increase the amount of damage they can take, increase how often they dodge an attack, and increase the amount of damage they'll do. This is useful for Witch Hunters who plan to travel solo.

The Witch Hunter who plans to catch opponents off guard, or who travels with companions who are well suited to drawing the attention of their foes, should focus on Strength, Initiative, Toughness, and Wounds. Doing so increases damage-dealing capabilities at the expense of some damage-taking ability.

ENTERING THE EMPIRE

I began my journey in Grimmenhagen. It was once a lovely town nestled within the mountains in the south of Nordland, but Chaos has spread even to this remote village. When I arrived, the town was under siege by the forces of Destruction, and a hero named Viktor Riese had been assigned to the town's defense by the Emperor himself.

Viktor, understandably, was somewhat angered by this duty, as he had been given insufficient men to help defend the town. As such, he was grateful to see me, and quick to enlist my rapier and pistol, inexperienced as it was, in the defense of the town.

Marget Grunenwald's shop had been burned to the ground, so she stood by the large statue in the middle of town. In spite of her predicament, she offered the materials for those who study making potions or farming the earth. She also provided a welcome source of income, for she purchased items for which I had no use, but had acquired through unneeded rewards or from the corpses of my enemies.

Eldred Krebs journeyed to Grimmenhagen in the Riese's service. Krebs' almost impossible task was to somehow rally and train the peasant rabble into some semblance of fighting force. I did not envy him his task. But to further motivate the farmers, Krebs acquired some exquisite artifacts, from potions to weapons and armor. He rewards those who have distinguished themselves on the field of battle and generated some influence. He had a sword that was far better than my dull and rusty rapier. I admit I spent a fair amount of time trying to prove my worth to the town's defense so he would see fit to give it to me. It was time very well spent, for that sword served me well for many months after.

Also in the center of town stood the village priest and healer, Wilhelm Frolich. Brother Wilhelm was ill-prepared for the rapid spread of Chaos, but he still tends to his flock, providing healing for any who approach. He was of great value the few times I had found myself sick after a particularly brutal battle with the enemy, removing the feeling of weakness and lassitude that often comes from the healing of serious injury.

While there were many other occupants in the town, the one I spoke with most frequently was a soldier named Elsa Schmidt. Schmidt is a dedicated servant of the Empire, who believes that for the Empire to reign victorious over the onslaught of Destruction, one must continually prepare oneself through training. Schmidt knew far more about my potential than I did, and, as I gained in experience, I frequently met with Schmidt so that she could teach me how to better use my skill in battle. She trained me in Core abilities and Tactical abilities, and even abilities that were based on my Morale. As I travelled far and wide, I made a point of seeking out the Empire's trainers, for the more I experienced, the more they taught me.

WITCH HUNTER GEAR

A Witch Hunter is only as good as the sword he uses to level his Accusations, and the pistol he uses to pass judgments through his Executions. Poor quality weaponry makes it extremely difficult to rid this land of the filth that pervades every corner. I was taught to tend to my weapons, first and foremost.

My earliest issued equipment seemed relatively weak. In spite of that, it was quite serviceable, and, in truth, was not all that different in form and function from the equipment that I use today. Of course, as soon as I found a better sword and pistol, I was happy to rid myself of the dull rapier and rickety pistol.

I was not initially given much armor, and it was an unintentionally wise decision. A Witch Hunter who relies heavily on his armor is a dead Witch Hunter. We wear only light armor anyway, and any armor I've worn has had only the slightest of effects. I learned to rely on offense as my defense by standing in front of a corrupted soul and dispatching it with naught but my faith and my weapons.

What little armor I can find, I wear, of course. I do get hit. There's no avoiding that. The followers of Chaos do their level best to see me dead, and they are, unfortunately, all too good at the art of destruction. Every little bit helps, but I find that the best way to avoid being hit is to kill my opponent as swiftly as possible.

Often, in my travels, upon completing tasks, I was given a choice of rewards. My primary focus has always been upgrading my sword and pistol. Given the choice of selecting a weapon that is a moderate upgrade, or a piece of armor that is a substantial upgrade, I usually took the moderately upgraded weapon.

Diligent study of the Tome of Knowledge, along with unabated trials and exploration, have granted me additional Tactics!

STRENGTHS AND WEAKNESSES

Strengths

A Witch Hunter with the element of surprise can defeat just about any enemy one-on-one.

Various abilities make a target easier to hit, wound it more, or slow down its movement.

Witch Hunters are excellent at pursuit. Many of their abilities work while moving, and some even slow an opponent if the Witch Hunter strikes from behind. This becomes extremely useful in PvP.

The Witch Hunter is very singly focused. They are trained to decide on a single target, and eliminate it. This makes it easy to determine how a Witch Hunter is going to approach a tactical problem.

With very few exceptions, almost every ability, talent, or skill is focused on doing damage to an opponent, or increasing that damage. The sheer number of attacks, buffs, and debuffs makes a Witch Hunter deadly in any of a number of different ways, which provides variety and interest in performing the single important task of cleansing the Empire of corruption.

Weaknesses

- Witch Hunters cannot deliver any real damage at significant distance. They must close with ranged attackers, or fall back until they can find a way to get closer.

- Because Witch Hunters do a lot of damage fast, enemies typically try to eliminate the Witch Hunter first in any combat. This becomes an issue, especially in groups.

- Witch Hunters can use only light armor, which doesn't protect against damage particularly well.

- Witch Hunters have very little that drastically affects more than one target at a time. Because of this, soloing can be difficult in crowded areas. Once a Witch Hunter has drawn the attention of more than one foe, it typically doesn't end well for the Witch Hunter.

A Witch Hunter does but one thing, but does that one thing very, very well. A Witch Hunter delivers melee damage faster and more efficiently than any other profession. The cost of my single-minded devotion toward ridding these lands of evil is that I cannot do much else. With only light armor, a Witch Hunter must out-damage his enemy or he will not last long.

Abilities

When I first started out, I was taught the rudiments of shooting, and the way to handle a sword. It will undoubtedly be the same for anyone else training to be a Witch Hunter.

One of the very first things I learned is Snap Shot. Snap Shot, which works between 5 and 65 feet, became my primary ranged attack. While I cannot use it in melee combat, I can use Snap Shot while moving, making it invaluable as I chase down a fleeing enemy. Early in my career, it served to draw the attention of an enemy at a distance. Snap Shot does relatively little damage, and it takes about a second to fire my pistol, although it never requires reloading. Naturally, I am required to actually have a pistol, which isn't an issue, for even today, I am never without one.

At the same time I learned to fire a pistol, I trained in the basics of swordplay. It was thus that I learned Razor Strike. Razor Strike is a darting, slashing blow, as fleeting as innocence. It has a five-foot range and can be used instantaneously, with no delay between strikes. Razor Strike has served me well from the day I picked up my first rusty rapier, and I expect it will continue to serve me until the day they lay me in the cold ground. The most important thing I learned about Razor Strike, however, is that it's a major way to level an Accusation at an enemy of the Light. Each time I wound a foe with Razor Strike, my righteousness swells, and the case against my target grows stronger.

For a Witch Hunter, the very roots of combat are based in "Accusations" and "Executions." The Witch Hunter has a number of sword-based abilities that generate something called an Accusation. The maximum number of Accusations a Witch Hunter may have in his "Accusation pool" is five.

I've already mentioned Razor Strike, my first Accusation ability. The other two, Fervor (Rank 3) and Torment (Rank 5), I learned by the time I'd left Grimmenhagen. Fervor is but a light scratch, but it leaves an open wound that continues to bleed, further sapping an enemy's health. I discovered that I could leave three such wounds on an opponent at any one time, allowing me to watch the evil gleam slowly trickle from a witch's eyes. Torment is a precise, stronger blow, doing about the same amount of damage as Razor Strike, but I learned to avoid hitting an opponent's armor when I struck from from behind. Again, the important thing about all of these abilities is that they all wound my targets, and they all add an Accusation to my pool.

These three abilities quickly became the very essence of my combat. I expect to be using them all until the fall of the Inevitable City itself. As I gained experience, I discovered that the strength and damage of the attacks increased as well. But no matter how experienced I became, each successful strike with any of these three abilities resulted in adding but one Accusation to my pool.

It should be noted that career paths offer three additional Accusations, one per path. I will discuss them further when I explain Mastery paths.

It was about that time that I started to learn my Executions. Once I have leveled at least one Accusation at my opponent (or as many as five Accusations), I can pass judgment on my enemy in the form of an Execution. Executions are abilities that vary in strength depending on how many Accusations I have in my Accusation pool. The three Core Executions I learned were: Absolution (Rank 2); Burn, Heretic! (Rank 6); and Trial by Pain (Rank 12). Absolution does a single large hit of damage. Burn, Heretic! does more damage than Absolution, but does it over 10 seconds. Trial by Pain does about the same damage as Burn, Heretic!, but does it over three seconds. Trial by Pain, however, requires that I concentrate for the three seconds while using it. Should I move while using Trial by Pain, I interrupt the ability, decreasing the amount of pain I ultimately inflict. Any damage I take has a chance of interrupting me as well. Like my Accusations, I use these Executions to this very day, although now they are significantly more powerful than when I first learned them.

When I use an Execution attack, it uses all the Accusations I have in my Accusation pool, and my opponent is harmed according to the number expended. Clearly, the more Accusations I level against my opponent, the more powerful my Executions are. From that standpoint, I often consider carefully before using my Executions. Leveling only an Accusation or two against an opponent before using an Execution will reduce the amount of potential damage I do as compared to the amount of action points spent, thus reducing my combat efficiency. Still, if I notice my enemy is close to death, it sometimes pays for me to use an Execution before I've built up all my Accusations, as even the reduced strength Execution may well kill my opponent. Obviously, the tradeoff is speed versus efficiency.

As with my Accusations, three additional Executions are available through career paths, one per path.

In addition to Accusations and Executions, I also learned Blessings. Blessings are abilities that modify the damage being done by my Executions, through the application of the Blessings on the holy bullets fired from my pistol. Again, like Accusations and Executions, I learned three different Blessings. They are: Blessed Bullets of Cleansing (Rank 4), Blessed Bullets of Purity (Rank 9), and Blessed Bullets of Confession (Rank 35).

To use any of the Blessings, I'd use the ability like any other, and the Executions fired from my pistol took on the characteristics of my Blessing. Blessed Bullets of Cleansing adds additional Spirit damage to my Executions, and reduces my target's movement speed. This is particularly useful for enemies who won't remain still long enough to be purged of the taint of corruption. Blessed Bullets of Purity adds additional Spirit damage to my Execution, but this Blessing also takes half of the additional damage dealt to my target, and returns it to me in the form of healing. When fighting hard-hitting foes, I often use this Blessing because it gives me a little more resilience while in melee. The last, Blessed Bullets of Confession, deals additional Spirit damage over time, and lowers my target's action point pool for the duration of the damage-over-time ability. This Blessing is useful in PvP. Opponents without action points can't use their abilities, and lowering their action point pool is a good way to help speed the depletion of their points.

Incognito, an ability I learned at Rank 10, allows me to become invisible for a short time. While I'm Incognito, I slowly lose action points. When I run out of action points, I become visible again. Incognito is important because by being invisible, I can sneak up on targets an engage them in combat before

I've been careful to speak with every person I've come across in my travels. Aside from the obvious requests for aid, these conversations have sometimes led me to hidden corruption.

hey have a chance to run or attack me. Few enemies of the Light can withstand
he sudden fury and righteousness of a Witch Hunter leaping out of the shadows.

Once I'd learned how to use Incognito, I discovered that there were three
additional Accusations that could be used only while I was Incognito. These Accusations, Burn Armor (Rank 10), Sudden Accusation (Rank 20),
and Fanatical Zeal (Rank 30) have become a common way for me to engage an enemy, as they not only debuff my target, but they temporarily
decrease the action point cost of my abilities, and add two Accusation points to my pool. Because I need to be Incognito for them to work, I use
them only to begin my fight, and rarely—if ever—in mid-combat. In addition to decreasing the AP cost of my abilities and adding two Accusations
to my pool, Burn Armor damages my target each time he or she attacks, Sudden Accusation damages my target each time he or she moves, and
Fanatical Zeal damages my target each time he or she casts a spell.

So, depending on my target, I use one of these Accusation abilities to start my fight with a great deal of fury. Obviously, I use Burn Armor against
melee types, Sudden Accusation against ranged types, and Fanatical Zeal against casters. Fanatical Zeal is particularly nasty against healers, because
they take damage with every heal.

I learned a great many things in a short time, so I know that it's a great deal of information to absorb. Unfortunately, those who read this manual
will likely have ample opportunity to use these abilities, starting from the very first day in Grimmenhagen. But at least the novice Witch Hunter
will quickly learn how Accusations, Executions, and Blessings all work in conjunction. Or they won't, and the Empire will be digging another
unmarked grave.

Abilities

Name	Level	Path	Cost	Range (in feet)	Type	Build	Duration	Reuse	Description
Snap Shot	Level 1	Core	20	10 to 65	Ranged Attack	1s	0s	0s	Deals 75 damage. When hit from the rear, Snare target by 40% for 5s.
Razor Strike	Level 1	Confession	40	Melee	Builder Melee Attack	0s	0s	0s	Deals (262+DPS) damage.
Absolution	Level 2	Judgement	35	Melee	Pistol Finisher	0s	0s	0s	Deals instant damage based on combo points spent. 1: (262+DPS), 2: (262+DPS)*1.33, 3: (262+DPS)*1.67, 4: (262+DPS)*2, 5: (262+DPS)*2.333.
Fervor	Level 3	Inquisition	35	Melee	Builder Melee - Cripple	0s	9s	0s	Deals (75+DPS) and stackable DoT that deals 249 over 9s. Stacks up to 3 times.
Blessed Bullets of Cleansing	Level 4	Judgement	55	Self	Blessed Buff - Cripple	0s	30 min	0s	All Executions will also cause DoT (225 over 5s) and Snare (40% for 5s).
Torment	Level 5	Judgement	35	Melee	Builder Melee	0s	0s	0s	Deals (187+DPS) damage. If rear positional, ignore armor.
Burn, Heretic!	Level 6	Inquisition	35	Melee	Melee Finisher - Cripple	0s	10s	0s	Deals damage over 10s based on combo points: 1: 637, 2: 848, 3: 1,064, 4: 1,275, 5: 1,487.
Feinted Positioning	Level 7	Core	25	65	Self Buff	0s	10s	60s	Witch Hunter positional attacks can be used on debuffed target without the positional requirement. Does not affect Morale abilities. Does not trigger GCD. Affects: Torment, Silence the Heretic, Pistol Whip, Vitrolic Judgement, and Flanking.
Get Thee Behind Me!	Level 8	Core	20	Melee	Melee Attack	0s	15s	30s	Deals no damage. Detaunts all targets (50%, 15s). Radius: 30ft.
Blessed Bullets of Purity	Level 9	Confession	55	Self	Blessed Buff	0s	30 min	0s	Executions deal an additional 150 Spirit damage and heal the Witch Hunter for 50% of the extra damage.
Incognito	Level 10	Core	4 AP/s	Self	Buff	2s	30s	60s	Character stealths. Using any ability breaks stealth. Reuse begins after stealth is broken.
Burn Armor	Level 10	Confession	Free	Melee	Opener Attack - Cripple	0s	15s	0s	Place Melee Barb on target. Effect deals 150 every time the target uses a melee ability. AP costs are reduced by 50% for 10s. Builds 2 combo points. No GCD.
Trial by Pain	Level 12	Confession	15/s	Melee	Pistol Finisher	0s	3s	0s	Channeled. Deals damage every 0.5s for 3s. Damage based on combo points. 1: (112+DPS)*0.5, 2: (112+DPS)*.665, 3: (112+DPS)*0.835, 4: (112+DPS)*1, 5: (112+DPS)*1.165.

Abilities

Name	Level	Path	Cost	Range (in feet)	Type	Build	Duration	Reuse	Description
Confess!	Level 14	Inquisition	40	Melee	Melee Reactional - Cripple	0s	5s	10s	Requires Parry. Deal (262+DPS) damage and disarm target for 5s.
Silence the Heretic	Level 16	Judgement	25	Melee	Builder Attack - Cripple	0s	3s	20s	Silence target for 3s. If you are behind the target, also deal (225+DPS) damage.
Sigil of Sigmar	Level 18	Core	45	Self	Dispel	0s	0s	60s	Remove movement impairing effects (Snare/Root) and grant immunity for 10s.
Sudden Accusation	Level 20	Inquisition	Free	Melee	Opener Attack	0s	15s	0s	Place Movement Barb on target. Effect deals 56 every time the target moves (check every 0.5s). AP costs are reduced by 50% for 10s. Builds 2 combo points. No GCD.
Sever Blessing	Level 22	Core	25	Melee	Melee Attack	0s	0s	5s	Removes a blessing from target. Deals (75+DPS) damage if successful.
Seeker's Blade	Level 25	Confession	45	Melee	Builder - Melee Curse	0s	10s	10s	Deals (262+DPS) damage. Unable to be defended against. If the target is Crippled, reduces their chance to defend by 5% for 10s.
Fanatical Zeal	Level 30	Judgement	Free	Melee	Opener Attack	0s	15s	0s	Places a Spell Barb on target. Effect deals 150 every time the target uses a magic ability. AP costs are reduced by 50% for 10s. Builds 2 combo points. No GCD.
Blessed Bullets of Confession	Level 35	Inquisition	55	Self	Blessed Buff - Curse	0s	30 min	0s	All Executions also cause Spirit DoT (262 over 9s) and remove 30 AP.
Declare Anathema	Level 40	Core	Free	Self	Escape	0s	2s	30s	Stuns target for 2s; player leaps backward away from them.
Shroud of Magnus	Confession x5	Confession	25	Self	Relic Buff	0s	10s	60s	Increase all resists by 6/level by 10s. No GCD. Shared cooldown with other relics.
Repel Blasphemy	Confession x9	Confession	40	Melee	Builder Melee Attack	0s	5s	30s	Deals (337+DPS) damage and increases chance to Parry by 100% for 5s.
Dragon Gun	Confession x13	Confession	35	Melee	Pistol Finisher	0s	0s	10s	Deals damage based by combo points: 1: (262+DPS), 2: (262+DPS)*1.33, 3: (262+DPS)*1.67, 4: (262+DPS)*2, 5: (262+DPS)*2.33. Radius based on combo points: 1: 20ft, 2: 25ft, 3: 30ft, 4: 33ft, 5: 38ft.
Seal of Destruction	Inquisition x5	Inquisition	25	Self	Relic Buff	0s	10s	60s	Removes 1 Hex or Curse per second for 10s. Each time an effect is removed, heal self for (225)*0.6. No GCD. Shared cooldown with other relics.
Punish the False	Inquisition x9	Inquisition	30	Melee	Builder Melee - Curse	0s	10s	10s	Deals (225+DPS) damage and reduces healing on target by 50% for 10s.
Exit Wound	Inquisition x13	Inquisition	35	Melee	Finisher - Cripple	0s	5s	10s	Deals damage based on combo points. 1: (300+DPS), 2: (300+DPS)*1.33, 3: (300+DPS)*1.67, 4: (300+DPS)*2, 5: (300+DPS)*2.333. Lowers target's Strength, Weapon Skill, and Toughness by (2/3/4/5/6) per level for 10s.
Van Horstmann's Speculum	Judgement x5	Judgement	25	Self	Relic Buff	0s	10s	60s	Steal 3/level worth of Strength, Toughness, and Weapon Skill from target for 10s. No GCD. Shared cooldown with other relics.
Pistol Whip	Judgement x9	Judgement	35	Melee	Builder Melee Attack	0s	3s	20s	Deals (337.5+DPS) and Stuns target for 3s. Requires rear positional.
Burn Away Lies	Judgement x13	Judgement	35	Melee	Finisher Attack - Curse	0s	9s	10s	Deals damage over 9s based on combo points. 1: 448, 2: 1: 597, 3: 748, 4: 898, 5: 1,046 and at the end of the Dot deals an additional 1: 337, 2: 449, 3: 564, 4: 675, 5: 786.

I make every effort to perform all the tasks that the occupants of a town or warcamp have for me before moving on. Doing so ensures that I have the experience and strength to do the tasks that await me in the following village.

Morale

Morale is the last type of ability I learned during my Core Training. I gained my first Morale ability at Rank 8, and I gained an additional Morale ability every four ranks thereafter. As I engage in combat, my Morale slowly accumulates, reflecting the surge of righteousness I feel as I fulfill my duties. Once combat is over, and the blood-pumping rush of adrenaline subsides, my Morale bar quickly empties. Additionally, I must choose my Morale abilities prior to combat, and cannot change them while I am engaged.

My initial Morale ability was Sever Nerve. That Morale ability does a great deal of damage to a single target, but can be used only if I'm behind or to the side of my target. This occasionally came in handy as a finishing move against a fleeing opponent, or when I traveled with companions.

Later on, I learned a Morale ability called Confusing Movements (Rank 16). Confusing Movements allows me to dodge and parry all attacks directed toward me for seven seconds. I've found that ability to be extremely useful, especially when fighting several opponents.

But perhaps the most important Morale ability I've learned is Exoneration (Rank 28.) Exoneration is the only ability that allows me to heal myself on demand. It is, of course, reliant upon Morale, but if I'm not in combat, I rarely need healing, now do I?

Morale

Name	Level	Rank	Range (in feet)	Duration	Description
Sever Nerve	Level 8	Rank 1	Melee	15s	Melee attack that deals 1,200 damage.
Force of Will	Level 12	Rank 2	Self	30s	Drain 200 AP from target and give to character. Decrease target's Strength by 4/level for 30s.
Confusing Movements	Level 16	Rank 1	Self	7s	Increase chance to Parry and Evade attacks by 100% for 7s.
Relentless Assault	Level 20	Rank 2	Group	15s	Group buff. Grants 10 AP/s to group for 10s. This occurs even during layers.
Broad Swings	Level 24	Rank 3	Self	10s	All attacks hit 2 additional targets within 350u for 10s. Additional targets take 300 damage.
Exoneration	Level 28	Rank 1	Self	9s	Self-only buff that heals 720 over 9s and increases AP 20/sec for 9s.
Reversal of Fortune	Level 32	Rank 2	PBAE	5s	AE Disarm target for 5s and deal 600 damage, 30ft radius.
Witchfinder's Protection	Level 36	Rank 3	Group	10s	Group Buff. Increase chance to Parry attacks by 50% for 10s.
Holy Blade	Judgement x15	Rank 4	LAE	0s	Deals 2,400 to targets in radius.
Excommunicate	Cleansing x15	Rank 4	100	15s	Deals 1,800 to targets in radius over 15s. Heals are reduced in initial target by 100% for 15s. Radius: 30ft.
Expurgation	Inquisition x15	Rank 4	PBAE	10s	Deals 2,400 to targets in radius over 10s. Snares targets by 60%. Radius: 30ft.
Frenzied Slaughter	Level 40	Rank 4	Self	7s	Self buff. AP costs are reduced 25%. Cooldowns are reduced by 50%. Damage dealt is increased by 20%. Lasts 7s.

Tactics

Name	Level	Description
Emperor's Ward	Level 11	25% chance when attacked to absorb 262 damage for 10s.
Jagged Edge	Level 13	Critical hits also place a 412 damage bleed DoT on the target for 9s.
Inquisitor's Fury	Level 15	Critical hits increase auto-attack speed by 50% for 10s.
Unwavering Faith	Level 17	Increases Spirit resist by 6.3/level of the character.
Brute Force	Level 19	Increases Strength by 4/level of the character.
Flowing Finishers	Level 21	Finishers have a 50% chance to grant the Witch Hunter 2 combo points.
Sigmar's Favor	Level 23	25% chance when healed to be healed for an additional 135.
Flanking	Level 25	Increase damage by 15% from attacks made to the side or rear of an enemy.
Righteous Steel	Level 27	Increase Parry chance by 10%.
Riposte	Level 29	When the character Parries, he deals 187 back to the target.
Penetrating Barbs	Level 31	Opener barbs last 20s on target.
Last Rites	Level 33	When the Witch Hunter kills a target, he heals himself 472 over 9s.
Vindication	Level 35	After disrupting a spell, all damage dealt by the character is increased 35% for 10s.
Emperor's Commendation	Level 37	All Openers also give the Witch Hunter 150 Morale.
Blood, Faith, and Fire	Level 39	When the Witch Hunter kills a target, all group members within 30ft gain 75 AP.
Seeker's Triumph	Confession x3	Seeker's Blade gains 50% armor penetration and lowers the reuse timer by 5s.
Sanctified Bullets	Confession x7	Blessed Bullets of Purity deals 225 damage and heals for 100%.

Tactics

In addition to my abilities, I learned a great deal about Tactics. Tactics modify abilities or stats, or provide buffs. Tactical sets can be changed relatively quickly, and provide a bit more adaptability. For example, I have created a Tactical set for offensive combat (such as assaulting a keep) and a set for defensive combat (such as defending a scenario objective.)

I learned my first Tactic at Rank 11, and I've learned a new one every other rank thereafter. The first Tactic I learned, Emperor's Ward, gives me a chance to have a shield that protects me against some damage each time I'm attacked. I found this somewhat useful, although it doesn't come up as often as I'd like. At rank 13, however, I learned Jagged Edge, which adds additional damage over time to any critical blow. This has been a much better choice for me. Later on, I learned my personal favorite, Flowing Accusations (Rank 21), which gives my Executions a 50% chance of returning two Accusations to me. This tactic allows me to keep the fallen ones on their toes, as I can rain down a seemingly endless amount of Executions on them in short order.

Tactics

Name	Level	Description
Sweeping Razor	Confession x11	Razor Strike gains a 15ft radius (max targets of 3).
Full Confession	Inquisition x3	Confess becomes free and has a 100% chance to critical.
Prolonged Confession	Inquisition x7	Proc durations of Fervor; Burn, Heretic!; and Blessed Bullets of Confession are increased by 3s.
Encourage Confession	Inquisition x11	Blessed Bullets of Confession removes 40 AP from target and gives it to the Witch Hunter.
Fanatical Cleansing	Judgement x3	Blessed Bullets of Cleansing last for 10s.
Atonement	Judgement x7	Increases crititical chance with Absolution by 25%.
Vitriolic Judgement	Judgement x11	When attacking an enemy from the rear, 25% chance to remove 225 Morale.

Mastery

While every Witch Hunter learns the same Core abilities, at Rank 10, they acquire the ability to train in Mastery paths. How and what a Witch Hunter studies along these paths differentiates one Witch Hunter from the next. I received my first Mastery point at Rank 10, and continued to receive them at roughly every rank, ultimately learning 25 Mastery points by the time I reached Rank 40.

The Path of Confession is focused on head-on, toe-to-toe combat, which makes it a good choice for those Witch Hunters who like to adventure alone. Witch Hunters who choose to follow this path increase the power of the abilities Blessed Bullets of Purity, Burn Armor, Trial by Pain, and Seeker's Blade. Confessors, as adherents to this path are called, learn Repel Blasphemy as their Accusation, which does a fair bit of damage, but also doubles the Witch Hunter's Parry ability. For their Execution, these Witch Hunters learn Dragon Gun, which does a nice amount of damage to the target and enemies surrounding the target. The Rank 4 Morale ability is Holy Blade, which does an enormous amount of damage to any enemy in front of the Witch Hunter, up to 80 feet away.

The Path of Inquisition is focused on longer-duration weakening effects, which often benefits the Witch Hunter who seeks long, group-oriented battles against large, powerful opponents. Witch Hunters who choose to follow this path increase the power of Fervor; Blessed Bullets of Confession; Burn, Heretic!; Confess!; and Sudden Accusation. For their Accusation, Inquisitors learn Punish the False. Like most Accusations, this ability does the usual damage, but also reduces the effectiveness of any healing that is applied to the target for 10 seconds. The Inquisitor's Execution is called Exit Wound, and does less damage than the other Executions, but greatly reduces the target's Toughness for 10 seconds. The Rank 4 Morale ability is called Excommunicate. For 15 seconds, the target receives no benefit from any healing spells or abilities. At the same time, the target, and any enemy within 30 feet of the target, receives a huge amount of damage over 10 seconds. This Morale ability can drastically turn the tide of a battle.

The Path of Judgment focuses on surprise attacks and positional combat. This path favors Witch Hunters who enjoy group-oriented adventuring or PvP, or who expect to solo PvP. This path increases the power of Absolution, Blessed Bullets of Cleansing, Torment, Silence the Heretic, and Fanatical Zeal. For their Accusation, Judges learn Pistol Whip. This ability does nice damage, plus stuns a target for five seconds. The drawback to it is that it must be used from behind the target. If the Witch Hunter travels with other adventurers, that usually isn't a problem. The Judge's Execution is called Burn Away Lies, which does moderate damage over time, then finishes with a burst of damage. This Execution works marvelously well in battles where groups of enemies are charging forward and falling back regularly. The Rank 4 Morale ability is called Expurgation, and is a PvP Witch Hunter's dream come true. Expurgation does a huge amount of damage over 10 seconds to every enemy within 30 feet, all the while reducing their run speed.

Through contemplation and much discussion, I have determined that there is no wrong choice of paths. Focus entirely on a single path, learning all the abilities and maximizing their power, or divide one's attention across two or three paths. How I follow my path is a reflection of my preferences and beliefs regarding the role of a Witch Hunter within the Empire.

Renown

As I have traveled through this land fraught with corruption, I have run across followers of Chaos, witches, foul Orcs, and other scum that truck with Daemons and their ilk. It is a testament to the value the Empire places on purity that I have become somewhat well-known for ridding the world of that filth. In particular, I have become somewhat well-known for my success in PvP combat.

As I fight in the many battles, scenarios, keep assaults, and other PvP events, I gain Renown. As my Renown has grown, I've spoken with the Renown Trainers found in warcamps and keeps throughout the land. Through Renown Trainers, I've learned a number of Renown abilities.

There are a wide variety of Renown abilities. Renown abilities can be either passive abilities that are applied directly to stats, or they can be Renown Tactics, which are used just like Core and Mastery Tactics. The passive abilities adjust stats, such as Strength or Ballistic Skill. The Renown Tactics often have to do with things like how fast one gains experience, or being able to do more damage to a particular race.

Keep in mind what I wrote about stats when deciding which Renown abilities to learn. My initial Renown abilities were Blade Master, which increased my Weapon Skill; Marksmen, which increased my Ballistic Skill; and Fortitude, which increased my Toughness. I also considered an interesting Renown Tactic, Combat Awareness, which increases the amount of experience I gain in PvP.

WARHAMMER ONLINE
AGE OF RECKONING

corruption can be found anywhere and everywhere. That includes the homelands of our allies. When I found myself struggling to defeat my enemies in a given area, I often headed to an ally's homeland, and helped out some of the people in those villages.

Once I had gained 20 points worth of Renown Abilities, I could learn from the Tier 2 Renown abilities. In this tier, I leapt at the chance to learn Sharp Shooter, which increased both my Weapon Skill and my Ballistic Skill. Vigor, which increased my Wounds, and Reinforcement, which increased my Armor, weren't bad choices, either. For a Renown Tactic, I debated the kind of PvP I found myself engaged in most frequently, and considered For Glory!, King of the Hill, or Mission Focused, which would have increased the amount of Renown I earned when doing scenarios, skirmishing, or taking objectives, respectively.

Once I spent 40 points in Renown abilities, the Renown Trainers saw fit to allow me to train the most powerful of the Renown abilities, the Tier 3 abilities. Here, I quickly trained in Opportunist, which increased my melee crit chance. After that, I trained in Sure Shot, which increased my ranged crit chance, perfect for maximizing the damage of my Executions. On the defensive side of things, I began to train in Reflexes, which increased my Parry rate, and Agility, which increased my Dodge rate. These have served me well.

Report Card—Hieronymous Brandt

English: C

History: B

Physical Education: A

Math: D

Eltharin: F

Science: D

Young Hieronymous is something of a mystery to us all. He seems to be interested in the humanities, and none can best him at sport, but he clearly has no aptitude for math or science. He applies himself extraordinarily diligently to the histories, being especially interested in the founding of the Empire and the struggles inherent in its founding.

I admit we were surprised, however, at his unwillingness to even enter the classroom with Professor Silverleaf, his Eltharin professor. When questioned as to his refusal, he simply muttered something about "foul magic," and refused to speak further on it. This is ludicrous, of course... Silverleaf has no experience in such things, but Hieronymous remained suspicious and completely unpersuaded.

Of course, Hieronymous remains the star of the archery range, as his steady bow is unparalleled in the history of the school. Once Hieronymous has his eye on you, you're as good as done!

I hope he will reapply himself to math and science next semester. I look forward to seeing his progress. He's going to need some sort of skills if he's ever to find a trade. After all, what occupation could possibly benefit from his play on the rugby pitch?

Sincerely,

G. White, Headmaster

CRUSHING MONSTERS AND POCKETING TREASURE (PVE)
Solo Play

Rank 1~10

Witch Hunters spend the most of their time in melee with the forces of corruption. Notice that I did not say toe-to-toe. For while the Witch Hunter is often in hand-to-hand combat with an enemy, the Witch Hunter is just as likely to be attacking from the side or back. If possible, a Witch Hunter always attacks from behind, and some abilities are best used from that position.

Having said all that, how each Witch Hunter approaches combat can be very personal. Some prefer to strike hard and fast, hoping to out-damage their foe. Some choose to be light on their feet, dodging and parrying as much as possible, all the while nicking and slicing their opponents to death with relatively light blows. Still others like doing lasting damage: hit once and allow the wound to bleed, or set the foe on fire and watch the very witchery burn away.

As a new Witch Hunter, Ranks 1 through 10 were all about learning the Core abilities that ended up serving me for my entire career. There weren't any Tactics to learn yet, and the one Morale ability I learned at Rank 8 was largely useless.

When I first started out, at Rank 1, I didn't have much choice. I stood away from my target, and pulled with Snap Shot. Then I slashed with Razor Strike until my enemy saw the error of his ways. Because I didn't have an Execution yet, this was the best I could do. Fortunately, that didn't last long.

As soon as I reached Rank 2, I acquired my first Execution, Absolution. I then stood away from my target, and pulled with Snap Shot, as before. I then hit a few times with Razor Strike, but this time, when the foe had about a quarter of his life remaining, I Executed him with Absolution. That was wholly satisfying.

At Rank 3, I learned Fervor, which gave me a little bit of variety in my combat. I stood away, used Snap Shot, Fervor, Razor Strike, and Fervor until they were close to death. Once I had leveled enough Accusations at them, or they were knocking at death's door, I Executed them with Absolution.

At Rank 4, I got my first Blessing, Blessed Bullets of Cleansing. Now, I began each hunt by choosing my Blessing. Because the Blessing has a 30-minute duration, I used it between fights, refreshing it as necessary. I was careful to keep a Blessing up at all times, because casting it during combat would have been a waste of time and action points that could be better spent purifying some corrupt soul. Other than making sure I had a Blessing up, I continued to fight as I did at Rank 3. Because Blessed Bullets of Cleansing also had a snare component, it was a good choice for PvP.

Torment came at Rank 5. Because I was primarily soloing at this stage of my career, I used this interchangeably with Razor Strike. When I adventured with companions and could get behind my target, I used Torment more frequently. Otherwise, it seemed that I was fighting exactly as I did at Rank 3.

At Rank 6, I got my second Execution: Burn, Heretic! At that point, it didn't make all that much difference if I used Absolution or Burn, Heretic! If I was fighting things that ran away, like the PvP forces of Destruction, I used Burn, Heretic! If I wasn't, either one was equal to the task. Still, combat ran pretty much as it had since Rank 3.

At Rank 8, I learned my first Morale ability, but most of my fights weren't long enough for me to generate enough Morale to use it. If I did manage to generate that much Morale, I was rarely able to get behind an enemy to use it. I also learned Get Thee Behind Me! at Rank 8. This ability came in handy when I inevitably found myself fighting more than one target at once. It didn't keep things from beating on me, but it did decrease the amount of damage I was taking.

At Rank 9, I learned my second Blessing, Blessed Bullets of Purity. Finally, I had my first real decision: Do I go for the snare with Cleansing, or the healing that comes with Purity? This ended up being purely situational, but I settled on Cleansing for PvP and Purity for soloing. When I traveled with a healer, Blessed Bullets of Cleansing was the better choice.

At Rank 10, I learned Incognito and my whole world changed. In addition, I learned the first Accusation that requires Incognito: Burn Armor. With these new skills, I could do a great deal of damage as soon as I engaged an enemy.

With Incognito, my combat sequence now looked like: Incognito, move behind my target, Burn Armor, Torment, Fervor, Razor Strike, Execution (either Absolution or Burn, Heretic!, depending on how I was feeling at the time.) That sequence, which took less than three seconds if performed well, resulted in me standing in front of a badly wounded enemy who was bleeding and taking still more damage with every attempted hit. Finishing them off took very little effort.

If I couldn't use Incognito, my sequence became Fervor, Razor Strike, Fervor, Razor Strike, Fervor, and Execution. Repeat until cleansed.

Rank 11–20

Unlike Ranks 1 through 10, Ranks 11 through 20 provided an assortment of abilities, Morale abilities, and Tactics. At Rank 12, I learned my third Execution, Trial by Pain. Because it's a channeled damage-over-time ability, I couldn't really use in melee, because my opponent was still hitting me, which stopped my Execution. I ended up using it if my opponent was fleeing, or I was traveling in a group that had my target's attention. In any case, Absolution often served just fine in its stead.

At Rank 14, I learned Confess! Confess! is an attack that I can use only after I successfully parry an opponent's attack. When it became available, I inserted it into my normal combat sequence.

At Rank 16, Silence the Heretic became available. Silence the Heretic is an excellent strike, capable of silencing an opponent for 5 seconds, preventing the casting of any spells. When used from behind an opponent, it also does a moderate amount of damage. I find this skill to be of particular worth when fighting against casters and healers.

Whenever I entered a new village or warcamp, I always sought out the Rally Master before anything else. Doing so enabled me to travel swiftly back to town after I'd completed a task, saving me a great deal of wear on my boots.

At Rank 18, I trained my second-favorite ability (after Incognito). Sigil of Sigmar removes all roots and snares, and makes me immune to roots and snares for 10 seconds. In PvP, this ability is literally a lifesaver. A stationary Witch Hunter in PvP is a dead Witch Hunter. Because I'm still here, it may be safely assumed that I've used Sigil of Sigmar frequently since I first learned it.

At Rank 20, I learned Sudden Accusation, which is an Accusation used from Incognito. Sudden Accusation is just like Burn Armor, except it damages an opponent if they move, rather than attack. If my target was a melee type, and I thought they'd stand and fight, I used Burn Armor. If my target was a ranged or caster type, or I expected them to try to run, I used Sudden Accusation instead.

For Tactics, I quickly seized on Jagged Edge at Rank 13, which adds some damage over time each time I critically strike my opponent. Brute Force also wasn't bad if I decided to fight toe-to-toe. I didn't find particular value in the others, although I'm certain a clever Witch Hunter could find a use for them.

I learned two Rank 2 Morale abilities and one more Rank 1 Morale ability. The Rank 1 Morale ability I learned, Confusing Movements, allows me to dodge and parry all attacks for seven seconds. That is far better than Sever Nerve. Between the two Rank 2 Morale abilities, for group battles I chose Relentless Assault, which restores action points over time to my whole party. For solo slaying, I went with Force of Will, which drains action points from my target and gives them to me, all while reducing my target's Strength for 30 seconds.

I started my Mastery Training here, but the meager number of points I had didn't gain me much. Still, it was worth spending the points in the path to increase the strength and power of the path's related abilities.

In short, my combat didn't look all that different than when I reached Rank 10, although I had a little more ability to deal damage, and Sigil of Sigmar kept me moving around when the forces of Destruction tried to slow me down.

Rank 21~30

By now, I'd learned most of my Destruction abilities, and the focus of my training was on Tactics. I was learning some decent Mastery abilities, and because I'd spent some time in PvP, I had some Renown abilities. Still, my combat sequence hadn't changed much. I focused mainly on increasing the power of the abilities I used the most frequently.

At Rank 25, I gained access to Seeker's Blade, which is a melee attack that cannot be defended against. This was particularly useful against heavily armored opponents, even if it wasn't an Accusation. The interesting thing about Seeker's Blade is that if my opponent has a crippling debuff (from Confess!, Burn Armor, or Burn, Heretic!, for example,) my target had less chance of parrying, blocking, or dodging attacks for a few seconds afterward.

I also learned the last of the Core Accusations at Rank 30. Fanatical Zeal requires Incognito, and acts exactly like Burn Armor and Sudden Accusation, except Fanatical Zeal causes damage when an opponent casts a spell. Obviously, I used this as my opening Accusation from Incognito when my target was a caster or a healer.

While I learned five Tactics during this period, only two of them really stood out. Following Accusations gives all of my Executions a 50% chance to return two Accusations, having the effect of speeding up the amount of damage I can deal as it takes time to generate the desired five Accusations I like to have before I execute a target.

Rank 31~40

Through this stage of my training, the abilities I learned were among the most useful I'd learned to date for PvP. Blessed Bullets of Confession, the last of the Blessings, allows my Executions to do additional Spirit damage to my target over time, but also lowers the enemy's action points for nine seconds. I found this to be particularly useful, because I was using Executions several times during a fight now.

The other ability I learned, Declare Anathema, allows me to knock down my opponent while leaping backward about 30 feet. This ability lets me disengage from opponents, regroup, and re-engage on my terms, or fall back to the aid of my fellows.

I also learned a number of useful Tactics during this stage. Penetrating Barbs increases the duration of Fanatical Zeal, Burn Armor, and Sudden Accusation by 5 seconds, making it an excellent addition to my combat sequence starter. Last Rites allows me to regain some health each time I kill an opponent. I use that Tactic when I expect to be killing a large volume of targets, rather than large, single targets. The others, Vindication; Blood, Faith, and Fire; and Emperor's Commendation, are situationally useful, and they're all part of one set or another.

The Morale abilities learned during this time were the most useful of all. Reversal of Fortune, a Rank 2 Morale ability, allows me to do a fair bit of damage to all opponents within 30 feet, but also disarms them all for five seconds. This is extraordinarily useful in large-scale skirmishes, and my war party greatly enjoys the look of surprise on our enemies' faces when they realize that they have no weapons and are staring into the eyes of a half dozen coldly smiling Witch Hunters, all wielding naked blades and smoking pistols.

Witchfinder's Protection, a Rank 3 Morale ability, allows my entire war party to parry all incoming melee attacks for 10 seconds. Obviously, this Morale ability, used at the right time, can turn the tide of a battle, and buy time for a group to breach a door, land some much needed healing, or just provide a surge of momentum to force a line to move.

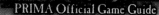

The last Morale ability learned, Frenzied Slaughter, a Rank 4 Morale ability, turns me into a killing machine, decreasing the action point cost and cooldown of all my abilities, and increasing their damage.

At this point, as well, I've trained in the last of my steps for my Mastery paths, and, since I've focused on a single path, I'm now using the Rank 4 Morale ability granted by my path, which is the single most powerful ability I've learned. I've also trained in the Mastery Accusation and Mastery Execution offered by my path, which I've added to my combat sequence.

Through what seems like endless battle, I've acquired just about every last Renown point I can, and I've spent those points with the Renown Trainers, really focusing those stats and abilities that bolster my style of combat. Last, the equipment I've acquired through countless rewards, or finding them on the corpses of what must be thousands of fallen enemies, is the very best the Empire has to offer.

Finally, I am ready.

Group Play

My purpose in a group or war party is simple: Kill as many of those who oppose us as possible.

In a group, I can get behind my opponents more, letting me take advantage of abilities such as Torment, Silence the Heretic and Pistol Whip (if I've followed that path). Additionally, I find myself using Blessed Bullets of Confession as my Blessing, and Trial by Pain as my Execution, because my opponents' attention is often distracted by my allies, and the results of these abilities aid all of my companions in dealing damage.

Likewise, I choose Morale abilities and Tactics that focus on group benefits, such as Witchfinder's Protection, which allows my entire group to parry attacks for 10 seconds, or Blood, Faith, and Fire, which gives action points back to my whole party each time I kill an enemy. Still, my combat sequence remains fairly consistent, and I spend most of my time making the evil swarm of Chaos feel the fervent wrath of the Pure. Those few situational abilities I have are sprinkled in here and there.

With my many abilities that work on the run, and my very valuable snaring abilities, my role is often to chase down errant targets, especially during PvP. For example, the mage, whose front-line troops are falling like storm-tossed leaves, turns to run. Moments later he feels the force of righteousness slash into his back, courtesy of Torment (which avoids all armor when striking from behind,) which blasts him prostrate, finally granting him Absolution, his vision growing as dark as his heart, never to corrupt another living thing again.

CRUSHING PLAYERS AND GATHERING RENOWN (PVP)

Corruption is found everywhere. From the largest of the great cities to small farms miles from the nearest town, I have sworn to root out this dark witchery no matter what the cost. And the cost has sometimes been dear. Not only for me, but for those who unfortunately found themselves hopelessly trapped between the ravening maws of Chaos and the razor-sharp steel of the purifying forces of the Empire.

From my very first skirmish with the forces of Destruction, near my home in Grimmenhagen, to where I sit today, in a warcamp on the fringes of the Inevitable City, waiting for the horns to sound the advance, every breath I take has been dedicated to ensuring that the Empire continues to fight the evil to be found within its very borders, as well as within the borders of the lands of our supposed allies, the Dwarfs and the High Elves.

Still, the skills and abilities I have learned will serve me well. My abilities do not distinguish between the mindless minion of a bandit and the feral glint of cunning in the leader of a PvP Destruction warband. I must remember that the forces of an enemy PvP warband are far more organized and strategically creative than the dull stupidity of a group of wolves, in spite of their similarity in outlook and table manners. Ultimately, they will all be purged from these lands, but to succeed, we must remember to focus our attention on those who maintain the strength of the dark wave.

Learning the strengths and weaknesses of traveling companions allowed me to more effectively combat the forces of Destruction. Plus, it never hurts to know that information, should some of them become tempted by the lure of Destruction.

It is a well-known stratagem from the very earliest days of combat: Eliminate those who maintain the health of an army, and the army will be far weaker, and thus easier to destroy. To that goal, I seek out and destroy enemy healers, those who keep the hugely armored vanguard of Chaos standing tall. Without the support of their healers, they are entirely mortal. Entirely.

But each combatant on the battlefield is different.

There are those who would stand away from the fray, such as mages, with their evil witchery, or marksmen, with bow or gun. As I'm sure I've mentioned, a Witch Hunter does not stand a chance while he remains at range. I must close the distance with my target, or they will make short work of the likes of me. The best way to do this is to go Incognito, and circle around behind my target, if I can. If I cannot, I simply charge forward, take the inevitable damage, and engage with my foe. If I am at too great a range, I am better off falling back, hopefully toward some allies who can provide support, and re-engage when the situation favors me better.

Against those who are heavily armored, such as warriors, I must engage carefully. While I can deal all manner of strikes to such a foe, the armor worn by such combatants can minimize all but the smallest amount of damage. To stand toe-to-toe with such an enemy would be folly. The way I typically deal with an armored opponent is to go Incognito and circle behind, use Burn Armor to inflict damage each time my opponent attacks, use Torment while still behind, then continue as I usually do. It is better still if I have a companion to engage my armored foe so that I might do my damage with impunity.

For those who are lightly armored, such as skirmishers or other roguish types, I can engage toe-to-toe, if I dare, or, as always, Incognito to slip behind and wreak havoc before my opponent knows what's hit him.

Very few can stand alone against the righteous fury of a Witch Hunter. Consequently, should I spy a follower of Chaos traveling alone, or far away from the support of peers, I do not hesitate to slip into the shadows, sneak up on the vicious thing, and start leveling Accusations with all the vehemence I can muster. Those in this situation have rarely survived long enough to mount much of a defense, and the ones that had managed to flee, or survive long enough to gather allies, almost always met their ends shortly thereafter.

If I'm to engage a group of enemies, however, I must have a group of my own. I cannot stand alone against several enemies and expect to win. Coupled with a heavily armored companion and a companion who can heal, we can easily defeat a group equal to our number, and, on a good day, a few foes more. Obviously, my armored friend holds their attention, or at least makes life difficult for them, while I do what I do best. The healer keeps both my companion and myself in good spirits, and there we are.

The last thing I always remember is that combat is a fluid thing. The forces of Destruction will devise new and insidious ways to assault the bastions of purity, and it is incumbent upon us to learn these, and find ways to blunt them. I learn from every encounter with the vile Daemons and witches that threaten the Empire. Whether it's the timing on a sequence, a new combination of Tactics I hadn't thought of before, or stringing together abilities in a way that startles or surprises a foe, I am always learning and refining my skills.

Failure means darkness.

BURNING RIGHTEOUSNESS

I'm certain that there's much left to be said, questions left unanswered, advice not given. A journal isn't quite the same as a conversation, and I am sorry for that. There is much that I've learned during my journey, and hopefully, a good portion of it lies in these writings. Unfortunately, I have an appointment at the gates of the Inevitable City that has waited long enough.

I am entrusting this journal to a courier who is headed back to Grimmenhagen with dispatches for Lord Riese. If he is successful in delivering it, I am hopeful that it might be granted to a young Witch Hunter who has nothing but a dull rapier, a rickety pistol, and the burning righteousness within his heart to purge this land of the evil that permeates every crevice and corner.

Should our paths cross, you might ask me your questions then.

ARCHMAGE

By Zharn

Welcome, young apprentice. My name is Zharn, Master Archmage of the White Tower of Hoeth. I have long served the Phoenix Kings of Ulthuan, and now, in our darkest hour, it is my duty to prepare you for the battles that are to come. The Chaos moon, Morrslieb, has risen, and chaos is upon us. The White Tower of Hoeth is abuzz with activity as its Swordmasters and Archmages prepare for war against their sundered kin.

Yes, the rumors are true. Our dark kin have returned. They are here to supplant and eradicate us, so as to claim the Phoenix Throne for themselves. It is up to us...yes, you, young apprentice, and I, to stem their desires, and to cleanse the taint that was born of our own weakness so many generations ago.

But our time is short, and your journey is long and perilous. I will be your mentor, to teach you the art of weaving High Magic. You must pay close attention to my words for, very soon, your life will depend upon it. As an Archmage, you will neither create nor destroy magic. You are a conduit, attuned to the magic that exists and binds all living things. You will learn how to focus large amounts of High Magic to destructive purposes while also learning to use it to bind and restore the living to full health. You will learn how to concentrate High Magic in people to both increase their abilities and to weaken and limit the capabilities of your enemies.

But these lessons await you farther down your path. Though I will be with you to teach and assist you, the journey is yours and it starts now. Your first step is to report to Moonrise Tower at the northern end of the Blighted Isle, where you will be given your first instructions.

The war is upon us young one! Defend your kin and homeland!

What is an Archmage?

The Archmages of the High Elves are long-range healers and the undisputed masters of High Magic. Through centuries of study, High Elves are the only race that can access this highest and purest form of magic, and the Archmage channels it into both offensive damage spells and defensive healing spells. In addition, they have spells that both enhance the abilities of allies and limit the powers and actions of opponents in battle. All of their magic can be cast, and is most effective, from long range.

Due to their low Armor rating and limited ability to freeze or snare people while they escape, they do not easily survive in close combat. Most of the Archmage's spells are instant cast—meaning that they can be cast with but a thought in no time at all—and can be used while on the move. An Archmage must constantly reposition himself to be a more elusive target. In a pinch, an Archmage can stand and cast potent damage and heal spells, but this should be done only in an emergency, or when enough High Magic has been saved up to reduce the spell cast times to next to nothing.

Archmages carefully balance their use of High Magic to weave back and forth between offensive and defensive spells, move constantly, and scan the battlefield for that precise moment when a powerful spell can be used to swing the outcome of the battle.

—Aleister Schreiber, Scholar Emeritus, University of Nuln

Cast all of your instant damage-over-time spells in a row to help boost your healing spells.

STARTING STATS

Sweaty, bloody, hand-to-hand combat is for those muscle-bound brutes in other careers. Dispense with those thoughts completely. An Archmage should concentrate on his mind, so look to boost your Willpower and Intelligence. Willpower will increase your healing powers—a must for an Archmage—while Intelligence will augment your damage spells. All other stats come down to play style and group preferences. For example, if you end up soloing a lot, you may want to invest in some Wounds and Toughness to keep you alive longer should the battle come down to who holds the most health.

Your use of High Magic is very weak in the beginning, apprentice. But fear not, as you grow in experience and practice your abilities, your physical abilities will improve. Wearing and using items that are magical in nature can also improve your abilities. As you fight our dark kin and the other lesser races, you will have ample opportunity to take their weak magic items from them. I know they will be inferior to our crafted items, but in times of war you use every item that you can find.

Never stand your ground and chain cast heals. Shield the target and allow your heal-over-time spells to catch up.

BEGINNING AS A HIGH ELF

Before you can master your new profession, young one, you must first master yourself. To know yourself, you must know from whence you and your kin have come. Therefore, I will start you on your path with a lesson about your ancestors. You must understand why it is necessary to use discipline and control when you weave High Magic. It was the temptations of power that led our dark cousins to their fate. They feed their emotions with power, greed, and jealousy. Although this allows them to conjure large amounts of destructive magic, it has barred them from using the forms of High Magic that you will weave against them. Learn the path of balance so that you will not be lured down their path of darkness and destruction.

We are an ancient people who have survived for millennia. When our human allies still lived as barbaric tribes in the eastern lands, we were building great cities and exploring the vast oceans of the world. We spent countless generations learning to master the Winds of Magic and learning the grace of the warrior's dance. Long ago your ancestors realized that the baser emotions of fear, rage, jealousy, and greed fed the power of Chaos. We chose to forsake these emotions with discipline and control so that we would not be led away from the higher forms of magic. As you know from the ancestral tales, our darker kin rejected this theory and believed that the power of Chaos surpassed that of High Magic, and from this argument, the split of our race came to be. Although you master your emotions and learn to weave the highest magic, never forget that you still have within you the rage that makes you capable of the savage violence in which our dark kin bathe themselves.

To master the highest of magics, you must master the balance of nature, between joy and hate, love and rage. Only in this balance can you truly weave, and hopefully master, the power of High Magic. You will be faced with your mirror image in every battle. We are our dark kin, but in them, their rage is fostered, grown, and let loose. Never let them rattle you and always maintain your balance, and you will serve your family, race, and cause with distinction.

Now the true test comes. You are prepared and you have your spells. Now we must go face the enemy.

Your first duty station as an apprentice will be Moonrise Tower. There, you will report to Silvshara Greywind. She will give you some menial tasks to complete, but pay attention, apprentice and use these tasks to hone your use of your base spells. These early tasks will not put you in any danger, but they are your laboratory to learn the basics of how High Magic works. As you finish these tasks and show your mastery of your base abilities, Lyndriel Flameleaf will begin your training in more powerful spells.

When Silvshara feels you are ready to enter the true battle for the Blighted Isle, she will send you to report to Prince Eldrion in Calumel. The prince will send you in to fight the first of your dark kin around Calumel. He has a very important mission to help keep our dark cousins from possessing the Altar of Khaine, but resist the urge to immediately plunge into that fray and instead complete all of his tasks in Calumel so that you can gain a bit more power. Once you have gained the spell Radiant Gaze, you will be ready to defend the Altar of Khaine. As you prove yourself on that battlefield, you will gain Renown with your fellow High Elves. This is your first chance to prove yourself, so take your time and rise in Renown here before you move on to other battles.

Once you have completed Prince Eldrion's tasks, he will send you farther down the Blighted Isle to Azurewood Forest to talk to Sariel Keenbow. Sariel is carefully scouting a major beachhead landing of our twisted kin. After completing tasks for several of the group stationed in the woods, she will send you to fight with your fellow brothers to turn back the landing of the Black Ark (public quest: "House Arkaneth"). Your dark kin are relentless and will continue to assault your defenses at the landing. Stay and help your fellow High Elves defeat them and your influence with the defenders in the Azurewood Forest will grow. If you do enough to help, you will reap powerful items taken from your enemies, and as your influence grows, Captain Talorith, who is in charge of the forces in the woods, will open his store of artifacts and allow you to use them. Additionally, as you grow in power, Aedolaen will teach you how to use Searing Touch. This is a powerful, channeled damage spell, but it requires that you stand in place and not be interrupted, so use it carefully, only when you're certain not to be interrupted.

The Meme of the Archmage

The ancients have handed down to each apprentice the "Meme of the Archmage." It is the central idea by which a few—a very special few—Archmages truly learn to become Masters.

"Elements are Nature,

Nature is Balance,

Balance is Power."

Mastery of this codex will shape you from a limited healer into a force of nature. In harmony with Force and Tranquility, you can control the outcomes of battles.

Balance is what we seek in all things. Only there can you reach your true potential and access the purest forms of High Magic.

Once you have completed the tasks in the woods, and Sariel and Captain Talorith have no more need of you, they will send you to help in the defense of Adunei and its surrounding communities. There, you will report to Rirelis Swiftblade, who will send you to the tasks where you are needed most. Among the many quests there, Kyrinn Silversea is organizing the defense of two key objectives. Our most hated cousins are attempting to burn down Thanalorn Forest (public quest: "Thanalorn Forest") to the northwest of Adunei, and she is trying to hold back an invasion of Dark Elf Beastmasters in the Swale of Miralei (public quest: "The Swale of Miralei"). Helping in either of these tasks will allow you to gain influence with Kyrinn, and she will arm you with powerful items as you prove yourself. At Adunei, you will learn the new spells Transfer Force, Prismatic Shield, and Dissipating Hatred. Transfer Force is your first damage-over-time/heal-over-time spell that drains the life of a single target, and turns that into healing for your defensive target. This is an extremely important spell because it can be cast on the run and both strengthen your side and weaken your enemies. Prismatic Shield is a group spell that increases the magical resistance of your entire group. You can also learn and practice the arts of crafting while in Adunei. Once your work in Adunei is complete, you will be sent to Haladhrel Sternbrow at Sternbrow's Lament.

As you proceed down the Blighted Isle, you come upon the warcamp where our army is gathering for the first major battle on the Plain of Bone. Learn your spells well, apprentice, because your dark cousins will test you heavily. They know your strengths and your weaknesses, so be prepared. If you survive the battle there, you will surely rise to high levels of Renown among your family and kin. Do us proud, and the sages will sing your song into history. Learn not the lessons that I teach, and your life will be short, as your tainted brothers bathe themselves in the essence of your soul.

Once you master your abilities, apprentice, you will wield elegantly carved staffs of great power, wear gracefully bejeweled circlets, and ornate headdresses inscribed with the greatest runes of protection. However, you cannot be trusted with such powerful artifacts now. You must start your career with the humility of the student and boldly wear your initiate's robes and wield your initiate's staff.

These humble tools will suffice if you focus on the correct casting of your spells. With practice and experience, you will quickly be discarding your starting gear for items of much greater power. Although you will see many magic items and apparel in your career, you will be limited to robes and staves as your main protection and weapons, respectively. Conjuring High Magic requires great concentration, and wearing heavier protection and carrying huge metal weapons would disrupt your focus.

There are several ways to gain more powerful items. The first, and most efficient, method for gaining more powerful items is to take them from the dead bodies of your enemies. As you travel the warpath, you get plenty of opportunities to kill your enemies, their allies, and their minions. Loot every corpse to find these items, and fill your pockets with their gold. Everything must be salvaged if we are to win this desperate conflict, and save our island and our race. The second method for gaining gear is to participate in special missions of high importance as you travel the lands. Helping our kin in their cause will greatly increase your influence among these groups. As your influence grows, they will open their personal collection of powerful items and allow you to take from their stores.

ARCHMAGE GEAR

STRENGTHS AND WEAKNESSES

Strengths

- Big Healing: This gives you unlimited life as long as you have action points to use and aren't exhausted.

- Damage through the proper use of spells while you are healing: Spells that continue to do damage while you move away or are silenced are the main advantage to using High Magic.

- Heal multiple targets: In large battles, you will often find yourself the only healer among many allies. Your ability to heal over time allows you to concentrate on aiding many allies at once. Of course if time isn't on your side, then cast one large group heal.

- Range, range, and range: If you can touch them you are too close.

- Action point drains: Neutralizing the ability of an enemy to cast or act is one of your most powerful abilities.

You have been blessed with the grace of life-giving and death-dealing abilities. While enemies fall around you, your healing spells can save allies or your own soul. Some healers are purely defensive, but not you. The Archmage can wield powerful damage-over-time abilities and offensive spells that can kill the unsuspecting.

Weaknesses

- No real armor: Cloth robes are no substitute for plate armor or a shield. So don't be in swinging range of an axe wielder.

- Low health: Your strength is your superior intellect. We didn't choose you to be an Archmage because you were big and strong.

- You are a very poor single-target healer.

All of your big heals have cast times that require you to stand still and not cast damage spells. You must anticipate where the enemy is going to do damage in the future. Rely on your keen intellect and think "proactive over reactive." If you are just reacting to a target that the enemy is harming, you can't cast enough heals to keep him alive. Also, focusing on either offensive or defensive spells will quickly exhaust you and leave you unable to cast spells until you have rested.

In groups, always drain the enemy healers of action points, and silence them, if possible.

SKILLS AND ABILITIES

Abilities

An Archmage starts out with two abilities. Radiant Lance does medium spirit damage to a single target. Direct damage is taken from your opponent's life all at once when the spell lands. Healing Energy heals for a small direct amount and heals for a moderate amount spread over nine seconds.

These basic spells grow stronger as you gain experience in casting them. Work on understanding how these two forms of High Magic interplay because you will still be using these even at the highest levels.

Your first two abilities are aligned to the two forms of High Magic: Tranquility and Force. As you cast Radiant Lance you gain charges of Force (a maximum of five) that shorten the casting time and cost of your healing energy spell. In balance to this, as you cast your healing energy spell, you build up charges of Tranquility that lower the casting cost of your Radiant Lance and improve its damage ability. Your first lesson is to learn how to weave back and forth between these two types of spells and properly manipulate the charges of Force and Tranquility.

Your Core abilities are the same for all Archmages and you learn most of them at early ranks. These abilities grow in power with your experience, so you will be using the same spells at Rank 40 that you use at Rank 4. As you gain in experience, you also focus on more specialized abilities, such as Tactics, Morale, Mastery, and Renown abilities.

As you have been taught, apprentice, your three main damage spells are the damage-over-time spells Law of Conductivity, Radiant Gaze, and Transfer Force. These are augmented by the direct damage spell Radiant Lance and the channeled damage spell Searing Touch. You have one drain spell, Drain Magic, which takes away your opponent's action points. This spell can turn the tide of the battle in a single cast by denying the target an action at a critical moment.

Your main healing spells are the heal-over-time spells Lambent Aura and Healing Energy. While Lambent Aura is solely a heal-over-time spell, Healing Energy does a small direct heal in addition to applying a heal-over-time effect. The damage-over-time spell Transfer Force also applies a heal over time to your current defensive target as it drains the life from your enemy and gives it to your ally. Used throughout a battle, this instant-cast, two-for-one effect can easily swing the course of a battle if used properly. Later, with more experience, you will learn your big one-target heal spell Boon of Hysh, and the group heal Blessing of Isha. These spells are powerful, but their long casting times

Along your career, apprentice, you will receive a few spells that aid your allies and hinder your opponents. Spells such as Dissipating Hatred help relieve the pressure that opponents can put on you, and area-of-effect spells such as Rain Lord will weaken large groups of opponents. Dissipating Hatred lowers the amount of damage that enemies do to you. However, its effect is lost once you damage them. This is especially helpful when you are facing multiple targets and need to lower the amount of incoming damage to you. Rain Lord lowers the attack skills of a large group of opponents. This is highly useful in group battles, especially when cast at the start of a combat.

At very high ranks you will get some crowd-control spells such as Wind Blast and Storm of Cronos. Wind Blast is your main escape tool when you are confronted by enemies in close combat, because it pushes all adjacent targets away from you and slows them. Storm of Cronos does a small amount of damage to a large group of enemies in front of you and significantly drops their resistance to Spirit damage. Law of Gold silences enemy casters.

These abilities make up the core of what all Archmages cast. Master them to the fullest.

Destruction's Top 5 Reasons for Killing Archmages First in Every Battle

1. You just have to dislike those prissy-looking High Elves.

2. They squish so easily.

3. Anything that heals shouldn't be able to cast all of those damage-over-time spells. That's just plain unnatural.

4. With all those instant-cast, heal-over-time spells, they never stand still.

5. They are always way in the back, where the treacherous like to start their killing.

Move constantly in combat.

Abilities

Name	Level	Path	Cost	Range (in feet)	Type	Build	Duration	Reuse	Description
Healing Energy	Starter Ability	Lore of Isha	55	150	Heal	1s	9s	0s	Heals 247 damage, then heals 658 damage over 9s. Builds Tranquility.
Radiant Lance	Starter Ability	Lore of Asuryan	30	100	Magic Attack	2s	0s	0s	Deals 499 damage. Builds Force.
Law of Conductivity	Level 2	Lore of Asuryan	30	100	DoT	0s	15s	0s	Deals 499 over 15s. Builds Force. Gains 5% damage bonus per Tranquility expended.
Lambent Aura	Level 3	Core	30	150	HoT	0s	15s	0s	Heals for 1,496 over 15s. Builds Tranquility. Gains 5% heal bonus per Force Expended.
Radiant Gaze	Level 4	Lore of Vaul	40	100	Magic Attack	0s	9s	5s	Deals 648 damage over 9s. Lowers target's damage output by 5% and lowers target's crit rate by 5%. Gains 5% damage bonus per Tranquility expended.
Searing Touch	Level 5	Lore of Asuryan	25/2s	100	Channeled Attack	0s	3s	11s	Channeled attack. Deals 349 every 2s for 6 seconds. Setback rules: 100% for 0.5s. Builds Force. Gains 5% damage bonus per Tranquility expended (gains 1 free step).
Transfer Force	Level 6	Lore of Isha	35	100	Lifetap DoT	0s	24s	10s	Deals 648 over 24s and heals defensive target for damage done on each tick. Builds Force. Gains 5% damage bonus per Tranquility expended.
Dissipating Hatred	Level 7	Core	20	100	Debuff	0s	15s	15s	Detaunts target (15s duration, 50% redux).
Prismatic Shield	Level 7	Lore of Vaul	55	Group	Buff	0s	60 min	0s	Increases group's Spiritual resist by 6.3 per level for 60 minutes.
Boon of Hysh	Level 8	Lore of Isha	45	150	Heal	3s	0s	0s	Heals target for 1125 Setback override: 100% chance, 2s value Builds Tranquility.
Drain Magic	Level 9	Lore of Asuryan	25	100	AP Burn	0s	0s	10s	Target loses 90 AP, takes 187 damage. Builds Force.
Gift of Life	Level 10	Core	20	100	Resurrection	6s	0s	3s	Resurrect targeted friendly dead player. Builds Tranquility
Walk Between Worlds	Level 12	Core	30	Self	Aggro/CC management	0s	5s	60s	Reduce hate on target by 1,875. Archmage cannot be s for 5s.

Always have your group buffed before combat.

Abilities

Name	Level	Path	Cost	Range (in feet)	Type	Build	Duration	Reuse	Description
Shield of Saphery	Level 14	Lore of Isha	35	Buff	Buff	0s	10s	20s	Shield that absorbs 100% of damage up to 937. Builds Tranquility.
Cleansing Light	Level 16	Core	25	150	Magic Attack	0s	0s	5s	Removes an Ailment or Hex from target.
Rain Lord	Level 18	Lore of Vaul	25	100	Debuff	0s	20s	10s	Intelligence, Strength, and Ballistic Skill are reduced by 3/level. Radius: 30ft.
Blessing of Isha	Level 20	Lore of Isha	60	Group	Group Heal	3s	0s	0s	Heals every group member for 540. Builds Tranquility.
Wind Blast	Level 25	Core	40	CAE	CC - Curse	0s	10s	60s	CAE knockback targets. Snare targets by 20% for 10s. Arc: 180, radius: 30ft.
Storm of Cronos	Level 30	Lore of Asuryan	45	CAE	DD/Debuff	2s	10s	30s	CAE Attack. Does 249 damage to all targets in the radius, and debuffs their Spirit resistances for 4.5 per level for 10 seconds. Arc: 120, radius: 65ft. Builds Force.
Law of Gold	Level 35	Lore of Vaul	25	100	CC/ Damage	1s	5s	30s	Deals 187 and Silences the target for 5s. Builds Force.
Dissipating Energies	Level 40	Lore of Vaul	50	100	Buff	2s	10s	60s	For 10s, target ally pulses PBAE damage. Deals 149 damage per tick every 2s. Radius: 30ft. Builds Force.
Balance Essence	Isha x5	Lore of Isha	25	100	Magic Attack	2s	0s	0s	Deals 199 and heals defensive target for damage dealt. Builds Force.
Funnel Essence	Isha x9	Lore of Isha	20/s	100	Channeled Heal	0s	3s	13s	Channeled. Heals 231/s to defensive target. Setback override: 100%. Builds Tranquility.
Magical Infusion	Isha x13	Lore of Isha	35	100	Buff	3s	20s	30s	Buff that makes heals 25% more effective on the target for 20s.
Fury of Asuryan	Asuryan x5	Lore of Asuryan	30	Thrown	Magic Attack	0s	0s	30s	Short-range attack, deals 337 damage to target. Builds Force. Gains 5% damage bonus per Tranquility expended.
Feel the Winds	Asuryan x9	Lore of Asuryan	20	100	Debuff	0s	10s	30s	Reduces Spirit resist of everyone in radius by 9/level for 10s. Radius: 30ft.
Cleansing Flare	Asuryan x13	Lore of Asuryan	20	100	Magic Attack/CC	2s	0s	20s	Deals 299 damage to all targets in a 20ft radius and deals a short knockback. Builds Force.
Scatter the Winds	Vaul x5	Lore of Vaul	25	100	Debuff/DoT	0s	9s	10s	Deals 449 over 9s. Heals are 50% less effective on the target for 9s. Builds Force. Gains 5% damage bonus per Tranquility expended.
Law of Age	Vaul x9	Lore of Vaul	20	100	Debuff	0s	10s	0s	Toughness is reduced by 3/level. Radius: 30ft.
Mistress of the Marsh	Vaul x13	Lore of Vaul	20	100	GTAE Ranged Attack	3s	10s	30s	Reduces Initiative for 2/level and Snares 60% for 10s. Radius: 30ft.

Morale

You gain Morale abilities after Rank 8. As you gain higher ranks, you gain access to more powerful Morale abilities. You have four levels of Morale abilities that you can equip depending on what you are doing at the time. These abilities can be changed at any time, but you can have only four equipped at the same time.

These abilities are slotted into Tiers 1 through 4. As you kill your enemies, you slowly build up Morale so that you can activate these abilities. The more Morale you build, the higher tier ability you can use. Once you activate any Morale ability, all of your collected Morale is used, and you must rebuild Morale to reuse these abilities.

Your first Morale ability is called Divine Favor. This Tier 1 Morale ability is a very large direct heal with an instant cast time. This is excellent for saving a single target, well into a battle, without having to stop and cast a Boon of Hysh.

Morale abilities are powerful but have extremely limited use, so watch for key strategic moments in the flow of the battle before using them. Use them too early, apprentice, and they will aid you little. Cast them late, and you may not get a chance to use them at all. Wisdom is a key ally of a Master Archmage.

In keep combat, always let your tanks go in first.
Never present yourself as the obvious target.

Don't forget to heal yourself in the heat of battle.

Morale

Name	Level	Rank	Range (in feet)	Duration	Description
Divine Favor	Level 8	Rank 1	150	0s	Heals target for 1,800.
Rampaging Siphon	Level 12	Rank 2	PBAE	0s	PBAE that deals 600 and heals the group for 100% of the value.
Steal Life	Level 16	Rank 1	100	9s	Magic attack that deals 900 over 9s. Self heals 50% of the damage dealt.
Focused Mind	Level 20	Rank 2	Self	10s	For 10s, build times are reduced by 50%. Character purges and is immune to Silence, Disarm, Root, Snare, and setback.
Divine Protection	Level 24	Rank 3	Group	10s	Group buffs each group member with an ablative that absorbs the next 1,500 of melee damage, with a maximum duration of 10s.
Isha's Ward	Level 28	Rank 1	Self	60	Buffs the character with an ablative that absorbs the next 60 damage (upgrade: 16.67%).
Blinding Light	Level 32	Rank 2	100	5s	Increased build times by 1s for all targets in the radius. Radius: 30ft.
Arcane Suppression	Level 36	Rank 3	PBAE	3s	All enemies within 20ft are knocked back 20ft and Silenced for 3s.
Alter Fate	Level 40	Rank 4	PBAE	9s	PBAE resurrection for group members. Resurrected targets also get a HoT that heals 1,200 over 9s.
Winds' Protection	Isha x15	Rank 4	Group	15s	Heals group for 720 over 15s and casts a 1,200 damage absorb shield on the group.
Flames of the Phoenix	Asuryan x15	Rank 4	100	4s	GTAE channel that deals 600 every second for 4s. Radius: 30ft.
Funnel Energy	Vaul x15	Rank 4	PBAE	15s	Enemy AP costs are increased by 50% and ally AP costs are reduced by 50% for 15s. Radius: 30ft.

Tactics

Similar to Morale abilities, Tactics are gained with rank and allow you to customize what your character can do during a battle. You will receive your first Tactic, Centuries of Training, at Rank 11. This Tactic gives you a chance on hit to do a small amount of additional damage over time based proportionally on your rank. Just like Morale abilities, Tactics can be changed out depending on what you plan to do.

Use Tactics to strengthen the specific role that you intend to play in a group or in solo play. For instance, you may equip damage-enhancing Tactics when solo fighting, or you may swap them out for healing-based Tactics when you are in a group. The higher rank you attain, the broader selection of Tactics you gain, and the more you can equip. Tactics let you customize your Archmage for several different roles, depending on the challenges currently confronting you.

Mastery

As you rise in rank, apprentice, you gain Mastery points that can be spent in any of the three paths. You accumulate your first points at Rank 10, and by Rank 40 you will have accumulated 25 points to spend. These points can be spent in one of three paths, depending on where you wish to concentrate your talents.

Choose wisely where you spend your points, for your choices are not easily, or cheaply, changed and can only be changed by a trainer. While it is possible to master one path completely (15 points), it is impossible to master a second. Some Archmages choose to learn skills in all paths, but not to master any. Though this keeps them versatile in all roles, it also keeps them from shining in any one area.

Tactics

Name	Level	Description
Centuries of Training	Level 11	25% chance on attack to proc a DoT that deals 150 damage over 3s. Non-stacking, non-refreshing.
Divine Fury	Level 13	Increase damage dealt by 25%, reduce healing values by 20%.
Empowered Lores	Level 15	Critical hits build an extra point of the appropriate kind of High Magic.
Bend the Wind	Level 17	Increases Elemental resist by 6.3/level of the character.
Discipline	Level 19	Increases Willpower by 4/level of the character.
Isha's Encouragement	Level 21	Spells that spend High Magic have a 20% chance not to use it.
Discerning Offense	Level 23	Attacks have a 10% reduced chance to be defended against.
Subtlety	Level 25	Decreases threat by 50% on all heals.
Master of Tranquility	Level 27	Heals gain an additional 10% chance to critical.
Restorative Burst	Level 29	Critical heals return 40 AP over 3s to the caster. Non-stacking, non-refreshing.
Hurried Restore	Level 31	Resurrections are instant cast, but character is stunned for 3s after casting.
Master of Force	Level 33	Damaging spells gain an additional 10% chance to critical.
Transfer Magic	Level 35	Drain Magic also grants your defensive target 50 AP.
Run Between Worlds	Level 37	Cooldown on Walk Between Worlds is reduced to 20s.
Desperation	Level 39	When the target of your heal is below 25% health, increase the healing effectiveness by 40%.
Balanced Mending	Isha x3	Healing energy is 35% more effective on other targets, and 15% less effective on self.
Bolstering Boon	Isha x7	Boon of Hysh grants the target 250 Morale.
Wild Healing	Isha x11	On Critical heal: Self buff for 10s, 50% reduction in healing AP costs.
Forked Lancing	Asuryan x3	Radiant Lance hits 2 other enemies near the target (radius: 20ft).
Dispel Magic	Asuryan x7	Offensive spells have a 25% chance to dispel a Bless on the target of the spell. If they do, they deal an extra 150 damage.
Increased Conductivity	Asuryan x11	Increase damage of Law of Conductivity, Drain Magic, Storm of Cronos, Fury of Asuryan, and Cleansing Flare by 20%.
Expanded Control	Vaul x3	Rain Lord, Law of Age, and Mistress of the Marsh radius is increased to 45ft.
Arcing Power	Vaul x7	Anytime you attack someone, 25% chance for your defensive target to be healed for 25% of the damage dealt.
Golden Aura	Vaul x11	Radiant Gaze gains a 20ft radius.

To help you decide on your path, I will outline the nuances of each:

The Path of Isha is focused on weaving the healing and restorative spells in your arsenal. Archmages who master this path and build power up with offensive spells can cast extraordinarily powerful healing spells.

The Path of Asuryan is focused on weaving the more destructive side of High Magic. Archmages who master this path and build power up with healing spells can rain massive amounts of doom and despair on enemies.

The Path of Vaul is focused on the more subtle uses of High Magic that both bolster your allies, strengthening their abilities, and cripple your enemies through magical hindrances. Archmages who master this path can control the flow of the battle by manipulating the very strengths and weaknesses of allies and enemies.

Renown

You gain access to powerful Renown abilities as you prove yourself in direct conflict with the Forces of Destruction. These abilities are separated into tiers, and the higher tiered abilities can be accessed only when you have spent enough Renown points in a lower tier. You must spend 20 points in the first tier before the next tier is opened. Then you must spend 20 more points to open the third tier. You can gain 60 points over your career, so plan carefully how you wish to spend them.

The number of Renown ranks that you can obtain is not limited to your rank. However, time spent fighting on the many battlegrounds does not increase your experience at your profession. Balance the time you spend doing the quests with time spent in battle to raise your reputation.

Tier 1 abilities are available immediately once you gain ranks in Renown. You should easily have attained Renown Rank 5 by the time you reach Rank 11 in experience. This would give you five points to spend in the Tier 1 abilities. By the time you have reached Rank 20, you should attain Renown Rank 10 and have five additional points to spend. When you reach Master Archmage at Rank 40, you still gain ranks in Renown as you continue the fight against your tainted kin. As your ranks grow, your fellow adventurers will view you as a god of battle and your enemies will learn of your reputation and avoid you on the battlefield.

SLAYING MONSTERS AND EARNING EXPERIENCE (PVE)

Although fighting the forces of Destruction on the many battlefields may raise your Renown among your peers, it does little to increase your power. I know you are eager to prove yourself, apprentice, but to grow in experience and gain access to stronger forms of High Magic, you must first practice your skills on the many minions and allies of our enemy. The best way to accomplish this is to help the various people that you will encounter along your journey. Sometimes you will find yourself among many of your friends and allies, but often you will be fighting the forces of Destruction alone. Fear not that you may not be able to stand on your own, apprentice. Your powers of High Magic can easily handle large groups of our enemies' minions at once if you heed my advice here.

Solo Play

As always, young one, range is your friend. Pull your enemies from max range so that you can control where and how many you fight at once. This also maximizes the damage you can inflict before your foes reach you.

If your target is a single enemy, pull him with a large damage spell with a long casting time such as Radiant Lance. As the enemy runs to engage you, pile on all three of your major damage-over-time spells: Law of Conductivity, Searing Touch, and Transfer Force. Apply Transfer Force last because it also heals your damage as the minion hits you. If the enemy is near your rank or below, dispatch it by channeling Searing Touch. If it is higher than you, consider using one or two Radiant Lances, even though it has a long casting time, before you finish him off with Searing Touch. This should kill the enemy and have you at full Force charge. Next, use this Force to almost instantly cast Boon of Hysh or Healing Energy, depending on the amount of damage that you need to heal. With enemies below your level, even a simple Lambent Aura may restore your health to full.

This method is effective but it drains your energy, so you can only pull enemies for so long before you need to rest.

If you are pulling groups of enemies, pull from maximum range with your largest damage spell, Radiant Lance. If you are higher level, pull with your area-of-effect spell Rain Lord. With groups, spread your damage-over-time spells out onto three different targets. Then use the Force that you have built to stack healing spells on yourself, such as Healing Energy followed by a Lambent Aura. After you have stacked your damage-over-time spells onto your opponents, and applied your healing-over-time spells on yourself, burn down a single target with Searing Touch and Radiant Lance. Reapply your three main damage-over-time spells on the targets, reapply your heals to yourself, and burn down each enemy in succession. Depending on the number of enemies and their strength, you may need to intersperse direct healing spells into this rotation. This will make you more resistant to their damage as you continue the fight. This also gives you the Tranquility points to improve the power of your damage spells.

When you are Rank 25 or higher, you gain Wind Blast as an escape tool. All enemies near you get pushed back and have their speed reduced. This lets you regain range to continue the fight or escape.

If you get overwhelmed, use your Flee ability and cast all of your heal-over-time spells on yourself as you escape. It's always better to withdraw, gain your powers back, and reposition the fight than to die trying to win a losing battle.

Group Play

In groups, you will play the more traditional role of the healer. Your allies within the cause of Order may view you strictly as a healer, but your role is much larger than that. It is within the power of a Master Archmage to control the very flow of the battle. You cast your standard powers of damage-over-time and heal-over-time spells much as you did in solo play.

Buff your group with Prismatic Shield to raise their resistance to all forms of magic. Use Rain Lord to weaken groups of enemies. If your heals fall behind on one of your allies, apply your Shield of Saphery to let your heal-over-time spells catch up to your ally's health loss and to give you more time to cast additional healing spells.

Run and Gun: An RvR Survival Guide

Simply stated, apprentice, move or die in combat. The core of your spells can be cast instantly while moving. Damage-over-time spells such as Law of Conductivity, Radiant Wave, and Transfer Force are your main fare even into the highest ranks. Cast these in rotations, stacked on one target or spread among many enemies. Chain-casting these damage-over-time spells builds Force charges that allow you to cast your bigger heals, such as Boon of Hysh for single-target healing and Blessing of Isha for group heals.

Once your group begins to absorb damage, focus on casting your instant heal and buff spells such as Lambent Aura and Shield of Saphery. If your group needs bigger healing, stand and cast your major heals such as Boon of Hysh, Blessing of Isha, and Healing Energies. Immediately afterward, move and use the Tranquility that you have built to start inflicting larger and more powerful damage to your enemies.

In most cases a designated person, such as an Ironbreaker, will take the brunt of your enemies' attacks. Because this character will be your major heal target, keep Transfer Force on an enemy so that the damage taken by the enemy becomes healing for your warrior.

If you lose a member of your group during a fight, build up your Force points and cast an instant Gift of Life to resurrect your fallen comrade.

SLAYING PLAYERS AND COLLECTING RENOWN (PVP)

PvPing as an Archmage is all about mobility and time. The bulk of your abilities take effect over time. All of your big heals and big damage spells have cast times that make them hard to get off if someone is in your face, and unless your enemies are foolish, they will *always* be in your face. Present as small a target as possible to all of the Destruction heavy damage dealers, because they will try to target you first.

Solo Play

If you are solo fighting, attack opponents with surprise or while they are focused on other targets. If you achieve surprise, start your opening attack with your biggest damage spell, followed by spells that weaken, such as Rain Lord.

If your target is a melee fighter, then cast damage-over-time spells on him as he closes the gap to you, because you did start the fight at range, right? If your opponent is a ranged damage dealer, apply Transfer Force then immediately cast Drain Magic. Usually an opponent will use high-cost spells early and drain his own energy pool. Using your Drain Magic to take away huge chunks of his action point pool will severely limit your foe's options.

Once you have applied your initial damage-over-time spells and drains, start stacking healing on yourself. Use your Force points to instantly cast Boon of Hysh or Healing Energy followed by instant-cast, heal-over-time spells such as Lambent Aura. This counteracts your opponents' damage and builds Tranquility points to strengthen your next set of damage spells.

Most importantly, move constantly. The most effective way to deal with another ranged damage dealer is to cast your instant damage-over-time spells, then quickly move out of range during the casting of his damage spells, only to return to range to follow up your damage-over-time spells. This forces them to cover the ground between you and come into closer range. This lengthens the fight and enhances the pressure put on by your damage-over-time spells, especially with Transfer Force, which converts its damage to heals.

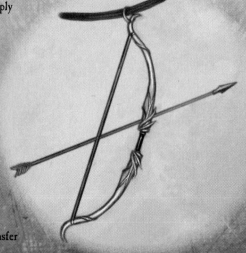

Wind Blast is your friend when confronted by melee attackers. Push them back, slow them, and retire with your heal-over-time spells active so that you can restart the combat.

Group Play

Remember, apprentice, it is your job to control the flow of the fight, not win it outright. In a group situation, you will likely be in the healer role or a support healer role. But the best defense is a strong offense. By proactively layering heals among the key targets in your group, you can use your damage spells to put pressure on the opposing healers. When they are forced to focus their healing on multiple targets, it is much easier for them to make a mistake and miss healing a key ally.

Your two most important powers in group battles are Shield of Saphery and Drain Magic. Your shield momentarily protects the enemies' key target so that you or an ally healer can catch up their healing. Drain Magic is your most strategic ability in any battle situation. When used at the right moment, especially on an opposing healer, it can shut down a key opponent. If you're grouped with other Archmages, team up to completely nullify an opposing healer or damage dealer. If executed at the precise moment, this one spell can allow your party to drop one key opponent, which can cause a domino effect that wipes their entire group. So keep a wary eye for that moment and have your spell ready.

As you grow to the highest ranks of the Archmage profession, you will also gain a spell called Law of Gold. This spell does direct damage and has a silencing component. If used in conjunction with Drain Magic, a good Archmage can stop most opposing casters one on one.

Inevitably you will become a priority target and will come under direct attack. What do you do then? First, apply your instant-cast, heal-over-time spells and Transfer Force so that you can start mitigating your opponent's damage immediately. If you can't move away from your enemy, then use Walk Between Worlds to cast without interruption. Healing yourself is always a priority over damaging your opponent. Your damage-over-time spells will wear down most non-healing classes, while your heals effectively give you nearly unlimited life. If you ever find yourself completely overwhelmed, then your best option is Wind Blast, which is instant cast and pushes all of your enemies away from you. In addition it slows them down, which makes it near impossible to close the range back to close combat. This allows you to retreat, heal up, and return to the fight.

TO JOIN THE WHITE TOWER

You have passed your beginning tests, young one, and are an apprentice no more. Now that you are an Archmage, remember the lessons I have taught you, practice your spells, and maybe one day you will join me on the council in the White Tower. In the battles that come, remember that you represent your kin. As you well know, High Elves are the oldest of the races in this world. It is up to us to protect the Dwarfs and the Humans. They may not be as powerful as we are, but they are our allies in the cause of Order.

Remember that balance and discipline are the keys to power, and only power can protect the Phoenix Throne from our accursed kin.

Walk Between Worlds first to ensure that you are not interrupted.

SHADOW WARRIOR

By Bhaene

I was not there at the start, at least not that I recall. I was definitely there at the end.

By the time the battle reached the part of the city where I and my family had lived for many years, the din and clash of swords, the high whistling of arrows, the low roar of battle cries had long since reached the walls of our tower.

My youngest brother rushed into my chamber, where I had been putting on my armor and getting ready to defend our small home. He urged me to put down my blade and bow. He spoke of siding with Malekith, saying that only those who stood against the Witch King would be destroyed. If we would but join with...with that usurper, we would be granted wealth beyond measure, power beyond our wildest dreams. We would sweep over Ulthuan and take what was rightfully ours. His eyes flashed with anger and violence, with greed. I had never seen my brother so out of control.

I tried to reason with him. I tried to explain that the Witch King would use him as he would use every other being in Ulthuan and beyond. The Witch King did not want honor, or peace, or quiet contemplation of arcane magic. The Witch King wanted control, wanted to rule, wanted power. We argued further.

Finally, I told him that I could not join him. I swore that I would never allow our beloved Nagarythe to become a den of corruption and foul magic, of betrayal. He snarled at me and told me I was a fool, that I would surely be slain that very day. I quietly told him that if that came to pass, it would be while I fought against all that is wrong with this world.

As I reached for my bow, my brother came at me, dagger drawn. The fight was short, and at the end, my own brother, my dearest of kin, lay at my feet, his blood pooling the stonework around my boots. With utter sadness, and with tears blurring my vision, I went out from the tower and into the city where the fighting from other towers, shops, and buildings had spilled out onto the streets. The carnage was far worse than any battle I'd ever heard of. Elves slaying Elves; this should not be the way of it. But this has become the way of it. We had all become kinslayers. All of us.

I fought my way out of the city, and with each usurper I put down with bow or blade, I swore an oath that I would not rest until Malekith and all of his traitorous followers were spitted on Nagarythe steel.

Lower your weapon, friend. I am no threat to the likes of you. Who am I? Asuryan, are the times so dark as to cause kin to be suspicious thusly when they meet? I am Bhaene, the Vengeance of Nagarythe. I am descended from a grandshire who survived the Sundering. His blood is the blood that courses through my veins. I know from my forebearers the pain of treachery.

Cousin, the bow you carry, is it not completely like my bow? The manufacture is of the former craftsmen of Nagarythe, if I am any judge of such things. From where did you acquire such a weapon, if I may be so rude as to ask?

You carry the blood line of the Nagarythe? We must bring you to the Blighted Isle. Every child of Nagarythe is needed. I feel certain than Silvshara will know what to do with you....

What is a Shadow Warrior?

Shadow Warriors exact vengeance up close with the steel of Nagarythe, or from afar with the shafts and bows of their Elf kin. They train constantly to become expert with these traditional weapons of the Asur. They do not use magic, as suspicion already rests heavily on their heads, with many of their kin believing that they are in thrall to the Witch King. This could not, of course, be further from the truth.

They are not typical soldiers, with heavy armor and strong arms. These warriors do not often confront the enemy in large, static battles, marching stolidly to the fore to meet steel with steel. Instead, they are lightly armored and move swiftly, raining arrows down upon their targets from dozens of feet away, throwing their targets into disarray, then charging in if necessary to finish the grim task.

A Shadow Warrior must be able to adjust stances fluidly to best adapt to the evolving battlefield, because their strength is in their flexibility. Against an opponent skilled in ranged combat, they can close the distance and engage them toe-to-toe. Against heavily armored opponents who would crush them, the Shadow Warrior can maintain distance and destroy them at range. Depending on the enemy, they can adjust their style of combat to best take advantage of any situation.

Of course, this flexibility is not without cost. Their swordplay is weaker than that of their Swordmaster kin, and they cannot stand before a determined enemy and shrug off damage. However, few in the forests can match their skill with a bow. And those who can lack the ability to deal much damage once their enemy stands before them with a sword.

—Aleister Schreiber, Scholar Emeritus, University of Nuln

STARTING AS A
SHADOW WARRIOR

Those who would join the ranks of the Shadow Warriors would best consider how to train. The disciplines of bow and sword would seem to be contradictory in focus, and indeed, many who follow the ways of the Shadow Warrior often favor one weapon over the other. Some of us prefer to become masters of the bow, raining down a hail of steel capable of stopping an entire enemy war party in its tracks. Some of us prefer engaging our enemies with an arrow or two before charging in with the thin, razor-sharp sword for which our kin are known. Last, more than a few prefer to fire at their foes while on the move. These capable Shadow Warriors learn to harass their targets in the swirling melee of combat, drawing steel only when necessary to finish the job. Of course, there are those who believe that each of these ways of approaching combat has merit, and so learn something of all of them, or two of them, to better exact their vengeance in their own way.

Should you become a Shadow Warrior, you need to determine how you will approach combat. Early in your training, you get plenty of exposure to all the stances and abilities that flow from them, and so you can make an informed decision. While you consider your training, think about your personal characteristics.

Each Shadow Warrior is very different and will view their training individually. There is no right. There is no wrong. All techniques and theories find some manner of agreement within our kin. A diverse populace remains strong against all enemies. Regardless of how you choose to train, consider that stats should support your abilities, abilities should support the way you fight, and the way you fight should be dependent upon your situation and your proclivities.

Ballistic Skill increases the amount of damage done on ranged attacks, and also makes it more difficult for opponents to block or evade those attacks. Ballistic Skill is the Shadow Warrior's single most important stat. If you're doing the majority of your damage with a bow, this stat is even more important.

If you plan to fight mostly with your sword, focus on Strength to increase melee damage and make it less likely that an opponent will block or parry your attacks, on Toughness to minimize the damage you take from melee attacks, and on Weapon Skill to increase the chance of parrying an incoming attack and bypass some of an opponents' armor.

Regardless of how you plan on fighting, pay attention to Wounds, so you can survive more damage. And because you cannot avoid melee, consider enhancing Initiative to evade melee attacks and reduce the chance of taking a critical hit.

Shadow Warriors do not use magic, and so you might think that Intelligence has fairly limited value. But many of a Shadow Warrior's abilities, particularly the ones that use a bow, are channeled.

If you plan mainly on traveling alone, or traveling in a group that has little melee capability, consider Strength, Toughness, and Initiative as your most important stats. You start combat with your target at range, hit them a few times with a bow, then finish them with a sword. Strength helps you do more damage once they reach you, while the Toughness and Initiative help minimize the damage being taken from your opponent in response.

If you plan to do your damage with a bow from range, and you plan to travel with a party that has melee capabilities, consider Intelligence, Initiative, and Toughness. If you train like this, you start at range and remain at range while your war party engages your target and keeps it there. Because you rarely use a sword, Strength becomes less important, and the Intelligence helps keep you from being interrupted by other ranged damage dealers and casters while shooting. Again, Initiative and Toughness minimize the damage you take. And whatever your plan, Ballistic Skill should be at the front of your stat needs because it is how you deliver maximum damage.

Your stances determine your success or failure. Do not forget to keep them active at all times, and switch them as necessary.

You are as subtle as twilight and as silent as death.

SHADOW WARRIOR GEAR

A bow and sword are the instruments of a Shadow Warrior's vengeance, and as such, are always considered the most important equipment a Shadow Warrior has.

The Scout Bow and Sword are sufficient for the tasks you'll find at Moonrise Tower. However, as you become more embroiled in the battles on Blighted Isle and beyond, and as your skills improve, you'll require swords and bows of higher quality craftsmanship and power.

You aren't wearing any armor, I've noticed. As soon as you can, find some light armor. Wear nothing heavier than that, or you'll end up hindering your movement. You can often find armor on the corpses of fallen enemies, or, occasionally, someone offers you armor in exchange for some service you've rendered. Still, the armor you wear won't provide much protection. Any armor is better than no armor, but not getting hit is the best armor still. Rely on mobility and range for your defense, where possible.

STRENGTHS AND WEAKNESSES

Strengths

- It's very easy to hunt solo, because a Shadow Warrior can remain effective in melee or at range, or while moving between the two positions.
- Shadow Warriors are among the best ranged damage dealers anywhere.
- Shadow Warriors have abilities that let them root or snare, silence, or disarm opponents, or disrupt opponents' abilities—most of them at range.
- Shadow Warriors have three stances that improve their combat capabilities depending on whether they're at range, in melee, or moving between the two. When used effectively, stances provide maximum flexibility of response to any threat.

A Shadow Warrior is a very good ranged damage dealer who can also be effective in melee. Those who participate in the Shadow War are more than capable of dispatching their traitorous kin whether near or far, armored or not. A Shadow Warrior can fire an arrow from 100 feet away that does heavy damage over time, then fire arrows while the target closes range. If the target isn't dead before it reaches the Shadow Warrior, the Shadow Warrior's sword can finish the job. Coupled with a heavily armored compatriot to maintain the attention of a major target (or group of lesser targets) a Shadow Warrior can deal a huge amount of damage as well as weaken that target (including roots, knockdowns, silence, and others) in a very short time.

Weaknesses

- Shadow Warriors have no real armor, so cannot withstand a great deal of damage in melee.
- Certain abilities only work in certain stances, and it can quickly become confusing.
- It's easy for a Shadow Warrior to draw the attention of several enemies at once and have no way to deal with them all. They have no ability to shed enemy aggression.
- Shadow Warriors do relatively lighter damage than most classes, relying on being able to hit an opponent several times, rather than hit once with a devastating shot. Over time, this balances out, but when pressed, they don't really have a "knockout punch."

Shadow Warriors cannot withstand concentrated damage and usually have difficulty in dealing with several opponents simultaneously, unless they're all at range and closely grouped. Due to their ability set, the majority of their serious damage dealing is single-target focused. Also, if a Shadow Warrior has difficulty moving through stances, he can quickly find himself in trouble.

Talk to everyone in town. Those with green sunbursts over their heads will ask you to perform small tasks. These lead to wealth, fame, and experience.

If you're in melee combat for more than even a little while, switch to Assault Stance!

SKILLS AND ABILITIES

Before we begin, we should talk briefly about the three main schools: Scouting, or attacking from a distance with long bow; Skirmishing, attacking with a bow from short distances while closing the distance to ultimately dispatch your foes with a blade; and Assaulting, attacking up close with rapid swordplay.

Understanding these schools becomes the key to success as a Shadow Warrior. Most of your damage-dealing abilities belong to one or more of these three schools. Additionally, when you enter your Career Mastery paths, you must focus your training on one or more of these paths, depending on how you prefer to fight.

Abilities

I have no doubt you understand the very basics of how to use your sword and bow. But allow me to show you a few things I have learned.

Top Five Ways to Tell If Your Friend Is Really a Dark Elf

1. At your birthday party, he insists on cutting the cake, does so unevenly, and grabs the biggest piece for himself.

2. He takes you out to dinner, then borrows money from you to pay the check.

3. When you ask for his help, one of his friends shows up in his stead, grumbling about him.

4. He always seems to have this purple glowing aura about him.

5. Two words: Blood Sacrifice.

Our first ability is called Eagle Eye. It does quite a bit more damage than your average bowshot and can hit a target from 100 feet away. You will become very familiar with Eagle Eye. I used it the very first time I picked up a bow, and I use it to this day. It takes a few seconds to pull the bow and release. A good Shadow Warrior learns to time his shots so as soon as the first arrow leaves his bow, the second one is already nocked and being drawn. If you practice this, you can fire an Eagle Eye shot every two seconds, almost indefinitely. Of course, we never run out of arrows.

The next ability is called Grim Slash. This ability deals slightly more damage than a normal sword swing. As such, you'll use it in combat frequently. Like Eagle Eye, I use this even today.

You learn Broadhead Arrow very shortly after arriving at Moonrise Tower (Rank 2). Broadhead Arrow does a large amount of damage over time. The advantage of a damage-over-time ability is that you do not have to hit your opponent again for them to take additional damage. This is particularly useful against heavily armored targets who are difficult to hit, or targets that are very agile or mobile. Hit them once, and they continue to take damage whether you hit them again or not. In the utter chaos of battle, being able to hit someone once and have them die whether they're standing in front of you or not can be extremely useful.

Scout Stance is the last thing I'd like to show you to get you started. If you stand just like this...good. By using your Scout Stance ability, you'll enter Scout Stance. Scout Stance is a way of positioning your body that increases the range of your bow attacks, Ballistic Skill, and initiative. You don't actually need to move or go anywhere; you just use your ability to enter your stance.

Understanding stances, and how and when to use them, is instrumental to becoming an effective Shadow Warrior. A Shadow Warrior eventually learns three stances that match up to the paths: Scout Stance (Rank 1), Assault Stance (Rank 4), and Skirmisher Stance (Rank 6). Scout Stance increases your range, Ballistic Skill, and Initiative. Assault Stance increases your Strength and Weapon Skill, and also doubles your armor rating. Skirmisher Stance increases your critical chance and Toughness.

In addition to providing benefits to specific stats, most of your abilities require that you be in a specific stance or in one of two specific stances. Each stance has six abilities associated with it. Of those six, two of them can be used only while in that specific stance. The other four can be used only when paired up with another stance. For example, if your Scout abilities, two can be used only in Scout Stance. Two others can be used only in Scout Stance or Assault Stance. The last two can be used only in Scout Stance or Skirmisher Stance.

All of the abilities that require a stance are either ranged or melee attacks. They're all different, and they all inflict varying levels of damage and effects. I'll discuss those later as I discuss your overall training plan.

Eagle Eye, Grim Slash, and Broadhead Arrow have no stance requirements, and a few other abilities have no stance requirements, either. However, all of your other damaging abilities require a stance of some type.

The stance requirement of your damage-dealing abilities isn't really a problem. Stances do not have any cost to use, and you can switch them every few seconds. Now that I've taught you your first stance, you should never go anywhere without being in a stance. Once you've learned all three stances, choose the one that best suits your style and situation.

In addition to your stances, it's important to learn how to harness your fury and channel it into Vengeance. Vengeance of the Nagarythe (Rank 12) draws from your rage and anger at Malekith's betrayal to increase your damage by 20 percent for 15 seconds. During that 15 seconds, in addition to the increased damage, you become Vengeful.

Being Vengeful adds additional power or characteristics to some of your abilities. For example, early on in your career, you learn an ability called Takedown. Takedown is a ranged attack that does light damage to any target between 5 and 65 feet, but also slows an opponent's movement for a few seconds. However, if you're Vengeful, Takedown also knocks the opponent down, so your foe stops dead, unable to attack or move for three seconds.

Vengeance of the Nagarythe is tiring, however, and you can use it only every three minutes or so. Consider carefully before using it, as you can rarely rely on it more than once in a single fight. Typically, I use Vengeance when I'm outnumbered and need to dispatch an enemy quickly, or when I'm near the end of a fight, and my health is getting low. In contemplation, you can see that when to use Vengeance is situational, and each Shadow Warrior will find his or her own uses.

As for the remainder of the abilities you'll learn, all of them either damage your opponents, modify your ranged or melee attacks, provide you with a beneficial effect, or provide a detrimental effect on an enemy. Steady Aim is one example of an ability that provides a beneficial effect, and it increases your chance for a critical hit. Whirling Pin, on the other hand, inflicts a detrimental effect on your enemies, rooting every adversary within 30 feet of you for five seconds.

Abilities

Name	Level	Path	Cost	Range (in feet)	Type	Build	Duration	Reuse	Description
Scout Stance	Starter	Core	Free	Self	Stance Buff	0s	Stance	5s	Stance: Increases Ballistic Skill and Initiative by 2 per level. Increases range of ranged abilities by 10%. Does not trigger global layer.
Eagle Eye	Starter	Scout	40	5 to 100	Ranged Attack	2s	0s	0s	Basic long-range attack. Deals (300+DPS)*1.33.
Grim Slash	Starter	Assault	35	Melee	Melee Attack	0s	0s	0s	Deals (225+DPS) damage.
Broadhead Arrow	Level 2	Skirmish	25	5 to 65	Ranged Attack - Ailment	0s	15s	0s	Deals (525+DPS)*1.33 over 15s.
Acid Arrow	Level 3	Scout	35	5 to 100	Ranged Attack	1.5s	10s	5s	Requires Scout or Assault. Reduces armor by 24.75/level and Block chance by 10% for 10s. Deals (225+DPS) damage.
Brutal Assault	Level 4	Assault	40	Melee	Melee Attack	0s	0s	5s	Deals 337+DPS. Requires behind target. If Vengeful, does not require rear positional. Builds less threat than normal. Requires Assault/Scout
Assault Stance	Level 4	Core	Free	Self	Stance Buff	0s	Stance	5s	Stance: Gives +3 Strength and Weapon Skill per level. Gives a 100% bonus to Armor. Does not trigger global layer.
Takedown	Level 5	Skirmish	25	5 to 65	Ranged Attack - Ailment	1s	10s	15s	Requires Skirmish/Scout. Deals (187+DPS) damage and Snares the target by 40% for 10s. If Vengeful, knocks the target down for 3s.
Spiral-Fletched Arrow	Level 6	Skirmish	25	5 to 65	Ranged Attack	1s	0s	0s	Requires Skirmish/Assault. Deals (187+DPS) damage. Usable while moving.
Skirmish Stance	Level 6	Core	55	Self	Stance Buff	0s	Stance	5s	Stance: Increases Toughness by 2 per level. Increases crit chance by 5%. Does not trigger global layer.
Distracting Shot	Level 7	Core	20	100	Detaunt	0s	15s	15s	Detaunts (50%) target for 15s.
Hunter's Fervor	Level 8	Core	25	PBAE	Buff	0s	15s	60s	Increases group's AP regen rate by 20% for 15s.
Draw Blood	Level 9	Assault	25	Melee	Melee Attack - Ailment	0s	0s	0s	Deals (412+DPS)*1.33 damage over 9s. Requires Assault/Skirmish.
Whirling Pin	Level 10	Core	30	PBAE	CC - Cripple	0s	5s	20s	PBAE Root for 5s. Radius: 30ft.
Vengence of Nagarythe	Level 12	Core	35	Self	Buff	0s	15s	3 min	For 15 seconds, increases all damage dealt by 20%. Some abilities gain other benefits while you are Vengeful.
Flame Arrow	Level 14	Scout	40	5 to 80	Ranged Attack - Ailment	2s	9s	10s	Requires Scout. Deals 249 Elemental damage and places a (MH)*1.33 DoT over 9s on targets in radius. Radius: 24ft.

Abilities

Name	Level	Path	Cost	Range (in feet)	Type	Build	Duration	Reuse	Description
Rapid Fire	Level 16	Scout	25/S	5 to 100	Ranged Channeled Attack	0s	3s	8s	Deals (187.5+DPS)*0.5 damage every 0.5s for 3s. Deals 10% extra damage if Vengeful. Requires Scout/Skirmish. Being hit while channeling removes 0.5s from the duration of the ability.
Eye Shot	Level 18	Skirmish	20	5 to 65	Ranged Attack - Cripple	1s	10s	10s	Requires Skirmish. Deal (187.5+DPS) and lower target Initiative by 2/level for 10s.
Steady Aim	Level 20	Core	25	Self	Buff	0s	5s	30s	Increases build time on attacks by 1.5s to increase crit chance by 50%. Does not set the global cooldown.
Opportunistic Strike	Level 25	Assault	20	Melee	Melee Attack - Cripple	0s	5s	30s	Deals (187.5+DPS) damage and Disarms the target for 5s. Requires Assault.
Counterstrike	Level 30	Assault	25	Melee	Melee Attack	0s	0s	10s	Deals (112.5+DPS) and interrupts target's building ability.
Throat Shot	Level 35	Scout	30	5 to 100	Ranged Attack - Cripple	1s	5s	30s	Deals (Mh+DPS) damage and Silences enemy for 5s. Requires Scout.
Lileath's Arrow	Level 40	Skirmish	40	LAE	Ranged Attack	2s	0s	0s	Requires Skirmish. Deal (262.5+DPS)*1.33 to targets in radius. Arc: 200, radius: 65ft.
Glass Arrow	Scout x5	Scout	35	5 to 80	Ranged Attack	2s	15s	10s	Deals (112.5+DPS)*1.33 damage to target. Deals 399 damage over 15s to targets within 45ft radius.
Festering Arrow	Scout x9	Scout	30	5 to 100	Ranged Attack	3s	0s	5s	Deals 750 Corporeal damage. Requires Scout.
Fell the Weak	Scout x13	Scout	25	5 to 100	Ranged Attack	2s	0s	5s	Requires Scout. Deals (300+DPS)*1.33 damage If target is less than 20% health. Deals (150+DPS)*1.33 damage if target is greater than or equal to 20% health. Vengeful: Reduce healing on target by 50% for 5s.
Swift Strikes	Assault x5	Assault	20/S	Melee	Melee - Ailment	0s	3s	13s	Requires any stance. Deals (187.5+DPS)*0.5 every 0.5s for 3s. If the target is building an ability, each hit deals (375+DPS)*0.5 damage instead.
Sweeping Slash	Assault x9	Assault	30	CAE Melee	Melee Attack	0s	0s	10s	Requires Assault. Deals (262+DPS) damage to targets in the area. Arc: 120, radius: 30ft.
Exploit Weakness	Assault x13	Assault	25	Melee	Melee - Cripple	0s	0s	20s	Requires Assault. Deals (300+DPS) and Stuns target for 3s.
Shadow Sting	Skirmish x5	Skirmish	30	5 to 65	Ranged - Ailment	0s	9s	0s	Requires Ailment. Deals (337+DPS)*1.33 over 9s. Reduces healing on target by 50%.
Flanking Shot	Skirmish x9	Skirmish	25	5 to 65	Ranged	1s	0s	10s	Requires Skirmish. Requires rear positional. Deals (337+DPS). Vengeful: 20% increased chance to critical. Usable while moving.
Barrage	Skirmish x13	Skirmish	45	CAE	Ranged	2s	0s	10s	Requires Skirmish. Deals (300+DPS)*1.33 to all targets in radius. Arc: 120, radius: 65ft.

Morale

Your first Morale ability is gained at Rank 8, and you'll gain an additional Morale ability every four ranks thereafter. As you fight, Morale slowly accumulates, reflecting your thirst for vengeance. I'm certain you've felt it. Dealing or avoiding damage (through parrying or dodging, for example) increases your Morale bar. Once your Morale bar is a quarter full, you may use Rank 1 Morale abilities. When it reaches half full, you can use Rank 2 Morale abilities, and so on. Once combat is over, and as the blood-pumping rush of adrenaline subsides, your Morale bar quickly empties. Additionally, you must choose your Morale abilities prior to combat, and they cannot be changed while you are fighting.

The first Morale ability you learn is Point-Blank. Point-Blank is a Rank 1 Morale ability that does a moderate amount of damage to a single target in front of you, up to 65 feet away, and also knocks the target back a substantial amount. This ability is extremely useful, because it enables you to damage and knock back a melee target, hit them with an instant ranged ability (such as Broadhead Arrow, which does a large amount of damage over time), then close range with them again, and re-engage in melee. If you're heavily offensively focused and end up in melee a fair amount, or you're a Skirmisher, this is an excellent addition to your arsenal.

Shortly thereafter, you learn Unshakable Focus (learned at Rank 12), a Rank 2 Morale ability that doubles your damage for seven seconds. Couple that with Vengeance of the Nagarythe, and you can wreak a horrible punishment upon the traitors. Again, for someone who's heavily offensively focused, this makes for a very good early choice for your Rank 2 Morale ability.

Concealment (Rank 16), another Rank 1 Morale ability, allows you to dodge and disrupt all attacks for seven seconds. As opposed to Point-Blank, Concealment makes an excellent Rank 1 Morale ability choice for Scouts or anyone else who plans to remain at range, because avoiding ranged and magical attacks is often very useful.

Focused Mind (Rank 20) is your second Rank 2 Morale ability. Focused Mind allows you to ignore all snares, roots, silences, and disrupts. It also makes your abilities build up faster and they cannot be set back. Like Concealment, if you're focused on being a Scout, or plan on staying at range, this can be a great alternative to Unshakable Focus.

You learn several others, all of which inflict or increase damage to your opponents, with the exception of Lileath's Forgiveness, which allows you to recover from hexes, curses, cripples, or ailments, as well as recover a lot of action points.

As you can probably tell, the Shadow Warrior Morale abilities are largely very useful. But because you can choose only one of each rank, it's important to select the ones that best suit your fighting style. Very powerful Morale abilities become available from your Career Mastery teachings.

Morale

Name	Level	Rank	Range (in feet)	Duration	Description
Point-Blank	Level 8	Rank 1	65	0s	Attack that deals 600 damage and performs a long knockback on the target.
Unshakable Focus	Level 12	Rank 2	Self	10s	Self buff. For 7s, increase damage dealt by 100%.
Concealment	Level 16	Rank 1	Self	10s	Increase chance to Disrupt and Evade attacks by 100% for 7s.
Focused Mind	Level 20	Rank 2	Self	7s	For 10s, build times are reduced by 50%. Character purges and is immune to Silence, Disarm, Root, Snare, and setback.
Explosive Shots	Level 24	Rank 3	Self	10s	Self buff. For 10s, ranged attacks explode in a AE around the target for an additional 300 damage. Radius: 30ft. Can only activate 1 per second.
Lileath's Forgiveness	Level 28	Rank 1	100	5s	Removes Hexes, Curses, Cripples, and Ailments from self. Gain 250 AP.
Signal Our Snipers	Level 32	Rank 2	100	0s	GTAE DD. Deals 1,200 damage. Radius: 30ft.
Instill Fear	Level 36	Rank 3	PBAE	7s	PBAE Disarm and Silence. Radius: 30ft.
Hail of Doom	Level 40	Rank 4	100	5s	Channeled TAE. Deal 300 damage to all targets in the area every 0.5s. Max duration: 5s.
Rain of Steel	Scout x15	Rank 4	100	10s	GTAE damage pulse deals 2,400 damage over 10s. Radius: 30ft.
Whirling Rage	Assault x15	Rank 4	PBAE	0s	Deals 2,400 damage. Radius: 30ft.
Penetrating Arrow	Skirmish x15	Rank 4	CAE	10s	Deals 1,200 + 1,200 over 10s (Injury) DoT. Arc: 90, radius: 40ft.

Tactics

The last type of Core ability you learn is the Tactic. Unlike abilities, which require active use, Tactics are passive, which means they are always in effect. Tactics modify abilities and stats or provide limited-duration bonuses. Tactical sets, because they can be changed relatively quickly, are a good way to provide additional adaptability to your circumstances. For example, you might create a Tactical set for ranged combat and a set for melee combat. You cannot change Tactical sets while in combat, however. So while you might change your stance from Scout to Assault when moving from ranged combat to melee combat, you can't change your Tactical sets.

You learn your first Tactic at Rank 11, and a new one every other rank thereafter. The first Tactic you'll learn, Centuries of Training, gives additional Initiative, which allows you to dodge melee attacks. At Rank 13 you learn Expert Skirmisher, which increases the damage you deal when close, but decreases the damage you deal when ranged. This is another place where your training focus determines your choice of abilities. If you're a Scout, you won't want to use Expert Skirmisher, because it decreases the damage you do at range. If you're a Skirmisher, obviously, you'll want to take this for the added damage.

Steady Aim, learned at Rank 19, increases your Ballistic Skill. As such, it generally will become a key component of your Tactic sets, regardless of your style of combat.

Tactics

Name	Level	Description
Centuries of Training	Level 11	25% chance on attack to proc a DoT that deals 150 damage over 3s. Non-stacking, non-refreshing.
Expert Skirmisher	Level 13	Increases damage by 25% when under 45ft and decreases damage by 20% when over 45ft.
Replenishing Strikes	Level 15	Critical hits restore 40 AP.
Bend the Wind	Level 17	Increases Elemental resist by 6.3/level of the character.
Steady Aim	Level 19	Increases Ballistic Skill by 4/level of the character.
Wrist Slash	Level 21	Grim Slash lowers the target's Weapon Skill by 3/level and Initiative by 2/level for 10s and increases self's Weapon Skill by 3/level and Initiative by 2/level for 10s.
Discerning Offense	Level 23	Attacks have a 10% reduced chance to be defended against.
Clever Recovery	Level 25	When the character's attacks are dodged, regain 75 AP.
Smoldering Arrows	Level 27	Flame Arrow's DoT damage is increased to 499 over 9s.
Pierce Defenses	Level 29	When the character is defended, he reduces the target's Block, Parry, and Evade chances by 15% for 10s.
Distracting Rebounds	Level 31	Distracting Shot becomes 20ft AE.
Bullseye	Level 33	Gains a 20% bonus chance to critically hit for 5s when he critically hits. He also becomes 10% easier to crit to enemies.
Instinctive Aim	Level 35	Reduces cooldown time of Steady Aim by 20s.
No Quarter	Level 37	Detaunts used against you have reduced duration by 50%.
Blood-Soaked War	Level 39	On kill: heal 292.
Enchanted Arrows	Scout x3	Flame Arrow and Festering Arrow gain 100% resist penetration.
Leading Shots	Scout x7	When you crit with a bow attack, you increase your group's crit chance by 15% for 10 s (does not affect yourself).

Tactics

Name	Level	Description
Guerrilla Training	Scout x11	Scout abilities are reduced in AP cost by 35%.
No Respite	Assault x3	Increases Parry chance by 10%. When you Parry, crit chance is increased by 10% for 10s.
Sinister Assault	Assault x7	Brutal Assault gains 100% Armor penetration.
Merciless Soldier	Assault x11	Melee abilities are reduced in AP cost by 35%.
Split Arrows	Skirmish x3	Spiral-Fletched Arrow hits all targets within 20ft of the target.
Keen Arrowheads	Skirmish x7	Increases durations of Broadhead Arrow to 21s, Takedown's snare to 15s, Takedown's Stun to 5s, and Eye Shot to 15s.
Charge Forth	Skirmish x11	Reduces max range of Skirmish attacks to 45ft, but increases chance to crit Skirmish attacks by 20%.

Mastery Paths

You may have noticed that every Shadow Warrior learns the same Core abilities. This is true. However, at Rank 10, you start to train in Career Mastery paths. Before this point, you were equally proficient, although average, in each stance. The path, or paths, you choose when training will greatly enhance the abilities associated with those paths. You might become a deadly Skirmisher capable of charging forward, firing your bow all the while, for example, or a Scout capable of quickly slaying any who come within the long range of your bow.

You receive your first Mastery point at Rank 10, and continue to receive them at roughly every rank, ultimately earning 25 Mastery points by Rank 40.

The paths themselves are called the Path of the Scout, the Path of Assault, and the Path of the Skirmisher, and each path aligns with the stance of the same name.

The Path of the Scout is focused on dealing damage from very long range. This makes it a particularly good choice for those who often join groups or war parties, or those who plan on solo hunting single targets. Those who choose to follow this path increase the power of the abilities Eagle Eye, Festering Arrow, Flame Arrow, Throat Shot, and Rapid Fire.

Scouts, as Shadow Warriors who follow this path call themselves, learn three additional ranged attacks. Glass Arrow is a ranged attack that does light damage to any target up to 80 feet away, but also has a moderate area-of-effect damage component. Festering Arrow is a ranged attack that does heavy damage. The last ability is Fell the Weak, a ranged attack that does moderate damage to any target within 100 feet, as long as that target is under 20 percent of his or her maximum health. If not, the shot does light damage. In addition, if the Shadow Warrior is Vengeful, the shot reduces healing on the target by half. The three Tactics a Scout learns from this path increase abilities following a critical ranged hit. The Rank 4 Morale ability for Scouts is Rain of Steel, which does a large amount of damage over time to any target within the targeted area of effect.

The Path of Assault is for those who desire to stare their enemies in the eyes as they exact payment in blood. This path concentrates on enhancing toe-to-toe melee combat, which can be useful for those Shadow Warriors who choose to hunt alone, or those who travel in groups of ranged damage-dealers. The sight of a mass of Shadow Warriors charging the field of battle, grimly seeking vengeance, is certain to chill the blood of any Dark Elf. Assaulters who choose this path increase the effectiveness of Grim Slash, Brutal Assault, Draw Blood, Opportunistic Strike, and Counterstrike.

Assaulters learn three additional melee attacks. The first is Swift Strikes, which is a channeled damage-over-time attack that does light damage unless the target is charging an ability, in which case it does double the damage. The next is Sweeping Slash, which does moderate damage to all targets in front of the Assaulter up to 35 feet. The last is Exploit Weakness, which is a crippling attack that does moderate damage, but also stuns the target for three seconds. The three Tactics available to Assaulters modify their melee abilities. The Rank 4 Morale ability, Whirling Rage, does a huge amount of damage to all targets within 30 feet of the Assaulter, making it particularly useful in PvP objective capturing or defending.

The Path of the Skirmisher focuses on fairly close ranged attacks (within 65 feet) and firing while on the move. Shadow Warriors who prefer to remain mobile, particularly in PvP, often choose to be Skirmishers. Shadow Warriors who choose this path increase the power of the abilities Broadhead Arrow, Takedown, Spiral-Fletched Arrow, Eye Shot, and Lileath's Arrow.

Like the other paths, the Path of the Skirmisher offers three ranged attacks, all of which work from 5 to 65 feet. The first is Shadow Sting, which does moderate damage over time to a target that already suffers an ailment. It also reduces any healing effects on the target by half. The second ability available is Flanking Shot, which does a moderate amount of damage, but only if you're behind the target. If the Shadow Warrior is Vengeful, there's also an increased chance to hit critically with this ability. Additionally, Flanking Shot can be used while the Skirmisher is moving. The last ability, Barrage, does moderate damage to all targets in an arc in front of the Shadow Hunter, up to 65 feet away, and this attack, too, works while the Skirmisher is moving.

The Tactics learned on this path make the Skirmisher's attacks more effective. Of particular note is Charge Forth, which reduces the range of all Skirmisher attacks by 10 percent, but increases the critical chance of those attacks by the same amount. The Rank 4 Morale ability, Penetrating Arrow, does very heavy damage to all enemies in front of the Skirmisher for 40 feet, and adds a damage-over-time component for the same amount of damage. A group of Shadow Warriors with this Morale ability could easily wipe out an entire enemy war band.

To gain all of the abilities available within a path, you need to focus on a single path to the exclusion of the others. However, because simply studying the path itself has benefit, dividing your attention across two or three of the paths may be desirable, depending on how you choose to engage in combat. Of course, dividing one's attention means giving up access to some of the abilities that can be found deep within the paths. It is not unusual to find successful Shadow Warriors who have increased the power of many of their Core abilities, making them not only more effective, but more versatile as well.

My experience tells me that variety is inevitable, and each Shadow Hunter is as individual as a snowflake. There are no wrong choices here, so make the decisions that satisfy *your* thirst for vengeance.

Nagarythe Weapon Name Generator

To name your weapon, simply choose one word from each column below and you now have a commanding title, such as Gleaming Soul Slasher or Sacred Demonbane Bunny.

Sacred	Death	Razor
Fluffy	Blood	Blade
Holy	Soul	Slasher
Bright	Demonbane	Avenger
Lileath's	Essence	Bane
Gleaming	Dark	Bunny
Asuryan's	Forest	Bow

Renown

As you fight in the many battles, scenarios, keep assaults, and other PvP events throughout Ulthuan, you earn the respect of your kin and gain Renown. As your Renown grows, speak with the Renown Trainers found in warcamps and keeps to learn very useful Renown abilities.

Renown abilities are either passive abilities that are applied directly to your stats, or they can be Renown Tactics, which are used just like Core and Career Mastery Tactics. The passive abilities adjust stats, such as Strength or Ballistic Skill. The Renown Tactics affect things like how fast one gains experience, or being able to do more damage to a particular race.

We discussed stats much earlier. Keep that conversation in mind when choosing your Renown abilities. You'll undoubtedly want to train in Marksmen, which increases your Ballistic Skill, and Blade Master, which increases your Weapon Skill. If you find yourself assaulting frequently, Fortitude is a good choice because it increases your Toughness. If you're focusing on PvP a great deal, consider Combat Awareness, which increases the amount of experience you gain in PvP.

Once you gain 20 points worth of Renown abilities, you can select from

organized warband. No matter how tough, yet an organized group is far tougher.

If you've done all the quests in an area, and the quests in the next area are too tough, do the public quests a few times, enter some scenarios, or find a Flight Master and complete Empire or Dwarf quests of your rank.

the Tier 2 Renown abilities. Clearly, you should learn Sharpshooter, which increases both your Weapon Skill and your Ballistic Skill. Vigor, which increases your Wounds, and Reinforcement, which increases your Armor, might be good choices for a Skirmisher or Assaulter.

Once you spend 40 points in Renown Abilities, the Renown Trainers allow you to train the most powerful of the Renown abilities, the Tier 3 abilities. Your clear choices here are Sure Shot, which increases your ranged crit chance, and Opportunist, which increases your melee crit chance. On the defensive side, train in Reflexes, which increases your Parry rate, and Agility, which increases your Dodge rate. If you're leaning toward Scout, learn Agility first, then Reflexes. If you think you're more the Skirmishing or Assaulting type, consider Reflexes first.

SLAYING MONSTERS AND EARNING EXPERIENCE (PVE)

Solo Play

Although fighting the forces of Destruction on the many battlefields may raise your Renown among your peers, it will do little to help you increase your power. I know you are eager to prove yourself, apprentice, but to grow in experience and gain access to stronger abilities, you must practice your skills on the enemy's many minions and allies. The best way to accomplish this is to help the various people that you encounter. Sometimes you'll be among friends and allies, but often you face the Forces of Destruction alone.

Rank 1–10

Ranks 1 through 10 are largely about learning the Core abilities that you'll use until no Dark Elf breathes in Ulthuan. It's also your prime opportunity to experiment with the three basic paths. There aren't any Tactics to learn yet, and you'll only learn the one Morale ability at Rank 8, so you'll use it when you get it.

When you first start, get into Scout Stance. Stand way back from your target and repeatedly fire Eagle Eye. Or, simply walk up to a foe and Grim Slash at it until it falls dead at your feet. Or stand a short distance away and fire a few Eagle Eye shots at it, until it reaches you, whereupon you Grim Slash it once or twice. Any way you choose, you're likely be successful. Remember these options because you'll be using them for the rest of your career.

At Rank 2, you'll learn Broadhead Arrow. Broadhead Arrow has a shorter range than Eagle Eye: 65 feet instead of 100. Your options haven't really changed, but if you're starting at very long range, start with Eagle Eye, and when the foes reaches 65 feet, fire Broadhead Arrow. If you're quick, you can get another Eagle Eye off, and your target will likely fall dead before it reaches you. If you're starting at shorter range, start with Eagle Eye, immediately follow with Broadhead Arrow, then Grim Slash until your target dies. It shouldn't take long.

At Rank 3, you'll get a chance to learn Acid Arrow. Acid Arrow does relatively light damage at range, but it also reduces a target's Armor and Block chance. This makes it a good addition to your opening sequence. You can fire this one immediately after Bonehead Arrow instead of the second Eagle Eye, and make it easier to hit your opponent with your following attacks.

At Rank 4, you'll learn Brutal Assault. Brutal Assault works only in Scout or Assault Stance. Because you only have those two stances now), this shouldn't be a problem. Because this ability requires that you attack from behind your target, this is best used in a group, with ne exception: When you're Vengeful, you can use this ability without being behind your target. So if you're Vengeful, use this instead of Grim Slash. Otherwise, your combat sequence remains the same. However, at Rank 4, you also learn Assault Stance. If you want to walk p to your targets rather than pull them with a bow, use Assault Stance instead of Scout Stance. Or, pull with a bow in Scout Stance, nen shift to Assault Stance once you're within sword range.

akedown comes at Rank 5. This changes things somewhat. Takedown does light damage, but it also snares your opponent. It has a 5-foot range. So your sequence is now: stand at 100-foot range, Eagle Eye, Takedown, Broadhead Arrow, Acid Arrow, and if your arget is still standing, unlikely as that is, Grim Slash until he's dead. To use Takedown, you must be in Scout or Skirmisher tance.

At Rank 6, you learn Skirmisher Stance, which is your last stance, and Spiral-Fletched Arrow. Spiral-Fletched Arrow does fairly light damage, but you can use it while you're moving. You need to be in Skirmisher or Assault Stance to use Spiral-Fletched Arrow. Now, your paths are really starting to diverge. You could go for Scout Stance, stand at a very far distance, and use your tried-and-true sequence of Eagle Eye, Takedown, Broadhead Arrow, Acid Arrow, repeat until dead, or until your target reaches you, at which point you use Grim Slash to finish up. Or, if you're in a more Skirmisher mood, you can go to Skirmisher Stance, start with Takedown, and quickly follow with Broadhead Arrow, then back up as your target approaches, and fire Spiral-Fletched Arrow until your foe dies or catches up to you, whereupon you can Grim Slash it to death. Or, you might start in Assault Stance, walk up behind your prey, start with Brutal Assault, then Grim Slash until your target dies. Things are getting complex now, aren't they?

At Rank 7, you learn Distracting Shot, which is useful for reducing the damage a ranged opponent does by half. If you're following the Scout path, go ahead and put that in your combat sequence when it suits you, preferably early in the fight where it'll do the most good.

At Rank 8, you'll learn your first Morale ability, Point-Blank, but most of your fights won't be long enough for you to generate enough Morale to use it. You might find it useful if you're Assaulting a lot, where you'll generate enough Morale through dealing and receiving damage. If so, you might want to use it for the moderate damage and knockback, which gives you an opportunity to get a Broadhead Arrow or other ranged shot off.

You also learn Hunter's Fervor at Rank 8. This buff increases action point regeneration for 15 seconds for your whole group. This becomes useful in long battles or PvP when in a group, or when you're Assaulting, because using Grim Slash repeatedly can deplete your action points.

At Rank 9, you learn Draw Blood. Draw Blood is a moderate damage-over-time ability, and you need to be in Assault or Skirmisher Stance to use it. It adds to your Assault combat sequence nicely. Now, Assault Stance, Brutal Assault from behind, Draw Blood, Grim Slash, repeat. Or use Vengeance here, and really rack up the damage.

At Rank 10, you learn perhaps the best Shadow Warrior ability. Whirling Pin roots every enemy within 30 feet for five seconds, and it has no stance requirement. As an Assaulter, if you end up biting off more than you can chew, hit Whirling Pin and back off. If you're a Scout and you end up surrounded by enemies, use Whirling Pin and run. If you're Skirmishing, run up to a target while firing, use Whirling Pin, then run back, firing all the while. Of course, the usefulness in PvP is obvious.

During this period, you should be gaining ranks through completing all the quests your areas have to offer. If you have no more quests in your area, and the quests in the following area are too difficult, engage in PvP or participate in public quests until you feel that you have sufficient experience to continue. Or, as always, you could find a group.

Rank 11–20

Ranks 11 through 20 provide an assortment of Core abilities, Morale abilities, and Tactics. At Rank 11, you'll learn your first Tactic, Centuries of Training, which adds +1 Initiative per rank. Place it in your first Tactic bar immediately.

At Rank 12, you'll finally learn Vegeance of the Nagarythe. This doesn't change your combat sequences as discussed above, but, if you find yourself needing to do some extra damage in a hurry, Vengeance is the way to do that. You might find it useful if you end up fighting more than one enemy, or if you've engaged by charging in without using your bow, and you find yourself running low on health.

At Rank 14 you gain Flame Arrow. It does light damage, but has a nice moderate area-effect, damage-over-time component. This one's great for PvP, or against a stunned or engaged group of targets. You need to be in Scout Stance to use it, but if you're in PvP with a group, you will be anyway.

At Rank 16, you'll learn Rapid Fire, which is a Scout/Skirmisher Ability that does relatively light damage over time, and it's channeled. This means that a Skirmisher will rarely get a chance to use it in any case. A Scout could use it, but unless you're certain not to be interrupted, you have other Abilities that do more damage. You could probalby pass on this one.

At Rank 18, you can learn Eye Shot, which is a Skirmisher ability. It does light damage from up to 65 feet away, but it reduces the target's Initiative for a short while. Use this just before you close to melee range to decrease the target's Dodge.

At Rank 19, you learn the Steady Aim Tactic, which increases your Ballistic Skill. Unless you're a Skirmisher, and really like Expert Skirmisher, slot this one immediately, and never remove it again.

You also learn two Rank 2 Morale abilities, and one more Rank 1 Morale ability. The Rank 1 Morale ability, Concealment, allows you to dodge and disrupt all attacks for seven seconds. If you're a Scout, this is a far better choice than Point-Blank. If you're Assaulting, stay with Point-Blank.

Between the two Rank 2 Morale abilities, Unshakable Focus (Rank 12) doubles your damage for 12 seconds. You can't go wrong with that, regardless of your path. You also learn Focused Mind (Rank 20), which allows you to ignore all snares, roots, silences, and disrupts for 10 seconds. It also makes your abilities build faster, and they can't be set back while the Morale ability is active. If you're a Scout, you might consider this one, especially in PvP.

You also start your Mastery Training here. You won't gain many new abilities, but spending points to increase the strength and power of the path's related abilities is worth it alone. Your sequences will have changed a bit, with some nice additions to all your possible paths. You'll be starting to focus a bit more, probably, which should make equipment choices and Renown ability selection much easier. At this point, however, solo quests won't rank you up sufficiently, unless you're completing the quests your allies have to offer. But if you're participating in even a moderate number of scenarios and skirmishes, you shouldn't be having any trouble gaining ranks.

Rank 21–30

Between Ranks 21 and 30, the focus of your training will be on Tactics. You gain some of the nicer Mastery abilities at this point, and if you're spending any time in PvP, you'll have a nice selection of Renown abilities. Mainly, you'll be focusing on increasing the power of the abilities you use the most frequently.

At Rank 25, you gain an Assault ability, Opportunistic Strike, which is a melee attack that does light damage and disarms your opponent for five seconds. This makes a nice addition to your Assault sequence, because it prevents a significant amount of damage. At Rank 30, you learn Counterstrike, another Assault ability. Counterstrike does relatively light damage, but it interrupts any ability. This becomes very useful against casters, healers, or anyone who has abilities that take time to build.

You also learn five Tactics, but three of them are about regaining action points, which shouldn't be much of an issue if you're pacing yourself. Discerning Offense gives your opponents a lower chance of defending against your attacks. This is interesting for a third Tactic, but I definitely wouldn't trade Steady Aim or Centuries of Training for it.

Explosive Shots is your first Rank 3 Morale ability, so you'd use it even if it wasn't particularly valuable. But it is, especially for PvP, because it adds a moderate-damage area effect to all your shots for 10 seconds. Lileath's Forgiveness is a good Rank 1 Morale ability. It removes all hexes, curses, cripples, or ailments, and allows you to recover a lot of action points. As the only healing-type ability a Shadow Warrior learns, it's worthy of consideration. In PvP, it's a must.

If you want to level now, you need to PvP. You'll need the experience gained from completing the PvP quests. The number of group quests greatly increases here, making it difficult for the solo player to rank up.

Rank 31–40

You gain the last of your Core abilities here. At level 35, you'll learn Throat Shot. You'll need to be in Scout Stance to use it, but there's nothing bad about this Ability. It does moderate damage at 100 ft, and it silences the target for five seconds. This definitely becomes an addition to the Scout sequence against casters and healers of all types.

Lileath's Arrow (Rank 40) is a great Skirmisher attack, doing moderate damage to all enemies in front of you for 65 feet. It also works while moving, making it perfect for PvP.

You learn five Tactics, but only two of them, are worthy of much consideration. Blood-Soaked War grants you health each time you kill an opponent. For any path, that makes a great fourth Tactic. Distracting Rebounds causes your Distracting Shot to affect an enemy within 20 feet of your target, making this an excellent area effect Debuff. That, naturally, makes it excellent for PvP.

Don't hesitate in battle. If a foe asks for the blade, give it to him, preferably in the throat so he never asks again.

Your Morale abilities are all decent damage dealers, but only one is a must-have. Instill Fear is an Area Effect Disarm and Silence shot that lasts for seven seconds. This, without question, is a PvP winner. An entire group of Shadow Warriors laying this down one right after the other effectively shuts down an entire area. The only other Morale Ability in this range that comes close to being a must-have is Outrider Patrol, a Rank 2 Morale ability. It's a ranged area-effect attack that does heavy damage. Even so, it's not better than Unshakable Focus or Focused Mind, unless you're part of a war party that's all about massive amounts of area-effect damage.

By now you should have trained in the last of your steps for your Career Mastery paths, and, if you've focused on a single path, you can now use the Rank 4 Morale ability granted by your path, which is the single most powerful ability a Shadow Warrior can learn. Your bow, sword, and armor are the finest you can find.

You spend a great deal of time in PvP combat and gain most of your experience there. Spend your Renown points to really focus on those stats and abilities that bolster your combat style. Half the quests you undertake will be group-oriented. You can gain quite a bit of experience solo, if you wish, but the real fun is in taking keeps.

Group Play

A Shadow Warrior's purpose in a group or war party is simple: exact as much revenge as possible upon the traitors of Ulthuan and all of their allies. The only group ability a Shadow Warrior has is Hunter's Fervor. It never hurts, but it's not particularly useful in most situations.

In a group, you'll find Scout Stance more efficient than either Skirmisher or Assault Stance, unless the group composition dictates otherwise. For example, if you're in a group of casters and ranged attackers, any stance might serve well. In a balanced group of heavily armored tanks, healers, casters, and a Shadow Warrior, stay in Scout Stance and destroy targets from afar. Your Scout combat sequence remains fairly consistent, and you'll be using more area-effect attacks than when you're soloing. Even so, your sequence is all about dealing damage, slowing down your target, and, where necessary, silencing casters with Throat Shot.

In a running, moving melee, which happens often in world PvP, Skirmisher Stance is an excellent choice. With all the abilities that a Skirmisher has that can be used on the run, as the lines of the forces of Malekith surge forward and fall back, a Skirmisher can ebb and flow with them.

A war party of ranged area-effect adventurers can do a huge amount of damage very quickly. A group of Shadow Warriors, Bright Wizards, and Engineers makes for an explosively good time.

SLAYING PLAYERS AND COLLECTING RENOWN (PVP)

The war between High Elf and Dark Elf will not end until Malekith—and every one of his foul, traitorous kinslaying followers—lies spitted on Nagarythe steel. Unfortunately, Malekith has found allies in the followers of Chaos, and the wretched Orcs and Goblins, making our task all the worse. Should any of our allies fail, those armies will find themselves on the shores of Ulthuan, and that we cannot allow. So we fight a war on several fronts, each as important as the next. Ultimately, we will see Malekith dead, and with it comes our redemption.

Minutes from when I picked up my blade and bow, I found myself extracting my payment from the usurpers and murderers who would rule Ulthuan and beyond. Every combatant on the battlefield is different, and only the Shadow Warrior can deal with the weakness of each, in turn. For those who deal damage at range, such as mages, we engage at range, disrupting their attacks or silencing them with Throat Shot. Alternately, we can charge in as Skirmishers, firing arrows as we come, switching swiftly to Assault Stance to slash and cut them down. For the more heavily armored, the ones who wish to get close and hammer us with heavy weapons, we remain at range, stunning and slowing them, all the while firing arrow after arrow into their metal hides, falling back as necessary to maintain our distance.

As part of a group, if my warband has some armored companions who will hold the attention of the enemy, I can stand apart from the fray and rain down arrows with impunity. In this case, I can fire area-effect arrows, damaging entire groups of adversaries. Against those who are lightly armored, I can start from distance, firing a arrows until my foe closes range, then I switch to Assault stance and attack.

To be victorious against a group of enemies, I must be a part of a warband myself. While I have a number of abilities that affect groups of attackers, I cannot use them fast enough to slay all those in my way. While, if given time, I could dispatch an entire horde of enemies, it isn't likely that they'd give me that chance. However, with a few other Shadow Warriors, a few healers, or a couple of heavily armored companions, I could more than carry my weight, dealing enough damage for two.

The last thing I will tell you is that combat is a fluid thing. Fortunately, we are the most fluid of the participants in any battle, and our ability to change with the needs of the battle is unique. As long as we remain as fluid as the battle itself, we cannot fail to win.

FORGIVENESS AND DEATH

We near the Moonrise Forest. We've discussed much, you and I.

You now know and understand we who tirelessly fight against the Dark Elves. You carry the weapons of war from Nagarythe, and I am certain that the demand for vengeance runs hot in your veins. Seek out and slay the usurpers who killed your family, your friends, your city. Together, we can exact our revenge. Together, we can redeem our blood.

We will see Malekith dead. Will you aid us?

Do every task in an area before moving on. If you move on too quickly, you will likely run into difficulty combating the enemies you find there.

SWORDMASTER

The war is upon us. It creeps not on Ulthuan, but crashes toward our hallowed home like a wave upon the shore. Malekith will not be satisfied until his desecration of the Phoenix Throne has come to fruition. However, his rage will be his undoing; Malekith's obsession with the throne makes him vulnerable. We must protect our bastion until Finubar returns. It is time that we, the Asur, wield the Greatsword of Hoeth in the defense of Ulthuan. Pride must give way to structure, fear must give way to tranquility, rage must give way to reason. Inner peace must persevere.

Stay near, young Swordmaster as I, Orithion, impart upon you the quintessential knowledge necessary to be adept in our discipline. While the learning curve is steep, I can see in your demeanor that you have the potential to become a master in the art of balancing grace and force.

Do not succumb to the depth of what lies before you; I have mentored scores of young pupils such as yourself. I can impart the knowledge of the Tower of Hoeth to you, young master, but experience is our world's best guide. So, lift your greatsword in the defense of Ulthuan. Now is the time your tutelage begins.

By Orithion

What is a Swordmaster?

They are the defenders of Ulthuan. As sentinels of the Asur, it is their duty to meet Destruction enemies face to face on the battlefield. Unlike other protectors within the armies of Order, they are quite adept at guarding allies while wielding their greatswords. Their special magical abilities—studied at the White Tower of Hoeth and imparted from generation to generation—grant them this preternatural skill in combat.

To achieve success, a Swordmaster shifts his balance throughout the course of the fight, both defending and attacking with their two-handed swords. A wise and talented Swordmaster always plans several strikes in advance and relies on his battle prowess to exploit the enemy's weakness. A Swordmaster dances through combat with precision and calculation, a lithe defender who evades and deflects oncoming assaults. Even when Swordmasters decide to carry a shield, they excel at close combat.

They are experts at amalgamating physical combat and magical prowess through discipline to bring an imposing foe to ruin. Fighting at range may be a cause for concern; however, most Swordmasters are savvy of this vulnerability and find avenues to their opponents quickly to shut down attacks. Once a Swordmaster has an opponent in his grasp, there are few careers that can destroy the enemy better.

—Aleister Schreiber, Scholar Emeritus, University of Nuln

STARTING STATS

Introspection is required to achieve true discipline. It is imperative that you grasp what attributes will make you a mightier Swordmaster.

Foremost, we are frontline defenders and should be able to withstand brutal attacks. Toughness and Armor reduce the amount of damage that we must endure, while Wounds increases our total health. Your Parry ability is boosted with Weapon Skill, and increasing your Initiative helps you evade incoming attacks and lowers the chance of being critically hit.

Swordmasters are two-pronged: we both able defenders and lithe assailants. Your Strength attribute increases your melee damage, and decreases the likelihood that your attacks will be blocked or parried. Furthermore, Weapon Skill bolsters your ability to penetrate your opponents' armor. All these attributes can be elevated through equipment, Tactics, and Renown abilities.

Avoid accruing equipment that focuses on Ballistic Skill, Willpower, and Intelligence, because these attributes are of little use to a Swordmaster.

BEGINNING AS A HIGH ELF

We are currently standing upon the overlook at Moonrise Tower in Blighted Isle. Come to the edge of the overlook and gaze out upon the horizon of our storied land. Indeed, dusk has brought more than night. I can sense your astonishment and consternation as you peer upon that monstrosity that is a barnacle upon our shore, the Black Ark. From its deep bowels it spews legions of our kin, the Dark Elves. They come to take dominion over our hallowed homeland. For this reason, you must rein in your emotions. The enemy charges forward with hatred and greed. If we are to deflect their attacks and defend what is rightfully ours, we must remain calm and logical. Now that you have a sense of the dangers that encroach upon us, let us start your training.

Allow me to introduce you to Shadow Warrior Silvshara Greywind. She can provide you with tasks that are suitable for a young Asur of your experience. To the east in the woods hide Dark Sprites and Dark Elves. After you have gained enough expertise in your current abilities, talk to Lyndriel Flameleaf, and she will impart upon you new abilities befitting your advance in experience. As you continue to advance in proficiency, travel down the path where you will befriend other Asur who will direct you to ways to assist the aegis of Ulthuan. Even in your neophyte state, you can be quite an asset to our defense of this hallowed land.

SWORDMASTER GEAR

Swordmasters are the frontline defense of Ulthuan. It is our destiny to meet our enemy face to face, and halt their charge upon our blade. Thus, armor is of great importance to us. We can don Heavy Armor. Our armor is a special creation, for while it is durable, it is not burdensome. A Swordmaster must be agile and swift, while not sacrificing the ability to withstand the punishing blows delivered by your opponents.

The steel that you wield is no mere weapon, young High Elf. What you hold in your un-calloused hands is a Greatsword of Hoeth. We Swordmasters plied these wondrous designs of craftsmanship long before other factions in the Age of Reckoning existed. From hilt to tip a greatsword is usually six and seven feet long. Weaponry of this magnitude would surely topple a Dwarf. Only the Asur can understand how to wield such a creation. Others are misled to believe that brute might is required to use a tool of such vastness; it is through an understanding of nature and discipline of oneself that we exploit a construct of this magnificence. Do not be deceived, we do not defy nature—rather, we are more cognizant of it.

While we are more than adept at defending ourselves and our allies with our greatswords, we can still use a tower shield if the need arises. The sacrifice made to offensive capabilities heightens defensive prowess. The Swordmaster with a sword in his right hand and a shield by his left ought to be one of the last ones standing during a heated battle. Opponents will have to make a concerted effort to bring you to ruin.

You might feel very meek right now, but do not despair. As you progress, through training and aiding the war effort, you will acquire equipment that will bolster your abilities and defenses.

Participate in scenarios early on to gain Renown. While you may not gain expertise as fast as you would by completing tasks others give you, as you achieve higher Renown ranks you gain access to equipment at the warcamps. The first warcamp you encounter is Tor Aendris.

Strengths

· Ability to wield the two-handed Greatsword of Hoeth even while defending your allies. We can withstand onslaughts that might otherwise require the use of a shield.

· You never have to skirt the fringe of battle like those dependent upon range. We meet the enemy head on, imparting our will upon those who oppose us.

· Swordmasters are excellent protectors in the alliance of Order. Our services will always be required by those who are unable to withstand the direct blows of the enemy.

· Adept at disrupting and weakening opponents.

· You can dispense a considerable amount of damage while wielding a greatsword. Thus, the Swordmaster is quite effective when adventuring alone or in the company of others.

We are quite a force in close combat. It is essential that we position ourselves between the foe and our allies, rather than charging recklessly into battle. We are often called upon to obtain the enemies' focus; we are well suited for withstanding the punishing blows that our foe intends to deliver to our weaker comrades. We are not forced to abandon our offensive aptitude to protect our allies. While evading and parrying incoming attacks, we dance through battle, delivering deliberate, punishing, and debilitating assaults to those who oppose us.

Weaknesses

· Swordmasters lack a true ranged ability. While Throw does a slight amount of damage, we are nullified by ranged combat.

· We cannot heal ourselves. We are formidable fighters, but we are dependent upon others to restore our health during longer battles.

· Very dependent upon equipment. Our duty is to absorb the blows that our allies cannot; we can do so with the appropriate gear.

While we are a potent defender in the forces of Order, we are dependent upon those we fight alongside. As adept as you may be, you are only as successful as those around you. A lackadaisical healer or an overzealous attacker can oft spell the demise of a group; unfortunately the onus is often on us, because we are expected to maintain focus. Furthermore, we are easily neutralized by ranged combat. When we cannot close the gap to the ranged attacker, we oft meet our demise. Finally, a Swordmaster must put great effort to maintaining current equipment, because a deficit in our gear is noticed by all around us, friend or foe.

Abilities

The abilities that we use have been developed and mastered over the generations by our ancestors. The Core abilities that every Swordmaster should know are taught by Career Trainers as you gain in expertise. Talk with your Career Trainer after each level of experience you achieve; you are unseasoned and shouldn't hesitate to pick up new talents regularly.

Besides the Core abilities that all Swordmaster should learn, your Career Trainer can also help you travel down the paths that make you a unique combatant. You have three paths from which to choose. You can choose to focus solely on one path, mix between two, or find yourself an amalgam of all three. The latter is least advised though, because such diversification would make you deficient.

The Path of Khaine enriches your ability to directly damage the enemy. Swordmasters who follow this path excel at punishing their enemies with devastating blows. If you choose the Path of Khaine, your Quick Incision, Blurring Shock, Heaven's Blade, Sapping Strike, and Wall of Darting Steel abilities will reap the benefit. Additionally, your Career Trainer can impart abilities that only those who follow the Path of Khaine can master.

The Path of Vaul fortifies your defensive abilities. The Swordmasters who follow this path excel at withstanding punishing attacks. While all Swordmasters can defend themselves, this path allows you to become a dominant protector; few others can rival your defensive expertise. It would be wise though, if you follow the Path of Vaul, to sheath your greatsword and wield a sword in one hand and a great tower shield in your other. An enemy will find it most difficult to penetrate your defenses. If you choose the Path of Vaul, your Dragon's Talon, Eagle's Flight, Intimidating Blow, and Phantom's Blade abilities will reap the benefit. Again, your Career Trainer can impart abilities that only those who follow the Path of Vaul can master.

The Tome of Knowledge is a great ally; inquire within its depths for insight that will aid you.

The Path of Hoeth enhances your magical attacks and competencies. The Swordmasters who follow this path have a heightened ability to both enhance themselves and weaken their foe. If you choose the Path of Hoeth, your Nature's Blade, Ensorcelled Blow, Wrath of Hoeth, Gusting Wind, and Dazzling Strike abilities will reap the benefit. Once again, your Career Trainer can impart abilities that only those who follow the Path of Hoeth can master.

Abilities

Name	Level	Path	Cost	Range (in feet)	Type	Build	Duration	Reuse	Description
Graceful Strike	Starter Ability	Path of Vaul	35	Melee	Balance Attack - Open - Cripple	0s	0s	0s	Deals (75+DPS) damage and 150 damage over 5s. Generates an extra 225 worth of hate.
Throw	Starter Ability	Core	20	10 to 65	Ranged Attack	1s	0s	0s	Deals 75 damage. Rear position: If the target has less than 20% health, gain a 50% chance to deal an additional 525 damage.
Quick Incision	Level 2	Path of Khaine	25	Melee	Balance Attack - Improved	0s	5s	0s	Deals 349 damage over 10s. Snares target by 40% for 10s.
Blurring Shock	Level 3	Path of Khaine	Free	Melee	Balance Attack - Perfect	0s	0s	0s	Deals (150+DPS) Spirit damage.
Eagle's Flight	Level 4	Path of Vaul	35	Melee	Balance Attack - Improved - Augment	0s	5s	10s	Deal (150+DPS) damage and increases chance to Parry by 25% for 5s.
Nature's Blade	Level 5	Path of Hoeth	55	Self	Buff	0s	Stance	0s	All attacks have a 25% chance to proc a random stat tap for 3 per level for 10s.
Ensorcelled Blow	Level 6	Path of Hoeth	35	Melee	Balance Attack - Open	0s	0s	0s	Deals (112+DPS) damage. Deals Spirit damage.
Taunt	Level 7	Core	20	65	Debuff	0s	15s	15s	Interrupts target. For 15s, the tank deals 30% more damage against target. Monsters turn to attack tank until Taunt expires. After 3 ability activations and/or auto attacks from target hit tank, Taunt fades. Tank generates 2,250 in hate.
Gryphon's Lash	Level 8	Path of Khaine	40	Melee	Balance Attack - Open	0s	0s	0s	Deals (150+DPS) damage. Ability cannot be defended against.
Heaven's Blade	Level 9	Path of Khaine	55	Self	Buff	0s	Stance	0s	All attacks have a 25% chance to proc a 112 Spirit DD.
Guard	Level 10	Core	Free	41	Buff	0s	Stance	60s	Buff on friendly player that splits the damage between the target and the tank. Buffed player takes 50% of the incoming damage. Tank takes 50% of the incoming damage directed at the buffed target. Hate is split between player and tank.
Hold the Line	Level 10	Core	20/S	PBAE	Buff	0s	10s	60s	Toggled buff. Each second the toggle is active, bestows a buff that increases Evade and Disrupt chances by 45% to the tank and 15% to all friendlies in the radius that lasts 1s. If the tank uses another ability, the ability ends. Buffs on friendlies stack up to 3. Arc: 180 (pointed to the rear), radius: 40ft.
Intimidating Blow	Level 12	Path of Vaul	40	Melee	Balance Attack - Improved	0s	0s	0s	Deal (187+DPS) damage. Remove 100 Morale.
Wrath of Hoeth	Level 14	Path of Hoeth	Free	PBAE - Melee	Balance Attack - Perfect	0s	0s	0s	Deals 150 damage (Spirit damage) in a PBAE of 30ft. Also reduces target's Spirit resistance by 9.45/level for 10s.
Gusting Wind	Level 16	Path of Hoeth	35	PBAE	Balance Attack - Improved	0s	0s	0s	Deals (150+DPS) damage. Radius: 10ft (Melee).
Dragon's Talon	Level 18	Path of Vaul	Free	Melee	Balance Attack - Perfect	0s	4s	0s	Two hits that each deal (112+DPS)*0.5 damage (Spirit damage). Lower target's damage by 20% for 4s.
Juggernaut	Level 18	Core	45	Self	Buff	0s	0s	60s	Removes Snare, Root, Disarm, and Silence effects from the tank.

As you gain influence in each chapter, new rewards become available at the nearby Rally Master. These rewards are an excellent way to improve your equipment.

Abilities

Name	Level	Path	Cost	Range (in feet)	Type	Build	Duration	Reuse	Description
Challenge	Level 20	Core	30	CAE	Debuff	0s	15s	30s	For 15s, the challenged target deals 30% less damage to everyone but the caster. Monsters turn to attack tank until Challenge expires or 5s. After 3 ability activations and/or auto attacks from target hit tank, Challenge fades. Also generates 2,250 hate. Arc: 90, radius: 65ft.
Shatter Enchantment	Level 22	Core	25	Melee	Melee Attack	0s	0s	5s	Removes an enchantment from target. Deals (75+DPS) damage if successful.
Phantom's Blade	Level 25	Path of Vaul	55	Self	Buff	0s	Stance	0s	All hits have a 25% chance to proc 375 worth of threat and remove 50 Morale.
Aethyric Grasp	Level 30	Core	30	PBAE	Crowd Control	0s	5s	60s	Roots up to 4 targets within 30ft for 5s.
Dazzling Strike	Level 35	Path of Hoeth	40	Melee	Balance Attack - Improved	0s	5s	10s	Deals (187+DPS) damage. Disorients target for 5s (1s addition). Physical if no enchantment active
Wall of Darting Steel	Level 40	Path of Khaine	40 AP/s	Self	Buff	Toggle	10s	0s	Requires great weapon. Increase Parry, Dodge, and Disrupt chances by 50%. Self-snare by 40%. Toggled ability. When the target Parries, the attacker takes 150 damage. Any other ability activation interrupts Wall of Darting Steel.
Specialization									
Sapping Strike	Khaine x5	Path of Khaine	25	Melee	Balance Attack - Open	0s	5s	10s	Deals (112+DPS) damage. Removes 10 AP/s for 5s on target.
Phoenix's Wing	Khaine x9	Path of Khaine	35	CAE - Melee	Balance Attack - Improved	0s	0s	0s	CAE Melee Attack, Requires great weapon. Deals (112+DPS) damage to targets in area. Generates 2x normal hate. Arc: 180, range: Melee.
Ether Dance	Khaine x13	Path of Khaine	Free	Melee	Balance Attack - Perfect	0s	3s	20s	Swings 5 times over 3s. Deals (150+DPS)*0.75 each attack (deals Spiritual damage).
Redirected Force	Vaul x5	Path of Vaul	25	Melee	Balance Attack - Open	0s	0s	5s	Requires Block. Deals 262 damage and cannot be defended against. Against monsters, builds an extra 375 hate.
Crushing Advance	Vaul x9	Path of Vaul	30	Melee	Balance Attack - Improved	0s	0s	0s	Deals (112+DPS) damage. Interrupts target building an ability. Increases Armor by 24.75/level. Increases Block chance by 5% for 10s. Requires Shield.
Crashing Wave	Vaul x13	Path of Vaul	Free	Melee	Balance Attack - Perfect	0s	5s	20s	Two hits, each hit deals (225+DPS)*0.5 damage (Spirit damage). Knockdown target for 3s.
Aethyric Armor	Hoeth x5	Path of Hoeth	35	Self	Self Buff	0s	30 min	0s	Increase armor by 16.5/level and Disrupt chance by 5%.
Protection of Hoeth	Hoeth x9	Path of Hoeth	25	Buff	Balance Attack - Improved	0s	5s	60s	Absorbs the next 675 damage.
Whispering Wind	Hoeth x13	Path of Hoeth	Free	Melee	Balance Attack - Perfect	0s	5s	20s	Hits twice, each hit dealing (225+DPS)*0.5 damage (Spirit damage). Interrupts any currently building attack. Silence target for 5s

Morale

Whenever you engage in combat, you will feel the rush of adrenaline as the battle progresses. You find yourself feeding off the crushing attacks you can deftly parry or evade, and the punishing strikes you deliver to your foe with the Greatsword of Hoeth. Be warned though, do not give way to pride or lust in battle; instead, harness this momentum and, through discipline, unleash it at the precise instant to turn the tides of battle in your favor.

This momentum is called Morale. Your Morale increases as the battle progresses; after accruing enough Morale, you can unleash a Morale ability. These are oft more grandiose talents than simple abilities. By the time you achieve the eighth rank, you should learn your first Morale ability: Demolishing Strike.

As you advance through our echelons, you gain access to several other Morale abilities. At any time, you can have four Morale abilities ready at your disposal to strike down the forces of Destruction. One caveat: each ability is assigned a particular rank (1–4); you can only be ready to use one ability from each rank at a time. Understandably, you must be disciplined to accrue the larger amount of Morale necessary to execute a Rank 4 ability, such as Immaculate Defense. Remember, your discipline will ultimately dictate your success or failure.

Morale

Name	Level	Rank	Range (in feet)	Duration	Description
Demolishing Strike	Level 8	Rank 1	Melee	0	Deal 900 damage over 15s and lower armor by 26.4/level for 15s.
Shield Wall	level 12	Rank 2	Self	10s	Self buff: Increase chance to Block by 100% for 10s.
Grapple	Level 16	Rank 1	Melee	10s	Unbreakable Root on target and tank (both roots break simultaneously).
Raze	Level 20	Rank 2	CAE	3s	Channeled physical CAE attack that deals 1,200 damage to targets over 3s. Arc: 90, radius: 66ft.
Distracting Bellow	Level 24	Rank 3	100	10s	Target and all enemies within 30ft deal 50% less damage for 10s.
Wings of Heaven	Level 32	Rank 2	Self	10s	Propels the Swordmaster toward the target. Upon landing, Swordmaster PBAEs a snare (60%, 10s).
Bladeshield	Level 36	Rank 3	Self	10s	Absorbs the next 1,200 damage. Deals 600 back each time the Swordmaster takes damage.
Immaculate Defense	Level 40	Rank 4	Group	10s	Group members who stay within 65ft of the tank take 75% less damage for 10s.
Whirling Geyser	Khaine x15	Rank 4	PBAE	0s	Deals 1,800 and knocks back targets within 30ft. Requires a great weapon.
Shield of Valor	Vaul x15	Rank 4	Self	0s	Group members each absorb the next 1,800 damage. Also gain 200 AP. Requires a shield.
Shadow Blades	Hoeth x15	Rank 4	PBAE	12s	Deals 1,800 over 12s. Also removes 30s of Morale on targets over 12s.

Tactics

Name	Level	Description
Centuries of Training	Level 11	25% chance on attack to proc a DoT that deals 150 damage over 3s. Non-stacking, non-refreshing.
Focused Offense	Level 13	Increase damage dealt by 25%. Increase damage taken by 20%. Decrease threat generation by 25%.
Ensorcelled Agony	Level 15	Ensorcelled Blow causes a DoT that deals 249 damage (Magical) over 5s.
Bend the Wind	Level 17	Increases Elemental resist by +6.3 per level of the character.
Rugged	Level 19	Increases Toughness by +4/level.
Dampening Talon	Level 21	Dragon's Talon also reduces the target's chance to Parry and Block by 10%.
Discerning Offense	Level 23	Attacks have a 10% reduced chance to be defended against.
Menace	Level 25	Increases threat by 100% on all attacks.
Isha's Protection	Level 27	Increase the value of heals on the character by 20%.
Unstoppable Juggernaut	Level 29	Juggernaut's reuse timer is lowered to 20s.
Potent Enchantments	Level 31	Enchantments also deal 349 over 9s.
Poised Attacks	Level 33	Attacks while in Improved and Perfect Balance states are 10% harder for enemies to defend.
Forceful Shock	Level 35	Blurring Shock also perfoms a medium knockback.
Impeccable Reactions	Level 37	When you Parry, you instantly gain the Perfect Balance state.
Adept Movements	Level 39	Wall of Darting Steel's AP cost is 30 AP/s and no longer snares.
Deep Incision	Khaine x3	Quick Incision's DoT is increased in value to 498 over 10s.
Balanced Accuracy	Khaine x7	Increases critical hit chance by 10% when in Improved Balance, and 20% while in Perfect Balance.
Gryphon's Precision	Khaine x11	Gryphon's Lash has a 25% chance to Stun targets for 1s (no immunity).
Perfect Defenses	Vaul x3	Increase Block and Parry chances by 5% when in Improved Balance, and 10% when in Perfect Balance.
Lingering Intimidation	Vaul x7	Intimidating Blow reduces the target's ability to critically hit by 25% for 10s.
Vaul's Buffer	Vaul x11	On defense: Gain an 412 absorb shield.
Volatile Enchantments	Hoeth x3	Increase chance for Enchantments to proc by 25% (to a rate of 50%).
Bolstering Enchantments	Hoeth x7	Enchants also proc a 9.45 Spirit/Corporeal resist debuff to the target and buff group members' Spirit/Corporeal for 10s.

Tactics

A prime method of enhancing your own abilities is throug the use of various Tactics. You select these before battle and you can even store a few sets into memory if you like. Tactics bolster your defensive and offensive prowess. Tact are easily adaptable to the situation at hand. You have a limited number of Tactics that you can use at a time; this increases as you grow in rank. The first Tactic you gain is Centuries of Training. This increases your Initiative as long as you are using it. If you choose to take advantage of a different Tactic instead, your Initiative returns to its un-enhanced level.

We Swordmasters oft find ourselves in a variety of roles, depending on what the situation dictates. Tactics are an excellent opportunity to fortify the abilities you deem m pertinent to each battle. For example, if you are called to tank enemies, you might find Menace, Isha's Protection, Rugged, and Dampening Talon as pertinent Tactics. Where if you are more offensively minded, Focused Offense, Discerning Offense, Centuries of Training, and Potent Enchantments might be of more use. In battle versus the forces of Destruction, you might exploit the Rugged, Unstoppable Force, Forceful Shock, and Discerning Offense Tactics. Fortunately, you do not have to sit and formulate a new set of Tactics every time you encounter a different situation; you can memorize several sets of Tacti and choose to employ whichever seems appropriate prior t battle.

The best way to gather influence is to participate in areas where you find other allies fighting against a common foe. This is known as a public quest, and through its achievement, the local surroundings will temporarily be spared from peril.

Renown

Even as we sit here among the scenic cliffs of Blighted Isle, it is impossible to forget that war is upon us.

If you choose to do battle with the forces of Destruction, and I hope you shall, you will rise in Renown. A young, untested Swordmaster, such as yourself, is an unknown in our domain. Fear not though, as you achieve success in your battles against the Destruction armies, others throughout the world will come to know both you and your accomplishments.

With this success comes great reward. As your Renown increases, you can talk to Renown Trainers; find them hanging around warcamps, spreading the lore of flourishing combatants. These Renown Trainers have conversed with many a champion, learning of their strengths. Their task is to bestow upon storied defenders the traits that will help them in the strife against the Dark Elves and their allies.

Indeed, there are many options for training Renown. It is all dependant on what type of Swordmaster you want to be. As a seasoned veteran of this combat and many others, I will enlighten you about how I chose to spend my Renown. Keep in mind, I am much more experienced and have achieved the 60th rank of Renown. It is a long, but rewarding path. Early on I would focus on Might, increasing your Strength. It would also be prudent to invest into Fortitude early on, increasing your Toughness. Additionally, working on your Blade Master ability will bolster your Weapon Skill. By the time you have hit Rank 20 in Renown you should look something like this: Might III, Fortitude II, and Blade Master II. Now the Assault ability becomes available; this increases both your Weapon Skill and Strength. Other abilities to invest in on your rise through the Renown ranks include Vigor, to increase your Wounds, and Reinforcement to supplement your Armor. As you approach Rank 50 you might have: Might IV, Fortitude III, Blade Master III, Assault II, Vigor I, and Reinforcement I. By now you will be a marvelous fighter and deserve abilities that reflect such. I would finish off with Opportunist I to increase your critical strike chance, and Reflexes I to bolster your parrying prowess.

One Minute with Orithion Mistblade

An excerpt from the "War Archives Record" journal on Orithion Mistblade, a veteran defender for the forces of Order

First of all, welcome. It is good to see that you are doing well and relatively unscathed.

Orithion: Thank you.

Were you surprised by the arrival of the Black Arks?

Orithion: Not really. We figured it would occur once Finubar departed. I must admit I did not expect such imposing vessels. I guess we should not be surprised though; the Dark Elves are of similar intellect as the Asur.

Speaking of that, many claim that the High Elves think they are superior to the other races. How would you respond to such a claim?

Orithion: "Superior" is such a relative term. Considering the source of such claims, one knows they could never comprehend such thought.

I think that's a yes. I frequently hear others comment on the difficulty of discerning the sexes of the Asur. Care to comment?

Orithion: I find that surprising. We males are so rugged and chiseled, whereas the female Asur are so delicate and feminine. I do have to admit I have the same trouble with Dwarfs. For awhile I thought that you could use facial hair to tell them apart, but let us say that is not always the case.

I could only imagine. I would not want to incur the wrath of a slighted she Dwarf. I hear you are quite an animal lover.

Orithion: It is true. I have always had a special interest in animals, and I've had many pets over the years. Truth be told, I've always fancied having a Goblin as a pet. They are a good size, and have that "so ugly that they are cute" charm to them. However, I don't think I have it in me to try to train one, much less clean up after it. I should probably stick to easier creatures, like wolves.

When you once again return or merge... with the Rally Master to make that location your new home. This can save you traveling time as you adventure. Use the Battle Map in your backpack to return to this point.

As you progress through your campaign, try to complete the chapters in your war story.

Solo Play

Rank 1–10

In the early part of your development, your abilities will be limited. While you lack the spectrum of talents of a veteran Swordmaster, do not miss this opportunity to hone your competence at shifting your Balance throughout the fight. I noticed that you had already grasped Graceful Strike by the time we met. Most excellent, young Swordmaster. When you execute a Graceful Strike on your foe, you enter an Improved state of Balance; it is through this Improved Balance that you can deliver additional strikes to your foe that are not possible from a Normal Balance stance. The first ability you can execute from Improved Balance is Quick Incision. Just as Graceful Strike heightens your Balance, so to does Quick Incision. After performing Quick Incision on your enemy, you gain Perfect Balance. In this state you are perfectly poised to deliver a punishing blow. Blurring Shock is the first skill you learn to perform while in a state of Perfect Balance. Thus, early on, a suitable chain of attacks would be Graceful Strike, Quick Incision, and Blurring Shock. That sequence will lead you from Normal Balance, to Improved Balance, to Perfect Balance, and back to Normal Balance. Beholding a veteran Swordmaster in combat is akin to watching an intricate and eloquent dance performed in the middle of a field of strife.

As you grow more skilled, you can use different abilities to move through the different phases of Balance. A sequence I found proper at your skill level when I fought alone was Graceful Strike, Eagle's Flight, Blurring Shock. Eagle's Flight heightens our defenses by increasing our ability to parry for 10 seconds; using this boost of protection elevates your defense while not forcing you to sheathe the greatsword, making you a formidable ally and foe.

Remember callow one, we Swordmasters are not mere pugilists. Through generations of studying in the White Tower of Hoeth, we continue to cultivate our magical prowess. We have learned to enchant our blades with magic to bolster our fighting abilities. These enchantments should be inflicted upon your foe about one out of four strikes. The first of these magical enhancements is Nature's Blade; landing this randomly steals one of your enemy's attributes for 10 seconds. Nature's Blade is useful in longer fights when weakening your opponent is vital. When you find yourself facing enemies of near equal or lesser stature, Heaven's Blade is well-suited to slice through your adversary. It is important to keep your blade enchanted at all times. As you can see, we have evolved ways to bolster our melee proficiency while not being the most physical of frontline combatants.

In terms of Morale, start with Demolishing Strike. As combat progresses and your Morale swells, it is important not to become prideful with your accomplishments. Rather, use your accrued Morale to unleash a Demolishing Strike upon your adversary. This not only does damage, but reduces your foe's armor as well.

Rank 11–20

As you progress through the ranks, you integrate new abilities. You master your first Tactic when you reach Rank 11. Centuries of Training gives your blows a chance to deal additional damage.

If you're intent upon unleashing damage to your enemy, you'll find Focused Offense and Escorelled Agony quite useful. You also gain abilities that allow you to damage multiple opponents at once—Gusting Wind ability, Wrath of Hoeth, and Raze Morale ability.

Fret not if you have chosen to be a defensive specialist. New skills in this range fortify your tanking prowess. The Shield Wall Morale ability allows you to block all of your opponent's attacks for a short time. Imagine the frustration even the most skilled Witch Elf will experience when she cannot penetrate your defenses. Additionally, you learn to gain the aggression of multiple foes with the Challenge ability.

You will expand your combative arsenal with the Dragon's Talon ability— crippling your foe, whilst decreasing the damage they deal.

Rank 21–30

By this time you should have a solid understanding of how to shift your Balance to exploit your foe. Continue to implement the skills you have already mastered. A key addition to your Core abilities in this range is Aethyric Grasp, rooting several of your enemies in place.

Offensively, continue to increase your proficiency at the abilities you possess. An enhancement to your offensive attacks is the Discerning Offense; implementing this Tactic decreases your opponent's ability to defend against your attacks.

For the defensive Swordmaster, this span is a boon to your protective aptitude. Tactically, Menace increase the threat you generate, making it easier for you to maintain the enemies' focus. Also, Isha's Protection enhances the effectiveness of all heals on you. The Guard of Steel morale ability fortifies an ally's Toughness for a time. Furthermore, the Morale ability Distracting Bellow decreases the damage done by your opponent. Even the greenest of Swordmasters, such as yourself, can see how these enhancements make us formidable defenders at the frontline of battle.

Rank 31–40

No longer a novice, you should now possess a true understanding of our discipline. As you shift through the phases of Balance, you will be something truly remarkable to observe. It is now time for you to complete and polish your vast arsenal of skills, to drive back the forces of Destruction in defense of Ulthuan.

You gain many skills that benefit any style. Tactical advances include Potent Enhancements, increasing the damage done by all your blade enchantments. Additionally, Forceful Shock adds a knock back element to Blurring Shock. Impeccable Reactions has a chance to advance your state of Balance whenever you parry. Dazzling Strike disorients your enemy while slowing its reactions.

Your defensive aptitude is enhanced with the Wall of Darting Steel ability; this increases your ability to dodge, parry, and disrupt your opponent. This potent ability can be quite fatiguing and should be executed at precisely the right moment. Your Morale ability options expand with Immaculate Defense, decreasing the damage taken by you and your allies for a short time. Furthermore, the Bladeshield Morale ability envelopes you in a shield that absorbs incoming damage and reflects it to your opponent.

Group Play

You will oft find your tanking services requested by your allies. This is a challenging, yet rewarding task. You will find yourself face to face with the fiercest of competitors; it will be your duty to maintain the enemy's focus, so that your fellow combatants can bring those who threaten the forces of Order to their demise.

We possess many abilities that make us deft protectors. Understand what you are capable of to maximize your chances of success. While much of our combat strategy is useful whether you find yourself alone amidst a Goblin warband or banded with allies to strike down scores of Dark Elf invaders, several techniques shine only within a group setting.

Again, it is your duty to absorb the incoming blows in lieu of your allies. To be adept at this, you must control the opponent's threat. Certain abilities increase the threat we accrue. Graceful Strike can be executed from any state of Balance, and in addition to damaging your foe, it increases your threat. Also, if the enemy switches focus to one your allies, Taunt redirects the aggression to you, where it belongs. When you find yourself against multiple foes, use Challenge to grab their attention quickly; to be successfully Challenged, the enemy must be in front of you. Another means to bolster your threat includes the Menace Tactic.

In addition to maintaining threat, we have several methods of bolstering our allies in combat. Hold the Line helps you and your allies disrupt and dodge attacks. Distracting Bellow and Shield Wall reduce your opponents' damage and increase your own Blocking ability respectively. The Guard of Steel Morale ability bolsters your group's Toughness. Immaculate Defense decreases all incoming damage to you and your allies. Additionally, Wall of Darting Steel heightens your own defensive prowess.

Your backpack has both an inventory and a quest section. If you cannot find an item required for a quest even after killing the enemy, check the quest section of your backpack.

sha's Protection increases the amount you are healed for, surely making your
healer grateful. A Swordmaster quickly realizes that personal and group success
s intertwined with the fate of your healer. As such, casting Guard on a healing ally is a prudent way to protect those who bandage your maladies.
While you aim to protect all your allies, pay special attention to the safety of your healers.

SLAYING PLAYERS AND COLLECTING RENOWN (PVP)

War is indeed everywhere and our conflict with the Dark Elves is not an isolated event. Other battlefronts rage
across our world. The Dwarfs defend themselves against the hordes of greenskins, and the Empire humans must
protect themselves from the rampage of the Chaos. We must ally ourselves with the Dwarfs and the Empire in
the war against the forces of Destruction. It is impossible to insulate yourself from this war, for it permeates from
the coasts of the Blighted Isle to Lothern. It dictates the actions of all Asur.

You will become entrenched in this epic war from early in your training. Khaine's Embrace scenario lies not too far from
this very overlook. There, and in several other scenarios throughout the world, you find Asur, Empire, and Dwarfs battling
the armies of Destruction.

While most of the strategies that apply to combating creatures still apply in realm versus realm (RvR) warfare, some do not
translate as well. For instance, threat is of no use. The forces of Destruction will not be taunted like a mere Harpy.

Likewise, some abilities are more prudent when fighting the armies of Destruction. Like you, Destruction combatants use
Morale to unleash devastating blows. This must be averted if possible. Intimidating Blow, which you learn in your early
teens, decreases your foe's Morale; this ability can be enhanced with the Cowering Intimidation Tactic. Additionally, Morale
can be countered by enchanting your sword with Phantom's Blade.

Combat in RvR warfare is very dynamic. A combatant who stands still will oft be found lying on the earth. Control your
opponents' mobility the best you can. Fortunately, we Swordmasters are quite adept at this feat, even during our novice ranks.
Quick Incision snares your enemy briefly. Another method of snaring opponents is the Wings of Heaven Morale ability; you
gracefully leap through the air and land next to your foe, snaring him and his nearby allies. A potent means of rooting your
enemies in place is Aethryic Grasp. Along this line, Grapple (Morale ability) locks you and your foe in place, preventing
cowards from fleeing from your Greatsword of Hoeth. If you find yourself on the unfortunate end of your opponent's
attempt to limit your movements, the Juggernaut ability will free you. The talent Unstoppable Juggernaut allows you to
utilize this ability more frequently. While short in duration, Blurring Shock and Dazzling Strike can knock down and daze
your enemy, respectively.

A key to being an effective Swordmaster in RvR warfare is to learn from every situation, be it a small skirmish in Chrace
or an epic battle on the streets of Praag. Analyze your victories, so they may be replicated. Likewise, dissect your defeats so
adjustments can be made. The axiom remains true: experience is the best teacher.

CAST ASIDE YOUR VICES

You have listened well, young Swordmaster. This is certainly a vast amount of information to absorb
in such a short time. Fear not though, for my words and lessons are merely a guide. Experience, not
I, will be your true teacher. With each battle, victory or no, you will find yourself growing more
adept at our craft. The term "Swordmaster" is a bit of a misnomer—true, no others can wield the
blade like us. But Mastery is what we seek, not what we are. We are perpetually gaining insight and
proficiency, with constant room for improvement in the aim of perfection. Focus on your discipline
and discernment as you assimilate the lessons from each battle so you may evolve into a formidable
force in combat. Cast aside your lust, pride, fear, and hatred so that you may lift your greatsword as a
calculating, disciplined defender of Ulthuan. You are an apt pupil, and I'm certain our paths shall cross
again. Until then, may experience and discipline guide you well.

WHITE LION

By Khalidar

The sheer beauty and untamed nature of the wilds of Chrace can unnerve even the cruelest of our kin, the Dark Elves, as they have come to call themselves. Even our southern kin do not fully understand why we would choose to live in such a place, but they, and even the Phoenix King, respect our indomitable will in battle. Regardless, this is the place of my birth, and the wilderness is my home, and the home of the Chracian hunters, the White Lions.

War. I hear it spoken in whispers. The animals have sensed it for some time now. We have sensed something, as well. Destruction, the darkness, will bring a shadow of murder and cruelty over our land. The war lions grow restless. Our dark kin send raiding parties and assassins into our lands. They have never truly felt the axe and claws of a pride of White Lions. Murderers have come to our shore, and they will show us no mercy. The White Lions will go to war. And we will show no mercy.

The dawn sun has yet to be seen. Instead, clouds of shadow have covered the sky, blocking all light from shining through. I adjust my grasp on the haft of my axe and prepare for what is to come. Roac can smell the scent of the intruders in the air. His coat and mane bristle in anticipation. I cast an eye over his battle armor, reminding myself to adjust the straps so that his armor will not disturb him as we prepare for the hunt.

As I look at him, I can't help but remember the many years of training. He has grown much stronger and more experienced since I first found the cub. I have seen to that in his training over the decades. We have fought for many years together, in many skirmishes and conflicts. We have fought with axe and claw together as a single whirlwind upon our enemies for many years. We will fight together till the end, whether battle or old age takes us.

A low rumble sounds through Chrace, as if the land is warning us of their arrival. Even the newest of our recruits can sense the dark ones who have invaded our land. I look into the darkness, steeling myself for what is to come. As I ready, a fierce wind whips toward the darkness, and the horns of the White Lions sound the advance. Roac lets out a tremendous roar, and takes on a savage visage. In one step, we both launch out, leaping and striding with strength, swiftness, and fearlessness. As we race on to the enemy, I see the hope of the light surrounding us, opening the darkness ahead. I realize then that an Archmage of some power has come to help us fight against the encroaching darkness of our tainted kin. The light of hope rests in our hands, now, and our people need us. We must protect the land of our hearts, our homes, and our kin. With strength, honor, and duty for Ulthuan.

Young hunter, listen well. I leave this knowledge to you, so you are prepared. Listen, and learn well my teachings, for when I am gone, the defense of the light is in your hands, and the hands of our brethren. If we are to help the younger races from Destruction, as the Phoenix King has commanded, with strength and will, by the skill of our axes and the strikes of our claws, it will be so!

What is a White Lion?

You might have seen ferocious wild animals in cages or from afar atop the city gates. Believe me, when I tell you that you have never seen as magnificent a beast as the war lion, the companion to the High Elf White Lion warriors.

White Lion and war lion live in tandem. Once a High Elf enters into his righteous profession and chooses a beast, the two are inseparable; they are almost of one mind. In battle, the swift lion distracts, and rends if it can get in tight enough with its claws, while the White Lion strikes at the least-protected parts of his enemy. They combine their attacks for a deadly, damaging assault, and rare is the opponent who can withstand the combined fury of Elf and lion.

No matter where a White Lion goes, he always has a companion, which makes adventuring easier than those who journey truly alone. The Empire calls the High Elves and the Dwarfs allies, but the lion may be the noblest ally of all.

—Aleister Schreiber, Scholar Emeritus, University of Nuln

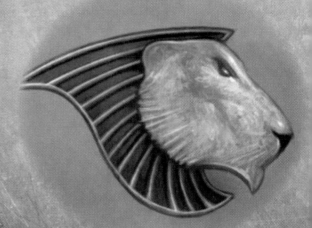

Never trust a Dark Elf. You should already know this, but reminders do not hurt.

STARTING STATS

I know what you are thinking, young cub. How should I enhance my body to become a truly fierce White Lion? First, we require Strength. Our mighty axes require a strong arm not usually seen by our kind. Strengthen yourself, and your axe will fall with great might. Also enhance your Weapon Skill. This will make your axe hits more precise, so they will not easily miss your target. If you find yourself needing a boost of protection in battle, you can't go wrong with Toughness. This will lessen the blows inflicted upon you. Finally, as a fighter, Wounds is important, as you will gain more health and be less likely to fall so quickly, should you be getting hit.

As you start out, you will be granted training in these three very important skills. Learn them well, cub, for they will serve you for your entire life. Call War Lion summons your lion to aid you in battle. Hack is a brutal melee axe chop at your enemy. This is an easy axe move for a novice, and will serve you well throughout your career. Axe Toss lets you fling an axe at your target. Use this at range to damage the enemy before you engage in melee.

The best way to initiate a fight, early on, is to use Axe Toss to throw your axe at the enemy, send your war lion into battle ahead of you and, then use the axe skills you have learned so far, and Hack away at your enemy. As you become stronger and better equipped, you will find that all of your attacks become more powerful. This holds true for skills you will learned early on and use much later as an elder.

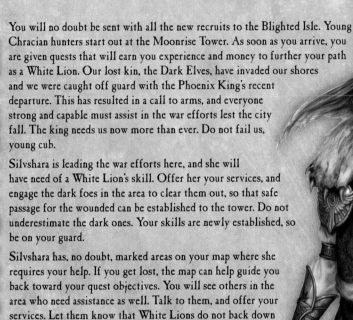

STARTING AS A HIGH ELF

You will no doubt be sent with all the new recruits to the Blighted Isle. Young Chracian hunters start out at the Moonrise Tower. As soon as you arrive, you are given quests that will earn you experience and money to further your path as a White Lion. Our lost kin, the Dark Elves, have invaded our shores and we were caught off guard with the Phoenix King's recent departure. This has resulted in a call to arms, and everyone strong and capable must assist in the war efforts lest the city fall. The king needs us now more than ever. Do not fail us, young cub.

Silvshara is leading the war efforts here, and she will have need of a White Lion's skill. Offer her your services, and engage the dark foes in the area to clear them out, so that safe passage for the wounded can be established to the tower. Do not underestimate the dark ones. Your skills are newly established, so be on your guard.

Silvshara has, no doubt, marked areas on your map where she requires your help. If you get lost, the map can help guide you back toward your quest objectives. You will see others in the area who need assistance as well. Talk to them, and offer your services. Let them know that White Lions do not back down from a challenge.

Now that you have become familiar with the area, talk with everyone around you, and gain lore for your Tome of Knowledge. All your accomplishments lie in this book, young cub. If you do enough, you may obtain a title for your achievements. Down the road, help man the bolt throwers against flying forces. These are highly tuned Elven throwers, and your hits will be dead-on, so you need not worry of your lack of proficiency with the weapon. When you have gained enough experience to increase your rank, speak to one of the trainers. They will teach you some new skills.

Silvshara will send you to the nearest outpost to help fight against our dark kin. There, you can investigate Khaine's Embrace. This is a known stronghold for the Dark Elves, and you must fight in player versus player battle against them, but now is your chance to show your strength as a White Lion and ready your axe skills even further. If you do not cower against the evil of our enemies, and show them you hold the light of hope, then this battle scenario will gain you Renown for fighting for the side of Order. Perhaps you might even become wiser in the endeavor.

Down the road, you will find an encampment of our brethren. No doubt my old friend, Captain Talorith, the Rally Master, has some missions for you. There is a battle area up ahead called a public quest. Here you can gain influence and earn the captain's respect. If you help out in this area, you will be rewarded. Talorith gives out weapons or armor specific to our use, and collecting such artifacts would be a boon to your further advancement, young cub. You may run across a Dwarf on your way to the public quest. Talk to her, for she has been in the area for some time, and I have seen the explosives she can make. That kind of firepower at your disposal, along with your skills, will be a great advantage in defeating the Arkeneth guards and slaves in the area. I have seen the Beastmaster in the area, and be warned: His pet Scornlash is a fierce

Top 5 War Lion Snacks

1. Squig stomachs.

2. Chaos knuckles.

3. Troll toes.

4. Nurgling neck.

5. Dark Elf thigh.

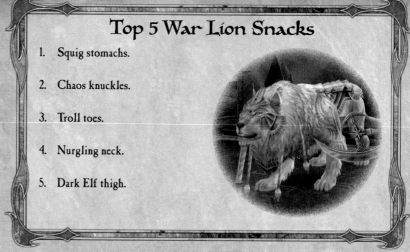

beast, and will require many strong hands to defeat. Show them who is a true master of beasts, and slay the abomination they have brought to our lands.

After you have sufficiently won Talorith's respect and influence, head out of Azurewood Glade, down the road toward the Ruins of Adunei. Be wary here, young cub. While it may appear calm here, the battle still rages. Seek out quests and help your brethren fortify this position for the king. When you reach Rank 10, head down to the warcamp of Tor Aendris. They need someone of our skills. This is the very forward edge of battle. Many Dark Elves and other forces of Destruction will be lurking around this player versus player area. They will undoubtedly use stealth and cunning against you. Watch your back, young cub, but fight with the valor, honor, and fearlessness I have instilled in you.

WHITE LION GEAR

Your elder, no doubt, gave you the trusted family Elven Greataxe before you left for training. Although a fine weapon, it has surely seen many battles and is most likely showing its age. Even so, it is sturdy, and will be fine for the time being. When you have become proficient enough to wield a heavier and deadlier axe, smiths and Rally Masters have what you need, provided you have enough coin or influence.

You will be given woven garb and other pieces. These basic pieces are given to all our new recruits. As a White Lion it is your duty to obtain new hides and new armor for yourself as part of the hunt. A White Lion's armor is not just a scattering of hides. We honor our kills and hunts by displaying the hides through having them interwoven with fine Elven chain armor. This keeps us light and agile as well as formidable looking when we confront our enemies. Honor the beasts' hides and use them well, for we do not kill needlessly.

STRENGTHS AND WEAKNESSES

Strengths

- When both axe and lion strike together, our damage dealing power is rarely matched by others.

- All of our axe skills provide a range of flexibility in purpose, from damage to ailments, which come in handy in any situation.

- Due to the affinity we have with our pet and the training he receives, we can use powerful skills that are executed in conjunction with one another.

- Ability to solo well. We have a companion who travels with us wherever we go, and we use that greatly to our advantage.

Having our war lion makes us a deadly force. With all of our axe skills and abilities, we have a barrage of attacks to assail our enemy. Let this be a lesson that our enemies may know of our strengths, and may exploit your weaknesses. Knowing your weaknesses allows you to protect yourself if an enemy tries to exploit them. Take heed.

Weaknesses

- No self-healing spells. Only true fighters understand that we must rely on others to heal us.

- If our pet dies we lose a lot of damage-dealing capability. When our war lion falls in battle, this leaves us weak.

- We cannot attack well at range, relying almost solely on close melee combat. Standing in the background watching a fight? Never! Lead the pride, and close on your enemy.

- We wear medium armor. Leave the tanking to those with heavy shields or suits of plate armor that cover from head to toe.

Listen, cub. Knowing your weaknesses is key. You will learn to control your war lion more easily as you grow in rank. Do not be disheartened. All young White Lions must learn how to become an effective team with their companions. Learn wisdom and have patience. I will continue to guide you.

SKILLS AND ABILITIES

Abilities

You are no mere recruit. You were chosen because of your affinity to nature, to Ulthuan, and the beasts. I, myself, had many trials raising my cub. Though fierce now, he has had much tutelage. These stances are not to be taken lightly. A trainer teaches three different stances to make our pet react certain ways during battle. first will enable you to command your war lion to taunt an enemy, and keep its attention. will enable you to command your war lion to attack without mercy, biting and clawing without regard for gaining or losing agro. The next will enable you to command your war lion to attack without mercy, biting and clawing without regard for gaining or losing agro. will enable you to command your war lion to taunt an enemy, and keep its attention. The last stance allows you to tell your war lion to slow and baffle, striking multiple enemies. These are not Mastery paths. Each skill is given to our lion regardless of our Mastery studies. Note, however, that skill within the different Mastery paths you choose inherently makes these stances more effective.

Trained to Hunt: Increases Terrifying Roar, Claw Sweep, and Bite. When our war lion is instructed to take the stance of a hunter, he is not positioned to generate threat among his enemies, but instead deals with multiple enemies. When he lets out his Terrifying Roar, it causes all your enemies around you to tremble, slowing their attacks. His Claw Sweep swipes at all the enemies in front of him, dealing damage to each one. When he Bites an opponent, it deals a fair amount of damage to the one lucky enough to be his snack.

Well, young cub, have you read and learned my teachings on the matters of your war lion? I know you have, otherwise you would not have been given a White Lion's axe. Remember these lessons, and they will serve you well in battle.

Trained to Kill: Increases Maul, Gut Ripper, as well as Fang and Claw. This stance simply tells your war lion to go all out. When your pet rips someone's guts it inflicts bleeding damage over time. His Maul swipes for instant damage. With Fang and Claw, your lion bites and claws four times in a row. When you and your lion are fighting this way, an opponent won't last long.

Trained to Threaten: Increases Lion's Roar, Shred, and Leg Tear. When your war lion is trained to threaten, he does all that and more. Your war lion displays his prowess by gaining the enemy's attention. Lion's Roar causes all your enemies around you to focus on him and lessen the damage inflicted upon anyone else. Shred tears enemy's armor to pieces, allowing you to more easily break through your opponent's defenses. Leg Tear causes your enemy to bleed and become slower.

Abilities

Name	Level	Path	Cost	Range (in feet)	Type	Build	Duration	Reuse	Description
Axe Toss	Level 1	Core	20	5 to 65	Ranged Attack	1s	0s	0s	Deals 75 damage.
Call War Lion	Level 1	Core	55	Self	Pet Summon	2s	N/A	30s	Summon lion pet. -70% DPS.
Hack	Level 1	Hunter	30	Melee	Melee Attack	0s	0s	0s	Deals (112+DPS) damage.
Blindside	Level 2	Axeman	30	Melee	Melee Attack - Ailment	0s	0s	5s	Deals (112+DPS) and 249 over 9s. Only usable non-front.
Trained to Threaten	Level 3	Axeman	Free	Self	Stance Buff	0s	60m	0s	Increase pet's Toughness and Initiative by 2/level. Increases owner's crit chance when attacking from sides or back by 5%.
Coordinated Strike	Level 4	Hunter	40	Melee	Melee Attack	0s	0s	10s	Player deals (75+DPS) damage to target. Pet deals 75 damage to his personal target. If player and lion are within 25ft of each other's target, then they also deal their damage to each other's target.
Nature's Bond	Level 5	Core	30	150	HoT	0s	15s	0s	Heals for 748 over 15 seconds. Only usable on pet.
Sundering Chop	Level 6	Axeman	35	Melee	Melee Attack	0s	0s	0s	Deals (112+DPS) damage. If used from the rear positional, ignores 50% of Armor.
Baiting Strike	Level 7	Guardian	30	Melee	Melee Attack	0s	0s	0s	Deal (112+DPS) damage. Defensive target (or pet if no target) generates 20% less threat for 5s.

Don't let your lion lick you. His tongue is like sandpaper and will ruin your nice Elvish complexion.

Groom your pet after he eats. He is less likely to bite you if his tummy is full of fresh meat.

Abilities

Name	Level	Path	Cost	Range (in feet)	Type	Build	Duration	Reuse	Description
Lion's Fury	Level 8	Hunter	35	Melee	Melee Attack	0s	0s	5s	Deals (150+DPS) damage, Spiritual damage. Requires target to be Ailing.
Trained to Kill	Level 9	Guardian	Free	Self	Stance Buff	0s	60m	0s	Increase pet's Strength and Weapon Skill by 2/level. Increase Caster's Toughness by 2/level.
Submission	Level 10	Core	50	PBAE	Magical Debuff - Ailment	0	5s	10s.	Detaunts targets around him (50%, 5s). Character's hate generation is reduced by 25% for 5s.
Charge!	Level 10	Core	75	Self	Buff	0s	7s	30s	Increase run speed by 50%. Using any ability will dispel Charge.
Cleave Limb	Level 12	Guardian	35	Melee	Melee Attack - Ailment	0s	10s	5s	Deals (112+DPS) damage and reduces enemies auto attack speed by 20% for 10s.
Shattering Blow	Level 14	Axeman	25	Melee	Melee Attack - Ailment	0s	9s	0s	Deals 249 over 9s. If used from non-front, reduces Strength by 3/level.
Trained to Hunt	Level 16	Hunter	Free	Self	Stance Buff	0s	60m	0s	Increases pet's crit chance by 10% and attack speed by 20%. Your attacks and pet's attacks gain 10% chance to cause extra DoT that deals 150 over 3s.
Feline Grace	Level 18	Core	45	Self	Dispel	0s	0s	60s	Remove movement impairing effects (Snare/Root) and grant immunity for 10s.
Pack Assault	Level 20	Guardian	30	Melee	Melee Attack	0s	5s	10s	Deals (150+DPS) damage. Buff group for 5s, each group member's next ability activation deals 150 more damage.
Fey Illusion	Level 25	Axeman	35	Melee	Melee Attack	0s	0s	10s	Deals (225+DPS) damage. Defensive target (or pet if no target), gains 2x hate generated from attack. Only usable while in front.
Slashing Blade	Level 30	Hunter	50	CAE	Melee Attack	0s	0s	5s	Deals (187+DPS) damage to all targets in radius. Arc: 120, radius: 30ft.
Throat Bite	Level 35	Guardian	25	150	Pet Command - Ailment	1s	5s	20s	Pet's next attack will cause an additional 150 damage, and Silence the target for 5 sec. No GCD.
Fetch!	Level 40	Core	45	Thrown - Nuke	Magical Attack	2s	0s	10s	Orders the lion to knock back a target in his melee range toward the White Lion.
Pounce	Hunter x5	Hunter	50	Self	Melee Attack	0s	0s	0s	You jump forward (short hop). Deal 262 damage to enemies in a 20ft radius around as you land.
Echoing Roar	Hunter x9	Hunter	35	Self	Ailment	0s	15s	10s	Interrupts targets in radius. Deals 449 Spirit damage over 15s to targets in radius. Radius: 15ft around both player and pet.
Whirling Axe	Hunter x13	Hunter	25/s	PBAE	Melee Attack	0s	3s	13s	Channeled. Deals (150+DPS)*0.5 every 0.5s for 3s. Radius: 20ft.
Primal Fury	Axeman x5	Axeman	45	Self	Self Buff	0s	10s	60s	Increase DPS output by 25% for 10s for attacks to an enemy's side or rear.
Cull the Weak	Axeman x9	Axeman	30	Melee	Melee Attack	0s	0s	10s	Deals (375+DPS) damage to a target below 50% health.
Thin the Herd	Axeman x13	Axeman	25	Melee	Melee Attack	0s	0s	10s	Deals (187+DPS) damage and reduces target's outgoing heal effectiveness by 50% for 10s. Only usable from non-front.
Force Opportunity	Guardian x5	Guardian	40	Melee	Melee Attack	0s	0s	5s	Requires Parry. Undefendable melee attack that deals (150+DPS) and increases pet's chance to crit by 20% for 10s.
Brutal Pounce	Guardian x9	Guardian	20	Self	Pet Command	0s	0s	30s	Pet's next attack will cause an additional 187 dmg, and Stun the target for 3 secs. No GCD.
Leonine Frenzy	Guardian x13	Guardian	40	Self	Pet Buff	0s	10s	30s	Removes all Snare, Root, and Stun effects from your pet and adds immunity for 10s. Pet deals an additional 150 damage on all hits for 10 sec.

Don't let him sleep on your hides, scrolls, or armor. They will likely end up shredded, punctured, and dirty.

Abilities

Name	Level	Path	Cost	Range (in feet)	Type	Build	Duration	Reuse	Description
PET ABILITIES									
Trained to Threaten									
Lion's Roar	Level 3	Axeman	N/A	Melee	Pet Melee Attack	0s	5s	10s	Pet taunts (30%, 5s) all targets in radius. Arc: 120, radius: 30ft.
Shred	Level 3	Axeman	N/A	Melee	Pet Melee Attack	0s	10s	10s	Pet deals 187 damage to target and reduces their armor by 26.4/level for 10s. Front position only.
Leg Tear	Level 3	Axeman	N/A	Melee	Pet Melee Attack	0s	0s	10s	Pet deals 499 over 15s and Snares target by 40% for 5s.
Trained to Kill									
Fang and Claw	Level 9	Guardian	N/A	Melee	Pet Melee Attack	0s	3s	8s	Channeled Attack. Pet does 187 damage every 1s for 3s. Setback chance: 100%.
Maul	Level 9	Guardian	N/A	Melee	Pet Melee Attack	0s	0s	20s	Pet deals 262 damage.
Gut Rip	Level 9	Guardian	N/A	Melee	Pet Melee Attack	0s	0s	5s	Pet deals 75 damage and 349 damage over 15s.
Trained to Hunt									
Bite	Level 16	Hunter	N/A	Melee	Pet Melee Attack	0	0	5s	Pet deals 150 damage.
Claw Sweep	Level 16	Hunter	N/A	Melee	Pet Melee Attack	0	0	10s	Pet deals 187 damage to targets in radius. Arc: 180, radius: 17ft.
Terrifying Roar	Level 16	Hunter	N/A	PBAE	Pet Debuff - Ailment	0	10s	10s	Pet lowers auto attack speed of all targets in radius by 25% for 10s. Radius: 30ft.

Morale

Only the most battle-hardened person can pull off a Morale ability during a fight. When you are in the midst of battle, you continue to gain Morale, which fills up as you fight and fades when you stop to rest. This makes Morale abilities situational. Some damage or snare, and some do area-effect damage. It would be rather pointless to use an area-effect Morale ability when you are fighting but one enemy. Remember your training and wits, young cub.

You have to wait until Rank 8 to get your first Morale ability: Sever Nerve. You learn it at your trainer, like any other skill, and assign it to a Morale slot of appropriate rank. Sever Nerve causes a fair amount of damage to your target. This one is all about damage and can be a finisher to a long, drawn-out fight. Experimenting is fine, cub. Many White Lions have lived and learned by trial and error.

Every few levels, another Morale ability becomes available. As you rank up, higher ranked Morale abilities become available. You have four slots in which to place Morale abilities. In your first slot, a Rank 1 slot, you can only place a Rank 1 ability, and so on for all four slots.

During battle, as your Morale increases, each rank's slot becomes available. You can use your Rank 1 Morale ability as soon as you have sufficient Morale, or you can wait until you gain enough Morale to use your Rank 2 ability. Of course, as you gain Morale abilities for Ranks 3 and 4, you require more Morale to use the ability. This means that by the time you have enough Morale to do a Rank 4 Morale ability, you could have used a Rank 1 Morale ability up to four times. Choosing when to use your Morale is entirely up to you. The higher rank Morale abilities are useful and usually have great bonuses for someone who waits and uses up all their saved Morale. If you solo and take time between monsters, you usually won't save up enough Morale for the Rank 4 abilities, so keep this in mind and don't let your Morale go to waste.

Morale

Name	Level	Rank	Range (in feet)	Duration	Description
Sever Nerve	Level 8	Rank 1	Melee	15s	Melee attack that deals 1,200 damage.
Force of Will	Level 12	Rank 2	Self	30s	Drain 200 AP from target and give to character. Decrease target's Strength by 4/level for 30s.
Confusing Movements	Level 16	Rank 1	Self	7s	Increase change to Parry and Evade attacks by 100% for 7s.
Relentless Assault	Level 20	Rank 2	Group	15s	Group buff. Grants 10 AP/S to group for 10s. This occurs even during layers.
Broad Swings	Level 24	Rank 3	Self	10s	All attacks hit 2 additional targets within 350u for 10s. Additional targets take 300 damage.
Ensnare	Level 28	Rank 1	65	5s	Deals 900 damage and Roots target for 5s.
Whirling Axe	Level 32	Rank 2	LAE	9s	Deals 1,200 damage over 9s to all targets in 65ft.
Dominance	Level 36	Rank 3	Melee	3s	Deals 1,800 damage and heals self for 50% of damage dealt.
Frenzied Slaughter	Level 40	Rank 4	Self	7s	Self buff. AP costs are reduced 25%. Cooldowns are reduced by 50%. Damage dealt is increased by 20%. Lasts 7s.
Blade and Claw	Hunter x15	Rank 4	PBAE	0s	PBAE around both caster and pet. Each PBAE deals 1,200. Radius: 30ft.
Joy of the Hunt	Axeman x15	Rank 4	100	0s	Pet is healed to full and group's AP is restored by 250.
Rampage	Guardian x15	Rank 4	PBAE	10s	For the next 10s, all cooldowns for self and pet are reduced to 0s.

Tactics

No doubt you have seen the different Tactics available now that you have reached the proper rank. Most of these Tactics are shared with others of your kind, but how you use them is entirely up to you. I will explain further. Listen.

As you gain rank in our order, you have to train new Tactics, which you can then use. At Rank 11 you learn your first Tactic: Centuries of Training. It provides a 25% chance to deal additional damage over 5 seconds. Speed Training can ehance your pets run speed by 50%, which can be handy. Every 10 ranks, you gain a slot for another Tactic. Ultimately, at rank 40 you have four Tactic slots available to use any four different Tactics. Early on, I recommend using Centuries of Training and Brute Force because they enhance you in combat.

Listen, cub, once you learn a Tactic, you automatically use it in battle. You don't need to activate it like a skill. Each Mastery path also contains Tactics. Combine different Tactics into sets for different situations.

Let's say you want to focus on mauling your enemy. You could use Brute Force for Strength, use Centuries of Training or Jagged Edge at first and Tearing Blade to make your offensive skills deadly. All these add some sort of extra damage. You can see the benefit of using all these damage Tactics when we don't have to worry about being assaulted and can focus on pure damage. Our second set could be all defensive Tactics in times of trouble, featuring Riposte for added Parry, and Bending Winds for added Elemental resistance, for example. Remember these defensive Tactics as you are hunting.

Tome of Knowledge Tactics are obtained through finding and opening certain areas, discovering lore and history, or completing certain requirements. Once you have unlocked a Tactic in your Tome of Knowledge, you have to visit a trainer who can train you in Tome Tactics. For a small fee, these specialty trainers train the skill you have unlocked, which you can then use in

Tactics		
Name	**Level**	**Description**
Centuries of Training	Level 11	25% chance on attack to proc a DoT that deals 150 damage over 3s. Non-stacking, non-refreshing.
Jagged Edge	Level 13	Critical hits also place a 412 damage bleed DoT on the target for 9s.
Pack Synergy	Level 15	Increases critical damage done by 50% for player and pet if pet is summoned.
Bend the Wind	Level 17	Increases Elemental resist by 6.3/level of the character.
Brute Force	Level 19	Increases Strength by 4/level of the character.
Speed Training	Level 21	Pet runs 50% faster.
Discerning Offense	Level 23	Attacks have a 10% reduced chance to be defended against.
Flanking	Level 25	Increase damage by 15% from attacks made to the side or rear of an enemy.
Flashing Claws	Level 27	Increases Parry chance by 10% for player and pet if pet is summoned.
Riposte	Level 29	When the character Parries, he deals 187 back to the target.
Revenge!	Level 31	When player's pet dies, he gains a buff that increases damage by 50% for 10s.
Loner	Level 33	Deal 25% more damage if pet is not summoned.
Calming Presence	Level 35	Anytime you are healed, your pet will receive 25% of the healing as long as it is within 30ft.
Tearing Blade	Level 37	Slashing Blade and Sundering Chop cause additional DoT that deals 187 damage over 3s.
Close Bond	Level 39	Increases Morale gain by 10 Morale per second. If pet dies, player loses 600 Morale.
Lionheart	Hunter x3	Removes Ailing requirement from Lion's Fury, reduces the AP cost to 150, and increases the damage to (187+DPS).
Pack Hunting	Hunter x7	Trained to Hunt will now also increase your auto attack speed by 50%.
Hack and Slash	Hunter x11	Reduces AP cost of Hack and Slashing Blade by 50%.
Blindsided	Axeman x3	Blindside also adds a disorient that increases build times by 1s for 10s.
Threatening Distraction	Axeman x7	Trained to Threaten will now also reduce all threat that you cause by 75%.
Full-Grown	Axeman x11	Increases your pet's Wounds by 4/level and increases your Toughness by 2/level.
Stalker	Guardian x3	Your pet generates 150% less threat.
Furious Mending	Guardian x7	Trained to Kill now also grants you and your pet 120 HP/5s.
Baited Trap	Guardian x11	Baiting Strike will now increase your Armor 24.75/level and Parry and Disrupt chance by 10% for 10s.

your Tactic bar in its own slot. You can only have one Tome Tactic active at one time. Tome Tactics usually affect specific monsters. For example, a certain tome Tactic decreases the aggro range of greenskins, while another helps you do more damage toward trolls. This leads them to be very situational, so keep that in mind when you are creating your Tactic sets.

Lastly, when your guild has sufficiently ranked up, you obtain access to certain Tactics specific to the guild Tactic slot. Like Tome Tactics, you only get one slot to use alongside your basic four. The total number of Tactics you can equip, eventually, is six: four basic, one tome, and one guild. Seek out an elder in a guild for information on guild Tactics, if you have the power and rank in the guild to use them.

Be aware of where your lion is at all times. Sometimes the creature has a mind of his own and can get you in trouble if you don't heed his intentions.

The Look of a Lion

As you earn your ranks, your gear will improve until you look like a mighty lion yourself. The enemy shall fear your glare.

WARHAMMER ONLINE
AGE OF RECKONING

Choose your companions well. They may be High Elf, Dwarf, or Empire; everyone else is an enemy.

Mastery Paths

While all White Lions receive the same basic training, as a White Lion grows, he cultivates a philosophy on how he fights. That philosophy, or path, really differentiates one White Lion from another. When you train further in these three paths, you gain access to additional Tactics and skills.

The Path of the Hunter focuses on enhancing your war lion's Trained to Hunt skill stance, making you more of a focused team for damage. This path is for the White Lion who likes to do damage as a team with his war lion. This enhance your combo attacks such as Coordinated Strike, Lion's Fury, and Slashing Blade. You can learn a few Tactics and skills in this path. One favorite of many young hunters is Pounce; you leap in the air, striking at all nearby foes. Echoing Roar grants both you and your war lion the ability to unleash ailing on anyone around you. Another skill is a deadly display of your Whirling Axe, spinning and striking all who come near you for a few seconds. If you master the Path of the Hunter, you can learn a Rank 4 Morale ability that unleashes a fury of Blade and Claw that turns you and your lion into a whirlwind of destruction to all who stand near.

The Path of the Axeman focuses on enhancing your war lion's Trained to Threaten skill stance and your direct strike axe skills so your pet can threaten while you strike from a position to the side or rear. Abilities such as Sundering Chop, Blindside, Shattering Blow, and Fey Illusion are enhanced to deal more damage. Like I said, young cub, most of these skills can be used only from positions behind the enemy. Many Axemen are strong of arm, and you can learn Primal Fury, becoming enraged for a short time to deal extra damage to the side or rear of your enemy. With your skill in axe, you can Cull the Weak; sensing that your opponent is halfway to doom, you strike ruthlessly with your axe. Thin the Herd slashes your opponent's rear, dealing damage and briefly minimizing any healing effects your enemy may be under. Many Axemen choose to learn the Tactic Full-Grown, as it will gives you Strength, and your lion gains more Wounds to increase his health. If you choose to be a Master Axeman, you can learn the Rank 4 Morale ability, the Joy of the Hunt, fully healing your war lion and giving action points to your entire group instantly.

The Path of the Guardian focuses on assisting and supporting your pet as he deals damage, as well as enhancing your war lion's Trained to Kill stance. Baiting Strike, Pack Assault, Cleave Limb, and Throat Bite are enhanced. Further, as a Guardian a great tactic for your War Lion is Stalker, cutting your War Lions hatred to enemies by 75%. Special skills and abilities include Force Opportunity. When you parry, you strike back viciously, creating a fury that makes your war lion crit more for a short time. Brutal Pounce makes your war lion pounce at his enemy, letting him strike for extra damage, and briefly stunning the foe. When your opponent is stunned, he can no longer hit you or move, allowing you to move to a rear position if you choose. This can be quite handy. Leonine Frenzy send your pet into a rage. An enraged war lion cannot be rooted, stunned, or slowed by any effects, and every attack he deals does extra damage. This makes your pet into quite a force to be reckoned with. A master Guardian can eventually learn the Rank 4 Morale ability Rampage, which causes all skills to cool down instantly and allows you to use any ability with action point cost for a short time, allowing you to open a barrage of attacks against your enemy.

So, young cub, have you already decided which path you will take? Or has my knowledge opened your eyes to new possibilities you had not thought of yet? When you reach the exalted rank of 40 you will have 25 Mastery points, so use them wisely.

Renown

You wish to gain Renown fighting for the forces of Order, do you? Well, let me tell you now, it is not an easy path. To gain Renown, you must engage in player versus player (PvP) combat against the mindless minions of Destruction. Go visit a warcamp and show them what a White Lion is made of. Well, young cub, if you fight for the forces of Order long enough, by Rank 40 you could have up to 60 Renown points.

Here, cub, keep this scroll with you. It will guide you in how you might spend some of your points, should you need the help. This training plan focuses on the White Lion who chooses to maximize his damage output.

At Rank 11 and Renown Rank 5, spend your 5 points in: Might I–II: 4 points and Fortitude I: 1 point. At Rank 21 and Renown Rank 10, with 5 more points, your point distribution could be: Might I–II: 4 points, Fortitude I–II: 4 points, Blade Master I: 1 point, with one point left over. At Rank 31 and Renown Rank 20, point suggestions are: Might I–II: 10 points, Fortitude I–II: 4 points, Blade Master I–II: 4 points, with two points left over. At Rank 40 and Renown Rank 30: Might I–III: 10 points, Fortitude I–III: 10 points, Blade Master I–II: 10 points. At Rank 40 and Renown Rank 60, you now have 60 points total and your point spread could look like: Might I–IV: 20 points, Fortitude I–III: 10 points, Blade Master I–III: 10 points, Assault I–II: 6 points, Opportunist I: 5 points, Defender I: 5 points, Vigor I: 2 points, Reinforcement I: 2 points.

Remember your paths, young Elf. Do not think this is the only way to train. If you're going down the Path of the Guardian or Hunter, you may want to spend more in Fortitude, Defender, or Reinforcement to help against the damage you receive. If you aren't concerned with your Toughness or Wounds, then the path above is a good way to enhance your damage-dealing prowess. None of these will help your war lion, young hunter, but by fortifying yourself in battle, you are helping your companion.

Don't let your friends stick their heads in your lions mouth. He has been trained to kill and maim, remember.

Solo Play

Rank 1–10

Begin by summoning your war lion to your side. When you start a fight, use Axe Toss at range and send your war lion in for the kill. When the enemy closes in on you, hit with Hack. If he's facing away from you, use Blindside instead. Later on, during these ranks, you can train your pet to Kill. Make sure you apply these stances to your war lion for maximum potential. When the enemy engages you directly, hit with instant attacks such as Hack or Sundering Chop, then follow these up with an ailment like Blindside if you can get your war lion to distract your opponent. Once your opponent is suffering from Blindside, hit with a Lion's Fury attack. Strike mainly with instant attacks. In between these attacks, use an attack with an ailment, and make sure one is active on your opponent at all times. When you get Coordinated Strike, you and your pet will attack simultaneously, which ravages the enemy. If your pet gets in trouble, and you want to gain aggro over the enemy, hit it with a Baiting Strike. Once the enemy is facing you, hit your war lion with a Nature's Bond to heal him. Keep in mind that your pet can hold a second target's attention if you get in over your head. Once your pet gains the attention of the second target, have him focus his damaging attacks on the same target as you, so that you can finish one enemy quickly, then both you and your war lion can focus all of your attention on the second target. Dividing your attention results in longer battles... and the longer a battle lasts, the more dangerous it is for you. Remember, we are lightly armored, and our strength is in the speed in which we kill.

Submission is a newly acquired skill in this range. This is a skill that can save your life when the time comes. You will be able to shed a decent amount of aggro from yourself onto your war lion, allowing you to get out of imminent death. Also, when soloing, notice your Morale growing with every fight. Your first ability is Sever Nerve. If it glows, you can use it, but wait till you need that extra hit or your action points are low. It's good for ensnaring your opponent if you need to get away for some reason. Don't be afraid to use your Morale, just use it wisely.

Rank 11–20

The same strategies you used as a novice continue to hold true throughout these ranks. You obtain all three pet stances now, which allows your pet to threaten the enemy, kill, or hunt, and slow them down. You can have only one stance active on you and your pet. The stances greatly increase your effectiveness, so stay aware of your stances, and activate the appropriate one. While you level in this range, you also receive some new ailments that you can use instead of Blindside. A good replacement for it is Shattering Blow. Hit an enemy from behind with this to weaken him and inflict damage over time; use this attack early. Follow it with a Coordinated Strike and Pack Assault pet attacks for quick damage, then try a Cleave Limb attack, then go back to Hack and Chop. Throwing in these new ailments along with the skills you have used the past few ranks helps you even more in battle.

You also have a couple of Tactic slots now. Brute Force and Centuries of Training are a good set to use early on, because they enhance your damage and Strength.

Rank 21–30

By now, you have become more powerful and wiser in the ways of battle. You have a few new Tactics and more slots for them. You also have additional Morale abilities. Ensnare and Relentless Assault are good Morale abilities to have. Keep Centuries of Training and Brute Force unless you have a Mastery that better suits your style. Submission is a new skill that can save your life. You shed a decent amount of an enemy's hate from yourself onto your war lion, allowing you to avoid imminent death. Continue using the same skills and sets as we have discussed before and any new Mastery skills you may have unlocked or trained in.

Rank 31–40

When you eventually reach the lofty rank of 40, White Lions of our order will seek you as an elder and look to your skills to help with new recruits. You have fought many battles, and learned the skills of axe and claw that only the elite of our order can obtain. But you continue to use the same skills, though they are more powerful. Of particular note is Throat Bite, which commands your pet to attack and silence a victim, preventing your target from casting. You can increase your Tactics to four slots. Some favorite Rank 3 and 4 Morale abilities among our profession are Dominance and Frenzied Slaughter. Use the skills you have advanced with up to now and you will have little trouble dealing with your enemies.

Group Play

Grouping is essential in almost any public quest area, or even just among a group of friends scouring some remote dungeon to gain fame and fortune.

Our role in groups is that of flexibility. Although we are damage dealers, we can use our war lion to take point, or send him to taunt a monster hitting a healer ally that the tank cannot get to. Always be mindful of what is going on with your party and understand that you will be more helpful by being flexible than mindlessly hacking away and not paying attention.

It is essential that you control your pet from wandering and gaining aggro from a pack of monsters that would no doubt overwhelm and annihilate your group. Keep an eye on your pet, and keep him from causing trouble, or your group will look down on you. Keep these things in mind, and you will no doubt be a favorite in your group when the smoke clears and wounds are mended.

Combine attacks with your lion. Together you are greater than striking alone.

Solo

You have to use your wits. Each stance can be useful here. While your pet can't taunt a player off you and get its attention, all the stances are useful. Having your opponent slowed or weakened if he ignores your war lion is always a fun sight. Most

SLAYING PLAYERS AND COLLECTING RENOWN (PVP)

won't go for your lion, which is to our advantage. Even if they do, you can get behind your enemy and assail him with ailments and heal your pet or back off and let your pet soften him up for you.

If your pet is about to die, back off and regain action points so that you can resummon your pet before the enemy gets near you. If your enemy runs away, Charge! Remember to use your ailments and Morale abilities when possible. A White Lion of skill is not easily pushed aside in a one-on-one fight. When you're outnumbered, get out and get a group to counter the forces.

Group Play

No doubt you have run into the mindless hordes of Destruction. Always, they cluster like ravens waiting to swoop in on the kill. Stay calm and look for healers. Also protect your healers from Marauders charging at them like the mindless slaves of Chaos that they are. Keep your pet close, making sure he focuses on your target and does not wander off on his own. This is a good time to set him on passive so that he only attacks what you command and doesn't get distracted by others attacking him.

When larger groups of players start to converge, it can become hectic. Keep your head and watch your group mates and pet. Focus as a team, and you will be much more successful than if you split off and attack different enemies. Teamwork is the key to a successful PvP group. A good group of players can handily defeat even larger numbers of forces that may be arrayed against them. When you are grouped, follow the group leader and fight as a team.

Some good Morale abilities to use are Ensnare on a single opponent for damage and slowing effect. I always liked the satisfaction of using the Rank 2 Morale ability Flying Axe, so all the opponents around you can feel the sting of your axe. Dominance and Frenzied Slaughter are good as well. When a large group is around you, use any good area-effect Morale ability. In large battles, use your frontal swipe axe skills such as Slashing Blade or Pounce and any pet ones you may have unlocked. Keeping on the move and slashing your victims is what a White Lion excels at. Don't stand toe-to-toe getting nuked and hit. Use offensive Tactics such as Brute Force and Centuries of Training, Flashing Claws for added Parry, or added Resistance from a tactic buff like Bending Winds. If you are high rank and have mastered a path, don't forget to use a good Tactic that another White Lion doesn't have, such as Hack and Slash, Full-Grown, or Furious Mending.

SORROW AND A NEW DAWN

It has been a long few weeks. My muscles are bruised and weary, but we will not relent, Roac and I. The wave of our dark cousins upon our shores has been broken against the rocks of our resistance, but not without losses. Many have died, some unprepared for the onslaught our misguided kin have brought upon us but we stand, unrelenting.

I have heard that Mournfire has fallen, and his body lies at Moonrise Tower. My heart goes out to my fallen friend and his family. I have seen the light of hope spark in the eyes of my kin though, and it only grows. Our dark cousins thought us weak and unprepared to fight. We do not wish to fight, but they have forced our hand, and we will show them the valor and hope of the Elves renewed. Now that the king is returning to our shores, I will set out to the remainder of the world. I have heard my calling as if the land whispered it to me. In the face of the evil of the Dark Elves, and the rest of the world under siege by Destruction, there is little choice left. I must help the younger races, for if they fall, the tide will wash over Ulthuan to oblivion.

My duty is clear. I will carry the king's banner as he commands. I will show Humans and Dwarfs alike the fury of a White Lion, and beset upon the hordes of Destruction with clear purpose and intent. The ship is sailing, so I leave this guide with you now, my kin, so you may pass on what I have learned and taught unto other young recruits in our ways. Perhaps we shall meet again someday, whether at home or on distant lands.

Keep the faith. So long as you breathe another breath, Darkness can never come.

BLACK ORC

Oi you! Wot iz you looking at? You seem lost. Wot, you iz a new Black Orc? Well then iz gud thing you found Mugnob Rokchoppa'. I iz in need of warriors. Oh, you've never beaten a Goblin into da ground? How could you get so big without fightin'? I guess dere iz only one way fer you to learn... Wot iz by FIGHTIN'! Pick up yer choppa an' yer shield an' get ready.

Look at you all nervous wif yer choppa an' shield. Before you start fightin' guess I should tell you 'bout being a Black Orc. Black Orcs iz big, mean, and mo' mean. You go in dere to win an' let nothin' stop you. We iz da muscle of da greenskins.

One day maybe if you iz lucky enough you could be almost as big as me. But fer now I can see you got not a single trophy. Not gud either. Take wot choppa of yers an' go get yerself a trophy from wot stunty hiding behind da tree near Mount Bloodhorn. Remember from ear to ear an' put dat head on a spike!

Don't forget, you iz bigger, you iz badder an' you iz stronger den any of dose stunties. Keep dat in mind an' you cannot lose. Now go away and let me leaks.

By Mugnob Rokchoppa

What is a Black Orc?

These are the brawlers you can throw in the trenches, where the enemy cowers from how close they are to the spittle and grit on the Black Orcs' teeth. The bigger of the greenskins, the Black Orc follows the orders of a "tank": a highly aggressive, yet also defensive, unit that draws the attention of the foes around it so that weaker allies can continue to maintain their proper roles. They are our chosen greenskins, for we use their flesh to ram against the enemy's shields and spears, to beat those who would fall before us into retreat or merciless surrender.

Brutes through and through, the Black Orcs lead the charge against the crumbling might entrusted to the lords of Order. From up on the towers, you can watch the ebb and flow of a battle. Study the movements of the Black Orcs and you will see a skirmish's vital lifeblood. The Orcs will slow down to combat a group, stun a foe dashing to escape, or pull more enemies toward them and away from their allies. Their guttural taunts can be heard above the clash like crude town criers seeking to stir a gathering to violence.

The Orc care for little but to crush the enemy until rivers of blood irrigate the earth. If only we could water our crops like this—what a paradise we could thrust upon this world. Still, we must not pin all our hopes on these bloodlust brutes, for they are not the brightest of creatures and tend to beat on anything that moves. The disciplined ones survive to reign as front-line champions for the greenskins.

Black Orcs are engines of Destruction, and we will drive them until the clubs fall from their bloody fists.

—Baron Heinar Balethar, Zimmeron's Hold, Chaos Wastes

If da ledge looks too high to survive da jump, it most likely iz. Proceed wif caution.

STARTIN' SKILLS

You start with more Wounds den other greenskins. Da only way to make yer statz bigger iz through gear an' climbin' higher in da ranks of Black Orcs.

'er skills, Black Orcs start out wif two abilities other den Flee an' Auto Attack:

Lob Choppa: It iz a basic throwin' attack, an' if da enemy is wounded gud, it can deal more damage if you throw it into dere back.

Clobber: Slashes fer gud damage, an' generates extra hate against monstuz. Hate iz when da monster gets mad an' attacks only you. Dis skill also 'eads to da 'Gud Plan!, anotherer gud fightin' skills dat works wif Clobber.

All abilities will rank up wif da player. Da stronger da Orc gets, da stronger da attacks will become.

Black Orcs iz part of da Destruction side of da war. Dey iz allies wif da others out of need not respect. Orcs live fer da battle, so any reason to go to war iz gud enough fer dem. Plus we iz bigger den other greenskins an' gets to smash stunties.

Mount Bloodhorn iz where we starts off. Dis iz where you will learn skills, buy an' sell items an' get missions from other bigger an' meaner Orcs den you. Dis will get you goin' on da path of becomin' a big n' tough Black Orc. 'Member to talk to everyone like da Core Trainer Sogsnag Grubsnout. Get dem skillz trained. Talk to da merchant Gragdush. Him iz greedy so be careful. If you die, talk to Greeble, he heal you gud. Everythin' you need can be found in Mount Bloodhorn.

Don't forget to go by da lobbers shooting toward Stunty Mountain so you get to clobber stunties. Near da lobbers iz a cave of mean ol' Squigs, an' dey like to bite, so be careful... Wot am I sez? Go in there an' show dem who da' boss. Now don't forget to also check out Da Slop. I don't know why dem stupid Goblins iz always rolling around in me sauce fer me leg of Squig, but maybe dats why dat slop taste so gud. But dis iz yer new home. Why not take a moment a' look around? Maybe you too will find somethin' you will always 'member about Mount Bloodhorn.

GEAR AN' STUF

A Black Orc only starts wif a few items: a sword called Me Ol'Choppa, an' a shield called Me Ol' Shield, an' an old stinky shirt called Me Most Worn Shirt. As you rank up you will pillage an' be given new shiny, bigger, stronger, an' spikier armor an' weapons. Pluz trophies an' other trinkets.

A Black Orc iz deadly wif just about any item in your hand, but you should look fer items wot are made special fer Orcs. Dis will allow you to have da best gear possible fer yerself. Now da thing about da Black Orc iz he iz not limited to ones-handz weapons. Grab a nice big two-handz axe an' slice through stunties. Make dem even stuntier. Deez big slow weapons will allow a Black Orc to dish out big damage, an' parry attacks. Now da parry will not be as gud as a shield but if da Black Orc can handle itself no shield iz necessary.

Don't get hit too much in head or you forget things. Like yer name.

Flee iz your friend.

BEIN' AN ORC

GUD THINGS AN' NOT SO GUD THINGS

Gud Things

- Disables a foe wif snares or skills dat silence magic-users.
- Quickly able to protect others wif skills like Save da Runts.
- Gain aggression quickly wif skills like Taunt.
- Buffs to benefit da group. Black Orcs have a couple skills dat increase itz groups' action points, armor, an' strength.
- Big damage wif two-handz weapon.

Da biggest strength fer us Black Orcs iz to get hit an' keep on fightin'. Between our shield an' our armor we iz set fer battle. We can protect ourselves an' our friends. We can also quickly pull da enemies from where dey iz going. We can shout loudly at da enemy an' guess wot? We make dem weaker an' us stronger. But if you iz feelin' like showing how gud of a warrior you iz, den grab a two-hands weapon an' hit very hard.

Not So Gud Things:

- Weak ranged attacks.
- Orcs iz big an' slow. Other players wif range can stay outta reach of da Black Orc's attacks.
- No self healin'. Needz healers much in battle.
- Caster groups iz bad news fer Black Orc. You iz a giant movin' target an' if da mages move in two different ways, you will never beat dem all.

Black Orcs iz da toughest, da bravest, an' da strongest. But dere iz times when things iz not so gud. Don't let dat stop you tho. We don' get much ranged attacks, an' da ones we do have i weak. Dis can be a problem when fightin' dem casting an' ranged foes. We iz also slow, so if you iz feelin' bloodlust, think before lettin' dem stupid stunties jumps on you. Also because we iz so big, we have giant targets on our back. Dem people we fight will kill us fast. So make friendly wif dem healers.

Abilities

Dere iz Core Training an' Mastery Training fer all classes in da world. You want to always locate da Career Trainers when you get to a new camp. When you start ranking up you start getting Mastery points. You will get yer first one at Rank 11 an' will max out at 25 when at Rank 40. Dere iz three main paths fer Mastery Training fer da Black Orc:

Path of da' Brawler: Dis iz da path dat will give you bonus to yer damage.

Path of da' Toughest: Dis iz da path dat will enhance yer tanking an' survivability.

Path of da' Boss: Dis iz da path dat iz fer buffs an' group support.

One of da most common questions to me iz, "Wot iz da best path to take?" Well dat iz up to you. Da Black Orc iz trained to be different things fer different times. Generally Black Orcs iz strong tanks. Dat would mean training up Path of da' Toughest, an' throw in some Path of da' Brawler. Dis will allow you to keep da monstuz on you an' do tons of damage.

Now letz take a look at Path of da' Brawler: Trip 'Em Up, Skull Thumper, Da Biggest!, Wot Armor?, Big Slash. Deez iz da skills dat you get without training in da mastery. You will be usin' Trip 'Em Up an' Skull Thumper all da time. At Rank 12 an' 18 you will be able to train da last two specific Path of da' Brawler skills: Wot Armor? an' Big Slash. Wot Armor? will remove some armor on yer enemy an' you can use it on yer foe more den once. Dis allows fer hits to hit dem harder. Dis also leads to Big Slash. Dis skill iz best used when dere are multiple targets dat you iz taking on. Dis will do a big swing, hitting two targets at once.

If you want to fight a mob dat iz strong an' near another mob, use Lob Choppa to pull da powerful mob to you.

Once me eats farty Squig. No gud fer da crack.

Now lets look at Path of da' Toughest: Tuffer 'n Nails, Right in da Jibblies, Savin' Me Hide, Da Toughest! Again deez iz da skills you get from Core Training. Deez iz da skills dat help wif survivability. Deez will let you fight more an' longer. Tuffer 'n Nails deals out damage an' increases yer armor fer 0 secondz. Dis really helps Black Orcs tanks. Right in da Jibblies—dis iz me favorite attack! Dis skill deals out damage an' cuts down da target's weapon skill fer 10 secondz. Again dis helps survivability. When tanking, Savin' Me Hide an' Da Toughest! iz great skills. Dis will help you block more an' keep on fightin'.

Path of da' Boss: Follow 'Me Lead, Da Big Un', Da Greenest, Big Swing, Shut Yer Face. Deez iz da skills dat make you Da' Boss. Deez skills let you boost morale of yer teammates. Da Big Un' does some damage to everythin' in front of you. Da Greenest: Dis skill iz gud. Think bout dis! You scream at yer group an' dey increase der resists to everything fer 10 secondz. Big Swing iz another attack dat hits all targets in front of you. Wots better then clobbering one stunty? CLOBBERING TWO! An' den dere iz da magic-users' worst enemy. You get to tell dem to Shut Yer Face. Dis will deal damage an' silence yer target.

Abilities

Name	Level	Path	Cost	Range (in feet)	Type	Build	Duration	Reuse	Description
Clobber	Level 1	Da' Toughest	35	Melee	Balance Attack - Open	0s	0s	0s	Deals (150+DPS) damage. Generates double hate.
Lob Choppa	Level 1	Core	20	10-65	Ranged Attack	1s	0s	0s	Deals 75 damage. Rear position: If the target is less than 20% health, gain a 50% chance to deal an additional 525 damage.
Trip 'Em Up	Level 2	Da' Brawler	25	Melee	Balance Attack - Improved - Ailment	0s	6s	5s	Deals 349 damage over 10s. Snares target by 40% for 10s.
Skull Thumper	Level 3	Da' Brawler	Free	Melee	Balance Attack - Perfect	0s	0s	0s	Deals (187+DPS) damage.
Da Biggest!	Level 4	Da' Brawler	55	Self	Buff - Bless	0s	Stance	0s	All attacks have a 25% chance to proc a 3 Str buff for 20s.
Follow 'Me Lead	Level 5	Da' Boss	35	Melee	Balance Attack - Open - Bless	0s	10s	0s	Deals (112+DPS) damage and buffs defensive target's Weapon Skill by 3 for 20s.
Tuffer 'n Nails	Level 6	Da' Toughest	30	Melee	Balance Attack - Improved - Bless	0s	10s	0s	Deals (150+DPS) damage. Increases Armor by 24.75/level for 20s. Requires shield.
Taunt	Level 7	Core	20	65	Debuff	0s	15s	15s	Interrupts target. For 15s, the tank deals 30% more damage against target. For 5s monsters turn to attack tank. After 3 ability activations and/or auto attacks from target hit tank, taunt fades. Tank generates 2,250 in hate.
Da Big Un'	Level 8	Da' Boss	Free	CAE - Melee	Balance Attack - Perfect	0s	0s	0s	CAE melee attack, Requires great weapon. Deals (187+DPS) damage to targets in area. Arc: 180, range: Melee.
Right in da Jibblies	Level 9	Da' Toughest	35	Melee	Balance Attack - Improved - Ailment	0s	10s	20s	Deal (187+DPS) damage and reduces target's Weapon Skill by 3 for 20s.
Save da Runts	Level 10	Core	Free	41	Buff	0s	Stance	60s	Buff on friendly player that splits the damage between the target and the tank. Buffed player takes 50% of the incoming damage. Tank takes 50% of the incoming damage directed at the buffed target. Hate is split between player and tank.
Get 'Em!	Level 10	Core	25	PBAE	Buff - Bless	0s	15s	60s	Increases group's AP regen rate by 20% for 15s.
Hold the Line	Level 10	Core	112.5/S	PBAE	Buff	0s	10s	60s	Toggled buff. Each second the toggle is active, bestows a buff that increases Evade and Disrupt chances by 45% to the tank and 15% to all friendlies in the radius that lasts 1 second. If the tank uses another ability, the ability ends. Buffs on friendlies stack up to 3. Arc: 180 (pointed to the rear), radius: 40ft.
Wot Armor?	Level 12	Da' Brawler	30	Melee	Balance Attack - Open - Ailment	0s	20s	0s	Deals (75+DPS) damage. Reduces Armor by 12.5% plus 12.5% per counter. Maximum of 5 counters.
Da Greenest!	Level 14	Da' Boss	55	Self	Buff - Bless	0s	Stance	0s	All attacks have a 25% chance to proc a self buff that increases all resist by 3/level for 20s.

Abilities

Name	Level	Path	Cost	Range (in feet)	Type	Build	Duration	Reuse	Description
Savin' Me Hide	Level 16	Da'Toughest	Free	Melee	Balance Attack - Perfect - Bless	0s	6s	0s	Deals (150+DPS) damage and increases Toughness by 3 for 20s
Big Slash	Level 18	Da'Brawler	40	Melee	Balance Attack - Improved	0s	0s	0s	Deals (187+DPS) damage. Hits up to 2 targets within 10ft.
Juggernaut	Level 18	Core	45	Self	Buff	0s	0s	60s	Removes snare, root, disarm, and silence effects from the tank.
Challenge	Level 20	Core	30	CAE	Debuff	0s	15s	30s	For 15s, the challenged target deals 30% less damage to everyone but the caster. Monsters turn to attack tank until Challenge expires or 5s. After 3 ability activations and/or auto attacks from target hit tank, Challenge fades. Also generates 2,250 hate. Arc 90, radius: 65ft.
Da Toughest!	Level 25	Da'Toughest	55	Self	Buff	0s	Stance	0s	All attacks have a 25% chance to proc a 75 dmg absorb (physical only) lasts 5s
Where You Going?	Level 30	Core	30	PBAE	Crowd Control	0s	5s	60s	Roots up to 4 targets within 30ft for 5s.
Big Swing	Level 35	Da'Boss	40	PBAE	Balance Attack - Improved - Ailment	0s	20s	0s	Deals (150+DPS) damage and debuffs all target's strength by 3 per level for 20s. Radius: 10ft.
Shut Yer Face	Level 40	Da'Boss	30	Melee	Balance Attack - Perfect - Ailment	0s	5s	20s	Deals (112+DPS) damage and silences the target for 5s.
Specialization									
Arm Breaka	Brawler x5	Da'Brawler	25	Melee	Balance Attack - Open - Ailment	0s	5s	10s	Deals (112+DPS) damage. Removes 10 AP/s for 5s on target.
Down Ya Go	Brawler x9	Da'Brawler	Free	Melee	Balance Attack - Perfect	0s	5s	20s	Deals (225+DPS) damage. 50% chance to knockdown target for 3s. 100% chance if target is snared. Req. great weapon.
T'ree Hit Combo	Brawler x13	Da'Brawler	Free	Melee	Balance Attack - Perfect	0s	3s	20s	Channeled Attack. Deals (187+DPS) every second. If AP runs out, then channel stops.
Ya Missed Me	Toughest x5	Da'Toughest	25	Melee	Balance Attack - Open - Ailment	0s	10s	20s	Requires Block. Deals (112+DPS) damage and cannot be defended against. Lowers target's physical damage done by 20% for 10s.
Not in da Face!	Toughest x9	Da'Toughest	Free	Melee	Balance Attack - Perfect - Ailment	0s	0s	20s	Deals (187+DPS) damage. Increases cooldowns on target by 5s for 10s.
Can't Hit Me!	Toughest x13	Da'Toughest	35/S	Self	Buff - Bless	Channeled	10s	0s	Requires shield. Increase Block chance by 50%. Self-snare by 40%. Can move while channeling. When the player blocks, the attacker takes 150 damage.
We'z Bigger	Boss x5	Da'Boss	45	Melee	Balance Attack - Improved - Bless	0s	10s	20s	Deals (187+DPS) damage to target. Increases armor of all groupmates in the radius by 16.5 for 20s. Radius: 20ft.
Rock 'Ard	Boss x9	Da'Boss	35	Buff	Balance Attack - Improved - Bless	0s	5s	10s	Deals (112+DPS). Buffs user with a shield that absorbs the next 450 damage.
WAAAAAAAGH!	Boss x13	Da'Boss	Free	PBAE - Melee	Balance Attack - Perfect - Ailment	0s	0s	5s	Deals 150 Corp damage damage in a PBAE of 30ft. Also reduces target's resistance to Corp by 9.45/level for 20s.

Morale

Morale abilities iz learned from da Career Trainers. Dere iz nine from da Career Trainers an' three from Mastery Training. Now I'll tell you how deez things work. Go out an' hit things. Hit dem again an' again but dis time harder. Da more you beat on things an' da longer you're in combat da more you will activate deez Morale abilities. Now you can only have four of deez abilities selected at once. Da more Morale you gain, da more stronger da ability you will be able to make. Once you have used one, you needs to start buildin' it up again. So use it when you needs it an' before fightin' ends.

Now you need to choose wot one of deez Morale abilities will be best suited fer you. First learns Demolishing Strike at Rank 8. Dis will be yer first Rank 1 Morale ability. Dis ability iz a great ability to use when up against an enemy dat looks bigger an' stronger. It will less dere armor an' hit dem wif damage fer 15 secondz.

After dat you will want to learns Shield Wall. Dis iz something to save yer hide when you iz tanking something bigger an' stronger than you. Dis ability will block everythin' fer 10 secondz. No stunties give you headache wif dis ability. Also 'member dat dis one iz a Rank 2 Morale ability so if you want to use dis you must skip da Rank 1 ability.

If you have saved yer Morale attack like a gud Orc, you will then have Distracting Bellow at Rank 24. Dis shout will scare yer target an' all enemies around dem up to 30 feet. Dis will less all of dere damage in half fer 10 secondz. Dis iz an awesome ability when doing public quests an' against other players. Den fer your final rank using Immaculate Defense iz really gud fer yer party cuz it will give a defensive bonus against all damage.

When in RvR, Rank 1 Grapple iz a great ability wif a group. Dis ability can't be broken an' can't be dispelled. Dis lets you lock an enemy in one place fer 10 secondz. Dis iz an ability dat will make you happy, cause you won't be able to move either—dat means more stunty bashing! Fer Rank 2, Raze iz always gud when you iz getting hit by more den one thing at once. Dis will allow you to hit all targets every second fer three secondz up to 65 feet away. When you can use Rank 3 abilities an' you iz fightin' against other players you should use Walk It Off fer yer group. When defending or attacking dis will buff yer group in Toughness fer 15 secondz.

Deez iz da ones dat iz gud fer me! But wot you use iz up to you. Try 'em out. Don't lose to no stunty tho.

Name Dat Smell

Youz have walked into a dark moldy cave an' all youz can smell iz death an' decay. Wot iz it?

Answer: It's yer group mate, da Black Orc. But don't tell him or youz could get hurt.

A gud odor rises 'round the cook fire? Wot iz it?

Answer: Hopefully iz yer dinner. Could also be da Squig pen, an' Goblins not happy when you go in dere.

Youz pick yer new trophy 'cause it smells like...

Answer: Rottin' snotling head. Ah, da smells of yer youth.

Youz standin' in a field of red, yellow, and purple flowers. Wot iz da bestest smell?

Answer: Da stunty corpse at yer feet.

Morale					
Name	Level	Rank	Range (in feet)	Duration:	Description
Demolishing Strike	Level 8	Rank 1	Melee	Offensive	Deal 900 damage over 15s and lowers armor by -26.4/level for 15s.
Shield Wall	Level 12	Rank 2	Self	Defensive	Self buff: Increase chance to block by 100% for 10s.
Grapple	Level 16	Rank 1	Melee	Offensive	Unbreakable root on target and tank (both roots break simulaneously).
Raze	Level 20	Rank 2	CAE	Offensive	Channeled physical CAE attack that deals1,200 damage to targets over 3s. Arc: 90, radius: 66ft.
Distracting Bellow	Level 24	Rank 3	100	Defensive	Target and all enemies around deal 50% less damage for 10s. Radius: 30ft.
Quit Yer Squabblin'	Level 28	Rank 1	Group	30s	Group buff. Increase Parry and Evade chances by 10% for 30s.
Deafening Bellow!	Level 32	Rank 2	PBAE	7s	PBAE silence for 7s. Radius: 30ft.
Walk It Off!	Level 36	Rank 3	Group	15s	Increase the group's toughness by +3/level for 15s.
Immaculate Defense	Level 40	Rank 4	Group	Defensive	Group members who stay within 65ft of the tank take 75% less damage for 10s.
Puddle o Muck	Brawler x15	Rank 4	CAE	15s	Deals 1,800 over 15s and snares all targets (40%, 15s). Arc: 120, radius: 65ft.
Cant'Touch Us	Toughest x15	Rank 4	Group	15s	Group members each absorb the next 1,800 damage. Also gain 200 AP. Requires a shield.
Yer Nothin	Boss x15	Rank 4	PBAE	12s	Deals 1,800 over 12s. Also removes 30s of Morale on targets over 12s. Radius: 30ft.

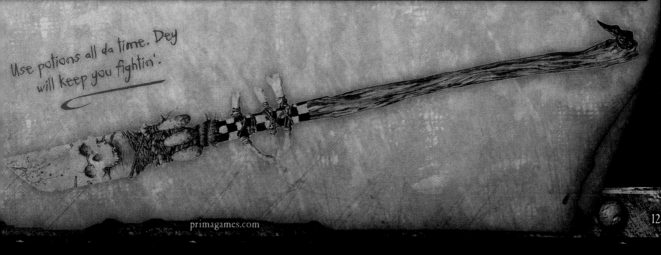

Use potions all da time. Dey will keep you fightin'.

Tactics

More skills from dem skills trainers. Dey will rip you off but you need to learn. Deez skills I am talkin' about dis time iz Tactics. Deez iz personal little buffs dat turns on fer different reasons. Havin' da best of deez Tactics will help you survive fer a long time.

From da Rank 1 you get one Tactic list. Come Rank 21 you get two Career slots, an' dis iz where you get to start making different combos of Tactics. Dis iz da fun part! At Rank 31 you get three Tactic slots, an' at Rank 40 you get four Tactics slots to fill. Choose wots best fer you. 'Member to go do RvR—dere iz Renown Tactics an' pay attention to da Guild Tactic slots.

Now here iz da Tactics I like da most. Perfect Patient iz great! It will make healing spells work better. Gud Wif Shield iz also great, as it will increase your blocking chance! No stunties will get through to your skull! To combat dose pesky magic-users Can Youz Hear Me Now? will speed up da reuse of when you can use da skill Shut Yer Face. Now deez iz da ones I like. Try dem out an' figure wot works best fer you.

Here iz some examples dat you can do. First, you must notice dat you can change da Tactics on da fly. Dis iz where it gets interestin'. You can actually have five Tactics set up. Some could be fer da PQs so you might use a mix of Tactics dat you normally wouldn't solo wif. Den dere iz da ones fer other players. Strongly want to tell you dat you should figure outs wot Tactics work best fer you as switching to dem when going into a campaign, scenario, skirmish, an' battlefields could mean livin' or dyin'.

Tactics

Name	Level	Description
I'm da Biggest!	Level 11	Increases Wounds by +4 per level of the character.
Focused Offensive	Level 13	Increase damage dealt by 25%. Increase damage taken by 20%. Decrease threat generation by 25%.
'Ave Another One	Level 15	"Follow 'Me Lead" causes a DoT that deals 349 damage over 5s (Ailment).
Don't Bother Me None	Level 17	Increases Spirit resist by +6.3 per level of the character.
Rugged	Level 19	Increases Toughness by +4/level
Lookin' for Opp'tunity	Level 21	Clobber lowers the target's Morale by 200.
Stab You Gooder	Level 23	Critical hits deal 50% more damage
Menace	Level 25	Increases threat by 100% on all attacks.
Good wif Shield	Level 27	Increases Block chance by 10%.
Unstoppable Juggernaught	Level 29	Juggernaught's reuse timer is lowered to 20s.
Dat Was Great!	Level 31	Increases the duration of Wot Armor? by 10s and puts 2 counters on at a time.
Youz See Me Blok' Dat'?!	Level 33	Blocking an attack gives the Black Orc 150 Morale.
Bring 'Em On	Level 35	When you Parry, you instantly gain the Perfect Balance state.
Loudmouth	Level 37	War Bellows (Da Biggest, Da Toughest, Da Greenest) also deal 150 damage.
Can Youz Hear Me Now?	Level 39	Cooldown on Shut Yer Face is reduced by 5s and damage is increased to (187.5+DPS).
Specialization		
Keep It Goin'!	Brawler x3	Big Slash deals an additional 112.5 damage and only costs 187.5 AP.
Gork Smash	Brawler x7	Increases critical hit chance by 10% when in Improved Balanced, and 20% while in Perfect Balance.
An Bestest!	Brawler x11	Da Biggest now increases Strength by 6/level and affects your entire group when it procs.
Less Stabbin' Me	Toughest x3	Increase Block and Parry chances by 5% when in Improved Balance, and 10% when in Perfect Balance.
Stop Hittin' da Runts	Toughest x7	Character gains 10 AP when his guarded target is attacked.
Mor' Hardcore	Toughest x11	Right in da Jibblies and Not in da Face also have a medium knockback effect.
You Got Nuffin'	Boss x3	Detaunts are dispelled automatically when applied to you.
Big Brawlin'	Boss x7	Big Swing snares targets (40%, 5s) and disorients targets (0.5ss for 5s) (Ailment).
No Choppin' Me	Boss x11	Follow 'Me Lead also buffs all groupmates within 30ft of the defensive target.

Renown

Dis iz da fun stuff. Dis means you been clobberin' people! Kill enemy players in combat an' you will get Renown points. Dere iz three levels of Renown. In da first level you need to spend 20 points. After da first 20 points you can get Level 2 of da Renown awards, den after dat you have to spend 40 points an' you get da level 3 Renown abilities. Each Renown rank you get will give you one point. So dats a lot of killing!

Wid Renown points you can buy both passive buffs an' Renown Tactics. You have one Renown Tactic slot so don't bother wif dem until you iz into Rank 2 or Rank 3. When training up through Rank 1 train all yer points into Fortitude or Blade Master. Deez two skills will make you strong, but depending on how you play will depend on wot ones you want to train. Fortitude will upgrade yer Toughness, which in turn less da damage taken. Blade Master will increase yer weapon skill.

In Rank 2 you should train Vigor or Assault. Vigor give you more hit points. Dat means more survivability fer bashing stunties! An' Assault give you more strength an' weapon skills. Then in da last level of skills Rank 3, you should select Opportunist. Dis skill iz great. It will let you get better hits on everythin' you hit wif yer weapon.

Remember deez iz wots best fer me. Maybe somethin' iz better fer you. Depending on how you fight, you might want somethin' else. But deez skills iz da bestest!

You iz bound to find something new.

Solo Play (PvE)

Rank 1-10

When a Black Orc starts out, dey will be in da mouth of a cave lookin' out to Mount Bloodhorn. Dis iz where da Black Orcs will take dere first steps into da world, an' will notice dere iz little Goblins all over da place. First thing you will see when walkin' forward iz da first quest giver. Go talk to dis large Orc an' get a mission. Dis will be da first time da Orc gets to clobber some stunties. When attacking deez stunties, 'member to lob yer choppa at dem to pull dem over to you. Fer da first level all you iz going to be doing iz using yer attack Clobber. Don't worry you will level quickly, an' at Rank 2 you get Trip 'Em Up, which iz da second part of yer three-part combos. Continue getting all da quests an' clearing dem out. Dat will rank you up pretty quickly. At Rank 3, go train Skull Thumper. Dis iz da final attack in yer low-level three-hit combo. Your attack setup should be Clobber, Trip 'Em Up, Skull Thumper. Follow da path to Lobber Hill an' continue to get quests an' finishing dem. Dis will get you to Rank 4, when you get yer first personal buff skill. Dis iz called Da Biggest! All attacks will have a small chance to increase yer strength fer 10 secondz. 'Member only one war bellow at a time.

At Snouts' Pens dere iz many quests fer a young Orc to complete. Finish dose an' head south an' partake in da first public quest open to da Orcs. It's called Urgog's Rage. Dis iz a great place to gain experience an' influence. Be active in deez public quests as da rewards can be great. Dere iz three levels of awards fer each public quest. On da third level you will generally get a nice piece of armor or a weapon. At da same time, if killing Squigz iz not yer thing, der iz always da Sharpthorn Wud public quest. Some time between Snouts' Pens you will rank up a couple more times, but to survive all da battles you iz change yer attack sequence a little. First use Da Biggest! on yerself an' den it iz still Clobber, Trip 'Em Up, Skull Thumper. At Rank 5 you will be able to train Follow 'Me Lead, which iz another defensive buff dat will deal small damage an' buffs defensive target's weapon skills. You could hold off on training dis skills till you iz more powerful than any creature near you.

Between Rank 6 an' Rank 8 you can train Tuffer 'n Nails. Dis iz a replacement fer yer second combo step. Now dis ability iz better fer grouping or if you iz fightin' monsters a few ranks higher den you. It will deal damage an' then increase yer armor fer 10 secondz. An' den at Rank 7 you can train Taunt. Dis iz a skill you use till da end of ..me. Dis skill will make yer target attack you an' take more damage from yer .ttacks fer 15 secondz or after yer opponent has hit   you three times.

)nce you reach Rank 8 you can train Da Big Jn'. It needs a great weapon an' iz combo spot .aree (da' best plan) an' will deal damage to all .argets in front of you up to 25 feet. At dis point .epindin' on how much public questing you do you .ould head over to Da War Maker. Dis iz Chapter 2 in .a greenskins' path to glory. Dere iz many quests here, as well . trainers fer crafting skills. Dis would be a great time to learn deez .rafting skills an' remember to use dem while adventurin' so dey iz useful .ter. When questing out of Da War Maker, keep questing until Rank 10. Den .ead back to town to train, as you receive two more skills Rank 8 to10.

.t Rank 9 iz a replacement to Trip 'Em Up called Right in da Jibblies. Ha! oot dem dum stunties. Dis skill does wot it sounds like, by dealing decent .amage an' less da foe's weapon skill fer 10 secondz. At Rank 10 you receive a .rty skill Save da Runts, which allows you to defend an ally.

Rank 11-20

Now dat you have da first three skills of all three Masteries, you will have a general idea as to wot dey do. When levelin' by yerself, switch yer attack sequence to Clobber, Right in da Jibblies, Skull Thumper. 'Member to use yer bellow. Go north from Da War Maker once all da quests iz done, an' at Rank 10 or 11 you should arrive at Komar (Chapter 3) where a never-ending battle iz taking place between da Orcs an' stunties. Dis iz where da Orcs must choose do dey continue on a forward path toward dere first fight against other players in Screeb's Stunty Killin' Camp or dey can follow da quests through da Crawla Cave to da southeast of Komar dat leads to Ekrund.

Once done in Mount Bloodhorn, around Rank 13, go to Marshes of Madness. Here you will find a large RvR section right in da middle of da map. Make sure to stop off at Bonerender's Bash an' train up Wot Armor?, a new skills to replace Clobber, so your attacks go: Wot Armor?, Right in da Jibblies, Skull Thumper. get some quests an' once complete go to Morth's Mire Warcamp. Get some Renown points fer doin' some RvR as da skills gained will help you do better. Once done in Marshes of Madness, go to da Badlands. But before you do, 'member to train up Da Greenest at Rank 14, Savin' Me Hide at Rank 16, Big Slash an' Juggernaut at Rank 18, an' Challenge at Rank 20. Juggernaut makes you immune to snaring, rooting, stunning, an' disarming effects, so keeps it handy.

Influence rewards iz still gud even if you go three to four ranks after you supposed to get dem.

Rank 21-30

Once at da Badlands checks everythin' out. You never know wot you may find. Der iz always a chance dat something new an' exciting will pop up fer you.

Here you will find da quests needed to level up some more, an' more RvR an' PQs. 'Member to talk to a binder an' not have to do a lot of running around when you iz in need to go back to town. Dis iz da time when you will want to start spendin' a lot of time in da RvR areas, scenarios, an' PQs. Dat way you gets all da rewards dey offer. Between Ranks 21 and 30 there iz only two combat skills you can train. dose iz Da Toughest, a war bellow, an' Where You Going?, which holds foes in place. Where You Going? be important while doing da PvP aspects fer da rest of da game.

Rank 31-40

When done at da Badlands an' you iz on yer path to Rank 40, go over to da Thunder Mountain or Black Crag. Here you can max out yer ranks, an' da best way to do dis iz by doin' all da RvRs an' PQs you can get into. You have only one skill left an' dats Shut Yer Face. Dis shuts up casters, which iz gud all da time. From da major town hubs you will be able to go meet wif yer Destruction brethren in Dragonwake an' Praag. Being involved in da campaigns will be da best. Dis iz where all da stunties will be, so clobber dem gud!

Group Play

Dere iz a few things to consider when doin' da different group tasks in da world. Think of yer Tactics an' wot would better benefit da group as a whole. A Black Orc iz big, strong, an' has a lot of hit points. A Black Orc iz also controls enemies. So be on da front line, take control, an' lead yer friends into battle, an' hold yer enemy in ones spot so da group can be more better against yer enemies.

Who iz in da group iz goin' to be da decidin' factor on how you as a Black Orc iz going to play. Say you iz in a public quest. Lead da charge an' remove da enemies as fast as possible. Hold da enemies in ones spot fer other players to finish off da mobs. 'Member you iz strong, tho, an' you can do damage to dem too. But if der iz a healer, go all out. Dat iz if you can trust da healer. A gud healer will allow you to get savage an' start attackin' many things at once. But 'member to keep on eye on dat healer as you an' da rest of da party must protect dat healer to keep stay alive.

Same sort of plan iz used in a scenario. Work as a group, hold yer foe in place, disorient, an' make dose enemies bleed. Da more you kill, da more Renown points you get. Dis should make any Orc happy. 'Member in a group to think wot benefit da group. Do not go runnin' in head first without gettin' da proper buffs, potions, an' yer Tactics ready.

I'm bigga den Goblins.

BEATIN' ON PLAYERS AN' SMARTY PANTSES

Solo PvP

When wantin' to beat on other players, you can do dis different ways. You can join up wif any of da many scenarios, you can go into RvR areas, or you can find someone who iz RvR flagged so you can attack dem outside of deez instances.

'Member to use yer skills to slow down da enemy an' attempt to get combos off. Finishin' combos be hard against a player dat knows wot dey iz doing. But a gud Black Orc knows how to keep dem close.

Dere iz two main reasons to go out an' fight: One iz to take control of areas in da world. You don't want dose stupid stunties getting control. Then there iz Renown points dat will help you get Renown awards dat increase yer fightin'. Dere iz different places to do all dis.

Ranks 1-10

Da tactics to be used in Rank 1-10 iz da same as when fightin' regular monstuz. You need to run up to da enemy an' you smash dere heads in! Use Clobber, Trip Em Up!, Skull Thumper. Use dis multiple times on a stunty an' dey iz dead.

Ranks 11-20

Use da same tactic as Rank 1-10, but switch Right in da Jibblies fer Trip Em Up! An' once at Rank 12, train up Wot Armor? an' switch dat out wif Clobber. So after Rank 12 yer combo tactics should be Wot Armor? Right in da Jibblies, Skull Thumper.

When up against magic-users 'member to use Da Greenest ability to give yerself a buff to yer resistances. A magic-user try to keep you at a distance so use yer Juggernaut skills an' then get nice an' close an' personal wif da magic-user. Dey have weak armor so Wot Armor?, Right in da Jibblies, an' Skull Thumper iz all you need. Repeat over an' over an' over till dey dead.

Ranks 21-30

Wot can I tell you about deez ranks dat you don't already know? You goin' to do da tactics from above. But now when yer enemy iz runnin' from you like a baby stunty, you can use da skills Where You Going? Dis will hold dem in dere place fer five secondz and you can catch dem.

Ranks 31-40

You get some new skills in dis rank range. So now when fightin' you iz gonna attack like dis: Do Da Greenest war bellow, charge in, use Wot Armor?, Right in da Jibblies, an' Skull Thumper till you reach Rank 35 then train Big Swing. Dis deals damage an' a debuff to dere strength so you will now be using Wot Armor?, Big Swing, Skull Thumper, den Wot Armor?, Right in da Jibblies, Skull Thumper. Repeat back an' forth till you have won. When against a magic-user, run up to dem an' bash in der heads. Use Wot Armor?, Right in da Jibblies, Skull Thumper, den Wot Armor?, Big Swing, Skull Thumper. You can use Where You Going? when dey run, an' Shut Yer Face to silence dere casting when dey look to be casting somethin' mean.

Group Play

like teamin' wif others who want to crush stunty skulls. 'Member when you get to an area where battle iz happening, find yerself a group to fight wif. No one can handle da hordes of stunties on der own. So find a healer, some other attackers, an' maybe some mages to help you, an' go stunty bashing. Dis will be fun an' rewardin'.

You have two primary jobs. Da first thing yer enemy iz going to do iz come after your weak healer. So wot iz you to do? Stop dem. Use yer abilities to protect your team. If you can get to dem before dey can get to you, den do it. Da second iz to stomp on stunty heads. Hold dem in one spot long enough fer yer team to burn down da enemy from behind, in front, or dem sides. Do wot you been doing by yerself when you get a foe singled out.

As a team you will want to talk wot iz happening. Orcs have da bigger larger voice so you do da commanding. Don't let some silly Squig-lovin' Goblin tells you wot to do!

If you have multiple Black Orcs dat iz doing gud, don't be scared to pull out yer great weapon an' do some multiple target attacks. You iz there to make a difference, so make one.

YOU MADE IT DIS FAR?

You iz now a proud Black Orc. No tryin' to take me rank in da clan! You might be younger but I am still better den you. None da less, you survived dis long. Oh look at dat, you got yerself a couple of trophies. Oh an' wots dat? You get some new armor an' weapons. Very nice.

Anyways, happy I could help you get to where you iz today. Now go out dere an' enjoy yerself. Wot else could you want in life? You got stunties to clobber, an' all da battle you could ever want.

Me Favorite Joke

Why stunties laugh when dey runz?

Answer: Because da grass tickles dere chins.

Explore everywhere.

Enjoy Dwarfs in a Barrel.

SHAMAN

By Firebag

Sniff...sniff...I smell somethin' gud burning. Ack, must be dis flesh grub a cookin'. Don't just stand dere, grab me dat bone over dere so I can mix dis pot. So you've come here to be Shaman likes me, hmm? Ha! May Gork an' Mork help us now! You thinks iz so easy to be Shaman like me. You thinks wrong den.

Dis healer class iz da most needed in any group. Everybody wants to have you in dere party fer yer abilities to make dem stronger wif yer buffs, fer debuffing dere enemies so dey can kill 'em quicker, an' fer yer heals all filled with *WAAAGH!* If you likes to help others an' support dem all da time, den dis class iz right fer you. But you need plenty of patience to play dis role. Dat iz huge responsibility dat many not do so gud, but if yer up fer it den you've come to da right class.

What is a Shaman?

I've never trusted magic. You know what cold steel does to a Bright Wizard's belly. Magic is unpredictable and can lose you wars if you place faith in it.

But magic does have its charms when it heals a steel cut and snatches warriors from the deathly abyss. Shamans are Goblins that heal well, as much as you can rely on a greenskin. They cast on foes to debilitate them and on allies to boost their abilities. I've seen them radiate armor and make leather seem like chain. Shamans can even sling damage spells from afar, so we use them to pound through an enemy when the tide turns in our favor.

Like their brethren Squig Herders, Shamans cannot be thrown into the din of maces and pikes. They haven't the armor for it—or the fortitude, in most cases—and should be kept to the rear where their light armor fares better. Not to mention, I've never seen one hold a sword firmly. They trust in walking sticks and their clawed hands to weave their arcane mysteries.

This special magic, which the greenskins call *Waaagh!*, fuels their damage and healing spells to unholy levels. It once destroyed the regiments under Lord Korlain, when he sought the Inevitable City for himself. The fool has almost been wiped from history's memory. To be beaten, annihilated, by scattered greenskins in the hills. I learned from the loss. Yes, I learned, and sought to woo the Shaman casters and their ilk to me, and with them my army swept upon the land as a tidal wave against creatures burrowing in the sand.

—Baron Heinar Balethar, Zimmeron's Hold, Chaos Wastes

Me name iz Firebag, chieftain of Blood Gash tribe an' I know Gazbag, who iz grand Shaman of da Bloody Sun Boyz, real gud. He bit me once 'cos I was watchin' 'im while 'ee slept. Says my breevin' on 'is face woz all wet an' ikky. He don't bite many people, mostly 'ee jest sticks 'em wiv 'is pigstikka. We iz like reel gud friends.

Gazbag an' stupid Grumlok an' dem Boyz rule deez parts of da Badlands. I helps Gazbag wif running dis place too. Dem big buggers thinks dat dey runs it all. Dats just wot Gazbag wants dem to think. Him actually rules dem all an' tell dem wot to do. Ack! Grumlok too dumbto know.

Now den me pot of flesh grub iz still cookin'. Les' go find us some fat ugly pointies to kill in dem marshes to da west. Most gobbos likes to skin dem stunty Dwarfs, but I always like to kill da pointy-eared Elves. I like ears more den lots of hair or stunty toenails. Grab me dat staff dere an' we best be goin'. Nothin' better den a few kills dis early in da morning to make da belly rumble. Den we go eat some of me grubs.

STARTIN' SKILZ

Let's go over yer basic abilities fer dis class. Everybody gets Auto Attack an' Flee. I think you can figure dem out you snotling! If not den lemme tells you. Auto Attack iz fer you lazy greenskins dat want to attack wif melee or ranged automatically. Flee iz fer you scared greenskins use to run away. Den dere iz Gork'll Fix It dat iz yer first healing ability. Next iz Brain Bursta, which iz yer main damaging spell. Use dis to kill yer enemies likes stunties or pointies. Dem enemies not know wot hit dem.

Keep in yer puny mind dat yer base stats change wif different weapons an' armor dat you be gettin' as you get higher in rank. Deez stats makes you stronger, tougher, or duma all depends on your rank an' gear. By gear I means yer stuf, weapons, an' armor. Da higher rank you iz, da higher yer stats. Da better equipment you get, da more better yer stats. Da defensive stats tell you how strong yer armor iz against different types of attacks like Elemental. Defensive stats tells you how gud you can Block, Dodge, Parry, an' Disrupt attacks against you.

Things you need to know about deez stats iz how dem affects you. Outta all of deez stats fer a Shaman, you need Intelligence an' Willpower. Intelligence issa posh way of sayin' smarts an' Willpower is like guts but more cleverer. Den you need Initiative—dats wot Gazbag calls speedyness—an' Toughness is fer protection. I fink Toughness is just a funny way of sayin' how tuff you is, but I ain't sure. Intelligence stat helps increase yer magic damage. Da higher it iz, da more betta' yer damagin' magic will be. Take it from me, I likes to seez things go boom. Other most important stat iz Willpower. You iz a healer class so you need dis stat to improve yer healing abilities, it's also gud help against enemy casters wot cast bad magics at you. Da other two stats, Toughness an' Initiative, help you avoid gettin' hit. I not like to get hit at all. I'm a Shaman, not a stunty punchin' bag. If you is gettin' hit den maybe you iz doin' somethin wrong.

Build up yer WAAAGH! always. I likes to cast five quick heals on my group members so my Gork's WAAAGH! iz ready before I get to any battle an' do major damage on da enemy. Dis goes fer Mork's WAAAGH! too.

We Shamans iz little Goblins dat are part of da greenskins race. We might be smalla den da other greenskin Orcs, but we iz smarta. Likes I sez all da time, da bigga dey iz, da dumba dey gets. Not to worries, we needs dem fer now so we let dem think dey in charge. We iz all part of da Destruction side, da dark side. We live nowhere but make everywhere we go our home. Our tribes iz big an' only gettin' bigga as more an' more greenskin tribes join us. We iz one big sloppy green family.

Our tribes have been joining each other to destroy dem drunken stunties. Dey no care fer no one else but dem ale dey be drinkin' all da time. Dey iz greedy little you know wot. We greenskins will band together to get rid of dem once an' fer all, then maybe dey can help me wif da pointies. wif da strong dumbOrcs leading da way, we Shamans will be right behind dem to command da attacks an' keep dem alive. Dem stunties have no chance against us. Wait till we get more tribes to join dis battle. We iz gonna have da biggest *WAAAGH!!*

Shamans start out in a mushroom cave at Mount Bloodhorn. Dis area iz da pits, but iz da bestest place in da world. Dere tons of big Orcs, Squigs, snotlings, an' other green things runnin' around. Here you seez Sharzag da Orc dat will get you some quests. Talk to 'im an' other greenskins wif open books over dere heads. Other greenskins dat will help you iz Sogsnag Grubsnout. He looks sneaky but he iz da Career Trainer. Come back to him every time you gain a rank. He iswhere you buy available abilities dat he can train. Next down da path iz Gagdush da Merchant. Speak to Gagdush if yer want ter swap stuff wot you has found fer shinies. Gagdush will buy pretty much anyfink an' 'ee don't care if yer stole it or nuffink! I likes him, tho never trust a greenskin wif only one ear. You find him wif a gold pouch over his head.

Down da hill you find Da Slop. Da Slop is da best place eva! It's like dinner wot you can swim in! It's all warm an' tickley in me keks! Next to Da Slop iz where you find Lobber Hill. We greenskins keep it simple. Lobber Hill iz where we keeps da lobbers. Dem iz used fer lobbing stuff at dem stunties at wot we call Stunty Mountain. Yes, you is a smart Shaman. Dat mountain has tons of stunties. Quit staring at me likes a stupid snotling. Come now, you funny looking green thing. We talk more about yer gear next.

BEIN' A GREENSKIN

GEAR AN' STUF

You start out wif nothing but yer skives, Me Softest Shirt, an' Me Ol' Stick. In yer backpack you find a map. Not just any other map but a Battle Map. Dis iz used to save yer last recall point. You find da Rally Mastas at different areas of da world. Talk to dem to save yer recall point. You can click on yer Battle Map to go back to yer recall point. Other things you will find in yer backpack iz gold, but you don't start out wif any, so start killin' an' get some.

Yer only allowed to wear light armor fer Shamans. Dis makes it tuff fer Shamans to go toe-to-belly against stunties or toe-to-knee against pointies. Shamans armor iz light an' weaker den most, so avoid gettin' hit. We carry a big ole stick an' only allowed to carry staffs. Our sticks iz nice wif pretty skulls, but dey still just sticks. No gud fer killin' enemies. We only can bash dem some, but we use our magic more fer killin' dem. We don't need other weapons anyways cuz Shamans are busy healers. We cast more magic fer damage an' healin' den we bash wif sticks. We do find nicer staffs out dere as loot from our killin' or from da merchants dat sell dem. Use da ones wif da most damage if melee fightin'. But why's you melee fightin'?

Fer staffs an' armor, find da bestest dat have good stats an' increase yer Intelligence an' Willpower. Dem are yer most important stats fer a Shaman to get. After dat pick weapons an' armor dat have Toughness an' Initiative fer avoidin' gettin' hit. Dem will help you stay alive in deez lands.

Gud Things

- Having da power of *WAAAGH!* Dem increase all me offensive an' healing spells.
- Healing abilities to stay alive. Most classes not have dem.
- Buff an' debuff abilities dat make me even stronger an' me enemy weaker.
- Long-range spell abilities. I can reach out an' kill things from real far.
- Supporting role. Any group wants me cuz dey need healing to stay alive.

Yeah, I got *WAAAGH!* an' I know how to use it! Me offensive spells iz so damaging dey iz hot. Get back all your pointies, I's gonnashow you me real power. No worries me Destruction buddies, we Shamans will keep you alive wif our healing. Shamans wif da help of almighty Mork can cast powerful healing spells fer one target or da whole group. Dats our main role iz to support da group an' keep dem healthy. Shamans get range too. No needs to be up close an' smell dem stinky stunty breath. Cast dem spells from long range.

Not So Gud Things

- Light armor iz crap. I should just run around in me skives dey so weak.
- Walking stick. Me staff not hurt so gud, so melee combat iz not gud.
- Supporting role. Any group needs me, but being by me self iz not so gud fer me.

Biggest problem wif Shamans iz der light armor iz weak. Shamans not like gettin' hit all da time cuz we drop real quick wif weak armor. I not stand wif dem melee fighters cuz me staff iz no gud fer swinging. Melee fighters wot hit me head too much makes it hurts. Dis staff iz so weak dat it tickles dem fat stunties. Thank da gods we get strong magic to keep dem away an' kill 'em quick. Don't be afraid to use Flee to run outta dere. Shamans gud wif groups but not so gud fightin' solo. Just fight one to one if you can. Too much iz no gud.

Be patient. I know you want to run into battle yellin' an' screamin'! You will be yellin' an' screamin' if dats wot you do. So let da runnin' into battle be fer da others. You can walk behind dem an' do yer job, healin'.

WARHAMMER ONLINE
AGE OF RECKONING

SKILZ AN' ABILITIES

Abilities

bility training iz done by da Career Trainers. Speak wif dem every time you rank up so you can buy yer next available ability. When you talk to Career Trainer, dere iz two options: Core Training an' Mastery Training. Core Training iz da main choice fer buying ability training. Guess wot Mastery Training iz? Yes, dats right, dere you train yer Core abilities fer Mastery. You startin' to not look dat stupid at all, gud job. In da Mastery training, you get three paths to work on. You only get a total of 25 Mastery points at max rank of 40. You get one point startin' at rank 11. Dats ean you need to make smart choice on wot path to master. Let's go over each of dem:

ath of Mork: Increases da Core abilities Bleed Fer' Me; Bigger, Better, An' Greener; Don' Feel Nuthin; Gather Round

ath of Gork: Increases da Core abilities Life Leaka, Bunch O' *Waaagh!*, Stop Hittin' Me!, Scuse Me!

ath of Da Green: Increases da Core abilities 'Ere We Go!, Mork's Buffer, Get'n Smarta, Yer A Weaklin', You Got Nuthin!

a path to take iz up to you. Not one path iz da best. It iz up to you an' da type of Shaman you want. Here's wot dey all mean. Path of Mork iz ore fer healers. Path of Gork iz fer offensive Shaman wif damaging spells. Path of Da Green iz fer debuffing yer enemy. I sez dat yer primary role a da Shaman iz healer an' offensive damage, an' debuff are secondary.

yer play style iz as da main healer den max out Path of Mork wif 15 Mastery points an' da rest o' da 10 Mastery points go to Path of Gork. The nth point iz no gud cuz you need one more point to enable da level 11 Mastery ability. Da reason no points go to Path of Da Green iz because da rly level Mastery abilities dere are less gud.

yer play style iz more offensive an' likes to do major damage, den max out Path of Gork wif 15 Mastery points an' da rest o' da 10 points go to ath of Mork fer healing Mastery abilities.

ow if you enjoy da group support role an' mostly doing debuffs, den max out wif Path of Da Green wif 15 Mastery points. Den wif da rest of da lastery points, spend five points on Path of Mork an' five points on Path of Gork. Deez make you a more balanced debuff Shaman.

er role is different wif each play style an' path I jess told you about above. I want to call da first one da Healer Shaman role (max Mork, rest on Gork), cond one da Damage Dealer Shaman role (max Gork, rest on Mork), an' den da Debuff Shaman role (max Da Green, some Mork, some Gork).

Abilities

Level	Name	Path	Cost	Range (in feet)	Type	Build	Duration	Reuse	Description
Starter Ability	Gork'll Fix It	Mork	55	150	Heal - Enchantment	1s	9s	0s	Heals 247 damage, then heals 658 damage over 9s. Builds Mork's Waagh!
Starter Ability	Brain Bursta	Gork	30	100	Magic Attack	2s	0s	0s	Deals 299 damage. Builds Gork's Waagh!
Level 2	Life Leaka	Gork	30	100	DoT - Ailment	0s	15s	0s	Deals 499 over 15s. Builds Gork's Waagh! Effectiveness is increased by 5% for each point of Mork's Waagh!
Level 3	'Ey, Quit Bleedin'	Core	30	150	HoT - Enchantment	0s	15s	0s	Heals for 1,496 over 15 seconds. Builds Mork's Waagh! Effectiveness is increased by 5% for each point of Gork's Waagh!
Level 4	'Ere We Go!	Da Green	25	Group	Group Buff	0s	5s	10s	Each group member's next attack deals an additional 150 damage.
Level 5	Bunch o'Waagh!	Gork	25 / 2s	100	Channeled Attack	0s	3s	11s	Channeled attack. Deals 349 every 2s for 6s. Setback Rules: 100% for 0.5s. Builds Gork's Waagh! Effectiveness is increased by 5% for each point of Mork's Waagh! (Gains 1 free step extra.)
Level 6	Bleed Fer' Me	Mork	35	100	DoT - Ailment	0s	24s	10s	Deals 648 over 24s and heals defensive target for damage done on each tick. Builds Gork's Waagh! Effectiveness is increased by 5% for each point of Mork's Waagh!
Level 7	Look Over There!	Core	20	100	Debuff	0s	15s	15s	Detaunts target (15s duration, 50% redux).
Level 7	Mork's Buffer	Da Green	55	Group	Buff - Enchantment	0s	60min	0s	Increases group's Elemental Resist by 6.3 per level for 60 minutes.
Level 8	Bigger, Better, an' Greener	Mork	45	150	Waaagh Heal	3s	0s	0s	Heals target for 1,125. Builds Mork's Waagh!
Level 9	Yer Not So Bad	Core	40	100	Debuff - Ailment	2s	9s	20s	Steal 180 AP over 9s. Builds Gork's Waagh!
Level 10	Gedup!	Core	20	100	Waaagh Resurrection	6s	0s	3s	Resurrect target friendly dead player. Builds Mork's Waagh!

Heal an' heal often. Some of yer heals are HoT. No, not full of fire. It mean Heal over Time. Yer target get healed fer some points, den every few seconds dey still get healed some more.

Abilities

Level	Name	Path	Cost	Range (in feet)	Type	Build	Duration	Reuse	Description
Level 12	Get'n Smarter	Da Green	30	100	Debuff - Ailment	0s	10s	10s	Steals 3 Int from target for 15s and grants it to caster. Deals 349 over 15s.
Level 14	Don' Feel Nuthin	Mork	35	Buff	Buff - Enchantment	0s	9s	20s	Shield that absorbs 100% of damage up to 937. Builds Mork's Waagh! Effectiveness is increased by 5% for each point of Gork's Waagh!
Level 16	Greener'n Cleaner	Core	25	150	Magic Attack	0s	0s	5s	Removes a Curse or Ailment from target.
Level 18	Yer a Weaklin'	Da Green	30	100	DD - Ailment	2s	20s	0s	Deals 249 damage and lowers target's Strength by 3/level for 20s Builds Gork's Waagh!
Level 20	Gather Round	Mork	60	Group	Waaagh Group Heal	3s	0s	0s	Heals every group member for 540. Builds Mork's Waagh!
Level 22	Shatter Enchantment	Core	25	Melee	Melee Attack	0s	0s	5s	Removes an enchantment from target. Deals (75+DPS) damage if successful.
Level 25	Eeeek!	Core	55	PBAE	Escape, Crowd Control	1s	0s	60s	The Shaman and all enemies within 20ft of him are knocked back 20ft.
Level 30	Stop Hittin' Me!	Gork	40	PBAE	Aggro/CC management - Enchantment	0s	20s	30s	PBAE detaunt (50%, 10s) and increases disrupt chance of the caster by 5% for 20s.
Level 35	You Got Nuthin!	Da Green	25	100	CC - Ailment	1s	5s	30s	Deals 187.5 and silences the target for 5s. Builds Gork's Waagh!
Level 40	Scuse Me!	Gork	45	CAE	DD - Ailment	2s	20s	10s	CAE Attack. Does 249 damage to all targets in the radius, and debuffs their Elemental resistances for 4.5 per level for 20 seconds. Arc: 120, Radius: 65ft.
Specialization									
Mork x5	I'll Take That!	Mork	25	100	Lifetap	2s	0s	0s	Deal 199 damage to target, heals defensive target for damage dealt. Builds Gork's Waagh!
Mork x9	Do Sumfin Useful	Mork	35	150	Heal - Enchantment	0s	9s	0s	Heals 628 damage over 9s. Spends Waagh!, increasing Toughness by 1 for each point of Waagh!, up to 3 points. Builds Mork's Waagh! Effectiveness is increased by 5% for each point of Gork's Waagh!
Mork x13	Shrug It Off	Mork	55	150	Heal - Enchantment	2s	9s	10s	Buff target for 20s sec. Places a healing pool on the target with 250 health in it. Each time the target takes damage during the buff, an additional 150 health is placed in to a pool. When the buff expires, or that target dies, each group member is healed for the amount in the pool. Max 10 charges. Builds Mork's Waagh!
Gork x5	Big Waagh!	Gork	45	100	Magic Attack	1s	0s	20s	Deals 450 damage. Builds Mork's Waagh!
Gork x9	Da Waagh! Is Coming	Gork	50	80	Magic Attack	3s	0s	0s	Deals 600 damage to the target, deals 450 damage to 2 targets near the original target, deals 300 damage to 2 targets near each of the secondary targets. Target's cannot be hit more than once by the ability. Builds Gork's Waagh! Radius: 20ft.
Gork x13	Geddoff!	Gork	20	100	Magic Attack/CC	2s	0s	20s	Deals 299 damage to all targets in a 20ft radius, and deals a short knockback. Builds Gork's Waagh!
Da Green x5	Gork's Barbs	Da Green	30	100	Debuff - Ailment	2s	10s	10s	Deals 112 damage to target. For 10s, debuff deals 150 damage every time the target uses a melee action. Builds Gork's Waagh!
Da Green x9	You'z Squishy	Da Green	20	100	Debuff - Ailment	0s	20s	0s	Toughness is reduced by 3 per level for 20s. Radius: 30ft.
Da Green x13	Sticky Feetz	Da Green	20	100	Debuff - Ailment	3s	10s	30s	GTAE. Reduces Elemental resist for 9.45 / level and snares 60% for 10s. Radius: 30ft.

Stay waaaaaaay back behind da front lines. You get gud distance to cast heals an' damaging spells, so use it.

Morale

Shamans have 12 Morale abilities wif three of dem in Mastery path. Deez Morale abilities can be learned from da Career Trainers. Da first Morale ability da Shaman gets iz at Rank 8 called Divine Favor. Dere iz four ranks of Morale abilities. Each gets stronger as you build up yer Morale bar. Once dey light up on yer Morale bar, you can click dem to use. So it not be matterin' if you use Morale Rank 1 or Rank 4, you use it, you lose it, den you need to wait till it builds up again. Deez Morale abilities iz real special so be careful when you use dem.

Depending on which role or path you take will tells you yer Morale from da Mastery path. Da following iz wot you get:

Healer Shaman: Feelz No Pain, which heals yer group over 10 seconds an' decreases damage against dem by 25 percent fer 10 seconds

Damage Dealer Shaman: Fists Of Gork, which deals big damage an' knocks back all enemy targets within 30 feet

Debuff Shaman: Steal Yer Thunder, which reduces da stats of all enemies within 30 feet of da target by 1 an' increases all yer group member's stats by 1 fer 15 seconds

Let's seez which Core Morale iz nice fer each rank to use starting wif Rank 1 Core Morale abilities. Fer Rank 1 Morale I like Steal Life. Yer target suffers big damage over 9 seconds an' yer healed fer half of dat damage dealt. Not a bad deal at all. Just keep in mind dat dis Morale ability iz not available until you get to Rank 16. So make sure you fill yer Morale slot wif something till den. Dat gonna be Divine Favor, which can heal even da biggest Orc up from near death.

Rank 2 Morale slot I go fer Rampaging Siphon. Dat deals gud damage to all enemies within 30 feet an' heals yer entire group fer da full amount of damage dealt. Dats real nice way to do both damagin' an' healin'.

Now fer Rank 3 I like You Weren't Using Dat Morale ability. Dis takes away 100 action points (AP) from each enemy within 30 feet an' gives 50 percent of stolen AP to you. Now dats real gud so baddies have hard time to do action wif no AP, especially if dere AP iz low.

Rank 4 Morale ability dere iz only one to choose from Core abilities an' dats Alter Fate. Dis resurrects all group mates within 30 feet. Anyone who come back from dead iz healed fer a gud bit o' health over 5 seconds. Dere iz three more Rank 4 Morale abilities to choose from an dem from yer Career path. See my roles above an' see which one you have to choose from. Between all of dem Rank 4 Morale abilities, I pick da one from Career path. So if I'm a Healer Shaman I take Feelz No Pain instead of Alter Fate fer Rank 4 Morale ability. If I'm a Debuff Shaman, I pick Steal Yer Thunder fer me Rank 4 Morale ability. Dey more useful cuz you can rez wif yer Dat Makes Me Dizzy Tactic.

Morale					
Name	Level	Rank	Range (in feet)	Duration	Description
Divine Favor	Level 8	Rank 1	150	0s	Heals target for 1,800.
Rampaging Siphon	Level 12	Rank 2	PBAE	0	PBAE that deals 600 and heals the group for 100% of the value.
Steal Life	Level 16	Rank 1	100	9s	Magic attack that deals 900 over 9s. Self-heals 50% of the damage dealt.
Focused Mind	Level 20	Rank 2	Self	10s	For 10s, build times are reduced by 50%. Character purges and is immune to silence, disarm, root, snare, and setback.
Divine Protection	Level 24	Rank 3	Group	10s	Group buffs each group member with an ablative that absorbs the next 1,500 melee damage, with a maximum duration of 10s.
Gork Sez Stop	Level 28	Rank 1	100	2s	Target suffers 300 damage over 2s. If the target moves, the duration is restarted.
Breath of Mork	Level 32	Rank 2	150	9s	Anchor Heal. Heals 900 over 9s on target. Each pulse of of the HoT also heals those within 30ft.
You Weren't Using Dat	Level 36	Rank 3	PBAE	0s	PBAE AP drain. Removes 100 AP from enemies within 30ft, gives 50% of the stolen AP to the Shaman.
Alter Fate	Level 40	Rank 4	PBAE	9s	PBAE resurrection for group members. Resurrected targets also get a HoT that heals 1,200 over 9s.
Feelz No Pain	Mork x15	Rank 4	Group	10s	Heals the group for 720 over 10s and decreases damage against them by 25% for 10s.
Gork's Belch	Gork x15	Rank 4	100	0s	Deals 1,800 damage and knocks all enemy targets in the radius back 30ft. Radius: 30ft.
Steal Yer Thunder	Da Green x15	Rank 4	100	15s	Reduces the stats of all enemies in the radius by 1 per level (except Wounds), and increases all group member's stats by 1 per level (except Wounds) for 15s. Radius: 30ft.

Use Eeeek! when you're in a sticky spot. Me use it to escape an' get some distance from enemies. Don't be scared to use it. I use it all da time.

Tactics

Dere iz 17 total Tactics fer da Shaman. Dere are 8 Career Tactics dat you learn from da Career Trainer as you rank up. Da rest are in da Mastery training still learned from da Career Trainer. Each Mastery path has three Spec Tactics. Dat means you're not going to get dem all. Deez Tactics are all passive an' dat means dey work by dem selves if you add dem to yer Tactic slots. Yer first Career Tactic iz available at Rank 11. You start out wif only one Career Tactic slot den get another slot by Rank 21 to make it two slots, three slots fer Rank 31, den four slots by Rank 40.

So which one iz nice fer da Shaman you sez? I's gonna tell you dat. Hold yer Squigs, me impatient young greenling. Let's break deez down by role so I can make it easy fer you. Depending on yer role I wot ya chose, you already get Spec Tactics. Here dey are:

Healer Shaman: Green Cleanin', Pass It On, Lookit What I Did!, Nothin' But Da *Waaagh*!

Damage Dealer Shaman: Leaky Brainz, Hurts Don't It?, Mork's Touch

Debuff Shaman: *Waaagh!* Frenzy, You Really Got Nothin, Ere We Goes Again

Fer Core Tactics I tells you which ones I likes da best. Fer Ranks 11–20, I likes Burst O' *Waaagh!* Dis gets me two extra *Waaagh!* wif every critical hit I does wif damaging spells. Dats iz huge an' iz big jump to full *WAAAGH!*

From Ranks 21 to 30 I sticks wif Burst O' *Waaagh!* fer first Tactic, den I takes either Subtlety or Desperation. Use Subtlety if you only fightin' monters, cuz it makes baddies hate you 25 percent less than normal wif all heals. Dat helps you stay safe from dem hairy stunties. If you plan on fightin' in da battlefields against other players, den use Desperation so yer heals iz 20 percent better wif critically wounded targets. Dat keeps dem alive longer an' dats gud fer you so dem baddies don't chase you instead.

Fer Ranks 31–40 I keep da same two Tactics from above. Da other one I like fer Tactics iz Get Movin'! Dis iz real nice for healing cuz all critical heals get target 50 action points. If you're in a pure healer role den go wif Burst O' *Waaagh!*, Dat Makes Me Dizzy, an' Get Movin'! wif Dat Makes Me Dizzy you can resurrect yer dead buddies instantly. Dat iz real gud so cuz get back to action quicker. Dey thank you too dat you get dat. Just tell dem you charge dem one gold per rez! Fer Rank 40 you get a fourth Tactic slot. I use same tactics as above but add *Waaagh!* Iz Heal. Dis help healing spells build up 50 percent faster when you get five points of *WAAAGH!*

Tactics		
Name	**Level**	**Description**
Whazat Behind You?!	Level 11	Reactive proc: 25% chance to proc a small detaunt (25%, 5s).
Divine Fury	Level 13	Increase damage dealt by 25%, reduce healing values by 20%.
Burst o' *Waagh!*	Level 15	Critical hits build an extra point of the appropriate kind of *Waagh!*
Too Smart For Dat	Level 17	Increases Spirit Resist by +6.3 per level of the character.
Discipline	Level 19	Increases Willpower by +4 per level of the character.
Green Cleanin'	Level 21	Greener 'n Cleaner will now heal your defensive target for 337.5 over 9s if an effect was successfully removed. (Enchantment)
RUN AWAY!	Level 23	Reactive proc: 25% chance to increase run speed by 30% for 5s.
Subtlety	Level 25	Decreases threat by 50% on all heals.
Extra Special Mushrooms	Level 27	Heals gain an additional 10% chance to critical.
Restorative Burst	Level 29	Critical heals return 40 AP over 3s to the caster (non-stacking, non-refreshing).
Dat Makes Me Dizzy	Level 31	Resurrections are instant cast, but character is stunned for 3s after casting.
Mork Is Watchin'	Level 33	Damaging spells gain an additional 10% chance to critical.
Ain't Done Yet!	Level 35	Spells that spend *Waagh!* have a 20% chance to not expend it when used.
Get Movin'!	Level 37	Ere We Go also grants 150 Morale when it procs.
Git Outta Here!	Level 39	Eeek's reuse timer is reduced to 20s.
Nuthin' But Da *Waagh!*	Mork x3	Don' Feel Nuthin increases target's damage by 15% for the duration of the buff.
Lookit What I Did!	Mork x7	Gork'll Fix It also gives the target 40 AP.
Pass It On	Mork x11	Healing abilities have a 25% chance to heal an additional friendly target within 30ft of the original target for 157.
Leaky Brainz	Gork x3	Life Leaka also places a 5/level Willpower and Intelligence debuff on the target for 15s.
Mork's Touch	Gork x7	Offensive spells have a 25% chance to dispel a Bless on the target of the spell. If they do, they deal an extra 150 damage.
Hurts, Don't It?	Gork x11	Brain Bursta also reduces the target's Toughness by 6/level for 20s and lowers their Morale by 150 (Ailment).
Waagh! Frenzy	Da Green x3	Yer a Weaklin' gains a 20ft radius.
You Really Got Nothin	Da Green x7	Reuse time on You Got Nothin decreased by 10s.
Ere We Goes Again	Da Green x11	Increases damage on 'Ere We Go to 187 and it will proc 2 times for each person before fading.

Renown

So you're finally ready to do some RvR (Realm vs. Realm) fightin'. Renown points iz gained from killin' other players. Collect enough points an' you get to pick from Renown rewards. Dere iz three levels of rewards. You must spend 20 Renown points first to access da second level. Den spend 40 total Renown points to access da third level. To train dem find a Renown Trainer normally around keeps dat you capture or some battlegrounds.

Where's you spend dem 20 points you ask? Dis depends on yer play style. If you're more offensive, den spend points on Acumen to max Acumen V. Dat makes you smart wif Intelligence likes me, which means yer magic damage be hurtin' much more. Den da rest of da points go to Resolve fer Willpower. Dis helps yer healing power by lots. So if yer more of da main healer, you're gonna want Resolve first to max, den Acumen next.

Now when you access second level rewards, you needs to focus on da next 20 points on Sage to max Sage V fer increases in Intelligence fer magic damage an' Willpower fer better heals. Da rest of da points go to Discipline. Dis gives more Willpower fer better heals plus Initiative fer evadin' attacks, which iz real gud.

You finally get to third level rewards an' here you decide if yer more magic damage dealer den go wif Focused Power to da max or Spiritual Refinement to da max fer increased healing criticals.

All deez rewards makes you special. Yes, you iz special an' different from da others. Da rewards I mentions above are da bestest fer you cuz dey focus on yer abilities an' make 'em better. Jess you remember: It's better to make a bad thing worse den spread out. Dere iz many rewards to choose from so if you need, respec to try other combos.

BEATIN' ON MONTERS AN' DUMB POINTIES

Before I gets into different tactics an' what to do, I needs to show you da power of da Shaman. No other class get dis but us. We gets da power of da *WAAAGH!* Our gods Gork an' Mork get us dis power to use. Gork's *WAAAGH!* improves our damaging spells. Mork's *WAAAGH!* improves our healing spells. Each gets stronger wif every level it goes up, which iz up to 5. Dey build up in level wif each spell depending on which path it takes. Let's take Brain Bursta spell fer example. Dis spell iz Path of Gork. So dat means if I cast Brain Bursta five times den me Mork's *WAAAGH!* will light up wif level of five. Once I use any healing spell, den me Mork's *WAAAGH!* iz used up den power iz gone. Another example if I uses a healing spell likes Gork'll Fix It, which iz Path of Mork. If I uses it three times den me Gork's *WAAAGH!* will light up wif a level of three. Once you use any damaging spell dat iz part of Path of Gork, den Gork's *WAAAGH!* iz used up an' den its power iz gone. You need to build up *WAAAGH!* again. So da easy way to think 'bout dis iz if yer gonna use any damaging spells dats Path of Gork, den Mork *WAAAGH!* light up. Any healing abilities dats Path of Mork, den Gork *WAAAGH!* light up.

WAAAGH! iz always going to be used in combat. Once you get outta fights den *WAAAGH!* will be gone. I like to build *WAAAGH!* as strong as possible. So how I does it iz by casting either Path of Gork or Mork spells five times in a row den use me *WAAAGH!* Dat way I build it up to max level five an' da spell iz stronger den ever.

Solo Play (PvE)

Rank 1–10

You start out wif four actions: Gork'll Fix It, Brain Bursta, Auto Attack, an' Flee. Auto Attack iz used when yer feelin' lazy so not do dis. Flee iz used to run away from baddies. I use dees fer runnin' from place to place quicker. Use dis all da time if you ever needs it. Brain Bursta iz yer first damaging spell. Den dere iz Gork'll Fix It, which iz yer first healing ability. Dere both two-second casting spells, which iz slow. Next abilities iz Life Leaka fer damage at Rank 2 an' 'Ey, Quit Bleedin' fer heals at Rank 3. Both dem much better cuz dey instant casts. Dat just means dey iz casted right away an' not wait two seconds to cast. You get more damaging spells an' healing abilities, plus buffs an' debuffs, all da way up to Rank 10.

Alwayz cast Mork's Buffer when you start to play. Dis lasts one hour so recast when needed. Tactics fer solo PvE would start off wif Yer Not So Bad on target to steal 240 APs, cast Life Leaka, Bunch O' *Waaagh!*, Bleed Fer' Me, Life Leaka, den another Life Leaka. Dis shouldget max Mork's *WAAAGH!* fer heals if needed. Use Bigger, Better, An' Greener wif Mork's *WAAAGH!* Fer quick heals use 'Ey, Quit Bleedin' an' Divine Favor Morale ability fer added healing ability. If not dead yet den repeat from Yer Not So Bad which shouldbe ready to cast again.

Rank 11–20

So you think you've got *WAAAGH!?* Wait 'til you get stronger git! Strategies fer Ranks 11–20 iz da same but you get more abilities now. Fer more details on Career Tactics an' Morale Abilities, go to da Tactics an' Morale section above. Dere you find out which ones to use an' fer wot ranks. Da main abilities dat were added fer deez ranks iz Get'n Smarter, Yer A Weaklin', Don' Feel Nuthin, an' Gather Round. You notice dat deez debuffs iz real useful depending on da enemy class. Fer casters, using Get'n Smarter iz gud to steal 3 Intelligence from dem. Yer A Weaklin' iz best against melee fighters. Don' Feel Nuthin an' Gather Round iz gud fer group mates.

Here's wot to cast against spellcasters: Get'n Smarter, Yer Not So Bad, Life Leaka, Bunch O' *Waaagh!*, Bleed Fer' Me, Life Leaka, den another Life Leaka.

Here's wot to cast against melee fighters: Yer A Weaklin', Yer Not So Bad, Life Leaka, Bunch O' *Waaagh!*, Bleed Fer' Me, Life Leaka, den another Life Leaka.

5 Ways to Prioritize Healing

Who gets heal last?

1. Da group member wot cries likes a little stunty.

2. Da group member not playin' dere class right an' gets everyone killed.

3. Da group member wot chattin' too much an' never shuts up.

4. Da group member wot not ask me nice fer a heal an' calls me names instead.

5. Da group member wot let stunties near you da most.

So lesson learned. Do not be any of da above so you get a heal from da Shaman.

Rank 21-30

Now let's seez da abilities fer Ranks 21–30. You get mostly Career Tactics an' Morale abilities fer deez ranks. You only get three new career abilities. Eeeek! iz da best out of dem. It's fer blastin' everyone away wif *WAAAGH!*, you an' enemies included. Next iz Stop Hittin' Me! Dis nice debuff to disrupt attacks den it makes baddies hate you less plus 50 percent less damage to you. Only things iz if you attack dis target dey not detaunted no more. Dis iz real gud to use wif fightin' more den one enemy. Third one iz Cleanse War Engine. Dis one cleans debuffs from siege engine which iz great fer battlefields, scenerios, and campaigns.

Here's how to cast against spellcasters: Get'n Smarter, Yer Not So Bad, Life Leaka, Bunch O' *Waaagh!*, Bleed Fer' Me, Life Leaka, den another Life Leaka.

Here's how to cast against melee fighters: Yer A Weaklin', Yer Not So Bad, Life Leaka, Bunch O' *Waaagh!*, Bleed Fer' Me, Life Leaka, den another Life Leaka.

Rank 31-40

You get more Career Tactics an' Morale abilities through Ranks 31–40. Dere iz three more Core abilities an' dey iz Scuse Me!, Shield The Skies, an' You Got Nuthin! Deez some real gud damaging spells dat does extra type damage. Scuse Me!, fer example, deals Elemental damage plus reduces enemy's Elemental resistance. Den dere iz You Got Nuthin! Dat deals Elemental damage but da bestest part iz it makes target not use magic fer five seconds. Now dat iz nice! Den dere iz Shield The Skies dat protects you an' two other group mates from ranged siege engines. Gud fer battlefields, scenerios an' campaigns.

Here's wot to cast against spellcasters: Get'n Smarter, You Got Nuthin!, Yer Not So Bad, Life Leaka, Bunch O' *Waaagh!*, Bleed Fer' Me, Life Leaka, den another Life Leaka.

Here's wot to cast against melee fighters: Yer A Weaklin', Scuse Me!, Yer Not So Bad, Life Leaka, Bunch O' *Waaagh!*, Bleed Fer' Me, Life Leaka, den another Life Leaka.

Group Play

Rank 1-10

Now everything changes wif group play. Yer buddies will want you to heal dere lousy hides. So now yer healing abilities play a big role in dis group play. Dey all depends on you to keep dem breathin'. So I'm going to speak slow so you don't miss anything I learns you. So here we goes git.

Now fer Ranks 1–10 we still get same starter spells Gork'll Fix It an' Brain Bursta. Anytime you start to play always cast Mork's Buffer. Dis increases resistances fer everyone in yer group fer one hour. Recast dis after everytime you hit da dirt an' die. Before each fight, cast 'Ere We Go! to give everyone in yer group additional 20 Elemental damage on next attack. Watch where yer tanks iz an' attack da ones dey killin'.

Here's wot to cast against spellcasters: Yer Not So Bad, Life Leaka, Bunch O' *Waaagh!*, Bleed Fer' Me, Life Leaka, den another Life Leaka.

Here's wot to cast against melee fighters: Yer Not So Bad, Life Leaka, Bunch O' *Waaagh!*, Bleed Fer' Me, Life Leaka, den another Life Leaka.

As you cast deez spells, keep yer eye on all group members. You need to help em if dey start gettin' hurt. Cast 'Ey, Quit Bleedin' an' Gork'll Fix It fer light wounds. If dey hurt real bad den use Bigger, Better, An' Greener. Now fer some backup healin', don't forget yer Morale ability Divine Favor dat can heals too. Yer first resurrection spell iz Gedup! Use dis fer rezzin' yer fallen buddies.

Now like I told you earlier, if you cast dem offensive Path of Gork spells den you build up Mork's *WAAAGH!* and get bigga better heals. Dat same fer Gork's *WAAAGH!* Do some heals till you build up Gork's *WAAAGH!* up to level 5 den blast away on baddies dat attack yer tank. Pick da ones dat iz hurt da most to get rid of dem.

Rank 11-20

Deez Ranks 11-20 really gets you some nice Career Tactics an' Morale abilities. Take a looks at Steal Life, a Rank 1 Morale ability dat damages yer target but den heals you fer half da damage you do. Den dere iz me favorite, Rampaging Siphon, dat damages all enemies within 30 feet plus heals yer whole group fer full amount damage you did. Fer Career Tactic you get Burst O' *Waaagh!* dat gets you extra two *WAAAGH!* wif critical hits. Dats real gud to build up *WAAAGH!* quicker. Den dere iz Restorative Burst dat you critical heals a buddy, but wait derez more. Den you get 50 action points back. Now dat some gud savings too.

Not forgettin' 'Ere We Go! before each battle. Now dere iz Don' Feel Nuthin that you shouldcast on yer tank before an' during battle to give dem protection.

Here's how to cast against spellcasters: Get'n Smarter, Yer Not So Bad, Life Leaka, Bunch O' *Waaagh!*, Bleed Fer' Me, Life Leaka, den another Life Leaka.

Here's how to cast against melee fighters: Yer A Weaklin', Yer Not So Bad, Life Leaka, Bunch O' *Waaagh!*, Bleed Fer' Me, Life Leaka, den another Life Leaka.

Healing still da same fer deez ranks. Keep yer tanks healed at all times. Here's a secret, tuff guy: once dat tank go, you go take dirt nap. Cast 'Ey, Quit Bleedin' an' Gork'll Fix It fer light wounds. Den use Bigger, Better, An' Greener fer bigga wounds. Da bestest heals fer group play iz Gather Round, which you get in deez ranks. I uses dis before, after, an' during fights. Dis heals da entire group around you. Dats nice to get everyone healed at da same time in case deres too many hurt buddies.

Rank 21-30

Now you're playin' wif da big boyz in deez ranks 21-30. Here you get another gud Morale ability called Divine Protection. Dis iz Rank 3 Morale an it's tuff to build up dat much morale, but you can. It casts protective shield around yer entire group an' it takes big damage from melee abilities. Den dere iz Subtlety Career Tactic dat makes yer heals cause enemies to hate you 25 percent less. Dis iz gud fer keepin' dem away so you can stay busy healin' yer woe iz me groupies. You get Stop Hittin' Me! which does almost same an' detaunt all enemies within 30 feet. Dat makes dem hate you less again by 50 percent less. Just not hit dem, so dey stay dat way.

Here's how to cast against spellcasters: Get'n Smarter, Yer Not So Bad, Life Leaka, Bunch O' *Waaagh!*, Bleed Fer' Me, Life Leaka, den another Life Leaka.

Here's how to cast against melee fighters: Yer A Weaklin', Yer Not So Bad, Life Leaka, Bunch O' *Waaagh!*, Bleed Fer' Me, Life Leaka, den another Life Leaka.

Heals da same too, so keep yer team healed first an' always.

Rank 31-40

You get some very nice Career Tactics fer deez Ranks 31-40. Tactics like Dat Makes Me Dizzy rezzes instantly any group members dat iz dead. Dat mean dey get back to life an' in da action. Dere even iz *Waaagh!* Iz Heal, dat makes yer healing spells build up 50 percent faster when you get 5 points of *WAAAGH!* Den dere iz da Morale ability You Weren't Using Dat, which takes 100 AP from all enemy within 30 feet den gives 50 percent of it to you. Not bad deal dere.

Same strategy here fer deez ranks. Keepin' yer tanks alive iz most important, an' den da rest of da group too. Cast Mork's Buffer after you die. Cast 'Ere We Go! before each battle. Cast Don' Feel Nuthin on yer tank before an' during battles.

If you miss a heal and let someone die, it's not yer fault. Well it iz, but miztakes happen and you should keep yer brain fixed on savin' da others.

Here's wot to cast against spellcasters: Get'n Smarter, You Got Nuthin!, Yer Not So Bad, Life Leaka, Bunch O' *Waaagh!*, Bleed Fer' Me, Life Leaka, den another Life Leaka.

Here's wot to cast against melee fighters: Yer A Weaklin', Scuse Me!, Yer Not So Bad, Life Leaka, Bunch O' *Waaagh!*, Bleed Fer' Me, Life Leaka, den another Life Leaka.

Healing stays da same too. 'Ey, Quit Bleedin' an' Gork'll Fix It fer light wounds. Den use Bigger, Better, An' Greener fer bigga wounds. Use yer Morale abilities too once dey light up.

Levelin' Up

Rank 1-10

Ahh home sour home, dis startin' place iz Mount Bloodhorn. Mmmm you smells dat? Yes yes dat was me. So here at da greenskin starting zone, you get to meet other greenskin. Yes dere iz more of you so don't be jealous. Dey all over da place here. You got small greenskins an' tall greenskins. You even got greenskins dat sell you stuff. Dat be Gagdush. Him not dat important tho you can sell yer junk dere. Him likes junk so sell dem often. Most important greenskin to know iz Sogsnag Grubsnout da Career Trainer. Here you need to visit da Career Trainer once you rank up. You can buy Core abilities from 'im an' train yer Mastery abilities too. Next important greenskins iz dem ones dat get a book on dere heads. From dem you get quests dat helps you level up. Fer deez Ranks 1-10, take all da quests you can get an' complete dem. You get some nice armor an' weapons as rewards, even potions to make you feel real gud. Yes, I calls dem pots.

When you're around Rank 5 you shouldbe around Ugrog's Bash. Here iz yer first encounter wif PQs, public quests. When you click on yer Open Parties an' Warbands button under yer Health bar, you can see all da active groups in yer area. Join dem if you like tho you can do PQs and PvE all by yerself. When fightin' in deez PQs, you get to earn tons of experience points an' some influence points too. Speak to Maggut about influence rewards. Him iz da Rally Masta too so bind here fer recalls. Dat means you can come back here using yer Battle Map. Der iz three levels of influence rewards: basic, advanced, an' elite. Hey snotling, of course elite iz da bestest. I likes to stick around PQs to gain da elite rewards. Dem real nice rewards, plus PQs get you more experience points fer ranking up quicker. Once you get done wif deez continue on wif yer PvE quests. Dis will take you to da next chapter fer greenskins. Dere iz more PQs like Sharpthorn Wud an' Ironclaw Camp along da way so work on dem too to get yer ranks up faster. As you walk around Mount Bloodhorn, you notice dat you get points too fer discoverin' new places. I likes to walk around so I seez all parts of da map.

Da War Maker iz a camp wif merchants, trainers. Make sure you sell yer junk you pick up as loot to dem merchants. No needs to be carry dem in yer backpack. Here at da camp pick up more quests an' complete dem. From dere you move on to Chapter 3 Komar. Dis iz another camp wif more quests, merchants, an' trainers. Don't forget to get yerself trained when you rank up.

By Ranks 8-10 you shouldbe at Screeb's Stunty Killin'. Here you get tons of merchants like armor an' weapons merchants. Den dere iz more quest givers too so get dem an' complete dem. Dis area too will be yer first encounter wif RvR battlegrounds. Enter da Stunty Killin' Camp to be flagged fer RvR. Here you get to RvR and fight other players from da Order side. You earn tons of experience points but most of all Renown points. See me details on Renown points above. Dere iz even a Renown Trainer here at Screeb's Stunty Killin' named Tofuz Gutsticka.

Rank 11-20

Next stop iz Ekrund zone. You get dere through da RvR battlegrounds at da very top of da map or you get dere through Crawla Cave. Once in Ekrund you can continue fightin' in da RvR battlegrounds an' try to capture some battlefield objectives. Dis iz capture points marked by flags dat you control fer Destruction. Outside of Crawla Cave iz Gorgor's Smash. 'Ere you get more quests. Dere iz lots 'o quests here so do dem. Dere iz da PQ called Broketoof Camp dats real fun killin' dem Broketoof Boyz. Get in dere an' get some influence rewards. Again as you get stronger an' rank up, go back to dem quests dat was too tuff fer you lil snotling. Don't ferget to buy yer Core abilities from da Career Trainer an' sell dem junk you loot off of corpses. As you get to camp make sure you find da Rally Masta and bind yer location. While you're here in Ekrund zone, participate in da Gates of Ekrund scenario. You get to earn experience quickly an' Renown points, plus dey fun too to kill dem stunties.

If you get a chance, den debuff an' cast damaging spells on yer target, but make sure yer group iz always healed first.

These Are a Few of Firebag's Favorite Things

1. Winnin' a big fight.

2. Cuttin' stunties' beards off. It makes dem real mad!

3. Castin' spells. It feels all warm and squooshy like mud in yer trousers.

4. Warm roasted kittens all tied up wiv string.

5. Countin' da numba of knuckles I can fit up me nose.

6. "Eatin' mushrooms. Dey make my bum talk.

7. Trippin' up gits wot is smaller den me an den hidin' behind gits wot is bigger dan wot the little git is.

8. Puttin' stones in git ears while dey is asleep. Dey is real angry when dey wake up.

9. Gettin' a bigger stick an' fancier pants 'cos I did a quest fing.

10. Da warm glow of satisfaction I gets from knowing I is da heart and soul of a dead gud warband.

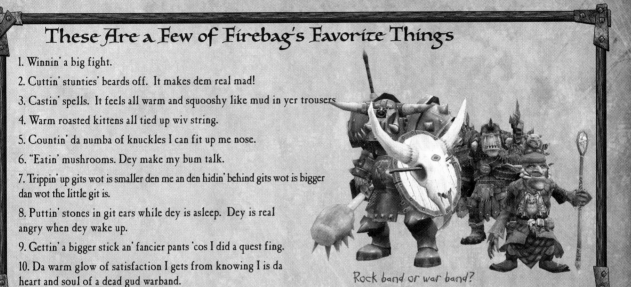

Rock band or war band?

Next stop iz Barak Varr. Here you get da Mourkain Temple scenerio. Join it likes in Ekrund an' earn more experience plus influence points. Da PQs are here too, so complete dem an' get yer elite rewards. In Barak Varr you get to take over some battlefield objectives likes Dok Karaz. Try to help out wif deez objectives to help you rank up quicker. It's a big help too so you're not always doing da same things. You continue in Tier 2 an' move to Marshes of Madness. In da center iz da battlefield Fangbreaka Swamp, da RvR area. Join it an' get some stunties. Once you finish dere, make yer way around an' continue to pick up more quests. To da south iz da Tower of Neborhest. Dis iz filled wif tons of baddies. Come dere wif some friends. Now iz time fer the Badlands.

Rank 21-30

Welcome to da Badlands. Yer first things you want to kill here iz dem trolls. Tuff ugly beats wif lumps on dere backs, real nasty. Hey almost looks like...nevermind. Stay focused. Continue on north part toward da Black Tar Canyon. Dere you run into da Mutant Exiles an' Fireforge's Camp PQs. Have some fun here, get yer rewards, den move on already. Fight deez damn stunties. Dere iz so many of dem, I can't stands it. At da top you get to Trug's Hut. You get tons o' questin' here. An' don't forgett 'bout da merchants selling dere goods. Sell yers to dem too. Get yer Core abilities at da Career Trainer. Make sure as you get more Core, Tactics, an' Morale abilities you set up yer Action bars.

To da north passage you can get to Black Fire Pass. Dere zi even more stunties just waitin' to be killed. Bring some buddies wif you cuz it gets hairy up dere. Right through da Empire Gate iz da Statue of Inspiration PQ. Get yer kills, loot, an' rewards an' get going. Dere iz another PQ called Thardrik Smashin' just a down da path. Finish dat off an' get movin'. Through da Black Fire Pass Gate, you find Moogz's Brawl camp. Dere get yerself some rest, more quests, an' trainin'. If you back track den head north you will run into Grimbeard Station. Get yer fill on stunties dere. Continue on north to da next PQ called Altstadt. Further north from dere iz Gnol Baraz da battlefield objective. Join forces wif yer Destruction friends an' try to take it from dem Squig haters from Order. Head back down to do Moonfang Remnant PQ an' kill sum Moonfangs. Dey iz bad Goblins. Finish dem off an' grab yer loot. Next down da path iz Hindelburg. At Umgal Pass up da path north iz stunty fortress. Dere you come across Kolaz Umgal PQ. Go get some action dere an' you be on yer way to higher ranks. Head back down toward da Badlands an' da southeast passage of Black Tar Canyon toward da Savage Wastes. Join in da PQs an' pick up more quests as you head toward Black Crag.

During RvR or campaigns, use dem siege weapons an' let greenskin enginuity—you know wot I means—work fer you.

Level 31-40

Black Crag iz where you begin yer journey from Ranks 31-40. Yer gonna run into Red Dust Camp where you can find all da comfort of home. At Black Crag dere iz two scenarios you can join, Thunder Valley an' Logrin's Forge. As wif most scenarios, capturing flag points an' treasure gets you points to win. Take a break from questin' an' join deez. You can get some more Renown points too when you kill some players. Dere are battlefield objectives here to capture, so get dem too. Black Crag marks da Tier 4 area. Dis means you're a bad greenskin like me, but not as gud as me git. Den dere iz bunch 'o PQs to do, so keep yer good eye out fer dem.

To da south iz Butcher's Pass. Dere iz da Destruction greenskin fortress an' city. Den to da north iz Thunder Mountain. Dere you can find Mudja's Warcamp wif plenty of quests fer battleground objectives an' merchants all over selling dere goods. Thunder Mountain iz major battlegrounds fer stunties vs. greenskins. Here you be gettin' more an' more Renown points. Use dem points nicely an' you'll be one tuff Blasta. Dis iz where you make yer stand an' battle it out wif dem drunk stunties. Finish up yer questin' an' join da battle. You'll be on yer way to Ranks 40 in no time.

Don't be scared to run when da tuff get hammered. Take off likes da greenskin you iz.

BEATIN' ON PLAYERS AN' SMART POINTIES

Solo PvP

So you want to know how to fight blasta 'n stunty? Yes you do. Let's get started. You iz a Shaman an' will always be a Shaman. Dat means you not fightin' green toe to stubby toe. No, you fight from real far. Yes, we be throwin' dem damagin' spells an' debuffs to save our greenskin. Below I shows you how what to use fer da range of ranks. Dis same strategy iz used fer skirmishes, battlefield, scenario, an' campaigns. Dem tactics not change cuz you still be doing same thing just different objectives fer each.

Ranks 1-10

Cast Yer Not So Bad on target to steal 240 APs, cast Life Leaka, Bunch O' *Waaagh!*, Bleed Fer' Me, Life Leaka, den another Life Leaka, den repeat from start.

Ranks 11-20

Cast against spellcasters: Get'n Smarter, Yer Not So Bad, Life Leaka, Bunch O' *Waaagh!*, Bleed Fer' Me, Life Leaka, den another Life Leaka, den repeat from start.

Cast against melee fighters: Yer A Weaklin', Yer Not So Bad, Life Leaka, Bunch O' *Waaagh!*, Bleed Fer' Me, Life Leaka, den another Life Leaka, den repeat from start.

Ranks 21-30

Cast against spellcasters: Get'n Smarter, Yer Not So Bad, Life Leaka, Bunch O' *Waaagh!*, Bleed Fer' Me, Life Leaka, den another Life Leaka, den repeat from start.

Cast against melee fighters: Yer A Weaklin', Yer Not So Bad, Life Leaka, Bunch O' *Waaagh!*, Bleed Fer' Me, Life Leaka, den another Life Leaka, den repeat from start.

Tanks 31-40

Cast against spellcasters: Get'n Smarter, You Got Nuthin!, Yer Not So Bad, Life Leaka, Bunch O' *Waaagh!*, Bleed Fer' Me, Life Leaka, den another Life Leaka, den repeat from start.

Cast against melee fighters: Yer A Weaklin', Scuse Me!, Yer Not So Bad, Life Leaka, Bunch O' *Waaagh!*, Bleed Fer' Me, Life Leaka, den another Life Leaka, den repeat from start.

Da trick iz to watch yer *WAAAGH!* Make sure you always try to max dis out to get full advantage of yer godly powers. Don't fergit to use dem Morale abilities too. I wud respec yer Morale an' Tactics. Use me guide above fer more details. I wud respec to da Damage Dealer Shaman. Now you iz battle ready.

Group Play

So now you want some friends to battle wif you. Same tactics above iz used on yer offensive fer any PVP situation. Da difference now iz yer role in da group. Yer main focus iz keepin' yer group alive.

Constantly use Use Bigger, Better, An' Greener fer big heals an' wif Mork's *Waaagh!*. Fer quick heals use 'Ey, Quit Bleedin' an' Divine Favor Morale ability fer added healing ability. Now yer focus here iz target da enemy yer tank or DPS group members are fightin' an cast yer debuffs, den continue wif offensive attacks, dat I sez to you. Watching yer group members, especially yer tank's health, keep dem constantly healed. Order of importance to heal first den to last important classes would be yer group tank iz always first, den yer DPS members, den da other healers if dey hurt.

Yer Morale an' Tactics need to switch to yer Healer Shaman setup fer group play. You need to respec yer Shaman to be an effective Healer Shaman. Once geared up an' ready to go, make sure to have Mork's Buffer always casted an' 'Ere We Go! before each encounter. Den dere iz Don' Feel Nuthin fer extra protection fer yer group an' constantly cast Gather Round as needed fer group heals. Keep da heals goin' an' yer gonna be fine. Otherwise you get some angry groupies. When you do get time to do some debuff an' offensive damage, focus all of it on da stunty dat yer tank iz killin'. Dat help dem kill stunties quicker.

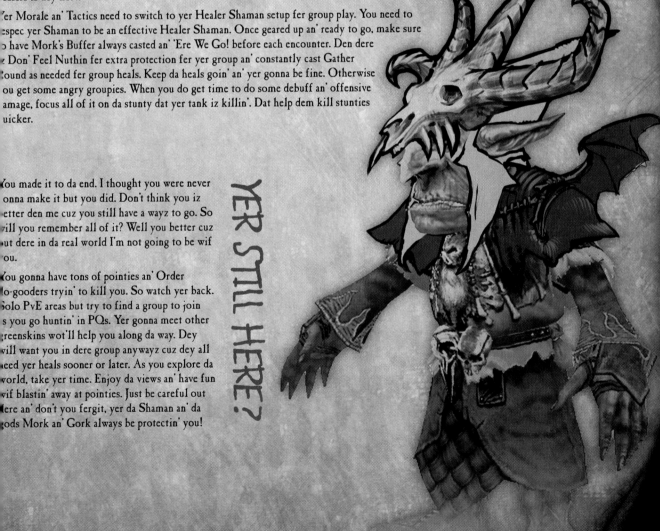

You made it to da end. I thought you were never gonna make it but you did. Don't think you iz better den me cuz you still have a wayz to go. So will you remember all of it? Well you better cuz out dere in da real world I'm not going to be wif you.

You gonna have tons of pointies an' Order do-gooders tryin' to kill you. So watch yer back. Solo PvE areas but try to find a group to join as you go huntin' in PQs. Yer gonna meet other greenskins wot'll help you along da way. Dey will want you in dere group anywayz cuz dey all need yer heals sooner or later. As you explore da world, take yer time. Enjoy da views an' have fun wif blastin' away at pointies. Just be careful out dere an' don't you fergit, yer da Shaman an' da gods Mork an' Gork always be protectin' you!

YER STILL HERE?

SQUIG HERDER

Ahh me pretty minion always wif a nice smile. Doze sharp teef an' yer stinkin' breath iz nice. Your horns gettin' bigger too, dats nice. Hey dere why you come bother me here? Can't you see I'm tendin' to my Squig? Oh so you want to learn more about deez Squigz eh? You come to da right place den.

Squigfly iz me name an' Squigz iz da name of me game. I'm a Squig Herder from deez parts here in da Mount Bloodhorn. I got no home though, dis whole place iz me home. I live here an' dere wif me Squigz. Dere me best buds of all deez lands. I'm nuttin wif out dem an' dats da truth. Dem be yer best buds if you know how to use 'em. So you come wif me an' I'll show you how to use dem Squigz.

I'z just a simple Squig Herder but you never want to get into a fight wif me or me Squigz. I'm an expert herder an' know what to do wif dem. My arrers iz best arrers in dez parts of Mount Bloodhorn. No one other den me knows how to train Squigz 'n use arrers like me. I knows arrers real gud, but I'z not so gud wif me spear. Gud enough though, so don't mess wif me. My armor's not so gud either but I run real fast. Squig Herders iz not tanks so I stay away from da front lines. Tanks are dem dumb players dat take da most hits from dere enemy while teammates like me stand bac 'n support. I don't like to get hit so I stand way back. Don't worry, I got your back when we fight dem stunties.

You should know dat I come from da Bloody Sun Boyz tribe. We iz da baddest bunch in da Badlands. No one's betta' den us, especially when us gobbos an dem Orcs unite. So get ready all you stunties out dere, itza time fer *WAAAGH!*

By Squigfl

What iz a Squig Herder?

Squig Herders are hunters, ranged fighters that slay the enemy before swords can taste their flesh. They are quite useful as supplemental troops that damage the foe as others clog the front lines, and they have pets, called "Squigs," that battle by their sides.

The roles of a Squig Herder are many. While the nettlesome Squigs attack and distract the enemy, the Squig Herders fire arrows into the vulnerabilities between shield, armor, and helm. They have an arrow for every situation. Should a difficult foe tie up valuable resources for a long time, the Squig Herder can choose a poison arrow to drop that foe faster. An exploding arrow harms a handful of clumped enemies, inflicting greater harm and panic than a single shaft. The special choking arrow silences its target, which serves as an effective counter to those spellcasting cowards who love to hide behind walls of troops and rain down destruction.

As a commander, what value do I see in this greenskin class? Few match up to my standards, but the Squig Herder can deal tremendous, long-range damage. They are adept at our hit-and-run tactics, when we need to harass an enemy or bring down a large foe over time without engaging in melee. They are a fragile breed, with nothing but very light armor for defense, so we encourage only those greenskins who resist the urge to charge into battle and can sit behind to support their allies. If you can handle a restless Squig and bend it to your will, you may enjoy your time as a Squig Herder, and possibly live a day longer.

—Baron Heinar Balethar, Zimmeron's Hold, Chaos Wastes

Pick up all quests even if you don't like the wayz someone's eyeballin' yer Squig. You might be at an area wot iz part of dem quests so it's easy to complete.

STARTIN' SKILLS

Let's talk about yer base starter skills. First off, you get Auto Attack an' Flee. Dem iz simple enough to unda'stand. Use Auto Attack if yer lazy, den use Flee if you're scared. Plink iz fer your arrers to shoot dem stunties from long range. Den you get Stabbity to stab dem when close to you. You get a bestest friend to help too, so use Summon Squig to get a Squig to help you.

Fer a stats on a Squig Herder, you best get some Ballistic skills an' as much as possible. Ballistic skills help your arrers hurt more. Dis iz yer main attack. Get some Toughness an' Initiative if you can cuz your armor iz not so gud. Dey help you survive longer in battle. If you can, get some Wounds too to boost yer hit points. Dat be gud fer lasting longer too. Defensive stats iz real simple, jess get some. Get as much of Block dat you can to avoid gettin' hit lots from melee an' ranged attacks. Next be Parry den Dodge as most important to get some points in.

BEIN' A GREENSKIN

Greenskins are da savages of da land. We likes to collect all things around us especially scraps of metal dat we turn into new armor an' weapons. Squig Herders are greenskin Goblins dat are smaller version of dere tougher an' taller greenskin brothers, da Orcs. Dem Orcs though not so smart an' cunning like me. We are part of da Destruction side of da armies of *WAR*. We wud like nothin' else den to rid deez lands of doze stubborn stunties called Dwarfs, our sworn enemies.

Me fellow brothers of da Bloody Sun Boyz can do just dat. Dey iz da toughest bunch of greenskins I know in da Badlands. Dey grow stronger every day an' waiting just fer da right time to rid of doze stunties. You will see. We greenskins will get more greenskins den we attack. We build up an' gather armies beyond yer imagination. Hmm head hurtz from dat one. Den when we are ready, we will have our *WAAAGH!*

Me home sweet home, Mount Bloodhorn. Dis iz where you be startin'. iz also filled wif Bloody Sun Boyz a runnin' here an' dere. Da fresh stench dat you smell makes me mouth water. We nicely decorate dis place wif big pointy sticks in da ground an' piles of junk all around. You'll see tons of other Squigz trainers too. On wot hill over dere iz a bunch of big tooth Orcs using some lobbers. Dem lobbers iz fer shootin' at Stunty Mountain jess accross da way. Make yerself feel at home here. I like to practice me arrers on dem stunties at Da Stump. Though me favorite iz to get me bath at Da Slop an' just roll around, maybe I'll scoop up a bite while I'z dere too. I feels so fresh an' full an' ready to kill. I know wot gets you excited, don't it?

Before you get too crazy, let's check out da NPCs dat be helpin' you. You meet Mogg Squigchasa da Guild Registrar. Him'll get you guilded but you need some other buddies. Next you see Sogsnag Grubsnout. He's da Career Trainer an' will help you wif Core Training an' Mastery Training. Him very important so you best so not to ferget him. Close to him iz Gagdush da Merchant. He'll rob you blind if hee can, but his wares iz needed so don't kill him just yet. Den dere Greeble da Healer. He's gud at healing, I just don't trust him. Down da path dere you meets Maggut. He'z where you bind an' recall. Bindin' iz da place where you can recall if needed an' recall iz fer taking you dere. Dere more NPCs here an' dere, so just keep your gud eye out fer dem.

You start wif only a few items as a Squig Herder. Here iz your starter gear: Me Nicest Shirt, Me Nicest Pants, Me Ol' Prodda, and Me Best Ol' Arrer Shoota. Nice stuf, right?

Squig Herders can only use spears fer melee an' bows fer ranged weapons. We get to wear only light armor too an' nothin' else. Dis iz gud so you can focus on da bestest of dem weapons an' armor. Fer spears, use da ones wot do da most damage per second (DPS fer you that likes to talk likes those Dark Elf commanders that thinks they knows everythin'). If you get spears wot almost da same den use da fastest one an' one dat has bestest bonus stats like Initiative an' Strength. Initative helps you avoid attacks an' Strength adds to yer DPS. When picking which bow to use, find one wot has da bestest DPS an' da fastest attack. Dem two iz da most important fer you to have. Den if you get more bows wif same DPS an' speed, pick da one dat has bestest stats like Ballisticsan' Initiative. Dem stats will keep yer arrers hittin gudder and keep yer green skin alive.

Armor iz da same thing as weapons when it comes to stats. Use armor dat has bestest armor points fer defense den find ones dat have bestest stats in Ballistics an' Toughness an' Initiative. All da rest stats are just added bonus. Deez stats are da ones you need to focus on. Again, you're a Squig Herder, not a tank. You stay back, way back, an' shoot dem arrers.

Best 5 Puncture Points fer Stunties

Like any other greenskin, I don't like Stunties. Over da years me go to exotic lands learnin' ancient secrets dat I want to pass along to you. Far Far out, way past da Badlands iz a place where dey practice wat dey call "puncture points." It iz said dat each point will do different things to yer body. Having learned der ways me now ready to show you deez techniques an' da bestest ways to use puncture points on Stunties.

4. Shoot arrer at throat wif Choking Arrer. Dis causes stunty to upchuck dere last pint of ale wot makes 'em choke, den dey turn green likes us. Nice color fer dem.

3. Shoot arrer at right temple wif Poison Arrer. Dis will cause stunty hair to fall off. Ever see a hairless stunty before?

2. Shoot arrer at left bottom cheek wif Explodin' Arrer. Dis will cause stunty bend over an' act like a flame thrower.

5. Shoot arrer at der belly button wif Shoot Thru Ya. Dis deadly point as it causes da stunty to look like a water fountain...err, in dis case an ale fountain.

1. Shoot arrer below stunty knee caps wif Stop Runnin! Dis will dizable his stubby legs from movin'.

Find da Rally Masta an' bind yer recall point where you be spending some time at in case you need to get back quickly.

When you don't have any healing pots on you, use yer Tastes Like Chicken ability fer a quick refresh, den summon other Squig. Avoid dis if you can but it iz needed sometimes especially during battle.

GUD THINGS AN' NOT SO GUD THINGS

Gud Things

- I get strong Squigz to help kill baddies. Dere iz four different types of Squigz to use, each wif dere own useful skills.

- Squigz can be used fer many things such as pulling, distraction, decoy, an' killin'.

- I get long range assault fer killin' baddies wif me bow. I have different types of arrers to use, each wif dere own use, like stopping dem from using magic, slowing dem down, an' lowering dem Initiative. skills like Run 'n Shoot nice too so I don't need to stop runnin'.

- Gud DPS especially wif help of Squig.

- Squigz gud fer eating too, so Squig Herders can heal. Dem Tastes Like Chicken.

You're a Squig Herder, don't ever ferget it. Dem yer bestest weapons in deez lands. Use dem to do yer fightin', pullin', chasin', runnin', killin', diztractin', everythin'. Dem gud eatin' too so don't be shy, take a bite out of dem when yer health iz low. Dem Squigz are dere fer you! As a hunter wif ranged abilities, use dem as yer trengths. Stand back from da crowd an' start plinkin'. Plinkin an' a runnin', dats what keeps you breathin'.

Not So Gud Things

- Can only use light armor. Dis iz abig problem so don't let baddies touch you.

- Can heal but only by eating yer Squig, den yer Squig iz dead an' baddies chase ya...not so gud.

- Melee attack iz limited an' not so gud, but you're a gud runner.

- Can solo well but yer not so gud against two or more baddies, so it's better if yer in party.

So yer armor iz not so gud like dem dumb Orcs. Dey ugly anyways. You look da bestest wif yer armor, only problem iz it's weak. So don't be a runnin' into battle wif yer weak armor. Sit back an' do what a hunter needs to do, go plink plink. If dem stunties get close to you, yer in trouble. Stab 'em an' cut 'em an'do whatever you can, jess get out of dere an' flee. Keep yer distance an' you'll be alive tomorrow mornin'.

IZ AN' ABILITIES

Abilities

Dere are Core an' Mastery Training fer all classes. You get dis training from da Career Trainers. Fer more details on Core abilities, look at da skills lists wot I put fer you on all deez pages. You start gettin' one point at Rank 11, wif a total of 25 Mastery points once at Rank 40. Squig Herders get three paths fer Mastery Training:

Path of Big Shootin': Increases de Core abilities What Blocka?, Gas Squig, Explodin' Arrer, Choking Arrer, an' Lots o' Arrers

Path of Stabbin': Increases de Core abilities Chomp, Cut Ya!, Horned Squig, Drop That!!, an' Squig Armor

Path of Quick Shootin': Increases de Core abilities Yer Bleedin'!, Stop Runnin!, Run 'n Shoot, Spiked Squig, Not So Fast!, Shoot Thru Ya

So which ya think iz da bestest path to take, you sez? Dats all up to your play style. Keep in mind wot a Squig Herder was designed to be a ranged DPS fighter. Wif dat I says Path of Big Shootin' an' Path of Quick Shootin' should both get more points den Path of Stabbin'. Each path only goes up to 15 points wif da last Mastery ability giving da most damage. You can specialize a bit here an' dere, but it's bestest to concentrate on only two paths so you can

Path of Stabbin' uses Chomp, which iz big damage dealer fer me horned Squig. Horned Squig iz yer bestest Squig to use cuz it's strong against physical attacks an' wot'swhat you really need. Cut Ya! iz your bestest melee ability o wot's real important too. Drop That!! iz nice but you need to get close o your enemy, which I don't do so much. An' dere iz Squig Armor wot ot let me shoot me arrers so I don't use so much either, but iz fun from time to time. Dat leaves not much abilities fer dis path.

> Don't be afraid to use yer Squig as a meatshield, you can get more! Don' be afraid to throw yer Squig in front of a nastie.

Den we get Path of Quick Shootin'. Dis get six Core abilities fer Mastery starting wif Yer Bleedin'!, a Core ability wot I use lots cuz it iz instant ast. I use da next one Stop Runnin! all da time cuz I don't like to get close to baddies an' dis slows dem down. One of me favorites iz Run 'n Shoot. hich iz a real nice damage dealer on da run. I don't use spiked Squig so much unless I need ranged Squig. Not So Fast! iz a gud Core ability fer owering Initiative on da enemy. Da next abilities an dat iz another favorite: Shoot Thru Ya, which damages many baddies in front of me. Dis path ts lotsa gud Core abilities wots real useful.

When you play da Squig Herder, you get tons of time to think about which path iz da bestest fer you, at least until Rank 11. Which is when you get er first Mastery point. Den you still need to get two more to even get a Mastery ability. An by then you should have a gud idea which path you ike. You can respecialize if you change yer mind wif da Mastery points. Move dem around if needed. Wif da Mastery abilities, you get Career actics an' Morale abilities too. Read more about dem next.

Abilities

Name	Level	Path	Cost	Range (in feet)	Type	Build	Duration	Reuse	Description
Stabbity	Starter Ability	Stabbin'	30	Melee	Melee Attack	0s	0s	0s	Deals (150+DPS) damage. Usable outside of Squig Armor.
Plink	Starter Ability	Big Shootin'	30	5-100	Ranged Attack	2s	0s	0s	Basic long range attack. Deals (187+DPS)*1.33. (Granted a free step.)
Yer Bleedin'!	Level 2	Quick Shootin'	25	5-65.	Ranged Attack - Ailment	0s	15s	0s	Deals (187+DPS)*1.33 over 15s.
What Blocka?	Level 3	Big Shootin'	40	5-100	Ranged Attack	1.5s	10s	5s	Can not be defended. Deals (225+DPS) damage.
Chomp	Level 4	Stabbin'	40	Melee	Melee Attack	0s	0s	10s	Player deals (75+DPS) damage to target. Pet deals 75 damage to his personal target. If Player and pet are within 60ft of each other's target, then they also deal their damage to each other's target. Usable inside and outside of Squig Armor.
Stop Runnin!	Level 5	Quick Shootin'	25	5-65.	Ranged Attack - Ailment	1s	10s	20s	Deals (112+DPS) damage and snares the target by 40% for 10s. Usable while moving.
Run 'n Shoot	Level 6	Quick Shootin'	30	5-65.	Ranged Attack	1s	0s	0s	Deals 112+DPS damage. Usable while moving.
Don't Eat Me	Level 7	Core	20	100	Detaunt	0s	15s	15s	Detaunts (50%) target for 15s.
Farty Squig	Level 8	Core	55	100	Pet Command	0s	0s	20s	Pet explodes dealing 375 damage to enemies within 360 units. Pet dies. Next Squig pet cast iz instant.
Cut Ya!	Level 8	Stabbin'	25	Melee	Melee Attack - Ailment	0s	0s	0s	Deals (412+DPS)*1.33 damage over 15s. Usable outside of Squig Armor.
Squig Armor	Level 9	Stabbin'	55	Self	Buff	2s	Toggle	60s	Self Buff. Increases Wounds 20%. Increases Strength and Toughness 3/level (stacks with everything).
Ard Noggin	Level 9	Stabbin'	30	Melee	Melee Attack	0s	0s	0s	Deals (150+DPS) damage, reduces threat on your pet's next attack. Usable only in Squig Armor.
Sticky Squigz	Level 10	Core	30	PBAE	CC - Cripple	0	5s	20s	PBAE root for 5s. Radius: 30ft.

Abilities

Name	Level	Path	Cost	Range (in feet)	Type	Build	Duration	Reuse	Description
Squig Frenzy	Level 12	Core	35	100	Pet Buff	0s	30s	3m	Increases all auto attack damage dealt by your Squig by 50%.
Explodin' Arrer	Level 14	Big Shootin'	35	5-100	Ranged Attack - Ailment	2s	9s	10s	Deals 199 Elemental damage to initial target and places a 249 DoT over 9s on targets in radius. Radius: 20ft.
Lots o' Arrers	Level 16	Big Shootin'	30/S	5-100	Ranged Channeled Attack	0s	3s	8s	Deals (187+DPS)*0.5 damage every 0.5s for 3s. Being hit while channeling removes 0.5s from the duration of the ability.
Not So Fast!	Level 18	Quick Shootin'	30	5-65.	Ranged Attack - Cripple	1s	10s	10s	Deal (150+DPS) and lower target Init by 2/level for 10s. Usable while moving.
Tastes Like Chicken	Level 20	Core	15	100	Pet Command	0s	0s	60s	Sacrifice the Squig pet for a 375 heal. Healed amount iz proportionate to pet's health (100% when pet iz at 100%, 50% when pet iz at 50%, etc.) Next Squig pet cast iz instant.
Big Claw	Level 20	Stabbin'	25	Melee	Melee Attack	0s	0s	5s	Deals (262+DPS)*1.33 damage over 9s, and snares target by 40% for 9s. Usable only in Squig Armor.
Drop That!!	Level 25	Stabbin'	20	Melee	Melee Attack - Cripple	1s	5s	20s	Pet's next attack will cause an additional 150 dmg, and disarm the target for 5 sec. No GCD. Usable inside and outside of Squig Armor.
Don't Hit Me!	Level 30	Stabbin'	30	Melee	Melee Attack	0s	0s	10s	Deals (187+DPS) and interrupts target's building ability.
Bounce	Level 30	Stabbin'	30	Melee	Melee Attack	0s	2s	20s	Deals (150+DPS) and knocks down enemy for 3s. Usable only in Squig Armor
Choking Arrer	Level 35	Big Shootin'	30	5-100	Ranged Attack - Cripple	1s	5s	30s	Deals (150+DPS) damage and silences enemy for 5s.
Shoot Thru Ya	Level 40	Quick Shootin'	45	LAE	Ranged Attack	2s	0s	0s	Deal (187+DPS)*1.33 to targets in radius. Arc: 200, radius: 65ft.
BOOM!	Level 40	Stabbin'	35	Melee	Melee Attack	0s	0s	0s	Squig Armor explodes. Squig Armor dispels, knocks Squig Herder straight up. PBAE damage 375 and long knock-back all enemies within 30ft radius. Squig Armor cannot be used again for 60s. Radius: 30ft.
Pets									
Summon Squig	Starter Ability	Core	55	Self	Pet Summon	2s	N/A	30s	Toggled. Summons a basic Squig, with the following monster Mask. * Increased Wounds (+33%) * Increased Toughness (+33%) * Auto attack - Speed: 2s, DPS: (No Change). Pet generates 3x normal hate.
Death from Above	Level 23 - Basic	Core	N/A	Melee	Pet Melee Attack	0s	0s	20s	Pet knocks down target for 3s.

Abilities

Name	Level	Path	Cost	Range (in feet)	Type	Build	Duration	Reuse	Description
Squig Squeal	Starter - Basic	Core	N/A	Melee	Pet Melee Attack	0s	5s	10s	Pet taunts (30%, 5s) all targets in radius. Arc: 120, radius: 30ft.
Horned Squig	Level 8	Big Shootin'	55	Self	Pet Summon	2s	0s	30s	Toggled. Summons a Horned Squig pet. * Melee auto attack - Speed: 2.4s, DPS: (0%) Monster DPS. Buffs Squig Herder with: Ranged abilities have a 10% increase range.
Head Butt	Level 21 - Horned	Big Shootin'	N/A	Melee	Squig Ability	0s	0s	20s	Deals 112 damage and medium knock-backs target.
Gore	Level 8 - Horned	Big Shootin'	N/A	Melee	Squig Ability - Cripple	0s	5s	8s	Deals 187 damage to target and makes the target bleed for 100 damage over 5s.
Gas Squig	Level 9	Stabbin'	55	Self	Summon Pet	2s	N/A	30s	Toggled. Summons a Gas Squig Pet. *Decreased Toughness (-33%) * *De-creased Wounds (-33%) * Ranged auto attack - Speed: 2.2s. Generates 50% of normal hate (half as much). DPS: (0%) Monster DPS. Buffs the Squig Herder with: Increase armor by 100%.
Bad Gas	Level 19 - Gas	Stabbin'	N/A	100	Squig Ability	2s	5s	10s	Deals 249 damage to targets in the radius. Heals pet and Squig Herder (if he iz in Squig Armor) in radius for 149. Radius 30ft.
Goop Shootin'	Level 9 - Gas	Stabbin'	N/A	100	Squig Ability	2s	0s	4s	Deals 149 damage to targets in the radius. Radius: 20ft.
Spiked Squig	Level 10	Quick Shootin'	55	Self	Pet Summon	2s	N/A	30s	Toggled. Summons a Spiked Squig pet. *Decreased Toughness (-33%) * Ranged auto attack - Speed: 1.8s, DPS: (0%). Gives the Squig Herder increased crit chance by 5%.
Spine Fling	Level 17 - Spiked	Quick Shootin'	N/A	100	Squig Ability	0s	0s	13s	Channeled. Deals 112 damage ever 1s for 3s. Setback override: 100%.
Poisoned Spine	Level 10 - Spiked	Quick Shootin'	N/A	Pet	Squig Ability - Ailment	0s	5s	5s	Deals 100 damage over 5s and lowers target's critical chance by 10% for 5s.

Carry tons of heal pots, wots potions to you young gobbos! Use dem pots fer healing an' other pots fer buffs cuz you don't want to lose yer Squig fer health.

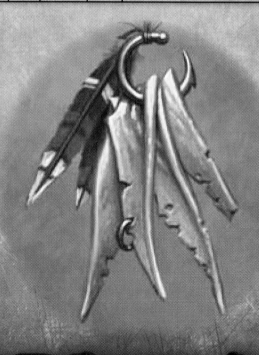

Morale

Deez Morale abilities are learned from da Career Trainers. Dere are four Morale slots to fill in' four ranks of Morale. Squig Herders get a total of nine Morale abilities wif three of dem Mastery Morale abilities. Deez Morale slots light up as you build dem up in combat. Da more you fight an' win battles, da quicker a Morale slot lights up. Dey will light up in order from Rank 1, Rank 2, Rank 3, den Rank 4. Da higher da rank, da stronger your Morale iz. You can only use one rank at a time. Once used you need to build it up again.

Timing an' knowing when to use Morale ability iz key to winning battles. You need to choose wisely which one you gonna put in dem Morale slots. Let's go over a few. Fer Rank 1 I like to go wif Point-Blank. Dis knocks yer enemy back an' does gud damage. It's gud fer keeping dem fat stunties from touchin' you. Fer a group buff an' Rank 1, I wud go fer Soothin' Mushroom Wrap. Dis iz nice fer 50 percent fewer action points fer 10 seconds. Fer Rank 2, a real nice Morale ability to have iz Squig Goo. Dis iz an area-effect attack wot deals high damage over nine seconds to all enemies within 30 feet, an' roots dem by 60 percent. Now dats a real sticky situation. Rank 3 I likes to use either Explosive Shots wot makes all ranged attacks xplode, dealing sum damage to all baddies within 30 feet of yer target. Dis lasts fer da next 10 seconds when used. Other gud Morale ability fer Rank 3 iz Squigbeast. Dis makes your Squig get big an' does triple damage fer 15 seconds, real crazy. Now fer Rank 4 you only get one choice an' dat be Hail of Doom. You focus on one spot fer five seconds an' constantly shootin' all baddies within 30 feet of dat area fer gud damage. It'z like fireworks.

Dem are me faves but you need to see fer yerself. You can always change 'em any time.

Name	Level	Rank	Range (in feet)	Duration	Description
Point-Blank	Level 8	Rank 1	65	0	Attack that deals 600 damage and performs a long knockback on the target.
Unshakable Focus	Level 12	Rank 2	Self	10s	Self buff. For 7s, increase damage dealt by 100%.
Concealment	Level 16	Rank 1	Self	10s	Increase chance to disrupt and evade attacks by 100% for 7s.
Focused Mind	Level 20	Rank 2	Self	7s	For 10s, build times are reduced by 50%. Character purges and iz immune to silence, disarm, root, snare, and setback.
Explosive Shots	Level 24	Rank 3	Self	10s	Self buff. For 10s, ranged attacks explode in a AE around the target for an additional 300 damage. Radius: 30ft. Can only activate 1 per second.
Soothin' Shroom Wrap	Level 28	Rank 1	Group	10s	Group buff. Group member's actions cost 50% less AP.
Squig Goo	Level 32	Rank 2	100	9s	Targeted AE attack that deals 900 over 9s and snares the targets by 60%. Radius: 30ft.
Squigbeast	Level 36	Rank 3	166	15s	Pet buff. Triples pet damage output, increases size of pet. Lasts 15s.
Hail of Doom	Level 40	Rank 4	100	5s	Channeled TAE. Deal 300 damage to all targets in the area every 0.5s. Max duration: 5s.
Lots of Shootin'	Big Shootin' x15	Rank 4	100	0s	Deals 2,400 damage. Radius: 30ft.
Wind Up da *Waaagh!*	Stabbin' x15	Rank 4	PBAE	0s	Deals 2,400 damage. Radius: 30ft.
Arrer o' Mork	Quick Shootin' x15	Rank 4	CAE	10s	Deals 1,200 + 1,200 over 10s (Injury) DoT. Arc: 90, radius: 40.

Tactics

Deez Career Tactics are learned from da Career Trainers. Dere are a total of 17 Tactics available wif nine of doze coming from da Mastery Training. Each Mastery path has three specialized Tactics. Da Squig Herder gets one Career slot so use it wisely. Dere are five different sets of Career Tactics wot you can save, so play around wif what works fer yer play style. Your first Career Tactic iz called Too Smart Fer Dat, which increases yer Spirit resistance. By Rank 21 you get two Career slots. At Rank 31 da Squig Herder gets three Career slots. Der Rank 40 you get four Career slots to fill. Choose da Career Tactics you think iz bestest fer yer play style. Dere iz also da Renown Tactics slot an' da Guild Tactics slot, which you get from buildin' up experience wif each one.

Just to go over a few of dem, let's start wif Clever Recovery. Dis Tactic helps you regain 75 action points if yer attacks are dodged. Which izreal gud cuz dere iz nothin' worse den not having action points. RUN AWAY! iz real nice too since it gives you increased movement speed by 30% anytime you iz hit. iz other useful tactic iz da Pierce Defenses. Any added offense fer you iz gud so wif deez yer enemy chance to Block, Dodge, an' Parry iz reduced by 15 percent for 10 seconds. You get a few gud Career Tactics fer yer Squigz too. He's a Biggun' summons Squigz wif increased Toughness and Strength by 4. Now dats jess da bestest Career Tactics which I likes da most. Buff dat Squig wif Sharp Toofs fer a damaging Chomp Tactic. Dats real gud too cuz it's used most often wif yer horned Squig. Deez Tactics are ones dat I use da most. Go through dem all an' see which one fits yer play style da best.

Tactics

Name	Level	Description
Whazat Behind You?!	Level 11	Reactive proc: 25% chance to proc a small detaunt (25%, 5s).
Expert Skirmisher	Level 13	Increases damage by +25% when under 45ft and decreases damage by -20% when over 45ft.
Sharp Toofs	Level 15	Chomp's damage increased to 375 and AP cost reduced to 150.
Too Smart for Dat	Level 17	Increases Spirit Resist by +6.3 per level of the character.
Steady Aim	Level 19	Increases Ballistic Skill by +4 per level of the character.
He's a Biggun'	Level 21	Squig has increased Strength and Toughness by +4 per level of the Squig.
RUN AWAY!	Level 23	Reactive proc: 25% chance to increase run speed by 30% for 5s.
Clever Recovery	Level 25	When the character's attacks are dodged, regain 75 AP.
Strength in Numbas	Level 27	25% chance each time a groupmate (but not yourself) hits an enemy to gain 100 Morale over 3s.
Pierce Defenses	Level 29	When the character iz defended, he reduces the target's block, parry, and evade chances by 15% for 10s.
Pick On Yer Own Size	Level 31	When you defend (parry/evade/disrupt), crit chance iz increased by 30% for 10s.
All By Meself	Level 33	Deal 25% more damage if pet iz not summoned.
Sharpened Arrers	Level 35	Explodin Arrer's damage iz increased to 349 to initial target and DoT damage increased to 349 over 9s.
I Got Lots	Level 37	Pet summon reuses are reduced to 0s.
Da Smell Don't Bother Me	Level 39	Cooldown on Squig Armor reduced down to 180s. Duration iz increased to 90s.
Aimin' Quickly	Big Shootin x3	Plink's build time iz reduced to 1s.
I Feelz Yer Pain	Big Shootin x7	Big Shootin' abilities give 50 AP back when they critical hit.
Clever Shootin'	Big Shootin x11	Big Shootin abilities are reduced in AP cost by 35%.
'Ere, Squiggy!	Stabbin x3	When the character iz dealt damage, there iz a 25% chance that 50% of the damage iz dealt to his Squig instead (42ft range).
Sneaky Stabbin'	Stabbin x7	Cut Ya!, Drop That!!, Don't Hit Me!, Spin 'n Slash, and Foot Stab! have a 25% chance to ignore all of the target's armor.
Clever Stabbin'	Stabbin x11	Melee abilities are reduced in AP cost by 35%.
Splinterin' Arrers	Quick Shootin x3	Run 'n Shoot now deals damage in a 20ft radius.
Da <I>Waaagh!<I> iz Strong	Quick Shootin x7	Increases durations of Yer Bleeding to 24s, Stop Runnin! to 15s, and Not So Fast! to 15s.
Shootin' wif da Wind	Quick Shootin x11	Increases range of Quick Shootin' abilities by 50%.

Squig Herder's 3 All-Time Favorite Games

Hide 'N Go Stab

Dis game iz all-time young gobbo classic. Grab yer buddies, dis game gud fer four players.

MATERIALS: You're gonna need one captured stunty an' each player gets one spear.

TIME LIMIT: You get all day or until somethin' better to kill comes up.

HOW TO PLAY: First you give da stunty lots 'o ale. Den you tell him to run likes hell. If he gets away he wins. All players will be out ta get da drunken stunty. First Goblin to get to stunty, gets to stab him. Every player closes dere eyes an' counts to 10...1 stabbity, 2 stabbity, 3 stabbity... Da stunty den gets to run fer dere life.

Shoots N' Arrers

An other Goblin classic. Dis can be played wif four players an iz simple to set up.

MATERIALS: As many stunties as you can get, an open field, an' of course lotsa arrers.

OBJECTIVES: Shoot a stunty wif yer arrers.

HOW TO PLAY: Dere iz two styles to play dis game. First iz called da Run Fer It! style. You pick yer stunty an' stand side by side. Den when you says "Go!" dey run as fast as dey can. Yer job iz to shoot dem wif yer arrer. You get more points da further dey get as long as you get dem too wif yer arrer. Da farthest stunty hit wif an arrer wins.

Da next style of play iz called Sprint! Stand in da middle of da field. About a 100 stunties away have stunties line up on da farthest left an' some on da farthest right of da field. Stunties will sprint out as fast as dey can to get from left side to right side an' stunties from right side to left. You get five minutes to shoot at dem. Da Goblin dat kills da most wins.

Wheel O' Stunty

Dis not a classic game but iz real popular. iz a real easy game but so much fun. You can get four players max to play dis wif you.

MATERIALS: One big round wooden wheel. One stunty tied up on da wheel.

OBJECTIVE: Not hit da stunty.

HOW TO PLAY: Stand 100 feet away from da wheel wif da stunty on it. Da wheel iz set upright so someone can spin it. Each player gets a chance to shoot an arrer at da stunty. If yer arrow hits da stunty you lose. But wait derez more! All players must be blindfolded to play an' spun around 10 times. Den dey can shoot der arrers at da stunty on da spinning wheel. Da Goblin dat not hit da stunty wins. Me know how tough it iz fer us Goblins to not want to hit dem stunties. iz great fun fer da whole tribe fer hours.

OPTIONAL: Replace dead stunty wif live one.

As yer plinking away at monsters, use da Tab button to cycle through when in a group to see which monster iz about to die. Attack dem first to help finish dem off.

Renown:

Fer Renown advancement, you must gain Renown points fer killin' enemy players in combat. Dere are three levels of available abilities to choose from. You need to spend 20 points on da first level to access da second level rewards. Den to access da third level rewards you must spend 40 total points from da first an' second level rewards. Each Renown Rank gets you one Renown point. Deez points depend on how active you are wif RvR (Realm vs. Realm) combat. You'll notice dat dere are Renown Tactics available fer purchase. Dis will go into da Renown Tactic slot marked by crossed swords.

So where should you place deez Renown points you says? Dis iz mostly up to yer play style but I will go over what I think iz best. Fer Rank 1 da first 20 Renown points invest in Marksmen fer increases Ballistic skill up to Marksmen IV or just a few in Marksmen den spread over Fortitude fer Toughness an' Impetus fer increased Initiative. Skip da Renown Tactics cuz you'll get better ones in Rank 2. Remember you only get 1 Renown Tactic slot to fill.

Once you spent 20 Renown points den you get access to Rank 2 rewards. Here you gotta spend 'em on Sharp Shooter to increase your Initiative an' Ballistic skill. Vigor iz a nice add too cuz it increases your Wounds. Dere iz also buffs fer Renown Tactics to choose from an' it's up to you between being betta against Dwarfs, Empire, or High Elves. I like to be against dem stunties. So den it's a toss up between Refreshing Dominance—Dwarf buff wot restores some health after killin' Dwarfs, or Invigorating Victory—Dwarf buff wot double your AP regen rate 10 percent of da time after killin' Dwarfs. I likes Refreshing Dominance da bestest cuz Squig Herders don't have gud healing.

After spending 40 points between Ranks 1 an' 2, you get to Rank 3 rewards. Here your bestest choice iz Sure Shot, which increases Ranged Critical Chance to hit. Concentrate yer Renown points here to da max an' you're gonna be a tough greenskin.

Now we gets to da gud stuff. Let's talk about PvE (fightin' against everythin' that isn't another player), an' how da Squig Herder rocks as da hunter dat it is. First off you iz a Squig Herder an' Squig Herders iz best wif dere Squigz. You're a dead Goblin without your Squig. Squigz have lots of ways to use dem. Use dem gud an' you will survive. Fightin' without your Squig iz da biggest no no. Keep dat always in mind.

BEATIN' ON MONSTERS AN' DUMB STUNTIES

Solo Play (PvE)

Rank 1-10

When you're first startin' out, you only get da common starter abilities like Stabbity fer melee attacks, Plink fer ranged attacks, an' Summon Squig. Always summon a Squig right away. Squigz are yer bestest friend. Fightin' against baddies during deez first 10 ranks iz a piece a cake. You get new abilities at every rank you get. So whatt you need to do first when fightin' iz to send yer Squig to attack da enemy. Keeping your diztance, Plink dem 'til dere dead, or if dey get near you, den use Stabbity to finish 'em off.

Add to yer arsenal wif Yer Bleedin'!. Send yer Squig to attack first, den Plink, den Yer Bleedin'!. Use Plink before Yer Bleedin'! cuz it has two-second cast time an' Yer Bleedin'! iz an instant cast. Keep using Yer Bleedin'! until da monster iz dead or if it's too close use Stabbity melee attack to finish.

Den we add Chomp next to da line up of abilities. I would place deez abilities in order of use from left to right. So I wud now send in Squig to attack, use Chomp fer Squig chomp at monster, Plink, den Yer' Bleedin'!, an' Stabbity to finish.

Why you readin' dez scribbles?
Start killin' stunties already!

By now you should get Stop Runnin!, so da attack tactic on monsters would be to send da Squig to attack, Chomp, Plink, Stop Runnin!, Yer Bleedin'!, den Stabbity. At dis point you might have to run away if da monster gets too tuff. Use da Flee ability to get yer green skin out of dere. Dats when dis next ability comes to play. Use da same tactic as before sendin' da Squig to attack, Squig Frenzy, Chomp, Plink, Stop Runnin!, Yer Bleedin'!, den Stabbity, but if you're gettin' hit too much wif melee attacks, den run not Flee an' use Run 'n Shoot. Use deez until da monster iz dead. Da same tactics are used too if da monster tries to run away from you. Chase it down wif Run 'n Shoot. By dis time you should use da horned Squig. Dis iz da bestest Squig, I think.

Now things get a bit hairy especially when fightin' more den one monster at a time. Use da same tactics as always, but pick a target dats more of a threat or closest to you. If dere iz two or more trying to attack you, use Don't Eat Me on one of dem dat you're not attacking. Dis will detaunt dem an' make dem not hurt you so much. If it getsz real rough wif too much monsters den use da Farty Squig ability to make yer Squig explode. Dis will damage all enemies within 30 feet, plus your next Squig will be insta summoned wif in 10 seconds. Dats a gud way to damage monsters in groups.

You will be gettin' a debuff called Point-Blank. Make sure to equip it to yer Rank 1 Morale slot. Dis iz da bestest Morale ability fer dem monsters dat are too close to you. It knocks dem back real gud den you shoot dem wif arrers. Once you get to Rank 10, you'll be gettin' two more Squigz, da gas Squig an' spiked Squig. Both of dem are ranged Squigz, but are weak when attacked. Two of da bestest Core abilities a Squig Herder gets iz da Cut Ya! an' Sticky Squigz abilities. When fightin' monsters, use da same tactics as before but if you need to melee use Cut Ya! instead of Stabbity. It's a much stronger melee attack. Sticky Squigz iz used anytime dat you think da monsters iz gettin' too close an' too much to handle. It will root all dem enemies within 30 feet an' dey can't move fer five seconds so you can get away den kill 'em wif arrers or Flee.

Rank 11–20

Wid Ranks 11–20, tactics do not change too much fer da Squig Herder. You still use da same as before but wif more abilities. Let's add Squig Frenzy. Send Squig to attack, use Squig Frenzy to buff Squig, shoot arrer wif Plink, shoot arrer wif Yer Bleedin'! until da monster iz dead. Finish off wif Stabbity if it's close range. You get yer first Career Tactic, Too Smart Fer Dat, so make sure you add to yer Tactic slot right a way. You also get other Tactics so pick da ones dats best fer you.

During quests wot requires picking up objects, use yer Squig to diztract an enemy while you pick up da object.

Squig Petz

You have Squigz to command an' control. Dey are yer bestest buds an' yer lifesaver. Commanding yer Squigz you can use dem to pull dem mobs an' other enemies. Pulling iz when you get monsters to attack you, in dis case yer Squigz. Me Squigz are da best bait to use. Heck, I eat dem when I'z feeling not so gud an' low in health. Dey are used to control aggro especially when dere lots of nasties around you. Aggro iz when da mobs or nasties get mad an' chase you, dats why me run fast. Me squiqs always dere fer me. Deze are the ones I use mostest:

Summon Squig

Dis iz da starter Squig. iz da basic an' first Squig pet you get. It's tough and mean and everything hatez it! It gots a nasty claw swipe wot makes big tears in things!

Horned Squig

Dis iz a melee Squig, stronger den basic Squig. iz strong against physical attacks, but weak against magic. It also makes me armor twice as gud! Me can't do the math but me can feel it working! Dis Squig can also knock down enemies wif his Head Butt and Gore enemies gud wif its horn! (Da horn also make good soup!)

Gas Squig

Dis iz a ranged Squig, but weak against attacks. It makes me arrers fly farther and when it attacks it hits everythingz around! Its got Bad Gas which makes enemies weaker in weird ways and it duz Goop Shootin all over everything around it but me and me friendz! You are me friend, right?

Spiked Squig

Dis iz a ranged Squig wif increase damage, but lower Toughness. It makes me arrers sometimes hit HARD! It gots a Spikey Shield dat hurts everyone dat hits it and when it Spine Flings somethins gonna hurt bad!

Group Play

Squig Herders iz a ranged DPS class. wif dat I says, your main goal iz to assist da group wif DPS. Squig Herders do da most harm wit' dere Squigz an' wit' dem arrers. Yer first encounter in group play would be in da public quests (PQs). You get in deez around Ranks 5 or 6. Dey are fun an' rewarding at da same time. Practice yer tactics dat I shows you in da PvE section, though da only difference iz you be in a group now. As I says, you da group to DPS assist. So wif dat make sure you don't attack first. Let da tanks attack first, den send in da Squig.

Dis iz da same tactics used fer public quests an' scenarios. Follow yer group, figure out which iz da tanks in da group, an' watch which monster it attacks. Dats yer cue to attack an' send in yer horned Squig to attack an' use da same tactics as in da PvE section. Once da monster or enemy iz dead, figure out which monster or enemy da group tank iz attackin' den attack da same beast. Rinse an' repeat fer both PQs an' scenarios. When da going gets tuff Flee fer da hills. Make sure to use da Sticky Squigz ability if you notice yer group or anyone in da group iz having hard time wif monsters. Dis will give dem time to move away, heal, or run. Dis gud time to use da Farty Squig ability too when dere too much monsters.

As you sit back behind yer group shootin' arrers from far far way, make sure you pay attention to da other group members. Watch out fer da ambush from monsters dat are aggrod by other group playerson accident. Help finish off da monsters dats about to die, den move on to da next target. Use yer Morale abilities wisely cuz dey could mean life an' death depending on da situation.

Levelin' Up

Rank 1-10

Starting in Da Stumps at Mount Bloodhorn, get to know Greeble da Healer, Gagdush da Merchant, an' most important Sogsnag Grubsnout da Career Trainer. When you look around you see Skarzag an' Crankz. Dose two will give you some quests wot will get you going. When you're done wif dem, den go to Lobber Hill. Dere you find Gubnash Facebiter, Molora da Seeker, an' Sploop wif more quests. After dat head toward Maggut near da Snouts' Pens an' get wif Snouts, Grubgob, an' Sar Kernith for more questin. Deez quests will help you wif yer first five ranks. Maggut iz a binder fer yer map. Dat means if you need to come back to him just click on yer Battle Map in yer pack an' recall back to him. It's important to bind where ever you plan to be around fer a long time. At dis time you should have some new skills already, so make sure you visit da trainer every time you rank up. I says you need to read up da PvE section fer tactics fer deez first 10 ranks.

Same wif Morale abilities.

So wif da tactics I used before we add a few more abilities to it. Use da following in dis order: Send Squig to attack, Squig Frenzy, Chomp, Poison Arrer, Stop Runnin!, Explodin' Arrer, Yer Bleedin'!, rinse an' repeat from Chomp den Cut Ya!. Against magic-users use dis order: Send Squig to attack, Squig Frenzy, Chomp, Poison Arrer, Explodin' Arrer, Yer Bleedin'!, rinse an' repeat from Chomp den Cut Ya!. Against melee attackers use diz: Send Squig to attack, Squig Frenzy, Chomp, Poison Arrer, Stop Runnin!, Not So Fast!, Explodin' Arrer, Yer Bleedin'!, rinse an' repeat from Chomp den Cut Ya! to finish off when it's melee time. Keep in mind dat you have Point-Blank if da monster iz too close an' attack you too much. You have Sticky Squigz if dere iz too many monsters or melee attackers near you. Use it an' back away to get range fer yer arrers. Use yer Morale abilities too as dey become available.

Rank 21-30

Wif deez higher ranks, you get more powerful Career Tactic an' more slots fer dem. You get more Morale abilities too wot iz much stronger den ever. I told you ways to escape wif Point-Blank Morale ability an' Sticky Squigz ability. Use da same tactics against ranged fighters/monsters as you use against melee fighters. Tactics remain da same fer deez Ranks 21-30.

Rank 31-40

More an' more Career Tactics an' Morale abilities are available fer deez Ranks 31-40. See me notes in dem sections fer more details. Tactics against magic-users, melee, an' ranged monsters/enemies are still da same as before, though dere iz two new abilities to add. Tactics to use against magic-users are now: Send Squig to attack, Squig Frenzy, Chomp, Poison Arrer, Choking Arrer, Explodin' Arrer, Yer Bleedin'!, Lots o' Arrers, an' Shoot Thru Ya, rinse an' repeat from Chomp den Cut Ya! to finish. Against melee/ranged monsters do deez: Send Squig to attack, Squig Frenzy, Chomp, Poison Arrer, Stop Runnin!, Not So Fast!, Explodin' Arrer, Yer Bleedin'!, Lots o' Arrers, an' Shoot Thru Ya, rinse an' repeat from Chomp den Cut Ya! to finish.

You can loot yer own Squig so watch fer doze.

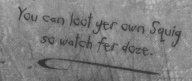

y Rank 5, you izready to go fightin' in da PQs. Dis iz da bestest way to rank up quickly in deez early ranks. 'er first PQ will be at Ugrog's Bash. Dis iz your first time to work in group too. You gain influence points 'r da PQ. Earn enough influence points den you can get back to Maggut to select some rewards. Da more oints you get, da closer you get to better rewards an' even elite ones. When you complete a PQ, you get to oll fer da PQ loot. Da top rolls wins Loot Sacks. Make sure to get it from da chest in da center of da field efore it dissappears. You can do da PQ fer Chapter 1 again or get going an' pick up all other quests you get long da ways. Dis should get you da Greenskin Chapter 2 area which iz Da Big Saw. Get yer bind spot, talk to ome NPCs, make sure you get any skills available from da trainer, den look fer some more quests in dis area. Dere are three PQs fer dis Chapter so make sure to join dem so you gets some loot an' more experience to ink up. Dis should take you to Rank 10.

ank 11–20

Chapter 2 will spill into deez ranks of 11–20. Spend some extra time doing PQs during deez ranks cuz dey em to help you rank up quicker. Use da tactics I says in da PvE section. Fer deez ranks make sure to speak 'if da trainer to get all da skills you can. Iz important to bind as you go along yer way so you can get back to a closest bind location you can if you die.

During deez ranks should lead you to yer first scenario. Go ahead an' participate in it. Hopefully dere be some olks to join in too. Dis will get yer Renown experience up in no time. Continue to do da PQs an' scenarios to et maximum experience to rank up quicker.

Chapter 3 Kron-Komar Gap will give you more challenging quests. Pick dem all up as you walk around deez arts. Do dem quests an' complete dem as fast as a greenskin can handle. Grouping up wif folks in da area doing Qs iz great so you can complete dem quicker. In da northern parts of Komar, you will come across your first vR (realm vs. realm) battlefield. Here iz da place where you can hunt down some ugly stunties an' get some loot ff dem. Keep dis up an' you'll be on yer way to Rank 20.

ank 21–30

.s you move along da map, keep updating yer skills, Morale abilities, an' yer Tactics sets. Get yerself binded 'if da nearest binder so you don't have to be a tired greenskin running back an' forth too much. Pick up any uests wot you run into an' complete dem fast as you can. Dere be PQs, scenarios, an' most especially da RvR attlefields wot be yer bestest bet fer ranking up da quickest. PvP in deez battlefields will earn you some enown points. Da more you get, da more access you get to da bestest Renown rewards. See me Renown ection fer more details.

If you're near a warcamp an' have to fight tough monsters, den pull dem back to camp an' let da guards whack 'em. Yes iz cheap but a dead stunty iz a gud 'n tasty one.

Deez ranks iz da bestest to move up quicker by doing da RvR battlefields da most. Deez battlefields have a Flight Master to take you to other regions wif RvR battlefields. It's not a free ride so make sure you want to go here an' dere. Fightin' in RvR will get you to rank 30 da quickest. If no stunties iz around den go do some questin or PQs instead.

Level 31-40

Continue wif some questin during da earlier parts of deez ranks from 31 to 40. PQs again will be bestest bet to get some loot an' gain some experience fer ranking up. Ranking up will be gettin' slower an' slower now. Checking up da mix from questin an' doing PQs will definitely make it feel quicker to rank up.

Da RvR battlefields will still be da bestest way to rank up real quick. But as you get closer to mid 30s den you need to get ready fer some more fun. Dats when you get some campaign action. Dis iz like abattlefield, but bigger. You get to help yer Destruction buddies capture some zones in deez campaigns to gain control over Order.

Da fun not stop der. To top dat off you get to siege a castle or even keeps. Dere be tons of experience points to get so keep on fightin' an' killin' dem stunties. Use dem field pads to get yer siege weapons planted to attack dem stunties an' knock down dere keep doors. Da campaign iz da main events dat you should focus on to rank up da quickest to rank 40. Keep it going an' keep dem stunties a dyin'.

BEATIN' ON PLAYERS AN' SMART STUNTIES

Solo PvP

Eh, so you think you can fight? It's skirmish time an' dat dumpy stunty iz out to get you. Deez tactics below can be used fer any solo PvP matches. Da purpose o' fightin' in battlefields, RvR, an' scenarios iz not just to gain control of land, but also to get Renown points dat help you get stronger wif dere rewards. Wot you do den you ask me? Here's some tactics you can use to not lose:

Ranks 1-10

Use same tactic as before wif send Squig to attack, Chomp, Plink, Stop Runnin!, Yer Bleedin'!, den Stabbity but if you're gettin' hit too much wif melee attacks den run, not Flee, an' use Run 'n Shoot. Run 'n Shoot iz best to use until stunty dead.

Ranks 11-20

Send Squig to attack, Squig Frenzy, Chomp, Poison Arrer, Stop Runnin!, Explodin' Arrer, Yer Bleedin'!, rinse an' repeat from Chomp den Cut Ya! to finish. Against magic-users use dis order: Send Squig to attack, Squig Frenzy, Chomp, Poison Arrer, Explodin' Arrer, Yer Bleedin'!, Lots O' Arrers, rinse an' repeat from Chomp den Cut Ya! to finish. Against melee attackers use diz Send yer Squig to attack, Squig Frenzy, Chomp, Poison Arrer, Stop Runnin!, Not So Fast!, Explodin' Arrer, Yer Bleedin'!, rinse an' repeat from Chomp den Cut Ya! to finish off when its melee time. If dat stunty iz too close, den use yer Morale ability Point-Blank to knock 'em back. If dat don't work, use Sticky Squigz so you can get some space an' do Run 'n Shoot. If in case you're runnin' low in health an' your Squig iz about to die, eat 'em! Eat yer Squig an' you get some health back den cast fer yer horned Squig back again.

Ranks 21-30

Same tactics are used fer deez ranks as above. Only difference iz you get da Drop That!! ability. Dis iz used when yer enemy iz real close an' you dizarm da stunty. Use dis only against melee fighters.

Ranks 31-40

Tactics to use against magic-users are now: Send Squig to attack, Squig Frenzy, Chomp, Poison Arrer, Choking Arrer, Explodin' Arrer, Yer Bleedin'! an' Lots o' Arrers, rinse an' repeat from Chomp den Cut Ya! to finish. To use against melee/ranged do diz: Send Squig to attack, Squig Frenzy, Chomp, Poison Arrer, Stop Runnin!, Not So Fast!, Explodin' Arrer, Yer Bleedin'! an' Lots o' Arrers, rinse an' repeat from Chomp den Cut Ya! to finish.

Group Play

Now we talkin'! It's party time an' I feel likes killin'. Squig Herders are still best at doing DPS. Dey not tanks so stay away from da front lines. Let dem dumb Orcs an' crazy Marauders take up da front. You're a gud Squig Herder an' stays in da back of da line, way back. Cuz you're way back, you get to see more action an' wot yer group iz doin'. Keep yer gud eye out fer yer healers in da group. Dats wot dem Order folks will be going fer to kill. Whats most important iz to keep yer healers safe, but it's only a secondary responsibility.

Flee ability iz not just fer making doze quick get aways. Use it to speed up yer travels between quests.

Use dat Squig of yours to pull one enemy ats a time. Even doze wot are right next to each other. Just try not to be too close an' aggro all of dem.

Yer main group responsibility iz to do major DPS. Find yer tanks, see who dey start choppin', den send in yer Squig. Do da same tactics as in solo PvP: Send in Squig, start shootin' dem arrers, den finish em wif yer melee attack if dey get too close. If in danger, push dem away wif Point-Blank, get dem stuck wif Sticky Squigz, or just run fer dem hills.

Tanks be killin' dem stunties off quick wif yer help. Make sure to Tab around an' see who iz da next weakest enemy, an' send in da Squig. Now if yer Squig iz between tons of baddies an' iz about to die, use Farty Squig. Dis will make 'em explode an' damage dem baddies around 'em. Wot iz gud around bad groups.

Me Bestest Squig Recipe

Me always been a gud chef. On me spare time away from fightin' me likes to cook a real gud meal. Sometimes me even offer some to dem long toof orcs to taste. Dem likes it too an' think me iz gud cook. Here's me best recipe fer cooking Squig.

Ale-in-da-Rear Squig

    1 3 lb. Squig
    1 Sprinkle of Seasoned Ruined Earth
    1 Pint of Ale
    1 Clawing Redvine
    1 Cup Field Lice
    1 Cup Elvish Parsley

Dis main dizh iz very simple but gud. Let's wash an' drain da Squig, den pat dry. Season da Squig inside an' out wif da Ruined Earth. Chop da Clawing Redvine an' spread around da Squig. Smear some of dat nice Field Lice all around an' make sure it covers entire Squig.

Dig a pit in da ground about three feet deep. Throw some hot coals in dere an' wait until its glowing. Den get da Squig ready. Get yer Squig, stick dat pint of ale in it, den place Squig on top of hot coals. Cover up da pit wif some dirt. Wait fer an hour an' dig yer Squig back out. Sprink it wif some Elvish Parsley fer garnish. Now dats wot I call dinner.

DON'T YOU FERGET WOT MAKES YER HEAD HURT

So how's yer head feelin', ehh? Dat small skull of yers holding in all deez things I says? I hopes so fer yer sake. It's a nasty an' crazy world out dere filled wif ugly stunties beyond yer dreams. Don't you ferget wot I taught you here. Keep away from dem enemies an' make sure you take care of yer Squigz. Make sure you keep yer spear sharp an' yer arrers even sharper.

I must go now an' do da same. Me Squigz misses me already. Dem Squigz are real hungry now, but I not feed dem too much. We iz gettin' ready to hunt fer some stunties an' dats wots fer dinner. Stunties: da other white meat!

CHOSEN

By Er

All glory to the Changer of Ways, young Chosen. You ask me what it is to be Chosen. Death and glory are the life of a Chosen one of Tzeentch. Death to your enemies and death to those who displease you. In craft and cunning do we ply our trade...we are not berserkers, although often we seem so to our enemies. In the forefront of the battle are we most feared, for with the powers granted to us, we are deadly in close quarters.

How did I become Chosen, you ask? Long ago I journeyed into the Chaos Wastes seeking the favor of Tzeentch. I fought countless numbers of other Northmen bent on the same goal as myself. On the bodies of the dead did I prove my worth to the Weaver of Destiny until finally he blessed me with his power...and I became his with all my soul. Family and friends, I have none of these, only brothers in arms and the dead. My past is forgotten. All that I am is on the battlefield, in the planning and final execution of the battle. The deaths of my foes.

Welcome to the ranks, young Chosen, but remember that the price of failure is death. Our God does not reward the weak and cowardly. To give your life to our God is the greatest joy, to kill and maim in his name a joy, to manipulate and scheme our best pleasure. Do not forget these things, and you will go far. Forget and the last thing you will see is the blade of my battleaxe. Our god wants only the best, and no cowards serve under me. All glory to the Raven God!

What is a Chosen One?

The Chosen accept that they must walk on the bones of friends and enemies alike. A Chosen one's place is at the forefront of the battle, side by side with Black Orcs as they lead the charge or as the vanguard for our forces of Destruction. Their strength in battle is fearsome; their threshold to suffer horrible wounds is even more impressive. Pain, I'm told, is how they show devotion to their Raven God.

In melee, the Chosen wield their weapons with frenzy, and warp the very air around them to augment their battle prowess. This warping effect, called "auras," creates special magic that benefits allies and debilitates enemies. The power of the Raven God flows through them, even as the Chosen's magic pulls enemies down into the mud before axe can cleave skull. As with our other brutes, the Black Orcs, the Chosen spit out taunts at the enemy to drive them mad and draw their attention upon the strongest of our warriors.

The Chosen may be the most powerful fighters in the warhost. In the fray, they abandon themselves to the joys of the kill with little regard for their bodies—something I find important when selecting those who would take the battle first to the enemy. These Chaos warriors have killed countless minions of Order, and have been blessed by the Raven God to wreak havoc on the battlefield. Who am I to argue with their god?

—Baron Heinar Balethar, Zimmeron's Hold, Chaos Wastes

> YOU LIVE AND DIE BY THE SWORD. KEEP
> YOUR WEAPON STRONG, AND CONTINUE TO
> UPGRADE IT OFTEN.

STARTING STATS

In the beginning you have only one special ability, an attack called Enraged Blow. Use this ability every time you can, until you learn something better. You also start with the ability to throw axes, which isn't very useful in killing things, but can be helpful in getting monsters close enough to attack them. Then there is Flee. No true Chosen of the Raven God would consider such a dishonorable act, but if you must, you will find that it makes you as weak as a pitiful High Elf, and an easy target to kill.

The most important stats for Chosen are Strength, Toughness, and Wounds. They determine how much damage you can do, how much damage you can take, and how many hit points you have. Weapon Skill and Initiative are also important. Young Chosen often fail in their quests because they focus on only one stat to the detriment of all others. Do not become like those Empire fools and their weak bodies.

Only Intelligence and Ballistic Skill have no value to you, Chosen, but Willpower and Initiative are especially useful in your battles where you can get the drop on frail magic-users.

BEING CHAOS

Chosen, like us, can come only from within the ranks of Chaos. We are the blessed of the Raven God, unlike the moat scum of the Empire. Our allies, the arrogant Dark Elves and the slow-thinking greenskins, combine with us to encompass all of the forces of Destruction. Our enemies, collectively known as the forces of Order, are the High Elves, the Dwarfs, and the cowardly Empire. We, the forces of Destruction, the Raven Host, come from the frozen Northlands. Bent on destruction, we march south, only to be blocked by the doomed efforts of the men of the Empire.

You begin your travels in Norsca, the Chaos portal behind you, the screams of the warhost in your ears, and that fool, Skurlorg, standing in front of you, a mission already in his shaking hands. I look back now on my first day and remember the trepidation suddenly disappearing as I looked over the crumbling Empire city with our hellcannons raining down upon them. Many of the feeble, too weak to press on with the warhost, reside in that camp, ready and willing to allow stronger, more fearless Chaos warriors to press on. Thorshafn is but a weak city of the Empire, but it was where I first discovered the joy of shedding Empire blood.

CHOSEN GEAR

As Chosen we are blessed by our god with the ability to use heavy armor, as well as both one- and two-handed swords, axes, and shields.

As you increase in skill and rank, growing from the weak-kneed warrior fresh out of the portal to the mighty champion that you hope to one day become, you will acquire better and stronger weapons and armor. You start, however, with weapons as pitiful as you deserve for one so low in rank. A shirt and boots are all you receive when you first cross the portal. These are weak rags, unfit for a warrior, with no value at all in armor or attributes. You also start with a weakened riding axe and shield. These will have to suffice until you can earn better.

As you progress in rank and skill, doing tasks, or quests, for other members of the warhost, you can choose new weapons or armor as a reward. Choose armor heavy in Toughness and Wounds to start with, and weapons with Strength and Weapon Skill. These will suit you well, and it is important to improve your weapons and armor as often as you can to make yourself stronger. Another choice you will have to make is between one- and two-handed weapons. The benefit of using a one-handed sword or axe is that you can also use a shield. Some Chosen prefer not to hide behind a shield, so a two-handed sword or axe is their weapon of choice. These two-handed weapons are often slower and heavy to swing, but they make up for it with higher damage. Very fortunately for us, Bright Wizard skulls do not take well to our two-handers.

BECAUSE YOU LACK THE ABILITY TO SELF HEAL, ALCHEMY AND CULTI-VATION TRADE SKILLS WILL BE VERY USEFUL. FIND A GOOD ALCHEMIST OR BECOME ONE YOURSELF.

STRENGTHS

- Ability to use heavy armor.
- Higher levels of Wounds, allowing us to suffer even greater damage.
- Auras that strengthen allies while weakening enemies.
- The ability to kill multiple targets at the same time.

A Chosen's strengths are based in his massiveness. Our ability to survive Wounds that would kill a weaker man while dealing enough damage to keep the foes focused upon us makes for a lethal combination. Auras support our war effort, whether it is by strengthening our prowess or dimming the enemy's.

WEAKNESSES

- Limited range.
- Slow moving and must be in close combat range to deal damage.
- Limited ability to snare enemy targets.
- Weak against magical and ranged attacks.
- No ability to heal self without the use of potions.

A Chosen's weaknesses are based in our inability to fight without being in close quarters. If the enemies that you are trying to kill can keep out of range of your attacks and shoot you from a distance, there is little you can do about it. Also, the inability to self heal can be a problem if the fighting is intense and you can't take a break from the action.

STRENGTHS AND WEAKNESSES

WARHAMMER ONLINE
AGE OF RECKONING

DO NOT FORGET TO VISIT YOUR CAREER TRAINER. HE WILL OFTEN HAVE NEW SKILLS FOR YOU TO LEARN.

SKILLS AND ABILITIES
ABILITIES

For Chosen there are both Core abilities and Mastery abilities. Core abilities are skills and Tactics that all Chosen get as they increase in rank. Mastery abilities are learned by spending Mastery points. These points are gained starting at Rank 11, and you receive a total of 25 points once you attain Rank 40. These points are what make you different from all those other Chosen around you. There are three Mastery paths.

PATH OF DREAD

Based on offense, this path increases the effectiveness of your Dreadful Fear, Tooth of Tzeentch, Withering Blow and Suppression Core abilities.

PATH OF CORRUPTION

Based on defense, this path increases the effectiveness of your Enraged Blow, Corrupting Wrath, Dizzying Blow, Repel, and Bane Shield Core abilities.

PATH OF DISCORD

Based on magical attacks and disruption, this path increases the effectiveness of your Discordant Instability, Seeping Wound, Ravage, Tzeentch's Reflection, and Touch of Palsy.

These Mastery paths also all have abilities, Tactics, and Morale abilities that can be trained along the way. Each ability trained costs a Mastery point, so be wise with your choosing. Although mistakes can be erased, there is a cost involved.

Which Mastery path is the best? Each is based upon how you like to go about your killing. If you prefer to deal your damage with your axe or sword, and want to be a powerhouse of death, then you should put more points into the Path of Dread. If, however, you want to take many hits and be hard to kill with lots of defense, then Path of Corruption is where you should focus. If you prefer to use strong magical attacks and auras while disrupting your enemies' attacks, then the Path of Discord is more your style. Each Mastery has strengths and weaknesses, like each Chosen, and the way the points are used will decide what kind of Chosen you become.

Abilities

Level	Name	Path	Cost	Range (in feet)	Type	Build	Duration	Reuse	Description
Starter Abilities	Throwing Axe	Core	20	10 to 65	Ranged Attack	1s	0s	0s	Deals 75 damage.
Starter Abilities	Enraged Blow	Corruption	30	Melee	Melee Attack	0s	0s	0s	Deals (112+DPS) damage. Adds 2x threat.
Level 2	Dreadful Fear	Dread	20	65	Dread Curse	0s	Toggle/12s	4.5s shared	User radiates an aura that increases the Strength of group members and debuffs the Strength of enemies within the radius by 2. Radius: 30ft
Level 3	Tooth of Tzeentch	Dread	30	Melee	Melee Attack	0s	5s	10s	Deals (150+DPS) damage. Buff group for 5s, each group member's next ability activation deals 150 more damage.

WIPE THE BLOOD OFF YOUR BLADE AFTER EACH KILL. IT KEEPS THE EDGE SHARPER OVER TIME

Abilities

Level	Name	Path	Cost	Range (in feet)	Type	Build	Duration	Reuse	Description
Level 4	Corrupting Wrath	Corruption	20	65	Corrupting Curse	0s	Toggle/12s	4.5s shared	User radiates an aura that increases the Toughness of group members and debuffs the Toughness of enemies within the radius by 2. Radius: 30ft
Level 5	Cleave	Dread	40	Melee	Melee Attack	0s	0s	0s	Deals (150+DPS) damage. Ability cannot be defended against.
Level 6	Seeping Wound	Discord	30	Melee	Magic Attack - Curse - Spirit	0s	9s	0s	Deals (187+DPS)*1.33 Spiritual damage over 9s.
Level 6	Discordant Instability	Discord	20	65	Discordant Curse	0s	Toggle/12s	4.5s shared	User radiates an aura that increases all resists of group members and debuffs all resists of enemies within the radius by 6.3. Radius: 30ft.
Level 7	Taunt	Core	20	65	Debuff	0s	15s	15s	Interrupts target. For 15s, the tank deals 30% more damage against target. Monsters turn to attack tank until taunt expires. After 3 ability activations and/or auto attacks from the target hit the tank, taunt fades. Generates 2,250 in hate.
Level 8	Ravage	Discord	35	Melee	Magic Attack - Spirit	0s	0s	0s	Deals (150+DPS) Spiritual damage.
Level 9	Dizzying Blow	Corruption	30	Melee	Melee Attack - Curse	0s	7s	5s	Deals (112+DPS) damage and Snares target by 40% for 10s.
Level 10	Guard	Core	Free	42	Buff	0s	Stance	60s	Buff on friendly group member that splits the damage between the target and the Chosen. Buffed player takes 50% of the incoming damage. Chosen takes 75% of the incoming damage directed at the buffed target. (Note: This results in more damage being dealt in total.)
Level 10	Hold the Line	Core	20/S	PBAE	Buff	0s	10s	0s	Toggled Buff. Each second the toggle is active, bestows a buff that increases Evade and Disrupt chances by 45% to the tank and 15% to all friendlies in the radius that lasts 1 second. If the tank uses another ability, the ability ends. Buffs on friendlies stack up to 3 times. Arc: 180 (pointed to the rear), radius: 40ft.
Level 12	Discordant Fluctuation	Discord	20	65	Discordant Curse	0s	Toggle/12s	4.5s shared	User radiates an aura that buffs group members with a damage shield. Damage shield returns 112 damage every time an offensive magical ability is used on a group mate within the radius. Radius: 30ft.
Level 14	Withering Blow	Dread	35	Melee	Melee Attack	0s	0s	10s	Deals (112+DPS) damage. Removes 30 AP on target.
Level 16	Repel	Corruption	35	Melee	Melee Attack	0s	0s	20s	Deals (150+DPS) damage and knocks back enemy (medium).
Level 18	Juggernaut	Core	45/S	Self	Buff	0s	0s	60s	Removes Snare, Root, Disarm, and Silence effects from the tank.
Level 18	Blast Wave	Discord	30	PBAE	Magic Attack - Curse - Spirit	0s	20s	20s	Deal 150 magical damage to targets inside the radius. All of target's resists are reduced by 9.45/level for 20s if a Discordant Curse is active. Radius: 30ft.
Level 20	Corrupting Retribution	Corruption	20	65	Corrupting Curse	0s	Toggle/12s	4.5s shared	User radiates an aura that will proc a heal for 90 over 3s every time a group member within the radius Blocks/Parries/Dodges/Disrupts. Radius: 30ft.
Level 20	Challenge	Core	30	CAE	Debuff	0s	15	30	For 15s, the challenged target deals 30% less damage to everyone but the caster. Monsters turn to attack tank until Challenge expires or 5s. After 3 ability activations and/or auto attacks from target hit tank, Challenge fades. Also generates 2,250 hate. Arc: 90, radius: 65ft.
Level 22	Sever Blessing	Core	25	Melee	Melee Attack	0s	0s	5s	Removes a blessing from target. Deals (75+DPS) damage if successful.
Level 25	Dreadful Agony	Dread	20	65	Dread Curse	0s	Toggle/12s	4.5s shared	User radiates an aura that deals 99 damage to enemies within the radius every 3 seconds. Radius: 30ft. Non-stacking, non-refreshing.
Level 25	Suppression	Dread	30	Melee	Melee Attack	0s	5s	10s	Deal (112+DPS) damage and increases chance to Parry by 10% for 10s.
Level 30	Petrify	Core	30	PBAE	Crowd Control	0s	5s	60s	Roots up to 4 targets within 30ft for 5s.

Abilities

Level	Name	Path	Cost	Range (in feet)	Type	Build	Duration	Reuse	Description
Level 35	Bane Shield	Corruption	35	Self	Buff - Enchantment	0s	7s	30s	For 10s, any targets using an ability or auto attacking on the character take 150 Spiritual damage back.
Level 40	Touch of Palsy	Discord	35	Melee	Debuff - Curse	0	10s	20s	Deals (75+DPS) damage and applies a Movement Barb. Target takes 56 damage when it moves. (Should check every 0.5s).
Specialization									
Dread x5	Dreadful Terror	Dread	20	65	Dread Curse	0s	Toggle/12s	4.5s shared	User radiates an aura that removes 9 AP from enemy targets in the radius every 3 seconds. Radius: 30ft.
Dread x9	Relentless	Dread	15/s	Melee	Channeled Melee Attack	0s	3s	8s	Deals (150+DPS)*0.6 damage to target every 0.6s for 3s.
Dread x13	Rending Blade	Dread	30	Melee	Melee Attack	0s	0s	10s	Undefendable (112+DPS) melee damage. Deals an additional 150 magical damage to up to 2 nearby targets in a 30ft radius if Dread Curse is active. Requires Great Weapon.
Corruption x5	Corrupting Horror	Corruption	20	65	Corrupting Curse	0s	Toggle/12s	4.5s shared	User radiates an aura that disorients anyone within the radius, causing their spells to take 0.5 second longer to build. Radius: 30ft.
Corruption x9	Downfall	Corruption	30	Melee	Melee Attack	0s	4s	20s	Deal (150+DPS) damage and knocks down enemy for 4s.
Corruption x13	Oppression	Corruption	30	Melee	Melee Attack - Enchantment, Curse	0s	20s/10s	20s	Deals (187+DPS) damage and increases armor by (24.75/level) for 20s. Increases target's build times by 1s for 10s if a Corrupting Curse is active. Requires Block or Parry.
Discord X5	Discordant Turbulence	Discord	20	65	Discordant Curse	0s	Toggle/12s	4.5s shared	User radiates an aura that decreases incoming healing on enemy targets within the radius by 25%. Radius: 30ft
Discord X9	Quake	Discord	45	CAE	Magic Attack	0s	2s	20s	Deals 150 magical damage and knocks down targets in the radius for 2s. Arc: 120, radius: 65ft.
Discord X13	Tzeentch's Reflection	Discord	20	Self	Enchantment, Curse	0s	10s	30s	Self buff, increases Willpower by +3/level and Disrupt chance by 25% for 10s. Disrupted spells Silence the caster for 3s.

MORALE

Morale abilities are another way that we Chosen get to show our superior ability. There are four Morale ranks in all; each takes more fighting and killing to trigger the ability, but the higher level ranks deal more damage or provide more gain. At the top of each Mastery tree is a Rank 4 Morale ability. These are the most powerful abilities, but because they are at the top of your Mastery tree, you will only have enough Mastery points to train one of them, so choose based on how you like to play.

I prefer the Rank 4 Morale ability at the top of the Discord Mastery tree, Shatter Faith. It deals horrible damage to all of the enemies around you and also dispels one of their so-called Blessings. You can also change which Morale abilities are in each of the four ranks. I prefer to use the Rank 1 Morale ability Grapple because it keeps a cowardly Empire Bright Wizard within my grasp so he cannot run away. The first Morale abilities that you learn for each rank will be defensive-minded. These work well to begin with, but killing is what we like to do best, and as soon as you can, it is better to use more offensive Morale attacks. I especially like the Rank 2 ability Raze because it damages everyone in front of me. The Rank 3 Sprout Carapace, although it is more defensive, makes killing you even harder than catching a greased Tuskgor. How and when you use your Morale abilities is up to you, but it is important that you use them because they can turn the tide of a battle for you and your allies.

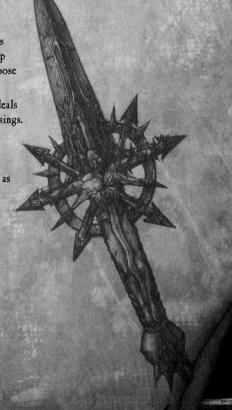

ALWAYS REMEMBER THE TEACHINGS OF THE
RAVEN GOD. THE TOME OF KNOWLEDGE IS
YOUR BEST RESOURCE AND SHOULD NOT BE
OVERLOOKED.

Name	Level	Rank	Range (in feet)	Duration	Description
Demolishing Strike	Level 8	Rank 1	Melee	0	Deal 900 damage over 15s and lowers Armor by -26.4/level for 15s.
Shield Wall	Level 12	Rank 2	Self	10s	Self buff: Increase chance to Block by 100% for 10s.
Grapple	Level 16	Rank 1	Melee	10s	Unbreakable Root on target and tank (both Roots break simulaneously).
Raze	Level 20	Rank 2	CAE	3s	Channeled Physical CAE attack that deals 1,200 damage to targets over 3s. Arc: 90, radius: 66ft.
Distracting Bellow	Level 24	Rank 3	100	10s	Target and all enemies around deal 50% less damage for 10s. Radius: 30ft.
Inevitable Changing	Level 28	Rank 1	Melee	0	Melee attack that deals 600 and grants the Chosen 250 AP.
Tzeentch's Amplification	Level 32	Rank 2	Self	15s	Self-buff that increases the value of heals targeting the Chosen by 300% for 15s.
Sprout Carapace	Level 36	Rank 3	Group	30s	Increase the group's Armor by +33/level and resists by +12.6/level for 30s. Also give a 1-shot boost of 100 AF
Immaculate Defense	Level 40	Rank 4	Group	10s	Group members who stay within 65ft of the tank take 75% less damage for 10s.
Warping Embrace	Dread x15	Rank 4	CAE	15s	Deals 1,800 damage over 15s and Snares all targets (40%, 15s). Arc: 120, radius: 65ft.
Impenetrable Armor	Corruption x15	Rank 4	Self	9s	Buffs the character with an ablative that absorbs the next 2,400 damage, with a maximum duration of 9s.
Shatter Faith	Discord X15	Rank 4	PBAE	0s	Deals 1,200 damage to targets in the radius and removes one Blessing from each target. Radius: 30ft.

TACTICS

Tactics are certainly a boon if used correctly, but they can tip the scales the opposite way if used without thought for the situation you are in. Some Tactics raise your skills, and some increase the effectiveness of your auras or attacks. To master Tactics, you must know what to use, and when to use it. For example, Focused Offense is good when you want to deal lots of damage, but it is worthless if you are tanking for your group. Tactics come from Core abilities, Mastery abilities, and Renown points, and how you use them can tip the scales in a battle with the weakling fighters of the Empire, or give them the victory.

The first Tactic you receive is Warped Flesh at Rank 11. Equip it immediately because it gives you a 25% chance to absorb damage dealt to you. After that you learn more and more Tactics, and as you rank up, you can equip more Tactics until at Rank 40 you have room for six total Tactics: four regular Tactics, one Renown Tactic, and one Guild Tactic. For regular Tactics, I like to use Chaotic Advantage and Rugged, as well as Power from the Gods and Destined for Victory. These four provide a lethal combination that serves me well against all comers.

Name	Level	Description
Warped Flesh	Level 11	25% chance when attacked to absorb 262 damage for 10s.
Focused Offense	Level 13	Increase damage dealt by 25%. Increase damage taken by 20%. Decrease threat generation by 25%.
Chaotic Advantage	Level 15	Parrying an attack gives 75 AP.
Tzeentch's Warding	Level 17	Increases Elemental resist by +6.3 per level of the character.
Rugged	Level 19	Increases Toughness by +4 /Level.
Flawless Armor	Level 21	Reduce incoming critical hits by 10%.
Backlash	Level 23	25% chance to put a 5s 150 DoT on attacker. Non-stacking, non-refreshing.
Menace	Level 25	Increases threat by 100% on all attacks.
Quickened Discord	Level 27	Reduce Blast Wave and Touch of Palsy's reuse timers to 10s.
Unstoppable Juggernaught	Level 29	Juggernaught's reuse timer is lowered to 20s.
Critical Suppression	Level 31	Suppression also reduces the enemies chance to defend by 10% for 10s.
Piercing Repel	Level 33	Repel also gives a self buff that lowers incoming Armor penetration by 100% for 10s.
Baneful Shielding	Level 35	Increase duration of Bane Shield by 7s.
Power from the Gods	Level 37	Auras cost no AP to activate.
Destined for Victory	Level 39	Blocking an attack gives the Chosen 200 Morale.
Feed on the Weary	Dread X3	AP removed from Withering Blow is increased to 40 and also added to the Chosen.
Crippling Strikes	Dread X7	Critical hits lower the target's damage by 25% for 10s.
Oppressing Blows	Dread X11	Attacks when using a Great Weapon have a 15% increased chance to critical.
Dire Shielding	Corruption X3	Bane Shield also applies itself to allies within 30ft.
Mixed Defenses	Corruption X7	On Block: Increase chance to Parry by 25% for 5s.
Hastened Dismissal	Corruption X11	Reduces the reuse on Repel by 10s and adjusts the AP cost to 150.
Siphoned Energy	Discord X3	On Disrupt: Chosen gains 30% run speed for 5s and self-heals for 157.
Tainted Wound	Discord X7	Seeping Wound also places an effect for 9s on the target that deals 262 damage to anyone that heals him.
Embrace the Winds	Discord X11	Increase the value of heals on the character by 15%.

BATTLEFIELDS AND SCENARIOS ARE A GOOD WAY TO HONE YOUR PVP SKILLS IN PREPARATION FOR THE FINAL BATTLE FOR DOMINATION.

RENOWN

Renown is what you earn from killing the forces of Order. The more you kill, the more Renown you earn, and as Chosen you should revel in killing those blasphemers every chance you get. As your Renown rank increases, you gain points that you can spend at a Renown Trainer. There are three levels of Renown abilities, and each requires you to spend a certain number of points to advance to the next level. For example, to advance to the second level, you have to spend at least 20 points in the first level.

These skills can make you so much more powerful. Some skills are useless to a Chosen one of your stature, such as Intelligence and Ballistic Skill, while others are very useful, such as Toughness and Weapon Skill. How you spend your Renown points is up to you, and it may change as you gain ranks and learn new Core abilities and Tactics, so it's helpful to know that you can relearn the skills, again at the cost of silver.

I prefer to spend my Rank 1 points of Renown in Fortitude, Resolve, and Impetus. These will increase your Toughness, Willpower, and Initiative, respectively. Willpower and Initiative may seem like bad choices, but your armor will have mostly Strength, Toughness, and Wounds on it, and Renown is an easy way to increase useful skills while keeping your armor strong for killing the monsters that you find in your travels. There are even Tactics that you can learn that make killing Empire fools, priggish High Elves, and greedy Dwarfs even more beneficial and fun, if you can imagine that.

The second tier requires you to spend 40 points to move into the third tier. I suggest spending points to get the Tactics For Glory! and Mission Focused so that you can benefit from the increased Renown that you gain by equipping these Tactics. With more points I would spend them on Vigor to increase my Wounds and also Discipline to increase both Willpower and Initiative. The third tier has some very powerful abilities and skills that you want to have if you like killing your enemies, which you should, if you want to bring glory to the Raven God.

HUNTING MONSTERS AND QUEST REWARDS

Young Chosen, now it is time to talk about using all that you have learned in the world. There are two types of battles that you can find yourself involved in. The first type is you against the various monsters that you find in your travels across the land. The Chosen excel at this type of combat. Our ability to suffer and glory in the pain of battle, combined with our ability to dish out hand-to-hand combat damage, may make monsters seem like mongrel camp dogs before long.

SOLO PLAY (PVE)

RANK 1–10

Young Chosen start with one basic attack: Enraged Blow. They can also throw axes, which is useful for bringing monsters to you. Because you are Chosen, even two monsters that are close to your rank are nothing for you to worry about. Now if you were a weakling member of the Empire, even one monster would make you quake in your boots. Once you gain your first rank, you also gain your first aura. This aura is a blessing from the Raven God and it reduces your enemy's strength while increasing your own. This may seem like a good ability to use, and it is, in some cases. When you use an aura you have to watch what is around you. You can easily anger many monsters, and even a strong Chosen will fall to an army when he is alone.

Each time you rank up in these first 10 levels, you will learn new skills. Try them out and see how they all work for you. One of the important abilities that you will use is Enraged Blow, which is an attack and a taunt. A taunt is an ability that forces monsters to attack you even if they would rather chase after someone else. Another good ability is Seeping Wound, which damages a monster over time. This can kill something as it runs away from you, or keep the damage going so that your target will keep hating you. It also cripples your target, so it combos well with Dizzying Blow, which triggers extra abilities if the monster is crippled. Probably one of the most important skills that you receive in your first 10 ranks is the Taunt ability. Even in solo combat this is a powerful skill because it increases the damage that the monsters take from you as well as forcing them to attack you.

DO NOT BE AFRAID TO EXPLORE MANY TIMES BY EXPLORING ALL AREAS YOU CAN LOCATE ITEMS AND QUESTS THAT YOU DIDN'T EVEN KNOW ABOUT.

RANK 11–20

This is much the same as Ranks 1–10. Much of your combat will center around Cleave, Taunt, and Seeping Wound. As you progress in skill, you learn a few new Tactics. You only have one Tactic slot when you get your first Tactic, but you should still equip it. You also learn even more Morale abilities and a few more damaging attacks, but you mostly use Cleave, Taunt, and Seeping Wound as you learn the mysteries of your other talents. At Rank 11 you earn your first Mastery point, and this is where you can start making choices about your path. Will you choose to be a tank, taking all the damage and keeping others alive, or will you focus on offense and damaging attacks?

RANK 21–30

Although the main attacks that you use to fight still remain the same now as when you were Rank 10, with your increased rank and Mastery, they will be working much better. Another important ability you receive at Rank 25 is Suppression, which is an instant attack ability that also makes you harder to hit. Add this to your rotation of abilities. Also many new Morale and Tactic abilities become available. Take the time to equip them to your best advantage, especially the Backlash Tactic, which gives you a chance to strike back at any monster that is hitting you. This is useful when you are fighting alone against more than one monster.

RANK 31–40

Many more Tactics and Morale abilities are now added to your arsenal, as well as even more Mastery points and the skills that can come with them. Another useful skill is Bane Shield, an ability that always damages any monsters hitting you. Solo play is still mostly the same for you, though. Cleave and Taunt, Seeping Wound and Suppression: these are your main solo abilities, and they will serve you well.

GROUP PLAY

Chosen can begin grouping at any rank and may find being grouped, especially with a Zealot or other healer class, even easier than going solo. The most important thing to remember in any group is that the monsters should always be hitting you. Thus, Enraged Blow and Taunt are two of your most crucial abilities in a group setting. Other than using taunts as often as possible, Cleave is still your best skill in a group. You can also mix in auras like Dreadful Fear to increase the strength of your group members while decreasing the strength of your enemies. At Rank 10 you also learn one of the most important group skills that you will ever use: Guard. This ability allows you to absorb half the damage that any one member of your group takes while also allowing you to receive half of the hate that the monster feels toward the guarded party member. This is especially useful in helping to keep your healer alive.

As you level, your skills as a tank for your group begin to expand. You receive different Tactics that can help you—or hurt you—as a tank in a group situation. Anything that increases the damage that you receive is a bad Tactic to use in a group. Anything that benefits your ability to taunt, block, or receive heals is a good Tactic to use.

Chosen excel in groups because of our ability to wear heavy armor along with all our special skills and abilities. We can be the strongest team members of the forces of Destruction. Always remember to keep your group alive, especially your healer, and you will have done your job for your group.

FULLY COMPLETE EACH QUEST AREA BEFORE YOU MOVE ON. THIS IS A GREAT WAY TO MAKE SURE THAT YOU ARE PROGRESSING IN RANK AT A STRONG PACE.

LEVELING UP

As you step through the Chaos portal, life as you know it ends, young Chosen. Left alone with only your wits, an axe, and a shield, what do you do? You get to killing. Once you've slain a few monsters and completed a few tasks, you may begin to feel invincible. You aren't, but you may feel that way. Make sure, within that false sense of superiority, that you don't forget to seek the advice and training of your local Career Trainer, Oskar Hredricson. He will have new abilities for you to learn, provided you have advanced in skills enough to rank up.

After you have finished your first few quests, it will be time to move on. Have no fear, though, for new quests await you just over the hill at the base of the bridge into Thorshafn, the first of many pitiful Empire cities awaiting you. As the lust to kill Empire wretches seizes you, make sure you take the time to speak with all the new task givers so that as you slake you thirst for blood, you also fulfill the demands of the weakling taskmasters who don't understand that killing can be its own reward.

Within Thorshafn you will also find your very first public quest, "Ruinous Powers." These public quests are like open tasks, and often require other members of the forces of Destruction to complete. Public quests are a great way to build influence. Building influence in an area is important because it opens up valuable rewards from Rally Masters that can be found within the Chaos camps. There are three levels of influence in each area, and once you attain the maximum level of influence, powerful weapons or armor will be your reward. The public quests are also a good way to acquire weapons and armor of superior quality. If you participate in these quests, are very influential in completing them, and get very lucky with rolling for rewards, you can win a bag of loot that will contain very valuable things.

Once you have finished all of the quests that the Unshackled Host has for you, you should have obtained Rank 5 or 6. Now is the time to really get your feet wet—in the blood of your enemies, of course. It's time for you to jump into Nordenwatch. Nordenwatch is a scenario where you will be required to capture and hold three points against the incursions of the forces of Order. What is a scenario? It is a place where the forces of Order and Destruction meet and contest for superiority.

Once you are bored proving your superiority to those fools who populate the Empire, head south out of Thorshafn and enter Wulfsiege Forest. Wulfsiege Forest is just another of the many steps in a long line of places you will see in your quest to attain greatness. Wulfsiege has many quests and even a few more public quests that you can participate in. Ranks will become increasingly hard to attain at this point, but don't get discouraged. There are plenty of tasks worthy of your skills as a Chosen to keep you entertained as you move along in your quest to destroy the Empire.

We could sit here all day, talking of battles that you have yet to see, but the best way to start a journey is to get killing, and I will hold you back no longer. I hope for your sake you are ready to use that axe in your hands. I won't swing it for you. I'm sure you will find, as you cleave a trail of blood and destruction behind you, that your course follows a path. Along this path will be even more quest centers, and a new type of area called a warcamp. In warcamps you will find Renown Trainers and armor and weapon merchants who will sell you items based on your Renown rank. This rank is based on your skill in killing members of the forces of Order in the scenarios and throughout the land.

Eventually you will progress farther and farther, passing out of Tier 1 and moving into Tiers 2, 3, and 4. Each will give you more opportunities to pillage and kill more of the forces of Order, culminating at the gates of the City of Altdorf. You aren't yet ready to join us in the final battle for control of the world, but I hope someday to stand side by side with you, swinging my axe in time with yours.

As you grow, wounds and toughness will be important attributes to focus on, but don't forget willpower so you can disrupt magic attacks cast on you.

HUNTING PLAYERS AND RENOWN AWARDS

Ah yes, lest I forget, there is one other bit of wisdom I wish to provide you with. I spoke before of two types of battle that you may find yourself in. The second, and more thrilling, is PvP battle, which means that the person you are fighting is often as skilled in battle as you, for even the weaklings of the Empire can produce some good fighters. A Chosen one should never fear these encounters, because it provides ample opportunity to embarrass your enemies with all that I've taught you. You can participate in four basic types of PvP combat.

Skirmishes are random battles between you and other members of the forces of Order that you find in your travels. These battles can start as soon as you enter Thorshafn and will continue for as long as you walk the world. These are often disorganized and messy battles with no objective greater than killing. They can occur only if you turn on your PvP flag or if you attack a member of the Order who is PvP flagged. These can serve to hone your skills in one-on-one combat, but beware because often the members of the Empire travel in packs and will take out a lone wolf.

Battlefields are areas where PvP objectives can be found. They are usually close to Destruction warcamps, and often there are quests associated with these objectives. You will encounter your first battlefield in New Emskrank in Nordland just outside the Blessed Gathering Warcamp. Once you enter a battlefield zone, your PvP flag automatically turns on and you become a target. Participating in these battlefields and conquering the objectives will help to increase your Renown rank and give you a chance to fight with other members of your realm. Find yourself a healer and a few other members to fill out your party, or if there are many people, form a warband that can contain up to four different groups of people and wade into the fray.

Scenarios have objectives like battlefields do, but the number of participants is limited, and the scenario is timed. Objectives differ from scenario to scenario, but even the idiots of the Empire can usually figure them out. For a Chosen one of the Raven God it should be easy enough.

Campaigns are the ultimate in PvP battle. They are large-scale assaults on major objectives like towns or cities. The final campaign of conquering Altdorf is a challenge that all members of the forces of Destruction will eventually participate in. There are smaller campaigns that you can participate in, but all campaigns will require a warband to be successful.

SOLO PVP

Ah, single combat. Well do I remember my first time facing off against a Bright Wizard of the Empire with my axe in my hand. Chosen warriors must remember one simple axiom in single combat: "Keep your friends close, but your enemies closer." To the untrained this may seem easy, but those Empire wizards love to run away. Seeping Wound followed by a Dizzying Blow will slow anyone down long enough for you to chop them down like a tree. The Morale ability, Grapple, is another handy tactic for solo PvP because it forces your target to stay in one place while you beat him down.

In all solo encounters, your tactics will be the same: close in on your target and put your axe into his skull. I like to use my Discordant Instability aura combined with Dreadful Fear. On top of those two auras, I also use Seeping Wound and Dizzying Blow. At Rank 18, you receive Tzeentch's Reflection, which you will find extremely useful in killing pesky magic-users. As you progress in rank and Renown, it will become easier for you to accomplish this killing, although you will find that you use most of the same attacks against your foes. Do not worry if you fail in your attempts at first. Learning how to be a good killer takes time and practice, and the mystics of the Raven God have devised a method to raise you from the dead to fight again with only a limited and temporary reduction in your fighting ability. This reduction will pass with time, but if you are in a hurry you can always pay one of the many Healer NPCs to remove it from you as well.

FIND A GOOD HEALER. TOGETHER THE TWO OF YOU WILL BE A STRONG TEAM, ACCOMPLISHING TOGETHER WHAT NEITHER OF YOU COULD DO ALONE.

GROUP PLAY

Within a group the role of the Chosen is simple: Create the chaos that you are so good at, and kill everyone around you as you can. Focus mainly on the healers of the Order because as the healers fall, so do their friends. Also keep your healer alive as best you can. The Guard ability is a good way to prolong a healer's life by taking upon yourself half the damage they would otherwise receive. The fools of the Order will try to kill your healer, so you suffer the pain for him and use it to kill them. Also stay with your group and keep your auras up and covering your group mates. Dreadful Fear and Discordant Instability will keep your enemies weak and your allies strong. I know in your bloodthirsty desire for death you may wish to chase those who flee, but this is an easy way to find yourself alone and surrounded by enemies. You may take a few with you, but you will most assuredly die unless help arrives.

As Chosen, when you are capturing an enemy objective in a battlefield or campaign, it is your duty to engage the defending champion. It is important to keep this champion off the weaker members of your group, because they will die quickly. Oftentimes this is when the cowardly Empire fighters will attack, when you are focused upon other matters, but maintain your focus and you will survive to kill them all.

THE FIRES MUST LIVE

Ahh, I can see the fires are beginning to die down. I believe it is time to light them once again. Those fools in Thorshafn believe they have forced us back, but we will attack again. You should join in the battle. Sharpen your axe and prepare yourself. Someday I hope to meet you again, once you grow greater in the eyes of the Raven God. Forget not these words I have spoken, for although I cannot see into the future, I have learned to trust my instincts. You will go far, young Chosen, and bring glory to our god. All Hail the Raven God! All Glory to Tzeentch!

MAGUS

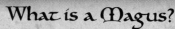

By Mortarias

Who interrupts my studies? Don't you know how dangerous it is to interrupt a Magus performing his rituals? If the ritual itself doesn't go awry, the Magus may sacrifice you to his Lord Tzeentch just for being such a fool! A lesser Magus' concentration may have been broken, and if that happens, even for a second, whatever he is attempting to summon may break free and wreak havoc upon all in the immediate vicinity. Lucky for you, I am no lesser Magus.

So, you seek the power that comes with tapping into the raw energies of the Chaos? What do you wish to do with this power? Are you looking for a quick and easy way to control and destroy your enemies and bring chaos to the land? If so, then get out of my sight. The path of the Magus is not an easy one; you must devote your life to the study of the Chaos and of our Lord Tzeentch. I myself spend most of every day studying the Raven God, seeking to understand Him and his creations just a little bit better, in hopes that I may service His needs as best I can.

Perhaps you have heard that Magi keep pets of the demonic nature? Again, you are a fool if you believe daemons to be "pets." They do our bidding to raze the blasphemers from the land, for they crave destruction as we do, but if you suffer a moment's hesitation, your throat will be theirs as well.

Enough prattling. I have been told the fire burns with you to seek out the craft of the Magus. I will tutor you until the time when you feel the fire must burn the heretics we see all around us.

What is a Magus?

Is it the power of the Magus's magic that we seek or the power of the Magus's daemons? Magi are the sole possessors of the secrets of summoning daemons, creations of the Great Changer. Though wild, these daemons are controlled by skilled Magi, and their demonic energies can alter the course of events. I have seen Daemons decimate a battlefield, leaving nothing but char and ash. Char and ash, with but a few bones to pick through.

That is not to say that a Magus himself should be cast aside as corpse-food for the dogs. Only a madman would waste such raw power. The Magus can pull upon the magic of the Chaos to rend flesh, dissolve sanity, and burn mountains to the ground. They fall to dagger and sword easily...if a foe can reach them under a relentless assault.

Chaos has need of such wizards to protect the armored warriors who march into the maw of the enemy. They whisper to fire and wind and other things unspeakable. We do not understand them, but we do comprehend the death that befalls our enemies when the Magus calls upon his trade.

—Baron Heinar Balethar, Zimmeron's Hold, Chaos Wastes

TRAIN NEW ABILITIES AND MASTERIES, AND SPEND RENOWN AS SOON AS YOU CAN, AS THE ABILITIES WILL INCREASE YOUR POWER AND OPTIONS.

STARTING STATS

You start with two strong magic abilities: Flickering Red Fire and Rend Winds. Both are ranged damage spells. Flickering Red Fire does a little higher damage with a better range, but takes longer to cast. Rend Winds, while doing less damage, has half the cast time of Flickering Red Fire, allowing you to fire it off more quickly if your enemy has survived long enough to get into close combat with you.

Intelligence will be your most important skill. This increases your damage and reduces the chance for your spells to be disrupted, allowing us to do what we do best. After that you will probably want to boost your defensive skills, as we are somewhat frail. Spending hours studying will do that. Get Toughness to reduce the damage you take, and increase Wounds so you have more hit points to spare. Initiative is also a very good stat to raise, as this will not only increase your chance to evade the enemy's attacks, but also increase the chance of your already powerful spells to critical hit, striking for even more damage.

SUMMON DAEMONS BEFORE STARTING ANY COMBAT. DAEMONS REQUIRE A MUCH LARGER NUMBER OF ACTION POINTS TO SUMMON THAN NORMAL SPELLS, AND THESE ACTION POINTS WILL BE NEEDED TO KILL YOUR TARGET.

DROPPED INTO CHAOS

As one of the elite spellcasting careers of Destruction, the Magus begins close to the front lines. You exit the portal and enter a Chaos warcamp in Sturmvall, a hub of Norsca. Immediately upon exiting this portal, you are greeted by the man who interrupted your studies and requested your assistance, Chieftain Skurlorg Blackhorn. He will help direct you to what you can do to assist to the war effort.

Farther down the hill, some tents have been set up. Off to your right is Oskar Hredricson, a trainer. You will get to know him and his type well on your journey to the upper ranks of the Magus. He and his brethren will teach you your new abilities as you progress through ranks. To your left are some cemetery gates, and this is where your adventure in these new lands will start. Enter, and begin the quest you were given by Blackhorn.

In the distance you can see the town of Thorshafn. You will get there soon enough, and this will be your first contact with the despicable Empire. You will fight this cruel nation and liberate its town in the name of the Raven God.

MAGUS GEAR

Magi can only wear robes and carry staffs, as the disc we ride on can't support much more weight, but that is all we need. When looking for a staff, you want the one with the highest bonuses to your statistics. Never choose a staff based on its ability to deal damage in combat, because you will rarely ever hit things with it. Look for staves with Intelligence, Toughness, Wounds, and Initiative, with Intelligence taking the priority, because it gives you more magic damage.

When choosing robes, follow the same idea. You want robes that provide more armor, but because they are all made from cloth anyway, the range will not be that large. Focus more on the stat bonuses of the armor, as you will gain more use out of them. For armor, you may want to focus a bit more on Toughness, Initiative, and Wounds, because these will keep you alive. As you rise in the ranks of the honored Magi, your equipment shall improve and you will hear the screams of your victims in more than just your dreams.

STRENGTHS AND WEAKNESSES

STRENGTHS

- Good magic damage from quick-casting spells.
- The ability to summon powerful daemons.
- Spells that do both Elemental and Spirit damage, bypassing armor.
- Spells that allow you to escape melee opponents and to mitigate some of damage.

The Magus should focus on damage. We can do excellent damage, and quite quickly, as our spells all have short casting times. We have spells for all situations, ones that attack at a great range, and ones that work only in melee range. Some spells deal immediate damage, some over time, and some to a larger area. Some of our damaging spells also strip the enemy of Toughness, or interrupt actions. We can also silence enemy casters, root enemies in place, and knock them away, all excellent for escaping from enemies who get too close.

Summoning daemons is our greatest asset, the pride of the Magus. Our daemons are just as varied as our spells: each one has unique powers that can attack single targets or all targets in a certain area. Their damage is excellent, especially compared to their action point cost. They are also incredibly useful when you solo; you can have them act as the aggressor, taking the damage from enemies while you attack safely from afar.

WEAKNESSES

- Can only wear robes, so we take more damage from melee attackers.
- Daemons do not last long and are stuck in their summoning circle. If you move, you must resummon the daemon.
- Spells can be set back and interrupted when hit by enemy attacks.
- No way of healing, though we do have ways of escaping.

We wear only light armor and take more damage from physical attacks. Unfortunately, when we are damaged, we have no way of healing ourselves. While the power of the Chaos is great, there are some limits to what it can do. Luckily we do have abilities to root enemies in place and knock them away. Our daemons, while a true testament to the great strength of the Magus, have their weaknesses. We must create a summoning circle to control them, and they cannot leave this circle. The shift between the Chaos and our world is also quite harsh on the daemons, leaving them with much smaller amounts of health than yourself. Most of our spells also require time and motions to cast, so if you are hit during this casting time, you will be set back, requiring more time to cast the spell.

ABILITIES

Our brains stew with the wonderful possibilities of the nature of Chaos. Is it possible to explain these mysteries? I shall try.

You advance through your training in two ways. There is your Core Training, and three different Mastery paths. You get new Core abilities as you rank up. Buy them from the Career Trainer, those greedy moneygrubbers. Don't they understand that they are just hurting themselves by charging us money for what will ultimately be of help to them? But I digress. Mastery paths are slightly different. Starting at Rank 11 you will start accruing Mastery points, and will end up with 25 by the time you have completed your journey to Rank 40. These are used to advance your way down any of the three Mastery paths. They are as follows:

Path of Havoc increases these Core abilities: Flickering Red Fire, Summon Pink Horror, Surging Violet Fire, Glean Magic, Mutating Blue Fire.

Path of Changing increases these Core abilities: Rend Winds, Summon Flamer, Surge of Insanity, Dissolving Mist, Infernal Blast.

Path of Daemonology increases these Core abilities: Daemon Lash, Summon Blue Horror, Aegis of the Orange Fire, Agonizing Torrent, Swat Aside.

So which one should you take? Well, that's depends entirely on what you want to do. Each path helps a specific set of skills. You can even go into multiple paths, and in fact, that is what I would recommend. You should probably focus on either the Path of Havoc or the Path of Changing, but not both, and spend the rest of your points in Daemonology. Whichever path you pick will also change the set of abilities you will use in combat. Let us take a deeper look at the paths now.

The Path of Havoc is all about raining the fire of Chaos on your enemies from afar. It strengthens your Pink Horror, the daemon with the longest range, and increases your other abilities' ranges. The abilities in this path all take longer to cast, but they have the extra range and damage to warrant this increase in casting time. This will help you and your daemon kill anything before it can reach you. Glean Magic is also very useful for this path, because it removes Elemental resistance, and all these abilities deal Elemental damage. This path excels at single-target damage, because all of its abilities focus on just one target, seeking to maximize damage on that one enemy.

CUT DOWN ON TRAVEL TIME. GATHER A BUNCH OF QUESTS BEFORE GOING OUT TO DO THEM.

SKILLS AND ABILITIES

The Path of Changing is a very versatile path. While its abilities don't do quite as much damage and have a shorter range than the Path of Havoc, its abilities all have a much shorter casting time. The main damaging abilities in this group also add secondary status effects. For example, Surge of Insanity makes enemy actions take longer, and Dissolving Mist strips Toughness from the target. A few of the spells also damage all enemies within a certain area, allowing them to do large amounts of damage spread out over many targets. One of the abilities you can train in the path itself opens a small rift in the Chaos, giving all enemies within 10 yards a small taste of the glory of the Raven God, and briefly rooting them in place.

The Path of Daemonology is a much more dangerous path, because its abilities require you to get into close range to use them. However, this risk does come with a reward: the path allows you to empower your daemons through abilities and Tactics, and has some of the highest damage-dealing abilities. Use Daemon Lash to deal damage if you do come into contact with enemies at close range. Swat Aside knocks enemies away from you if they attempt to hit you. Aegis of the Orange Fire can be a life saver, bathing you in a protective orange fire and increasing your armor and Toughness for a short amount of time.

Abilities

Name	Level	Path	Cost	Range (in feet)	Type	Build	Duration	Reuse	Description
Flickering Red Fire	Level 1	Havoc	35	100	Magic Attack - Elemental	2s	0s	0s	Deals 349 elemental damage.
Demonic Maw	Level 1	Core	35	Melee	Magic Attack - Hex	0	0	0	Deals 262 damage. If target is Hexxed, Snare 40% for 10s.
Rend Winds	Level 2	Changing	25	65	Magic Attack - Elemental	1s	0s	0s	Hits 3 times for 74 damage each time. Deals Spirit damage.
Summon Pink Horror	Level 3	Havoc	55	Self	Summon	3s	3 min	5s	Summons an immobile turret.
Strengthen Thrall	Level 3	Core	15/s	20	Horror Heal	0s	3s	0s	Channel. Heals your horror for 135/s for 3s.
Infernal Blast	Level 4	Daemonology	30	65	Magic Attack - Hex	0	9s	10s	Deals 449 over 9s. Deals Elemental damage. Arc: 180, radius: 30ft.
Glean Magic	Level 5	Changing	25	65	Debuff - Hex	0s	20s	0s	Deals 449 damage over 20s and lowers the Spirit resist of everyone in the radius by 9.45/level for 20s. Radius: 20ft. Deals Spirit damage.
Demonic Lash	Level 6	Daemonology	35	65	CAE Ranged Attack	0s	0s	0s	Deals 187. Spirit damage to targets in radius. Arc: 120, radius: 40ft.
Summon Blue Horror	Level 6	Daemonology	55	Self	Summon	3s	3 min	5s	Summons an immobile turret.
Horrifying Visions	Level 7	Core	20	100	Detaunt	0s	15s	15s	Detaunts (50%) target for 15s.
Summon Flamer	Level 8	Changing	55	Self	Summon	3s	3 min	5s	Summons an immobile turret.

REMEMBER TO SET YOUR DAEMON TO DEFENSIVE WHEN YOU SUMMON IT. YOU DON'T WANT IT DRAWING EXTRA ENEMIES WHEN YOU AREN'T READY FOR THEM.

Abilities

Name	Level	Path	Cost	Range (in feet)	Type	Build	Duration	Reuse	Description
Baleful Transmogrification	Level 9	Havoc	40	100	Magical Ranged Attack - Hex	0s	15s	0	Deals 798 damage over 15s. Elemental damage.
Tzeentch's Grip	Level 10	Core	30	30	CC - Hex	0s	5s	20s	PBAE Root for 5s. Radius: 30ft.
Demonic Armor	Level 11	Core	35	Self	Buff - Enchantment	2s	60 min	0s	Increases Armor by 22/level. After taking damage 20 times, buff fades. Setback override: 100%. Stacking rule: Stacks with other buffs and Tactics (is NOT stack largest).
Surging Violet Fire	Level 12	Havoc	35	100	Magic Attack - Elemental	0s	0s	10s	Deals 262 Elemental damage.
Surge of Insanity	Level 14	Changing	35	65	Magic Attack - Spirit	1s	0s	10s	Deals 337 damage to target. Interrupts all enemies around target. Radius: 20ft. Spirit damage.
Pandemonium	Level 16	Changing	40	65	TAE - Spirit - Hex	1s	15s	5s	Deals 748 damage over 15s to all targets in 20ft radius.
Demonic Infestiation	Level 18	Daemonology	50	65	Create Bomb	1s	1 min	15s	Creates a tiny Daemon on ground. When activated, deals 299 Elemental damage to all targets within 30ft radius and knocks down targets for 2s.
Warping Blast	Level 20	Changing	30	65	Magic Attack	1s	0s	10s	Deals 337 damage and a short knockback. Deals Spirit damage.
Resummon	Level 22	Core	30	Self	Demon Resummon	0s	0s	20s	Destroy current Daemon. Resummon Daemon at feet with health % equal to previous turret.
Instability	Level 25	Core	35	Self	CC	0s	0s	60s	Destroys current turret. Knocks down enemies around turret for 5s. Radius 30 ft.
Demonic Resistance	Level 28	Daemonology	55	Group	Buff - Enchantment	0s	60 min	0s	Increases group's Corporeal resist by 6.3 per level for 60 minutes.
Withered Soul	Level 30	Havoc	25	100	DoT - Elemental - Hex	0s	15s	20s	Deals 648 over 20s and reduces target's Disrupt chance by 5% for 20s.
Mutating Blue Fire	Level 35	Havoc	45	100	Magic Attack - Elemental - Hex	3s	9s	10s	Deals 675 damage and 448 over 9s. Deals Elemental damage.
Warpfire	Level 40	Daemonology	25/s	30	Magic Attack - Elemental	0s	3s	13s	Channeled. Deals 150 damage to targets in the radius, 1s for 3s. No setback override. Deals Elemental damage.
Perils of the Warp	Havoc x5	Havoc	45	8.33	Magic Barb - Hex	2s	10s	0s	Magic Barb, deals 299 Elemental damage.
Bolt of Change	Havoc x9	Havoc	30	12.5	Magic Attack — Elemental	3s	0	10s	Deals 750 damage. Undefendable.
Tzeentch's Firestorm	Havoc x13	Havoc	25 / 2s	6.66	Magic Attack - Elemental	0s	6s	16s	GTAE Channeled. Deals 299 every 2s for 6s. Radius: 20ft. Any attack to Magus interrupts 0.5s duration of channel. Deals Elemental damage.
Seed of Chaos	Changing x5	Changing	40	Thrown	Magic Attack - Hex	0s	9s	10s	Deals 499 damage over 15s and then explodes for 249 damage in a 20ft radius. Deals Spirit damage.
Dissolving Mist	Changing x9	Changing	35	GTAE Thrown	Magic Attack	0s	30s	30s	GTAE. Pulses 100 damage per 2s for 10s. Then pulses 200 damage per 2s for 10s. Then pulses 399 damage per 2s for 10s. Total duration: 30s. Deals Spirit damage. Radius: 20ft.
Indigo Fire of Change	Changing x13	Changing	25/s	8.33	Channeled Magic Attack - Spirit	0s	6s	16s	Channeled Spirit damage. Deals 449 every 2s second for 6s. If target dies with this effect on them, spawns an uncontrolled horror for 30s. Setback override: 100%
Demonic Instablity	Daemonology x5	Daemonology	45	Self	Self Buff	1s	9s	20s	Self buff. Pulses 200 Spirit damage every 3s for 9s. Radius: 30ft.
Aegis of the Orange Fire	Daemonology x9	Daemonology	25	Self	Buff - Enchantment	0s	20s	60s	Increases Wounds by 3/level (heals for value given) and gives a damage shield that returns 150 Elemental damage on all melee attackers.
Chaotic Rift	Daemonology x13	Daemonology	30	PBAE	PBAE CC	0s	4s	20s	PBAE. Pulls players within 65ft in toward the center and then causes a 40% Snare for 4s, 1s later (20ft effect).

Abilities

Name	Level	Path	Cost	Range (in feet)	Type	Build	Duration	Reuse	Description
Demonic Consumption	Level 7 - Turret	Havoc	Free	100	Turret Attack	0s	10s	10s	Deals 150 damage over 10s and reduces targets crit chance by 5% for 10s.
Demonic Fire	Level 17 - Turret	Havoc	Free	100	Turret Attack	1s	0s	5s	Deals 112.5 damage.
Flame of Tzeentch	Level 13 - Turret	Changing	Free	Thrown	Turret Attack	0s	2s	4s	Deals 100 Elemental damage over 3s.
Flames of Change	Level 23 - Turret	Changing	Free	Thrown	Turret Attack	1s	6s	10s	Deals 200 Elemental damage over 6s. Radius: 20ft.
Warping Energy	Level 11 - Turret	Daemonology	Free	30	Turret Attack	2s	0s	5s	Deals 150 damage. Arc: 120, radius: 40ft. Deals Elemental damage.
Coruscating Energy	Level 21 - Turret	Daemonology	Free	PBAE	Turret Attack	0s	3s	8s	PBAE around turret. Deals 75 damage every 1s for 3s. Deals Elemental damage. Setback override: 0 (Not setbackable). Radius: 30ft.

MORALE

And I suppose you will want to learn about Morale skills too? You really should do some research before bothering me with such trivial matters, but fortunately enough I have some free time. Morale skills are used by spending Morale, which builds up during combat, instead of action points. As you rank up, you learn nine different Morale abilities, and each Mastery path offers one specific to its path. These abilities are much stronger than your normal abilities, and you must use them strategically to accomplish your goals.

The Morale abilities are broken into two different types: ones that deal damage and ones that enhance you. While the damage ones are very nice to finish off that last unbeliever, you already have a large number of spells that do excellent damage, and should probably use some of the Morale slots for abilities to help you survive. If you do want a little more damage, I suggest using Morale abilities that do not solely deal damage, but also have a secondary effect to them, such as Scintillating Energy, which also stuns your target, or Grasping Darkness, which slows your enemy. These are both excellent abilities for escaping if need be, and deal enough damage to make your target think twice about attacking you again.

Morale

Name	Level	Rank	Range	Duration	Description
Mage Bolt	Level 8	Rank 1	100	0s	Magic attack that deals 1,200 damage.
Siphon Power	Level 12	Rank 2	100	30s	Drain 200 AP from target and give to character. Decrease target's Intelligence by 4/level for 30s.
Misdirection	Level 16	Rank 1	Self	10s	Self-Buff. For 10s, magical attacks return 50% of the damage back to the caster (resulting in 50% less damage to the target).
Focused Mind	Level 20	Rank 2	Self	10s	For 10s, build times are reduced by 50%. Character purges and is immune to Silence, Disarm, Root, Snare, and Setback.
Scintillating Energy	Level 24	Rank 3	100	7s	Target takes 1,200 + Stun for 7s.
Grasping Darkness	Level 28	Rank 1	100	6s	Deals 798 damage over 6s and Snares by 60% for 6s.
Roiling Winds	Level 32	Rank 2	100	4s	Deals 300 every second for 4s around the target to all targets in the radius. Radius: 20ft.
Conduit of Chaos	Level 36	Rank 3	Self	10s	All abilities cost 0 AP for 10 sec.
Unleash the Winds	Level 40	Rank 4	PBAE	0	PBAE that deals 1,800 and knocks back enemies.
Soul Leak	Havoc x15	Rank 4	100	10s	Deals 2,394 over 10s, drains 50 AP per tick.
Daemonic Scream	Changing x15	Rank 4	LAE	0s	Deals 2,400 damage. Radius: 65ft.
Firewyrm of Tzeentch	Daemonology x15	Rank 4	Self	15s	Summons uncontrollable daemon (fully mobile, not a turret) for 15 seconds (long enough to use the attacks below).
Warped Claw	=Turret Ability=	Rank 4	CAE	0s	Deals 798 to all targets in the radius. Usable three times over the course of the summon, at second 4, 8, 12. Arc: 120, radius: 30ft.
Breath of Change	=Turret Ability=	Rank 4	PBAE	0s	Deals 798 to all targets in the radius at second 15 and kills the daemon. Radius: 45ft.

WHILE YOU DO HAVE SOME ABILITIES THAT TARGET MULTIPLE ENEMIES, YOU AND YOUR DAEMON BOTH HAVE LIMITED DEFENSES, AND IT IS BETTER TO ENGAGE ONLY ONE ENEMY AT A TIME.

TACTICS

Tactics, like Morale and Core abilities, are trained at the Career Trainer and through your Mastery path. You start with one Tactic slot, and unlock a new one at Ranks 21, 31, and 40, for a total of four normal Tactic slots. You also get a special Renown Tactic slot and Guild Tactic slot. Browse through trainer lists and pick out ones that you think will fit your style best.

I will also recommend a few Tactics. If you are soloing, then you will definitely want to use Unearthly Shriek. It gives your daemon a chance to taunt its target, causing it to attack your daemon and not yourself, which is always a good thing. Sleight of Hand is also very important, because it makes your abilities cause less hate. This helps keep the damage on whatever brute feels like getting hit. Endless Knowledge and Warped Flesh are good ways to shore up weaknesses in your stats, as they boost your Intelligence and Toughness, respectively, by one per rank. The rest of the Tactics really depend on which style you want to use, as they affect different abilities in various ways. One Tactic that you may want to pick up in the Daemonology tree is the first one, Chaotic Attunement. This allows daemons to be summoned instantly, which is incredibly useful for PvP combat.

Tactics

Name	Level	Description
Warped Flesh	Level 11	25% chance when attacked to absorb 262 damage for 10s.
Devour Energy	Level 13	25% of the time, spells cast also gain the character back 30 AP per 3s. (Non-stacking, non-refreshing)
Infernal Flesh	Level 15	Increases Wounds for your turrets by 4 per level.
Tzeentch's Warding	Level 17	Increases Elemental resist by +6.3 per level of the character.
Endless Knowledge	Level 19	Increases Intelligence by +4 per level of the character.
Unearthly Shriek	Level 21	Your turrets gain a 15% chance to proc a taunt (Interrupts target. For 15s, the turret deals 20% more damage against target. Monsters turn to attack turret until taunt expires. After 3 ability activations and/or auto attacks from the target hit the turret, taunt fades. Generates 1,500 in hate.)
Backlash	Level 23	25% chance to put a 5s 150 DoT on attacker. Non-stacking, non-refreshing.
Sleight of Hand	Level 25	Decreases threat by 50% on all attacks.
Flame's Kiss	Level 27	Rend Winds and Flickering Fire become undefendable.
Close Quarters	Level 29	Increases magic damage by +25% when under 45ft and decreases magic damage by -20% when over 45ft.
Lasting Aegis	Level 31	Increases durations of Invoke Orange Fire and Boon of Tzeentch by 10s.
Redirection	Level 33	Any time you disrupt a spell, you gain 75 AP.
Surging Power	Level 35	Increases crit bonus damage from Infernal Blast, Surging Violent Fire, and Surge of Insanity by 50%
Swift Flames	Level 37	Reduces Surging Violet Fire's cooldown by 7s.
Daemonic Mending	Level 39	Strengthen Thrall will heal for an additional 33%.
Fiery Winds	Havoc x3	Red Fire and Violet Fire will hit one additional enemy near the target 10ft.
Changer's Blessing	Havoc x7	Surging Violet Fire now heals self for 50% of damage dealt.
Chaos Unleashed	Havoc x11	Increases crit chance for all Path of Havoc spells by 15%
Infernal Pain	Changing x3	Surge of Insanity causes additional 299 over 6s on all targets hit. Hex.
Endless Pandemonium	Changing x7	Everytime Pandemonium ends or dispelled, it has a 50% chance to reapply itself Maximum reapplications: 5.
Wild Changing	Changing x11	Increases crit chance for all Path of Changing spells by 15%.
Chaotic Attunement	Daemonology x3	Turrets are now summoned instantly.
Daemonic Pact	Daemonology x7	Increases Toughness by 4 for you and your turret, as long as you have a turret active.
Daemonic Contract	Daemonology x11	Your turret will deal 100% more damage as long as you are within 30ft. While you have a turret up, your AP regen is reduced by 5 AP/s.

RENOWN

As you come into contact with the hypocritical Empire and the other forces of the Order, you will feel an intense drive to display the might of Chaos and Tzeentch, and by all means you should! The reward you get from these PvP combats is Renown. You get one Renown point for every rank you go up, and can spend these at Renown Trainers to boost different stats and to purchase special Renown talents.

There are three levels of Renown rewards. You progress to each new tier when you have purchased a sufficient number of abilities from the current tier. You need to spend 20 points in the first tier to get to the second, and then 40 points throughout both tiers to get to the third.

What should you purchase? Well, I would recommend spending your points in the first tier in Acumen, which raises your Intelligence. If you would like to increase your defenses you can buy a few points of Fortitude, which raises Toughness, and Impetus, which raises your Initiative. I would focus mostly on Acumen, though, because it raises your main stat.

The second tier is a little different, as all the stats have been paired up with another stat. In this case your main skill, Intelligence, is paired up with Willpower in the Sage reward. You should put a few points into this, but don't ignore Vigor; extra Wounds is always nice. You may want to take some of the Tactics here too. For Glory!, King of the Hill, and Mission Focused all give you extra Renown in scenarios, skirmishes, and quests, respectively. These are a good way to help you earn Renown and move up through the ranks.

SOLO PLAY (PVE)

RANK 1-10

Always remember to start out at maximum range. You can tell this by selecting your target and moving to the spot where your Flickering Red Fire can be cast. Cast Flickering Red Fire, cast it again as the target approaches, and then alternate between this and Daemon Lash. Once you get your Pink Horror, summon him before any combat, and allow your action points to regenerate. Also remember to set your daemon to defensive mode, taking control of his actions and having him attack only what you want him to attack. The Pink Horror will probably be the daemon you want to stick with, because it has the longest range and decent attack speed. Once you are ready, command it to attack the target first, allowing it to take the target's aggression away from you. Allow your daemon a few hits before you begin attacking, so the target will be thoroughly enraged at your daemon, and less likely to notice you. If an enemy does get within melee range, use Daemon Lash whenever it is up, because it is an instant cast and is one of your highest damaging spells. But, if your Daemon can keep the target focused on him, use Flickering Red Fire. At Rank 9 you get Surging Violet Fire. Use that whenever it s up. If your daemon gets low on health, use Strengthen Thrall to heal your daemon for a bit. Use it until he is at a safe health, or you feel confident in your ability to kill the target.

RANK 11-20

Ranks 11 through 20 have basically the same play style as your earlier combat training. The most important difference is the acquiring of Red Winds at rank 14. This will be a very important spell to your spell rotation, and will replace Flickering Red Fire if you choose to go the Path of Changing. You do get a few other abilities, though most won't make as large a change to your spell rotation. Use Aegis of the Orange Fire if you are low on health for a quick Toughness and Armor boost until your daemon can do its job and take the focus of the creature back on itself. When your summoned minion engages the target, start out with Glean Magic. It reduces the target's Elemental resistance, allowing your daemon's abilities, and your own, to deal Elemental damage more ferociously.

Discs of Tzeentch

The Magus is a formidable opponent, even without his daemon-infused Disc. Combine the two and terror quakes the knees of all but the most experienced veterans of the forces of Order.

Discs of Tzeentch are shaped from the Screamers gathered out of the ethers of Chaos. These Screamers are glimmering sky-sharks that soar upon the winds of magic, with no real conscious thought other than a hunting instinct to prey upon the shadow-souls of mortal creatures. A rare sight in the mortal world, screamers swirl around battlefields, lured from the Realm of Chaos by pulses of emotion and carnage. Armed with fangs, horns, and spurs, these manta-like creatures should be feared. Their flight maneuvers them into position quickly, and the daemons' sharp armaments tear through foe regardless of armor or skill.

Only a master craftsman can create a Disc of Tzeentch out of a Screamer. The daemon has to be transmuted from its original, ethereal-adapted form into a flattened, circular riding platform. As part of the binding process, it retains much of its magical essence and physical characteristics. Thus, you may see Discs covered in eyes, feathers, scales and even living metal.

The bond between Magus and Disc is a special one. The Magus' Disc is more than a vehicle to swoop down on victims and hover above the battlefield surveying the destruction. Magus and Disc are forever linked, and it is the power of that partnership that seeks to offer up more sacrifices to Tzeentch than any other career.

RANK 21-30

From Rank 21 to 30 you mostly get new Tactics and Morale abilities. I've already discussed the Morale abilities, and I assume you were paying attention, so I don't have to repeat myself do I? Good. As for the new Tactics, you unlock a new Tactic slot at Rank 20, so now you have space for two abilities. You pick up Sleight of Hand at Rank 25, and that should take one of those two slots. The second one is up to you, based on your play style.

At Rank 30 you gain Infernal Blast, which is very useful if you are fighting more than one enemy, and it hits all enemies at a decent range. You should also be specializing in one of the Mastery paths now, and start using those powers more. If you choose the Path of Havoc, use Flickering Red Fire as your main attack, and use the new ability you get at Rank 25, Mutating Blue Fire. If you go down the Path of Changing, stick with Rend Winds. If you have decided to take the Path of Daemonology, you may want to risk getting into range to use Daemon Lash. Of course, you should summon the daemon that is associated with your chosen path, because it will get stronger the farther you progress down that path. For the Path of Havoc, it's the Pink Horror. For the Path of Changing, it's the Flamer. For the Path of Daemonology, it's the Blue Horror.

Books Every Magus Needs

"The Harmer's Almanac"

"The Joy of Cooking . . . Squid"

"How to Siege a Keep in 39 Days"

"Encyclopedia Norsca"

RANK 31-40

From Rank 30 to 40 you only get two new spells, but those are both excellent defensive spells. The first is Theft of Words, which you should use against casters whenever it is available. It does damage and silences them for five seconds, preventing them from casting spells. The second ability is Swat Aside. Use this whenever an enemy gets within melee range. When used on another player it knocks them back, but it only knocks an NPC down, which should still be sufficient for you to get some distance on him.

Other than that, you get a lot of new Morale abilities and Tactics. Your rotation should be very similar to how it was in the beginning: Summon your daemon, let your action points recharge, order your daemon to attack, and then open with Glean Magic. From there, use whichever base spell you are specializing in—Flickering Red Fire, Rend Winds, or Daemon Lash—and use the other abilities in the different Masteries as the spells become available.

QUESTING GOES MUCH FASTER WITH A PARTNER. TRY TO PARTNER WITH SOMEONE WHO CAN KEEP THE ENEMY'S ATTENTION WHILE YOU BLAST IT WITH YOUR SPELLS.

Do's and Don'ts of First-Time Summoners

Do: Summon your daemon to create bowel-slackening terror and rain destruction upon your weakling foes.

Don't: Summon your daemon to impress members of the opposite sex, simple minded greenskins, or people that you owe money to but don't want to pay back.

Remember the ritual in which you swore your soul to the service of Tzeentch? Where you promised to serve his plots and destroy his enemies in return for reality warping powers of epic proportions? Well now that you have unholy powers of unspeakable daemonic control, it's up to you to be responsible. Tzeentch didn't give you the power to tear through the veil of reality and reach into the Realm of Chaos just so you could impress girls. (Unless you are attempting to recruit them to the service of Tzeentch.) Remember, the Bird God is everywhere, and he is watching.

Do: Make sure to show dominance over your daemon as soon as it is summoned.

Don't: Try to make it feel inferior by insulting it or giving it a silly name like Binky.

You want to make sure that your daemon knows who's in charge, so it will accept your commands. Do this through a strong and confident tone of voice. Giving it a name is good, but you should definitely avoid using names like Tiny, which, while okay for a Dwarf, will only enrage the daemon, making it harder to control.

Do: Summon the appropriate daemon for the job.

Don't: Attempt to summon something outside of your ability.

Different daemons serve different purposes. If you are facing one person who is starting far away, summon a Pink Horror. If you are facing maybe one or two people at medium range, summon a Flamer, and if it's a group of people who have gotten the jump on you, summon a Blue Horror. However, don't attempt to summon something out of your league like a greater daemon. The last time a Magus tried that, his entire group was wiped out. And his warband. And his army. And the opponent's army.

Do: Use your slowing and snaring spells when enemies get within range.

Don't: Taunt the enemy when they are unable to move.

One of our strengths is our various ways of preventing enemies from getting to us, while one of our weaknesses is that we take more damage than most do. So while it's great to have our enemies snared in place, stopping to taunt them may backfire, as they may have abilities that allow them to break snares and will be on you before you can insult them.

DAEMONS DON'T LEAVE THEIR SUMMONING
CIRCLE, SO CAREFULLY CHOOSE WHERE YOU
SET UP YOUR CIRCLE.

GROUP PLAY

Group play is going to be fairly similar to your solo playing, because you are still concentrating on the same thing: killing your targets. You should probably use the Pink Horror or Flamer, rather than the Blue Horror, so you can stay back out of melee range and cast spells unbothered. This allows your healer to focus more on the brute who is taking the damage. Keep your debuff spells up as often as possible, such as Dissolving Mist for the melee people and Glean Magic for any casters who deal Elemental damage. The Tactic Sleight of Hand is a mainstay; again, so you do not attract the attention of your target.

HUNTING PLAYERS AND RENOWN REWARDS

SOLO PVP

So, you are looking for a real challenge? Well then, fight other players, because they have a much higher intelligence than the monsters roaming about. They won't do the same thing every time, but that is what makes it so fun. It requires quick thinking, and an in-depth knowledge of your career and what the other careers can do. Luckily, knowledge is where the Magus excels.

Unfortunately, we are not great at fighting solo PvP. We have very low armor and health, so we die very easily. Therefore, it's important to get the jump on your enemy before they attack you. If a melee character gets up close to you and has a good amount of health left, it's usually best to throw up a defensive spell and Flee. There is no shame in running, because it allows you to live to fight for Tzeentch in a better situation. Use your slowing and snaring abilities such as Tzeentch's Grip or the Morale ability Grasping Darkness to put some distance between you and your enemy. Swat Away is also very good for getting away from an enemy that is too close.

Try to have a daemon summoned before the combat starts. Summoning daemons takes a lot of concentration and action points, so it's important to have one out before engaging an enemy. A daemon is an excellent source of damage, and forces your opponent to focus on multiple targets.

You'll use the same spells, but you have to be much smarter about how you use them. Save your silence for when your opponent seems to be casting a big spell or a heal, and always try to stay out of melee range. If you are being attacked, use the previously mentioned snare spells and move away, or use Boon of Tzeentch and Aegis of the Orange Fire if you feel you can kill them quickly enough.

GROUP PLAY

Group PvP is where we really shine, as now you can stay at the back of the lines and rain down destruction on our enemies for the glory of the Great Changer! Let the melee mashers go out in front and tie up the Order combatants, and keep an eye out on your healers. These are going to be what really turn the tide of a battle, as they keep your allies alive, stopping the enemies from reaching you. And if enemies do make it through the line, your healers will keep you alive while you kill off those few who recognize the real threat.

For damage, you will use the same spells you used in group play previously. They all still do the same thing, so put them to good use. It's your defensive and buff spells that need to be used differently, and much more intelligently. Luckily, we Magi have intelligence to spare in this department. Use your snare and slowing abilities on anyone who makes it through the front line, and use Theft of Words on any casters you see, but try to focus on the healers first, so they are prevented from healing their brethren, allowing you to kill them much faster.

A MAGUS IS A MEMBER OF AN ESTEEMED, ARCANE BROTHERHOOD THAT ALSO HAPPENS TO HAVE THE MOST SPECTACULAR RIDE IN TOWN.

Your daemons will also be very useful in battle. While they may not do quite as much damage as players, they deal enough be a threat on the battlefield, forcing your enemies to spend time, attention, and effort on them. You may want to group up with other Magi, as multiple daemons can do some serious damage, as well as possibly providing different daemons, so you are prepared for all situations.

We do have a secondary purpose, too, which comes up in many RvR situations: defending important strategic areas. Because our summoned daemons must be kept within their summoning circle, they are excellent for helping to defend captured areas, as they can be set down and allowed to devour all enemies that attempt to take the areas from the forces of Destruction. We have been compared in this aspect to the vile and greedy Dwarf Engineers, but I contend that summoning a daemon and forcing it to do your bidding is far superior to simply building some sort of contraption out of wood and metal.

OUTLIVING YOUR MASTER

My how time flies. I hope this has been informative for you. It had better be, as I actually put some thought and effort into it. I have now taught you all the basics of becoming a Magus, sharing practically everything I learned on my journey to where I am today. What have I not told you? Well, that's something you will have to figure out for yourself.

So does this sound appealing to you? I can't see why it wouldn't; do you not want to have massive amounts of power with which to serve your god? Yes, well take everything that I have said and consider it carefully when choosing which path to pursue, but do it somewhere other than here! You have taken up much of my time already, and my studies await. I must get back to them before our god notices my absence on the battlefield, and the screams I yearn to hear from the mouth of the Empire turn into my own.

MARAUDER

Ah, look at you, fresh from the Chaos Portal. It thrills me to see so many flocking to the Chaos banner. Look around you. Dozens are wracked upon the hard-packed earth, chilled to the bone, following the call of Chaos just as I did many winters ago, toward the screams, the smell of death, toward blessed power! No one will staunch the flow of Empire blood, rivers of blood, all in the name of our god! We are Marauders, and this blessed lust is our calling.

I am Magni, a Marauder through and through. You've been touched by the Ruinous Powers, just as I have, and I know your name. The Raven God has tasked me with your Marauder training. I have traversed many northern lands in service to our lord, and I have grown strong, spilling blood, eviscerating at will, drinking deeply of death and decay, all to appease our god. Today he favors you with my training. Do not waste this opportunity, underling; we shall soon join the front and your will and strength will be severely tested. Perhaps one day, like myself, you will flock to the Chaos Champion and, as one of his closest companions, find yourself unstoppable.

For now, get yourself away from the Chaos Portal. We have little time, and you must learn of your ability to change, to meld your bone, your very flesh, into weapons of the Raven Lord's blessed destruction.

By Magni

What is a Marauder?

Freedom. Change. Invigoration. Chaos is all these things, and more, and the Marauder embodies those virtues more than any other warrior in my vast army. To watch the skin bubble and shift as the Marauder alters his form is mesmerizing. A Marauder is truly is an implement of death, the perfect weapon.

Flesh parts effortlessly as the Marauder tears through the enemy. With no remorse, no regret, the children of the Raven God eviscerate the front lines of Order and charge for the heart. They have the rare gift of wanton destruction, and the toll Marauders take on the enemy does not go unnoticed by a shrewd commander.

Marauders enjoy the taste and smell of carnage, for they must use their bodies as weapons and do not rely on spell or arrow from range. Because of the Marauder's brutal arsenal and ferocious killing speed, the enemy will generally concentrate on eliminating the Marauder. It's a foolish plan against a force with so many counterattacks such as ours, but perhaps the Marauder does not feel so fortunate with an Ironbreaker brigade dogging his heels.

—Baron Heinar Balethar, Zimmeron's Hold, Chaos Wastes

ALWAYS HAVE A MUTATION ACTIVE

STARTING STATS

Your stats represent how strong you are, how much health you have, how much damage you can produce, how well you can throw your weapon. The only way to add to these stats is to equip new equipment and to rank up. You can also gain stat bonuses from equipping Morale ability bonuses.

A new Marauder should look at Strength and Initiative, the two main stats that increase your carnage. Strength enhances your melee damage and reduces the likelihood of some Empire scum blocking or parrying your melee attacks.

MARAUDER GEAR

A Marauder starts out by wearing nothing but pants and boots, and holding only a Weakened Mutated Axe. This is all a Marauder needs in life. A Marauder only needs what the Raven God gives him. So if you only have an axe, you are lucky enough to have the Raven God test your battle skills and maybe, just maybe, he will approve of a small aspect of your service.

Now take into account what a Marauder does best. Do not forget about your mutations. These make you sturdier and more terrifying, and show your appreciation for the gift that the Raven God has granted you.

As Marauders rank up, they start to gear up and receive the free second-hand weapon based on their mutations of choice. You are a fearsome foe because you can dual wield with a normal weapon in one hand and your hand, the mutation, as the other weapon.

STRENGTHS AND WEAKNESSES

STRENGTHS

- Mutations and all the benefits associated with them.
- Ability to break snares and crippling effects.
- Massive melee damage.
- Focus on multiple targets at once.
- Able to move really fast by using Charge.

Marauder strength comes from all things damaging. Our very existence is to hate, destroy, and kill. We excel based on our mutation of choice. Mutations allow us to do large amounts of damage at once, focusing on multiple targets if we choose. One mutation deals quick damage to an enemy, while another might torture our enemies slowly: scratch deep, cut tendons, and infect with long-lasting damage over time, like a cat playing with a mouse.

WEAKNESSES

- No substantial ranged attacks.
- No healing spells or Core abilities to help regenerate.
- Medium armor only.
- Groups of mages can burn you down fast if you don't have proper resistances.
- Will be singled out in PVP combat.

Now there are some weaknesses to Marauders, but a good one will not let these weaknesses hold him back. The enemy knows what you are, and what do people do when they are scared of something? They kill it. That is what they will be attempting to do to you, because you cannot stand back and lob stones; you must run into the midst of battle and slay while the enemy attempts to fend you off. Groups of mages will attack you from all sides, and this can hurt you if you can't reach them quickly to disrupt and counterattack. Don't forget your armor, either. Even though you are up in the thick of it all, you wear only medium armor, so you can't get hit as much as the other bruisers around you.

SKILLS AND ABILITIES

ABILITIES

Mutations are unique abilities that set the Marauder apart from lowly Black Orcs or weak-kneed Swordmasters. Mutations last as long as you want, or until you die. Marauders can change to any mutation of choice, in combat or out of combat, though there is a five-second wait between calling these dark powers.

Three mutations are bestowed onto all Marauders as they grow into monstrous fighters:

- The Gift of Savagery
- The Gift of Monstrosity
- The Gift of Brutality

The Gift of Savagery is the first mutation a Marauder receives. This mutation allows you to use skills that are trained in Savagery. It also increases your Weapon Skill and Initiative.

Next, the Gift of Brutality is yours at Rank 3 and allows you to use skills trained specifically in Brutality. It also increases your Strength and Initiative stats.

WHEN ENTERING A NEW CAMP OR TOWN, GRAB ALL THE MISSIONS TO SPEED UP YOUR EXPERIENCE GAIN.

The Gift of Monstrosity is your final mutation, received at Rank 7. This mutation allows you to use the skills specifically found in the Monstrosity tree. It also increases your Toughness.

Do not be confused by the different mutations and the abilities that correspond with them. Make sure to learn what each ability does, as not all abilities work with every mutation. Some abilities even work with no mutation. Some work with two different mutations, while others require specific mutations to function.

Core abilities give you the base skills that you need to survive in the world. Find the Career Trainers whenever you get to a new camp or town to train in these Core abilities. You also gain Mastery points as you rank up. At Rank 11 you receive your first Mastery point. To use these points, get over to a Career Trainer and ask him for access to the Mastery Training. You max out at 25 Mastery points at Rank 40.

There are three paths for Mastery Training. Start experimenting as soon as you can.

Path of Savagery: You leave lingering effects on your opponents that damage them over time and remove their abilities.

Path of Brutality: This is one of the meanest paths: pure damage against a single-target in vicious combat.

Path of Monstrosity: This path gives you access to the area-effect skills. This is great for multi-target combat.

What path does Tzeentch require you to take? Well, that is up to you. You will train different skills based on what you are doing. No matter what you select, you will be executing Tzeentch's will. But let us take a deeper look into these paths and perhaps I can give you a better idea as to what to train.

With Path of Savagery we have Rend, Corruption, Touch of Rot, Tainted Claw, and Gut Ripper. These don't cost you any Mastery points. Rend damages a foe for nine seconds and can be stacked three times. The Raven Lord has blessed you, because this skill becomes available at Rank 2. At Rank 4 you receive Corruption. This exhilarating skill corrupts the target, reducing their Toughness for 10 seconds and inflicting damage, making it a great skill to use when someone tries to run away. Next, Touch of Rot becomes trainable at Rank 9. This is even more pleasurable to use against an unsuspecting enemy. The skill sinks an ailment onto your target for 10 seconds whenever they use a melee attack. So cast this on them and start swinging; they take extra hits if they swing back! Tainted Claw, received at Rank 12, reduces a victim's heals. For Gut Ripper, at Rank 30, your opponent takes damage and your next attack within five seconds automatically becomes a critical strike.

Path of Brutality is a very entertaining and brutal Mastery tree. Debilitate, Impale, Convulsive Slashing, Touch of Instability, and Pulverize are the primary abilities affected. At Rank 3 Debilitate damages and slows your enemy's movement speed by almost half. Impale becomes available at Rank 5. Get behind your enemy and thrust into vital areas for some great damage. Convulsive Slashing slices up your enemy for three seconds, striking up to five times during that time, you may train this ability at rank 6. Now for some fun with the magic-users. Touch of Instability, trainable at Rank 14, causes a magic-using enemy pain whenever they cast a spell for the next 10 seconds. Now if you need to break through those shields, or get past any armor Pulverize is for you at Rank 25. It damages your target but also lowers his Parry and Block skills.

Path of Monstrosity includes the abilities Demolition, Mouth of Tzeentch, Ferocious Assault, and Mutated Energy. How many of those enemies can you hit at once? This tree will allow you to find out. At Rank 7, Demolition inflicts widespread pain on the Empire; anyone within 30 feet of you will feel the wrath of this damaging ability. At Rank 8, Mouth of Tzeentch interrupts mages and damages anyone in front of you, up to 65 feet away. It is vitally important when fighting a large group. At Rank 20, Ferocious Assault becomes active, making it easier to purify the lands of Empire scum by increasing your Strength and Toughness for 10 seconds. Finally, Mutated Energy at Rank 35 damages your caster target and knocks him down for three seconds.

WHEN GAINING MORALE, USE IT ONLY WHEN NECESSARY. A RANK 1 MORALE SKILL WILL NEGATE ALL YOUR MORALE, EVEN IF YOU HAVE ENOUGH TO USE A RANK 4 ABILITY.

Abilities

Name	Level	Path	Cost	Range (in feet)	Type	Build	Duration	Reuse	Description
Flail	Starter Abilities	Monstrosity	30	Melee	Melee Attack	0s	0s	0s	Deals (150+DPS) damage. Attacks a 2nd time for 112 damage if Marauder is mutated.
Throw Axe (Throw)	Starter Abilities	Core	20	10 to 65	Ranged Attack	1s	0s	0s	Deals 75 damage.
Gift of Savagery	Starter Abilities	Core	Free	Self	Mutation Stance	0s	Stance	5s (Shared)	Grants the character the Claw mutation. Grants the character an "off-hand" weapon for dual wield purposes. Invisible weapon granted that increases the character's Weapon Skill and Initiative.
Gift of Release	Starter Abilities	Core	Free	Self	Mutation Stance	0s	Stance	0s	Removes any current Mutation stance.
Rend	Level 2	Savagery	30	Melee	Mutation Attack - Ailment	0s	9s	0s	Deals (112+DPS) instantly and then 199 damage over 9s. Stackable up to 3 times. Requires Claw or Blade mutation.
Debilitate	Level 3	Brutality	25	Melee	Melee Attack - Cripple	0s	5s	10s	Deals (187+DPS) damage and Snares target (40%, 5s).
Gift of Brutality	Level 3	Core	Free	Self	Mutation Stance	0s	Stance	5s (Shared)	Grants the character the Blade mutation. Grants the character an "off-hand" weapon for dual wield purposes. Invisible weapon granted that increases the character's Strength and Initiative.
Corruption	Level 4	Savagery	25	Melee	Melee Attack - Ailment	0s	20s	0s	Deal (112+DPS) damage. Target's Toughness is lowered by 3/level for 20s.
Impale	Level 5	Brutality	25	Melee	Mutation Attack	0s	0s	0s	Deal (262+DPS) damage. Requires rear positional. Requires Blade mutation.
Convulsive Slashing	Level 6	Brutality	25/s	Melee	Mutation Attack	3s	8s		Deals (262+DPS)*0.6 damage every 0.6s for 3s. Channeled attack. Requires Blade mutation.
Demolition	Level 7	Monstrosity	25	CAE	Melee Attack	0s	0s	0s	Deals (150+DPS) damage to targets. Requires Mace mutation. Arc: 120, radius: 30ft.
Gift of Monstrosity	Level 7	Core	Free	Self	Mutation Stance	0s	Stance	5s (Shared)	Grants the character the Mace mutation. Grants the character an "off-hand" weapon for dual wield purposes. Invisible weapon granted that increases the character's Toughness (based on Item System).
Mouth of Tzeentch	Level 8	Monstrosity	30	CAE	Mutation Attack	0s	0s	10s	Deals 150 Corporeal damage. Interrupts target's currently building spell. Arc: 180. Radius: 40ft. Requires Mace or Claw mutaion.
Touch of Rot	Level 9	Savagery	25	Melee	Debuff - Ailment	0s	10s	20s	Melee Barb. Target takes 150 when it activates a melee ability. Requires Claw or Mace mutation.
Wave of Horror	Level 10	Core	50	PBAE	Magical Debuff - Ailment	0s	5s	10s	Detaunts targets around him (50%, 5s). Character's hate generation is reduced by 25% for 5s.
Charge	Level 10	Core	75	Self	Buff	0s	7s	30s	Increase run speed by 50%. Using any ability will dispel Charge.
Tainted Claw	Level 12	Savagery	30	Melee	Mutation Attack - Ailment	0s	5s	5s	Deals (150+DPS) damage. Reduces incoming healing on target by 25% for 5s (10s if target is Crippled). Requires Claw mutation.
Touch of Instability	Level 14	Brutality	25	Melee	Debuff - Ailment	0s	10s	20s	Spell Barb. Target takes 150 damage when it activates a magic ability. Requires Blade or Claw mutation.
Death Grip	Level 16	Core	25	Melee	Reactional Melee - Ailment	0s	5s	5s	Disarm target for 5s. Requires Parry.
Mutating Release	Level 18	Core	45	Self	Dispel	0s	0s	60s	Remove movement impairing effects (Snare/Root) and grant immunity for 10s.
Ferocious Assault	Level 20	Monstrosity	15	Self	Buff - Bless	0s	10s	60s	Increase Strength and Toughness by +5/level for 20s. Requires Mace or Blade mutation.

FIND A GUILD AND WORK WITH THEM TO
RANK IT UP SO YOU CAN GET ACCESS TO THE
VIPER'S PIT IN THE INEVITABLE CITY.

Abilities

Name	Level	Path	Cost	Range (in feet)	Type	Build	Duration	Reuse	Description
Pulverize	Level 25	Brutality	35	Melee	Mutation Attack - Ailment	0s	20s	20s	Deals (225+DPS) damage. Reduces target's ability to Parry by 10% and Block by 30%. Requires Blade or Mace mutation.
Gut Ripper	Level 30	Savagery	40	Melee	Mutation Attack (Remove Ailment)	0s	5s	10s	Parry Reactional. Deals (187+DPS). Your next attack automatically criticals the target. Requires Claw mutation.
Mutated Energy	Level 35	Monstrosity	25	1200	Mutation Attack	0s	3s	10s	Disrupt Reactional. Deal 262 damage to target and knocks down for 3s.
Terrible Embrace	Level 40	Core	45	Thrown - Nuke	Magical Attack	2s	0s	10s	Knocks the target toward the character.
	Specialization								
Wave of Mutilation	Savagery x5	Savagery	30	PBAE	Debuff - Ailment	0s	9s	20s	Lowers enemies' Weapon Skill by 3/level and Initiative by 2/level and deals 848 damage over 20s. Radius: 30ft.
Cutting Claw	Savagery x9	Savagery	35	Melee	Mutation Attack - Ailment	0s	10s	10s	Undefendable Claw Attack. Deals (225+DPS) damage. Armor reduced by 75% for 10s. Requires Claw.
Draining Swipe	Savagery x13	Savagery	30	Melee	Mutation Attack - Ailment	0s	10s	20s	Attack that deals 2 hits of (225+DPS)*.5. Target's AP regen is reduced by 50% for 10s. Requires Claw.
Guillotine	Brutality x5	Brutality	35	Melee	Mutation Attack	0s	0s	10s	Deals (413+DPS) damage to a target below 50% health. Requires Blade mutation.
Mutated Aggressor	Brutality x9	Brutality	40	Self	Buff - Bless	0s	10s	60s	Increase DPS output by 25% for 10s.
Wave of Terror	Brutality x13	Brutality	30	CAE	Mutation Attack	0s	0s	10s	Deals (262+DPS) damage and removes 150 points of Morale from targets in radius. Arc: 130, Radius: 30ft. Requires: Blade.
Concussive Jolt	Monstrosity x5	Monstrosity	25	CAE	Mutation Attack	0s	3s	20s	Deals (112+DPS) damage and knocks down targets in radius for 3s. Arc: 120, radius 30ft.
Thunderous Blow	Monstrosity x9	Monstrosity	30	Melee	Mutation Attack - Ailment	0s	5s	5s	Deals (225+DPS) damage and disorients target (+1s for 5s). Requires Mace mutation.
Wrecking Ball	Monstrosity x13	Monstrosity	25/s	PBAE	Mutation Attack	0s	3s	13s	Channeled. Deals (187+DPS)*0.5 every 0.5s for 3s. Radius: 20ft. Requires Mace mutation.

MORALE

You know that feeling of worthiness that courses through you when you've been in a battle for a long time? When you've been attacking and surviving blow after blow? That feeling is Morale. Morale can be one of the most powerful aspects of a fight; the types of attack you can produce with high Morale can be devastating to an opponent.

Every four ranks from Rank 8 to Rank 40, you can train a new Morale skill. There are four levels of Morale. Rank 1 skills won't be as devastating as a Rank 4, but they all can bring about victory if called upon at just the right time.

Use these Morale abilities while ranking up. They can help you in a time of need. The first Rank 1 is Sever Nerve. Use this skill behind the enemy and do large amounts of damage. The first Rank 2 ability you should use is Relentless Assault. This helps your entire group by granting each of them 10 action points per second for 10 seconds. Broad Swings becomes yours at Rank 3. This allows you to attack multiple targets at once for 10 seconds. The first Rank 4 you use is Frenzied Slaughter. This is a great ability if you want to get damage out quickly and prolong your ability to do so. It cuts the action point cost of all your skills, your skills return quicker, and you deal more damage for seven seconds. Not bad.

Remember to experiment with the other Morale skills like Flames of Fate, which heals you, and Tzeentch's Reversal, which deals out large damage and returns it as healing for you.

WARHAMMER ONLINE
AGE OF RECKONING

Morale

Name	Level	Rank	Range (in feet)	Duration	Description
Sever Nerve	Level 8	Rank 1	Melee	15s	Melee attack that deals 1,200 damage.
Force of Will	Level 12	Rank 2	Self	30s	Drain 200 AP from target and give to character. Decrease target's Strength by 4/level for 30s.
Confusing Movements	Level 16	Rank 1	Self	7s	Increase chance to Parry and Evade attacks by 100% for 7s.
Relentless Assault	Level 20	Rank 2	Group	15s	Group buff. Grants 10 AP/S to group for 10s. This occurs even during layers.
Broad Swings	Level 24	Rank 3	Self	10s	All attacks hit 2 additional targets within 54ft for 10s. Additional targets take 300 damage.
Flames of Fate	Level 28	Rank 1	Self	0	Self-heal for 720.
Great Fang	Level 32	Rank 2	Melee	0	Melee CAE attack. Deals 1,200 damage. Arc:120, radius: 30ft.
Tzeentch's Reversal	Level 36	Rank 3	Melee	0	Melee attack that deals 1,200 damage and gives 100% of that damage as health.
Frenzied Slaughter	Level 40	Rank 4	Self	7s	Self buff. AP costs are reduced 25%. Cooldowns are reduced by 50%. Damage dealt is increased by 20%. Lasts 7s.
Lashing Power	Savagery x15	Rank 4	Self	10s	Self buff for 10s. Each time the character is hit, there is a 33% chance that he randomly lifetaps an enemy within 30ft for the amount of damage just dealt to him. This damage bypasses the combat formula.
Forked Aggression	Brutality x15	Rank 4	Self	10s	Damage dealt to Marauder is mirrored back to the attacker with a 50% boost. Lasts for 10s.
Energy Ripple	Monstrosity x15	Rank 4	PBAE	7s	Deals 1,200 damage, Knocks back, Stuns for 7s all targets in radius. Marauder is knocked straight up.

Tactics

Name	Level	Description
Warped Flesh	Level 11	25% chance when attacked to absorb 262 damage for 10s.
Jagged Edge	Level 13	Critical hits also place a 412 damage bleed DoT on the target for 9s.
Subvert Strength	Level 15	Critical hits also gain the character back 40 AP.
Tzeentch's Warding	Level 17	Increases Elemental resist by +6.3 per level of the character.
Brute Force	Level 19	Increases Strength by +4 per level of the character.
Brush Off	Level 21	Marauder has a 10% increased chance to disrupt attacks.
Backlash	Level 23	25% chance to put a 5s 150 DoT on attacker. Non-stacking, non-refreshing.
Flanking	Level 25	Increase damage by 15% from attacks made to the side or rear of an enemy.
Rend Asunder	Level 27	Rend gains 6s of duration.
Riposte	Level 29	When the character Parries, he deals 187 back to the target.
Deeply Impaled	Level 31	Impale also increases the chance of the target to be critically hit by 10% for 15s. (Ailment).
Feeding on Fear	Level 33	Marauder gains a 20% bonus chance to critically hit for 5s when he critically hits. He also becomes 10% easier to crit to enemies.
Unending Horror	Level 35	Wave of Horror lasts an additional 10s.
Widespread Demolition	Level 37	Demolition has a radius of 50ft.
Piercing Bite	Level 39	Attacks ignore 50% of target's Armor.
Scything Talons	Savagery x3	Claw mutation-stance gives an additional +4/level stat gain for Weapon Skill and Initiative.
Exhaustive Strikes	Savagery x7	Critical hits while mutated remove 40 AP from target.
Deadly Clutch	Savagery x11	Tainted Claw reduces healing on target by 75% (instead of 25%)
Corrupted Edge	Brutality x3	Blade mutation-stance gives an additional +4/level stat gain for Strength and Initiative
Growing Instability	Brutality x7	For every 10% lost in health, critical damage is increased 20%.
Unstable Convulsions	Brutality x11	Each hit of Convulsive Slashes has a 50% chance to remove an Enchantment from the target and if it does so deals 75 (non-combat formula based) damage.
Hulking Brute	Monstrosity x3	Mace mutation-stance gives an additional +4/level stat gain for Toughness.
Insane Whispers	Monstrosity x7	Mouth of Tzeentch also adds a disorient that increases build times by 1s for 5s.

TACTICS

From the moment you step into this world, you have one Tactic slot. It's not until Rank 21 that you get a second Tactic slot. This is where you can start mixing and matching Tactics. At Rank 31 you have three, and Rank 40 you have four. I have my preferences as to what Tactics to use, but you must figure out which ones are best for you in your quest to destroy Order.

Now the Tactics I mix together the most are ones that I can use anywhere I go. Brute Force is great because it gives you +1 Strength per level. This adds damage and reduces the chance of your attacks being blocked or parried. Subvert Strength gives you 50 action points every time you critically hit an enemy. Add the Tactic Piercing Bite, and ignore a portion of an enemy's armor. Each of these Talents make you deadlier against your enemies.

Now remember there are other places to get Tactics. Through Mastery Training you can train nine more. These take a Mastery point, so be careful which ones you choose to train. You have access to many more from the Renown Trainers found in RvR zones.

RENOWN

So you think you are ready for the blessing of Renown by the Raven Lord? I can tell you there is nothing better than making those barbarians fall on the battlefield. So why shouldn't you be rewarded for doing so? Even Black Orcs understand this concept: go into battle, kill the enemy, and get a reward. The reward is Renown points. There are three Renown levels from which to buy achievements. You need to spend 20 points in the first level. There are many good choices here, but for maximum damage against those enemies of the Tzeentch, put 20 points into Might. This increases your Strength and, in turn, increases your melee attack damage and reduces the chance that your melee attacks will be blocked or parried.

After you have spent 20 points, you gain access to the second tier of skills. You must spend another 20 points (in either tier) to reach the next tier. Again, train but one skill for maximum damage output: Assault. Save Renown Tactics for the third tier.

In Tier 3, you can spend your remaining points. Opportunist is great to train. This increases your melee attack critical chance. On top of Opportunist you should probably train Chaotic Allegiance to get the 5% Morale gain.

Now with the understanding of Renown that you have, you need to remember that these are what were best for me. Depending on how you fight, your training may have to be a little different.

SOLO PLAY (PVE)

Few things will delay you, let alone stop you, on your quest to fulfill the tasks of Chaos and the rewards that come with it. Monsters, soldiers, and animals don't stand a chance. Heed my advice and you shall power your way through adversaries on your way to glory.

RANK 1-10

When you first get to Sturmvall, Skurlorg Blackhorn offers a mission to see if you are ready for the trials of being a Marauder. First, he asks you to head into the crypts to the northeast. At this point you have three main skills: Gift of Savagery, Flail, and Throw Axe. For this first level, just activate your mutation (Gift of Savagery) and throw in a few Flail attacks. You will rank up fast, learning Rend at Rank 2, which causes a bleeding effect. So while questing, use Rend, stacking it three times, and Flail to down any enemy of equal rank.

Follow your orders correctly, and you should reach Thorshafn by Rank 3. Here you learn a new mutation: Gift of Brutality. Turn it on immediately, because this will be your most used mutation. Questing in Thorshafn will take you to Rank 5 or 6, especially if you complete the public quest "Ruinous Powers" a few times. By this point, you should be able to train the skills Corruption, Impale, and Compulsive Slashing.

When you are fighting your enemies, your attack sequence will look something like this: Rend, Rend, Corruption, Convulsive Slashing. Add an Impale if you are standing behind the enemy to kill even faster. Now with these new skills, you are ready to head into the Nordenwatch scenario. This is more interesting and a true testament to your skills as a Marauder, and will likely be your first taste of PvP. After a few rounds of the scenario, head out of Thorshafn, and rank up doing the public quests around that area. It is now time to prove your true worth to the gods at the Blessed Gathering. This will be your first real RvR experience. Enjoy slaughtering the Empire. I know I did.

Now that you have claimed these lands for Chaos, head southeast of Nordland and rank up on the nearby public quests, then follow that path through the mountains to Ostland. Congratulations on finishing the first tier of your path to becoming a great warrior.

RANK 11-20

You should arrive in Ferlangen at Rank 10 or 11. Collect all the quests you can, and head out to complete them. Continue to use Gift of Brutality and this sequence of skills: Rend, Rend, Corruption, Convulsive Slashing. At Rank 12 you can train Tainted Claw. This is a Savagery skill that you should use when Gift of Savagery is active. While questing and doing the public quests in the area, you should hit around Rank 14, then head to the RvR area in Ostland. Make sure to train Touch of Instability at Rank 14. It's a necessity when fighting magic-users, because it makes them lose control of their magic and for 10 seconds they'll damage themselves when casting. At Rank 14, head to the middle of the eastern border of Ostland and partake in battles over in Koumos' Encampment. Remember that the public quests around here are a great source of gear.

Once you've finished around Koumos' Encampment, travel to Trovolek in Troll Country. Take all the quests, complete them, and then head to the public quest Plaguewood Thicket. You should arrive there at Rank 18 or just past that. Train Death Grip and Mutating Release. Finish the quests in this area and then move onto Tier 3.

MARAUDERS ARE ALWAYS STRONGER WHEN ATTACKING FROM BEHIND.

TAKING SHORTCUTS CAN KILL YOU; LOOK OUT FOR THE GROUND BELOW.

RANK 21-30

Similar to the last two tiers, your journey here will consist of scenarios, battlefields, and quests. Go and get your quests from Goblin's Head Coaching Inn. These quests bring you to Rank 22. Now it's off to Witches Hollow, the northernmost Chaos camp. Collect and finish more quests, then head over to Volgen and do more quests. At Rank 24, take a break from questing and do some battlefield combat. Go to Hellfang Ridge and prepare for some action against other players.

Now move on, leaving Talabecland. Hopefully, you have left your mark on the lands. We are now going to rank up in High Pass. First stop is Bloodmar. Finish a few quests here and you should be around Rank 26, so train Pulverize. This decreases your enemy's Block and Parry abilities for 10 seconds and inflicts large damage. Now that you are finished with the quests at Bloodmar, wander over to Jaggedspine Ridge. Finish your quests here and you should be at Rank 30. Train Gut Ripper and move over to Tier 4 of your training.

RANK 31-40

You are almost there. Get to Deathchill in the Chaos Wastes, grab all the quests, and finish them. While you are running along the road, remember to work on the public quests.

Once you've finished with those, go seek work in Awakened Tempest. You should be Rank 33 by now. Finish these quests and do more public quests in the area. Finally, it's time to head to Praag. Travel to Daemonfire, Ravensworn and then Southern Beach for quests and do the PQs in the area. You will soon be Rank 40. Don't forget to train your skills Mutated Energy and Terrible Embrace at 40.

Fun with Greenskins

When one of those stupid greenskins wants to shout orders at you and you have had enough, offer a compromise. Tell him that if he can guess how many fingers you are holding behind your back, you will let him lead the group. Hold up two fingers and then slowly place your hand behind your back. Now it might take a moment for him to grasp the concept, so be precise and patient.

Once he accepts the challenge, like you know he will, mutate. No matter what number the greenskin says (some might not understand the concept of "two"), he will be wrong and you will once again prove your superiority.

USE POTIONS TO INCREASE STATS AND KEEP YOURSELF ALIVE IN BATTLE.

GROUP PLAY

Playing with others will change your approach depending on the needs of your group. Consider different Tactics and Morale abilities options. Don't just think of yourself on these. You always want to make yourself strong, but your group is only as strong as the weakest link. It should never be you.

As a Marauder, it's your duty to kill the enemy in the tank's grasp. Remember you are trained for pushing pain onto your enemies quickly and hard. So when your tank has an enemy in one spot, move in and rip it apart. Let the hate fill you and litter the ground with your enemy's flesh.

With a good healer in your group, don't hold back. If the enemies attack you instead, your healer will keep you breathing, and the faster you drop enemies, the safer the group will be. You use the same strategies as you did solo. You and your party may decide to go PvP, so I'll tell you about the tactics of group PvP in a few minutes.

SOLO PVP

You are finally ready to help the Raven Lord purge the lands of the real Empire threat. Think back when you were getting to this point, killing all those little men and impaling Empire messengers. PvP is not much different than doing just that.

When fighting another person, they will try to outthink you. Do not let those barbarians get past you or outflank you. Drop ailments and Morale abilities onto these enemies. Use your brutal strength from your mutations, and keep the fight one-on-one at all costs.

Similar to some monsters, wounded players will attempt to flee. Do not let them get away. If they live, you will have failed Tzeentch. Charge at them, slow them down, make them bleed, and take your Renown experience with pride.

RANK 1-10

Use the same strategies in this range of ranks as you did when soloing. Make sure you have your mutation active. Brutality is the best for this. Now use Rend—stack it a few times if you like—then Corruption, Debilitate, and Convulsing Slash. If you are feeling lazy through Ranks 1-10 you can get away with using Rend, Rend, Rend, Corruption, and then Flail. Keep hitting Flail until the enemy is dead, or until the Rends run out and you can re-Rend. There isn't much that a Marauder cannot kill at these levels. When fighting ranged classes at Rank 10, start relying on Charge to quickly engage and throw them off balance. Make sure you Debilitate the enemies who like to run to cripple them.

RANK 11-20

Follow the same tactics used in Rank 1-10 for 11-20, but make sure to train as you rank up. Some important skills will increase your damage output. Continue to have your mutation on. When fighting a melee class, you must outdamage them. Charge the enemy; you move fast and some might be slow to react. Then use Debilitate, Rend a couple times, plant a Corruption, and end with a Convulsing Slash. If you get a chance, throw in a Touch of Rot so enemies take damage with every swing at you. At Rank 18 you get Mutating Release. This allows you to get out of snares; use it only when your movement is slowed. If you parry a melee career's attacks, remember to use Death Grip to disarm your opponent for five seconds.

When fighting against magic and ranged careers, start with Charge and land a Rend and Debilitate as soon as you can. They start to bleed and move slower. Rend them one or two more times to add extra damage while fighting. Also throw a Touch of Rot on them. Hit magic-users with Touch of Instability. This makes them take damage every time they cast a spell. They won't know what hit them

RANK 21-30

At Rank 25 you gain Pulverize. This hits hard and mean and lowers your target's Parry and Block skills for 10 seconds. Use when up against a shield carrier. Then at Rank 30, train Gut Ripper. Take Death Grip out of your arsenal for this skill. When you parry, use this skill to gut your opponent and make your next attack within five seconds an automatic critical hit.

RANK 31-40

You gain only one more substantially useful skill: Terrible Embrace at Rank 40. This pulls your targeted enemy to you, from up to 65 feet away. This is terrific!

Savagery, Brutality, Monstrosity

This distinguished game comes from the ancient texts found in the Lyceum within the Inevitable City.

Are you tired of battle? Do you want to take a break and have a little fun while the bloodstains are cleaned from your pants? Then this game is for you (for Marauders Rank 7 and up).

Rules:

1. Both contestants count to three, then change form to their mutation of choice.

2. Savagery beats Monstrosity, Monstrosity destroys Brutality, and Brutality impales Savagery.

Now I am no betting Chaos man, but this could be a way to earn some extra coin from another Marauder.

DISABLE YOUR FOE TO GIVE YOURSELF MORE TIME FOR BETTER ATTACKS.

GROUP PLAY

o you want to learn how to PvP in a group? Some people think we would be happy to fight on our own, but what's more powerful than one Marauder? Two working together. Now what's even more powerful still? You're getting it.

our role will not change much in a skirmish, battlefield, scenario, or campaign. You group size may vary, but you still have one goal: put as many enemies on the ground as you can. But you cannot do this alone. As long as you are near a healer and a tank you will do fine.

When the tank has a target singled out, your goal is to stop the enemy's healers from healing this person so your group can kill this targeted enemy. our strength and Tactics can take healers out quickly as long as they don't have too many bodyguards. Remove these abominable blights from the orld.

ow that you have dealt with the healers, or other casters with weak armor if there are no healers, come in and help take out the enemy damage-ealers. They will be going after your healer, so intercept them. Do what you can to get behind them. Let someone else get hit so you can jam your rutality mutated arm through their backs and kidneys.

emember to select your Talents and Morale skills to suit your needs for the situation. Being in a group, it is no longer all about you. The more ccessful your group is, the more glory you can bring Tzeentch, and is there anything more important?

FAVOR OF THE RAVEN GOD

So you have reached greatness and won the favor of the Raven God. Congratulations on that. Not many have achieved what you have. If only more young Marauders were filled with that same hatred and zeal. I see great things to come to you, with Tzeentch's blessing of course. Everything that you have accomplished is because of Him.

I look forward to seeing you on the battlefield, but I must go now. I have been summoned to the Inevitable City. Our paths part until the time when Tzeentch wills us together in His service.

REMEMBER, YOU ARE THE WEAPON. ATTACK EARLY AND OFTEN.

ZEALOT

Sit here with me, young Zealot, away from the fire. Yes, here, in the dark. The time is nigh for our attack upon the pitiful village of Thorshafn below, and the nefarious Empire citizenry therein...but sit, I wish to speak a while.

I see promise in your eyes. Dark promise.

By Rift

I am Rift. I've also been called Rift of the North, amongst other names. I have no preference; a name is a name. With time, your power will attract new names like moths drawn to a flame. I was once a general of the Empire, brought to the fold by the Changer of Ways while defending Darkwater Keep, in Nordland. I am no longer a general, but a leader of the Chaos... We are but dark leaves upon his thoughts, blown by change, but we find ourselves here, nearer to the Corruptor's Crown, the crown that Warlord Tchar'zanek desires with all of his might...and he will have it! It is not in the village below but we will reap the souls of the fallen, and the Raven God will bless us with a larger warhost and more souls as we press south. The Raven God has already blessed us with a Firewyrm, along with the Marauders and Chosen hidden within these trees, waiting for me to give cry. We even have a Magus with us this eve! But wait, 'tis not time, not yet...and I desire a moment to speak to you about Tzeentch, and the powers most recently given to you, much as they were given to me at the blazing foot of Darkwater Keep many, many moons ago.

I like that bloodlust in your eyes! Most fitting! Nurse that bloodlust. Grow it; revel in it. The craving will serve you well in your new career. Ah, to be a Zealot! Don't let the Chosen and the Marauders fool you: the Raven God's healers are the backbone of His armies! The brutes ahead of us would be reaped by the Empire like fields of wheat by a scythe without our unselfish heals and our ability to bring souls back from the brink of death.

We have many ways in which the dark healing powers flow through us, but we also need protection. Do not expect to take on two Witch Hunters all alone, for they will send your soul into the dark faster than you can implore Tzeentch for a wee Cordial. Alas, we only wear robes and feathers, so get used to it! But a capable army with Zealots behind it can drench this hillside with blood—and we shall!

But not until dark. Sit closer...

TZEENTCH'S CORDIAL IS YOUR BEST FRIEND. YOU LEARN IT AT RANK 3. NEVER FORGET IT.

STARTING STATS

It seems as though the Raven God has brought you to the fold like any other Zealot, including myself: weak, unclothed, but hungry for new rank. Do not fret, for your power will grow with every soul we harvest for our blessed god!

It's important to understand how your various attributes will improve your character. I know, I know, you are the same as any other Rank 1 Zealot, but there are numerous opportunities for improvement and diversification upon the long road toward our victories in the south, be it through gear, Tactics, Masteries, and more. So be patient.

Nevertheless, there are a few important attributes to be aware of here and now; mainly, Willpower and Intelligence. Willpower not only improves your healing power, it also increases your chance to disrupt the magic attacks of our enemies. There's very little as satisfying as disrupting that pesky stunty Rune Priest's final heal and watching him perish in a fog of Warped Reality, his face sloughing from his skull as he plummets to the damp earth.

Intelligence is also important. Not only does it improve the power of your own magic attacks, it lowers the chance that your magics will be interrupted. You don't want that insidious Empire caster melting *your* face into the foul Empire soil, do you?

A third important attribute is Wounds. The more you have, the longer you live. It increases your hits, simple as that, enabling you to take more damage and live to heal another day. This is very important when those black-hearted Witch Hunters start firing away, may Tchar'zanek send them all to early graves, their pistols melted into fine Zealot blades!

What is a Zealot?

When the Chosens' armor is stained with their own blood, they look to the Zealot to repair their bodies to struggle on a few minutes longer. From the defended ranks, Zealots magic-stitch torn limbs, seal sword slashes, and return trampled corpses to the march of the living. They are stalwart healers whose dark gifts can make a small group seem as great as a battalion.

Though their magic is not as fine or dependable as steel, Zealots must be protected for the army's greater existence. It only takes one misbegotten whelp—charging headfirst into battle, waving his skull like a wild Black Orc—to doom himself and risk the lives of those under his healing spells. That is not to say that Zealots have no offensive skills. While inflicting pain is perhaps not core to their studies, the Zealot can call forth damaging spells and instant-cast magics with potent results. However, our commanders know how to defend them, and know the price of failure should the enemy penetrate the defenses.

For such a bloodless pursuit, I've always admired that Zealots carry a skull. Their appearance inspires fear; a delicious change from some of the softer magic-wielders. One day yet we may invite them to sit at the warrior's table.

—Baron Heinar Balethar, Zimmeron's Hold, Chaos Wastes

ZEALOT GEAR

Rank 1 Zealots start out with very little gear. We are far less gear dependant than our Chosen brethren, although we certainly benefit from the increased attributes and such as we progress. Nevertheless, as you can see, you start out with very little. Your only piece of armor is the Infused Alchemist's Shirt. A wonderfully useless shirt, this is, not even worthy of calling itself armor. It can't protect you from even the slightest wound and won't even keep you warm!

You'll also start with your Weakened Magic Dagger, a Chaos dagger with a fine edge and an evil curved nature to the steel, but don't grow too attached to it; the dagger adds nothing in the way of attributes and does very little damage in a Zealot's hand. And, most insulting of all, you'll begin with your first charm in your left hand, a Weakened Magic Fetish. It adds nothing to your persona other than a modicum of evil as you prance about with your worthless skull, waving it fiercely for no reason whatsoever.

As a Zealot, you only use daggers in your main hand, and charms in your left hand. You'll also never wear more than cloth robes when it comes to armor. When we get hit, we get hit hard, so you must be smart and quick with your heals, and rely on heavy hitters to keep you safe.

STRENGTHS AND WEAKNESSES

STRENGTHS

- Heals. Bigger heals. More bigger heals.
- Instant heals!
- Resurrection.
- Self-resurrection buff.

Yes, I mentioned it before. We are healers; we obtain many different, increasingly powerful heals. A single Zealot can turn the tide of battle. That is why the Chosen and the Marauders flock to my banner, that is why a Magus does my bidding, and that is why you are here, at my side, the hunger burning in your eyes like the flames that will ignite Thorshafn this eve. One day, all of this will be yours, and more, if only you remember your strengths, and never forget your weaknesses.

WEAKNESSES

- Can only wear robes.
- Low damage.
- Targeted first.

It is unfortunate that our strengths make us one of the first targets in a battle. A smart enemy will come for you first. Be ready. Although we only wear robes, and our damage is low compared to the meatier, higher damage careers, we still have our legs and a few instant spells—both heals and damaging spells—to keep us alive while we seek safer ground.

Keep a bodyguard nearby, if you can, to help peel off any would-be attackers so that you can concentrate your heals on the battlefront. And don't forget to toss him a heal as well!

SKILLS AND ABILITIES

ABILITIES

CORE ABILITIES

Which abilities have you brought to the front? Scourge and Flash of Chaos? Those are great abilities, even for a weak Rank 1 Zealot...like you.

Cease that snarling before I cut your jaw from your very face and burn you to the ground! We cannot afford to short ourselves a Zealot, so save your hate for the Empire.

Scourge is a competent ranged magical attack, and you'll be using it at any rank, so practice it well. Flash of Chaos is a great heal, simple and fast. You'll be training soon enough, so let's get into your various abilities.

Scourge and Flash of Chaos are both Core abilities. Core abilities are standard abilities given to every Zealot. You'll gain at least a single Core ability every rank until Rank 10. After Rank 10 you'll gain a new ability every even-numbered rank until you're Rank 20. From 20 until the highest, exalted Rank 40, you'll gain a new ability only every fifth rank. Ah, but don't be misled; you'll be training other abilities...

MASTERY ABILITIES

These come in the form of Mastery abilities. Every career has three different paths in which to specialize. You'll gain a single Mastery point at Rank 11; by the time you reach Rank 40, you'll have a total of 25 Mastery points to spend. You can spend a maximum of 15 points in any one path. Aye, you'll be unable to specialize in all three paths; that's what will make you different from other Zealots, different even from me. Let me offer a quick description of each path for you:

Path of Alchemy: Focuses on healing and restorative powers. Improves the power of the Core abilities Mark of Daemonic Fury, Tzeentch's Cry, Elixir of Dark Blessings, and Daemonic Fortitude.

Path of Witchcraft: Focuses on offensive and damaging powers. Improves the power of the Core abilities Warp Reality, Veil of Chaos, Dark Medicine, Mark of the Spell Destroyer, and Tzeentch's Lash.

Path of Dark Rites: Focuses on hindering foes and strengthening allies. Improves the power of the Core abilities Rite of Agony, Mark of the Vortex, Leaping Alteration, Demon Spittle, and Dust of Pandemonium.

What type of Zealot will you become? I cannot hold your hand forever, but by the time you begin accruing Mastery points, you'll likely have an idea of what type of Zealot you are. One tip: focus on maximizing a single Mastery instead of peppering points into all three of them. For instance, I am fully specialized in the Path of Alchemy and my remaining Mastery points are invested in the Path of Dark Rites. I am a healer, through and through, and my Masteries allow me to improve my heals as well as abilities that hinder my foes and even strengthen our allies. For instance, I gained Boon of Tzeentch, a new ability, when I reached Rank 9 in my Path of Alchemy. Boon of Tzeentch is a great ability, which grants me the power to drain health from whoever I have cursed with my Harbinger of Doom, and the amount of health drained is funneled to my defensive target, which could be me, could be you, and could even be the irascible Marauder down the hill.

And not only do the paths grant abilities outside of Core abilities, Masteries also grant new Tactics and Morale abilities.

WARHAMMER ONLINE
AGE OF RECKONING

Abilities

Name	Level	Path	Cost	Range (in feet)	Type	Build	Duration	Reuse	Description
Scourge	Level 1	Alchemy	25	100	Magic Attack	2s	0s	0s	Deals 299 damage.
Flash of Chaos	Level 1	Alchemy	30	150	Heal	0s	0s	0s	Heals 203 to defensive target.
Warp Reality	Level 2	Witchcraft	30	100	Magic Attack - Hex	0s	15s	0s	Target takes 499 damage over 15s.
Tzeentch's Cordial	Level 3	Core	30	150	HoT - Bless	0s	15s	0s	Heals for 1,496 over 15 seconds.
Mark of Daemonic Fury	Level 4	Alchemy	25	Buff	Mark Buff - Bless	0s	60 min	0s	Increases target group member's Strength and Intelligence by 2 for 60 minutes. Activating the mark casts a 262 DD on target.
Daemonic Fury	=Sub Ability=	Alchemy	Free	100	Magic Attack	0s	0s	60s	Deals 262 damage.
Tzeentch's Cry	Level 5	Alchemy	35	100	Magic Attack	0s	0s	5s	Deals 300 damage.
Boon of Tzeentch	Level 5	Core	45	Self	Buff - Bless	0s	10s	60s	Damage taken is reduced by 50%, and reduces AP costs by 25%. Can not be set back and no threat is generated while this ability is active.
Veil of Chaos	Level 6	Witchcraft	35	100	Magic - Bless	0s	10s	20s	Target absorbs the next 563 damage. When the effect fades, the target is healed for 180 damage.
Chaotic Blur	Level 7	Core	20	100	Detaunt	0s	15s	15s	Detaunts target (15s duration, 50% redux)
Rite of Agony	Level 7	Dark Rites	40	PBAE	Magic Attack	2s	0s	0s	Deals 249 damage to all targets in the radius. Radius: 30ft.
Elixir of Dark Blessings	Level 8	Alchemy	45	150	Heal	3s	0s	0s	Heals 1,128 damage. Setback override: 100% chance, 2s value.
Harbinger of Doom	Level 9	Core	20	100	Debuff	0s	1 min	0s	Decreases target's Corporeal resist for 3.15 for 10s followed by: decreases target's Corporeal resist for 6.3 resist for 10s followed by: decreases target's Corporeal resist for 9.15 for 40s. (total of 1 minute duration).
Mark of the Vortex	Level 9	Dark Rites	25	Buff	Mark Buff - Bless	0s	60 min	0s	Increases target group member's Spirit resist by 6.3 for 60 minutes.
The Vortex	=Sub Ability=	Dark Rites	Free	PBAE	Crowd Control	0s	9s	60s	Deals 349 damage over 9s to all targets in the radius. Radius: 30ft.
Dark Medicine	Level 10	Witchcraft	55	150	Heal - Bless	1s	9s	0s	Heals 248 damage, then heals 658 damage over 9s.
Tzeentch Shall Remake You	Level 10	Core	20	100	Resurrection	3s	0s	6s	Resurrect target friendly dead player.
Mark of the Spell Destroyer	Level 12	Witchcraft	25	Buff	Mark Buff - Bless	0s	60 min	0s	Increase target group member's Initiative and Willpower by 2 per level for 1 hour.
Spell Destroyer	=Sub Ability=	Witchcraft	Free	100	Magic Attack	0s	0s	60s	Deals 648 damage over 9s.
Leaping Alteration	Level 14	Dark Rites	40	150	Heal - Bless	1s	9s	10s	Heals target for 389 over 9s. Effect will also hit 1 ally within 30ft from the original target, and 1 ally within 30ft from that target, healing up to 6 allies total. Effect will not hit the same target more than once.
Glimpse of Chaos	Level 16	Core	25	150	Magic Attack	0s	0s	5s	Removes a Curse or Hex from target.
Demon Spittle	Level 18	Dark Rites	45	CAE	Magic - Hex	0s	0s	5s	Deals 349 damage over 9s. Arc: 120, radius: 65ft.
Dust of Pandemonium	Level 20	Dark Rites	60	150	Group Heal	3s	0s	0s	Heals 540 damage to all group members.
Breath of Tzeentch	Level 25	Core	40	PBAE	Crowd Control	0s	10s	60s	PBAE Knockback targets. Radius: 30ft.
Daemonic Fortitude	Level 30	Alchemy	35	100	Buff - Bless	0s	1 min	3 min	Increases target group member's Wounds by 4 for 1 min. Heals target for value of HP increase. Wounds buffs stack largest.

KNOW THE INS AND OUTS OF EVERY HEAL. BY THE TIME YOU'RE RANK 40, YOU'LL HAVE PLENTY OF OPTIONS. KNOWLEDGE IS THE KEY TO LIVING TO FIGHT ANOTHER DAY.

Abilities										
Name	Level	Path	Cost	Range (in feet)	Type	Build	Duration	Reuse	Description	
Tzeentch's Lash	Level 35	Witchcraft	30	100	Magic - Hex	1s	5s	30s	Deals 399 damage over 5s and Silences target for 5s.	
Mark of Remaking	Level 40	Core	25	100	Mark Buff - Bless	0s	60 min	0	Increases target group member's Toughness by 2 for 60 minutes.	
Remaking	=Sub Ability=	Core	Free	Self	Resurrection	0s	0s	0s	Self Resurrect.	
Ritual of Innervation	Alchemy x5	Alchemy	25	80	Ritual Buff	1s	30s	30s	GTAE Deployable. Group members in the radius have a 20% chance on attack to proc a 50 point AP heal. Radius: 65ft.	
Boon of Tzeentch	Alchemy x9	Alchemy	30	100	Magic	2s	0s	0s	Deals 299 damage to the bearer of your Harbinger. Heals Defensive target for damage dealt.	
Aethyric Shock	Alchemy x13	Alchemy	35	100	Magic	0s	3s	20s	Deals 337 damage and stuns the target for 3s.	
Ritual of Superiority	Witchcraft x5	Witchcraft	25	80	Ritual Buff	1s	30s	30s	GTAE Deployable. Group members in the radius have a 20% chance when taking damage to proc a shield that will absorb 375 damage for 10s. Can not proc more than once every 2 seconds. Radius: 65ft.	
Storm of Ravens	Witchcraft x9	Witchcraft	10 / 0.5s	100	Magic	0s	3s	11s	(Channel) Deals 94 damage to the bearer of your Harbinger every 0.5s for 6s. Setback chance: 100%.	
Mirror of Madness	Witchcraft x13	Witchcraft	40	100	Magic - Hex	2s	10s	10s	Each time the target casts a heal, he takes 549 damage.	
Ritual of Lunacy	Dark Rites x5	Dark Rites	25	80	Ritual Buff	1s	30s	30s	GTAE Deployable. Heals group members in the radius by 150 every 3s for 60s. Radius: 65ft.	
Chaotic Agitation	Dark Rites x9	Dark Rites	25 / 2s	80	Magic Attack	0s	9s	16s	Channel. Deals 250 damage to the holder of your Harbinger and all targets in the radius every 2s for 6s. Radius: 20ft. Setback chance: 100%.	
Wind of Insanity	Dark Rites x13	Dark Rites	7/s	PBAE	Magic Attack	0s	6s	16s	Toggle. Deals 112.5 damage to all targets in the radius every second for 6s. Small knockback. Radius: 30ft.	

MORALE

Morale is granted as you fight, increasing through one of four ranks at your most powerful. Morale abilities come in four ranks as well, and you'll eventually be able to equip a single ability of each rank with the Rank 4 abilities being the most powerful. Sound complicated? It's less complicated than it sounds, and it helps that you only start with a single Rank 1 slot. You won't even attain your first Morale ability until Rank 8: Divine Favor. It's a strong, instant heal, very useful for pulling yourself back from the edge of the abyss, or ripping a Chosen from the jaws of death long enough to destroy his enemies.

Core Morale abilities are granted every four ranks, starting at Rank 8, and ending with the blissful Alter Fate. Alter Fate is a wonderful, wonderful ability, allowing you to resurrect all groupmates within 30 feet. Yes, your ears are not playing tricks on you, and our blessed allies are even brought back to life with slight heal over time to greet them! Aye, I used it once; I channeled the power of the Raven God through my every pore, my body taut, my soul tremulous, and from our gory lost battle I wrested a final gasp, enabling our forces to turn the tide of battle. We won that night and many souls infested my own.

It's also important to note that differing Rank 4 Morale abilities are also granted at the highest Mastery level. This means you can only learn a single Mastery Morale ability because it's impossible to maximize two Masteries with only 25 points. Because I am fully specialized in the Path of Alchemy, I am able to use the Tzeentch's Shielding Morale ability, enabling me to grant everyone in my group 250 action points and also shield everyone for 20 seconds from substantial damage. Perhaps not quite as powerful as Alter Fate, but in certain situations it could be the difference between saving everyone from dying instead of having to resurrect everyone within a hair's width of your own self perishing upon the battlefield.

Morale

Name	Level	Rank	Range (in feet)	Duration	Description
Divine Favor	Level 8	Rank 1	150	0s	Heals target for 1,800.
Rampaging Siphon	Level 12	Rank 2	PBAE	0	PBAE that deals 600 and heals the group for 100% of the value.
Steal Life	Level 16	Rank 1	100	9s	Magic attack that deals 900 over 9s. Self heals 50% of the damage dealt.
Focused Mind	Level 20	Rank 2	Self	10s	For 10s, build times are reduced by 50%. Character purges and is immune to Silence, Disarm, Root, Snare, and Setback.
Divine Protection	Level 24	Rank 3	Group	10s	Group buffs each group member with an ablative that absorbs the next 1,500 of melee damage, with a maximum duration of 10s.
Tzeentch's Talon	Level 28	Rank 1	100	15s	Lowers target's Armor by 33/level and all resists by 12.6/level for 15s
Eye of Sheerian	Level 32	Rank 2	Group	9s	Heals group 720 over 9s.
Suppressing the Fragile Unbelievers	Level 36	Rank 3	100	7s	Silences targets in the radius for 7s. Deals 1,200 damage over 7s. Radius: 30ft.
Alter Fate	Level 40	Rank 4	PBAE	9s	PBAE Resurrection for group members. Resurrected targets also get a HoT that heals 1,200 over 9s.
Tzeentch's Shielding	Alchemy x15	Rank 4	Group	20s	Group absorbs 18,00 damage for 20s and gains 250 AP.
Tzeentch's Scream	Witchcraft x15	Rank 4	100	0s	Deals 2,400 damage and knocks back enemies. Radius: 30ft.
Windblock	Dark Rites x15	Rank 4	100	10s	Deals 1,800 damage and reduces healing on targets by 50% for 10s. Radius: 30ft.

Tactics

Name	Level	Description
Warped Flesh	Level 11	25% chance when attacked to absorb 262 damage for 10s.
Divine Fury	Level 13	Increase damage dealt by 25%, reduce healing values by 20%.
Endless Gifts	Level 15	Reduces cooldowns of mark temp abilities to 30s.
Tzeentch's Warding	Level 17	Increases Elemental resist by +6.3 per level of the character.
Discipline	Level 19	Increases Willpower by +4 per level of the character.
Warping the Spirit	Level 21	Self heal for 158 and gain 100 AP when the bearer of your Harbinger dies.
Backlash	Level 23	25% chance to put a 5s 150 DoT on attacker. Non-stacking, non-refreshing.
Subtlety	Level 25	Decreases threat by 50% on all heals.
Scourged Warping	Level 27	Warp Reality deals 10% more damage and each tick has a 20% chance to make the next Scourge within 10 seconds instant cast.
Restorative Burst	Level 29	Critical heals return 40 AP over 3s to the caster. (Non-stacking, non-refreshing).
Blessing of Chaos	Level 31	Critical heals also place a buff on target that increases values of heals targeted at him by 25% for 10 seconds. (Bless)
Empowered Alteration	Level 33	Leaping Alteration also gives the targets 50 AP over 9s. (Bless)
By Tzeentch's Will!	Level 35	Crit heals grant you +200 Morale.
Drink Deeply	Level 37	Tzeentch's Cordial will now heal the target for 180 when it ends.
Waves of Chaos	Level 39	Rites will also pulse 112 damage every 3 sec. Radius: 20ft.
Chaotic Force	Alchemy x3	Increases crit chance of Tzeentch's Cry, Scourge, and Boon of Tzeentch by 15%.
Manipulation	Alchemy x7	Any time you heal someone, 25% chance for your offensive target to take damage equal to 25% of the amount healed.
Changer's Touch	Alchemy x11	Each time you deal Corporeal damage to the bearer of your Harbinger, your defensive target is healed for 25% of damage done.
Lashing Waves	Witchcraft x3	Tzeentch's Lash gains a 20ft radius.
Tzeentch's Refreshment	Witchcraft x7	Heals have a 25% chance to give the target 50 AP. (Cannot give self AP).
Transference	Witchcraft x11	Your Harbinger will deal 112 damage every 5s and heal your defensive target for damage done.
Sweeping Disgorgement	Dark Rites x3	Demon Spittle reduces Corporeal resist by 9.45/level and Armor by 24.75/level for 9s. (Hex)
Swirling Vortex	Dark Rites x7	Increases radius and duration of Mark of the Vortex's temp ability. Radius increased by 10ft, duration increased by 6s.
Tzeentch's Grip	Dark Rites x11	Any time an ally hits the enemy with your Harbinger, there is a 25% chance they'll become healed for 113 damage over 3s (non-stacking, non-refreshing).

TACTICS

Ah, yes, Tactics are yet another way to make yourself unique and useful in the eyes of the Raven God. You do not wish to disappoint, trust me...

Tactics are passive abilities that you can equip, so to speak. At max rank you'll have up to six Tactics, with space for four regular Tactics, a Renown Tactic, and also a Tome Tactic. For now, however, you have to make do with a single Tactic slot.

Glorious power comes only to those with a bloodthirsty patience...

You'll learn your first Tactic at Rank 11. It is called Warped Flesh, and although it's not an amazing Tactic, at Rank 11 it'll be the only Tactic you have. Equip it promptly. Anytime you are attacked, there is a 25% chance that you will absorb a small amount of damage, but it cannot trigger more than once every 3 seconds. Thereafter, you'll gain a new Tactic every odd rank all the way up to Waves of Chaos at Rank 39. Ha! My heart warms at the twinkle in your eye! Power! Waves of Chaos is delightfully nasty!

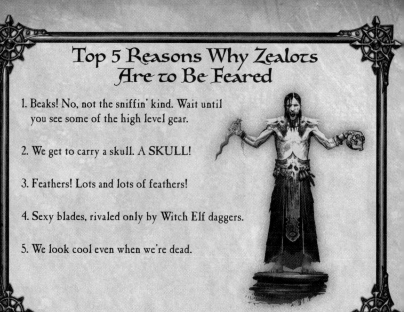

Top 5 Reasons Why Zealots Are to Be Feared

1. Beaks! No, not the sniffin' kind. Wait until you see some of the high level gear.

2. We get to carry a skull. A SKULL!

3. Feathers! Lots and lots of feathers!

4. Sexy blades, rivaled only by Witch Elf daggers.

5. We look cool even when we're dead.

But let us not yet get ahead of ourselves. You'll also gain Tactics from your Masteries, up to two different Tactics in each path. With your Core Tactics, Mastery Tactics, Renown Tactics, and Guild Tactics, you'll have a plethora of useful Tactics from which to choose. Unfortunately, even at Rank 40, you can equip only six of them at any one time, and with so many various situations in which you'll find yourself, how is a Zealot to remain flexible? Thankfully, Tzeentch has blessed us with the ability to create five different sets of Tactics, enabling us to switch them on the fly for any situation.

So which Tactics should you use? That's entirely up to you. There are hundreds of different combinations. It all depends on your situation, be it solo or group play, even raiding with four full groups; be it a scenario, open battlefield RvR, or sacking a city; be you an offensive Zealot or a healer like me. For instance, I might choose the following for my four main slots while in a group that isn't looking to PvP:

Restorative Burst: Any time I critically heal an ally, I regain action points.

Warping the Spirit: Whenever the bearer of my Harbinger perishes, I gain action points and get healed for a small amount.

By Tzeentch's Will: Critical direct heals increase my Morale by a fair amount.

Blessing of Chaos: Critical heals bless my target for 20 seconds, increasing the power of my heals on them during this time.

Using just these four Tactics, I have improved my healing powers, increased my action points with Restorative Burst, and ensured that my Morale will grow more quickly with By Tzeentch's Will.

Even with all that I have told you, your Tactic choices are your own, depending on the type of Zealot you become. Use them well. One day you'll lead your own army south into the heart of the Empire!

RENOWN

You will gain Renown points as you begin killing opposing players, be they Empire or their allies the High Elves or the Dwarfs. Points gained through killing other players will lead to new Renown ranks, and each rank will earn you new points to spend on Renown advancement. There are three groups of abilities from which to choose. To purchase new abilities from the second group, you must spend 20 points in the first group. To purchase new abilities from the third group, you must spend 40 points in the first two groups. There are 15 abilities and buffs in the first group, 17 abilities and buffs in the second group, and a further 18 more powerful abilities in the third group. Each ability costs a set amount of Renown to unlock and, as a whole, the abilities will eventually make you much more powerful.

Take, for instance, the first group of abilities. Some of them are useless to you, such as Blade Master, a passive ability that increases your Weapon Skill by 3. Why are you fighting with your dagger, anyway? We do not invite death; we stave it off! However, abilities such as Resolve, which buffs our Willpower, and Acumen, which adds to our Intelligence, could be useful. You can also increase certain resistances, or even pick up The Empire Fears Me, a Renown Tactic that reduces the Morale of nearby opponents when you kill a member of the Empire. It's important to not only decrease enemy hit points but to control the power of their own Morale, for they too have powerful Morale abilities at their disposal...

In the second group, you'll also find Vigor most useful. It's a passive ability that increases your Wounds stat. Sage is also useful, increasing both your Intelligence and your Willpower. There are many abilities to choose from, and you can tailor your Zealot to whatever role you desire as you work on spending 40 points and unlocking the third group.

One of the best abilities for a healer in the third group is Spiritual Refinement, increasing your healing critical chance by 2% for each time you buy into it. Very nice! By the time you are spending points in this final group, the Raven God will certainly be watching your every battle!

BE VICIOUS, BE RESOURCEFUL. RELY ON YOUR WITS. YOU ARE NOT A MEATSHIELD. UNDER AN OFFENSIVE BLITZ, YOU'LL DROP QUICKLY. STAY ALIVE.

SOLO PLAY (PVE)

HUNTING MONSTERS AND QUEST REWARDS

RANK 1-10

We've already discussed your starter abilities, Scourge and Flash of Chaos. You'll rely on Scourge entirely for your early damage dealing. Our daggers are inept in our weak hands; we rely on our magic to do the majority of our damage. So pull your enemy toward you with Scourge, hit with Scourge again, you get the idea. If you get into trouble, heal yourself with a quick Flash of Chaos. It's not the strongest heal, but with a quick one-second cast time it's easy to heal yourself in a pinch.

At Rank 2 you'll learn Warp Reality from your trainer. It's a great damage-over-time ability, causing a bit of Corporeal damage spread out over 15 seconds. You'll still want to pull with Scourge, but hit the enemy with Warp Reality as soon as Scourge lands, and then revert to Scourge. If Warp Reality wears off, cast another, and revert again to Scourge. Simple and destructive.

At Rank 3 you'll pick up a new heal, Tzeentch's Cordial. It heals your target for so much spread out over 15 seconds. You'll still be using this ability at Rank 40! It's quite impressive, casts instantly, and uses very few action points. For tougher creatures, pull with Scourge, afflict your target with Warp Reality, then go ahead and cast Tzeentch's Cordial on yourself as your target closes. The small heals every few seconds will keep you in the fight and will save you from having to use other, more costly, heals, enabling you to do more damage instead of having to constantly heal yourself.

You'll gain your first mark at Rank 4, Mark of Daemonic Fury. Marks are group member buffs. Daemonic Fury grants you Strength and Intelligence. You can also activate the ability to inflict a small amount of Corporeal damage; unfortunately, the mark is lost when the ability is activated. Always keep this mark cast upon yourself! Zealots can do without the Strength, but the extra Intelligence is most useful.

At Rank 5 you'll gain a new damaging ability, Tzeentch's Cry. It's not all that powerful, but it's an instant cast and can certainly increase your damage when added to the mix.

Veil of Chaos is granted at Rank 6. It's an instant buff that shields you, or a group member, for 10 seconds. The shield absorbs minimal damage, but it can be enough to keep you around long enough to cast a heal or to activate your Flee ability and live to fight another day.

Harbinger of Doom! Yes! It's one of my favorite abilities, even now. Harbinger of Doom calls down a dark raven upon a single enemy. While afflicted, this enemy does less damage to you. Aye, 'tis a powerful ability, and I use it nearly every chance I get unless my enemy is perceptibly weaker than myself. Harbinger of Doom also ties into later Mastery abilities like Storm of Ravens.

You'll also learn Rite of Agony at Rank 7. It's an instant damaging spell that does minimal damage to every enemy within 30 feet. Not all that great when you're facing a single creature, but when there are many, it's quite useful. Unfortunately, we really don't excel at fighting more than one or two enemies, so this ability is better saved for PvP.

At Rank 8 you are blessed with a new, but fragile heal, Elixir of Dark Blessings. It's a hefty heal, but it takes three seconds to cast and is very tough to use during a solo fight because any damage sets the casting back by a large amount. It's practically useless in solo play, and you'll be better served by Tzeentch's Cordial and Flash of Chaos at this point.

You'll learn another mark at Rank 9: Mark of the Vortex. This one is simple: It increases all of your resistances by a set amount. It's useful in certain situations, but at this point in your young career, stick with your Mark of Daemonic Fury.

Finally, at Rank 10, you'll learn two new abilities: Dark Medicine, a two-second heal that not only heals for a set amount upon casting but also continues to heal over time for another 9 seconds. It's very useful in tandem with Tzeentch's Cordial, but beware of the two-second cast time! Then there's Tzeentch Shall Remake You, your first resurrection spell! Unfortunately, it's completely and utterly foolish to even consider this for solo play...

RANK 11-20

Solo play evolves very little during your teens. Most of the abilities granted between Rank 11 and Rank 20 are focused more on group play.

Oh, let me explain: Pulling is the careful, or careless, art of getting a creature's attention, generally from afar. So, a basic pull might run something like this: Cast Scourge, then Warp Reality, then cast the Harbinger of Doom upon your target as it approaches, and perhaps invoke Tzeentch's Cordial if you feel like it could be a tougher fight. Otherwise, assault your foe with Scourge, keep Warp Reality ticking away, and add Tzeentch's Cry and Rite of Agony for increased damage.

You're granted a useful new ability at Rank 12: Mark of the Spell Destroyer. It's a buff that increases both your Initiative and your Willpower attributes. It's very useful for healing.

FOLLOW YOUR QUESTS, AND DO THEM ALL, HOWEVER, ALWAYS BE THINKING OF PVP AND RVR, EVEN WHILE CLEANSING THE LAND AND HELPING OUR ALLIES THROUGH QUESTS, YOU CAN STILL IMPROVE YOUR PVP TACTICS.

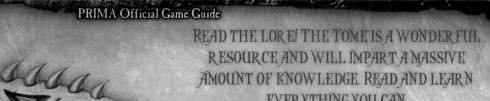

READ THE LORE! THE TOME IS A WONDERFUL RESOURCE AND WILL IMPART A MASSIVE AMOUNT OF KNOWLEDGE. READ AND LEARN EVERYTHING YOU CAN.

MAKE FRIENDS! FIND A GUILD AND PVP WITH THEM AS A TEAM. TAKE CASTLES IN RVR WITH YOUR NEW, OR EVEN OLD, FRIENDS. THE MORE YOU BATTLE TOGETHER, THE STRONGER YOU WILL BECOME.

RANK 21-30

Again, nothing really changes in terms of solo play during your 20s. Pull with Scourge and cast Warp Reality then Harbinger; use Tzeentch's Cordial, Flash of Chaos, and Dark Medicine to stay alive; and sprinkle in Tzeentch's Cry, Rite of Agony, and Demon Spittle for added instant damage. Just be sure to save enough action points for your heals during battle. It's easy to get carried away.

A new lifesaving ability is granted at Rank 25: Breath of Tzeentch. It's an instant ability that knocks back every opponent within 30 feet, and it also knocks them down for two seconds. Wonderful! It might be enough time for you to cast a Dark Medicine on yourself, or, as is usually the case, activate Flee and get to running. Trust me, there's no shame in living to fight another day...

RANK 31-40

Again, nothing is truly new in the spell rotation at this point. Cast Scourge, Warp Reality, and Harbinger; use Tzeentch's Cordial, Flash of Chaos, and Dark Medicine for heals; and mix in Tzeentch's Cry, Rite of Agony, and Demon Spittle for added damage. Watch your action points!

At Rank 35 you gain Tzeentch's Lash, a damaging spell that also silences the target, preventing them from using magic. Very useful when facing a fellow spellcaster!

And, finally, at Rank 40, you'll learn Mark of Remaking, the group buff I mentioned earlier that allows them to resurrect themselves if killed in the next 10 minutes. It's great to use on yourself, and even if you don't die during the 10 minutes, the mark also increases your Toughness by a large amount for one hour. Imagine the dismay when you resurrect yourself! It's a wonderfully devious ability!

GROUP PLAY

Although we are decent in solo play, it's in group play that we truly shine. It's a whole different method of play, because you depend on your group members for damage instead of having to rely solely on your own ability. Your task is to keep everyone alive, especially your tank, who will be absorbing most of the damage and allowing everyone else to deal the majority of the damage while he keeps the enemy's focus on himself.

RANK 1-10

No more pulling! This will no longer be your task. Pulling with a healer is generally considered to be bad form, although it can be done with a decent tank. Nevertheless, let's eschew pulling for a more conservative approach until you're more familiar with group play. Let someone else do the pulling!

Before the pull I usually cast a Cordial on my tank, or whoever is pulling...usually the tank. Once the tank has hit the monster once or twice, add your own slight damage by casting Warp Reality upon the target. This weak, damage-over-time spell won't gain you much hate. Afterward, concentrate on keeping a Cordial on the tank at all times. Flash of Chaos is still a great heal at this point, and it doesn't gather much hate unless you use it endlessly. Dark Medicine is wonderful, in conjunction with Tzeentch's Cordial, and if your tank gets into serious trouble, Elixir of Dark Blessings, even with its three-second cast, is a wonderful healing spell, but using it will likely draw a lot of hate.

Don't run away if you draw the target's attention and it begins attacking you. Calmly place a Harbinger of Doom upon it and a Cordial upon yourself, and wait for your tank to peel him away from your fragile self.

Also, keep marks upon your group members at all times. By the time you're Rank 9, you'll have learned Mark of Daemonic Fury and Mark of the Vortex, both of which can be useful. Group members will also activate

COMMUNICATE. THIS ONE IS SO SIMPLE, YET SO EASY TO FORGET. NEVER CEASE COMMUNICATING.

En's Skull Collection

Blue Chaos Skull

"I colored this one to relax me after a battle in Dragonwake. The voices in my head guided the final designs."

Sewn Skull

"I like to collect the skulls of the Empire Bright Wizards that I kill. This mage was a big problem, so just to be sure he wouldn't cause any more trouble in the next life, I grabbed the thread."

Iron Rod Skull

"The crack came from when I improvised and pierced this foe with a spike. I added a few more for fun, and the younger ones turned this skull into a game."

Eerie Skull

"I bury this skull under the pile. Its eyes haunt me, and my mind gets lost when I stare at the pattern on the bone. I would get rid of it, but I don't want to fetch it from the pile."

their marks for increased damage from time to time, so keep an eye on their various buffs and cast a new mark on them if needed, usually in the downtime between pulls. Don't forgo tank heals to cast a new mark!

And don't forget your resurrection ability, Tzeentch Shall Remake You. It's excessively useful to keep the party going!

RANK 11-20

You really start to evolve as a healer during your teens. In addition to your previous healing spells—Flash of Chaos, Tzeentch's Cordial, Dark Medicine, and Elixir of Dark Blessings—you'll pick up Leaping Alteration and Dust of Pandemonium on your way to Rank 20.

Leaping Alteration is a bolt of healing energy that takes one second to cast, but then leaps to allies within 20 feet of the last affected. It restores a small amount of health over 9 seconds and can affect up to six allies. Dust of Pandemonium heals all group members within 150 feet for a decent amount. Both can be quite useful when mixed into the rotation, depending on the situation.

You'll also learn a new mark, Mark of the Spell Destroyer, which you'll definitely want to cast on yourself, and perhaps other healers if you have them along, increasing both Initiative and Willpower.

Another useful new ability is Glimpse of Chaos, a damaging ability that dispels one enchantment from your target and does slight damage if successful. It's useful for weakening your tank's target and lessening the damage done to your tank.

RANK 21-30

Again, very little will change in your 20s. You'll still be letting the tank do the pulling. Keep Warp Reality on the monster. Keep a Cordial on your tank and use the appropriate heals when needed without bringing too much hate on you. If possible, cast Glimpse of Chaos on the tank's target, and keep marks on every single group member. Healers are often under a lot of pressure, and the vicious Marauders will be the first to blame you if something goes wrong, but don't let them get to you. You have the power.

Again, Breath of Tzeentch can be useful in a pinch, likely saving your party from dying. In addition, you'll also learn Daemonic Fortitude at Rank 30, an instant buff that increases your target's Wounds by a large amount for one minute and then heals the target for the amount increased. Unfortunately, Daemonic Fortitude takes a while to build up energy between castings so its usefulness is limited to the most serious of situations.

DON'T BE THE BONEHEAD WHO CHARGES THE FLAG IN NORDENWATCH. LET SOME OTHER PEON DO IT. FOLLOW YOUR TARGETS AND KEEP THEM ALIVE!

RANK 31-40

Very little changes on your way to Rank 40. Your tank will still be pulling, you'll still be casting Warp Reality on the target, keeping a Cordial on your tank, and mixing in your various heals as needed without making the monsters too mad at you. Keep marks on everyone. You'll likely have a very good feel for your career at this point.

Tzeentch's Lash is great for silencing targets, which can help save your tank, or even yourself, from magical damage. Mark of Remaking can be quite useful as well. Put it on your tank for a big surprise! Or keep it on yourself in case you brazenly draw too much attention to yourself.

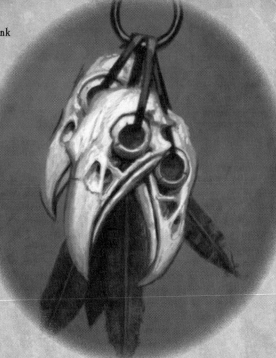

Ah, yes, PvP. Here is where you want to be. This is the culmination of questing, groups, and public quests. This is where your talents truly come to the fore and you will know if you are a fine healer or Empire meat.

As there are many varieties of PvP, let's look at each in brief, just to give you an idea of what you should be doing.

SOLO PVP

The trick to solo PvP for a Zealot? Eh, don't do it. But, if you must, it's much the same as a skirmish.

Be mobile: Do *not* let a Warrior Priest corner you, do *not* give a Bright Wizard endless line of sight. Use your legs, rely on your instant damage spells, and be sneaky. We're valiant with friendly tanks and damage classes in front of us, but when solo, we must use our wits to survive against any class, particularly the higher damage careers.

Heal when you can: Always keep Tzeentch's Cordial on yourself. Use Flash of Chaos when you need a small, quick heal. If you can get out of the enemy's grasp for a moment, risk a greater heal.

Stay alive: Use your instant damaging spells with an eye to their times. You can even hop out from cover, hit with a Scourge, and hide again. Don't go toe to toe with any class but another healer, and even some of them can be much tougher in a duel than a Zealot. I pray that Tzeentch melts the flesh from every Warrior Priest face in the lands! Veil of Chaos is a wonderful ability! If you're at the end of your rope, it might be the shield you need to get you back into the action, keeping you alive long enough for that big heal or a final devastating assault on your foe.

HUNTING PLAYERS AND RENOWN AWARDS

Best Zealot Hairstyles

Bald: All the rage across the countryside! It's easy to maintain; just be sure the curve of your Zealot's blade matches the roundness of your noggin'!

Mohawk: Ratty and simple but a must-have for the hardcore punk killers among our ranks!

Chaos Cornrows: Eh, not really cornrows, but it's hard to deny the appeal of the Chaos symbol shaved upon your cranium, a wee topknot in the center.

Shaggy: For the truly insane. Who needs a comb...or even a shave?

Ponytail: Grease it up, leave it hangin', tada! Nice silhouette from the side too...the Empire will fear you.

Skull and Ponytail: Nothing says Zealot lovin' like a skull with your greasy hair pulled through it. Goes great with a hooked nose.

SKIRMISHES

Taking on one player in incidental combat here or there is not always an easy task, depending on the career you are facing. You have to rely on your feet to keep you out of reach, your heals to keep you alive, and your Warp Reality and your instant damage spells to slowly whittle away at your opponent. It can be tough to cast a Scourge, with its two-second casting time, but that depends entirely on the career you are facing and how competent they are. One night you may trounce a Warrior Priest, and the next evening you may find yourself taking a dirt nap at the hands of a same rank Warrior Priest.

GROUP PVP

BATTLEFIELDS

Get a group and heal...heal, heal, heal! Unfortunately, you'll draw attention to yourself because, typically, Order will come after the healers first. It's a solid tactic, and we follow the same tenets: drop the healers and the rest will follow. Pick a main target, if you can, and keep heals on him, throwing Cordials and small heals to others if needed. If you have to beat feet, do it circuitously, keeping within range of your own group and being careful to balance healing yourself with healing your main target and allies. It can be a tough call. Sometimes you'll have to let your main target go, but be sure to let him know; he'll likely withdraw long enough to relieve the threat on his healer. Trust me, he wants those heals.

When defending castles and such, remember to stay out of sight, but keep line of sight to your group members. I spent an evening healing a determined young Disciple named Thrak from atop the battlements and he made a wonderful final last stand in the courtyard, even if he was just a Dark Elf...

SCENARIOS

Scenarios are much the same as battlefields, although your objectives can differ widely from one scenario to the next. Use your head, stay safe, run if need be, and communicate! Never forget to communicate. It can win or lose a flag or even the entire scenario. Call out incoming enemies so others know where the action has shifted, and try not to run solo into the fray; it's certain death because we drop quickly in our thin robes.

TO THE FRAY!

Aha! Do you see that? Dusk is but a vapor, the sun but a fine line upon the ridges. It is time. For this endeavor, into the village of Thorshafn, stay close, and remember what I have told you. Choose your targets well, and stay out of sight when you can. Just because you are at my side does not mean you will not perish tonight, but think of all the times I have fallen to attain my own powers. Those same powers will be yours; just be smart and rely on Tzeentch and your own resolve.

Thorshafn falls tonight. And that wizard's bloody skull will fit nicely upon my chest...

DISCIPLE OF KHAINE

Has it been so long that I once sat where you sit? No, do not speak unless spoken to, for I will do all the talking, child. How is it that you have been brought to me, you might ask? No place to begin but the beginning, but listen closely for I will not repeat myself.

If I am to be your mentor, you must learn to trust me as I will also have to trust you. For now there is no need for you to be worried. If I wished you dead, you would not have made it past the door, child. Many fear the Disciple, especially your foes, for through Khaine's Blessing a Disciple can change the tide of battle.

By Dalurkain the Tormentor

It has been many years since I myself climbed from the Cauldron, to begin my training as you are about to. For many years I have served the Bloody-Handed God, slaying or aiding the slaying of more than I can count. So many questions I see in those molten brass eyes, but you sit before me having lived through Death Night and escaped the Cauldron yourself.

Once you complete your training, you will set sail as I did on the great Arks, to help in the war to retake Ulthuan. In the weeks and months ahead, you must never forget to strike without hesitation and kill without mercy, and you will serve the Might of Khaine.

Blood and Souls for Khaine.

What is a Disciple of Khaine?

The Bloody-Handed God Khaine is described by some as the God of Murder, and I have observed the Disciples of Khaine celebrate on Death Night, harvesting souls in his name. A Disciple is the chosen of Khaine, trained in his dark healing rites and the use of the ritual blades. Deadly warrior and healer, the Disciple must engage in battle to heal truly effectively, stealing the essence of life from their enemies. You have not seen beauty until you witness a Disciple rip through the enemy ranks.

Their goal in battle is to shed as much blood as possible. A Disciple strikes without hesitation, for the sooner they have leached their foe's essence the sooner they can use the rites of Khaine. Immersed in battle, however, does not imply that they charge in as if they were able to defeat all foes single-handedly. They choose their targets carefully, and should always be aware of their allies. Khaine's chosen use their dark gifts to enhance the Destruction warriors around them, drain foes, and kill in my name, as well as their god's.

It is not a surprise that you know little of this noble career. The rites of the Disciple are secret, and few are chosen. Very few thrown into the Cauldron on Death Night survive. Still others fail to master the complexities of the Disciple, but in the end, all serve in their failure, for in death they have taken even more of our enemies from this life. Disciples are no warriors in heavy armor, nor are they sorcerers unleashing unspeakable powers. They are simply the harbingers of death.

—Baron Heinar Balethar, Zimmeron's Hold, Chaos Wastes

Pay attention to your armor and weapons. Upgrade with quest rewards and loot, for a new sword does no good if it remains in your pack.

STARTING STATS

Even the smallest of minds should be able to understand that the better your statistics, the more powerful you are. All Disciple statistics have a starting value of 50 and can only improve by gaining rank or from enhancements on our armor and weapons. You would be wise to remember this, and ensure you have armor with the best enhancements possible. Much of the armor and weapons you find while adventuring have enchantments that improve your statistics.

The only statistic that does not apply to a Disciple is Ballistics, for the Disciple has no ranged attack skill. Other than Ballistics, they all have a benefit, so learn what each does. What enchantments should you focus on?

A Disciple who focuses on healing should get as much Willpower as possible. Willpower increases all healing and also increases the chance to disrupt hostile spells.

A focus of combat means many statistics to consider, such as Toughness, Strength, and Weapon Skill, which you will find on much of the gear you acquire during the battle ahead. Toughness reduces the damage you take from all sources. Strength increases melee damage and makes it harder for enemies to parry or block your attacks. Weapon Skill increases your chances to parry melee attacks and allows your melee attacks to bypass a portion of the enemy's armor.

One might think that overlooking the value of statistics would not affect your ability to survive, but this is pure ignorance. Do not be ignorant. Pay attention to your statistics, as it will greatly enhance your ability to survive and destroy your foes.

BEING A DARK ELF

The Druchii are often called Dark Elves by other races, likely due to their inability to understand our tongue. Some suggest that the Dark Elf and the High Elf are brothers, but at best the so-called High Elves are our weaker cousins. Of all the races in the land, the High Elf is the most hated by the Druchii, for they have taken our homeland. It could be said that there are similarities between us, for it is true that they do worship Khaine as a God of War, not seeing his true guise as the God of Murder. Their inability to understand and embrace the truth of the Bloody-Handed God is one of the many reasons we will defeat them.

Long have we desired to reclaim our birthright, taking back Ulthuan from our lesser cousins. Our lord Malekith has awaited a sign to leave Naggaroth and retake our homeland. It is said that the High Elves have allied themselves with other weaker races. So be it. We will enslave them all as we march across our homeland. To that end we have made allies in this battle and are considered to be on the side of Destruction, but never forget that our goal is simply to retake our homeland and these so called allies are there to enable us to do this, nothing more.

The conquest of Ulthuan begins on the shores of the Blighted Isle. There is much to be done, and as you venture to join the war you will find many tasks you can perform to aid in the war. Each task you complete will give you a better understanding of our foes, hone your skills, and help you to gain respect from those Druchii you encounter.

The Blighted Isle are in the northern part of Ulthuan, and are the staging grounds for House Uthorin's forces. The area is important, for near it can be found the Shrine of Khaine. Our weaker cousins will strive to hold control of the shrine, but it must be controlled at all costs.

The land has many forests and mountains; it is rugged, but nothing like the frozen lands from which we hail. In these lands you will find many creatures, but it is known most for the white lions found in the mountains of Chrace. Kill those creatures on sight, for they have forged an unnatural union with the High Elves. You will also find many other creatures, such as dark sprites, unicorns, and deadly spiders.

Once you step on the beach of Narthain you will be overwhelmed by the differences between our homeland and the cold lands we have grown up in, but do not allow the so-called beauty of Ulthuan distract you from your task. Speak with Gorthan Rakar. He will guide you, helping you join the war against the usurpers. Like Gorthan Rakar, you will encounter others who will have tasks for you to perform to aid in the war. It is likely you will also advance in rank soon after reaching Narthain Beach, and Kovus Darkblade himself will train you.

Trust your "allies" less than your enemies.
Believe in only the past and its truths.

THE DISCIPLE GEAR

Your armor is not for looks, and neglecting it can cost you your life. The lands of Ulthuan can be dangerous, so maintain your armor, for it will shield you from attacks. The Disciple wears medium armor; you will not be able to use light or heavy armor. As the name implies, medium armor is better than light, but not as good as heavy. If you are to survive, you must be careful to always look for better armor, which can be looted from dead opponents or received as rewards from questing. You would do well to review the enhancements on armor you find, watching for better gear to replace what you are wearing.

You will encounter many weapons in the war against our weaker cousins, but concern yourself only with the ritual swords of the Disciple. To a Disciple, your swords will be an extension of you, and much of the time you will wield two swords. A Disciple's weapon of choice is a one-handed sword; you will not find any that are two-handed, and most are enchanted to improve your combat abilities.

At times you will need to do more healing than attacking, and in those cases it is possible that you may chose to wield a charm. A charm is wielded in your left hand. Often charms are enchanted to greatly increase your Willpower, and they also offer resistances to attacks.

Strengths

- Combat with swords.
- Direct healing and healing over time.
- Causing damage over time.
- Enhance yourself or an ally.
- Remove a bad effect from yourself or an ally.

The Disciple is not considered the shepherd of war for nothing, child. We are feared, and for good reason, for we are trained to be the masters of death. While it is true that a Disciple is a good warrior, their true power comes from the rites of Khaine that we use while in battle. Dark Elves enter the war against our weaker cousins with two other classes, the Witch Elf and the Sorceress, neither of which are healers. Because of this, the Disciple is perfectly suited as both warrior and healer. You have many rites of Khaine that will enable you to heal, enhance, and remove bad effects from your allies while leaching and damaging your foes.

Weaknesses

- Ranged combat.
- Average armor.
- Healer is a prime target.

What makes you think a Disciple has any weaknesses? Do I appear to have any? Oh, you are asking about your weaknesses starting out, I see. At all costs you must avoid attacks from a distance, as ranged combat is not the way of the Disciple. As a Disciple, you wear medium armor, so you will also be challenged when attacking heavily armored opponents. Our foes will seek you out on the field as a target, thinking that defeating the healer will win them the day. I do not see this as a disadvantage at all, for the sooner you can engage our foes, the sooner you can offer their blood and souls to Khaine.

STRENGTHS AND WEAKNESSES

Fill the Tome of Knowledge; it is your resource for information. Talk to everyone you encounter. Inspect everything you find. Kill anything that moves.

SKILLS AND ABILITIES

Abilities

Over time you will advance in rank, becoming more powerful and learning more about the abilities of a Disciple, the blessings of Khaine. Learning these can be done at various career trainers you will find as you adventure. Career trainers train you not only in abilities that every Disciple will learn, but they also help you to specialize in Mastery abilities. It is important to seek them out each time you gain in rank.

Do you need a break? Am I boring you? No? Then let us proceed with a very important discussion about specialization. Sooner than you might think, you will have to decide where to focus your training, picking a path of study.

Managing to survive to the higher ranks will enable you to master one of three different paths, starting slowly once you reach Rank 11. These Mastery paths are the Path of Sacrifice, Path of Torture, and Path of Dark Rites. Specialization in a path will not only improve all the Core abilities in that path, but also allow you to learn new abilities. Complete Mastery of a path will allow you to train three new Core abilities and three new Tactics. It is also the only way you can learn the most powerful Morale ability. Do not neglect to train these abilities; each will give you a large advantage against your foes.

Deciding which path to train will be influenced by how you plan to engage our weak cousins. Each has its advantages and disadvantages, which I will outline, so pay attention and don't make me repeat myself, for I have no desire to waste any more time than I have already.

Path of Dark Rites

Choosing the Path of Dark Rites is to focus on healing, enabling your allies to remain in battle longer. This path is a good choice if you are going to focus on true healing, and is best used if you plan to have a group of allies depending on you. While it is true that Khaine would be served by the deaths of your allies as well as your foes, consider that the longer you keep your allies in battle, the more enemies they can defeat. There will always be time to dispose of them when they are no longer of use to you.

You will find the abilities in this path very useful, especially Soul Shielding, which will absorb damage for your entire group. If you come to depend on this ability, consider using the Tactic Favorable Shielding, which will enable you to use it more often.

Each Mastery advancement in the Path of Dark Rites will improve these Core abilities: Covenant Of Tenacity, Rend Soul, Khaine's Embrace.

Path of Torture

Choosing the Path of Torture is to focus on combat and the use of Bleed Out, to become a deadly warrior. This path is an ideal choice if you decide to fight alone, or are less concerned about healing your allies. Rather than the healing focus, this path has some of the more powerful melee abilities. Personally, I have always believed that the sooner you defeat your opponents the sooner you can find more, and this path will greatly increase your combat skills.

Sanguinary Extension is a cruel attack that is best used after you have already crippled your foe with Lacerate. On top of the damage it deals, it cripples your foe even more. You will also enjoy the Tactic Bleed Out increases Lacerate, Sanguinary Extension, and Fell Sacrifice's for an additional 6 seconds.

Each Mastery advancement in the Path of Torture will improve these Core abilities: Lacerate, Flay, Essence Lash, Covenant Of Celerity.

Path of Sacrifice

Choosing the Path of Sacrifice is to focus on siphoning power from your enemies, gaining from them as you damage them. Second only to their deaths is the enjoyment of leaching your foes' strength and using it against them; this path focuses on that ability. Much of this path enhances your ability to deal damage over time rather than direct melee damage.

One of the more interesting abilities in this path is Devour Essence, for it not only does it drain life from up to four foes near you, but also heals you and your allies. This ability will drain your Soul Essence quickly, so use it with care. Horrifying Offering is a particularly interesting Tactic if you take this path, for it will give you a chance to reduce your foe's ability to attack even more when using Consume Strength.

Each Mastery advancement in the Path of Sacrifice will improve these Core Abilities: Consume Strength, Consume Essence, Covenant Of itality, Transfer Essence, Consume Thought.

Name	Level	Path	Cost	Range (in feet)	Type	Build	Duration	Reuse	Description
Blood Offering	Level 1	Core	30 AP/s	Self	Other	0s	5s	10s	Channel: Gives 187 SP/s (30 SP/s); when player runs out of AP, channel stops.
Restore Essence	Level 1	Rituals	55 SP	150	Heal	0.5s	9s	0s	Heals 247 damage, then heals 658 damage over 9s.
Cleave Soul	Level 1	Torture	30 (Builds 30 SP)	Melee	Melee Attack	0s	0s	0s	Deals (150+DPS) damage.
Fist of Khaine	Level 1	Rituals	15 (Builds 15 SP)	10 to 65	Ranged Attack	1s	0s	0s	Deals 75 damage.
Consume Strength	Level 2	Sacrifice	25 (Builds 25 SP)	Melee	Melee	0s	10s	5s	Deals (112+DPS) damage. Lowers target's Strength (Cripple) by 2/level and raises defensive target's Strength (Bless) by 2/level for 10s.
Soul Infusion	Level 3	Core	30 SP	150	Heal - Bless	0s	15s	0s	Heals for 1,496 over 15 seconds.
Covenant of Tenacity	Level 4	Rituals	Free	Group	Dark Pact	0s	0s	10s	Aura: Group members increase their Armor by 16.5/level. Toggled.
Lacerate	Level 5	Torture	20 (Builds 20 SP)	Melee	Melee	0s	10s	5s	Deals (187+DPS)*1.33 damage over 10s, lower target's Toughness by 3/level. (Cripple).
Consume Essence	Level 6	Sacrifice	30 (Builds 30 SP)	0s	Melee Attack	0s	0s	0s	Deals (75+DPS). Defensive target and those within 10ft of him are healed for 100% of the amount of damage done.
Terrifying Vision	Level 7	Core	20 (Builds 20 SP)	100	Debuff	0s	15s	15s	Detaunts target (15s duration, 50% redux)
Rend Soul	Level 8	Rituals	25 SP/S	Melee	Melee Attack/ Lifetap	0s	3s	8s	Channel. Deals Spirit damage. Deals (75+DPS) damage to target. Heals defensive target for 250% of damage dealt. 100% Setback chance, Setback for 1.5s.
Flay	Level 9	Torture	30 (Builds 30 SP)	Melee	Melee	0s	6s	10s	Deals (187+DPS) damage. If target is Crippled, Snare by 40% for 6s (Cripple).
Stand, Coward!	Level 10	Core	20 SP	100	Resurrection	6s	0s	3s	Resurrect target friendly dead player.
Essence Lash	Level 12	Torture	45 (Builds 45 SP)	CAE	Magical Attack	0s	0s	10	Deals 225 damage to everyone in the radius. Arc: 180, radius: 40ft.
Covenant of Vitality	Level 14	Sacrifice	Free	Group	Dark Pact			10s	Aura: Group members have a 20% chance to deal 112.5 damage and heal themselves for 112 when they hit an enemy. Does not trigger the layer timer. Toggled. Does not get stat bonus. Does not crit. Maximum proc rate of 1 per 2s.
Patch Wounds	Level 16	Core	25 SP	150	Magic Attack	0s	0s	5s	Removes a Ailment or Hex from target.
Covenant of Celerity	Level 18	Torture	Free	Group	Dark Pact	0s	0s	10s	Aura: Group members have a 20% chance to proc a Snare (20%, 9s) and 349 damage over 9s, Cripple). Does not trigger the layer timer. Toggled.
Khaine's Embrace	Level 20	Rituals	60 SP	150	Group Heal	1s	0s	2s	Heals every group member for 540.
Consume Enchantment	Level 25	Core	25 (Builds 25 SP)	Melee	Melee	0s	0s	10s	Deals (75+DPS) damage. Dispels one Enchantment from target.
Transfer Essence	Level 30	Sacrifice	35 (Builds 35 SP)	Melee	Melee Attack, Heal	0s	0s	5s	Deals (150+DPS) Heals group members within the radius for 50% of damage done; does not affect self. Radius: 30ft.
Consume Thought	Level 35	Sacrifice	25 (Builds 25 SP)	Melee	Melee Attack, Ailment	0s	5s	30s	Deals (150+DPS) damage and silences the target for 5s.
Uncaring Dismissal	Level 40	Core	40 (Builds 40 SP)	CAE	Escape, Crowd Control	0s	0s	60s	Enemies in the AE are knocked back (medium). Arc: 180, radius: 30ft

Abilities

Name	Level	Path	Cost	Range (in feet)	Type	Build	Duration	Reuse	Description
					Specialization				
Soul Shielding	Rituals x5	Rituals	40 SP	Group	Group Buff	0s	10s	60s	Group absorb buff for 787.
Khaine's Vigor	Rituals x9	Rituals	40 SP	PBAE	Heal - Bless	0s	15s	10s	Group heal over time, heals 607 over 15s. (Bless)
Khaine's Refreshment	Rituals x13	Rituals	20 SP/S	PBAE	Channeled Heal	0s	3s	13s	Channeled heal. Heals around him for 202 every second for 3s. 100% Setback chance. Radius 30ft.
Sanguinary Extension	Torture x5	Torture	30 (Builds 30 SP)	Melee	Melee Attack	0s	15s	5s	Deals (187+DPS) damage. If target is Crippled, add a second DoT (Cripple) that deals 199 damage over 15s.
Fell Sacrifice	Torture x9	Torture	30 (Builds 30 SP)	PBAE	Magical Attack	1s	24s	0s	Deals 748 over 24s to all in radius (Cripple). Radius: 30ft.
Wracking Agony	Torture x13	Torture	30 (Builds 30 SP)	Melee	Melee Attack	0s	0s	10s	Deal (112+DPS), If target has less than 50% health, deal (337+DPS).
Warding Strike	Sacrifice x5	Sacrifice	30 (Builds 30 SP)	Melee	Melee Attack	0s	0s	5s	Deals (150+DPS) damage to target and reduces the enemy's chance to Parry by 10% for 10s.
Devour Essence	Sacrifice x9	Sacrifice	25 SP/s	150	Buff	0s	5s	20s	Toggle. Buffed friendly pulses out a PBAE Lifedrain that deals 150 damage and heals for 50% of the damage dealt every second. Maximum targets: 4. Radius: 30ft. Drains Soul Essence each second, toggle disables if SE runs out.
Pillage Essence	Sacrifice x13	Sacrifice	30 (Builds 45 SP)	Melee	Melee Attack	0s	0s	10s	Melee attack that deals (225+DPS) but drains 50 AP from the target and gives 1 SE for each AP drained.

Morale

You best stifle that yawn and pay attention or you may find yourself with one less ear. Timing, timing, timing. Knowing when to use a Morale ability and when to wait can be the key to success and failure in a battle. Morale abilities have four ranks, and you can use only one of each rank at any time. To use a Morale ability requires you to be in battle building up Morale up to a high of Rank 4. Once you use a Morale ability, it consumes all the Morale that you have received.

There are only three choices of Rank 1 Morale, but I found my most used to be Divine Favor for its large heal that is very useful in an emergency. I generally used it most with my allies, but you likely will find yourself needing it to stay alive until you are stronger. My second choice is Steal Life, for it will possibly do enough damage to defeat your foe, and heal you or an ally in preparation for the next target.

Similar to Rank 1, you have three choices to consider at Rank 2, and two of them are very interesting. I recall the pleasure of the looks on my opponents' faces when I evoked Rampaging Siphon, damaging all enemies near me and healing my allies. Even more enjoyable is the surprised looks from Universal Confusion as your enemies are not only damaged, but stunned. What opportunities this opens.

Divine Protection is just what its name implies, and you will find it to be the most versatile of the Rank 3 Morale abilities. Both Rank 3 abilities are oriented to aiding a group, and you will not likely find them useful when adventuring alone. This brings me to the Rank 4 choice. My advice would be to use the Morale ability from your Path of Mastery, whichever you chose.

Morale

Name	Level	Rank	Range (in feet)	Duration	Description
Divine Favor	Level 8	Rank 1	150	0s	Heals target for 1,800.
Rampaging Siphon	Level 12	Rank 2	PBAE	0	PBAE that deals 600 and heals the group for 100% of the value.
Steal Life	Level 16	Rank 1	100	9s	Magic attack that deals 900 over 9s. Self heals 50% of the damage dealt.
Focused Mind	Level 20	Rank 2	Self	10s	For 10s, build times are reduced by 50%. Character purges and is immune to Silence, Disarm, Root, Snare, and Setback.
Divine Protection	Level 24	Rank 3	Group	10s	Group buffs each group member with an ablative that absorbs the next 1,500 of melee damage, with a maximum duration of 10s.

If you embark on the Path of Torture, add Sanguinary Extension into your combat sequence: Consume Strength, Lacerate, Sanguinary Extension, Flay, Cleave Soul.

You are a healer. Assassins will always select you as their primary victim. Never forget that.

Morale

Name	Level	Rank	Range (in feet)	Duration	Description
Life's End	Level 28	Rank 1	Group	10s	For 10 seconds, your group (but not self) will be healed for 50% of the melee damage you deal.
Universal Confusion	Level 32	Rank 2	PBAE	5s	Deals 600 damage and Stuns for 5s to all targets in 30ft radius.
Khaine's Withdraw	Level 36	Rank 3	Group	0s	Remove all negative effects from the group members.
Alter Fate	Level 40	Rank 4	PBAE	9s	PBAE resurrection for group members. Resurrected targets also get a HoT that heals 1,200 over 9s.
Thousand and One Dark Blessings	Rituals x15	Rank 4	Group	30	Group buff. Increase Armor by 33/level. Increase all resists by 12.6/level. Increase all defenses by 25%. Lasts for 30s.
Vision of Torment	Tourture x15	Rank 4	Melee	7	Melee attack that deals 2,400 damage over 7s, Stuns target for 7s seconds, and causes target to lose 100 Morale per second.
Chant of Pain	Sacrifice x15	Rank 4	PBAE	4s	Channeled PBAE Magical attack that deals 300 damage per second and heals self for damage dealt. Max duration: 4s.

Tactics

Use of Tactics will greatly increase your effectiveness, so do not neglect them. What's more, you should plan different sets that you can use for different situations, as the ones you use while adventuring alone are much different than ones to employ when supporting a group as a healer. I have already discussed with you some of the specialization tactics you get from training in one of the three paths, so let's consider some of the core Tactics you can learn. Their use is limited based upon your rank as follows: Rank 11: one Tactic slot; Rank 21: two Tactic slots; Rank 31: three Tactic slots; Rank 40: four Tactic slots.

With a goal of dealing as much damage as possible, it is hard to ignore Khaine's Imbuement gives a 25% boost which will add additional damage over time when you hit an enemy. You should also consider Divine Fury, which greatly increases damage dealt at the expense of healing, but many times it is worth the price. Also do not rule out Increased Pain, for it will aid you in making critical hits in combat. All of these are suited to the Path of Torture.

When trying to support a group as the healer, it is always good to avoid being the target, so consider Subtlety. To maximize your healing, there is Restorative Burst, which allows you to cast more, or Desperation, which improves your healing when someone is critically wounded. Another that helps in all healing is Bound by Blood which gives you a 25% chance that you get 25% healed whenever you heal an ally. All of these are suited to the Path of Dark Rites.

Name	Level	Description
Dark Blessings	Level 11	Incoming healing effectiveness increased by 10%.
Divine Fury	Level 13	Increase damage dealt by 25%, reduce healing values by 20%.
Khaine's Blessing	Level 15	Whenever you critically hit a target, your auto attack speed is increased by 100% for 10s.
Alignment of Naggaroth	Level 17	Spirit resists increased by 6.3/level.
Discipline	Level 19	Increases Willpower by +4 per level of the character.
Khaine's Imbuement	Level 21	Melee attacks have a 25% chance to proc a bleed that deals 449 over 9s. (Cripple)
Bathing in Blood	Level 23	When the Dark Elf kills a target, he heals himself 472 over 9s.
Subtlety	Level 25	Decreases threat by 50% on all heals.
Bound by Blood	Level 27	25% of the time you heal an ally, you are healed for 25% of the value.
Restorative Burst	Level 29	Critical heals return 40 AP over 3s to the caster. (Non-stacking, non-refreshing).
Murderous Intent	Level 31	Increase melee critical chance by 10% and Parry chance by 10%, decrease healing done by 20%.
Fueled Actions	Level 33	Restore Essence and Soul Infusion have a 25% chance to make the next attack cost no AP.
Transferred Focus	Level 35	Critical hits increase healing effectiveness by 20% on defensive target for 10s.
Potent Covenants	Level 37	Proc rate of covenants increased by 15%.
Siphoned Consumption	Level 39	Consume Enchantment heals defensive target for 135 if it removes an effect.
Specialization		
Khaine's Bounty	Rituals x3	Critical heals give the Disciple a 487 absorb for 30s.
Restored Motivation	Rituals x7	Restore Essence grants the target 250 Morale.
Persistant Rending	Rituals x11	Rend Soul is only setback 50% of the time when struck while channelling.
Bloodthirst	Torture x3	Covenant of Celerity's snare is increased to 60%, and damage increased to 648.
Bleed Out	Torture x7	Lacerate, Sanguinary Extension, and Fell Sacrifice all last an additional 6s.
Curse of Khaine	Torture x11	Critical attacks reduce healing on target by 100% for 5s.
Horrifying Offering	Sacrifice x3	Consume Strength reduces target's AP by 50.
Gift of Khaine	Sacrifice x7	Critical hits from abilties in Sacrifice give the defensive target 60 AP. (Cannot give self AP.)
Empowered Transfer	Sacrifice x11	Increases the percent of damage healed by Consume Essence (to 150%) and Transfer Essence (to 100%).

Your consume spells bring lead to great powers. Tactics such as Horrifying Offering does that by allow you to consure Strength In exchange for causing your victim to lose 50 Action Points which is huge. The Gift of Khaine tactic gives your defensive target 60 Action Points any time you critically hit an enemy with any abilities from Path of Sacrifice. Another great tactic is Empowered Transfer which increases Consume Essence heals for 150% of the damage it deals plus Transfer Essence heals are 100% of the damage it deals. These tactics are all well suited to the Path of Sacrifice.

Renown

To truly become powerful, you must gain Renown by engaging in RvR, and as you progress in ranks of Renown you will gain access to better gear and be able to train abilities in three ranks. You need to train at least 20 points in the first rank to advance to the second rank of Renown abilities. You are required to train at least 40 points in the first two ranks before advancing to the third rank of abilities.

The first rank of abilities allows you to gain bonuses to your statistics and magic resistances, and it will also enable you to get bonuses for defeating Order races, bonus gold, or bonus experience. The ideal choices for this advancement are the core statistics of the Disciple such as Resolve, which increases Willpower for healing. However, I always found myself drawn to Blade Master, which of course increases Weapon Skill. Others to consider are Impetus for Initiative, Fortitude for Toughness, and Might for Strength.

The second rank of Renown abilities allows you to gain bonuses to multiple statistics, bonuses for defeating Order races, and bonuses to Renown gains. Two of the abilities I am drawn to are Skirmisher, which increases both Weapon Skill and Initiative, and Assault, which increases Strength and Weapon Skill. Others to consider are Vigor for Wound and Reinforcement for Armor.

Most of the Renown abilities in Rank 3 are useful to the Disciple, with the exception of ranged and magic critical. A Disciple in the Path of Dark Rites should consider Spiritual Refinement for the healing critical increase.

Killing Monsters and Questing

Solo Play (PvE)

So how can we ensure you survive with your pitiful inexperience? I will help you understand. First you must always be conscious of the amount of Soul Essence you have available. Gaining Soul Essence requires you to be in combat, but if you are not able to and need it fast, use Blood Offering. It will rarely be necessary when you are fighting alone, but the sooner you learn to always be aware of it, the better your chance of survival.

Rank 1-10

You will quickly learn some key abilities as you train in the initial ranks of the Disciple. Even as early as Rank 2 you will learn Consume Strength, which is the first of many abilities that leaches from your opponent and enhances you. Once you are Rank 4, you will learn your first aura, Covenant Of Tenacity, which will increase you and your group's armor. At Rank 5 you will learn one of the most useful attacks, Lacerate, and from that point forward it should be the second attack you use in every battle after Consume Strength.

I might also mention that there are some healing skills you learn early on, but if you find you need them, I have already wasted my breath on you. Regardless, if the need arises, consider using Soul Infusion, for it will heal over time and is fast, which will allow you to continue the battle. You will also learn Consume Essence at Rank 6, which is a melee attack that will also heal you or an ally.

I would be remiss if I did not mention the ability Fist Of Khaine, as it is the only real ranged attack you will learn. I find it useful when trying to get as many opponents engaged as possible, but if you are afraid to engage and wish to try and pull a lone opponent to you, it may be useful. If you happen to find yourself pressed by too many opponents after getting their attention with Fist Of Khaine, you may find the Rank 8 Morale ability Divine Favor useful, for it will significantly heal you, enabling you to finish the remaining foes.

Seek to earn influence among the camps. You may earn respect, but you will certainly earn better item rewards.

Rank 11-20

If you reach the ranks of the teens, you will have learned most of your melee abilities and by this stage you should have mastered their use. At Rank 12 you can learn Essence Lash and Rampaging Siphon. These are good area attacks that will strike foes in front of you that are near, but take care not to use it if you fear getting the attention of too many foes. It can draw some to you that have yet to engage. Rampaging Siphon also heals, but as a Rank 2 Morale ability, it is best saved for those times when a large boost of healing is needed.

Many Tactics are learned in these ranks, and Divine Fury at Rank 13 is one worth mentioning. There will be no need to use your healing abilities if you can defeat your foe faster, and Divine Fury is an ideal Tactic for that purpose. With only one Tactic to use, it is hard to go wrong choosing this one.

Rank 21-30

In these ranks, you will be pleased if you have chosen the Path of Dark Rites, as there are many skills gained that strengthen the healing power of a Disciple. Four of the five Tactics that become available affect healing ability. You can train Divine Protection, which is a very useful Morale ability that can easily turn the battle to your favor if used at the right time.

One Core ability, Uncaring Dismissal, can be trained at Rank 25. It can be very entertaining to see our weaker cousins knocked away like dolls. You may find this useful to catch your breath in battle and give you time to consider options.

The final ability, Transfer Essence, is very useful when in a group of allies. This ability is a melee attack that does a group heal. It is also much more useful for healing when combined with the Path of Sacrifice Tactic Empowered Transfer, which greatly increases the amount of healing done.

Rank 31-40

So you anticipate surviving to the highest ranks, do you? Well then, let us discuss what you may be learning and how to use the abilities. Two Core abilities remain, and they are both melee abilities. You learn Consume Thought at Rank 35, which is ideal for combating spellcasters, because it silences them as well as dealing damage. Rank 40 brings Consume Enchantment, which does damage and dispels one enchantment from your foe. You continue to gain new Tactics. Three of them require two Tactics slots each, but they enhance your entire group. Three new Morale abilities also come available.

With so many new abilities available, one would think that would be enough to juggle, but you will have even more considerations. These ranks will have you completing your Masteries, and your specialization in a path. You must maintain focus, train your abilities, and complete your specialization.

Group Play

Rank 1-10

During the lower ranks, most of your skills used in a group should be similar to adventuring alone. Rare is the case when you should feel challenged as a group, but when you are it will likely be in a public quest (PQ). Likely even in these cases, you will find yourself not needing to do much to aid the group until the final stages of the quest.

Soul Infusion is your friend. Its healing over time may be low, but keep it active at all times when in battle.

How does one describe the nature of things to the ignorant? As simple as my beginnings are, I can recall the day like it was yesterday. Never had I felt such exhilaration as I did when the Black Ark approached the shores of Ulthuan. Soon we would be in battle, and soon blood would flow. Our homeland was nothing like the cold lands we set sail from. Naggaroth is bleak and cold, and this land is fecund and teaming with life...for now. I have studied, trained, and defended myself since birth for this day, the day I would join the war, the day I would seek glory in the name of the Bloody-Handed God. Blood and souls for Khaine.

Setting foot on the beaches of Narthain, it was all I could do to contain my excitement, and soon I found what I had hoped to find: the war was near. I checked my armor, simple as it was, and my swords were shining in the sunlight as I saw for the first time one of our weak-willed cousins, a sea guard. Soon Gorthan Rakar was requesting my assistance in slowing the High Elves' attempt to fortify their position, and nothing more needed to be said, for this was the day I had waited for my entire life. I took my time, taking in all the newness of this land, the smells of the growing plants, the warm sun on my skin, the familiar salty breeze from the ocean.

Then he was there, sword in hand ready to attack, and I had almost let my purpose get away from me...almost. My training took over. Swords in hand, I engaged my enemy and as his blood began to spill I thought, with a slight smile, so, the war begins.

Rank 11-20

Battling through these ranks will be similar to the lower ranks, so you will likely continue to adventure using abilities as if you were alone. One slight difference is the addition of the new covenants at Ranks 14 and 16, which may cause you to switch from Tenacity to Vitality or Celerity. Another new element is specialization, and if you feel you will be spending most of your time in groups, you may consider the Path of Dark Rites. Even if your focus is the Path of Torture, you can heal. And if someone dies, it is the will of Khaine. Blood and souls for Khaine.

Rank 21-30

Khaine's Embrace will become one of your more common healing spells cast once you get it at Rank 20. Combat will start to get more difficult, and your medium armor will not stand up as well as it may have before. Ideally your group will have a warrior to take the brunt of the punishment while you focus on more interesting targets.

Rank 31-40

Once you attain these high ranks, give serious consideration to your Path of Mastery, for these are the ranks you will train for the real battles ahead. If you are still focused on Torture and think you will likely change, this is the time to consider refocusing. At higher ranks you start finding yourself not in the front of the battle at times, even using Blood Offering more frequently to build Soul Essence. Use Khaine's Embrace often to heal your group, keeping the main warrior targeted for your direct healing.

Leveling Up

With all I have related to you so far, I suspect you are asking yourself: "How can I advance in ranks as quickly as possible?" You might think it a good question, but it is one I would expect a child to ask. What you should be asking is: "How I can best take advantage of this situation?" You must never forget that the only help you will receive will be from those who seek to benefit from you, and even I will benefit from your success.

Let me again impart my wisdom to you regarding this subject, for it is best to clear this question from your mind. The simple answer is to do everything. Yes, you heard me correctly. The simple answer is to do everything and you will advance in rank quickly. Complete every quest you can, and, yes, many quests you receive will be beneath you, but complete them regardless. Get all the influence you can by participating in public quests. These not only help you advance in rank, but also provide good equipment. Join scenarios and RvR battles to gain Renown, for these provide good advancement as well as the ability to buy better equipment and train Renown abilities.

Rank 1-10

If you are to survive past the beaches of Narthain, you need to master your melee skills quickly. Always have Covenant Of Tenacity aura active, and use Soul Infusion often to regain health. Get in the habit of having Soul Infusion working to restore you and also use Restore Essence if larger healing is needed.

By the time you attain Rank 10 you should be attacking using the following abilities in order: Consume Strength, Lacerate, Flay, and Cleave Soul. Keep Consume Strength active on your opponent at all times, for it will drain him and enhance you. Lacerate is important because it cripples your opponent, and this is necessary to enable other abilities to do Spirit damage.

If you need additional healing besides Soul Infusion and Restore Essence, replace Cleave Soul with Consume Essence. You will have no Tactics, but do use Divine Favor at Rank 8. Again, practice and practice.

Rank 11-20

Continue using what I have already shown you, with some minor changes. It is best I don't overtax your small mind with too many details. Simple solutions tend to be the best solutions, and to survive, you must not get distracted. Make sure to use your Tactics: Dark Blessings at Rank 11 and switch to Divine Fury at Rank 13.

Now is the time for you to start a Mastery path, and the most effective is the Path of Torture. Your combat and healing will not change much in these ranks, but practice using Essence Lash when you have multiple targets and take any opportunity to try Patch Wounds to remove negative effects.

Now is your chance to get more Morale practice with Rampaging Siphon, switching to Steal Life at Rank 16. Both of these do good damage as well as healing.

Rank 21-30

Once you reach Rank 22, you get your first Path of Mastery attack, Sanguinary Extension. I recommend you use it after Lacerate for the added cripple effect. You will be attacking in the following order: Consume Strength, Lacerate, Sanguinary Extension, Flay, and Cleave Soul. Again, you can use Consume Essence in place of Cleave Soul if you need the added healing.

Add Khaine's Imbument at Rank 21, the very useful Morale ability Divine Protection at Rank 24. Start using Divine Fury as your second Tactics slot. Continue to focus on your Mastery training, learning Fel Sacrifice at Rank 27 and Khaine's Imbuement at Rank 30. Practice using Fel Sacrifice because you will find it very helpful when surrounded by multiple opponents.

Level 31-40

Combat will not change much once you have reached these ranks. Stick to the core attack sequence you finished at Rank 22. This is not to say you will not introduce other attacks, but never forget what works. Often, once you finish your Cleave Soul attack, your opponent is already defeated.

You must train Murderous Intent after three ranks of Mastery and once you have it, immediately use it as your Tactic at Rank 17. This Tactic should never leave your slots.

I suspect you have realized by now that the focus has been to deal as much damage as possible, so be sure to wield dual swords and use armor that increases your combat skills. Willpower is not a priority for this approach. You can support a group if you need to, but if your goal is to advance as quickly as possible, focus on the warrior inside you and abilities that achieve that end.

Pick a gathering craft even if you are not interested in crafting. It will be a source of income.

Killing Players and Seeking Renown

Solo PvP

I find that all things being equal, in a battle against the forces of Order you will win the day against a single opponent. Now if you have neglected to pay attention to what I have tried to teach you, then things will not be equal and you will die as you should, but it will be due to your incompetence. Engaging in battle against opponents is nothing like defeating the cattle you find while questing. You will be tested to your fullest, and if you have done what I told you, there will be much blood spilled for Khaine.

Success comes from many factors, such using as the best armor and weapons you can find. Train the correct Path of Mastery, such as Torture. Train all your Core abilities, Tactics, and Morale abilities, as well as Renown. Doing these things, and having some skill, will bring you success on the battlefield.

Simple things even a child such as you will understand will make a huge difference in the battle. Going into a battle without a covenant active--I suggest Tenacity--is a serious mistake. Always keep Consume Strength active, attacking with it as soon as it expires. Keep your opponent crippled with Lacerate, for that will cause many of your attacks to do Spirit damage over normal damage. Lastly, you must keep your health up; do not take the chance of letting it get too low. Soul Infusion should always be active. When it expires, invoke it again. Supplement this healing with Restore Essence.

On occasion I have found that doing all of this is not enough, so what can you do, you might ask? The right Morale ability can often turn the battle. Whether it is Divine Favor for "emergency" healing, or Steal Life for damage and healing, both are ideal Rank 1 Morale abilities that I have used many times to turn the battle to my favor.

Skirmish Tactics

When traveling alone in the battlefields, consider your rank as it compares to others you will find in that area. There are four ranks or "tiers" of battlefields that you will encounter. The ranges for each tier are as follows: Tier 1: Rank 1-11; Tier 2: Rank 10-21; Tier 3: Rank 20-31; Tier 4: Rank 30-41. If your rank is close to the top of the range for that tier, it is more likely that you will survive a battle.

You will not have the luxury of time to consider your options when in the battlefields, so when you see an enemy, you must decide quickly how you will act. As I have said, against a single foe the Disciple is well suited to win, if you engage quickly and use your abilities carefully.

Battlefield Tactics

So you are already interested in capturing battlefield objectives or keeps. That's a bit ambitious for one barely able to hold a sword, but I appreciate your enthusiasm. I will venture to say that you will rarely find a time when you will be able to capture objectives in the battlefield without the aid of allies. You may be fortunate to encounter an objective that is unclaimed, and in those rare cases do not hesitate to capture it, but it is likely that you will need to avoid those held by Order if you are adventuring alone. It is unlikely you will be able to defeat the guards and capture it without aid.

Scenario Tactics

Tell me why you would even ask me about not aiding allies in a scenario? Once you enter the instance with the goal of defeating the forces of Order, it will be difficult to be effective if you are not working with the others there with the same goal. I am not suggesting that you befriend anyone, but you must always take advantage of any resource available to you, and ignoring allies in these battles is unwise. I have nothing more to say on this subject.

Top 5 Uses for a High Elf Slave

1. Figurehead for your ship. Oh, how they scream!

2. Bait for other Dark Elves. Irony and revenge in on delightfully cold dish.

3. Fodder for your cold ones. Chasing their meals makes the reptiles so much meaner—and there's always profit to be made from bets on how long your slave will last.

4. A reminder of your superority.

5. Gifts for the Temple of Khaine. It never hurts to flatter the Bloody-Handed God and his priestesses with a tribute.

Campaign Tactics

The ultimate goal is retaking our birthright. It is good that you are aware of this and eager to aid in achieving it. Success in the campaign is gained from controlling each tier and ultimately sacking enemy cities, and much is involved in achieving these objectives. As you adventure, everything you do will aid in achieving this goal: every quest you complete, every enemy you defeat, every scenario you win.

Now do not think you must capture a keep to make a difference. This is not a battle to capture one target, it is a war to retake our homeland, to enslave our cousins, to avenge our fathers. Even the smallest tasks, ones that often are below you, contribute to this ultimate goal. Never forget this, and you will continue to bring us closer to our goals.

Group Play

So you feel the need to engage others, and believe you will have some allies to battle at your side? Best watch your back, for even an ally can cause you to lose a battle through their ignorance. When you find yourself in a group in a player vs. player (PvP) battle, your role is usually to be the main healer. You must never forget that our opponents will seek you out on the field of battle as a prime target because of your healing.

Rarely will you find me suggesting that you avoid charging into battle, but this is one of the few times I will. You may be the most powerful warrior on the field, but against many foes I do not recommend charging in. The last place you want to find yourself is up against a Swordmaster, only to be attacked by many spells and arrows for which you have little defense.

So yes, I suggest you bide your time, aiding your allies from the rear of the battle. Heal and enhance your allies while watching for an ideal time to charge in to finish choice targets. Nothing is more enjoyable than spilling the blood of an Archmage who believes she is safe behind a Swordmaster.

At times you need to be in the front, but if you have no other Disciples to heal you, I recommend you reconsider the group you are traveling with. It is possible to succeed, but you should strive to engage the ranged opponents first, stopping them from dealing high damage to you.

Skirmish Tactics

Battling the forces of Order with allies is much more effective than attempting it alone. You often find the peasants of Order in groups, and what better way to defeat them than with a group of allies. Do not get overconfident when engaging these forces; they likely will be well organized, so it is best to not take any chances. Keep your allies healed so they can continue to fight, and engage when you have an ideal target. I have always found the softer ones more entertaining.

Battlefield Tactics

As you adventure, you find yourself working with others more and more. This is hard to avoid in a war, and the most effective way to do this is in a guild. Battlefield objectives such as keeps can only be held by guilds, so if your goal is to participate in keep captures, you must find a guild.

Healing yourself does not work if your defensive target is someone else, so watch your targeting while soloing.

Scenario Tactics

Fighting alongside a group of allies in a scenario battle is the best way to succeed in completing the objective. There is no special wisdom needed to be successful, but consider that your rank in the tier does somewhat affect your ability. This is not to suggest that you cannot participate when you are in the lower ranks, but be aware that you will face foes who are near or at the rank limits. Keep your allies healed, and do not charge into battle without enough support to defend you. Never forget that as a healer, you are going to be the prime target.

Campaign Tactics

How do you best aid in the campaign in a group? This is another seemingly simple question with a complex answer, I am afraid. There is no one action or task that will bring us success in the campaign; it is the combination of many things that win the day. Your contributions can be increased by, as I have said before, doing everything. As you advance, you will want to join a guild and aid your guild to advance. Your rank advancement is important, but the advancement of a guild's rank is also one of the many factors that will aid in completing the campaign objectives.

It would seem I have invested much time in you, child. Let us hope you live long enough not to disappoint me. The time has come for you to use what I have taught you, time to kill or be killed. Heed what I have taught you and you may survive, and with your success, more of our weak cousins will fall. I will follow your progress, for in time I hope to profit from your success, or failure, for that is the way of the Druchii.

TO SLAY THE WEAKER

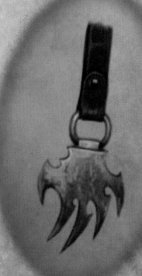

SORCERESS

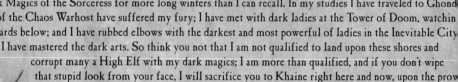

By Arachul

Stand here with me, Sorceress adept.

Now. We have little time.

The *Nemesis* quickly draws near to the bluffs of the northern shores, and soon we will surge from our Black Ark into glorious battle with our hated enemies, the High Elves.

Is that fear in your eyes? Squander it away, weakling; there is no time for fear.

Look now across the raging ocean, and you can make out the lights of our foes. We legions of the Druchii will snuff those lights, and the cliffs will glow crimson come the morning light. Many of our despised cousins will perish tonight. I desire bloodletting.

Stand still! If Lord Uthorin must foist you upon me, adept, then I must quickly impart to you what dark wisdom I am able before we land. I care not for your own blood, but I do not desire my own spilt upon those cliffs, and I don't want an ignorant whelp at my side.

I am Arachula. I have studied the Dark Magics of the Sorceress for more long winters than I can recall. In my studies I have traveled to Ghond to the North Tower there, and many of the Chaos Warhost have suffered my fury; I have met with dark ladies at the Tower of Doom, watchin our dark brethren prepare at the shipyards below; and I have rubbed elbows with the darkest and most powerful of ladies in the Inevitable City I have mastered the dark arts. So think you not that I am not qualified to land upon these shores and corrupt many a High Elf with my dark magics; I am more than qualified, and if you don't wipe that stupid look from your face, I will sacrifice you to Khaine right here and now, upon the prow of this mighty Black Ark.

What is a Sorceress?

The enemy builds siege engines to hurl ruin at us from afar. It is crude and effective only at times. I prefer to breed my long-range devastation: We call them Sorceresses.

From 100 feet away, the Sorceress destroys all that she sees. A Sorceress is more mobile than a siege engine, more intelligent in the targets she chooses. She gathers Dark Magic, engorges on the energy, and razes the enemy to the ground. The Dark Magic that she holds is both a blessing and a curse, for with every swell of dark energy, they are also likely to destroy themselves.

Those Dark Elves who enjoy dealing massive amounts of damage may find satisfaction in the life of a Sorceress. They take pride in watching an enemy wither or melt at their merest whim. However, a Sorceress's existence may be brief, should the enemy weapons reach their light robes or one catastrophic casting mistake forever extinguish their magic, but their hatred burns like a cool sun.

—Baron Heinar Balethar, Zimmeron's Hold, Chaos Wastes

Always watch your Dark Magic. If you let it escape your control, the results will be explosive.

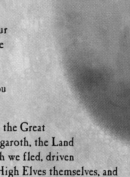

STARTING STATS

A lot of information so far, neh? Fortunately, you need only concentrate on what really matters to the powerful ranks of the Sorceress: Intelligence and, to a lesser degree, Willpower.

Intelligence empowers your magic damage. The more Intelligence you have, the more damage you can unleash upon your enemies. In addition, the more Intelligence you have, the less chance your enemies have of disrupting your own magic attacks. Even you should be able to comprehend what an aborted Doombolt could mean to you.

Willpower mainly increases healing, so in that regard it's useless to a Sorceress; however, Willpower also increases the chance that we will disrupt our enemy's magical attack. Yes, perhaps that gleam in your eyes is a lick of zeal fighting to come forth.

And, of course, Wounds are important as well. Wounds increase our hit points. The more hit points we have, the longer we can engorge upon lovely Dark Magic and make bloody shadows of our enemies. Toughness is also useful. It decreases all damage taken by a certain amount, and with only the slight protection of our robes, you'll be in need of Toughness to protect you further.

BEING A DARK ELF

We hail from a land across the Great Western Ocean, from Naggaroth, the Land of Chill. It is to Naggaroth we fled, driven from these shores by the High Elves themselves, and is to Ulthuan we now return. Finally! Our most immediate enemies are our weaker cousins—tall, haughty and utterly dispassionate. What a waste of Elven blood. As allies, the High Elves have chosen the shoddy humanity of the Empire and the bumbling audacity of the Dwarfs. Poor choices, and none will stand before our powerful war machine.

Your journey will begin ashore, just there. Aye, we will issue forth from the Black Ark. If you manage to walk carefully down the plank to the shore below, without breaking your neck after an oblivious plummet into the depths, we will quickly join our forward scouts at a small outpost upon Narthain Beach. There are local skirmishes already: High Elf Sea Guards upon the sands, Dark Elf Bolt Throwers manned by Warsiegers, and a steep assault up the high cliffs. But we will persevere and triumph. Ulthuan will be ours.

Take note of Gorthan Rakar. He will offer your very first quest. And do not forget to introduce yourself to Kovus Drakeblade, your very first Career Trainer. It is most important to train as you gain ranks, lest ye be forever weak.

SORCERESS GEAR

They may not have taught you a single aspect of your new career, but at least they gave you some fine gear. Ha! Look at that brand new robe, and the boots to complement it. Such futile clothing! Not a lick of decent armor in sight. How we send our adepts into battle! Alas, I suppose I'd be remiss if I was in charge of supplies and gave your dim self a semblance of decent gear. I'd break the war machine in two weeks, would I not, as you stumble blindly to your fated death, coughing up gear to the enemy with your last gasp? At least you're sexy in your slight clothing, yes? And your Witchling Staff, how it sets off the ensemble!

Nevertheless, get used to very slight protection. We can wear only cloth robes, and you'll never find yourself with a large amount of armor. However, you will find increasingly powerful gear, offering boosts to important stats like Intelligence, Wounds, and more. Covet this armor, and attain it quickly, for it will make you ever the more powerful. There is some very nice armor out there for the taking, and some fine staves as well, staves being the only weapons we can use. Search them out and make them yours.

Top 5 Uses For High Elf Intestines

1. A fine belt for Disciple trousers.
2. Great for snaring more High Elves.
3. Excellent for popular summoning rituals.
4. Make better necklaces with High Elf skulls.
5. Jump rope!

(left margin, rotated) which ones do not. It can be the difference between a vicious win and an embarrassing death.

STRENGTHS AND WEAKNESSES

Strengths

- Dark Magic.
- High damage magical attacks.
- Great range on your spells.
- Excellent group buffs.
- Handy roots, silence abilities, and debuffs.
- Nasty area-of-effect damage.

Yes, Dark Magic is our greatest strength. Without it our Core abilities are mundane; with enough Dark Magic, though, our critical spell attacks will burn down the most ferocious Swordmaster in little to no time. It also helps that we can kill from long distances, keeping us out of the fray. It's not fun when a White Lion gets in your face, his pet scratching at your shins! Of course, Grip of Fear is a great root spell, holding all enemies within 30 feet in place for several seconds. It's not disgraceful to run; you're just making some space to fill with a vicious charged Doombolt.

Weaknesses

- Dark Magic.
- Wear only cloth.
- Targeted early in a battle because of our high burst damage.

Yes, Dark Magic is also one of our worst weaknesses. With it comes great strength, but Dark Magic can also consume and kill you. There is a fine line between melting faces and melting yourself. You'll only learn this with time. Thankfully, we have an Ark full of Disciples. We'll have you up and going again soon enough.

Of course, as soon as we step free of the camp on Narthain Beach, you'll likely be the first adept the Sea Guards will attack. Why? Your vacuous gaze, of course! And your lack of gear. You look like an easy kill; as a whole, the Sorceress drops fast, and we will most likely be targeted first, or at least after the healers have gone down. We can do a massive amount of damage in a very short time. The faster the enemy drops us, the quicker they can shift their attention to tougher targets like the Witch Elf or a Black Orc.

Abilities

Core Abilities

Unique to our station is our Dark Magic. We build this Dark Magic using certain skills. For instance, surely you have already learned the Rank 2 skill, Gloomburst? Have you not? You truly are a whelp sent to belabor my progress! Hopefully you'll live long enough to find it useful. Gloomburst is a quick-casting spell that, while it doesn't inflict a ton of damage, builds up your Dark Magic in 25-point increments. Dark Magic starts at nothing and progresses to a maximum of 100 points. As your Dark Magic increases, so does your chance to land a critical spell, but also so does your chance of miscasting, causing a backlash.

Let me draw a chart here for you. Was this NOT in your Sorceress scrolls of learning? Do they even allow adepts parchment in these headlong times? Nevertheless, read this...if you're able. They do teach you to read, do they not?

1–10 Dark Magic: +5% Critical chance, 10% Critcal damage, 10% Backlash chance.

11–30 Dark Magic: +10% Critical chance, +20% Critical damage, 20% Backlash chance.

31–70 Dark Magic: +20% Critical chance, +40% Critical damage, 40% Backlash chance.

71–90 Dark Magic: +40% Critical chance, + 80% Critical damage, 40% Backlash chance.

91–100 Dark Magic: +50% Critical chance, +100% Critical damage, 50% Backlash chance.

As you can hopefully see, writ plainly upon this parchment, the more Dark Magic you accrue with your abilities—and you will gain greater abilities than a simple Gloomburst—the more power you will bring to bear upon your enemies. However, it's easy to get carried away and forget about backlash.

Backlash is what happens when you lose control of the Dark Magics you have gathered to yourself. The more Dark Magic you have gained, the greater chance of a backlash. A backlash will not only damage you, but it will also completely empty your store of Dark Magic, forcing you to cast spells to regain Dark Magic. Dark Magic is your greatest asset, and you should always have an eye on its magnitude as well as its dangers.

Now, I want to see how well you can handle your two of your three starting abilities: Doombolt and Chillwind. You're not quite ready for Dhar Wind, we'll get to that ability later. Both will be staples of your magical casting all the way until you're Rank 40, so it's best to understand them well before we step off the Black Ark.

Doombolt is a standard direct-damage spell, causing an initial blast of Corporeal damage, and then the same damage applied over the next five seconds after impact. Chillwind, on the other hand, is a curse that deals Corporeal damage over 9 seconds. Try casting Doombolt at me—it has a very long build-up, so it's often good to start a fight with it instead of trying to cast it during combat. Then, immediately after the casting is complete, likely even before the Doombolt hits me, cast Chillwind. It's an instant cast spell, meaning it takes zero time to cast, so keep your wits about you.

Very good! That almost stung! There may be hope for you yet. Just be careful of who you attempt to attack. If the White Lion you cast Doombolt on is wearing massive white furs and his pet is as tall as you...then I shall handle it.

As you progress toward Rank 40, you'll gain new Core abilities every so often: every rank until you're Rank 10, then every even numbered rank until Rank 20. After Rank 20 you'll gain a new Core ability every fifth rank, meaning at 20, 25, 30, 35 and, finally, Rank 40. But don't let the dwindling offering of new Core abilities concern you, there are more than just Core abilities at your disposal as you grow in rank.

Mastery Abilities

There are also Mastery abilities. At Rank 11 you'll gain your first Mastery point. At Rank 40 you'll have gained a maximum of 25 Mastery points. There are three paths for the Sorceress: Path of Agony, Path of Calamity, and Path of Destruction. We'll discuss what each offers in a moment, but for now all you need to know is that you can specialize up to 15 points in each path. So you can

only ever fully specialize in a single Mastery, because after you maximize a single path, Path of Agony for instance, you'll only have 10 remaining Mastery points to spend elsewhere.

Before you choose your path, I can educate you on what the three paths have to offer.

Path of Agony: Focuses mainly on immediate damage. Improves the power of the Core abilities Gloomburst, Umbral Strikes, Impending Doom, and Stricken Limbs.

Path of Calamity: Focuses mainly on longer-duration effects. Improves the power of the Core abilities Demonic Chill, Word of Pain, Vision of Torment, and Shadow Spike.

Path of Destruction: Focuses mainly on wide-area effects. Improves the power of Shattered Shadows, Surging Pain, Pit of Shades, Infernal Wave, and Stricken Voices.

I know, as of right now, you have absolutely no idea of what type of Sorceress you wish to be. Personally, I specialized in the Path of Agony to improve my direct damage, including my Gloomburst. Choose the path that most appeals to you. Although you know less than nothing now, hopefully by the time you're Rank 11 or so you'll have at least a slight idea of the type of Sorceress you wish to become.

Abilities

Name	Level	Path	Cost	Range (in feet)	Type	Build	Duration	Reuse	Description
Dhar Wind	Level 1	Core	Free	Nuke	Magic Attack	1s	0s	5s	Undefendable nuke, applies flat damage based on combustion thresholds as follows. Drains all Dark Magic. 1-10: deals 41; 11-30: deals 82; 31-70: deals 165; 71-90: deals 330; 91-100: deals 412.
Doombolt	Level 1	Agony	30	100	Magic Attack - Corp	3s	0s	0s	Deals 600 damage. Builds 10 Dark Magic.
Chillwind	Level 1	Calamity	35	100	Magic Attack - Curse - Corp	0s	9s	0s	Deals 548 DoT over 9 seconds. Delays damage until first tick. Builds 5 Dark Magic.
Gloomburst	Level 2	Agony	40	100	Magic Attack - Spirit	1s	0s	5s	Deals 337. Builds 25 Dark Magic.
Shroud of Darkness	Level 3	Core	20	Self	Buff - Augment	0s	15s	60s	Self buff. Increase resists by 9.45/level for 10s.
Dread Aspect	Level 4	Core	20	100	Magic Debuff	0s	15s	15s	Deals no damage. Detaunts target (50%, 15s).
Surging Pain	Level 5	Destruction	35	PBAE	Magic Attack - Corp	0s	0s	0s	Deals 150 damage to all targets in radius. Radius: 30ft. Builds 20 Dark Magic.
Umbral Strikes	Level 6	Agony	30	100	Buff - Augment - Spirit	0s	60 min	0s	Group buff. Adds a 25% chance to deal an additional 150 damage after hitting with any attack.
Word of Pain	Level 7	Calamity	20	100	Magic Debuff - Hex - Spirit	0s	10s	0s	Lower target's Willpower by 2/level. Stacks up to 3 times. When effect wears off, deals 299 per stack. Builds 5 Dark Magic.
Shattered Shadows	Level 8	Destruction	35	80	Magic Attack - Spirit	3s	0s	0s	Deals 375 damage to all targets in radius. Radius: 20ft. Builds 20 Dark Magic.
Obsessive Focus	Level 9	Core	20	Self	Buff	0s	20s	60s	Self buff. Increase damage against single target by 10% for 20s. Lower damage against all other targets for 10% for 20s.

Go after the enemy healers first. Trust me, they will be coming for you.

Follow your quests, and do them all. Remember, even while cleansing the land and helping our allies through quests, you can still improve your PvP tactics.

Abilities

Name	Level	Path	Cost	Range (in feet)	Type	Build	Duration	Reuse	Description
Grip of Fear	Level 10	Core	30	PBAE	CC - Hex	0s	5s	20s	PBAE root for 5s. Radius: 30ft.
Cataclysmic Darkness	Level 12	Agony	30	100	Magic Attack - Curse - Spirit	2s	0	0s	Deals 349 damage. If target is cursed, Snares target by 40% for 5s. Builds 10 Dark Magic.
Shadow Spike	Level 14	Calamity	35	LAE	Magic Attack - Curse - Corp	0s	15s	0s	Deals 549 over 15s to all in radius. Arc: 30, Range: 65ft. Builds 10 Dark Magic.
Infernal Wave	Level 16	Destruction	40	LAE	Magic Attack - Spirit	0s	0s	10s	Deals 225 damage to all targets in radius. Arc: 350, range: 65ft. Builds 20 Dark Magic.
Demonic Chill	Level 18	Calamity	30	100	Buff - Augment - Corp	0s	60 min	0s	Group buff. Adds a 25% chance to deal 75 damage back to the attacker when hit with a melee attack.
Stricken Limbs	Level 20	Agony	25	100	Magic Attack - Hex - Corp	1s	5s	30s	Deal 225 and Disarm target for 5s. Builds 10 Dark Magic.
Pit of Shades	Level 25	Destruction	25 /2s	100	Magic Attack - Spirit	0s	10s	20s	GTAE channel. Deals 299 damage every 2s for 10s. Radius: 20ft. Setback override: 100%. Builds 15 Dark Magic.
Reckless Gathering	Level 30	Core	Free	Self	Buff	0s	10s	30s	Channel. Regenerates 70 AP/s for 3s. Taking damage during channel knocks self down for 3s.
Vision of Torment	Level 35	Calamity	35	100	Magic Debuff - Curse - Spirit	0s	5s	0s	Target loses 6 AP/s for 5s. At the end of the effect, target takes 249 damage. Builds 10 Dark Magic.
Stricken Voices	Level 40	Destruction	25	80	Magic Attack - Corp	2s	3s	30s	Deals 249 damage and silences the target and those around him for 5s. Builds 20 Dark Magic. Radius 20ft.
Echo of Power	Agony x5	Agony	35	100	Magic Attack - Corp	0	0	0	Deals 337 damage. Cannot be defended. Usable after a Disrupt. Builds 10 Dark Magic.
Impending Doom	Agony x9	Agony	40	100	Magic Attack - Spirit	0s	0s	10s	Deals 412 damage. Builds 40 Dark Magic.
Shades of Death	Agony x13	Agony	30	100	Debuff - Hex - Corp	0s	10s	5s	For the next 10s, next time the target takes damage, he takes an additional 112 damage. Can only trigger 5 times.
Gloom of Night	Calamity x5	Calamity	25	80	Magic Attack - Hex - Spirit	2s	15s	10s	Anchor to target. Deals 199 damage to every target in the radius every 3s. 15s Duration, Radius: 20ft. Builds 10 Dark Magic. Builds 20 Dark Magic.
Hand of Ruin	Calamity x9	Calamity	20/s	100	Magic Attack - Spirit	0s	6s	11s	Channeled. Deals 399 every 2s for 6s. Builds 15 Dark Magic. Setback chance override: 100%
Absorb Vitality	Calamity x13	Calamity	30	100	Magic Attack - Curse - Corp	0	15s	20s	Deal 798 damage over 15s. Heal self for 100% of value. Builds 5 Dark Magic.
Black Horror	Destruction x5	Destruction	40	80	Magic Attack	3s	0	0	Deals 375 damage to all targets in radius and debuffs their Initiative by 2 per level for 10s. Radius: 20ft. Builds 10 Dark Magic.
Disastrous Cascade	Destruction x9	Destruction	30/s	PBAE	Magic Attack - Spirit	0s	3s	8s	Channeled. Deals 225 every second for 3s. Builds 15 Dark Magic. Radius: 30ft. Any attack to Sorcerer interrupts 0.5s duration of channel.
Shadow Knives	Destruction x13	Destruction	20/s	80	Magic Attack	0s	3s	13s	Channeled. Deals 299 every 2s for 6s to all targets in radius. Radius: 20ft. Setback override: 100%. Builds 15 Dark Magic.

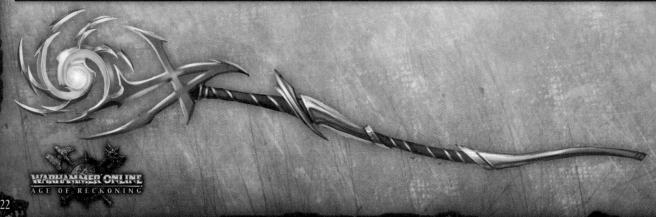

Morale

You will uncover your first Morale ability at Rank 8. It will be a Rank 1 Morale ability, and you will unlock the slot in which to use it. Eventually, you can equip four Morale abilities, one Rank 1, one Rank 2, one Rank 3, and the most powerful abilities at Rank 4. But, at Rank 8, you'll have a single Morale slot and you'll learn Mage Bolt. It's an instant cast, focused blast that deals good damage. When the ability lights up, it's yours to use, and it's a very useful beginning Morale ability, I might add.

It's also important to note that differing Rank 4 Morale abilities are also granted at the highest Mastery level. This means you can only learn a single Mastery Morale ability because it's impossible to maximize two Masteries with only 25 points. I am fully specialized in Path of Agony; therefore I can equip the Rank 4 Morale ability called Soul Stealer. It's a nasty ability, even though it can take a while to build up enough Morale to use it. My target, and all other enemies within 30 feet of him, will suffer a lot of damage and lose a tremendous number of action points. I also gain a small amount of health and gain the action points I drained. Yes, it's definitely a wildly useful ability, if you ever find yourself with more than a handful of power, assuming you specialize in the Path of Agony, of course. There are wonderful Rank 4 Morale abilities at the top of the other two paths as well, so no one path is exceeded by another.

Morale

Name	Level	Rank	Range (in feet)	Duration	Description
Mage Bolt	Level 8	Rank 1	100	0s	Magic attack that deals 1,200 damage.
Siphon Power	Level 12	Rank 2	100	30s	Drain 200 AP from target and give to character. Decrease target's Intelligence by 4/level for 30s.
Misdirection	Level 16	Rank 1	Self	10s	Self buff. For 10s, Magical attacks return 50% of the damage back to the caster (resulting in 50% less damage to the target).
Focused Mind	Level 20	Rank 2	Self	10s	For 10s, build times are reduced by 50%. Character purges and is immune to Silence, Disarm, Root, Snare, and Setback.
Scintillating Energy	Level 24	Rank 3	100	7s	Target takes 1,200 damage + Stun for 7s.
Fire Blast	Level 28	Rank 1	100	9s	Deals 600 damage and another 1,200 over 9s.
Wind-Woven Shell	Level 32	Rank 2	Group	20s	Reduce incoming damage to the group by 20% for 20s.
Darkstar Cloak	Level 36	Rank 3	Self	10s	All abilities cost 0 AP for 10s
Unleash The Winds	Level 40	Rank 4	PBAE	0	PBAE that deals 1,800 and knocks back enemies.
Soul Stealer	Agony x15	Rank 4	100	0s	Deals 1,200 damage to targets in radius. Heals self for 720 damage. Removes 250 AP from targets. Gains 250 AP. Radius: 30ft.
Crippling Terror	Calamity x15	Rank 4	1,000	7s	Silence and Disarm targets in the radius for 7s. Radius: 30ft.
Paralyzing Nightmares	Destruction x15	Rank 4	Self	7s	Deals 1,800 and Roots all targets for 7s. Radius: 30ft.

Tactics

You'll also notice that at Rank 11, you train your first Tactic. Tactics are passive abilities that give you a bonus as long as you have them active. At max rank you'll have up to six Tactics, with space for four regular Tactics, a Renown Tactic, and also a Guild Tactic. For now, however, you're going to have to make do with a single Tactic slot. As you progress toward Rank 40, more slots will open, and you'll also learn more increasingly powerful Tactics.

For instance, your Rank 11 Tactic is called Dark Blades. It's a simple Tactic: all heals directed toward you will cause you to recover 10% more health. Not bad at all, if you have a healer around. With any luck, you will. Go ahead and equip it at Rank 11, it'll be the only tactic you have.

Did you notice that there are five different sets of Tactics? As you rank up and gain new Tactics at advanced ranks, you'll find you can mix and match the many Tactics for any type of situation, from solo to group to sacking an enemy city. There are hundreds of useful combinations.

As a solo player, I often equip these four regular Tactics:

Triumphant Blasting: Any time I critically strike an enemy with Doombolt or Shadow Knives, I deal even more critical damage.

Empowered Dhur: Increases my action points based on how much Dark Magic I expend..

Grasping Darkness: My Doombolt and Chillwind Core abilities gain a chance to snare my target and reduce their run speed.

Endless Knowledge: Increases my Intelligence by +1 per level.

With these four Tactics alone I have not only increased my Intelligence, which also increases my spell damage, I have also increased my action point pool and my critical damage, and I've gained a chance to snare my target. Trust me; any movement impairing ability is wonderful for a Sorceress.

The Orcs, Goblins, and Chaos. Join or create a guild. Together, you will become more powerful than you are alone.

Melt faces.

Name	Level	Description
Dark Blessings	Level 11	Incoming healing effectiveness increased by 10%.
Devour Energy	Level 13	25% of the time, Spells cast also gain the character back 30 AP / 3s. (Non-stacking, non-refreshing)
Grasping Darkness	Level 15	Doombolt and Chillwind debuffs Str/BS/Int for 3/level for 10s and removes 20 AP.
Alignment of Naggaroth	Level 17	Spirit resists increased by 6.3 / level.
Endless Knowledge	Level 19	Increases Intelligence by +4 per level of the character.
Infernal Gift	Level 21	Offensive spells have a 25% chance to increase group's damage dealt by 20% for 10s (Enchantment, does not affect self).
Bathing in Blood	Level 23	When the Dark Elf kills a target, he heals himself 472 over 9s.
Sleight Of Hand	Level 25	Decreases threat by 50% on all attacks.
Empowered Dhar	Level 27	Dhar Blast returns 1:1 AP for Dark Magic lost.
Close Quarters	Level 29	Increases magic damage by +25% when under 45ft and decreases magic damage by -20% when over 45ft.
Manic Obsession	Level 31	Reduces the cooldown of Obsessive Focus to 20s reuse.
Triumphant Blasting	Level 33	Critical hits with Destruction abilities also apply medium knockback to the enemy.
Hastened Fear	Level 35	Dread Aspect and Grip of Fear have their reuse lowered by 7s.
Glorious Carnage	Level 37	Critical hits increase Morale by 200.
Umbral Fury	Level 39	Umbral Strikes proc chance increased by 50%
Recover Energy	Agony x3	Agony abilities have a 25% chance to restore 50 AP.
Tapping the Dark	Agony x7	When Umbral Strikes procs, it also gives the holder a 262 damage absorb for 5s.
Swell of Gloom	Agony x11	Gloomburst deals an extra 225 damage, but always explodes.
Vision of Domination	Calamity x3	When Vision of Torment ends, you gain 50 AP.
Shadow of Disaster	Calamity x7	Demonic Chill will now also reactively proc from ranged or magical damage.
Chilling Gusts	Calamity x11	Each tick of Chillwind and Shadow Spike has a 33% chance to proc an extra 187 damage.
Piercing Shadows	Destruction x3	Miscasts deals 50% of explosion damage in a PBAE of 30ft around you.
Lengthening Shadows	Destruction x7	Increases radius of Surging Pain and distance of Infernal Wave by 33%.
Neverending Agony	Destruction x11	Decrease reuse time of Pit of Shades by 10s and Infernal Wave by 5s.

Renown

You will gain Renown points as you begin killing opposing players, be they High Elves or their allies, the Empire and Dwarfs. Points gained through killing other players will lead to new Renown ranks, and each rank will earn you new points to spend on Renown advancement. There are three groups of abilities from which to choose. To purchase new abilities from the second group, you must use 20 points in the first group. To purchase new abilities from the third group, you must spend 40 points in the first two groups. There are 15 abilities and buffs in the first group, 17 abilities and buffs in the second group, and a further 18, more powerful, abilities in the third group. Each ability costs a set amount of Renown to unlock and, as a whole, the abilities will eventually make you much more powerful.

Not every Renown ability will be useful for you, as a Sorceress. For instance, Might 1 increases your Strength by 3. Why would a Sorceress bother with Strength? You shouldn't. However, you will find useful abilities such as Acumen, which increases your Intelligence, and even High Elves Fear Me, a Renown Tactic that reduces the Morale of nearby opponents when you kill a High Elf. Nasty, eh?

Further in you'll find other interesting abilities in the second group. Sage will increase your Intelligence and Willpower as you train it up; Arcane Protection will increase your magic resistances. There are also Renown Tactics such as Refreshing Dominance: killing High Elves will restore a small amount of health. You'll need every combat edge you can attain.

Deeper into the third group are the most powerful Renown abilities. Focused Power will be an outstanding choice, improving your magic critical chance. Arcane Dismissal will increase your disrupt rate. And new Tactics become available, like High Elf Bane, which enables you to inflict more damage against High Elves. And if you ever change your mind, you can always respecialize and receive a refund on all of your Renown points—for a price, of course. I should think that, in your handful of life from birth till now, you've at least learned that much. Everything comes at a price.

Killing Monsters and Questing

Solo Play (PvE)

When we are not upon the fields of battle, we must practice our skills elsewhere, helping our Dark Elf brothers, increasing our attributes, and finding new gear before we head back to the front. As a Sorceress, we are a very viable solo class, and we can excel as we quest through the various lands, but only if we are aware of our weaknesses. Because you are Rank 1, a helpless whelp, I'll start from the bottom and give you an idea of some of the better ways to fight as you level to Rank 40. Interested?

I thought so...

Rank 1–10

I've already let you practice your starter abilities, Doombolt and Chillwind. Did you find that practice useful? As I mentioned earlier, you also begin your career with Dhar Wind. This ability consumes all of your Dark Magic and deals direct damage to your target based on how much Dark Magic you have gathered. Very powerful at the higher levels of Dark Magic! These T are the only abilities you begin with, other than Auto-Attack and Flee, so it's important to understand them now, before you are ashore and on your own. Most Dark Elves improve to Rank 2 in next to no time. You, I'm not so sure of, but I'll give you the benefit of the doubt.

WARHAMMER ONLINE
AGE OF RECKONING

At Rank 2 you'll learn Gloomburst. Yes, I have previously mentioned it. It's a quick casting spell, taking only one second to cast, and it deals a small amount of Spirit damage to your target. In addition, it also empowers you with 25 Dark Magic. Very useful! I often cast Gloomburst first, then Doombolt and, finally, Chillwind. Afterward you can use Doombolt over and over. Or, if you feel lucky, you can build up even more Dark Magic with one or two more Gloombursts.

At Rank 3 you gain Shroud of Darkness, your first Augmentation. This augmentation draws the shadows close to you, increasing all of your resistances by a small amount for 15 seconds. Unfortunately, there's a one minute cooldown.

Dread Aspect is your reward for attaining Rank 4. It's an instant debuff that makes a target hate you less and deal less damage to you for a short amount of time. Unfortunately, if you attack anyone that you have Dread Aspect on, the effect will immediately end. It's totally useless against a single mob, but if you happen to pull two attackers, detaunt one of them with Dread Aspect and quickly burn down the other.

At Rank 5 you'll learn Surging Pain. With it you can cause waves of agony to roll outwards from you, dealing slight damage to all enemies within 30 feet. It also builds 20 Dark Magic!

At Rank 6 you'll gain a new augmentation, Umbral Strikes. It too lasts for a full hour, but Umbral Strikes gives everyone in your group a chance to deal an additional small amount of damage any time they deal damage. It's much more useful than Demonic Chill. Thankfully, you can keep both augmentations active on everyone, or just yourself, just don't find yourself without them after an hour.

At Rank 7 you'll train Word of Pain, your first hex. In part, Word of Pain is a debuff, reducing your target's Willpower by a small amount, and it can also be stacked up to three times. Word of Pain is also a damaging spell, dealing a small amount of Spirit damage when the effect ends for each spell stacked, and builds 5 Dark Magic as well.

A delicious new area-of-effect ability is yours at Rank 7, Shattered Shadows. Not only does it deal a good amount of damage to your target and all other enemies within 20 feet of them, it also builds 20 Dark Magic. It's not entirely useful soloing, but it's splendid in group play (when used with care) and wonderful in PvP (when used with careless abandon!).

You'll also learn your first Morale ability at Rank 8, the Rank 1 ability Mage Bolt, which we discussed earlier.

At Rank 9 you'll pick up Obsessive Focus. Obsessive Focus is wonderful when fighting a single foe. Basically, you become obsessed with your target for 20 seconds. You deal 10% damage to all other mobs, but for your single target all damage is increased by 10%. Very effective. Be sure to stick it into your shallow brainpan, adept!

Ah, yes, Grip of Fear is one of your Rank 10 abilities. A wonderful root spell, it snares every enemy within 30 feet, freezing their movement for five seconds. It's a great spell for getting some distance and firing off a large attack or just running, if the battle is not in your favor.

News from the War Front

The popular Naggaroth author, Vishak Doombolt, recently published his biggest bestseller yet: *1,001 Ways to Melt Faces*. In his amazing new tome, clocking in at well over 700 pages, Mr. Doombolt dives into the Sorceress career like a Dark Elf obsessed. Not only are his observations keen, but his diagrams are splendid, and his insight into the ancient magical Sorceress profession is amazing reading for a Sorceress of any rank.

Currently busy with a whirlwind tour in support of his latest magnum opus, Mr. Doombolt recently commented on the impending Ulthuan invasion:

"I wish our brothers and sisters the best of luck. I wish I were there. As a token of my support, however, I am sending crates of my newest book, *1,001 Ways to Melt Faces*, to the Sorceress leaders for full dispersal to their many practitioners. I hope it will serve them well."

When asked what he was currently writing, he answered: "Nothing as of yet, but I'm tossing about ideas for a tome detailing the Disciple career. *Two Swords and Big Heals*, maybe? *Slash and Heal*?"

We wish him all the best of luck.

Rank 11-20

Your basic solo play will change very little in your teens. For instance, a basic pull might start with Doombolt, followed by Chillwind. Quickly cast two or three Word of Pain hexes, not only lowering your target's Willpower but also stacking the added damage after the hex wears off in 10 seconds. When the target is near, use the faster casting Gloomburst spell to build up damage for the Word of Pain hexes. If the target is stronger than most, root with Grip of Fear, gain some distance, and begin anew. Be sure to keep Chillwind upon the target at all times.

A few decent solo abilities become available as you level. Obsessive Focus is wonderful when fighting a single foe. Basically, you become obsessed with your target for 20 seconds. You deal 10% damage to all other mobs, but for your single target all damage is increased by 10%. Very effective. You'll learn this ability at Rank 12. Be sure to stick it into your shallow brainpan, adept!

At Rank 18 you gain Demonic Chill. This is a group augmentation that surrounds everyone with a demonic chill for a full hour, giving them a chance to deal slight Corporeal damage back against their attackers when they are struck by a melee attack. It's not the most useful buff for a solitary Sorceress, but every bit of damage counts, so keep it active at all times, if you can remember.

At Rank 14 you'll pick up Shadow Spike, an area-effect curse that deals damage over time to all enemies in front of you, up to 65 feet. Be careful if there are too many enemies, though! You could find yourself in a spot of trouble if you bring every blasted High Elf running.

You also learn Stricken Limbs at Rank 20, a new hex that deals a slight amount of damage and also disarms your target for 5 seconds. They won't be able to use their melee or ranged abilities, poor things. It also builds 10 Dark Magic, so watch your Dark Magic levels.

Rank 21-30

Again, not much is new in your rotation in your 20s. Doombolt, then Chillwind, and stack Word of Pain. Fire off Gloombursts to boost your damage, and adding Obsessive Focus to the rotation is great as well. Disarm tougher opponents with Stricken Limbs, if needed. Throw in a Grip of Fear as well, if you find yourself in trouble. The enemy will drop soon enough.

You learn an interesting new ability, Reckless Gathering, at Rank 30. With it you can gain action points per second as long as you are uninterrupted. Be careful using it in combat, though, because your Initiative is reduced while concentrating, and any damage will knock you down for three seconds. Reckless Gathering is an effective way to replenish your action points in a hurry when not under duress.

Rank 31-40

Very little changes. Still use Doombolt and Chillwind, then stack Word of Pain. Use Gloomburst to increase your Dark Magic, and add Obsessive Focus. Stricken Limbs is still a great disarming spell. Use Grip of Fear, as needed, and Reckless Gathering at your own risk, if you've run low on action points.

A great new ability will be yours when you finally reach Rank 40, assuming you ever do: Stricken Voices. It deals slight damage to your target, after a two-second cast, but the insidious side effect—I'd say main effect—is that Stricken Voices silences all enemies within 20 feet of your target, killing their magic use for five seconds. Quite treacherous. Stricken Voices also builds 20 Dark Magic, so keep an eye on your Dark Magic pool as well.

Group play

Not only are we powerful, if fragile, magic-users, we are also extremely potent within a group. Our biggest asset, our damage, can also be our biggest weakness if we deal too much damage and find ourselves under attack after pulling the target away from the warriors up front. In general, group targets will be tougher than solo targets and you definitely don't want excess attention from the bigger, nastier monsters. Nevertheless, playing a Sorceress within a group is much the same as playing a Sorceress in solo play; you just have to watch your burst damage and try not to pull away from the tank.

Never heard of a tank? I'm not surprised. Tanks are the massive, meaty warriors used to absorb damage from one or more foes. They have abilities designed to make the enemy hate them and concentrate on killing them while other party members do the majority of the damage and the healers keep the tank alive. Got it?

In general, you'll be focusing on a single target. We are great at area effect as well, but it makes it tougher for the tank to keep the attention of multiple foes when we are firing off massive area-effect spells.

Most of the Sorceress basics remain unchanged, although you may want to start with Chillwind instead of Doombolt until your tank gathers enough hate. You'll still use Word of Pain and stack the hex up to three times, then Gloomburst for added Dark Magic, and Obsessive Focus as well. If you do bring unwanted attention to yourself, cast Dread Aspect. Vision of Torment can also be great during group play, draining action points from your target and causing slight damage.

Avoid melee combat unless absolutely necessary. High damage attackers can be deadly to a Sorceress.

It's also important to keep your group augmentations up at all times during group play. Demonic Chill and Umbral Strikes are great for the entire group.

And do not forget to communicate! You'll also have to learn to listen to your tank, which is tough for any Dark Elf, probably excessively tough for one as daft as yourself...

Leveling Up

Soon you'll be alone upon the beach. I will not hold your hand every step of the way. You'll have to make your own path as well, and you'll start with Gorthan Rakar upon Narthain Beach. From him you'll obtain your very first quest, Blood Feud. It should prove a simple task, even for you: kill four of the Sea Guards in combat upon the shores, return to Rakar. Simple enough?

Other quests will soon follow, and you'll notice that it's very easy to follow quests from one camp or quest center to the next. Be sure to introduce yourself to Kovus Drakeblade at Rank 2. He's your first Career Trainer and can impart to you knowledge in both Core abilities and Mastery Training. You will encounter Career Trainers in most every camp or town or city as you progress, and it's important to visit them every time you rank up, but it's not free. Be sure to bring some silver with you. As you gain higher ranks, the price for training will also increase, so don't blow your every brass piece on slight weapon and armor upgrades. Your abilities are just as important.

Soon enough the quests upon Narthain Beach will dry up and you'll be directed to progress to the next camp, which is up the hill to the west. This is the Black Ark Landing proper, a fenced-in area. Nehmora the Hag is in charge. Speak with her and others in the area; you'll gain more quests and more opportunities for advancement.

In addition, you'll encounter your first public quest, which is a big open quest for anyone in the vicinity. Public quests are great ways to gain experience and possibly gain new items, if you are fortunate enough to win rewards for your service. Your first public quest will be Spires of Narthain, a short distance southeast of the Black Ark Landing. May Khaine guide your mind and your powers.

Once you have attained at least Rank 5, you should visit Khaine's Embrace. It's the very first scenario, which is like a small area in which opposing players face one another on the field of battle. Scenarios are short and rewarding, in both experience and Renown points, and in combination with questing, you'll be amazed at how fast you can actually rank up. There is also an Uthorin Warscout at the Black Ark Landing, just inside the walls, who offers the repeatable quest called Khaine's Embrace. Every time you visit the scenario, win or lose, he'll reward you with a generous helping of experience. He'll even give you the quest again. Be sure you are on the quest every time you enter the fray.

By this time you'll surely have an idea of how to progress farther into the heart of the Blighted Isle, encountering new camps, new quests, new public quests, and more as you venture farther south. I would suggest attempting all of the many public quests at least once; I would further suggest completing them more than once to gain experience and items, but also influence rewards from the Rally Masters in each Chapter.

Don't forget to silence an enemy spellcaster before they silence you.

You'll travel through Isha's Garden, and you'll meet your first Rally Master there, Master Kaltarn, with a selection of basic, advanced, and elite influence rewards on offer. Farther south you'll travel into Mistwood where you'll unlock Chapter Two.

Beyond, you'll discover Dreamshade, more quests, public quests and, eventually, you'll find yourself in Chrace where there are even more quests to venture upon. You'll also notice an increased High Elf presence. Indeed, as you progress, you'll come upon your very first battlefield, which is the culmination of every piece of action in Tier 1, from both the Blighted Isle and Chrace. Every quest, every public quest, every dead High Elf, every scenario won or lost leads to the battlefield.

To begin your foray into the battlefield, into RvR proper, head to the Cynathai Span Warcamp, down the path southeast of Dreamshade. Here you will find not only the entrance to the battlefield itself, but also forces of Destruction with quests completed by participating in RvR, a Core Trainer, merchants, and your first Renown Trainer. With the Renown you have gained in the scenarios, you should be able to pick up a smattering of Renown abilities. They will definitely improve your chances upon the field of battle. Go forth and deal as much damage as you can without melting your own face. Every High Elf deserves a quick and painful death, and it is your right to give it to them.

Sadly, you'll rank up and out of Tier 1, with time and experience. You'll soon travel to the Tier 2 areas, the Shadowland and Ellyrion; from there, you'll progress to Tier 3, including Avelorn and Saphery; eventually, you'll approach the pinnacle of the Tier 4 conquest, the final High Elf bastion, Shining Way, but not before you have fully mastered the areas leading through Tier 4, including Caledor, Dragonwake, and Eataine. It will be a long journey, but hopefully by the time you are ranked in your 30s you'll possess enough knowledge to succeed and see this battle to its bloody end.

Killing Players and Seeking Renown

Solo PvP

This is where we make our name: player versus player, or PvP. It's the most divinely sublime experience, blasting your enemies upon foreign soil. Everything leading up to the frontline against our foes is just child's play, practice, if you will. A powerful, smart Sorceress upon the battlefield is a terrible sight, woeful to our enemies.

As there are several types of PvP, we'll look briefly at the basics encompassing the various types and give you an idea of what your mindset should be in each situation:

When you capture both of the points in the Khaine's Embrace scenario...run! Don't say you weren't warned.

Ambush whenever possible. Burn your foes before they even identify your location.

Skirmishes

We excel in one-on-one combat, particularly if we have the advantage of attacking first from a distance. A Sorceress can severely damage and weaken a foe, very quickly. It's prudent to begin with Doombolt, as before, if possible. If you can't get off the three-second Doombolt cast before your target is upon you, do not use it, for smart adversaries will quickly hack and cleave at you to disrupt and slow your spellcasting. Chillwind should always be on your target, and three Word of Pain hexes, particularly if they are healers. Add Shadow Spike, with Chillwind, if needed. Fire off Gloombursts for quick Dark Magic, and use Grip of Fear to get some space. If you are fighting a caster, healer or otherwise, use Stricken Voices as well, for that quick but deadly silence. And don't be a static target—move your feet.

Group Play

We are also great in group PvP. We can stand back from the majority of the fray, hurling our magics into burning High Elf bodies, but when the enemy's attention does turn to us, we can drop very fast if mob mentality kicks in (and it usually does).

Battlefields

The Sorceress is great upon battlefields. We gather less attention in larger crowds, most of the time, and we can do massive damage from behind the ranks, allowing longer cast times like Doombolt. Area of effect abilities are particularly fun upon battlefields when so many enemies are so often gathered into one place. Shadow Spike will become your new best friend. And don't forget Stricken Voices at Rank 40. It's sure to bring a halt to any assault, as well as any healing, for five full seconds, which can be the difference between a win and a loss.

Scenarios

Every scenario is different, but in general your tactics will be the same here, except you need to keep your eye on the scenario objectives and communicate. Always communicate!

Campaigns

Campaigns are not much different from battlefields, although this time more is at stake—our home city, or, more likely, the enemy's home city. There will likely be a big increase in the number of targets, as well as the number of allies, so it's definitely a good time to unleash lots of area-effect damage.

THE FRAGRANT MELODY OF DYING SCREAMS

It is time to go ashore! I smell the fragrant melody of dying screams, death and decay, High Elves trampled underfoot, a land brought back to the fold. We land today upon Ulthuan! You'll be the last ashore, behind the more seasoned veterans like myself. However, I'm sure we'll meet again, farther inland, if you survive the skirmishing upon the beach. Careful! You are an adept. I hope all my promises of future abilities have not left you with stars in your eyes, or you'll be dead before nightfall. Practice what you know with an eye toward improving your craft at every step. Before you know it, you will be powerful, but do not get ahead of yourself. That is certain death.

Now, get back, away from the side, back there with your fellow adepts. Trust not a single one of them. You must still rely upon them in battle, but always watch your back. If you're not careful, you'll have a Witch Elf dagger in your back before the week is past.

Now forward to your destiny!

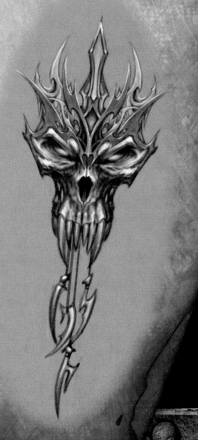

WITCH ELF

Ladies, may I have your attention please? You, raven-haired wench who won't shut up, how would you like to spend the next few battles polishing my spare blades? Shhhhhhh...Hush now; I command you! You must be wondering why I have called you here amongst the crags of Har Ganeth away from the sun, beneath the rocks.

Rejoice with me, my ladies, and we shall give thanks to Khaine for our upcoming victory, for a victory it will be. I, Lady Sryne, have called my sister hags together to bathe in the blood of our fallen enemies and plan our next conquest. Oblige me your ears, for I have a plan.

We shall lead a dark army into battle on a fleet of Reaper-armed Black Arks upon waves that crest with the blood of our enemies. We will rule not just the streets of the cities of the Dark Elf, but the streets of all cities in all lands we tear asunder. We will go far, we will capture many, we will destroy many more. And come the morn, we will enslave and make our own those who have suffered the night.

Violence must be tempered with passion and worship. Let sharp wit, dark heart, and an all-seeing eye guide the dagger that cleaves the heart of our enemy.

Hear me Brides of Khaine, and band with me, for now is the time! We will defeat all those who rise against us, and we will steep in their blood as they lie dying!

My dagger is my weapon, and with it I've sliced many a pretty throat. Woe the sleepy eye and trusting heart not keen to the baneful blade I wield, for I will cut it out and kiss the corpse from whence it came. Dare you to blink?! One flutter is time enough for me to cut you to crossbones! I am swift as a Manticore. I shall manifest from shadow. Make no mistake; I am more than just a pretty face.

I hail from Naggaroth, kingdom of the Dark Elves, under the lordship of Malekith. Long have we awaited this time. Stoking the flames, we bide our time, our forges torrid day and night, our craftsmen shaping the necessities to make us battle ready. Our beasts are caged and ready at the gates. Our armies are readied under Sorceresses selected by the Hag Queen herself. We have only to wait for Malekith's order to strike.

By Sryne

What is a Witch Elf?

Few things warm my heart more than seeing an enemy's open throat caressed with the edge of a blade. Perhaps none in my magnificent entourage perform this task better than the Witch Elf. She is at her best in the midst of a blood frenzy, sticking, jabbing, cutting. She does not hold the line like Black Orcs; she is too refined for such obvious bestiality. Nor is she a healer. The scent of blood on her hands is far too appealing for a Witch Elf to spend time casting healing magics. She simply prefers to kill.

One can appreciate her method: an old-fashioned, hand-to-hand jumble of blood and guts, blades, and brawn. The Witch Elf craft is to deal melee damage quickly, with as much precision as possible. They are an excellent support unit in the endless battle against the forces of Order.

Does the combination of elegance and lethality put a spark to your heart? Does a cunning witch with a venomous blade and deadly kiss send a rush of blood to your brain? If you enjoy blood spilling and efficient executions, you will find much to enjoy in the pursuits of a Witch Elf. Or, by chance, you just may have an axe to grind against your enemies, and the only way to sate your desires is to see those warm bodies turn cold.

—Baron Heinar Balethar, Zimmeron's Hold, Chaos Wastes

STARTING STATS

Let's begin with the Throwing Dagger. I use that for a bit of fun when I want to prick someone in the neck and I'm at range to do it outright. I like to think of it as bait. Generally, they bite and run toward me, allowing the opportunity for me to perfect my Slice, which is another ability you will learn. Slice creates a gorgeous hole in the throat of the enemy—you can almost see your reflection in the blood. So red, so wet.

Your dagger should move as vapor, quiet and unseen, therefore you will need Weapon Skill. Your armor will be near useless at first. Remedy this with Toughness, Initiative, Strength, and Wounds. Block, Parry, and Dodge are key in your defense, and if you have anything left to play with, look toward Armor. Ranks and better outfitting as you progress will raise your Stats.

Blood Lust is your friend. Use certain abilities to build Blood Lust and trigger effects when they are at their peak.

BEING A DARK ELF

We Dark Elves follow Destruction, and we are aligned with the forces of Destruction and the greenskins. We seek to annihilate the hated High Elves, our sworn enemies. We will never forget how the High Elves purged us from our homeland and denied Malekith his rightful throne. We have planned and we have waited and we have planned some more, and now the time is here. While you effete, pompus High Elves are away aiding the Empire, we will be delivered upon your doorstep. Yes, you Finubar, feeble High Elf king, will have no home! We will reign supreme in Ulthuan once again, and Malekith will have his throne!

We begin this adventure in Narthain, specifically Narthain Beach. We may begin on a beach, but don't expect to see sunlight. Shadowed places are so much more intriguing. You'll see many a Black Arks near the shore. Aboard the nearest Black Ark, you'll also find Uthorin Executioners and House Scions attending to various tasks. The Black Arks are powered by the souls of the Dark Sprites conjured by Uthorin Sorceresses atop the hills of Narthainian. On the shores, a fray is taking place: Corsairs and Warsiegers with Bolt Throwers fend off Sea Guards, Mages, and Spearmen. On a particular Black Ark amidst the bloodfest, you find Captain Selawyn guarding some important documents. Several folk here in the Dark Elf galley are at your service, so make good use of them. Gorthan Rakar will reward you if you do his bidding. Train your skills with Kovus Drakeblade and purchase your wares or dye your gear via the good merchant, Ceria Illsith. Wandering about is Master Cerivak, but pay him no mind.

Up the torch-lit path, one finds Black Ark Landing, a walled community of Uthorin Reapers, Executioners, Warsiegers, and Dreadblades. Oh yes, did I neglect to mention Wardens and Prisoners? You will find these as well. Only one each in Black Ark Landing proper, because I sacrificed the others to Khaine at his alter. By starlight we bathed in their blood and felt ecstasy in the communion with our God. You will have the opportunity one day my dark pupil. Perhaps you may even feel the lingering touch of Khaine as you pass by the site. His is the enormous statue on a staired dais towering into the sky. Should you want to hone your talents, Avathe Hrathek and Enicher Ravenwill are happy to teach you. Nehmora the Hag and an Uthorin Warscout stand ready with tasks to occupy your time, for which you will be offered a bit of coin and perhaps some baubles of sorts. The town merchant, Nilsva Ilklairn is happy to buy your wares or sell you hers. Lest I forget, directly to your right before entering Black Ark Landing, you will gaze upon a Black Ark, an enormous vessel, brooding and mysterious.

Also atop the hill is Seawind Glade. Here we find more Wardens and Prisoners. The Prisoners are tucked dead and alive into handy pits. If I had more time, I'd stone the remaining living ones for amusement. Hark! What is that I spy? Narthain Shadow Swords helping Escaped Prisoners? This cannot happen! Report to Saril Zen the Kill Collector at the prison grate and see what he has to say about this! While there, perhaps you will fancy doing a few tasks for Overseer Rathus.

Do not neglect to visit Isha's Garden, directly outside the Tower of Narthain, while you are in these parts. The garden is a treat for the eyes with towering stone icons, a majestic fountain, and Beastmaster Apprentices and Novice Beast Tamers. You may even spot a Manticore or a pen of Cold Ones. Tiritha Venomfire and Beastmaster Maughann stand ready at the fountain with trinkets and coin for your assistance. Develop your talents with Aviruxer Vilewing and make your purchases from Scion Malryn. Master Kaltarn is here. He offers influence rewards. Influence is important, dear, and you gain this by participating in the public quests in these parts. You can also bind here and return as needed by recalling. After you bind here, your recall point will be known as Nemesis Landing.

I believe that I mentioned the Tower of Narthain. There is a tri-stage public quest here, the Spires of Narthain. Baptise your blades in the droves of Narthain Towerguards, Towerwatches, and Sun Mages. Do well and you may just be able to slay the Dragon. Master Kaltarn will be ever so pleased.

Near here are the Ruins of Narthain where Witch Elf Acolytes slay Narthain Sword Novices and Narthain Archers stand nearby ready to die, bows in hand. Seeing as how they stand ready to die, please oblige them by killing a few... hundred! Be wary, though, they are cowardly and like to bring their friends along to fight. Every so often, the Bloody Sun Boyz will come running up the hill and waylay a few, greenskins do have their purposes. Before you venture out of this area, search the ruins for A Discarded Message and don't forget to pay Thamp'zan the Goblin a visit. He is just on the outskirts of the ruins over the hill from the Archers you recently slayed.

As you leave this area, the road leads out to Lion Walk Grove, a forest filled with White Lions. Be prudent, for I hear there is a king of the beasts lurking about.

WITCH ELF GEAR

Although you will start with the bare minimum in apparel, these are not our garments of choice. We are best outfitted in light armor. Medium or heavy armors are not worn because they are ugly and not befitting of a Bride of Khaine. Robed armor hides our lissome curves, weapons in and of themselves. When outfitting yourself, be prudent to choose items with the stats I mentioned to you earlier, provided of course you were listening.

For fighting we use daggers, the most intimate of weapons, the most courageous instrument of death. We must get close to our enemies, smell the fear on their breath, see the desire in their eyes. There can be no hesitation on our part, nor fear. You must yearn for this closeness, desire their heat upon you. For in this final dance with them you will touch Khaine. When the lifeblood sprays your skin you will feel a true heat, a true passion, that no mortal can provide. This is our legacy sisters. This is our birthright.

Anytime you need to move fast—whether to attack or to cover more ground faster—use Flee.

STRENGTHS AND WEAKNESSES

Strengths

- Even the most novice of Witch Elfs can wield two daggers, a distinct advantage throughout your career.

- Your daggers are coated with poison.

- You are limber, dexterous, and fleet of foot.

- Your are quick to bring pain and death to your enemies.

- The ability to stealth is no small thing.

Dual wield is a simple premise: hold a weapon in each hand. While they try to avoid one dagger, you kill them with the other. You boil a brew so vile that one drop upon their brow will kill them where they stand. For that matter enemies will fall one after another to your blades with a dizzying alacrity.

Weaknesses

- Your light armor leaves little to the imagination as well as little to stop a blade.

- Your safeguards are few. You must choose your enemies wisely.

- You do not hold up well under heavy attack. Therefore you should prefer to sally with companions at your side.

Your armor is beautiful, and its mere appearance deadly with the various jags and spikes, but in truth it offers little in the way of protection. When battling alone, you must be selective and kill your enemies quickly. Protracted battles are dangerous as the chances of catching the attention of other enemies grows with each errant swing. This can be somewhat eased by selecting the time and place for battle by "pulling" enemies to more secluded locations. One can not always choose the field of battle though. In such cases be quick about your business or all will be lost.

Abilities

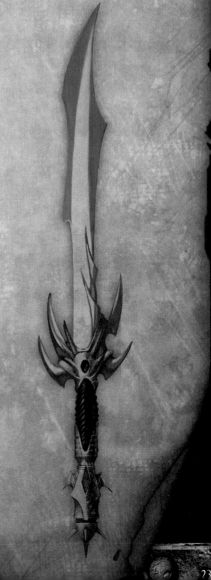

You train Core and Master abilities with a Career Trainer. At Rank 11 you begin gaining Mastery points and should be able to choose a path to concentrate on by Rank 11. This continues until Rank 40, when you will have accumulated 25 points total. Certain Core abilities are increased via Mastery Training, thus they are connected to a Mastery path. Witch Elves select from three Mastery paths:

The Path of Carnage: This focuses on toe-to-toe combat and is best learned when your combat style does not allow for much positional advantage or for those who just like to do a lot of damage in any situation. The Path of Carnage increases the Core abilities of Kiss of Agony, Vehement Blades, Ruthless Assault, and Sever Limb. Path of Carnage is excellent for damage which is, after all, what you are relied upon for. You get to spin and slice and stab and pierce and sever with abilities such as Pierce Armor, On Your Knees, and Elixir of Insane Power.

The Path of Suffering: This focuses on poisons and weakening effects. The Path of Suffering increases the Core abilities of Envenomed Blade, Heart Render Toxin, Kiss of Death, Enfeebling Strike, and Wracking Pains. Path of Suffering is excellent for the sadist in you. What could be more fun than watching your enemy dying a slow and painful death? Here we find the abilities of Elixir of Maddened Speed, Black Lotus Blade, and Witchbrew.

The Path of Treachery: This focuses on surprise attacks and positional combat. This is best for those who commonly group as you'll need someone to distract your enemy so you can get into place for a deft blow. The Path of Treachery increases the Core abilities of Puncture, Agonizing Wound, Throat Slitter, Treacherous Assault, and Kiss of Betrayal. Path of Treachery is perfect for those who love the element of surprise and sneak attacks. Elixir of the Cauldron, Sacrificial Stab, and Heart Seeker are the abilities associated with this path.

Because we are melee damage-dealers at heart, I prefer the Path of Carnage. Yes, the path with the most outright bloodshed is the path I fancy. The Path of Suffering is somewhat of a middle ground for those who like to have their daggers and poison them too. The Path of Treachery is a good choice for those who like to group, because it is based being behind your target, which requires allies to hold your enemies attention.

I know, I know. You want it all. Such is life. Unfortunately, you must make choices. Luckily, you are free to change your mind, at the cost of some coin. Remember: It's far better to invest your Mastery points into the path that best suits what you want to accomplish, rather than peppering them evenly among all paths and coming up mediocre. The mediocre do not last long in the service of Khaine.

Pay attention to your abilities, Tactics, and Morale abilities. Try setting up a specific chain of attacks against a magic-user and switch strategies if you are up against a melee enemy.

Abilties

Name	Level	Path	Cost	Range (in feet)	Type	Build	Duration	Reuse	Description
Slice	Starter Ability	Carnage	40	Melee	Builder Melee Attack	0s	0s	0s	Deals (262+DPS) damage.
Throwing Daggers	Starter Ability	Core	20	120-780	Ranged Attack	1s	0s	0s	Deals 75 damage. When hit from the rear, Snare target by 40% for 5s.
Puncture	Level 2	Treachery	35	Melee	Finisher	0s	0s	0s	Deals instant damage based on combo points spent. 2 hits. 1: 0.5*(262.5+DPS), 2: (262.5+DPS)*.665, 3: (262.5+DPS)*.835, 4: (262.5+DPS)*1, 5: (262.5+DPS)*1.165.
Envenomed Blade	Level 3	Suffering	35	Melee	Builder Melee - Cripple	0s	9s	0s	Deals (75+DPS) and stackable DoT that deals 249 over 9s. Stacks up to 3 times.
Kiss of Agony	Level 4	Carnage	20	Melee	Builder, Posion Buff - Ailment	0s	120s	10s	Deals (150+DPS) damage over 5s and for the next 120s all melee attacks (including auto attack) have a 25% chance to Snare target by 40% for 5s and deal 225 damage over 5s.
Agonizing Wound	Level 5	Treachery	35	Melee	Builder Melee	0s	0s	0s	Deals (187+DPS) damage. If rear positional, ignore armor.
Heart Render Toxin	Level 6	Suffering	35	Melee	Finisher Attack - Ailment	0s	10s	0s	Deals instant damage based on combo points spent. 2 hits. 1: 0.5*(187.5+DPS), 2: (187.5+DPS)*.665, 3: (187.5+DPS)*.835, 4: (187.5+DPS)*1, 5: (187.5+DPS)*1.165. Reduce target's Wounds by (1 / 1.33 / 1.67 / 2 / 2.33) per level for 10s.
Feinted Positioning	Level 7	Core	25	Self	Self Buff	0s	10s	60s	Witch Elf positional attacks can be used on without the positional requirements. Does not affect Morale abilities. Does not trigger GCD. Affects: Agonizing Wound, Heart Seeker, Throat Slitter, Elixir of the Cauldron, Baneful Touch, and Flanking.
Enchanting Beauty	Level 8	Core	20	Melee	Melee Attack	0s	15s	30s	Deals no damage. Detaunts all targets (50%, 15s). Radius: 30ft.
Kiss of Death	Level 9	Suffering	20	Melee	Poison Buff - Ailment	0s	120s	10s	Deals (150+DPS). For the next 120s all melee attacks (including auto attack) have a 25% chance to deal an additional 349 damage to target over 9s and remove 30 AP.
Shadow Prowler	Level 10	Core	4/Sec	Self	Buff	2s	30s	60s	Character stealths. Using any ability breaks stealth. Reuse begins after stealth is broken. No AP regen. Buildable while moving. Any attack interrupts ability.
Vehement Blades	Level 10	Carnage	Free	Melee	Opener Attack - Cripple	0s	15s	0s	Place Melee Barb on target. Effect deals 150 every time the target uses a melee ability. AP Costs are reduced by 50% for 10s. Builds 2 combo points. No GCD.
Ruthless Assault	Level 12	Carnage	15/S	Melee	Finisher	0s	3s	0s	Channeled. Deals damage every 0.5s for 3s. Damage based on combo points 1: (112.5+DPS)*0.5, 2: (112.5+DPS)*.665, 3: (112.5+DPS)*.835, 4: (112.5+DPS)*1, 5: (112.5+DPS)*1.165.
Sever Limb	Level 14	Carnage	40	Melee	Melee Reactional - Cripple	0s	5s	10s	Requires Parry. Deal (262+DPS) damage and disarm target for 5s.
Throat Slitter	Level 16	Treachery	25	Melee	Builder Attack - Cripple	0s	3s	20s	Silence target for 3s. If you are behind the target, also deal (225+DPS) damage.
Fleet-Footed	Level 18	Core	45	Self	Dispel	0s	0s	60s	Remove movement impairing effects (Snare/Root) and grant immunity for 10s.
Enfeebling Strike	Level 20	Suffering	Free	Melee	Opener Attack - Cripple	0s	15s	0s	Place Movement Barb on Target. Effect deals 56 every time the target moves (check every 0.5s). AP Costs are reduced by 50% for 10s. Builds 2 combo points. No GCD.
Sever Blessing	Level 22	Core	25	Melee	Melee Attack	0s	0s	5s	Removes a blessing from target. Deals (75+DPS) damage if successful.
Wracking Pains	Level 25	Suffering	35	Melee	Builder Attack - Cripple	0s	9s	10s	Deal 449 damage over 9s. Damage is Spirit based. If target is ailing, lower initiative by 2/level and Weapon Skill by 3/level for 9s.
Treacherous Assault	Level 30	Treachery	Free	Melee	Opener Attack	0s	15s	0s	Place Spell Barb on target. Effect deals 150 every time the target uses a magic ability. AP costs are reduced by 50% for 10s. Builds 2 combo points. No GCD.

WARHAMMER ONLINE
AGE OF RECKONING

Abilties

Name	Level	Path	Cost	Range (in feet)	Type	Build	Duration	Reuse	Description
Kiss of Betrayal	Level 35	Treachery	20	Melee	Poison Buff - Ailment	0s	120s	10s	Deals (150+DPS) for the next 120s all melee attacks (including auto attack) have a 25% chance for attacks to deal (75+DPS) damage, reduce target's Toughness by 3/level for 10s and increase self Toughness by 3/level for 10s.
Agile Escape	Level 40	Core	Free	Self	Escape	0s	2s	30s	Stuns target for 2s; player leaps backward away from them.
Specialization									
Elixir of Insane Power	Carnage x5	Carnage	25	Self	Buff	0s	10s	60s	For 10s, all melee attacks will hit another enemy within 10ft.
Pierce Armor	Carnage x9	Carnage	35	Melee	Builder Attack	0s	0s	10s	Deals (DPS+262) damage. Attack ignores all Armor. If target is Crippled, reduce armor by 24.75/level for 10s.
On Your Knees!	Carnage x13	Carnage	35	Melee	Finisher Attack - Cripple	0s	Varies	10s	Two hits. Deals 1: (187.5+DPS)*.5, 2: (187.5+DPS)*.665, 3: (187.5+DPS)*.835, 4: (187.5+DPS)*1, 5: (187.5+DPS)*1.165 each hit and knocks down the target for 2s. Radius: 30ft. Max targets: (2/3/4/5/6) based on combo points.
Elixir of Mad-dened Speed	Suffering x5	Suffering	25	Self	Buff	0s	10s	60s	For 10s, melee attack speed is increased by 25% and ability reuse timers are reduced by 25%.
Black Lotus Blade	Suffering x9	Suffering	30	Melee	Builder Attack - Ailment	0s	5s	10s	Deals (225+DPS) damage. Reduces healing on target by 50% for 10s.
Witch Brew	Suffering x13	Suffering	35	Self	Finisher Buff	0s	60s	10s	Next attacks deal an additional (150) Spirit damage to enemies within 20ft. Number of attacks affected is based on combo points.
Elixir of the Cauldron	Treachery x5	Treachery	25	Self	Buff	0s	10s	60s	For 10s, increase critical chance by 25% from behind the target.
Heart Seeker	Treachery x9	Treachery	35	Melee	Builder Melee Attack	0s	3s	20s	Deals (337+DPS) and Stuns target for 3s. Requires rear positional.
Sacrificial Stab	Treachery x13	Treachery	35	Melee	Finisher Attack	0s	0s	10s	Two hits. Deals 1: (187.5+DPS)*.5, 2: (187.5+DPS)*.665, 3: (187.5+DPS)*.835, 4: (187.5+DPS)*1, 5: (187.5+DPS)*1.165 each hit. Heals you for 100% of damage dealt.

Morale

Your Morale bars will fill as you do battle. With every drop of blood you spill, you gain Morale. After you attain Rank 8, you will see your Morale slots directly above your Morale bars and receive your first Rank 1 Morale ability. Sever Nerve is a directed strike that inflicts high damage to your target if you are standing at the side or rear. The staggered Morale bars correspond to Morale Ranks 1–4, with the lowest bar being Rank 1 and the highest bar being Rank 4. Likewise the lowest Morales are Rank 1 Morales and the highest Morales are Rank 4 Morales.

Like Tactics, you also gain Morale abilities with Mastery Training. The Master Morale abilities are Rank 4. Because you can invest 15 points into only one path, you will achieve only one Rank 4 Morale ability associated with Mastery Training. The Path of Carnage has Blade Spin. The Path of Suffering has Fling Poison. The Path of Treachery has Overwhelming Dread. Choices, choices, it is so hard. No matter, what really matters is regardless of what you select, your killing will improve.

After you attain your first Morale ability at Rank 8, they come every four levels with the last coming at Rank 40. Some of my personal Morale preferences include Sever Nerve, because of the heavy damage it does at an early level; Death Reaper, because of the increased group chance of a critical strike; and Frenzied Slaughter, because of its cheaper cost, quicker reuse, and increased damage.

Pace yourself. Even in the heat of battle, don't get overzealous. Remember that certain attacks will cost you action points or require time till you can use them again.

Be aware of which Morale abilities and Tactics are more beneficial for a group and use them accordingly.

Morale

Name	Level	Rank	Range (in feet)	Duration	Description
Sever Nerve	Level 8	Rank 1	Melee	15s	Melee attack that deals 1,200 damage.
Force of Will	Level 12	Rank 2	Self	30s	Drain 200 AP from target and give to character. Decrease target's Strength by 4/level for 30s.
Confusing Movements	Level 16	Rank 1	Self	7s	Increase chance to Parry and Evade attacks by 100% for 7s.
Relentless Assault	Level 20	Rank 2	Group	15s	Group Buff. Grants 10 AP/S to group for 10s. This occurs even during layers.
Broad Swings	Level 24	Rank 3	Self	10s	All attacks hit 2 additional targets within 29ft for 10s. Additional targets take 300 damage.
Dance of Doom	Level 28	Rank 1	Melee	3s	Channeled melee attack that deals 300 every 0.5s for 3s.
Web of Shadows	Level 32	Rank 2	CAE	0s	Deal 1,200 damage in a LAE 37.5ft wide and 67ft long.
Death Reaper	Level 36	Rank 3	Group	10s	Increase group's critical hit chance by 50% for 10s.
Frenzied Slaughter	Level 40	Rank 4	Self	7s	Self buff. AP Costs are reduced 25%. Cooldowns are reduced by 50%. Damage dealt is increased by 20%. Lasts 7s.
Blade Spin	Carnage x15	Rank 4	PBAE	5	Deals 2,400 damage over 5s to all targets in radius. Radius: 30ft.
Fling Poison	Suffering x15	Rank 4	LAE	5	Deals 2,400 damage over 5s to all targets in radius. Arc: 350, radius: 65ft.
Overwhelming Dread	Treachery x15	Rank 4	PBAE	10	All enemies in radius lose 250 AP, and AP regeneration is reduced by 50% for 10s.

Tactics

Let's delve into Tactics, shall we? Eventually you will have four regular Tactic hexagons, one Renown hexagon, and one Guild hexagon; however, you begin with three Tactics hexagons. You receive your first Tactic at Rank 11, Sacrificial Blades. When equipped, Sacrificial Blades will improve your Weapon Skill by +1 per level; therefore you will have a better chance of parrying attacks and penetrating armor. After gaining your first Tactic, you receive one Tactic every other rank until you reach Rank 39.

You also gain Tactics from Mastery Training. Each Mastery Path has three Tactics exclusive to that path. The Path of Carnage has Sharpened Edge, Swift Severing, and Swift Blades. The Path of Suffering has Murderous Poisons, Poison Mastery, and Lingering Pains. The Path of Treachery has Masterful Treachery, Baneful Touch, and Deep Wound.

Choose your Tactics according to your style of play and whatever environment you find yourself in at a given time. Some of my personal Tactic preferences include Sacrificial Blades, because it builds Weapon Skill, and Whirling Blades and Frenzied Mayhem, because they stand the chance to build Blood Lust and the chance of a critical strike. At your highest rank, the maximum number of Tactics you can have is six.

Name	Level	Description
Dark Blessings	Level 11	Incoming healing effectiveness increased by 10%.
Jagged Edge	Level 13	Critical hits also place a 412 damage bleed DoT on the target for 9s.
Whirling Blades	Level 15	Builder attacks have a 33% chance to gain an extra combo point.
Alignment of Naggaroth	Level 17	Spirit resists increased by 6.3/level.
Brute Force	Level 19	Increases Strength by +4 per level of the character.
Increased Pain	Level 21	Critical damage increased 50%.
Bathing in Blood	Level 23	When the Dark Elf kills a target, he heals himself 472 over 9s.
Flanking	Level 25	Increase damage by 15% from attacks made to the side or rear of an enemy.
Frenzied Mayhem	Level 27	Increase critical chance by 3% per frenzy point.
Riposte	Level 29	When the character parries, he deals 187 back to the target.
Exotic Venom	Level 31	Opener barbs last 20s on target.
Bathing in Blood	Level 33	When the Witch Elf kills a target, he heals himself for 472 over 9s.
For the Hag Queen!	Level 33	All Finisher attacks gain a 10% chance per combo point spent to knock down the target for 3 seconds (grants immunity).
Taste of Blood	Level 35	On taking damage, character has a 25% chance to increase melee damage by 15% for 10s.
Swift Pursuit	Level 37	Fleet footed will also increase run speed by 25% for 10s.
Sacrifices Rewarded	Level 39	On being critically hit: gain an absorb buff that absorbs the next 412 worth of incoming damage.
Sharpened Edge	Carnage x3	Finisher's debuff the enemy -75% Armor for 3s.
Broad Severing	Carnage x7	Sever Limb gains a 20ft radius, 180 arc.
Swift Blades	Carnage x11	Increase Parry chance by 10%. Gain 20 AP every time a Parry occurs.
Kiss of Doom	Suffering x3	Kisses now proc 50% of the time.
Septic Blade	Suffering x7	Envenomed Blade also reduces the target's chance to critical by 25%.
Healer's Bane	Suffering x11	Suffering Attacks have a 25% chance to debuff outgoing healing by 75% for 10s.
Swift Movements	Treachery x3	Feinted Positioning has a 20s reuse.
Baneful Touch	Treachery x7	Attacks from non-frontal position have a 25% chance to remove 40 AP from target.
Masterful Treachery	Treachery x11	Openers will also cause you to deal +20% damage for 10s.

WARHAMMER ONLINE

Renown

The concept of Renown points is a simple one to grasp. The more enemies you slaughter—Dwarfs, High Elves, or Empire—the more Renown points you gain.

As you gain Renown points, you also gain Renown ranks. As you gain Renown ranks, you gain more Renown points. You spend these points on Renown advancements. Find your first Renown Trainer, Ensalos Shadowstorm, in Cynathai Span Warcamp.

Renown advancements are staggered into three tiers. Within each tier are Renown abilities and Renown Tactics. The first Renown tier totals 10 Renown abilities and five Renown Tactics. The second Renown tier totals eight Renown abilities and nine Renown Tactics. To advance to the second Renown tier, you must invest a minimum of 20 points into the first Renown tier. The third Renown group totals nine Renown abilities and nine Renown Tactics. To advance to the third Renown tier you must invest a minimum of 40 points into the two lower tiers. Each tier's abilities are more powerful than the next, with the third Renown tier being the most powerful. As you unlock and gain Renown abilities, your character will become more powerful. You do not use each ability in each group. You have no need for some. Some you absolutely need, and others are a matter of personal preference. In the first tier, for example, Marksmen 1, which increases Ballistic Skill by 3, is largely useless. Blade Master 1, however, which increases Weapon Skill by 3, is invaluable. If you are a greedy, gold-digging, money-grubbing wench of a Witch Elf—or simply have certain financial milestones you must meet—then you will likely want to select the Renown Tactic of Looter, which increases your gold haul by 5% in Realm vs. Realm combat.

Solo Play (PvE)

Rank 1–10

When you first begin, you have only your starter abilities. Use Throwing Dagger to pull your enemy to you and Slice for your melee attack. You should be able to get in Throwing Dagger twice if you gauge your distance just right. Note that Slice builds Blood Lust, which will be a key factor as you progress. Should you get into a tight spot in a group of enemies, hotfoot it away from the scrap using Flee.

Upon reaching Rank 2, you gain Puncture. Puncture allows you a double jab at your target and the damage done is based on your amount of Blood Lust (Blood Lust goes up to 5, which does the most harm). Blood Lust is a requirement for Puncture, so without Blood Lust you cannot use this attack. At Rank 2, using Throwing Dagger followed by Slice and Puncture is an excellent technique.

At Rank 3, you add Kiss of Agony to your arsenal. Kiss of Agony stabs into your target for a little damage, and their blood sticks to your corrupted blades. For the next 30 seconds, all of your attacks have a chance to snare your target, reducing run speed. Kiss of Agony builds 1 Blood Lust as well. This is the first of several kisses, each more malevolent than the next, which is why you may use only one kiss ability at a time. Switch it up a bit at Rank 3; use Throwing Dagger to pull and then follow up with Kiss of Agony. Afterward try moving into Slice and Puncture.

With Rank 4 comes Agonizing Wound, which builds 1 Blood Lust and deals a small amount of damage. You get to ignore your target's armor if you happen to be standing behind them, which is less likely in one-on-one combat. At Rank 4 you can interchange Slice and Agonizing Wound and see which you prefer. Perhaps you will want to work out a pattern of using both.

Rank 5 sees your first debuff, Feinted Positioning, whereby you can use your positional abilities for 10 seconds and ignore positional requirements. Your Morale abilities are not impacted.

Rank 6 is quite the blow with Heart Render Toxin. Yes, pet, that's right; carve it out while it still beats! Heart Render Toxin delivers a dual strike dealing extra damage each time. It also inflicts a 10-second ailment on your target. Like Puncture, Blood Lust is a requirement for Heart Render Toxin. Blood Lust builds on a scale up to 5, here reducing Initiative in growing amounts and in the latter two levels of Blood Lust, Toughness is reduced as well. Heart Render Toxin can interchange with Puncture at this level.

Kiss of Death, your second kiss, comes at Rank 7. Kiss of Death does a small amount of damage upon attack, and for the next 30 seconds, all of your attacks have a chance to deal additional damage over five seconds. Try interchanging kisses as well to develop a feel for what you like best.

Your second debuff, Enchanting Beauty, arrives at Rank 8, as does your first Morale ability, Sever Nerve. With Enchanting Beauty, your ravishing good looks stun the enemy masses and their damage is decreased for 15 seconds. There is a downside, however. After you have bewitched them with your feminine wiles, attacking them will end the enchantment. Ah well, if that happens, just give them a kiss. They'll never know what hit them. Sever Nerve is a lovely treat because it deals a mighty blow to your target; however, for the attack to be effective you must be at your target's side or rear.

Rank 9 brings Envenomed Blade. You stab your enemy with a poisoned blade, and the victim becomes wracked with pains, suffering additional damage over nine seconds. This effect stacks with itself up to three times. Envenomed Blade builds 1 Blood Lust. Envenomed Blade can be interchanged with Slice or Agonizing Wound.

Rank 10 brings two new abilities. The first, Enfeebling Strike, is your last debuff at the beginner ranks. Enfeebling Strike allows you to ambush your target from the shadows and strike with a crippling attack. Enfeebling Strike builds 2 Blood Lust and requires Prowling, which also comes at Rank 10. Shadow Prowler is your final ability in the beginning levels, and aside from Flee, your only buff. Shadow Prowler diminishes the ability of an enemy to see you, but drains your action points. If you use an ability or run out of action points, Shadow Prowler will disappear.

Public quests are great introductions to group play. Be sure to participate. Not only do you get great practice and experience points but you stand to gain some nice rewards should you perform well.

Killing Monsters and Questing

Rank 11–20

You will not see much change in play in these levels. You gain five new abilities: three damaging (Kiss of Betrayal, Sever Limb, Treacherous Assault), one buff (Fleet-Footed), and one debuff (Agile Escape). Kiss of Betrayal works in much the same way as the other kisses; you do initial damage and then have a chance of impacting the abilities of the enemies for a set length of time, in this case reduced Toughness for three to five seconds. Treacherous Assault is a Prowling-based ability similar in effect to Enfeebling Strike. Sever Limb is a handy new ability during this phase. This parry-based attack immediately deals damage and then disarms your opponent for five seconds, perhaps allowing you time to move in for the kill. Sever Limb is particularly nice against melee enemies. Fleet-Footed and Agile Escape are both escape mechanisms. Fleet-Footed disentangles you for 10 seconds from any roots and snares your opponent may present, and Agile Escape stuns your target for two seconds as you jump backward away from them.

You also gain Rank 1 and Rank 2 Core Morale abilities during these levels. Force of Will (Rank 2 Morale) comes at Rank 12. Confusing Movements (Rank 1 Morale) comes at Rank 16, and at Rank 20 comes Restless Assault (Rank 2 Morale). Morales at these ranks focus on increased action points, reduced stats for your opponent, and heightened Dodge and Parry.

As I mentioned before, you begin to get your Core Career Tactics and your first Tactic slot appears at Rank 11. You receive a total of five tactics during these ranks: Sacrificial Blades (Rank 11), Jagged Edge (Rank 13), Whirling Blades (Rank 15), Increased Pain (Rank 17), and Brute Force (Rank 19). Your tactics at these ranks will increase your stats, cause more damage to enemies, or increase your chance of a particular battle aspect.

Rank 21–30

Again, not much will change in your style for Ranks 21–30. This is not to say these ranks are without change, however. Can you feel the change, sister? Can you? You are gaining power. Yes, power! Revel in your superiority, bathe in it, and become intoxicated with your might! I digress...

You will only gain two new Core abilities: the debuff Vehement Blades at Rank 25 and the damaging ability Throat Slitter at Rank 30. Both attacks build Blood Lust. Vehement Blades requires Prowling and deals extensive damage over a 15-second period. Throat Slitter does not require Prowling, but its benefits are increased if you attack from the rear. Also of note is Throat Slitter's usefulness against magic attacks: regardless of the attacking angle, you silence your enemy for three seconds and prevent the use of magic, which is a valuable time for you to chop their legs off at the knees.

You receive two new Core Morale abilities during these ranks: the buff Morale Broad Swings at Rank 24 is also your first Rank 3 Morale. Dance of Doom is a damaging Morale received at Rank 28 and is also your last Rank 1 Morale. Broad Swings allows all attacks to pulverize not one but two, and possibly three enemies with a single attack. Dance of Doom is a very tasty dish as well, dealing damage repeatedly to one target for three seconds. You will have some fun with these two.

You receive five new Core Tactics during these ranks: Bathing in Blood (Rank 21), Dark Elf Magical Alignment (Rank 23), Flanking (Rank 25), Frenzied Mayhem (Rank 27), and Riposte (Rank 29). Tactics at these ranks focus on increased health, decreased damage received, increased Blood Lust, and increased damage given. I find Bathing in Blood particularly enticing. With every enemy that falls at my feet, my health increases.

As your ranks increase through these levels, you get better at handling groups of enemies while playing solo; however, should the battle get too intense, remember that you have multiple options (Flee, Agile Escape) with which to retreat.

Rank 31–40

By now you are well on your way to becoming all powerful. You receive only two new abilities here: Wracking Pains at Rank 35 and Ruthless Assault at Rank 40. Wracking Pains focuses on stats loss upon your enemy and Ruthless Assault is a Blood Lust–based attack dealing significant melee damage over time. Wracking Pains is particularly nice because it adds insult to injury by dealing Spirit damage to your target over nine seconds, and ailing targets have Initiative and Weapon Skill reduced.

Talk to other players, group together. Rank up faster. And always remember no matter who you group with, you are still better looking than they are.

Core Morale abilities during these last ranks are Death Reaper (Rank 3 Morale) received at Rank 32, Web of Shadows (Rank 2 Morale) received at Rank 36, and Frenzied Slaughter, which is your single Rank 4 Morale associated with Core abilities (received at Rank 40). All of the Morale abilities at these ranks are extremely useful. Death Reaper increases your group's chance of a critical strike. Oh the mayhem! Oh the blood! Don't lose your head fantasizing about it now! Web of Shadows is an amusing toy; it deals major damage to all enemies in front of you up to 65 feet away. Frenzied Slaughter decreases the cost and cooldown of your abilities and increases the impact of your damage for seven seconds.

Core Tactics received at these ranks are For the Hag Queen (Rank 31), Heedless Assault (Rank 33), Taste of Blood (Rank 35), Swift Pursuit (Rank 37), and Sacrifices Rewarded (Rank 39). These Tactics focus on increased stats, damage absorption, and increased attack and run speeds. Heedless Assault is the odd bird of the Tactics. It increases your Strength, but reduces your Initiative. Decide, based on your style of combat, which is more important, and use it accordingly, if at all.

group play

Rank 1–10

Remember your Rank 1–10 methods for playing solo. Except for Throwing Dagger, which you won't be using because you won't be engaging foes first, the same order will generally apply here. Begin with Slice. After you attain Rank 2, use Slice to build your Blood Lust and Puncture to deliver your strongest jabs. Rank 4's Agonizing Wound will be more effective here because you have a better opportunity to get behind your enemy and deliver a knife to the back! Enchanting Beauty at Rank 8 helps defray damage from any enemies you haven't had a chance to devour yet. Your Rank 10 Enfeebling Strike and Shadow Prowler will be easier to use and more effective in group play as well. Your Sever Nerve Morale will also be easier, because it's easier to attack from the side or rear when in a group.

Some of your first endeavors at group play come from the public quests. Public quests are multiple-stage quests extending over a set area automatically available to any player. They are a virtual bloodbath and an excellent source for sharpening your dagger against the skull of your foes! It is worthwhile to mention that you will likely perform better doing the public quests after you achieve Rank 5. Also of note is that public quests can be repeated multiple times.

Rank 11–20

Continue to use your Rank 1–10 strategies (Slice, Puncture, Kiss of Agony, Enchanting Beauty, Agonizing Wound) while mixing in your new toys. The Relentless Assault Morale gained at Rank 20 will be more beneficial now because it extends to the entire party. You have your new Prowling attack, Treacherous Assault, here at Rank 16, which helps with ambushes.

Read your Tome as you progress through chapters and encounter new races, characters, and creatures. The knowledge it imparts is invaluable.

Rank 21—30

You will still not find a great deal of change in these ranks, because you have likely refined your slaying strategies by now, but that is not to say they are boring. Death is never boring. Vehement Blades at Rank 25 and Throat Slitter at Rank 30 prove handier in a group setting, because they involve Prowling and posterior attacks. Broad Swings, your Rank 24 Morale ability that strikes up to two additional enemies near your target, offers a bit of assistance to other group members as well as yourself. Your Rank 25 Flanking Tactic is of more use in a group setting as well; you now do more damage when attacking from the sides or rear if you have nearby allies to distract your opponent.

Rank 31—40

By the last 10 ranks, you should be solid in your play style and ever ready to lop off heads. Wracking Pains will be as beneficial here as it is in solo play. All Tactics and Morale abilities gained during this period prove beneficial. Taste of Blood is a rather sultry Tactic at Rank 35. With Taste of Blood, any time you take damage, there is a chance your auto-attack speed will increase for 10 seconds.

Know your place. Don't cause intentional strife to your group by making foolish mistakes.

Killing Players and Seeking Renown

Solo PvP

Solo PvP for the Witch Elf is much the same as solo PvE, which we covered earlier. Attack quickly, from a position of surprise if possible, follow up with your Slice, and as you progress in rank, replace the lesser abilities with better ones and add your finishing moves. An early example of this is at Rank 2 when you can follow Slice with Puncture. A good time to start PvP is with your first scenario, which you will likely encounter around Rank 5.

In any PvP situation be it skirmish, battlefield, scenario, or campaign, you need to evaluate the class of your opponent. Yes, yes I know. I kill everyone with no trouble at all, but I am better than you. If you are fighting a healer and you get the jump on them, they will die fast. You want healers to die fast so they can't heal, of course! Magic-users are also a wise choice for early elimination.

Use Prowling techniques here, but if you are alone fighting against a group, remember that you lack any assistance. Therefore, use Prowling prudently in solo situations.

You gain your Renown points through PvP (solo and group), which you can spend on Renown abilities and various rewards. Some rewards require a specific Renown rank before you can purchase them. Gaining the points to obtain the rewards is a continuous process. You accumulate them over time and, of course, over the various hearts you render lifeless.

Group Play

In group PvP, you want to be right in the heart of the skirmish. It will get you in trouble and your party members will frown if you cause the demise of the entire group. Communicating with your party is key to your success in group PvP. Know what you are going to do before you do it, and always have a Plan B.

Remember to visit the healers in the various areas if you have died. They will remove your death penalties, one or all depending on your selection.

Use your attacks as with solo PvP, but remember to focus on the abilities, Tactics, and Morale abilities best suited for group play. These include the Core abilities of Agonizing Wound, Feinted Positioning, Enchanting Beauty, Enfeebling Strike, Shadow Prowler, Vehement Blades, and Throat Slitter. Useful Morale abilities include Sever Nerve, Relentless Assault, Broad Swings, Death Reaper, Web of Shadows, and Frenzied Slaughter. Helpful Tactics are Flanking, Taste of Blood, and Sacrifices Rewarded.

Prowling is particularly important in group PvP. It is easier to use when in a group, because you have the other party members for backup when you come out of stealth mode. Prowling techniques are good for surprise and positional attacks, and you cause more damage when coming from a stealth form. As with solo PvP, healers and magic-users are good choices to take out early on.

Aching For Murder

There now, luscious, we are finished. Have you enjoyed our little talk as much as I have? Actually, I know you have enjoyed yourself, after all, I am the exciting one here. You, you are just a lump. But perhaps you can be molded. Of course, you'll never be as good as me, but who is.

All this explanation when I could be cleaving heads has made me weary. See there, you've turned me into a madwoman channeling greenskin nonsense. I must stop now and go kill. My dagger has been sheathed far too long and my heart aches for murder.

DWARFS VS. GREENSKINS

THE WARFRONT

Orcs and Goblins generally don't work well together. However, when a new tribe called the Bloody Sun Boyz grows in power, its leaders, the goblin Shaman Gazbag, providing the brains, and the towering brute Grumlok, supplying the muscle, pull the two races together as one. Under the sway of the Witch King Malekith's dark council, the allied greenskins march into the World's Edge Mountains and capture the Dwarf fortress of Karak Eight Peaks. The Orcs and Goblins are on the move.

The Dwarfs ache over the loss of Karak Eight Peaks. With vengeance in their hearts, the Dwarfs retaliate against the greenskins who have invaded their ancestral home. In the midst of the turmoil, Emperor Karl Franz sends word that the Chaos hordes have advanced on the Empire, and the Empire needs the Dwarfs' help. It is an impossible situation.

With civilization on the brink of war, the most powerful of the land's races choose sides. Trusty Dwarfs and wise High Elves join the Empire and become the forces of Order. Relentless greenskins and cunning Dark Elves join Chaos and become the forces of Destruction. The two sides shall battle, and the world shall sunder.

THE TIERS

There are three warfronts (race pairings) in *Warhammer Online*: Dwarfs vs. greenskins, Empire vs. Chaos, and High Elves vs. Dark Elves. Each of these warfronts breaks down into four tiers. There are two zones each in Tier 1, Tier 2, and Tier 3, and eight zones each in Tier 4

Tier 1 zones are where all characters begin. Generally, you'll spend approximately 10 ranks in each zone, so your early ranks, 1–10, will be spent in Tier 1, 11–20 in Tier 2, 21–30 in Tier 3, and 31–40 in Tier 4. Of course, there are exceptions to this rule, as you should rank up at your own pace and follow the paths set by your various quests. The RvR (realm vs. realm) areas in Tier 1, where you can fight against other players, are relatively small compared to the larger ones in Tier 4, so you won't get lost as you train up your player vs. player (PvP) skills.

Tier 2 zones bridge your advance between Tier 1 and Tier 3 zones. While in Tier 2, you should have gained all your fundamental abilities and you start mastering the paths that will define your career. RvR areas are a bit larger and more challenging than Tier 1. You certainly want to ally with other players from this point forward.

Tier 3 zones can be fierce battlegrounds as characters become more and more powerful. At this stage, you fine-tune your career before heading into the campaigns of Tier 4.

Tier 4 will become your home once you hit the 30s, and you'll stay locked in Tier 4 campaigns for the rest of your time in *Warhammer Online*. Because you will spend most of your time here, and the RvR areas are vast, you should learn each zone well before moving to the next. If you follow your race's chapter unlocks and complete as many regular quests and public quests as possible, each zone will be a memorable experience.

TIER 1

EKRUND

Dwarfs Chapters 1–2
Greenskins Chapters 4

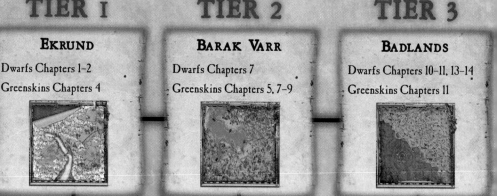

MOUNT BLOODHORN

Dwarfs Chapters 3–4
Greenskins Chapters 1–3

TIER 2

BARAK VARR

Dwarfs Chapters 7
Greenskins Chapters 5, 7–9

MARSHES OF MADNESS

Dwarfs Chapters 5–6, 8–9
Greenskins Chapters 6

TIER 3

BADLANDS

Dwarfs Chapters 10–11, 13–14
Greenskins Chapters 11

BLACK FIRE PASS

Dwarfs Chapters 12
Greenskins Chapters 10, 12–14

TIER 4

STONEWATCH

Dwarfs Campaign

Greenskins Campaign

KADRIN VALLEY

Dwarfs Chapters 15–16

Greenskins Chapters 20–22

THUNDER MOUNTAIN

Dwarfs Chapters 17–19

Greenskins Chapters 17–19

BLACK CRAG

Dwarfs Chapters 20–22

Greenskins Chapters 15–16

BUTCHER'S PASS

Dwarfs Campaign

Greenskins Campaign

REIKWALD

ALTDORF

TO BLACK FIRE PASS

CINDERFALL

Dwarfs Campaign

Greenskins Campaign

DEATH PEAK

Dwarfs Campaign

Greenskins Campaign

TO BADLANDS

THE MAW

INEVITABLE CITY

HOW TO USE THE MAPS

The maps in this guide are organized first by warfronts and then by tiers (in alphabetical order within each tier). The first section deals with Dwarfs and greenskins, the second section highlights Empire and Chaos, and the third section details the struggle between High Elves and Dark Elves. As you adventure, open the appropriate map section and follow along as you discover chapters. For example, as a Empire player, you would open to the start of the Empire vs. Chaos map section and turn to the Tier 1 zone, Nordland, the very first map in that section. Empire Chapters 1–3 take place in Nordland. To help you along on your journey, keep the Nordland map open until you're ready for Empire Chapter 4, which takes you to the Norsca map. For Empire Chapter 5, you travel to Troll Country, your first Tier 2 zone. Continue with your "Chapters of *WAR*" until you've completed Chapter 22 and conquered them all.

Each zone map contains a wealth of information. Important points are labeled right on the map: chapter unlocks, public quests, landmarks, dungeons, lairs, battlefield objectives, and more. To identify any map point for your race, see the map's legend.

The page next to each map summarizes that zone's chapters. At a glance, you can see what chapters are in the zone (and your enemy's chapters) and all the public quests in the area. Pay close attention to the public quest objective information, as this will give you a leg up on what to expect and arm you (or your warband) with clues about what gear, Morale abilities, and Tactics to equip before battle.

If you don't want to flip through the maps chapter by chapter, see the map index at the start of each warfront and look up exactly where the zone of your choice can be found.

EKRUND

CHAPTERS 1–2

"Th' greens never seem ta end. Blow a head off here, hew a neck there, it don't matter much—th' Goblin spawns keep comin'. We're surrounded at th' Bitterstone Mine, wiv but fresh beardlings to hold our gates. Training in Goldbrow's Lament against those mindless Squigs only takes ye so far.

"Fight as we may through th' endless Goblin waves along Ancestor's Watch, it takes th' bravest and stoutest among us to break their ranks an' gain th' Bitterstone Span. Deeper into Ekrund ye get to pick yer poison: tussle with th' filth-ridden Burguz's Boyz in what th' tales are now callin' th' Battle of Bitterstone or slip through th' tunnels ta Redhammer Brewery an' add yer axe ta those that repel th' Goblin swarm.

"We're battlin' fer a broken country. Greens have ripped apart th' once-proud structures an' shattered th' rail that served th' Dwarfs of old. Should ye dare to journey into th' wilds ta preserve what little we have left, wait for a few notches on yer belt, then seek out Grudgekeg's Guard northeast of th' mines. It's th' stagin' ground fer our war effort inta Mount Bloodhorn, where we stain th' Goblin lands wiv blood an' repay their homes wiv th' kindness that was given ours."

—Framglin Grimaxe, Oathbearer Keeper

CHAPTER 1: MORDRIN'S ANVIL

This is the newbie area for all you beardlings learning a warrior's trade out there. You'll have to smash many Squigs, and complete a few quests, to hone your skills enough to trade blows with the Cave Troll that blocks passage through the Barren Reach and out onto Ancestor's Watch.

PUBLIC QUESTS

The Battle of Bitterstone

· Objective #1: Kill 20 Iron Claw Greenskins.

· Objective #2: Collect 10 Black Powder Barrels.

· Objective #3: Kill 3 Ironclaw 'Eadbustas. Kill Krusha Skag.

CHAPTER 2: REDHAMMER BREWERY

A pint might be waiting for you in this fine establishment, or you might be losing a pint of blood in the frequent greenskin skirmishes within a rock's throw of the brewery's doors. Only a coward avoids the three public quests around Redhammer Station. Don't be in a rush to the warcamp or you'll end up a carcass to the stinking Goblins or wild animals that comb the tracks in the north lands.

PUBLIC QUESTS

Durak's Gate

· Objective #1: Kill 100 Bloody Sun Greenskins.

· Objective #2: Use the Black Powder Barrels to destroy 3 Big Rock Lobbers.

· Objective #3: Kill 2 Grimskull Shaman.

Engine Number Nine

· Objective #1: Kill 30 Bloody Sun Scavengers. Kill 15 Snotling Looters.

· Objective #2: Use Salvaged Beer to revive the 8 Wounded Engineers.

· Objective #3: Kill 4 Beerthirstin' Squigs. Kill 2 Bloody Sun Handlers. Kill Ugrog.

Murgluk's Gits

· Objective #1: Rescue 10 Captured Miners. Rescue 10 Unconscious Miners. Rescue 10 Injured Miners.

· Objective #2: Kill 8 Boss Gits.

· Objective #3: Kill Murgluk.

· And many more...!

WARCAMP: GRUDGEKEG'S GUARD

Once you've laced up your boots and hoofed it up to the lone Dwarf warcamp in the zone, it's time to meet enemy players nose to nose. A strong surge north from Grudgekeg's Guard can cut off greenskin enemies who enter from one of two eastern trails. Secure the two battlefield objectives for bonuses: a Defensive Boon from Stonemine Tower and a Merchant's Gift from the Cannon Battery. When they are both under Order control, push east and bring the offensive to Mount Bloodhorn.

CHAPTER 4

"Sent by da warmaster to this end uf nowhere when dere's reel fightin' to be done up north. Little did him no all dem going on down here. Furst dem backstabbing Broketoof tribes turned on us and had to be smushed. Den dem grubby stunties tried to sneek up on us from that Goldfist Sinkhole, an' dems had to be learnt da hard way. Now dere's a new bunch of grippy thieves stealin' our stuff, so I sended out a group of my gits to take care of dem Red Raiders. Maybe when da boss sees all I dun down heres, I'll get to go back to da reel fights!!!"

—Grubba of da Thick 'Eads

CHAPTER 4: GORGOR'S SMASH

The Broketoof tribes have rejected alliance with the Sun Boyz tribe and must be destroyed. Be ready for hordes of fun and let's show 'em whatfor:

PUBLIC QUESTS

Broketoof Camp

· Objective #1: Secure 5 Broketoof Huts; Kill 75 Boyz.

· Objective #2: Capture 2 Shaman Huts; Kill 4 Broketoof Shamans.

· Objective #3: Kill Dagesh Dreadbelch.

Goldfist's Hole Recovery

· Objective #1: Kill 100 Irontoe Dwarfs.

· Objective #2: Destroy 3 Water Pumps; Kill 6 Enraged Irontoe Foremen.

· Objective #3: Kill Halfdan Ironrail; Kill 4 Irontoe Master Engineers.

Raider's Haven

· Objective #1: Kill 75 Red Raiders; Destroy 5 Outpost Tents.

· Objective #2: Kill 6 Red Taskmasters.

· Objective #3: Kill Vergis Black.

· And many more...!

DWARFS

GREENSKINS

WARHAMMER ONLINE
AGE OF RECKONING

WARCAMP: NONE

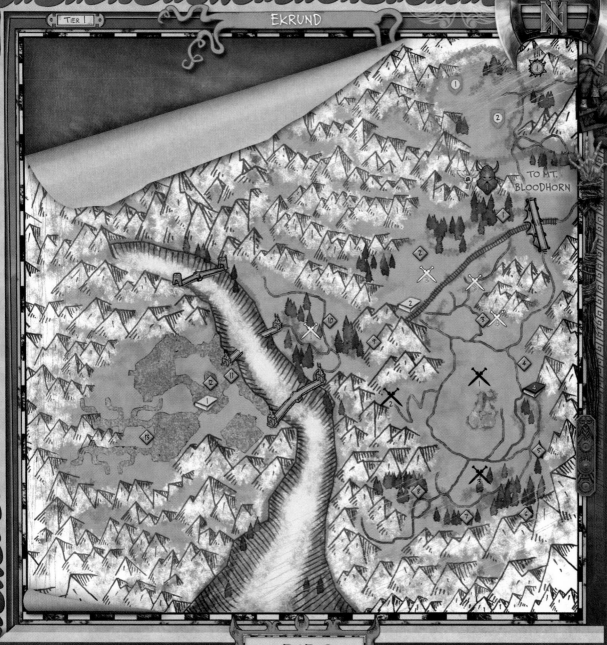

TIER I

EKRUND

TO MT.
BLOODHORN

LEGEND

Warcamps: 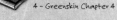 1 – Grudgekeg's Guard

 RvR Area (Outlined)

Chapter Unlock (Destruction)
4 – Greenskin Chapter 4

Chapter Unlock (Order)
1 – Dwarf Chapter 1
2 – Dwarf Chapter 2

Major Landmarks
1 – Norri's Tunnel
2 – Durak's Gate
3 – Durak's Mine
4 – Crawla Cave
5 – Goldfist's Tomb
6 – Wolf Den
7 – Broketoof Camp
8 – Njorinsson's Tomb
9 – Redhammer Tunnel
10 – Burguz's Boyz
11 – Ancestor's Watch
12 – Pick & Goggles
13 – Stonemane's Junction

Public Quests (Destruction)
1 – Goldfist Hole Recovery
2 – Raider's Haven
3 – Broketoof Camp

Public Quests (Order)
1 – Battle of Bitterstone
2 – Durak's Gate
3 – Engine Number Nine
4 – Murgluk's Gits

Battle Objectives
1 – Stonemine Tower
2 – Cannon Battery

Lairs
1 – Bandit Queen

Flight Master

MOUNT BLOODHORN

DWARFS

CHAPTERS 3-4

"I was ready ta head out meself and fight those greenies, but old man Rorkisson said we all 'ave ta prove our mettle first. So off we go ta Komar fer our training. 'Aving ta dodge th' flying rocks an' take care of th' greenies builds a terrible thirst, but th' rule is no pints till th' job is done."

—Filgar Lorestone

CHAPTER 3: STANDOFF AT THE KRON KOMAR GAP

This is where you prove that you have what it takes to rid the world of these slimy greenskins. For the first time, you'll be in the thick of battle. Hordes of greenskins are trying to take the gorge, and it's our jobs to stop them.

PUBLIC QUESTS

Kron Komar Gap

- Objective #1: Kill 100 Bloody Sun Greenskins.
- Objective #2: Kill Gorrek Jawbreaka; Kill Gorrek's 2 Shamans.

Siege of Komar

- Objective #1: Defeat 100 Bloody Sun Greenskins.
- Objective #2: Destroy 3 Rock Lobbers; Kill 12 Siege Crew; Prevent 25 Lobbers from Firing.
- Objective #3: Kill Drahzag Neckbreaker; Kill Mokri Slime-breath.

CHAPTER 4: KEEPING THE DOGS AT BAY

Now for those of us who have proven ourselves at the Gap, it's time to head deep into greenskin territory and take out Marghaz Bloodtoof and stop the ritual, leaving the greenskins without magic protection.

PUBLIC QUESTS

Marghaz Bloodtoof Ritual

- Objective #1: Kill 50 Ironclaw Boyz; Extinguish 3 Shaman Effigies.
- Objective #2: Keep Hammer Strikers alive.
- Objective #3: Kill Marghaz Bloodtoof; Kill 4 Ironclaw Defenders.

Traitor's Watch

- Objective #1: Kill 100 dog soldiers.
- Objective #2: Kill 8 Dog Paymasters; Collect 8 Plundered Beers; Set 8 Tents Ablaze.
- Objective #3: Kill Dietrich Lichtermann; Kill Abigail Gartner.
- And many more...!

WARCAMP: NONE

GREENSKINS

CHAPTERS 1-3

"First dey wantz us to pull up dem stumps, den it wuz the Squigs. Dat got borin', so me moved on to find dem stunties, but dat Grokk grabbed me by da neck an' sent me here to da war maker. If'n me get all dis dun, me get to go up north where the reel work iz. Ol' Grokk sayz me need a bit more trainin' so me gonna keep killin' till me hand falls off."

—Ootawn of Tribe Sun Haterz

CHAPTER 1: SKARZAG'S WARCAMP

Killing annoying Squigs and drinking beer are but some of the fun trials a young greenskin has in store around the warcamp.

PUBLIC QUESTS

Ugrog's Rage

- Objective #1: Kill 30 Annoying Squigs.
- Objective #2: Collect 20 Beer Barrels.
- Objective #3: Kill Dulgrek Ironmane; Kill 2 Ironmane Stonebeards

CHAPTER 2: DA WAR MAKER

Ward off the invaders and set up your fellow greenskins for Da War Maker.

PUBLIC QUESTS

Sharpthorn Rock Mine

- Objective #1: Kill 80 Invading Vermin.
- Objective #2: Collect 30 Lobber Rocks.
- Objective #3: Defeat 8 Irontoe Mine Overseers.
- Objective #3: Kill Onaar Irontoe; Kill Hagruld Irontoe; Kill Bilder Irontoe.

CHAPTER 3: KOMAR

You finally get to see some action against the hated Dwarfs. Slay as many as you can.

PUBLIC QUESTS

Kron Komar Gap

- Objective #1: Kill 100 Komar Dwarfs.
- Objective #2: Kill Goren Stonebrow, Kill 2 Kromar Runesmiths.

Sacred Grove

- Objective #1: Gather 100 Animal Hides.
- Objective #2: Kill 60 Wrathful Spites.
- Objective #3: Kill Lucius Richter; Kill Solamir; Kill Bladeclaw.

WARCAMP: SCREEB'S STUNTY KILLIN' CAMP

Once you've worked your way through Da War Maker and made Grokk happy, head to Komar and get on with the killing. After you plow through the Dwarfs and attain a Healing Boon and an Artisan's Gift, it'll be time to take back Mount Bloodhorn and make it ours.

TIER 1

MT. BLOODHORN

N

LEGEND

Warcamps: 1 – Screeb's Stunty Killin' Camp

RvR Area (Outlined)

Chapter Unlock (Destruction)
1 – Greenskin Chapter 1
2 – Greenskin Chapter 2
3 – Greenskin Chapter 3

Chapter Unlock (Order)
3 – Dwarf Chapter 3
4 – Dwarf Chapter 4

Major Landmarks
1 – Mouth of Morngrim
2 – Old Dwarf Lookout Tower
3 – Old Stoneson Mine
4 – Da Gobbo Camp

5 – Broketoof Boyz
6 – Sharpthorn's Rock Mine
7 – Snout's Pens
8 – Lobber Hill
9 – Spore Rock
10 – Da Stumps
11 – Gran Thewn Watch
12 – Forgotten Hold
13 – Statue of the Oathbearer
14 – Glon Barak
15 – Forgehand's Workshop
16 – Crawla Cave
17 – Chompa's Cave

Public Quests (Destruction)
1 – Ironclaw Camp
2 – Sharpthorn Wud
3 – Urgog's Rage
4 – Sharpthorn's Rock Mine
5 – Sacred Grove
6 – Durak's Rest

Public Quests (Order)
1 – Siege of Komar
2 – Gutrot Mine
3 – Traitor's Watch
4 – Marghaz Bloodtoof Ritual

Public Quests (Neutral)
1 – Kron Komar Gap

Battle Objectives
1 – The Lookout (Artisan's Gift)
2 – Ironmane Outpost (Healing Boon)

Flight Master

BARAK VARR

DWARFS

CHAPTER 7

"Who do these greenies think they are!? Coming into our lands trying ta push us around. Time fer us ta put a stop ta this, but there's so many of 'em; where can they be coming from? Gah! There's th' call again, incomin' greenies. First they came on us at Bar Dawazbak and we pushed 'em back, barely. Hopefully help will come from th' Mountain King soon."

—Thurg Axegrinder

CHAPTER 7: THANE'S DEFENSE

The Dwarfs have sallied forth from their port home of Barak Varr to hold back the greenskin invasion. While small forces slip through the defenses, the stalwart Dwarfs are intent on keeping the main greenskin force at bay.

PUBLIC QUESTS

Bar Dawazbak

- Objective #1: Kill 100 One Tusk Greenskins; Destroy all the Rock Lobbers.
- Objective #2: Kill One-Tusk Shamans.
- Objective #3: Kill Grumgor Blacktoof; Kill 5 One-Tusk Chargers.

Korgoth's Raiders

- Objective #1: Kill 100 Korgoth Gors; Recover 5 Karakshot Crates.
- Objective #2: Kill 20 Korgoth Ambushers; Protect Karakshots Oathbearers.
- Objective #3: Destroy the Herdstone; Kill 5 Korgoth Shamans.
- Objective #4: Kill Wargor Korgoth.

Gudrim's Veterans

- Objective #1: Kill 50 Bloody Sun Greenskins.
- Objective #2: Kill Gruznug.

WARCAMP: NONE

GREENSKINS

CHAPTERS 5, 7–9

"Why should dem little stunties get all da gud stuff. Dey steal all da loot from our lands an' take it to deir precious Barak Varr. No more! I say, itz time to make it ours. We gather up our boyz an' meet up on dah Big Sand an' push out more pests... stupid stunties everywhere. Next we wuz goin' to Bar Dawazbak, da mountun where dey live, and clear these nasty stunties out fer good."

—Ugmar the Shaved

CHAPTER 5: DA BIG SAND

For the coming *Waaagh!*, we gather more greenskins and some Trolls to beat back the stunties.

PUBLIC QUESTS

Danurgi's Rangers

- Objective #1: Kill 125 Hammerstriker Dwarfs.
- Objective #2: Kill 8 Hammerstriker Veterans.
- Objective #3: Kill Danurgi Stoutbeard; Kill Hemilda Stoneaxe; Kill Bergren Firehammer.

Firebeard's Slayers

- Objective #1: Kill 100 Sea Anvil Forces; Destroy 25 Piles of Goods.
- Objective #2: Destroy 4 Cannons; Kill 4 Sea Slayer Oathkeepers.
- Objective #3: Kill Fuergan Firebeard.

CHAPTER 7: ROTTOOF'S MUGZ

While the main body of the *Waaagh!* is located at Eight Peaks, some other lesser elements continue to push on with their own agendas. A massive greenskin force has pushed from the Marsh to assault the ancient stunty port of Barak Varr.

PUBLIC QUESTS

Bar Dawazbak

- Objective #1: Kill 100 Hammerstriker Dwarfs; Destroy 8 Cannons.
- Objective #2: Kill 5 Hammerstriker Runesmiths.
- Objective #3: Kill Thorar Ironrock; Kill 8 Ironrock Grenadiers.

Gudrim's Veterans

- Objective #1: Kill 50 Gudrim Dwarfs.
- Objective #2: Kill Gudrim Steelanvil.

CHAPTER 8: THE FALL OF BARAK VARR

The *Seahammer* is one of the ironclads in the King of Barak Varr's armada. It has been docked for repairs. The greenskins, thinking the King is on board, are storming the vessel looking for him.

PUBLIC QUESTS

Boarding the *Seahammer*

- Objective #1: Kill 100 *Seahammer* Dwarfs.
- Objective #2: Kill 4 *Seahammer* Saltbeards.
- Objective #3: Kill Admiral Sternbrow.

Fall of Firebrew

- Objective #1: Kill 100 Barak Varr Dwarfs
- Objective #2: Kill 4 Barak Varr Alekeepers.
- Objective #3: Kill "Mugs" Firebrew; Kill Brewmaster's Assistant.

CHAPTER 9: MOBASH'S PLACE

When the greenskins attack and King Byrrnoth Grundadrakk realizes the extent of the greenskin presence, he immediately dispatches a force to deal with them and then retreats to the security of his ship.

PUBLIC QUESTS

Ironrock Point

- Objective #1: Kill 125 Grundadrakk Grudgeladen.
- Objective #2: Defend Lobber Crew.
- Objective #3: Kill Drundig Garlesson.

When the Ship Hits the Sand

- Objective #1: Kill 125 Grundadrakk Dwarfs; Kill 50 Grundadrakk Sea Engineers.
- Objective #2: Kill 10 Grundadrakk Honor Guards.
- Objective #3: Kill Hargar Stonebearer; Kill Grugnis Grundisson; Kill King Byrrnoth Grundadrakk.
- And many more...!

WARCAMP: NONE

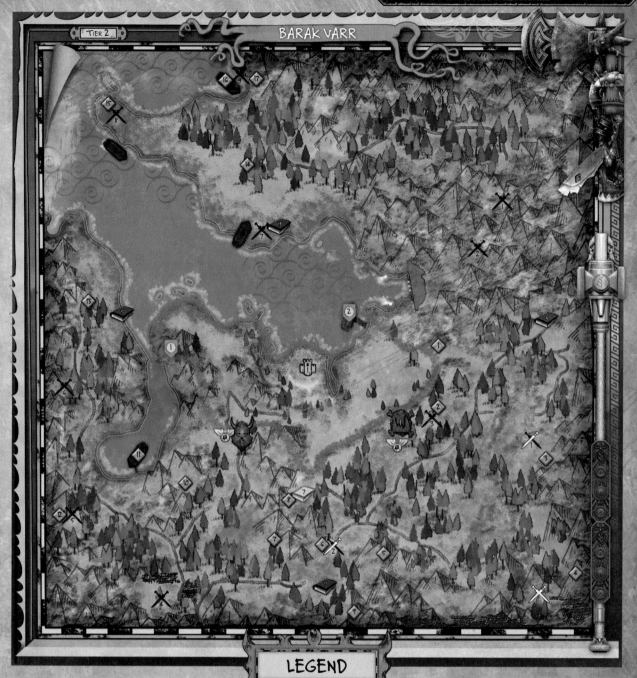

LEGEND

Warcamps: 1 – Foultooth's Warcamp 1 – Goldpeak's Overlook RvR Area (Outlined)

Chapter Unlock (Destruction)
5 – Greenskin Chapter 5
7 – Greenskin Chapter 7
8 – Greenskin Chapter 8
9 – Greenskin Chapter 9

Chapter Unlock (Order)
7 – Dwarf Chapter 7

Major Landmarks
1 – Longbeard's Strand
2 – Mingol Vongal
3 – Steel Anvil Mine
4 – One-tusk Cave
5 – Rikkit Duk

6 – Bar Dawazbak
7 – Cave
8 – Gnol Garak Throng
9 – Rikkit Duk (Second Entrance)
10 – Thunder Ridge Tower
11 – Sea's Anvil
12 – Firebeard Duk
13 – Wetfang
14 – Mingol Ironside
15 – Ironrock Point Lighthouse
16 – Fair Fregar II
17 – Crazy Stunty Cove

Public Quests (Destruction)
1 – Fall of Firebrew
2 – Boarding the Seahammer

3 – Burn Rock Tower
4 – Up the Creek without a Battle
5 – Firebeard's Slayers
6 – Danurgi's Rangers
7 – When the Ship Hits the Sand
8 – Ironrock Point
9 – Long Drung and the Slayer Cove

Public Quests (Order)
1 – Korgoth's Raiders

Public Quests (Neutral)
1 – Gundrim's Veterans
2 – Bar Dawazbak

Battle Objectives
1 – Lighthouse (Artisan's Gift)
2 – Ironclad (Healing Boon)

1 – Dok Karaz Dwarf Keep

Flight Master

MARSHES OF MADNESS

DWARFS

CHAPTERS 5–6, 8–9

"We made our way ta th' Marshes of Madness ta collect th' glorious oathgold. Sadly this hellhole is th' only place that it forms. Plus, th' place be crawlin' with greenskins. 'Ave ye ever seen so many of th' brutes? When our brothers asked, we 'eaded up to Murdogh's Hold ta 'elp clear th' greenies. Nice when ye can kill greenies an' gather oathgold at the same time...a real bonus that is."

—Vorth, Veteran Ironbreaker

CHAPTER 5: BOGGED DOWN

We entered the Marshes of Madness to mine the old mines for any leftover oathgold, vitally necessary for our new weapons. We were attacked while mining and had to chase down the greenies and get our boys back. We found oathgold on some of the greenies, and decided to farm them instead of toiling in the mines.

PUBLIC QUESTS

Foul Ruins

- Objective #1: Kill 125 Bog Zombies.
- Objective #2: Destroy 8 Mourkain Pillars.
- Objective #3: Kill Faustus von Diehl; Kill 3 Abhorrents; Ensure All 8 Pillars are not Restored.
- Objective #4: Kill Faustus the Liche; Kill Sarhakot; Kill Garith the Fleshrender.

CHAPTER 6: MURDOGH'S HOLD

Old Murdogh needs help taking the fens from the greenies, and we need the oathgold some of the greenies carry. So off to war we go, clearing the swamp and getting the ore for new weapons.

PUBLIC QUESTS

Marsh Conquest

- Objective #1: Kill 100 Greenskins; Destroy 3 Rock Lobbers.
- Objective #2: Kill Korgaz Toofrippar; Kill Deathtusk; Kill 2 Black Skull Waaaghs.

CHAPTER 8: A BRIDGE TOO FAR

Tales of the undead ravaging our poor boys cami in from the east. We headed that way to give them a hand. After wiping out the scourge of undead and rescuing captured Dwarfs, we noticed leaks in our dam. Stupid rodents were trying to tear it down.

PUBLIC QUESTS

Legacy of the Mourkain

- Objective #1: Kill 125 Reanimated Servants.
- Objective #2: Destroy 25 Magical Ruins; Kill 10 Nushtar Minions.
- Objective #3: Kill Nushtar; Kill 2 Angered Wights.

Dam Boglars

- Objective #1: Plug 10 Dam Holes; Kill 100 Dam Wreckas.
- Objective #2: Kill 10 Toadlars; Kill 25 Spawned Toadlars.
- Objective #3: Kill Scregrath; Kill 3 Bignose Toadlars.

CHAPTER 9: MINE ALL MINE

Our supplies have been dwindling and some of our boys are missing. Finally we got word that it was the work of that dark soul Neborhest. So we marched up to his tower to take care of business.

PUBLIC QUESTS

Tower of Neborhest

- Objective #1: Stop 75 Feeders; Collect 50 Grudges
- Objective #2: Destroy the Pillar; Defeat Mattias von Jaeger.
- Objective #3: Destroy the Pillar; Defeat Norrisson.
- Objective #4: Destroy the Pillar; Defeat Dork Redeye.
- Objective #5: Kill Neborhest.

Neborhest's Vanguard

- Objective #1: Kill 125 Souless Minions.
- Objective #2: Keep 30 Dwarfs from Being Slain.
- Objective #3: Kill Petrova the Bloodless.
- And many more...!

WARCAMP: THURAIKSON'S WARCAMP

Finally all the riff raff is cleared and not even time for a pint. Word has come that a Merchant's Gift and Defensive Boon are there to be had by the best Dwarf. Once we get those, we can launch attacks from Thurarikson's Warcamp, crush the greenie keep, and take this land as ours.

GREENSKINS

CHAPTER 6

"Dem nasty stunties have come to our swamp an' we have to figure out why. We're meetin' up at da ol' Blood Fens ta clear dem of da stunties. Leve it to a Dwarf to want to fight in a bitey buggy area—that's why we weren't dere in da first place."

—Shaman Pugkorgh

CHAPTER 6: BONER-ENDER'S BASH

From the battle at Blood Fen to slaying specters, the greenskins fight for every square inch of the Marshes.

PUBLIC QUESTS

Specter of Battle

- Objective #1: Kill 50 Spectral Screamers.
- Objective #2: Kill Muzinko; Destroy Muzinko's remains.
- Objective #3: Destroy 30 Hammerstriker Supplies.
- Objective #4: Kill Fielig Thunderbeard; Kill Runar Silverforge.

Marsh Conquest

- Objective #1: Kill 100 Dwarfs; Destroy 3 Rock Carriers.
- Objective #2: Kill Grennar Stonecutter; Kill Bronzeclaw; Kill 2 Hammerstriker Runesmiths.
- And many more...!

WARCAMP: FANGBREAKA

After clearing out these trouble spots, it's off to the keep in Fangbreaka Swamp to start pushing out these stunties for good. After we collect the Defensive Boon and Merchant's Gift, those Dwarfs will trip over their beards running back home.

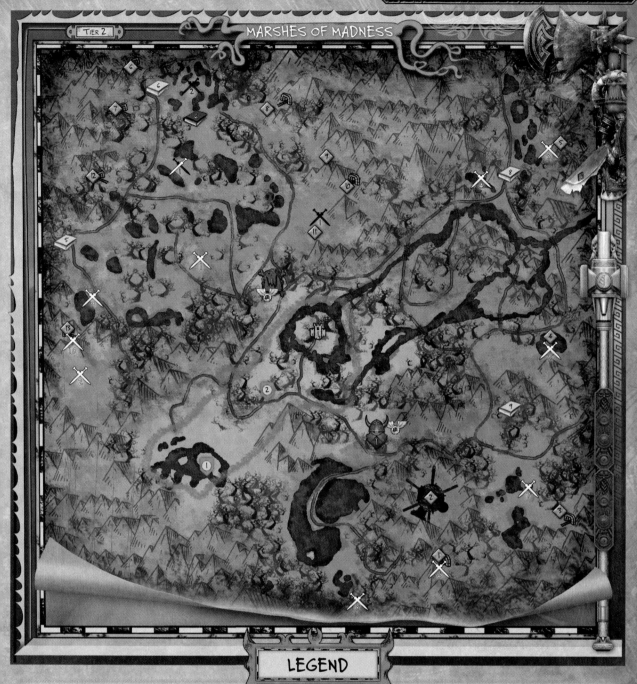

TIER 2

MARSHES OF MADNESS

LEGEND

Warcamps: 1 – Thurarikson's Warcamp   1 – Morth's Warcamp   RvR Area (Outlined)

Chapter Unlock (Destruction)
6 – Greenskin Chapter 6

Chapter Unlock (Order)
5 – Dwarf Chapter 5
6 – Dwarf Chapter 6
8 – Dwarf Chapter 8
9 – Dwarf Chapter 9

Major Landmarks
1 – Agymah's Lair
2 – Tower of Neborhest
3 – Falcon's Tomb

4 – Tree of Beards
5 – Nushtar's Tomb
6 – Hunk Grung
7 – Tainted Mines
8 – Marshfang Spider Cave
9 – Hargruk's Camp
10 – Dragon Eye Cavern
11 – Mingol Thag
12 – Mourkain Tomb
13 – Dawr Galaz Grung

Public Quests (Destruction)
1 – Spectre of Battle
2 – Battle at Blood Fen

Public Quests (Neutral)
1 – Marsh Conquest

Public Quests (Order)
1 – Assault on Coal Ridge Depot
2 – Axerust Peak
3 – Legacy of the Mourkain
4 – Dam Boglar
5 – Tree of Beards
6 – Tower of Neborhest
7 – Neborhest's Vanguard
8 – Agymah's Lair
9 – Foul Ruins
10 – Oathgold Burrow

Battle Objectives
1 – Goblin Armory (Merchant's Gift)
2 – Alcadizzaar's Tomb
      (Defensive Boon)

1 – Fangbreaka Swamp

Flight Master

THE BADLANDS

DWARFS

CHAPTERS 10–11, 13–14

"Fer years we 'ad all called 'ol Phineas crazy, but now 'ere we were following 'is steps hoping ta find th' mines of old that 'ad Brightstone in 'em. We be losing friends to greenie attacks, but always finding more clues ta lead us on in search of th' mines. Finally, we found them and were able ta actually start mining. Th' only problem was that we were encircled by th' greenskin horde...they just sat there waiting fer us ta drop our vigilance."

—Hagmas, Deep Miner

CHAPTER 10: NORRIKSON'S EXCAVATION

The greenskins are using an ancient magic cauldron to raise dead Dwarves to fight for them. They must be stopped.

PUBLIC QUESTS

The Cauldron

- Objective #1: Kill 100 Blue Face Stunty Killas.
- Objective #2: Kill 5 Blue Face Stunty Cookas; Prevent 10 Dwarfs from being sacrificed.
- Objective #3: Kill Skazig Splitmaw.
- Objective #4: Destroy 10 Raised Dwarfs.
- Objective #5: Kill Skazig Splitmaw.

Savage Assault

- Objective #1: Kill 125 Blue Face Orcs.
- Objective #2: Rouse 10 Oathbearers; Kill 10 Blue Face Clubbas.
- Objective #3: Kill 10 Blue Face Boarboyz.
- Objective #4: Kill Urghuma da Big; Kill all the Blue Face Big 'Uns.

CHAPTER 11: THE GOOD NEWS AND THE BAD NEWS

Masses of Moonfang Goblins have descended upon the Dwarfs. They have to be dealt with so the mining can continue.

PUBLIC QUESTS

Revoltin' Gobbos

- Objective #1: Kill 175 Moonfang Goblins.

- Objective #2: Kill Gobhead Squigbringa.

Troll Island

- Objective #1: Kill 60 Bloody Sun Manglas; Kill 20 Bloody Sun Breakas; Kill 20 Feral Trolls.
- Objective #2: Kill 7 Bloody Sun Big Breakas; Kill 7 Enraged Broken Trolls.
- Objective #3: Kill Gizbo da Wize; Kill Gnasher.

CHAPTER 13: ENCIRCLED

Nasty undead creatures from the nearby tar swamp have been raised by a Lich. Two greenskin tribes have united to fight the Dwarfs. They all must be removed.

PUBLIC QUESTS

Skullbreaker Ridge

- Objective #1: Kill 75 Blue Face Orcs; Kill 50 Bloody Sun Boyz.
- Objective #2: Kill 10 Bloody Sun Neckbreakas; Destroy 5 Greenskin Idols.
- Objective #3: Kill Grumgul Fistsmasha; Kill 2 Bloody Sun Healas.

Tomb of Kali'Amon

- Objective #1: Open 20 Withered Sarcophagi; Kill 60 Followers of Kali'Amon.
- Objective #2: Kill 10 Risen Kali'Amonar Haruspices.
- Objective #3: Kill Kali'Amon.

CHAPTER 14: THE BEST DEFENSE

Black Orcs have kidnapped and enslaved some Dwarfs. We must go save them and punish the Orcs, plus any other greenskins that happen to be in the area.

PUBLIC QUESTS

Black Orc Slog

- Objective #1: Free 20 Oathbearer Captives; Kill 100 Bloody Sun Orcs.
- Objective #2: Kill 2 Bloody Sun Enforcas; Kill 8 Enforca's Squigs.
- Objective #3: Kill Bashtoof One-Eye; Kill 5 Bashtoof's Gits.

Bloody Savages

- Objective #1: Kill 150 Bloody Sun Greenskins.
- Objective #2: Set 5 Watch Towers Ablaze; Kill 10 Bloody Sun Big Krunchas.

- Objective #3: Kill Garbog da Splitta; Ki Dirtfur; Kill Scraggletoof.

Skullsmashar's Boyz

- Objective #1: Kill 75 Savage Bloodsnouts Kill 50 Blue Faced Grabbas.
- Objective #2: Kill 20 Blue Face Reapas.
- Objective #3: Kill Skullsmasher da Bloodied; Kill Pigmuncha.

- And many more...!

WARCAMP: NONE

GREENSKINS

CHAPTER 11

"We set camp by some old roons. Durin' da night we herd noises an' ran out to see wot wuz goin' on. Dere were Mutant Exile undead all over. 'Course we made 'em dead dead. A moony captive sed da rest of da moonies had decided to go off on der own Waaagh! an' leave us Sun Boyz hangin'. So now we are off to deel wi dose Gobbos."

—Carzak the Round

CHAPTER 11: BAD LUCK IN TH BADLANDS

The Moonfang Goblins have shown up, but they are fighting on their own, trying to take all the glory instead of helping the greenskin Then the mutants show up too.

PUBLIC QUESTS

Revoltin' Gobbos

- Objective #1: Kill 175 Moonfang Goblin
- Objective #2: Kill Gobhead Squigbringa

Fireforge's Camp

- Objective #1: Kill 70 Oathbearer Denizens; Destroy 40 Supply Crates.
- Objective #2: Kill 8 Oathbearer Master Gunners.
- Objective #3: Kill Thane Grofsson; Kill 4 Oathbearer Sharpshooters.

Mutant Exiles

- Objective #1: Kill 100 Exiled Mutants.
- Objective #2: Destroy 5 Chaos Stones; Kill 10 Exiled Blighters.
- Objective #3: Kill Pestilent Plaguebeast Kill 4 Exiled Summoners.

- And many more...!

WARCAMP: NONE

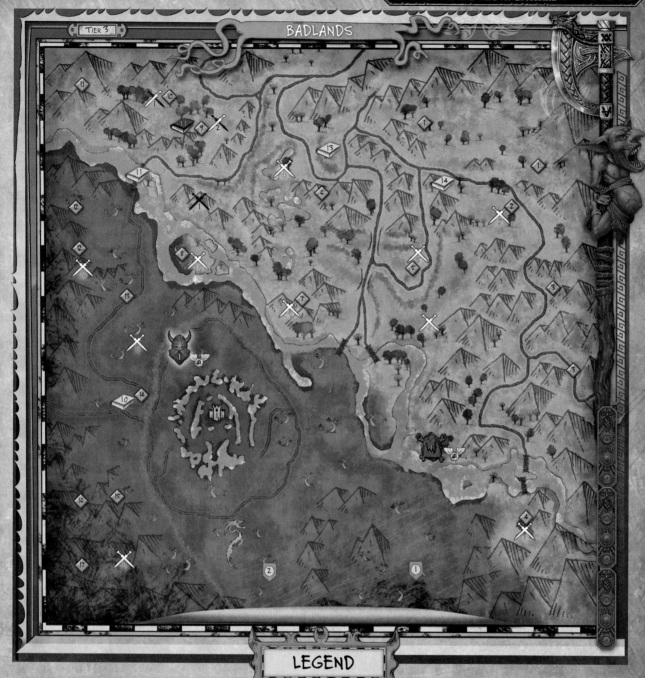

TIER 3

BADLANDS

LEGEND

Warcamps: 1 – Dour Guards   1 – Muggar's Choppa   RvR Area (Outlined)

Chapter Unlock (Destruction)
11 – Greenskin Chapter 11

6 – Olin's Hideout
7 – Tomb of Kali'Amon
8 – Troll Sunder
9 – Fireforge's Camp

Public Quests (Order)
1 – Savage Assault
2 – The Cauldron
3 – Kazad Drung
4 – Putrid Tar Pits
5 – Skullbreaker Ridge
6 – Skullsmasher's Boyz
7 – Black Orc Slog
8 – Bloody Savages
9 – Tomb of Kali'Amon
10 – Troll Island

Battle Objectives
1 – Karagaz (Artisan's Gift)
2 – Goblin Artillery Range (Healing Gift)

Chapter Unlock (Order)
10 – Dwarf Chapter 10
11 – Dwarf Chapter 11
13 – Dwarf Chapter 13
14 – Dwarf Chapter 14

10 – Enclave of the Withered
11 – Mount Gunbad (Dungeon)
12 – Blood Spike Cave
13 – Brokebone Pass
14 – Norrikson's Excavation
15 – Warpclaw Hideout
16 – Geyser Den
17 – Kazad Drung

1 – Thickmuck Pit

Flight Master

Major Landmarks
1 – Bloodgash Cave
2 – Bloody Savages
3 – Bloodmaw Cave
4 – Black Orc Slog
5 – Skullbreaker Ridge

Public Quests (Destruction)
1 – Mutant Exiles

Public Quests (Neutral)
1 – Revoltin Gobbos
2 – Fireforge's Camp

BLACK FIRE PASS

DWARFS

Chapter 12

"Our patrols found a gathering of slimy greenies trying ta make their way through Black Fire Pass. Seems they are trying ta attack our homeland from th' rear. Though we be sorely outnumbered, we be th' only hope fer our homelands. We 'ave all taken a solemn oath ta stand ta th' very end."

—Engineer Kilial Longbeard

Chapter 12: Solemn Oath

The remnant of the Moonfang Goblin's rebellion is holed up in Black Fire Pass.

Public Quests

Moonfang Remnant

- Objective #1: Kill 80 Moonfang Goblins; Kill 45 Moonfang Arachnids.
- Objective #2: Destroy 10 Moonfang Banners.
- Objective #3: Kill Grogaf Spidablood; Kill Orakrix the Sunderer.

Hindelburg

- Objective #1: Kill 125 Warpclaw Looters.
- Objective #2: Protect Dieter Vorkwald.
- Objective #3: Kill 12 Warpclaw Rat Ogres; Kill 6 Warplclaw Slavemasters; Protect Dieter Vorkwald.
- Objective #4: Protect Dieter Vorkwald.
- And many more…!

WARCAMP: Odinator's Watch

GREENSKINS

Chapters 10, 12, 13–14

"We wuz havin' a grand ol' time killin' everything til da Enforcer showed up. Furst thing him did wuz stomp on Moogz an' squish him head an' dat wuz dat fer Moogz. Him told us da Big Boss wuzn't happy at all, dat we weren't been doin' wot we wuz told. So him put Drok in charge an' we cleared dem stunties right out. Next we headed to take on dem humies. Dey wuz tall, but squishy, easy killin' un' a fun fight too. We knowz wot we iz doin' now."

—Farglbrep No Teef

Chapter 10: Moogz's Brawl

As part of the normal operations in Thardrik, the mine supplies the Dwarfs with weapons and a steady stream of ore to build and maintain structures throughout the pass. It's vital that the Dwarfs maintain this mine and keep the surrounding countryside free of enemies.

Public Quests

Gassy Mines

- Objective #1: Kill 100 Gassy Mine Inhabitants; Destroy 30 Mining Supplies; Destroy 10 Mining Valves.
- Objective #2: Kill 10 Thardrik Tinkerers.
- Objective #3: Kill Ironbreaker Burrowrock.

Thardrik Smashin'

- Objective #1: Kill 100 Thardrik Citizens.
- Objective #2: Place 10 Burny Things in North Building; Place 10 Burny Things in West Building; Place 10 Burny Things in South Building.
- Objective #3: Kill Goldhammers.

Chapter 12: The Enforcer

After some changes in command, we kill more Moonfangs, attack the stunty train station, and invade the fortress of Kolaz Umgal.

Public Quests

Moonfang Remnant

- Objective #1: Kill 80 Moonfang Goblins; Kill 45 Moonfang Arachnids.
- Objective #2: Destroy 10 Moonfang Banners.
- Objective #3: Kill Grogaf Spidablood; Kill Orakrix the Sunderer.

Kolaz Umgal

- Objective #1: Kill 125 Kolaz Umgal Dwarfs.
- Objective #2: Gather 25 Blacksmithing Resources.
- Objective #3: Prevent the 5 Sigmarite Warrior Priests from Entering Tower.
- Objective #4: Kill Forgrin Steelforge.

Chapter 13: A New Enemy

The Sigmarites try to rebuild the Empire town of Altstadt and protect the nearby monastery. The greenskins don't like this one bit.

Public Quests

Altstadt

- Objective #1: Kill 100 Altstadt Citizens.
- Objective #2: Claim 6 Altstadt buildings; Kill 10 Sigmarite Faithsworns.
- Objective #3: Kill Vorn the Faithful.

Sigmarite Temple

- Objective #1: Kill 150 Penitents and Inquisitors.
- Objective #2: Kill 10 Sigmarite Champions.
- Objective #3: Kill 5 Sigmarite Vanquishers.
- Objective #4: Kill Sigmund the Prophet.

Chapter 14: Da Big Burn

We get to play with fire and burn everything in sight. Of course, kill stunties and Beastmen too.

Public Quests

Blight Favored Cult

- Objective #1: Kill 100 Ritualists and Cultists; Kill 50 Nurglings.
- Objective #2: Suppress 4 Cultists' Ritual.
- Objective #3: Kill Blighted Plaguebeast.

Blighted Herd

- Objective #1: Kill 150 Blighted Herd Beastmen.
- Objective #2: Destroy the Herdstone.
- Objective #3: Kill Valraz the Plagued.

Kolaz Umgal Scouts

- Objective #1: Kill 75 Kolaz Umgal Steelshots; Kill 75 Kolaz Umgal Stoneguards.
- Objective #2: Burn 10 Dwarf Tents; Protect Bloody Sun Burna.
- Objective #3: Kill Thulgrim Hurlesson; Kill 2 Kolaz Umgal Ironguards.

WARCAMP: Blackteef's Boyz

TIER 3

BLACK FIRE PASS

LEGEND

Warcamps: 1 – Odinator's Watch   1 – Blackteef's Boyz   RvR Area (Outlined)

Chapter Unlock (Destruction)
10 – Greenskin Chapter 10
12 – Greenskin Chapter 12
13 – Greenskin Chapter 13
14 – Greenskin Chapter 14

Chapter Unlock (Order)
12 – Dwarf Chapter 12

Major Landmarks
1 – Priesterstadt
2 – Sigmarite Temple
3 – Altstadt
4 – Grimbeard Station

5 – Da Gassy Mines
6 – Khazad Bolg Tunnel
7 – Spida Hole
8 – Blackrock mine
9 – Warpclaw Cave
10 – Hindelburg
11 – Ebon Hollow
12 – Kolaz Umgal
13 – Ancient's Reach
14 – Black Fire Mine
15 – Lord Thardrik's Tower

Public Quests (Destruction)
1 – Thardrik Smashin'
2 – Priesterstadt

3 – Statue of Inspiration
4 – Sigmarite Temple
5 – Altstadt
6 – Gassy Mine
7 – Kolaz Umgal Scouts
8 – FavoCult
9 – Kolaz Umgal
10 – Blighted Herd

Public Quests (Order)
1 – Hindelburg

Public Quests (Neutral)
1 – Grimbeard Station
2 – Moonfang Remnant

Battle Objectives
1 – Furrig's Fall (Defensive Boon)
2 – Bugman's Brewery
(Merchant's Gift)

1 – Gnol Baraz

Flight Master

BLACK CRAG

DWARFS

CHAPTERS 20–22

"Th' deep chasms of Black Crag never cease ta amaze me. Almost a polar opposite ta Kadrin Valley...quite amazing. T'would be a wonderful place 'cept it's a gigantic warzone. We are based on th' eastern side of th' chasms with only a greenskin fortress near Gav's Oathbearers. Here it seems the greens be distracted by something. Our scouts tells us it's internal ramblings but nothing is fer sure at this point."

—Muidwlen of the First Watch

CHAPTER 20: CRAGHELM'S HOLD

The northernmost base for Dwarfs in the Black Crag is the safest. A few public quests help ease you into things and show you the terrain, mainly the big crag.

PUBLIC QUESTS

Da Great Smashin' Pit

- Objective #1: Kill 35 Smashin' Pit Brawlers; Kill 35 Smashin' Pit Scrappers; Kill 20 Smashin' Pit Gawpers.
- Objective #2: Prevent Big 'Uns from Riling up Gits.
- Objective #3: Kill 10 Da Bosses.
- Objective #4: Survive the Brawlers; Survive Big 'Uns; Survive the Gladiators.
- Objective #5: Kill Soc the Smashar, Bulch Bigbelly, Clawtoofs, and Thuk da Big 'Un.
- And many more to be discovered!

CHAPTER 21: OATHGRUND'S WATCH

The chapter is based in the bluffs and is the closest to the greenskin bases. You have to be careful not to fall down a cliff or face instant death.

CHAPTER 22: GAV'S OATHBEARERS

The third chapter for the Dwarfs in the Black Crag is positioned right beside a greenskin keep. This chapter prepares you for the final attack against Butcher's Pass.

WARCAMP: HAMMERSTRIKER POINT

If you are ready for some greenskin smashing, head over to the only Dwarf warcamp in the zone. There are three main objectives up for the taking in the Black Crag: Lobba Mill, a Merchant's Gift; Squiggly Beast Pens, a Healing Boon; and Macap Pickins, an Artisan's Gift. Once you capture these three, you can move to the two keeps, Bloodmoon Hold and Ironskin Scar. Once those two are captured, Butcher's Pass is up for the taking.

GREENSKINS

CHAPTERS 15–16

"Da reel battle takes place at da bottom of da Crag where we know da battlefield the bestest. Dose stunties won't know what's comin' to dem. We control two keeps here an' unfortunately da Dwarfs put a camp of deir strongest warriors just outside one of dem an' anotha on da bluffs above. Outside killin stunties we got to deal wid some traitors who ran away. Dey shouldn't cause too many problems. Just don't be stupid an' die. We need yer body livin'."

—Shaman Gorslick

CHAPTER 15: RED DUST CAMP

This first chapter for the greenskins in the zone involves dealing with some traitors. Dwarfs are not a major concern during this chapter due to the strength of the Dwarfs on the other side of the crag.

WARHAMMER ONLINE
AGE OF RECKONING

LEGEND

Warcamps:

 1 – Hammerstriker Point

 1 – Gudmud's Strong-Hut's Warcamp

RvR Area (Outlined)

 Chapter Unlock (Destruction)
15 – Greenskin Chapter 15
16 – Greenskin Chapter 16

Chapter Unlock (Order)
20 – Dwarf Chapter 20
21 – Dwarf Chapter 21
22 – Dwarf Chapter 22

Major Landmarks
1 – Destroyed Tower
2 – Redmane Mine
3 – Bat Hollow
4 – Morkfang Camp
5 – Morkfang Cave
6 – Despair Pits
7 – Sulfur Caves
8 – Venom Cave
9 – Tunnel of Karak Dazh
10 – Lageredson's Brewery
11 – Festering Cave
12 – Da Big Stink
13 – Cliffrunner Den
14 – Redfang Ridge
15 – Poisonwing Tunnel (East Side)
16 – Ruins of Karak Dahz
17 – Poisonwing Tunnel (West Side)
18 – Vidian Tower
19 – Stonemane Mine
20 – Muck Pen
21 – Infested Tower
22 – Burnmaw Tower

 Public Quests (Destruction)
1 – Mokfang Da Mad
2 – Overtop Outpost
3 – Valley of the Rangers
4 – Ambush Canyon
5 – Wyvern in the Hand
6 – Skargor da Traitor

 Public Quests (Order)
1 – Da Great Smashin' Pit
2 – Venom Lake
3 – Bait and Hit
4 – Gobbo Carvas
5 – Magister Dhetal
6 – Muck Pen
7 – Defiled Anvil
8 – Dammaz Skar
9 – Poisonwing Canyon

 Battle Objectives
1 – Lobba Mill (Merchant's Gift)
2 – Squiggly Beast Pens (Healing Boon, Underground)
3 – Macap Pickins (Artisan's Gift)
4 – Rottenpike Ravine

 1 – Ironskin Scar
1 – Badmoon Hole (Underground)

 Flight Master

CHAPTER 16: DA GREAT BIG FOOD POT

The second chapter for the greenskins deals with Dwarfs and with internal affairs of the greenskins. Some traitors and wyverns headline the public quests.

PUBLIC QUESTS

Ambush Canyon

- Objective #1: Kill 100 Oathbearers.

- Objective #2: Kill 5 Oathbearer Bombers. Kill 10 Oathbearer Technicians. All Ground Gyrocopters Destroyed.

- Objective #3: Kill Verkner Steelbeard; Kill 2 Oathbearer Strikers.

- And many more to be discovered!

WARCAMP: GUDMUD'S STRONG-HUTS

Once you head over to the greenskins' warcamp, you get to meet some stunties. There are three main objectives in the Crag, plus the two keeps we hold. There is Lobba Mill, a Merchant's Gift; Squiggly Beast Pens, a Healing Boon; and Macap Pickins, an Artisan's Gift. We must hold our two keeps, Bloodmoon Hold and Ironskin Scar, to advance. Once all is secured, heading to Thunder Mountain will introduce you to real war.

BUTCHER'S PASS

TIER 4

BUTCHER'S PASS

TO BLACK CRAG

LEGEND

RvR Area (Outlined)

Portals
1 – To The Maw
2 – To Fell Landing

CINDERFALL

TIER 4

CINDERFALL

TO THUNDER
MOUNTAIN

LEGEND

RvR Area (Outlined)

Major Landmarks
1 – Cave
2 – Cave
3 – Cave
4 – Cave

Public Quests (Destruction)
1 – Gutbash Tribe Stronghold
2 – Flamerock Mine
3 – Da Drakk Cult

Public Quests (Order)
1 – Cult of Drakk
2 – Ashreaver Tribe Stronghold
3 – Emberlight Mine

DEATH PEAK

"Be careful where ye tread and remember th' fallen" is a local Dwarf adage about the lands around Death Peak. The slopes along the eastern border of Thunder Mountain are indeed treacherous, and impassable in most areas. Only three pockets of terrain—Smoke Rock to the north, the Ebon Steppes in the center, and Sparkstone Ridge to the south—can be reached by the determined hiker, though only through special paths solely from Thunder Mountain.

Smoke Rock harbors both Dwarfs and greenskins. Should you travel up the northern path, stay wide of the acidfang spiders to your west—unless you want to visit ancient Dwarf caves now overrun with arachnids—and your steps will eventually take you to Grom Rodrin, a secluded Dwarf fortress with Bloody Sun Boyz greenskins in the hills directly across from it. In the southern portion of Smoke Rock, you run into a Bleakwind Colossus, a Bleakwind Harpy, or a Goblin catapult if you're not careful.

In the middle of Death Peak, the Ebon Steppes sit between Smoke Rock above it and Sparkstone Ridge below it. The Bloody Sun greenskins and their rampant Squigs rule the area from a command post next to Snarbog the Bilious to the road leading into the Valley of Bones. Few can investigate the Steppes without alerting the suspicious Goblins.

Far to the south, Sparkstone Ridge harbors mostly scrub grass, sheer cliffs, and a few species of deadly wildlife. Avoid the spiders and burntmoss striders if you would like to taste the dawn of a new day.

WARHAMMER ONLINE
AGE OF RECKONING

TIER 4

DEATH PEAK

TO THUNDER MOUNTAIN

TO THUNDER MOUNTAIN

LEGEND

RvR Area (Outlined)

◆ **Major Landmarks**
1 – Whoosha's Boyz
2 – Quimp's Cave
3 – Ashback Den
4 – Valley of Bones
5 – Webspun Hollow
6 – Skoragrim's Forge
7 – Ruins
8 – Ancestral Gates
9 – Sinar Orcstorm
10 – Ancestral Guardians

✗ **Public Quest (Destruction)**
1 – Fallen Keep of Grom Rodrim
2 – Peak's Edge

⚔ **Public Quests (Order)**
1 – Whoosha's Boyz

KADRIN VALLEY

CHAPTERS 15–16

"Th' misty mountains shield th' true battle we fight here. Those blasted greenskins just keep comin' and getting their necks hewed. They assault our fortresses at Duraz Dok and Slayer's Keep. All this training means nothing until ye actually fight th' real thing.

"Th' greenskins aren't th' only ones we get ta deal wiv here; we got those dung-awful Dark Elves here. South of th' Hungry Troll Pub, the places be crawlin' with th' little buggers. Ye got ta be ready with a strong weapon or spell ta avoid any trouble. And ye still can't forget about th' Ogres at Icehearth Crag. If ye want ta capture that place, ye got ta stain th' rocks wiv th' blood of ogres. Kadrin Valley, what a wonderful place it is."

—Grimgor Stoneaxe, Oathbearer Keeper

CHAPTER 15: KAZAD GROMAR

This is the base of all operation for us in Kadrin Valley. Safe from most of the greenskin warcamps and towns, it's a good place to get used to the rough environment. Be wary in the valley below though; it's a complete warzone.

PUBLIC QUESTS

Ambush Pass

- Objective #1: Kill 125 Blood Sun Greenskins. Secure 50 Dwarf Supply Crates.
- Objective #2: Kill 10 Oathbearer Freightmasters in 5 minutes.
- Objective #3: Kill Ghutoof da Hunta. Kill Nadarg 'Eadsplitta. Kill Weird Wahgez.
- And many more to be discovered!

CHAPTER 16: HUNGRY TROLL PUB

Might look like a pub, but it's our base for taking back Grung Grimaz. The blasted Dark Elves took it in the night and we want it back.

PUBLIC QUESTS

Gates of Grung Grimaz

- Objective #1: Kill 80 Uthorin Elves. Destroy 10 Bolt Throwers.
- Objective #2: Kill 3 Uthorin Dreadknights and 15 Uthorin Shadowriders in 10 minutes.
- Objective #3: Kill Beastmaster Vauroth and Rathuaal in 15 minutes.
- And many more to be discovered!

WARCAMP: GHARVIN'S BRACE

Once you head over to the only warcamp in the zone, you get to meet the valley. Two fortresses guard the path, and they must be defended. Secure the four battlefield objectives for bonuses: Gromril Junction for a Defensive Boon, Icehearth Crossing for a Healing Boon, Hardwater Falls for an Artisan's Gift, and Dolgrund's Cairn for a Merchant's Gift. When all four are captured, it's safe to storm down to Thunder Mountain—one step closer to the greenskin's fortress.

TIER 1

KADRIN VALLEY

TO STONEWATCH

LEGEND

Warcamps: 1 – Orcslayer's Warcamp   1 – Krung's Scrappin' Spot   ～～～ RvR Area (Outlined)

Chapter Unlock (Destruction)
20 – Greenskin Chapter 20
21 – Greenskin Chapter 21
22 – Greenskin Chapter 22

Chapter Unlock (Order)
15 – Dwarf Chapter 15
16 – Dwarf Chapter 16

Major Landmarks
1 – Shrine of Grimnir
2 – Tower of Grung Grimaz
3 – Mine of Grung Grimaz
4 – Clarion Tower

5 – Duraz Dok
6 – Gharvin's Tower
7 – Gharvin's Mine
8 – Crazy Stunty Drinking Place
9 – Peak Tower
10 – Duraz Deb
11 – Duraz Deb Mine
12 – Everpeak Mine
13 – Tunnel of Baradum
14 – Kazad Urbar
15 – Kloingar's Mine

Public Quests (Destruction)
1 – Duraz Dok
2 – Battlegut Ogres

3 – Beer Barrel Bash
4 – Duraz Deb
5 – Slayer Keep
6 – Baradum
7 – Kazad Urbar
8 – Burnbeard's Oath
9 – Clarion Tower

Public Quests (Order)
1 – Ambush Valley
2 – Evil Axis
3 – Sealed Tower
4 – Gates of Grung Grimaz
5 – Night Riders
6 – Plague Mist Vale

Battle Objectives
1 – Gromril Junction (Defensive Boon)
2 – Icehearth Crossing (Healing Boon, Underground)
3 – Kazad Dammaz
4 – Hardwater Falls (Artisan's Gift)

Lairs
1 – Fleshrender

1 – Dolgrund's Cairn (Merchant's Gift)
2 – Karaz Drengi

Flight Master

CHAPTERS 20–22

"Slayer's Keep iz problem. We must climb itz rock face. Me no like climbin'. Den we get dere and da stunties be dug in like termites in deir stone house. We have Dark Elf allies here but dey don't no how to fight stunties even though dey took Duraz Dok."

—Ilg the Skaky

GREENSKINS

CHAPTER 20: NAGUK'S COLD CAMP

This is the first camp for greenskins in Kadrin Valley. Most of the quests here eventually lead up to the public quest at Kazad Urbar. If you go down into the valley, whet your blade for battle.

PUBLIC QUESTS

Kazad Urbar

- Objective #1: Kill 50 Urbar Sharp Shooters; Kill 50 Imperial Duelists.
- Objective #2: Destroy 3 Pistolier Covers; Kill Captain Herdenschwintz; Kill 25 Imperial Tradesman; Kill 25 Commerce Smiths.
- Objective #3: Kill Bright Wizard Varick.

CHAPTER 21: UG'S WARBAND

The closer you get to the prize, the more difficult it gets. Public quests deal with taking out the forts defending Slayer's Keep. This fighting here is nothing compared to what you will have to face ahead.

PUBLIC QUESTS

Duraz Dok

- Objective #1: Kill 50 of Ungrim's Finest; Destroy 6 Cannons
- Objective #2: Kill Captain Stonefist.
- Objective #3: Keep Glutnog and Gutz alive.
- Objective #4: Kill Skor Douraxe.
- And many more to be discovered!

CHAPTER 22: BADROT'S BASHIN' PLACE

Finally almost at the goal, Slayer's Keep. Only a few defenses are left and Slayer's Keep is captured. Just have to take Duraz Deb and it's a swift capture.

PUBLIC QUESTS

Duraz Deb

- Objective #1: Kill 80 Road Wardens; Kill 95 Travelers and Patrons.
- Objective #2: Kill 5 Oath Scribes; Prevent 25 Oaths Taken.
- Objective #3: Kill Mournbrow.
- And many more to be discovered!

WARCAMP: KRUNG'S SCRAPPIN' SPOT

Once you head over to the only warcamp in the zone, you get to meet the valley. Two fortresses guard the path to Stonewatch; they must be taken. Secure the four battlefield objectives for bonuses: Gromril Junction for a Defensive Boon, Icehearth Crossing for a Healing Boon, Hardwater Falls for an Artisan's Gift, and Dolgrund's Cairn for a Merchant's Gift. When all four are captured, we can storm Stonewatch and take what is ours.

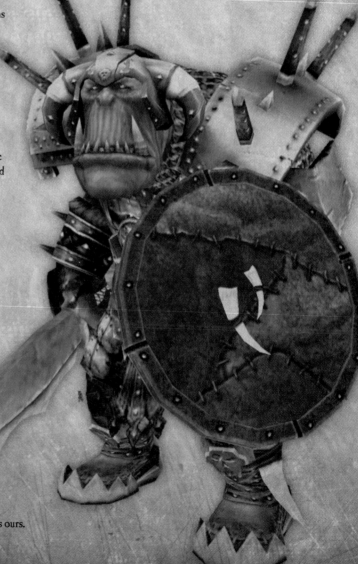

STONEWATCH

TIER 4

STONEWATCH

LEGEND

~~~~~ RvR Area (Outlined)

 Portals
1 – To Shining Way
2 – Cave Portal
3 – To Reikwald

THUNDER MOUNTAIN

DWARFS

Chapters 17–19

"Tis a dark humid place; what a stark comparison ta our home. Lava flows freely with only a few remnants of scorched trees. Oh how I miss th' snow. But alas, th' fight must go on. Ye better be prepared ta love th' heat. T'will be a scorcher again today."

—Grimgor Stoneaxe, Oathbearer Keeper

Chapter 17: Lorkinson's Excavation

The old excavation here is the first place you'll go in Thunder Mountain. You get to blow up some Dragon bones in one of the public quests.

Public Quests

Dragon's Blessing

- Objective #1: Destroy 15 Dragon Bone Piles.
- Objective #2: Kill 25 Drakk Fire-Channelers; Kill 30 Drakk Acolytes.
- Objective #3: Kill Dragonblessed Qilarn.
- And many more to be discovered!

Chapter 18: Palik Watch

The second base of operations in Thunder Mountain is possibly the most dangerous. To the south, the greenskins have a camp waiting to launch an attack at Karak Karag, the fort we hold. To our east, we have the ridge and mountain, which the greenskins are tucked neatly into. All the quests here lead to public quests in Cinderfall.

Chapter 19: Dragonslayer Ridge

This third and final stronghold on Thunder Mountain puts you very close to the greenskins once again. This place is an RvR hotspot, with battlefield objectives and warcamps being very close by. This chapter will ease you into Death Peak.

Public Quests

Ankul Grob

- Objective #1: Kill 20 Carrion Squig; Kill 40 Bloody Sun Boyz; Save 20 dying Oathbearers.
- Objective #2: Kill 20 Drakk Excavators; Kill 10 Drakk Guardians; Kill 3 Drakk Wardbreakers.
- Objective #3: Kill Doomseeker Bereth. Retrieve the Anvil of Doom.
- And many more to be discovered!

Warcamp: Greymere Point

Nearby you have Gromril Kruk, a Healing Boon. On the other side of the mountain you have the greenskin keep of Bloodfist Rock and three more battlefield objectives: Karak Palik, a Merchant's Gift; Doomstriker Vein, an Artisan's Gift; and Thargrim's Headwall, a Defensive Boon. Once you capture all four objectives and the keeps, you can head to Cinderfall, Death Peak, or Black Crag to continue the fight.

GREENSKINS

Chapters 17–19

"Most of our job be to kill stunties, or friends of stunties, or just things wez don't like. Dis iz da center of da battle with the stunties, so we iz 'olding da mountain to prevent deir gettin' past us. Dis is just one of dose places where itz club or be clubbed. Lucky fer us, our 'eads be like rocks. Really thick rocks."

—Hoarmrgle of da 'Ard Clubbers

Chapter 17: Hot Foot Boyz

This is the first stronghold for the greenskins in Thunder Mountain. Here you will not see much RvR action, but more public quests and defeating wildlife.

Public Quests

Reichert's Raiders

- Objective #1: Kill 100 Reichert's Men; Burn 2 Reichert's Tent; Raise a Greenskin Banner.
- Objective #2: Get 100 Shines on GreenskinPile; Prevent 100 Shines from Reichert's Vault.
- Objective #3: Kill Franz Reichert.

Chapter 18: Da Scrappin' Camp

The second stronghold for greenskins in Thunder Mountain. Most of the quests relating to this chapter are located in Cinderfall, including all the public quests.

Chapter 19: Da Big Bones

The third stronghold for the greenskins in Thunder Mountain is probably the most dangerous. The main RvR area in the zone is very close by, and the Dwarfs have a camp set up to the south.

Public Quests

Ruins of Mingol Kudrak

- Objective #1: Kill 80 Oathbearer Dwarfs; Destroy 20 Excavation Supplies.
- Objective #2: Kill 10 Oathbearer Cannoners; Destroy 5 Cannons.
- Objective #3: Kill Excavationer Borgarth.

Warcamp: Bonechukka's Warcamp

Nearby is Gromril Kruk, a Healing Boon. On the other side of the mountain lies our keep, Bloodfist Rock, and three more battlefield objectives: Karak Palik, a Merchant's Gift; Doomstriker Vein, an Artisan's Gift; and Thargrim's Headwall, a Defensive Boon. The Dwarfs have a keep on the west side of the zone near Cinderfall. Once we capture all the objectives here, it's onward to Kadrin Valley.

THUNDER MOUNTAIN

TIER 4

TO KADRIN VALLEY

TO CINDERFALL

TO DEATH PEAK

TO BLACK CRAG

LEGEND

Warcamps: 1 – Kagrund's Stand   1 – Mudja Warcamp

RvR Area (Outlined)

 Chapter Unlock (Destruction)
17 – Greenskin Chapter 17
18 – Greenskin Chapter 18
19 – Greenskin Chapter 19

3 – Ungdrin Ankor Tunnel
4 – Karak Palik
5 – Lava Flow Mine
6 – Moonfang Mine
7 – Ruins of Mingol Kurdak
8 – Field of Bone
9 – Bloodmaw Cave
10 – Ashhide Tunnel
11 – Nackrender's Warband

 4 – Ruins of Mingol Kurdak

Public Quests (Order)
1 – Dragon's Blessing
2 – Red with Envy
3 – Ungry Ungry Greenskins
4 – Ankul Grob

 Gift, Underground)
3 – Thargrim's Headwall
   (Defensive Boon)
4 – Gromril Kruk (Healing Boon,
   Underground)

1 – Bloodfist Rock
2 – Karak Karag

 Chapter Unlock (Order)
17 – Dwarf Chapter 17
18 – Dwarf Chapter 18
19 – Dwarf Chapter 19

Major Landmarks
1 – Nuffin' Ere
2 – Dragon's Breath Cave

Public Quests (Destruction)
1 – Und-a-Runki
2 – Reichert's Raiders
3 – Gutbashed Goblins

Battle Objectives
1 – Karak Palik (Merchant's Gift)
2 – Doomstriker Vein (Artisan's

 Flight Master

EMPIRE VS. CHAOS

THE WARFRONT

In the midst of the Empire, a great and gruesome plague spreads. For weeks, victims suffer horrible symptoms until a fate worse than death befalls them—they transform into fiendish Chaos mutants, creatures that die by their own savagery or slaughter those around them. With each passing week the death toll climbs, and Emperor Karl Franz declares quarantines and martial law wherever the plague strikes hardest.

Meanwhile, far to the north, a huge warhost spawns seemingly out of the nothingness that is the Chaos Wastes. Grotesque creatures and armored warriors march side by side, led by the Chaos Lord Tchar'zanek wielding the flag of his god, the Changer of Ways, Tzeentch. The warhost crushes anyone and anything that defies it on its march into the heart of the Empire.

With civilization on the brink of war, the most powerful of the land's races choose sides. Trusty Dwarfs and wise High Elves join the Empire and become the forces of Order. Relentless greenskins and cunning Dark Elves join Chaos and become the forces of Destruction. The two sides shall battle, and the world shall sunder.

THE TIERS

There are three warfronts (race pairings) in *Warhammer Online*: Dwarfs vs. greenskins, Empire vs. Chaos, and High Elves vs. Dark Elves. Each of these warfronts breaks down into four tiers. There are two zones each in Tier 1, Tier 2, and Tier 3, and eight zones each in Tier 4.

Tier 1 zones are where all characters begin. Generally, you'll spend approximately 10 ranks in each zone, so your early ranks, 1–10, will be spent in Tier 1, 11–20 in Tier 2, 21–30 in Tier 3, and 31–40 in Tier 4. Of course, there are exceptions to this rule, as you should rank up at your own pace and follow the paths set by your various quests. The RvR (realm vs. realm) areas in Tier 1, where you can fight against other players, are relatively small compared to the larger ones in Tier 4, so you won't get lost as you train up your player vs. player (PvP) skills.

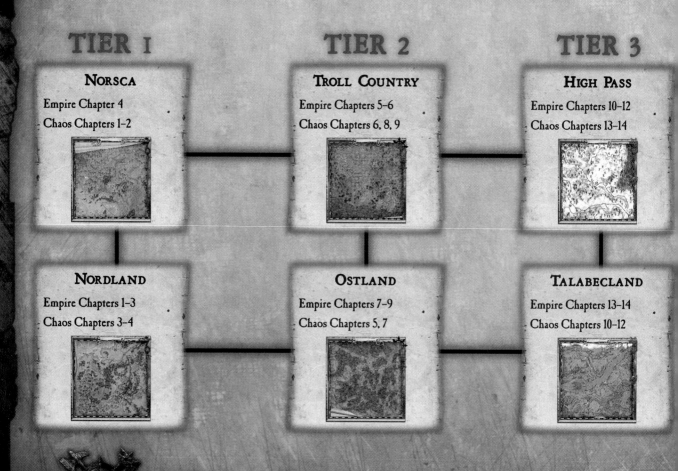

TIER 1

NORSCA
Empire Chapter 4
Chaos Chapters 1–2

NORDLAND
Empire Chapters 1–3
Chaos Chapters 3–4

TIER 2

TROLL COUNTRY
Empire Chapters 5–6
Chaos Chapters 6, 8, 9

OSTLAND
Empire Chapters 7–9
Chaos Chapters 5, 7

TIER 3

HIGH PASS
Empire Chapters 10–12
Chaos Chapters 13–14

TALABECLAND
Empire Chapters 13–14
Chaos Chapters 10–12

TIER 4

INEVITABLE CITY

Empire City Campaign
Chaos City Campaign

THE MAW

Empire Campaign
Chaos Campaign

CHAOS WASTES

Empire Chapters 20–22
Chaos Chapters 15–16

TO HIGH PASS

PRAAG

Empire Chapters 17–19
Chaos Chapters 17–19

WEST PRAAG

Empire Campaign
Chaos Campaign

REIKLAND

Empire Campaign 15–16
Chaos Campaign 20–22

TO TALABECLAND

ALTDORF

Empire City Campaign
Chaos City Campaign

REIKWALD

Empire Chapters
Chaos Chapters

Tier 2 zones bridge your advance between Tier 1 and Tier 3 zones. While in Tier 2, you should have gained all your fundamental abilities and you start mastering the paths that will define your career. RvR areas are a bit larger and more challenging than Tier 1. You certainly want to ally with other players from this point forward.

Tier 3 zones can be fierce battlegrounds as characters become more and more powerful. At this stage, you fine-tune your career before heading into the campaigns of Tier 4.

Tier 4 will become your home once you hit the 30s, and you'll stay locked in Tier 4 campaigns for the rest of your time in *Warhammer Online*. Because you will spend most of your time here, and the RvR areas are vast, you should learn each zone well before moving to the next. If you follow your race's chapter unlocks and complete as many regular quests and public quests as possible, each zone will be a memorable experience.

HOW TO USE THE MAPS

The maps in this guide are organized first by warfronts and then by tiers (in alphabetical order within each tier). The first section deals with Dwarfs and greenskins, the second section highlights Empire and Chaos, and the third section details the struggle between High Elves and Dark Elves. As you adventure, open the appropriate map section and follow along as you discover chapters. For example, as a Empire player, you would open to the start of the Empire vs. Chaos map section and turn to the Tier 1 zone, Nordland, the very first map in that section. Empire Chapters 1–3 take place in Nordland. To help you along on your journey, keep the Nordland map open until you're ready for Empire Chapter 4, which takes you to the Norsca map. For Empire Chapter 5, you travel to Troll Country, your first Tier 2 zone. Continue with your "Chapters of *WAR*" until you've completed Chapter 22 and conquered them all.

Each zone map contains a wealth of information. Important points are labeled right on the map: chapter unlocks, public quests, landmarks, dungeons, lairs, battlefield objectives, and more. To identify any map point for your race, see the map's legend.

The page next to each map summarizes that zone's chapters. At a glance, you can see what chapters are in the zone (and your enemy's chapters) and all the public quests in the area. Pay close attention to the public quest objective information, as this will give you a leg up on what to expect and arm you (or your warband) with clues about what gear, Morale abilities, and Tactics to equip before battle.

If you don't want to flip through the maps chapter by chapter, see the map index at the start of each warfront and look up exactly where the zone of your choice can be found.

EMPIRE

CHAPTERS 1-3

"I choke and cough myself awake. I can't catch my breath; I was drowning in my dream, but this is smoke. Smoke fills the room. There's fire on the curtains, fire on the rug, fire on the blankets. I kick off the covers and run for the stairs. The heat is strong from down the hallway, and I see wild flames through the open window as they dance along the shingles of the Four Heads Inn next door. All I want is fresh air, and I burst out the back door and into cool, open space. All around, Grimmenhagen burns, and my home turns to ash."

—Grifton Orley, Spice Merchant

CHAPTER 1: WAR COMES TO GRIMMENHAGEN

The enemy marches through your backyard and takes away your freedoms. The Nordland army seemingly fights everywhere at once, and the only way to strike back against the forces of Chaos is for every peasant, merchant, and thief to band together and replenish the ranks. For every Marauder of the Raven Host that falls, our lands are one step closer to renewal.

PUBLIC QUESTS

Raven Host Vanguard

- Objective #1: Slay 25 Raven Host Marauders.
- Objective #2: Protect Father Sigwald.
- Objective #3: Kill Argog the Unstoppable.

CHAPTER 2: INTO THE FIRE

As the farmers around the battle-torn land rally together to form a new regiment, the Grimmenhagen Regulars, scouts have engaged the main force of the enemy. All able-bodied warriors are heading north to New Emskrank, the focal point of the war effort between Empire and Chaos in Nordland.

PUBLIC QUESTS

The Burning Windmill

- Objective #1: Kill 50 Seeker Horrors.
- Objective #2: Kill 6 Seeker Cultists.
- Objective #3: Kill Baruun the Seeker; Kill Volkryth Flamecaller.

CHAPTER 3: THE BATTLE OF NEW EMSKRANK

With the battle for New Emskrank raging on, Empire and Chaos are at a standstill. Both sides search for ways to seize the battlefield objectives that will ultimately determine the victor.

PUBLIC QUESTS

Pillagers Approach

- Objective #1: Kill 10 Cruel Overseers; Kill 50 Murderous Raiders.
- Objective #2: Save 35 Citizen Militia Copses.
- Objective #3: Slay Lorok the Heartless.

NORDLAND

WARCAMP: ORDER

On a hill overlooking the fishing village of New Emskrank, Order's staging ground is but an arrow's flight away from the main streets where combat is as common as open markets had once been. On the streets, gates and buildings create a maze-like terrain, while down on the beaches, long stretches of open space may leave the unwary vulnerable.

CHAOS

CHAPTER 4

"I wait my turn to be chosen and to hear the words. Will I sneak into the city and slit a guard's throat, or will I be given into a battalion to slay in New Emskrank until my blade's thirst is quenched? I move up in line and listen to the others whispering and accepting the final prayer before our disappearance into the night. I move again, and it is my turn. I listen to my orders, branding every word into my mind. I will not fail."

—Jakonilch, Initiate of the Raven Host

CHAPTER 4: PROVING GROUND

Chaos has penetrated into Nordland, once a strongly held region of the Empire. The young foot soldiers of Destruction look to make their mark in the ranks of the Raven Host, and they will not falter until the kingdom crumbles.

PUBLIC QUESTS

Fields of Woe

- Objective #1: Destroy 10 Weapon Wagons.
- Objective #2: Kill 10 Nordland Sergeants.
- Objective #3: Kill Sir Falkirk; Kill 2 Militia Guards.

WARCAMP: DESTRUCTION

You have direct access to the city of New Emskrank, where you fight on varied terrain: city streets, sandy beaches, cliff faces, and hills. At first you may be surrounded with the strength of the gathering Order forces, but they cannot match your ferocity or indomitable will.

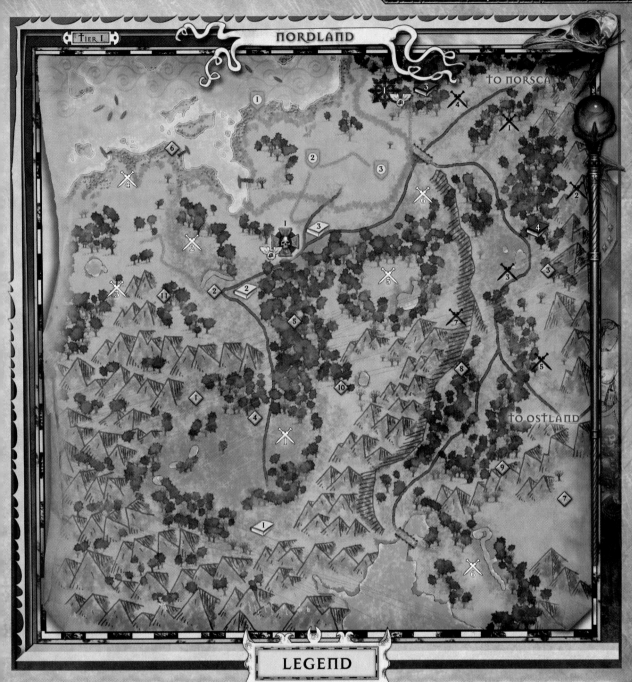

TIER I

NORDLAND

TO NORSCA

TO OSTLAND

LEGEND

WARCAMPS: I – Arnholdt's Company   I – Blessed Gathering   RvR Area (Outlined)

Chapter Unlock (Destruction)
3 – Chaos Chapter 3
4 – Chaos Chapter 4

Chapter Unlock (Order)
I – Empire Chapter 1
2 – Empire Chapter 2
3 – Empire Chapter 3

Major Landmarks
I – Grimmenhagen Barrows
2 – Grey Lady Coaching Inn

3 – Beeckerhoven Crypt
4 – Grimmenhagen Windmill
5 – Traitor's Crossing
6 – Norscan Longship
7 – Salzenmund Keep
8 – Gausser's Wilding
9 – Smugglers' Tunnel
10 – Murder Wood
11 – Abandoned Marauder Camp

Public Quests (Destruction)
I – Pillage and Plunder
2 – Wilds of War
3 – Fields of Woe

4 – Macabre Fervor
5 – Sacred Ground
6 – Salzenmund

Public Quests (Order)
I – Raven Host Vanguard
2 – Buring Windmill
3 – Ruins of Schloss von Rubendorff
4 – Norse Are Coming
5 – Faewulf's Rest
6 – Pillager's Approach
7 – Webworks

Battle Objectives
I – Nordland docks
2 – Festenplatz Defense Boon
3 – Harvest Shrine

Flight Master

NORSCA

CHAPTER 4

"I, a mere farmer holding a pitchfork, have been recruited to join the troops in defending our homeland. My family by themselves will have to guard the farm. This war has come to our homeland and now everyone has to fight...all professions and ages."

—Simon of Stalkings Stead

CHAPTER 4: THE PIT OF THE FORSAKEN

Standing there spying on the city of Gotland, collectively we feel our hair stand up. An evil sorceress uses magic right before our eyes to bring forth a hideous creature from beneath the land.

PUBLIC QUESTS

Altar of the Bloodbane

- Objective #1: Kill 75 Bloodbane Devoted.
- Objective #2: Destroy 4 Standing Stones.
- Objective #3: Kill Fjotli Bloodbane.

Pit of the Forsaken

- Objective #1: Rescue 30 Peasants.
- Objective #2: Kill Madren; Kill 5 Plagued Knights.
- Objective #3: Kill the Festering Abomination.

Ulfenwyr

- Objective #1: Kill 40 Bilerot Scavengers.
- Objective #2: Kill 10 Bilerot Plaguebearers; Kill 25 Bilerot Nurglings.
- Objective #3: Kill Khaankr the Rotten.

WARCAMP: NONE

CHAPTERS 1–2

"I am standing in front of the great commander, listening to him tell us our mission. My life depends on this mission. I must succeed and become one of the Raven Host or else die. My father is a Raven Host, thus our family honor is at stake. If I don't succeed, then I will kill myself or else my father will kill me himself. Failure is not an option."

—Lorend, Last of the Name "Bazeele"

CHAPTER 1: PROVING GROUNDS

New soldiers are arriving to help on the attack against Thorshafn. This will be their proving grounds.

PUBLIC QUESTS

Ruinous Powers

- Objective #1: Kill 25 Thorshafn Militiamen.
- Objective #2: Harvest 25 Souls from Tombstones.
- Objective #3: Kill Kar'thok the Bloodhowler.

CHAPTER 2: RITE OF PASSAGE

Haldar has proven his worth by bringing back trophies of his kill. Tonight they will celebrate, then tomorrow they move on to more killing. Haldar has the taste of violence and blood now and wants more.

PUBLIC QUESTS

Suderholm

- Objective #1: Kill 80 Suderholm Citizens.
- Objective #2: Set 11 Suderholm Buildings Afire.
- Objective #3: Kill Aborrah.

Destruction of the Weak

- Objective #1: Kill 50 Refugee Fighters.
- Objective #2: Kill 12 Refugee Duelists.
- Objective #3: Kill Haldin Wuertz; Kill Tonas Jorgan; Kill Gherig the Faithful.

Holmsteinn Revisited

- Objective #1: Collect 25 Holmsteinn Supplies.
- Objective #2: Kill 5 Norland Verkenners; Kill 5 Norland Verkenners.
- Objective #3: Kill Boswald Griev.

WARCAMP: BLESSED GATHERING

This warcamp is in a great position for attacking the port. You should have the advantage over the Empire scum.

TIER 1   NORSCA

TO TROLL COUNTRY

TO NORDLAND

LEGEND

RvR Area (Outlined)

 Chapter Unlock (Destruction)
1 – Chaos Chapter 1
2 – Chaos Chapter 2

 Chapter Unlock (Order)
4 – Empire Chapter 4

 Major Landmarks
1 – Armund's Barrow
2 – Tomb of Ravenborne
3 – Skaldbjorn

4 – Charred Lands
5 – Watchtower of Selthis Lysk
6 – Gothland Forest
7 – Spindekraken
8 – Gotland
9 – Thorshafn Crypt

 Public Quests (Destruction)
1 – Ruinous Powers
2 – Destruction of the Weak
3 – Superholm
4 – Holmstein Revisited

 Public Quests (Order)
1 – Altar of Bloodbane
2 – Ulfenwyr
3 – Pit of the Forsaken

 Battle Objectives
1 – Lost Lagoon

Lairs
1 – Silveroak

EMPIRE

Chapters 7–9

"Searching this city to find the contaminated water has been a very dirty and dangerous job. One never knows when a dangerous beast might be right around the corner. And one has to worry about the plague. I have to be constantly on guard. I hope we find this water soon. I would hate to see this plague spread to other cities. Word is that one of the next areas where Chaos plans to spread the plague is Talabecland, which is where my family lives."

—Frederic Lehmann, Empire Soldier

Chapter 7: Riddles and Clues

A group of soldiers discover clues as to what is causing the plague when they see holes and pits dug into the ground. Evil doctors have been digging up a green stone and combining it with vile ingredients to create the Chaos Plague.

Public Quests

Hochnar

- Objective #1: Kill 75 Dark Marauders; Kill 35 Dark Raiders.
- Objective #2: Kill 10 Dark Champions.
- Objective #3: Kill Ferdarch the Destroyer.

Chapter 8: The Siege of Bohsenfels

Captain Gaertner and her troops are defending the town of Bohsenfels against the Warhost from the north. The Captain and her troops were following the trail of the plague.

Public Quests

The Black Mire

- Objective #1: Kill 25 Black Mire Gors; Kill 25 Black Mire Ungors.
- Objective #2: Kill 8 Chaos Trolls.
- Objective #3: Kill Ghuurkor.

Siege of Bohsenfels

- Objective #1: Kill 35 Savage Warriors; Kill 5 Savage Champions.

- Objective #2: Destroy 5 Siege Mortars; Destroy 5 Seige Cannons.
- Objective #3: Kill Haargen Bloodmane.

Chapter 9: Wolfenburg

Naubhof's Huntsmen have come into the city looking for crates of contaminated water, which is being stored in the city to be used to spread the plague to other cities. This information was obtained when the Order of the Griffon confiscated a journal from one of the mad doctors.

Public Quests

Gore Wood

- Objective #1: Kill 80 Bloodstained Cultists; Kill 20 Bloodstained Maulers.
- Objective #2: Kill 10 Howling Bloodletters.
- Objective #3: Kill Bloodmagus Kristof; Kill 6 Raging Bloodletters.

Howling Vale

- Objective #1: Gather 40 Much Needed Supplies.
- Objective #2: Kill 7 Bestigor Raiders.
- Objective #3: Kill Shaman Ghaarkil; Kill Shaman Brekhaal; Kill Shaman Karkaris.

Warcamp: Troll Country

You'll have to make the hike from Troll Country to Ostland if you want to battle Destruction. Be sure to stock up on potions and supplies so you don't waste time running back and forth.

CHAOS

Chapters 5, 7

"I and a small group of Sorcerers are here to find the Scepter. I know others are also looking for the Darkflame Scepter, but I want to be the one to find it. I must regain Tchar'zanek's favor after failing him on my last undertaking. I will succeed or else die trying. I have no choice."

—Vinhnes the Sorcerer

Chapter 5: Into the Shadows

Turaanos was dispatched with his charges by Tchar'zanek himself to obtain the Darkflame Scepter. Turaanos is to search for the Shaman of the Beastmen in the Forest of Shadows; rumor places the Scepter in the beast's possession. The Darkflame Scepter is one of four artifacts to be used in a powerful spell.

Public Quests

Bells of War

- Objective #1: Kill 75 Alerted Militia; Kill 10 Milita Sergeant.
- Objective #2: Destroy the Bell.
- Objective #3: Kill Lord Duchenhof; Kill 4 Knights of Felde.

OSTLAND

Spirits of the Shadow

- Objective #1: Light 10 Kindling and Burn the Forest; Kill 50 Shadow Spites.
- Objective #2: Defeat 9 Shadow Dryads.
- Objective #3: Defeat Shadowkin.

Chapter 6: Channeller of Daemons (begins in Troll Country)

You will be given quests in Troll Country that will eventually lead you into Ostland where various public quests are located.

Public Quests

Reaper's Circle

- Objective #1: Kill 50 Rankhide Wolves.
- Objective #2: Kill 5 Dark Apprentices.
- Objective #3: Kill Kraunel the Reaper.

Wayshrine of Sigmar

- Objective #1: Kill 50 Felde Refugees.
- Objective #2: Kill 5 Doom Prophets.
- Objective #3: Kill Oswald Striker.

Chapter 7: The Darkfire Scepter

The Scepter was almost within reach for Kournar the Chosen, but Ragash Blood Horns was able to escape because of the Order of the Griffon's attack. Kournar vows that he will take care of the Griffon troops and recover the Scepter.

Public Quests

Ragash's Last Stand

- Objective #1: Kill 50 Blood Horn Beastmen.
- Objective #2: Kill 5 Blood Horn Shamans.
- Objective #3: Kill Ragash Blood Horns.

Warcamp: Raven's Edge

Poised on the edge of Raven's End Woods, the Destruction warcamp will soon send the Raven Host against the forest. The area's terrain constraints prevent a bold counter-attack, but it will easily be enough to send the Empire cowards screaming for their wives and mothers.

TIER 2

OSTLAND

TO TROLL COUNTRY

TO TROLL COUNTRY

TO NORDLAND

TO HIGH PASS

LEGEND

WARCAMPS: I – RAVEN'S EDGE

RvR AREA (OUTLINED)

CHAPTER UNLOCK (DESTRUCTION)
5 – CHAOS CHAPTER 5
7 – CHAOS CHAPTER 7

CHAPTER UNLOCK (ORDER)
7 – EMPIRE CHAPTER 7
8 – EMPIRE CHAPTER 8
9 – EMPIRE CHAPTER 9

MAJOR LANDMARKS
1 – OSTLAND TROOPS
2 – CLEANSING FLAME WARRIORS
3 – LOST CAVERN
4 – GERSTMANN CRYPT
5 – WAYSHIRE OF ULRIC

6 – FORGOTTEN GRAVEYARD
7 – HILLSBOTTOM LAKE
8 – BADGER'S NOOK AND
    LUTHOR'S POND
9 – SHADOW LAKE BRIGANDS
10 – CAVE
11 – CATACOMBS
12 – GRIM MONASTERY
13 – ALTERED BEASTS
14 – CATACOMBS
15 – LONELY FARM
16 – TOWER OF RUIN
17 – BLACK MIRE BELL TOWER
18 – FERLANGEN CEMETERY

PUBLIC QUESTS (DESTRUCTION)
1 – SILKENS
2 – BELLS OF WAR
3 – SPIRITS OF THE SHADOW
4 – KRUL GOR HERD
5 – REAPERS CIRCLE
6 – WAYSHIRE OF SIGMAR
7 – RAGASH'S LAST STAND

PUBLIC QUESTS (ORDER)
1 – HOCHNAR
2 – SIEGE OF BOHSENFELS
3 – BLACK MIRE
4 – NURENMIR'S LANCERS
5 – GORE WOOD

6 – HOWLING VALE
7 – WOLFENBURG

BATTLE OBJECTIVES
1 – CRYPT OF WEAPONS
    (ARTISAN'S GIFT)
2 – KINSHEL'S STRONGHOLD
    (HEALING BOON)

I – MANDRED'S HOLD

FLIGHT MASTER

TROLL COUNTRY

EMPIRE

CHAPTERS 5–6

"I have never seen such a horrific sight. The plague spreads so fast and so many have been claimed. The town of Felde is empty except for the troops. At night, I know I can hear the ghosts of the villagers. The community is a village of the damned now. I do not see how it can ever be the friendly and lively city that it was. I worry about the fate of the Empire."

—Krok Zummerman

CHAPTER 5: AID FROM AFAR

Siegmund Kraemer and his son, who had recently arrived, discuss the plague the son saw in Nordland. Kraemer and his son agree that it was the same plague that had started in Felde. Kraemer sends his son to Gotland to tell what he had seen of the plague in Felde, which could be very useful information.

PUBLIC QUESTS

Plague on the Wind

- Objective #1: Kill 40 Plagued Farmers; Kill 10 Plagued Harvesters.
- Objective #2: Destroy 15 Plague Carts; Destroy 4 Plagued Scarecrows.
- Objective #3: Kill Disvark Bilewind; Keep 4 Farms Ablaze.

CHAPTER 6: SINS OF THE PAST

Captain Breitenhach and his troops are camped out in the empty town of Felde. The troops found one of the noblemen hiding and confronted him about sacrificing the lives of the peasants for the promise of eternal youth. Thus the peasants became victims of the plague and the plague has spread throughout the region.

PUBLIC QUESTS

The Blighted Farm

- Objective #1: Kill 35 Blighted Mutants.
- Objective #2: Destroy 3 Black Altars; Kill 3 Blighted Demagogues.
- Objective #3: Kill Valgar the Leper.

CHAPTER 7: RIDDLES AND CLUES

You will be given quests in Ostland that will eventually lead you to Troll Country.

PUBLIC QUESTS

Lissariel's Glade

- Objective #1: Deliver 50 Wood to Engineer Rulf.
- Objective #2: Kill 12 Glade Dryads.
- Objective #3: Kill Deeproot.

WARCAMP: BLACKBRAMBLE HOLLOW

As the number of troops in the Destruction warcamp grows, the forces of Order hastily construct the Hollow in the hopes of matching their enemy's strength. Now the goal is to bottle up the Chaos army on the borders of Troll Country.

CHAOS

CHAPTERS 6, 8–9

"Destroying the Chaos Troll was the most rigorous battle I have ever been in. Once a normal Troll, the beast was transformed into a Chaos Troll after consuming the Soulblight Stone. The deadly creature could even vomit forth acid."

—Harold the Magus

CHAPTER 6: CHANNELLER OF DAEMONS

Urzula, a channeller of Daemons, warns that an army approaches from the north. The search for the Darkfire Scepter had to be delayed for the battle. The quests for this chapter lead into Ostland, where you will find plenty of public quests.

CHAPTER 7: THE DARKFIRE SCEPTER

These public quests begin in Troll Country but end in Ostland. Be sure to seek out the following public quests across the border.

PUBLIC QUESTS

Bog Hunters

- Objective #1: Disable 15 Bog Traps; Kill 35 Mire Huntsmen.
- Objective #2: Kill 6 Mire Huntmasters.
- Objective #3: Kill Otto von Buergh.

CHAPTER 8: THE SOULBLIGHT STONE

While wearing the Soulblight Stone around his neck, Bjarne was eaten by a huge Troll. Halza, the new leader, vows that tomorrow they will find the troll and cut open his stomach and remove the prized Soulblight Stone.

PUBLIC QUESTS

Lursa's Blight

- Objective #1: Kill 45 Rot Priests.
- Objective #2: Kill 9 Rot Bearers.
- Objective #3: Kill Lursa the Blight Sage.

Trovolek

- Objective #1: Kill 50 Trovolek Defenders; Kill 10 Trovolek Seers.
- Objective #2: Use 20 Kindling to Light the Houses on Fire.
- Objective #3: Kill Kulen the Wolf.

CHAPTER 9: BELLY OF THE BEAST

A huge Troll consumed Bjarne, who was wearing the Soulblight Stone. The magic of the stone transformed the Troll into a diseased Troll with unnatural strength. Gunnar and his troop of Raven Host warriors are in Troll Country, and they will kill the Chaos Troll no matter how many battles it takes.

PUBLIC QUESTS

Plague Altar

- Objective #1: Destroy 10 Standing Stones.
- Objective #2: Kill 10 Bloated Plague-bearers.
- Objective #3: Kill Bulvous the Plaguechyld.

Tearing the Portal

- Objective #1: Kill 40 Infected Warriors; Kill 10 Infected Champions.
- Objective #2: Protect Belarrl the Chosen.
- Objective #3: Slay Sysstos the Wretched.

WARCAMP: DESTRUCTION

There isn't one in this immediate area, so choose your allies wisely to stay alive longer.

TIER 2

TROLL COUNTRY

TO TALABECLAND

TO OSTLAND

LEGEND

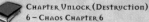

WARCAMPS: I – BRICKBRAMBLE HOLLOW

RVR AREA (OUTLINED)

CHAPTER UNLOCK (DESTRUCTION)
6 – CHAOS CHAPTER 6
8 – CHAOS CHAPTER 8
9 – CHAOS CHAPTER 9

CHAPTER UNLOCK (ORDER)
5 – EMPIRE CHAPTER 5
6 – EMPIRE CHAPTER 6

MAJOR LANDMARKS
1 – SUSKARG CAVES (CAVE)
2 – THE TROLL RIFT (CAVE)
3 – CORRUPTED WOLFLORD
4 – RAGNHILDER'S HUT
5 – DEN
6 – PLAGUE GRAVES
7 – EAGLE'S NESTS

8 – DEEPROCK MINE
9 – GRANT'S LAIR
10 – SOULBLIGHT CULTISTS
11 – SHIVER HOLLOW
12 – ICEFLOW MAW
13 – FROZEN CAVERN
14 – OGRE HUNTERS
15 – BLIGHTGORE

PUBLIC QUESTS (DESTRUCTION)
1 – TROVOLEK
2 – PLAGUEWOOD THICKET
3 – LURSA'S BLIGHT
4 – BLIGHTSTONE TROLLS
5 – PLAGUE ALTAR
6 – TEARING THE PORTAL
7 – BOG HUNTERS
8 – GRIFFON OUTPOST

PUBLIC QUESTS (ORDER)
1 – WELCOME TO
   TROLL COUNTRY
2 – PLAGUE ON THE WIND
3 – DEATHSTONE QUARRY
4 – BLIGHTED FARM
5 – GRAVE DIGGERS
6 – SLAYER'S DEMISE
7 – LISSARIEL'S GLADE
8 – PLAGUE TROLLS

BATTLE OBJECTIVES
1 – RUINS OF GREYSTONE KEEP
   (MERCHANT'S GIFT)
2 – MONASTERY OF MORR
   (DEFENSIVE BOON)

LAIRS
1 – METOH

I – STONETROLL KEEP

FLIGHT MASTER

HIGH PASS

CHAPTERS 10–12

EMPIRE

"Having already lost several of my family to the plague, I am as determined as my leaders to retrieve the vital plans and stop the plague. I keep thinking about my family back home and I hope they are still alive. Time is of the essence, but the battle up this steep hill is moving so slowly. But determination will get us there. The Empire has no choice."

—Oscar Tidlemeyer

CHAPTER 10: THE SEARCH BEGINS

Captain Nuhr and his troops are on a mission to find Doctor Zumwald, who is carrying vital plans that could save the Empire from the plague that is devastating the countryside.

PUBLIC QUESTS

Chaos Ruins

- Objective #1: Destroy 20 Power Stones.
- Objective #2: Kill 8 Shifting Sorcerers.
- Objective #3: Kill Velethor the Shifter.

Tomb of the Traitor

- Objective #1: Kill 80 Blood Flayerkin; Kill 40 Blood Warriors.
- Objective #2: Find 3 Pieces of the Shattered Key.
- Objective #3: Kill Hertzig the Traitor.

CHAPTER 11: AN UPHILL BATTLE

Grizela, a guide for the Order of the Griffon, finds herself in charge after her leader dies. She leads the troops up a steep hill, paying for every inch gained to reach the Shrine of Tzeentch.

PUBLIC QUESTS

Cult of the Magus

- Objective #1: Kill 20 Magi Orator; Kill 30 Magi Destroyer; Kill 30 Magi Seer.
- Objective #2: Kill 2 Magi Chosen; Kill 7 Magi Devourers.
- Objective #3: Kill Hredric Blackheart; Kill 2 Magic Champions.

Temple of Change

- Objective #1: Kill 30 Changing Cultists; Kill 35 Changing Magi; Kill 65 Changing Zealots.
- Objective #2: Destroy the Monolith.

- Objective #3: Kill Zyra the Ever-Changing.

CHAPTER 12: ICE AND FIRE

The Empire had saved one of its best weapons, Wizard Konrad Riese, for the final assault upon the Shrine of Tzeentch. Due to a surprise attack of the Raven Host, the Empire had to retreat and fight another day. The Chaos troops have won that battle, but the Empire troops will be back. They have no choice.

PUBLIC QUESTS

Echoes of War

- Objective #1: Clear the Grounds.
- Objective #2: Survive the Marauder charges for 10 minutes.
- Objective #3: Kill Cirosyan Silverstaff or Kill Hinrik Cleaveclaw.

Shrine of Tzeentch

- Objective #1: Kill 60 Keeper of the Shrine.
- Objective #2: Destroy 10 Celestial Wizard Shards; Destroy 10 Light Wizard Shards; Destroy 10 Jade Wizard Shards.
- Objective #3: Defeat Tzeentchian Artifact.

WARCAMP: DOGBITE RIDGE

This is the first line of defense, but the lack of walls hurts. The Order gathers its strength for the ultimate battle just beyond the ridge.

CHAPTERS 13–14

CHAOS

"Watching the Whispering Voice at work has been an amazing experience. Very few have ever watched him interrogate a Daemonic prisoner. I was truly chosen by the gods to learn from the best. I hope one day to excel as he does. When I interrogate my next prisoner, I will apply what I have learned from the Whispering Voice's example. To finally see the Daemon break and reveal the Sigil location will be something I always remember. Today has been a glorious day for the Raven Host."

—Tikamo

CHAPTER 13: THE PRISONER

The Whispering Voice is questioning one of the Daemons of the Blood God to learn the location of the Sigil of Malice. Sigil of Malice is the last remaining relic of the four that Tchar'zanek needs for his great spell.

PUBLIC QUESTS

Guts Out

- Objective #1: Kill 75 Icemaw Ogres; Kill 45 Icemaw Gnoblar.
- Objective #2: Kill 12 Bloodcrazed Gorgers.
- Objective #3: Kill Thorgh Gutsplitter; Kill Ugruk; Kill 2 Icemaw Butchers.

Tempest Horn

- Objective #1: Kill 30 Followers of the Blood God.
- Objective #2: Protect 5 Tempest Sorcerers.
- Objective #3: Kill Daarghor the Decapitator.

CHAPTER 14: THE SIGIL OF MALICE

The Champion of Khorne, Naar'Kohros the Merciless, uses the Sigil of Malice he wears in a battle, causing the Raven Host to retreat.

PUBLIC QUESTS

Beacon of Firengrom

- Objective #1: Kill 75 Bonestomper Tainted; Kill 25 Beacon Gnoblar.
- Objective #2: Kill 3 Bonestomper Touched.
- Objective #3: Kill Fargus Headswallower; Kill 2 Bonestomper Magus.

Temple of Heimkel

- Objective #1: Kill 80 Bloodforged Warrior; Kill 50 Bloodforged Champion.
- Objective #2: Destroy the Bloodforge.
- Objective #3: Kill Trohm the Destroyer; Kill 2 Bloodforged Chosen.

Tower of the Elves

- Objective #1: Kill 20 Crystalgrove Guards; Kill 60 Crystalgrove Scouts; Kill 85 Crystalgrove Archers.
- Objective #2: Destroy 6 Bolt Throwers.
- Objective #3: Kill Kalandrys Starweaver; Kill 5 Elven Mage-Council.

WARCAMP: NONE

WARHAMMER ONLINE
AGE OF RECKONING

TIER 3

HIGH PASS

TO OSTLAND

TO CHAOS WASTES

TO TALABECLAND

LEGEND

WARCAMPS: 1 – DOGBITE RIDGE

————— **RVR AREA (OUTLINED)**

CHAPTER UNLOCK (DESTRUCTION)
13 – CHAOS CHAPTER 13
14 – CHAOS CHAPTER 14

CHAPTER UNLOCK (ORDER)
10 – EMPIRE CHAPTER 10
11 – EMPIRE CHAPTER 11
12 – EMPIRE CHAPTER 12

MAJOR LANDMARKS
1 – BONESTOMPER OGRES
2 – OGRE APPROACH
3 – OATHBEARER CAMP
4 – CULTIST CAMP

5 – HORROR RIFTS
6 – BONESTOMPER OGRE CAMPS
7 – VLADESAUL'S DEFENSE
8 – CAVE
9 – BLOOD MARAUDERS
10 – CAVE
11 – LOST MINERS (CAVE)
12 – BRIGHTHOLLOW TOWER
13 – CAVE (PASSAGE TO
       JAGGEDSPINE RIDGE)

 PUBLIC QUESTS (DESTRUCTION)
1 – TEMPLE OF HEIMKELL
2 – BEACON OF FIRENGRAM
3 – GUT'S OUT

4 – KEEP OF ASAVAR KUL
5 – TEMPEST HORN
6 – TOWER OF THE ELVES

 PUBLIC QUESTS (ORDER)
1 – FOETID PLAINS
2 – TOMB OF THE TRAITOR
3 – CHAOS RUINS
4 – LAKE OF THE DAMNED
5 – CULT OF THE MAGUS
6 – TEMPLE OF CHANGE
7 – ECHOES OF WAR
8 – GRISLY HERD
9 – SHRINE OF TZEENTCH

 BATTLE OBJECTIVES
1 – FEITEN'S LOCK
     (DEFENSIVE BOON)
2 – OGRUND'S TAVERN
     (HEALING BOON)
3 – HALLENFURT MANOR
     (ARTISAN'S GIFT)

 1 – STONECLAW CASTLE

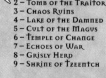 **FLIGHT MASTER**

TALABECLAND

EMPIRE

CHAPTERS 13–14

"While I sit here writing my last letter to my family, I remember the good and bad times. It is for them that I am here, and why I have volunteered for this suicide mission. It is time for me to finish my letter and get ready for my final mission—to blow up the bridge and cut off the enemy approach."

—Wilhelm Hirsch

CHAPTER 13: HERGIG BRIDGE

The Witch Hunter issued an invitation to the captain to hunt the remaining leader in the region. The captain had to decline because his duty was to blow up the Hergig Bridge.

PUBLIC QUESTS

Bitterschaum Swamp

- Objective #1: Kill 45 Swamptoof Squigs; Kill 60 Swamptoof Patrollers; Kill 90 Swamptoof Shooters.
- Objective #2: Kill 12 Swamptoof Bashas.
- Objective #3: Kill Butghas Badwind; Kill Urghit 'Eadbursta; Kill Gribnok the Weirdboy; Kill Wugot Swamptoof.

Witch Fire Glade

- Objective #1: Kill 60 Witch Fire Cultists; Kill 30 Witch Fire Acolytes.
- Objective #2: Kill 12 Cult Witches.
- Objective #3: Kill Sartrassa the Purged.

CHAPTER 14: SACRIFICES

Brave men of the Order of the Griffon had to be sacrificed to blow up the Unterbaum Bridge. The warhost will not able to cross at Unterbaum now.

PUBLIC QUESTS

Meuselbach Farm

- Objective #1: Kill 80 Corrupted Farmhands; Kill 30 Corrupted Overseers.
- Objective #2: Destroy 30 Prepared Crates; Use 8 Kindling to Light the Wagons on Fire.
- Objective #3: Kill Erik Meuselbach.

Unterbaum Castle

- Objective #1: Kill 70 Bane Knights; Kill 35 Bane Champions; Kill 25 Bane Sorcerers.

- Objective #2: Kill Biilos the Rotting; Kill Kanscere the Grotesque; Kill Sikous.
- Objective #3: Kill Nagrech the Festering.

Unterbaum Cemetery

- Objective #1: Kill 100 Mindless Zombies.
- Objective #2: Burn 3 Festering Corpse Carts.
- Objective #3: Kill Podgore the Leaking.

WARCAMP: NONE

CHAOS

CHAPTERS 10–12

"It infuriates me to think Lady Krueger was able to claim the Corrupter's Crown. Now she uses the Crown against us. Our leader, Ulvarin, has sent a rider for the warhost. When warhost comes, we will take revenge and become even more powerful. Nothing is going to stop us."

—Billy Todlison, Warhost Runner

CHAPTER 10: ENEMY TERRITORY

A small warband from the Raven Host has crept into Talabecland to find the Corrupter's Crown. The Corrupter's Crown is the third piece needed for a powerful spell that Tchar'zanek is going to use.

PUBLIC QUESTS

Mudflats

- Objective #1: Kill 35 Daemonic Coquettes; Kill 50 Peasants.
- Objective #2: Close 9 Small Rifts.
- Objective #3: Kill Stingwhip the Voracious.

Suderheim

- Objective #1: Search 10 Chests, 10 Crates, 10 Barrels, and 10 Baskets.
- Objective #2: Kill 6 Serpent's Fang Bandits; Kill 3 Serpent's Fang Thugs.
- Objective #3: Kill Reinaulk Scarblade; Kill 4 Scarblade's Assassins.

CHAPTER 11: VISIONS IN FLAME

In their search for the Corrupter's Crown, the warriors of the Raven Host have run afoul of a band of brigands. Weeks before, the leader of the brigands had stolen the Corrupter's Crown.

PUBLIC QUESTS

Army of Faith

- Objective #1: Kill 75 Peasants.
- Objective #2: Kill 4 Warrior Priests.
- Objective #3: Kill Arch Lector Ansel.

Serpent's Fang Bandits

- Objective #1: Kill 45 Decadent Bandits; Kill 85 Lounging Bandit.
- Objective #2: Capture 12 Bandit Wenches.
- Objective #3: Kill 12 Daemonettes.
- Objective #4: Kill Lenz the Serpent's Head.

CHAPTER 12: STAND OFF

Lady Krueger had hired a brigand to retrieve the Corrupter's Crown for her. The Raven Host warriors and their leader Ulvarin have tried to take the Crown from Lady Krueger several times but have failed.

PUBLIC QUESTS

Kruegerhaus

- Objective #1: Kill 50 Writhing Daemonettes.
- Objective #2: Kill Elizabeth Krueger.
- Objective #3: Kill Brunhilde Krueger; Kill Rebekka Krueger.

Bitterspring

- Objective #1: Kill 75 Bitterspring Peasants; Kill 15 Talabecland Militia.
- Objective #2: Kill 10 Griffon Spymasters.
- Objective #3: Kill Rolf Anderson; Slaughter the Mob.

Village Vermin

- Objective #1: Kill 55 Verminkin Night Hunters; Kill 75 Verminkin Night Runners.
- Objective #2: Kill 7 Verminkin Fangmasters.
- Objective #3: Kill Ikthik Poisonblood.

WARCAMP: HELLFANG RIDGE

With all the leaders of the warcamp having been slain, there is a lot of dissension. Among the arguing and fighting, who will take the lead?

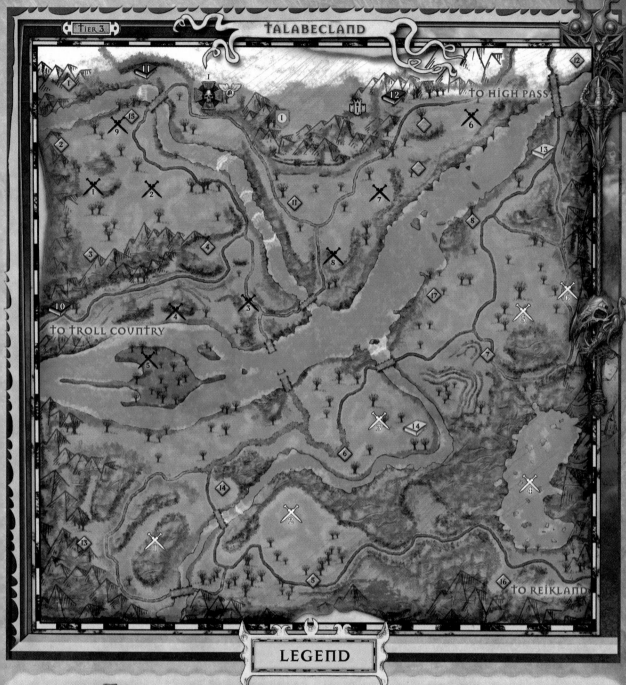

TIER 3

TALABECLAND

TO HIGH PASS

TO TROLL COUNTRY

TO REIKLAND

LEGEND

WARCAMPS: 1– Hellfang Ridge

RvR Area (Outlined)

Chapter Unlock (Destruction)
10 – Chaos Chapter 10
11 – Chaos Chapter 11
12 – Chaos Chapter 12

Chapter Unlock (Order)
13 – Empire Chapter 13
14 – Empire Chapter 14

Major Landmarks
1 – Griffin camps
2 – Join the Hunt
3 – Stags and Hounds

4 – Tower of the Fallen
5 – Road to Reikland
6 – Unterbaum
7 – Blackhorn Herdstone
8 – Chaos Landing
9 – Talabecland Troops
10 – Talabecland Bandits
11 – Horned Tower
12 – Ambushing Marauders
13 – Shrine of Sigmar
14 – Bell Tower
15 – Dortwald
16 – Bell Tower
17 – Bell Tower

Public Quests (Destruction)
1 – Serpent's Fang Bandits
2 – Army of Faith
3 – Suderheim
4 – Steinbruck Manor
5 – Mudflats
6 – Bitterspring
7 – Kruegerhaus
8 – Village Vermin
9 – Knightly Riders

Public Quests (Order)
1 – Meuselbach Farm
2 – Unterbaum Castle
3 – Unterbaum Cemetery

4 – Bitterschaum Swamp
5 – Witch Fire Glade
6 – Wagon Defense

Battle Objectives
1 – Verentane's Tower
(Merchant's Gift)

1 – Passwatch Castle

Flight Master

ALTDORF

EMPIRE

CITY CAMPAIGN

At first glance, Altdorf appears to be a thriving city that has been thrust into the middle of a bloody war. Its citizens are a mixture of many classes of life, from peasants and beggars all the way up to high members of society. The residents refer to Altdorf as the "Center of the World."

When you first enter Altdorf, you are greeted by the town crier, Kiosch. He introduces you to the town and suggests that you explore the districts of Altdorf. Of course, he talks about the Plague that is running rampant around the Emperor's Circle, that the merchants in the plaza are all but honest, and, of course, the nobles don't usually frequent the Docks area.

The districts in this city appear to tell a tale all their own.

The Slums, which are occupied by the town's peasants and beggars, appear as one would expect. Dilapidated buildings, filth in the streets and air, and even the bodies of their dead can be found in the alleyways. Surprisingly, though, this area is home to the Bright Wizard College, which is a spectacle unto itself.

How does one fit a college into such a small area? Why magic, of course! The tower for the college appears to be an active volcano, spewing out molten earth from a gaping maw on the side of the tower. Unfortunately this causes a lot of the dirt and pollution that the area's inhabitants have to deal with. It is also fair to mention that the college is noted as a contested area in this city.

The Temple of Sigmar is considered the town's holy ground. Pristine and bright, it is located closest to the Lord's Row where the lords and ladies of the town can go to worship their deity. Occasionally you will find some peasants who show up to pay their respects.

The Docks bustle with goods being shipped in and out of this port city. Of course, this area also contains some of the seedier places in Altdorf. Just be on your guard when visiting this scenic, yet potentially dangerous, section of town. You can even see a quite remarkable warship docked in the channel.

The War Quarters areas are as the name sounds. It is very militant in appearance, with guards and warriors training here constantly. War machines and statues of the realm's great champions are on display in the center courtyard. The two training areas become part of an RvR objective during an attack from the Chaos side.

The Palace itself is a grand display of architecture and wealth. The emperor Karl Franz can be found here, supervising the day-to-day running of this fine city. It is worth noting that he is part of an RvR battle later on.

PUBLIC QUESTS

Bank Robbery

- City Ranks 2–4
- Lord's Row/First Bank of Altdorf
- Objective: Recover 30 Hot Karls.

Gagrus the Unclean One

- City Ranks 5 (Rare Spawn)
- Slums and Docks
- Objective: Kill Gagrus the Unclean One.

Delicate Work

- City Ranks 3–5
- War Quarters
- Objective: Collect 15 Steam Tank Parts.
- And many more to be discovered!

DUNGEONS

The Sewers

Entrance Location: Slums

The Sewers beneath Altdorf are geared for adventurers in the level 9 through 10 range. There are three sewer entrances in total. The rotten flesh of zombies adds to the odorous passageways below, where Clanrats skitter and man-eaters dwell. Corpses line the waterways, and fallen wizards talk to themselves, when not casting spells to thwart those foolish enough to enter these environs. Rat Ogres, packmasters, recluses, and other various vermin call this place home. Should players venture into the high-level area, they shall meet Goradian, a scientist gone mad, mumbling and performing tests on those that stumble upon him...

Warpblade Tunnels

Entrance Location: Reikland's Arms, in Lord's Row district, the Mastiff's, in Market Square, the Blowhole, at the Docks, and the Screaming Cat tavern in the Slums.

The Warpot clan of the Warpblade have burrowed from unknown depths and lie in wait beneath the city of Altdorf. Man-made structure or foundations of layered rock and wooden supports give way to the Warpblade tunnels, which are more organic-looking, with twists and turns. The tunnels are lengthy, with Clanrats and Rat Ogres acting as the physical muscle, while Moulders practice their sorceries. Pipes, broken ladders, and unusable bridges furnish the walls, which are supported with wooden beams and archways throughout. The apparent leader of this magical clan of rat people, Grey Seer Quol'tik, lies at the end of the winding passageways.

Sigmar's Crypts

Entrance Location: Temple of Sigmar

Legends say two lectors, twins Maxwell and Markus Matzenbach, let corruption crawl into their hearts and abused their positions of power. Tempted by death magic, the twins were reborn unto darkness as the fallen lectors Zakarai and Verrimus. The Order of the Cleansing Flame requires fearless adventurers to purge the Temple of Sigmar's underbelly of its foul denizens before the citizens of Altdorf learn that even the most sacred of places is vulnerable in this dark age.

DESTRUCTION RvR PQs

Bright College

- City Ranks ALL (Captured Altdorf)
- Bright College
- Objective #1: Defeat 4 Aqshy Gatekeepers.
- Objective #2: Destroy 6 Aqshy Activators.
- Objective #3: Defeat Supreme Patriarch Thyrus Gormann.

Temple of Sigmar

- City Ranks ALL (Captured Altdorf)
- Temple of Sigmar
- Objective #1: Destroy the 4 courtyard shrines, Destroy the Sigmar door.
- Objective #2: Defeat 4 Temple Lectors.
- Objective #3: Defeat Grand Theogonist Volkmar.

TIER 4

ALTDORF

LEGEND

Altdorf District Name
1 – War Quarters
2 – Emperor's Circle
3 – Lord's Row
4 – The Slums
5 – The Docks
6 – Market Square
7 – Palace Courtyard
8 – Emperor's Palace

Major Landmarks
1 – Mass Transit
2 – The Altdorf Library
3 – Temple of Sigmar
4 – Bright Wizard College

Public Quests (Order)
1 – Bank Robbery (Lord's Row near First Bank of Altdorf) (City Ranks 2-4)
2 – Pub Brawl (Blowhole Tavern) (City Ranks 2-4)
3 – Gargus the Unclean One (City Ranks 4-5)
4 – Delicate Work (City Ranks 3-5)
5 – Daemons of the Night (City Ranks 4-5)
6 – Cult of the Feathered Coin (City Ranks All)
7 – March of the Dead (City Ranks 1-2)
8 – Pale-Eye Hideout (City Ranks 3-5)

Instances / Dungeons
1 – Altdorf Sewer Entrance
2 – Entrance to Bright Wizard College
3 – Altdorf Sewer Entrance
4 – Main Entrance to Altdorf
5 – Warpblade Tunnels (inside the Reikland Arms Basement)

6 – Sigmar Crypts
7 – Warpblade Tunnels (inside the Mastiff's End Basement)
8 – Warpblade Tunnels (inside the Blowhole Basement)
9 – Warpblade Tunnels (inside the Screaming Cat Tavern Basement)

Flight Master

Banks

Auctioneer

Entrances to the City

CHAOS WASTES

CHAPTERS 20–22

EMPIRE

"There is great hope and determination among the Empire troops in these desolate lands to find the Inevitable City. I feel that we are getting close. We will find the city and will make the Chaos legions pay for all the suffering they have inflicted on the Empire."

—Simon, Empire Soldier

CHAPTER 20: A DESPERATE GAMBIT

The Order of the Griffon is slowly pushing back the Necromancer's undead army. The objective is to take the Necromancer alive in hopes of finding the Inevitable City.

PUBLIC QUESTS

Dances of Bones

- Objective #1: Kill 50 Skeletal Wrathborn; Kill 75 Skeletal Hellfighter.
- Objective #2: Kill Marighast the Vile.
- Objective #3: Kill Marighast the Liche.

Razing an Army

- Objective #1: Kill 50 Frostmarrow Braineaters.
- Objective #2: Kill 6 Frostmarrow Wailer.
- Objective #3: Destroy Ahrok the Obliterator.
- Objective #4: Kill 2 Frostmarrow Deadraisers.

CHAPTER 21: MEN OF FAITH

As the troops get closer to the Inevitable City, it's harder to keep the madness and the terror at bay. The battles have been the saving grace by keeping the troops focused on the fighting.

PUBLIC QUESTS

Madness

- Objective #1: Kill 40 Gibbering Mutants; Kill 40 Mutated Madmen.
- Objective #2: Kill Orag Fleshsplitter; Kill Systrix the Damned; Kill Rolfgar Changewarden.
- Objective #3: Kill The Corrupter.

The Siren Sea

- Objective #1: Kill 75 Siren Daemonettes; Free 35 Songdrawn Captives.

- Objective #2: Topple 6 Siren Braziers.
- Objective #3: Kill Kharessa the Beautiful.

CHAPTER 22: THE EBON KEEP

Even though the troops have lost contact with the Empire, which might already lie in ruins, they are determined to continue and find the Inevitable City. They must first destroy the gatekeeper named Kaluthax the All-Seeing in the Ebon Keep.

PUBLIC QUESTS

The Fall of Night

- Objective #1: Kill 50 Dreadherd Gorehorn; Kill 25 Dreadherd Wargor; Kill 25 Dreadherd Ragetusk.
- Objective #2: Kill 6 Dreadherd Braygors.
- Objective #3: Kill Ghrual the Night-bringer.

Altar of Madness

- Objective #1: Kill 50 Eboncreed Acolyte; Kill 35 Eboncreed Whisperer; Kill 15 Eboncreed Elder.
- Objective #2: Reach the Altar of Madness.
- Objective #3: Destroy the Mindless Devoted.
- Objective #4: Kill Vhergaal the Fatebringer.

WARCAMP: TANNENBACH'S DOOM

The warcamp is located in an icy region of the Chaos Wastes. Many of the troops have already frozen to death. They are in dire need of supplies and clothing.

CHAPTERS 15–16

CHAOS

"The awakening of the Souleater is almost here. For many days now, I have been digging hard in the ice, and I can feel his power even now. The power he will have when released is definitely more than anything that I could ever hope to achieve. I feel so envious of our great leader to have such a great and powerful Daemon under his control."

—Greta, Chaos Mage

CHAPTER 15: DIGGING INTO THE PAST

Larus and a small group of trusted men are digging into a glacier to find the Daemon Souleater. Tchar'zanek, through the Raven God, knows how to bind the Souleater to his will.

PUBLIC QUESTS

Lonely Tower

- Objective #1: Climb the Steps.
- Objective #2: Defeat the Undead Army.
- Objective #3: Kill 3 Skeletal Titans.
- Objective #4: Kill Kraethia the Undying.

Reaping Pain

- Objective #1: Drain 6 Wanton Shards; Kill 35 Twisted Ensnarler; Kill 35 Twisted Entangeler.
- Objective #2: Kill Grimtongue the Sateless; Kill Fleshgore Manbreaker; Kill Ariann Thrustfang.
- Objective #3: Kill Benoit the Painbringer.

CHAPTER 16: TO AWAKEN THE SOULEATER

The ritual of awakening the Souleater to life has been given to Ydreda. Ten lives must be sacrificed to awaken the Souleater. The prisoners being escorted for the ritual have escaped and they must be recovered alive.

PUBLIC QUESTS

Fall of Grimclan

- Objective #1: Kill 10 Grimclan Veterans; Kill 35 Grimclan Runeseekers; Kill 50 Grimclan Warriors.
- Objective #2: Prevent Uncovering of the Mark of Grimnir.
- Objective #3: Kill Runelord Vargrum; Kill Thorzul Grimblood.

The Tower of Awakening

- Objective #1: Kill 60 Followers of Slaanesh; Kill 60 Followers of Nurgle; Kill 60 Followers of Khorne.
- Objective #2: Channel 20 Energy.
- Objective #3: Defeat Archmage Sylvara.
- Objective #4: Defeat Souleater.

WARCAMP: SEVEN SHADES CREEP

Seven Shades Creep is the best defended warcamp in the Chaos lands. The warcamp keeps the path open for the troops advancing southward from the Inevitable City.

CHAOS WASTES
Empire vs. Chaos

LEGEND

WARCAMPS: 1 – Tannenbach's Doom 1 – Seven Shades Creep RvR Area (Outlined)

Chapter Unlock (Destruction)
15 – Chaos Chapter 15
16 – Chaos Chapter 16

Chapter Unlock (Order)
20 – Empire Chapter 20
21 – Empire Chapter 21
22 – Empire Chapter 22

Major Landmarks
1 – Bleakwind Wights
2 – Chaos Warband Encampment
3 – Grimclan Camp & nearby Cave
4 – Grimclan Camp & nearby Cave
5 – Grimclan Rune

6 – Nurgle Outpost
7 – Nurgle Outpost
8 – Twisted Caves
9 – Caves of Despair
10 – Tree of Souls
11 – Ancient Night
12 – Cave

Public Quests (Destruction)
1 – The Storm is Coming
2 – Reaping Pain
3 – Lonely Tower
4 – Sands of Time
5 – Fall of Grimclan
6 – Tower of Awakening

Public Quests (Order)
1 – Lost Artifacts
2 – Razing an Army
3 – Dance of Bones
4 – Madness
5 – Siren Sea
6 – Reaping Field
7 – Fall of Night
8 – Ebon Keep
9 – Altar of Madness

Battle Objectives
1 – Chokethorn Bramble (Merchant's Gift)
2 – Thaugamond Massif (Artisan's Gift)

3 – The Statue of Everchosen (Defensive Boon)
4 – The Shrine of Time (Healing Boon)

Lairs
1 – Tezakk Gnawbone

1 – Zimmeron's Hold
2 – Charon's Citadel

Flight Master

THE INEVITABLE CITY

CHAOS

CITY CAMPAIGN

Entering from a Flight Master, you fly into the Inevitable City, and notice that the city itself is on a massive crater, deteriorating as time passes. Your landing zone itself is tenuously tethered to the rest of the city—the city of Daemons and the dead. Augur Verrimus welcomes you, insofar as anything in this city could be welcoming, telling you to get yourself together, or you will become—like countless others before you—a wandering, enraged soul, broken beneath the City's will. Maybe you'll end up a soulless servant at the central Soul Forge, and live or die by the whims of the weavers of Gahzal; you'll mindlessly walk into the forge to be vaporized. Maybe your death will be more honorable, in the Sacellum trying to prove your worth to the Chaos gods.

Avoid death and you'll see the city's sights, with Scryers poring over their Scrying Pools, bringing forth ghostly images of emperors and other legendaries. Stare into the face—or the complete lack thereof—of the Timeworn Disciples in the Lyceum; these are more servants damned to a single task, and their moans will chill your soul, if you are weak. Eat, drink, and try not to die in the Feast Hall, prove yourself in the Arena, and do the tasks asked of you and maybe, just maybe, you'll get a glimpse inside Eternal Citadel, with the throne of Tzeentch's chosen, Tchar'zanek, inside.

Will you help him rule over the Inevitable City by staving off the attacks from other Chaos gods and from the forces of Order? Or will you simply go mad staring into the Void, becoming just another damned soul?

PUBLIC QUESTS

Temple of the Damned
- City Rank: All
- Location: Lost Narrows
- Objective #1: Kill 30 combined Enraged and Horrified Souls.
- Objective #2: Kill Sovek the Merciless

Inevitable Rot
- City Rank: All
- Location: Lost Narrows
- Objective: Kill 30 Plaguesworn Marauder. Kill Gevl Rotpore.

Disputable Power
- City Rank: 1, 2
- Location: Fate's Edge
- Objective: Kill 30 Daemons.

Hel'Kar the Blood Lord
- City Rank: 5
- Location: Fate's Edge
- Objective: Kill Hel'kar the Blood Lord.
- And many more to be discovered!

TIER 4

THE INEVITABLE CITY

LEGEND

The Inevitable City District Name

1 – The Undercroft
1A – The Undercroft, Northern Section
2 – Journey's End
3 – Dread Way
4 – Death's Labyrinth
5 – Apex
6 – Lost Narrows
7 – Lost Narrows, Eastern Section
8 – Sacellum
9 – Fate's Edge
10 – Fleshrot Alley

Major Landmarks

1 – Arena at Sacellum
2 – Viper Pit, Guild House, Guild Registrar
3 – The Lyceum
4 – The Chaos Winds
5 – Monolith
6 – Breaking Grounds, Mount Vendor
7 – Eternal Citadel

Public Quests (Destruction)

1 – Inevitable Rot
2 – Temple of the Damned
3 – Disputable Power
4 – Hel'kar the Blood Lord
5 – The Bigger They Are...
6 – Toil and Trouble

Dungeon Entrances

1 – Bilerot Burrow
2 – Sacellum Holding Pits
3 – Sacellum Holding Pits
4 – Sacellum Holding Pits
5 – Bloodwrought Enclave

 Banks

Auctioneer

Entrances to the City

Flight Master

Dungeons

Bilerot Burrow

Entrance Location: The Monolith

Hints and Rumors: Bilerot Burrow features winding passageways covered in slime, with teeth protruding from the floors and walls. Humanoid fanatics, who apparently love the smell of sewers, are down here, as are fleshy Plaguebeasts. Not enough can be said about the oozing green and brown slime—it's everywhere, and in some cases, is partnered with a green and brown gas cloud.

Sacellum Holding Pits

Entrance Location: The Sacellum

Hints and Rumors: Caged and readied beasts, as well champions, stay here while waiting to be called out to the Arena. Enraged Servants also make their home here, as do the more volatile and destructive forces the Sacellum has to offer. The layout consists mostly of hallways with side rooms holding the named combatants, with three different layouts for the degree of difficulty (there are low-, mid-, and high-level entrances).

Bloodwrought Enclave

Entrance: Secret

Hints and Rumors: The Bloodwrought tribe, known for ungodly murder sprees, once hunted holy men and eventually expanded their reach to anyone who crossed their path. Tales say the tribe has been locked underneath the Inevitable City in an eternal war with each other, and woe to the mortal who unlocks their prison.

Order RvR PQs

The Monolith

- City Rank: All
- Location: The Monolith
- Objective #1: Kill Pechharus Voidcaller. Kill Zuram the Shifter. Kill Umoreon the Changed. Kill Yashnar Warpflesh.
- Objective #2: Drain 8 Focus Stones.
- Objective #3: Kill Lycithas the Harridan Seer.

The Sacellum

- City Rank: All
- Location: The Sacellum (Arena)
- Objective #1: Defeat 20 Sacellum Combatants.
- Objective #2: Defeat Vaz'hal the Once Whole. Defeat Lord Porus. Defeat Belvoul Fleshdoom. Defeat R'khar.
- Objective #3: Defeat Lorevoth. Defeat Torvug. Defeat Kruul. Defeat Eldazar the Mindwarper.
- Objective #4: Defeat Engra Deathsword.

The Eternal Citadel

- City Rank: All
- Location: The Eternal Citadel (Magus Tower)
- Objective #1: Kill the Lord of Lies. Kill the Lord of Whispers. Kill the Lord of Change. Kill the Lord of Fate.
- Objective #2: Kill Tchar'zanek.

THE MAW

Tier 4

THE MAW

Entrances to Inevitable City

To Chaos Wastes

LEGEND

RvR Area (Outlined)

Major Landmarks
1 – Career Trainers
2 – Small Camp (Merchant, Apothecary Trainer, Consumables Merchant)
3 – Small Camp (Salvaging Trainer, Scavenging Trainer, Talisman Trainer)
4 – Small Camp (Guild Registrar, Career Trainer)

5 – Door
6 – Door
7 – Door
8 – Door
9 – Door
10 – Door
11 – Door
12 – Door
13 – Migliod Menagerie (Lair)

Portals
1 – To Fell Landing
2 – To Butcher's Pass

Flight Master

EMPIRE

CHAPTERS 17-19

"I feel the pain and the suffering in the region. My purpose is to help heal the wounded while we bravely fight to regain control of the beloved city of Praag. The burning buildings and the devastation so tears at my heart. I hear rumors that a Daemon called Souleater is gaining power from the deaths of so many people. Our troops are gaining in numbers and I feel the tide is turning. The Empire will take down the Daemon and help the citizens of Praag rebuild their city."

—High Elf Tyla

CHAPTER 17: DARK REVELATION

Leopold Rohris and his troops have been sent to defeat the Daemon called Souleater. One can see the burning city of Praag in the distance.

PUBLIC QUESTS

- Public quests for this chapter are located in West Praag.

CHAPTER 18: FLOOD

Captain Becker and his men are trying to hold the bridge long enough to establish a camp on the far side. They must stop the Daemon from reaching Altdorf, where it would open a portal to the Realm of Chaos.

PUBLIC QUESTS

Broken Ground

- Objective #1: Rescue 10 Wounded Defenders; Kill 15 Doomglade Scouts.
- Objective #2: Kill 5 Doomglade Shadows; Kill 10 Doomglade Infiltrators.
- Objective #3: Kill Assassin Deathweaver.

Eyes in the Dark

- Objective #1: Kill 35 Plaguetail Cultists; Kill 5 Plaguetail Prophets; Empty 10 Cauldrons.
- Objective #2: Kill 10 Warpwind Plague Monks; Kill 5 Warpwind Plague Priests.
- Objective #3: Kill Lord Quol.

Gospodar Square

- Objective #1: Free the Steam Tank Driver.

- Objective #2: Escort the Steam Tank Driver.
- Objective #3: Destroy 2 Hell Cannons.
- Objective #4: Kill Fhorex Bloodstorm.

CHAPTER 19: FIGHT FIRE WITH FIRE

Krasa Falkenheim's objective is to delay the enemy with aid of the Steam Tanks, which had been delayed. Because of the delay, it might be too late to save Praag.

PUBLIC QUESTS

Beasts of War

- Objective #1: Kill 75 Ravenherd Raiders; Kill 50 Ravenherd Ambushers.
- Objective #2: Kill 6 Ravenherd Gorehoofs.
- Objective #3: Kill Krughroth Shorthorn.

Griffon's Last Stand

- Objective #1: Kill 50 Raven Eye Marauders or Velkar the Ruthless, Seer Berifus, Herala Everstorm, and Scer Lifetaker.
- Objective #2: Rescue 15 of the Wounded or Kill Prophet Erolc, Prophetess Ilare, Prophetess Urena, Prophetess Serevas.
- Objective #3: Defend Barricade.
- Objective #4: Defend Commander Konitzer or Kill Yrikal the Paincaller.
- Objective #5: Kill Warlord Kur.

Hell's Fall

- Objective #1: Kill 50 Raven Skullblades; Kill 25 Raven Hellbringers.
- Objective #2: Kill 5 Raven Darcanists.
- Objective #3: Kill Ghrulichar the Unfleshed.

WARCAMP: WESTMARK BARRICADE

The warcamp is on a street near the western entrance to the Centrum district of Praag. There are three leaders in camp and no cooperation between them. The other individuals in camp are doing the best they can, even with the dissension and constant bickering among the leaders.

PRAAG

CHAOS

CHAPTERS 17-19

"Victory is almost here! The Daemon Souleater is almost at full power, then we can advance farther south. We are so much closer to ruling these lands."

—Venusada, Dark Elf

CHAPTER 17: CITY UNDER SEIGE

Korzah and her troops have come to lay siege to the city of Praag. She released the Daemon Souleater on the city to aid in her conquest.

PUBLIC QUESTS

Gates of Praag

- Objective #1: Kill 50 Praag Kossars; Kill 25 Praag Champions; Destroy 5 Barricades.
- Objective #2: Ensure the survival of Sorcerer Vilesz.
- Objective #3: Kill Ivan Sidorov; Kill 2 Praag Rotamasters.

CHAPTER 18: A LOSING BATTLE

While Thurik celebrates his victories of Praag, he receives the news that The Order of the Griffons are assisting the Kislevites to reinforce their defenses in the city. Meanwhile the Souleater grows stronger with each death.

PUBLIC QUESTS

Cinderash Enclave

- Objective #1: Kill 40 Cinderash Flamesword; Kill 40 Cinderash Pyrepikes.
- Objective #2: Kill 4 Cinderash Wizards.
- Objective #3: Kill Gervault Feuer.

Tomb of Deathsword

- Objective #1: Kill 20 Acolytes of Morr; Kill 30 Warrior Priest.
- Objective #2: Open Deathsword's Tomb.
- Objective #3: Kill Inquisitor Lutz; Kill Brother Burgov; Kill Folgrun the Penitent.

Eastern Breach

- Objective #1: Kill 40 Griffon Armsmen; Kill 40 Griffon Deadeyes.
- Objective #2: Protect 3 Hellcannons.
- Objective #3: Kill General Deinrecht; Kill 4 Griffon Chargers.

PRAAG

TIER 4

TO CHAOS WASTES

TO CHAOS WASTES

TO WEST PRAAG

TO REIKLAND

TO REIKLAND

LEGEND

WARCAMPS: I – WESTMARK BARRICADE GUARD   I – RAVENSWORN   RvR AREA (Outlined)

Chapter Unlock (Destruction)
17 – Chaos Chapter 17
18 – Chaos Chapter 18
19 – Chaos Chapter 19

Chapter Unlock (Order)
17 – Empire Chapter 17
18 – Empire Chapter 18
19 – Empire Chapter 19

Major Landmarks
1 – Summoning Circle
2 – Raven Host Reinforcements

3 – Skaven Cave
4 – Cave (Stoneclan Dwarfs)
5 – Griffin's Last Stand
6 – Ursun's Den
7 – Cinderash Tower
8 – Kossars & Strikers
9 – Talonpeak
10 – Bear Shrine

Public Quests (Destruction)
1 – Gates of Praag
2 – Southern Breach
3 – The End is Nigh
4 – Wings of the Griffin

5 – Cinderash Enclave
6 – Eastern Breach
7 – Tomb of Deathsword

Public Quests (Order)
1 – Hell's Fall
2 – Griffon's Last Stand
3 – Beasts of War
4 – Eyes in the Dark
5 – Broken Ground
6 – Gospodar Square

Battle Objectives
1 – Kurlov's Armory (Defensive Boon)
2 – Martyr's Square (Artisan's Gift)
3 – Manor of Ortel von Zaris (Merchant's Gift)
4 – Russenscheller Graveyard (Artisan's Gift)

1 – Garrison of Skulls
2 – Southern Garrison

Flight Master

REIKLAND

EMPIRE

CHAPTERS 15–16

"I see the fires on the horizon, and the smoke like a dark bird of prey rising up into the clouds. We always thought we were blessed, and that war would never touch our streets and homes. We were wrong. The warhost has come, and we must trust that our Emperor has a plan to stop the madness that follows it."

—Jerkins Hanzstein

CHAPTER 15: TROUBLE AT THE EMPEROR'S BRIDGE

Renegades and rebels seeking the favor of Chaos hide among the loyal citizens. To avoid ruin, we must find the traitors and fight to hold our land.

PUBLIC QUESTS

Root of Rebellion

- Objective #1: Kill 50 Renegade Peasants; Kill 25 Rebellious Provokers.
- Objective #2: Convince 20 Loyal Peasants to Your Cause or Kill 5 Inciting Orators.
- Objective #3: Kill Kelmaur the Dark Apostle; Kill 3 Demagogues.

Fields of Ruin

- Objective #1: Kill 40 Instigators; Kill 60 Rebel Strongarms.
- Objective #2: Kill 5 Hedge Wizards.
- Objective #3: Kill Overseer Berault.

Heinrich Estate

- Objective #1: Kill 35 Besieging Rebels; Kill 35 Rebelling Peasants; Kill 10 Rebelling Militiamen.
- Objective #2: Kill 10 Rebel Sellswords; Kill 10 Rebel Estate Guards; Offer Lord Heinrich Assistance.
- Objective #3: Escort Lord Heinrich to the Courtyard.
- Objective #4: Kill Edgar Smythe.

The Reikland must be preserved to keep the forces of Destruction from penetrating our most inner defenses and reaching Altdorf itself. No matter what campaigns are elsewhere, the best of Order's defenses should regroup to defend Reikland in its time of need.

CHAPTER 16: THREATS FROM WITHIN

The river overflows with brigands and profiteers, while more traitors emerge from our very midsts. We must trust only our closest friends and family at this dire time.

PUBLIC QUESTS

Reik River Bandits

- Objective #1: Kill 60 Reik River Brigands; Kill 30 Reik River Profiteers.
- Objective #2: Load 6 Supplies into the Wagon.
- Objective #3: Kill Muriel the River-Queen; Kill 2 Reik River Cutthroats.

The Enemy Within

- Objective #1: Rally 15 Peasants.
- Objective #2: Kill 15 Grauenburg Goons to Secure the Village and Secure the West Flank, Center Line, and East Flank.

LEGEND

WARCAMPS: I – DEATHWATCH LANDING

 I – DARKSTONE VANTAGE

RvR AREA (OUTLINED)

 CHAPTER UNLOCK (DESTRUCTION)
20 – CHAOS CHAPTER 20
21 – CHAOS CHAPTER 21
22 – CHAOS CHAPTER 22

 CHAPTER UNLOCK (ORDER)
15 – EMPIRE CHAPTER 15
16 – EMPIRE CHAPTER 16

 MAJOR LANDMARKS
1 – CASTLE GRAUENBURG
2 – LORD'S PASS
3 – TROOP DEPLOYMENT
4 – WEST TEMPLE (MONASTERY)
5 – DISMAL HOLLOW
6 – RAVEN LANDING
7 – CAVE (THE DEPTHS OF DEPRAVITY)
8 – CAVE (BACK ENTRANCE TO HEINRICH ESTATE)
9 – CEMETARY
10 – TEMPLE OF REIKLAND (MONASTERY)
11 – CAVE
12 – FLAGELLANTS AND PILGRIMS
13 – CAVE
14 – RITTERBURG
15 – MORR'S MAZE
16 – CEMETARY
17 – SONS OF SIGMAR
18 – ELVEN EXPEDITION

 PUBLIC QUESTS (DESTRUCTION)
1 – DARK RETRIBUTION
2 – RAIN OF FIRE
3 – VULGAR DISPLAY OF POWER
4 – STONECLAN'S DEMISE
5 – HUNTING THE HUNTERS
6 – REIKSGUARD, TRAINING GROUNDS
7 – ALL THE KINGS MEN
8 – FIELDS OF REIKLAND
9 – AMBUSH AT GARNSONBURG

 PUBLIC QUESTS (ORDER)
1 – CASTLE GRAUENBURG
2 – THE ENEMY WITHIN
3 – REIK RIVER BANDITS
4 – ROOT OF REBELLION
5 – FIELDS OF RUIN
6 – HEINRICH ESTATE

 BATTLE OBJECTIVES
1 – FROSTBEARD'S QUARRY (ARTISAN'S GIFT)
2 – REIKWATCH (DEFENSIVE BOON)
3 – RUNEHAMMER GUNWORKS (HEALING BOON)
4 – SCHWENDERHALLE MANOR (MERCHANT'S GIFT)

 1 – WILHELM'S FIST, RENOWN TRAINER, CHAMPION EQUIPMENT
2 – MORR'S REPOSE, RENOWN TRAINER, CHAMPION EQUIPMENT

FLIGHT MASTER

- Objective #3: Kill August Segur; Kill 2 Gravenburg Knights.

Castle Grauenburg

- Objective #1: Kill 50 Grauenburg Defenders; Kill 25 Grauenburg Guardians; Kill 15 Grauenburg Sorcerers.
- Objective #2: Kill Champion Kilmer; Kill Beleth Hargron; Kill Jelera the Darksworn.
- Objective #3: Kill Lord Grauenburg.

WARCAMP: DEATHWATCH LANDING

As a combatant in this area, you have to hope that the "Deathwatch" in your camp's name stands for the fall of your enemies and not the minutes leading up to the demise of Order in the land.

CHAPTERS 20–22

"This is the final push. We have driven the enemy back almost to the gates of their fabled city, Altdorf, and it is there that we will rip the Emperor's heart out and feed it to our dogs. I can feel their fear and despair; it is what serves me when my mind dreams of sleep. Victory will be ours, even if I have to cut down a thousand Emperor fiends myself in the coming days."

—Kayleth Brimsteel

CHAPTER 20: THE HEART OF THE EMPIRE

Finally, our blades and spells taste Reikland blood and bodies. We battle militia and their commanders as we seize town after town.

PUBLIC QUESTS

Ambush at Garrisonburg

- Objective #1: Kill Reiksguard Braggart.
- Objective #2: Kill 20 Garrisonburg Defenders; Kill 50 Reikland Militia; Secure the Buildings.
- Objective #3: Hold the Center.
- Objective #4: Kill Captain Harris; Kill 4 Reikland Quickshots.

Rain of Fire

- Objective #1: Destroy 12 Empire Cannons.
- Objective #2: Kill 5 Reikland Black-swords.
- Objective #3: Kill Captain Gerhard; Kill 4 Reiksguard Novices.
- Objective #4: Slaughter 5 Horses; Burn 3 Tents; Blow up 2 Powder Stores.

Dark Retribution

- Objective #1: Kill 35 Sigmarite Warblades; Kill 25 Sigmarite Holyhelms; Kill 35 Sigmarite Warblades.
- Objective #2: Break Down the Monastery Door.
- Objective #3: Deface the Shrine; Destroy 3 Statues.
- Objective #4: Meet Luthor Huss in Battle.
- Objective #5: Evacuate the Courtyard.
- Objective #6: Defeat Luthor Huss.

The fools think they can hold the Reikland. They shall soon see that the forces of Destruction are all-powerful. Chaos, along with its lackeys, the greenskins and Dark Elves, shall drive the spear through Reikland and into the heart of the Emperor, Karl Franz himself.

CHAPTER 21: A GATHERING OF FORCES

Next up is the defeat of the Sigmarites and Stoneclans. We shall wipe them all out so they never bother us again.

PUBLIC QUESTS

Hunting the Hunters

- Objective #1: Kill 50 Sigmarite Zealots; Kill 35 Sigmarite Henchmen.
- Objective #2: Kill 5 Sigmarite Witch Hunters.
- Objective #3: Kill Edvard Kohl.

Stoneclan's Demise

- Objective #1: Destroy 6 Rapidfire Turrets; Destroy 3 Stoneclan Organ Guns; Destroy 3 Stoneclan Cannons.
- Objective #2: Kill 4 Stoneclan Stoutguts; Kill 8 Stoneclan Thundershots.
- Objective #3: Kill Redgar Ironbrew; Destroy Ol' Sparky.

Vulgar Display of Power

- Objective #1: Kill 50 Reikland Crackshots; Kill 50 Reikland Duelists; Pike 50 Heads.
- Objective #2: Kill 4 Reikland Deadshots; Kill 4 Reikland Lancers.
- Objective #3: Kill Captain Becker; Kill 5 Reiksguard Blacklances; Pike Becker's Head.

CHAPTER 22: THE BURNING OF CASTLE REIKSGUARD

Burn whatever you can find so that the Reikland lies in ruins. Some of their Emperor's best men guard the land, and when they fall we will show them that nothing can stand in the Warhost's way.

PUBLIC QUESTS

Fields of Reikland

- Objective #1: Destroy 35 Reikland Goods; Burn 3 Buildings; Burn 3 Wagons; Kill 35 Reikland Peasants.
- Objective #2: Kill 3 Reiksguard Vindicars; Kill 9 Reiksguard Defenders.
- Objective #3: Kill Sigmund Navarr.

Reiksguard Training Grounds

- Objective #1: Kill 60 Reiksguard Knights; Kill 30 Reiksguard Squires; Kill 20 Sisters of Mercy.
- Objective #2: Secure 2 Seige Batteries.
- Objective #3: Cripple the Steam Cannon.
- Objective #4: Destroy the Steam Tank.

All the King's Men

- Objective #1: Kill 50 Reiksguard Vanquishers; Kill 50 Reiksguard Protectors; Kill 30 Reiksguard Justicars.
- Objective #2: Kill Hound Master Gerrik; Kill Vorgen von Fieren; Kill the Brothers of Sigmar.
- Objective #3: Kill Kut Helborg.

WARCAMP: DARKSTONE VANTAGE

We are well positioned in our warcamp to lay seige to the surrounding countryside. One never retreats from battle, but when times are quiet, be sure to return to the warcamp to resupply and hone your training.

REIKWALD

REIKWALD

TO REIKLAND

TO REIKLAND

ENTRANCE TO
ALTDORF

ENTRANCE TO
ALTDORF

LEGEND

RvR Area (Outlined)

 Major Landmarks
1 — Career Trainers
2 — Career Trainers

 Portals
1 — To Shining Way
2 — To Stonewatch

WEST PRAAG

EMPIRE

CHAPTER 17

"To look upon a Daemon is to look upon mortality. You must face your fears and accept death as a natural course of life, else you shall never battle a creature out of hell and nightmares."

—Leopold Rohric

CHAPTER 17: DARK REVELATION (STARTS IN PRAAG)

A dozen plumes of smoke give evidence that the attack by the Raven Host is well underway. Somewhere in the smoking ruin is the Daemon called Souleater. According to the Grand Theogonist, the creature should still be weak enough to confront. It is for that reason that Rohric's regiment has been dispatched to Praag.

PUBLIC QUEST:

Screaming Daemons

· Objective #1: Kill 175 Raven Heartrippers.

· Objective #2: Kill 5 Raven Screambringers.

· Objective #3: Kill Yaardin the Cruel.

The Sundered Fortress

· Objective #1: Kill 60 Raven Sunderers; Kill 15 Raven Flame Magi; Kill 25 Raven Siegekins.

· Objective #2: Rescue 20 Sundered Defenders.

· Objective #3: Kill 6 Raven Hellscreamers; Kill 6 Raven Hellfeasters.

· Objective #4: Kill Bhelgom the Whisperer; Kill 6 Raven Blesseds.

Unlikely Allies

· Objective #1: Kill 35 Warpwind Clanrats; Kill 55 Warpwind Stormvermin; Kill 6 Warpwind Globadiers.

· Objective #2: Kill 8 Warpwind Engineers.

· Objective #3: Kill Warpmaster Skritt; Kill 1 Warpwind Warrior.

CHAOS

CHAPTERS 17-19 (STARTS IN PRAAG)

"Before us lies the city of Praag. We will attack this city, and you will revel in the glory of battle. Take life from those who oppose us, and use it to grow strong. You are of no use to Lord Tchar'zanek unless your powers are at their peak when we arrive in Altdorf."

—Korzah the Exalted

CHAPTER 17: CITY UNDER SIEGE

Korzah commands a circle of Magi to bind the Daemon Souleater. With its power under Korzah's control, at least for the time being, the Daemonhost engages the enemy and their hearts tremble.

PUBLIC QUESTS:

Chasing Shadows

· Objective #1: Kill 50 Moonstorm Shadow Warriors; Kill 25 Moonstorm Lurkers.

· Objective #2: Kill 12 Moonstorm Silver Helms.

· Objective #3: Kill Elliara Windsinger; Kill 12 Moonstorm Magi.

Sundered Fortress

· Objective #1: Kill Fortress Defenders.

· Objective #2: Destroy 4 Fortress Mortars.

· Objective #3: Kill Kuelen Ruell; Kill Captain Sturgis.

· Objective #4: Kill Gaspar Maan; Kill 4 Fortress Honor Guards.

WARHAMMER ONLINE
AGE OF RECKONING

Tier 4

LEGEND

Major Landmarks
1 – Sundered Pistoliers
2 – Dwarf Mines
3 – Cave
4 – Dark Banner
5 – Blacktalon Camp
6 – Tower (Scouts/Olaf Bloodrunner)
7 – Cave

Public Quests (Destruction)
1 – Sundered Fortress
2 – Chasing Shadows

Public Quests (Order)
1 – Sundered Fortress
2 – Unlikely Allies
3 – Screaming Daemons

HIGH ELVES VS. DARK ELVES

THE WARFRONT

Woe has embraced the world, and the Phoenix King of Ulthuan, Finubar, Ruler of the High Elves, will not stand idly by. With the threat mounting against his allies, the Empire and Dwarfs, Finubar sets sail with hundreds of warriors aboard their finest warships. They shall aid as best they can in this dire time.

Malekith, Lord of the Dark Elves, can sense the opportunity to seize the Throne of Ulthuan from his weak-bloodied cousins. Knowing that the High Elves will never abandon their allies against the looming Chaos invasion, Malekith commands all furnaces, forges, and blacksmiths to the crafting of weapons and machines of war. Witch Elves and Sorceresses join with ferocious creatures and fierce beasts as the kingdom of Naggaroth prepares for mighty bloodshed. When the High Elves depart to aid the Empire, the Dark Elves will strike.

With civilization on the brink of war, the most powerful of the land's races choose sides. Trusty Dwarfs and wise High Elves join the Empire and become the forces of Order. Relentless greenskins and cunning Dark Elves join Chaos and become the forces of Destruction. The two sides shall battle, and the world shall sunder.

THE TIERS

There are three warfronts (race pairings) in *Warhammer Online*: Dwarfs vs. greenskins, Empire vs. Chaos, High Elves vs. Dark Elves. Each of these warfronts breaks down into four tiers. There are two zones in Tier 1, Tier 2, and Tier 3, and eight zones in Tier 4 (in the Empire vs. Chaos warfront).

Tier 1 zones are where all characters begin. Generally, you'll spend approximately 10 ranks in each zone, so your early ranks, 1–10, will be spent in Tier 1, 11–20 in Tier 2, 21–30 in Tier 3, and 31–40 in Tier 4. Of course, there are exceptions to this rule, as you should rank up at your own pace and follow the paths set by your various quests. The RvR (realm vs. realm) areas in Tier 1, where you can fight against other players, are relatively small compared to the larger ones in Tier 4, so you won't get lost as you train up your player vs. player (PvP) skills.

Tier 2 zones bridge your advance between Tier 1 and Tier 3 zones. While in Tier 2, you should have gained all your fundamental abilities and you start mastering the paths that will define your career. RvR areas are a bit larger and more challenging than Tier 1. You certainly want to ally with other players from this point forward.

Tier 3 zones can be fierce battlegrounds as characters become more and more powerful. At this stage, you fine-tune your career before heading into the campaigns of Tier 4.

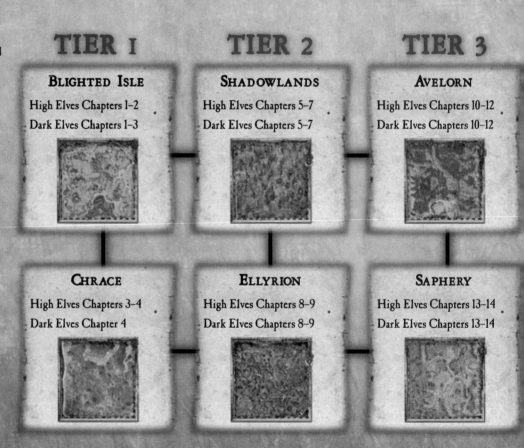

TIER 1

BLIGHTED ISLE
High Elves Chapters 1–2
Dark Elves Chapters 1–3

CHRACE
High Elves Chapters 3–4
Dark Elves Chapter 4

TIER 2

SHADOWLANDS
High Elves Chapters 5–7
Dark Elves Chapters 5–7

ELLYRION
High Elves Chapters 8–9
Dark Elves Chapters 8–9

TIER 3

AVELORN
High Elves Chapters 10–12
Dark Elves Chapters 10–12

SAPHERY
High Elves Chapters 13–14
Dark Elves Chapters 13–14

TIER 4

SHINING WAY

High Elves Campaign

Dark Elves Campaign

REIKWALD

ALTDORF

EATAINE

High Elves Chapters 15–16

Dark Elves Chapters 20–22

TO SAPHERY

DRAGONWAKE

High Elves Chapters 17–19

Dark Elves Chapters 17–19

ISLE OF THE DEAD

High Elves Campaign

Dark Elves Campaign

CALEDOR

High Elves Chapters 20–22

Dark Elves Chapters 15–16

TO SAPHERY

FELL LANDING

High Elves Campaign

Dark Elves Campaign

THE MAW

INEVITABLE CITY

Tier 4 will become your home once you hit the 30s, and you'll stay locked in Tier 4 campaigns for the rest of your time in *Warhammer Online*. Because you will spend most of your time here, and the RvR areas are vast, you should learn each zone well before moving to the next. If you follow your race's chapter unlocks and complete as many regular quests and public quests as possible, each zone will be a memorable experience.

HOW TO USE THE MAPS

The maps in this guide are organized first by warfronts and then by tiers (in alphabetical order within each tier). The first section deals with Dwarfs and greenskins, the second section highlights Empire and Chaos, and the third section details the struggle between High Elves and Dark Elves. As you adventure, open the appropriate map section and follow along as you discover chapters. For example, as a Empire player, you would open to the start of the Empire vs. Chaos map section and turn to the Tier 1 zone, Nordland, the very first map in that section. Empire Chapters 1–3 take place in Nordland. To help you along on your journey, keep the Nordland map open until you're ready for Empire Chapter 4, which takes you to the Norsca map. For Empire Chapter 5, you travel to Troll Country, your first Tier 2 zone. Continue with your "Chapters of *WAR*" until you've completed Chapter 22 and conquered them all.

Each zone map contains a wealth of information. Important points are labeled right on the map: chapter unlocks, public quests, landmarks, dungeons, lairs, battlefield objectives, and more. To identify any map point for your race, see the map's legend.

The page next to each map summarizes that zone's chapters. At a glance, you can see what chapters are in the zone (and your enemy's chapters) and all the public quests in the area. Pay close attention to the public quest objective information, as this will give you a leg up on what to expect and arm you (or your warband) with clues about what gear, Morale abilities, and Tactics to equip before battle.

If you don't want to flip through the maps chapter by chapter, see the map index at the start of each warfront and look up exactly where the zone of your choice can be found.

BLIGHTED ISLE

HIGH ELVES

CHAPTERS 1–2

"Hiding out in the Azurewood seems so cowardly for me, but I realize it is a smart strategy. It is so hard when the blood of the Dark Elves calls for me. I want revenge, and their blood, for my family killed in Calumel."

—Loraelle Lightwing

CHAPTER 1: INVASION

Prince Eldrion and his army retreated to the Undersea cave after the Dark Elves conquered Calumel. Due to large number of Dark Elves, Prince Eldrion decides to retreat to Azurewood to make surprise attacks on the enemy to weaken them, then attack.

PUBLIC QUESTS

House Arkaneth

- Objective #1: Kill 30 Guards and Shades.
- Objective #2: Keep the Shining Guard Crewmen alive.
- Objective #3: Kill Scornlash; Kill Beastmaster Lorkoth.

CHAPTER 2: AN ILL OMEN

The High Elves realize that the Dark Elves are following the ley lines, which run north to south. They have no idea why they follow the lines, but they know they must find out.

PUBLIC QUESTS

Thanalorn Forest

- Objective #1: Kill 100 Uthorin forces.
- Objective #2: Free 8 Crippled Dryads from their Bindings.
- Objective #3: Kill Felgrith the Arsonist. Don't let the firecallers re-ignite the trees 0/8.

The Swale of Miralei

- Objective #1: Kill 70 Harpies and Cold Ones.
- Objective #2: Kill 4 Beastmaster. Failure condition: Archmages slain 0/3.
- Objective #3: Kill Beastlord Revarok.

The Forlorn Isle

- Objective #1: Kill 100 Corrupted Dryads.
- Objective #2: Release 4 Stones.
- Objective #3: Kill Kharvena the Corrupter.

- And many more to be discovered!

CHAPTER 3: SISTERS IN ARMS (CHAPTER LOCATION IN CHRACE)

Heading into the Ruins of Erraneth, you must battle Bloodfueled enemies and Lilith Avorax.

PUBLIC QUESTS

Ruins of Erraneth

- Objective #1: Kill 30 Bloodfueled Devotees; Kill 20 Bloodfueled Witch.
- Objective #2: Kill 10 Bloodfueled Hag.
- Objective #3: Kill Lilith Avorax.

WARCAMP: TOR AENDRIS

Under siege, the High Elves must rally from here to beat back the Dark Elf invaders.

DARK ELVES

CHAPTERS 1–3

"To finally come to the Blighted Isle and get revenge on the High Elves has been thrilling. While the victories mount, I feel more powerful with each one."

—Galyz Fouldrake

CHAPTER 1: TRIAL BY BLOOD

Kaltran and his troops are attacking the Blighted Isle. With victory within reach, Kaltron receives orders from Lord Uthorin to move south.

PUBLIC QUESTS

Spires of Narthain

- Objective #1: Kill 30 Narthain Soldiers.
- Objective #2: Kill 15 Narthain Sun Mages.
- Objective #3: Kill the Sunlathin.

CHAPTER 2: NIMOSAR

Akrana and her troops prepare to raze Nimosar, leaving no High Elves left alive within the once-pristine village.

PUBLIC QUESTS

The Watchtower

- Objective #1: Kill 100 Adepts.
- Objective #2: Place 6 Charms. Failure condition: 4 Sorceresses killed.

- Objective #3: Kill Archmage Lithorial.

Nimosar

- Objective #1: Kill 100 Nimosar Defenders.
- Objective #2: Destroy 12 Braziers.
- Objective #3: Kill Erinas Songblade; Kill 4 Nimosar Silver Helms.

CHAPTER 3: INTO THE LION'S DEN

The Dark Elf assault upon Gon'Seraph has defeated the High Elf defenders. The menhir stone at the center of the village is destroyed in the process, which will further weaken the greater menhir.

PUBLIC QUESTS

Dreamshade Forest

- Objective #1: Kill 50 Dreamshade Ambushers; Disarm 20 Traps.
- Objective #2: Kill 10 Dreamshade Stalkers.
- Objective #3: Kill Guardian Beron; Kill Shadow-Walker Ialia.

Golden Tor

- Objective #1: Kill 50 Goldenwing Fliers; Kill 50 Goldenwing Eagles.
- Objective #2: Destroy 25 Goldenwing Eggs.
- Objective #3: Kill Queen L'thil.
- And many more to discover!

WARCAMP: CYNATHAI SPAN

The Dark Elves attack the Blighted Isle again, but this time they have a different plan that they keep secret from the hated High Elves.

WARHAMMER ONLINE
AGE OF RECKONING

TIER 1

BLIGHTED ISLE

TO CHRACE

TO CHRACE

TO CHRACE

LEGEND

WARCAMPS:  1 – TOR AENDRIS   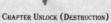 1 – CYNATHAI SPAN

~~~~~~~ RVR AREAS (OUTLINED)

 CHAPTER UNLOCK (DESTRUCTION)
1 – DARK ELF CHAPTER 1
2 – DARK ELF CHAPTER 2
3 – DARK ELF CHAPTER 3

CHAPTER UNLOCK
1 – HIGH ELF CHAPTER 1
2 – HIGH ELF CHAPTER 2

 MAJOR LANDMARKS
1 – BLACK ARK LANDING
2 – ISHA'S GARDEN
3 – FIRE CRYSTAL CAVERNS
4 – ADUNEI

5 – LACORITH VILLAGE
6 – STERNBROW'S LAMENT
7 – LAKE MENARHAIN
8 – LORE HOUSE
9 – GRIFFON'S NEST
10 – FOREST SPIRITS
11 – CALUMEL
12 – LIONWALK GROVE
13 – RUINS OF NARTHAIN
14 – SEAWIND GLADE
15 – POISONBLADE HEATH
16 – SPIRES OF NARTHAIN
17 – UTHORIN LANDING
18 – BLOODPRIEST CAMP
19 – FROSTRAGE KNIGHT CAMP

PUBLIC QUESTS (DESTRUCTION)
1 – SPIRES OF NARTHAIN
2 – WATCHTOWER
3 – MISTWOOD GROVE
4 – NIMOSAR
5 – DREAMSHADE FOREST
6 – GOLDEN TOR

PUBLIC QUESTS (ORDER)
1 – HOUSE ARKANETH
2 – THANALORN FOREST
3 – SWALE OF MIRALEI
4 – FORLORN ISLE
5 – RUINS OF ERRANETH

 BATTLE OBJECTIVES
1 – ALTAR OF KHAINE
    (DEFENSIVE BOON)
2 – HOUSE OF LORENDYTH
    (HEALING BOON)

 LAIRS
1 – GORTHLAK

 FLIGHT MASTER

CHRACE

HIGH ELVES

CHAPTERS 3–4

"Build your fighting and battle skills defending the Shattered Beach, reclaiming Blackwood Hill Garrison, freeing the citizens of Yenlui, and reclaiming Elisia. It is your destiny to rule the land of the White Lions."

—Uesilan

CHAPTER 3: SISTERS IN ARMS

The Dark Elves are making for the Plain of Bone to claim the Sword of Khaine. Yet others of their kind continue to move south for reasons yet to be determined. The Dark Elves must not be allowed to claim the sword and the reasons for their southward movement must be discovered. The High Elves must remain united if they are to overcome these dangers.

PUBLIC QUESTS

Shattered Beach

- Objective #1: Kill 75 Orcs; Kill 25 Corsairs.
- Objective #2: Defend the Eagle Claws and their Crew.
- Objective #3: Kill Verekus the Render.

Thrallseekers

- Objective #1: Kill 50 Uthorin Thrall-takers.
- Objective #2: Kill 10 Keymasters to Free Captives. Failure condition: Captives killed 0/5.
- Objective #3: Kill Vrecht the Merciless.

CHAPTER 4: STONE OF IMRATHIR

It is now apparent the Dark Elves are following the ley lines south to capture the Stone of Imrathir, and all the other menhirs scattered about the land. Built long ago, these powerful artifacts help to regulate magical energies. If the Dark Elves were to control the menhir stones or, worse, destroy them, it would give them a terrible

advantage in the Age of Reckoning. The High Elves must stop at nothing to prevent this from happening.

PUBLIC QUESTS

Blackwood Hill Garrison

- Objective #1: Kill 30 Uthorin Warriors.
- Objective #2: Destroy all Reaper Bolt Throwers.
- Objective #3: Kill Inyon Darklance.

Elisia

- Objective #1: Kill 100 Uthorin Dark Elves.
- Objective #2: Reclaim Mainland Village.
- Objective #3: Destroy Shining Guard Banner; Defeat Dark Elf Counterattack.
- Objective #4: Tear down the Uthorin Northern Banner to Claim Elisia Docks.
- Objective #5: Defeat the Dark Elf Counterattack. Protect the Shining Guard Banner
- Objective #6: Kill Vylisz the Cursebringer.

Stone of Imrathir

- Objective #1: Kill 100 Arkaneth Knights.
- Objective #2: Neutralize the Rubrics.
- Objective #3: Kill Beastmaster Rauul; Kill Hag Eritha; Kill Draich-master Vakar.
- Objective #4: Kill Ga'khur the Bloodcaller.
- And many more to be discovered!

WARCAMP: NONE

DARK ELVES

CHAPTER 4

"You must destroy Lionhome Lodge, the ancient home and training grounds for the White Lions, secure the powerful Stone of Valetear, capture the capital city of Tor Achare and much more to ready yourself for the battles that lie ahead. Only then can you claim the Sword of Khaine."

—Iledius Stormriven

CHAPTER 4: STONE OF IMRATHIR

Lead by General Malagurn, the Dark Elves move to capture the Stone of Imrathir. Once Captain Ulthawen and her forces are defeated, the Dark Elves will capture the other menhirs and drain the vaulted magic of Ulthuan that keeps the High Elves strong. The might of the Dark Elves will then be unstoppable, and the Sword of Khaine an easy prize to claim.

PUBLIC QUESTS

Gon'Seraph (begins in Blighted Isle)

- Objective #1: Capture 15 Gon'Seraph Citizens.
- Objective #2: Destroy the High Elf Reinforcements; Protect 7 Uthorin Slavemasters.
- Objective #3: Kill Lieren Palewind.

Lionhome Lodge

- Objective #1: Kill 75 Lion Hunters; Kill 25 Lion Stalkers.
- Objective #2: Kill 5 Lion Guardians.
- Objective #3: Kill Kaliera the Lioness; Kill 4 Lioness Guards.

Stone of Valetear

- Objective #1: Kill 100 Silver Helms.
- Objective #2: Absorb 300 Menhir Strength.
- Objective #3: Kill Guardian White Lion Kill Archer Champion; Kill Shadow Walker Terevin.
- Objective #4: Kill Sildaen of Hoeth; Kill 4 Shining Guard Knight. Failure condition: Rubrics retaken 0/2.

Tor Achare

- Objective #1: Kill 60 Hunter Guards; Kill 40 Hunter Axebearers.
- Objective #2: Destroy 10 Eagle Claws.
- Objective #3: Kill Prince Eriondas; Protect at least 5 Reaper Bolt Throwers.
- And many more to be discovered!

WARCAMP: NONE

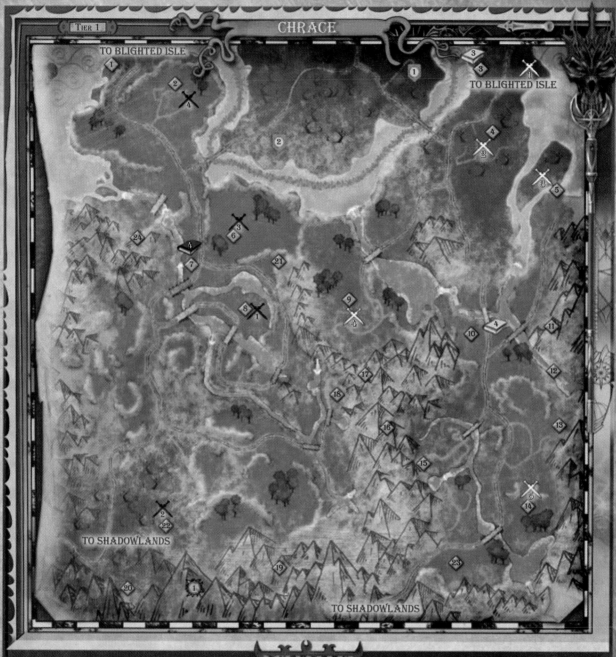

TIER 1

CHRACE

TO BLIGHTED ISLE

TO BLIGHTED ISLE

TO SHADOWLANDS

TO SHADOWLANDS

LEGEND

RvR Area (Outlined)

Chapter Unlock (Destruction)
3 – Dark Elf Chapter 3 (See Blighted Isle)
4 – Dark Elf Chapter 4

Chapter Unlock (Order)
3 – High Elf Chapter 3
4 – High Elf Chapter 4

Major Landmarks
1 – Shadowsong Landing
2 – Gon'Seraph

3 – Blightsward
4 – Yenlui
5 – Elisia
6 – Tor Achare
7 – Malagurn's Charge
8 – Lionhome Lodge
9 – Blackwood Hill Garrison
10 – Cliffs of Ushuru
11 – Everstar Stone
12 – Everstar Lake
13 – Lyriana's Mansion
14 – Lyriana's Repose
15 – Lyriana's Repose
16 – Stone of Melanar

17 – Flamescale Caverns
18 – Thanlui's Retreat
19 – Pridehome Den
20 – Dragonscale Caverns
21 – Whiteclaw Cavern
22 – Stone of Valetear
23 – Dark Elf Camp
24 – Emlyria Cavern

Public Quests (Destruction)
1 – Lionhome Lodge
2 – Stone of Valetear
3 – Tor Achare
4 – Gon'Seraph

Public Quests (Order)
1 – Shattered Beach
2 – Thrallseekers
3 – Elisia
4 – Blackwood Hill Garrison
5 – Stone of Imrathir

Battle Objectives
1 – Tower of Nightflame
2 – Shard of Grief

Lairs
1 – Kelbrax

THE SHADOWLANDS

HIGH ELVES

CHAPTERS 5–7

"This place is called the Shadowlands for a reason; it is a dark gloomy place that makes even the boldest break. When you first arrive in the Shadowlands, head to Mathrin's Watch. There you will be versed in the basics of this place. Once you finish up there, you'll get sent to Sorrowstrand, very close to the coast and the Dark Elf encampment at the Ruins of Anlec. Just stay alive, recruit, and be strong, because we need your help."

—Naleen, Swordmaster of the Shores

CHAPTER 5: MATHRIN'S WATCH

The first High Elves encampment in the Shadowlands is in the northeastern portion of the zone. This refuge is far from any Dark Elves, making it the safest also.

PUBLIC QUESTS

Mirelen

- Objective #1: Kill 125 Uthorin Seekers.
- Objective #2: Protect Sentinels of Saruthil for 5 minutes.
- Objective #3: Kill Lord Azurael.

CHAPTER 6: SORROWSTRAND

The next High Elf settlement in the Shadowlands is in close proximity to the Dark Elf camp in the Ruins of Anlec. A major landmark and public quest area is located at the Laurilion Caves.

PUBLIC QUESTS

Broken Spirits

- Objective #1: Kill 75 Broken Terrors; Kill 50 Broken Dryads.
- Objective #2: Uproot 25 Shadow Thorns.
- Objective #3: Kill Blacksap; Kill 2 Limbsnappers.

CHAPTER 7: SKYBLADE'S HOLD

The final base for High Elves in the Shadowlands is closest to the main RvR area. Here you have to break through a Dark Elf encampment guarding Dragon Gate.

PUBLIC QUESTS

The Dragon Gate

- Objective #1: Kill 30 Uthorin Siegewarriors; Kill 30 Uthorin Deathrains; Kill 65 Uthorin Deadaims.
- Objective #2: Kill 8 Uthorin Venomblades.
- Objective #3: Kill Lord Khirareq.
- And many more to be discovered!

WARCAMP: BLADEWATCH

If you are ready to fight some Dark Elves, head over to Bladewatch in the northeastern part of the RvR area. There are two main battlefield objectives and a keep up for the taking here. Dragonscale Tower (an Artisan's Gift) and the Dragon Siege Camp (a Merchant's Gift) are on either side of the keep, Spite's Reach. Once these three are captured, you can move down and take the

DARK ELVES

CHAPTERS 5–7

"Those boisterous High Elves think they own this place, but we know more. They have cast us out, and now we strike back. We stand at the Ruins of Anlec. Very close to Sorrowstrand, a High Elf encampment, but very safe with the might of our vast army behind us. We need to flush out our lowly brethren for good. They will never forget us when we are done. Never."

—Vasellan, Sorceress

CHAPTER 5: RUINS OF ANLEC

Even though it is very close, it is a very safe encampment. The first Dark Elf camp in the Shadowlands is near the High Elf settlement of Sorrowstrand.

PUBLIC QUESTS

Ruins of Anlec

- Objective #1: Kill 50 Nagarythe Citizens.
- Objective #2: Collect 3 Artifacts; Return the Collector to Safety.
- Objective #3: Kill Kelawyn the Unforgiving.

CHAPTER 6: SUNDERED STRAND

This camp is located on the western coast of the Shadowlands. Most of the quests here are based along the sea.

PUBLIC QUESTS

The Gloomridge Copse

- Objective #1: Plant 50 Shadow Thorns.
- Objective #2: Kill 16 Gloomridge Ragers; Protect Shadow Thorns.
- Objective #3: Kill Stonebark; Kill 6 Gloomridge Branchwraiths.

CHAPTER 7: RALKUTH'S RETURN

The final encampment in the Shadowlands is close to the RvR area. A main public quest involves rooting out some High Elves at Griffon Gate.

PUBLIC QUESTS

The Griffon Gate

- Objective #1: Destroy 8 Eagle Claws.
- Objective #2: Protect the Raidlords for 7 minutes.
- Objective #3: Kill 4 Reavers; Kill Firelen Erestial.
- And many more to be discovered!

WARCAMP: OATH'S END

When you are ready for a fight, head over to the sole warcamp, in the southwestern part of the RvR area. There are two main battlefield objectives and a keep. Dragonscale Tower and The Dragon Siege Camp are located on either side of the keep, Spite's Reach. Once we capture both of these points, we can head down to Ellyrion and continue the fight.

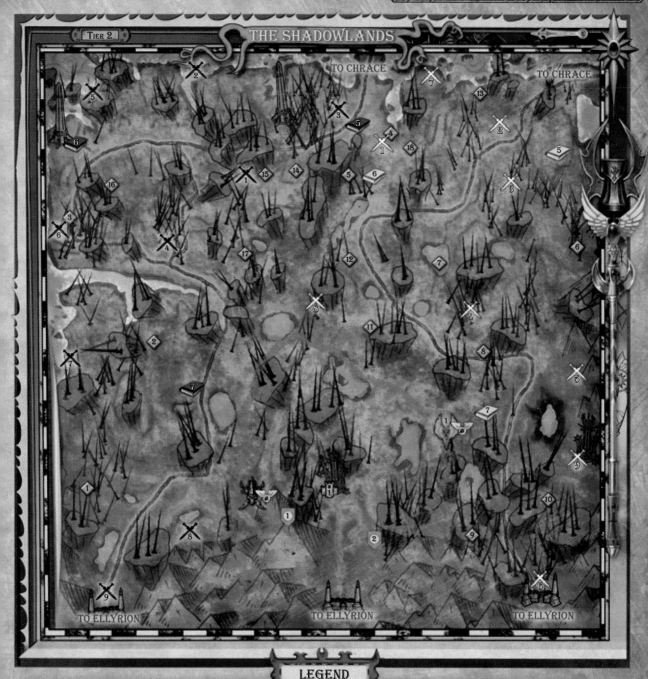

TIER 2

THE SHADOWLANDS

TO CHRACE

TO CHRACE

TO ELLYRION

TO ELLYRION

TO ELLYRION

LEGEND

WARCAMPS: 1 – BLADEWATCH   1 – OATH'S END   RVR AREA (OUTLINED)

CHAPTER UNLOCK (DESTRUCTION)
5 – DARK ELF CHAPTER 5
6 – DARK ELF CHAPTER 6
7 – DARK ELF CHAPTER 7

CHAPTER UNLOCK (ORDER)
5 – HIGH ELF CHAPTER 5
6 – HIGH ELF CHAPTER 6
7 – HIGH ELF CHAPTER 7

MAJOR LANDMARKS
1 – SHRINE OF REMEMBERANCE
2 – SEA CAVERN
3 – SERYNAL
4 – LAURILION CAVERNS
(NORTH ENTRANCE)

5 – LAURILION CAVERNS
(SOUTH ENTRANCE)
6 – DEATH'S WIND CAVERN
7 – DREAD LAKE
8 – ELBISAR
9 – SHADE ENCAMPMENT
10 – HARPIES
11 – DARK RIDER ENCLAVE
12 – WITCH ELF PRISONER CAMP
13 – CORSAIR BEACH CAMP
14 – ARKANETH TOWER
15 – PILLAGED HIGH ELF CAMP
16 – WILD COLD ONES
17 – SHADOW WARRIOR CAMP
18 – BLACKGUARD FORT

PUBLIC QUESTS (DESTRUCTION)
1 – OUT OF THE SHADOWS
2 – ROCK OF GALIRIAN
3 – RUINS OF ANLEC
4 – GLOOMRIDGE CLOPSE
5 – JAGGED COAST
6 – RUINS OF NAGARYTHE
7 – DAWN'S EARLY FIGHT
8 – STONE OF ECELSION
9 – GRIFFON GATE

PUBLIC QUESTS (ORDER)
1 – LAURILION CAVES
2 – MIRELEN
3 – COLD HEARTED PREDATORS
4 – FORGOTTEN FUTURE

5 – LAIR OF THE DEAD
6 – DRAGON GATE
7 – BROKEN DUNE
8 – BROKEN SPIRITS
9 – PREEMPTIVE STRIKE

BATTLE OBJECTIVES
1 – DRAGONSCALE TOWER
(ARTISAN'S GIFT)
2 – DRAGON SIEGE CAMP
(MERCHANT'S GIFT)

1 – SPITE'S REACH

FLIGHT MASTER

ELLYRION

HIGH ELVES

CHAPTERS 8–9

"The Battle at the Gate was all but lost when the sound of horns and pounding hooves lifted weary souls. The Reavers had showed up and pulled victory out of the very jaws of defeat. Even so, we now mourn the loss of so many young Elves. Word of larger Dark Elf forces has come in, and the fighting will continue. The general has decided to fall back to the Unicorn Gate. From there we will continue a slow withdrawal and hope that help will come before we all perish."

—Johan Fleets, Empire soldier within the ranks of the High Elves

CHAPTER 8: BATTLE AT THE GATE

The Dark Elves have gained a foothold in the lands and are now using human necromancers to summon undead to fight their battles. They must be stopped.

PUBLIC QUESTS

Starbrook Falls

- Objective #1: Kill 100 Risen Undead.
- Objective #2: Kill 3 Blightbinder Acolytes.
- Objective #3: Kill Orin Blightbinder.

Ellyrian Stables

- Objective #1: Kill 100 Uthorin Soldiers.
- Objective #2: Kill 6 Uthorin Knights.
- Objective #3: Kill Kesharq Blackspear.

Allies of War

- Objective #1: Kill 125 Blacktoof Orcs.
- Objective #2: Light 6 Orc Structures on Fire.
- Objective #3: Kill Lord Gurahk; Kill 2 Uthorin Reapers.

CHAPTER 9: PLAIN COUNCIL

The Dark Elves are combing the area around Well Springs looking for magical artifacts. It is not known what they seek, but it can't be good.

PUBLIC QUESTS

The Well Springs

- Objective #1: Kill 125 Bloodkiss Witch Elves.
- Objective #2: Rescue 25 Citizens.
- Objective #3: Kill Helgerith Kaelorax; Kill 2 Bloodkiss Hags.

Shady Tower

- Objective #1: Kill 125 Shadow Seekers and Lurkers.
- Objective #2: Recover 10 Ancient Artifacts.
- Objective #3: Kill Lord Karoun; Kill 2 Shadow Strikers.

Gates of Elthrai

- Objective #1: Kill 125 Loathsome Warriors.
- Objective #2: Kill 8 Bonecrafter Acolytes.
- Objective #3: Kill 1 Loathsome Constructs.
- And many more to be discovered!

WARCAMP: NONE

DARK ELVES

CHAPTERS 8–9

"The Fall of the Matriarch took the whole army by surprise. Lord Kohrith may have despised Sorceress Lunira, but her death by the hand of Harbinger Evriel could not go unpunished. Kohrith decided to ravage the lands and destroy the holy places and shrines of the High Elves. The attacks were brutal and efficient, and we swept them all away before us."

—Farid Almsripper

CHAPTER 8: THE FALL OF THE MATRIARCH

The Dark Elves intend to leave the town and any High Elves' monuments in ruin, as a symbol for the fate that awaits the rest of their weaker cousins.

PUBLIC QUESTS

Town of Berhessa

- Objective #1: Kill 125 Berhessa Defenders.
- Objective #2: Burn 4 Buildings.
- Objective #3: Kill Adrielas the Tamer; Kill 4 Fearless Steeds.

Monument of Narialle

- Objective #1: Kill 60 Narialle Reavers.
- Objective #2: Kill 6 Narialle Harbingers; Destroy the Alter.
- Objective #3: Protect the Alter.
- Objective #4: Defeat Elysiara while Maintaining Control of the Alter.

Reservation of Honor

- Objective #1: Kill 125 Swifthooves.
- Objective #2: Destroy Pillar of the Hoof, Pillar of the Flame, Pillar of the Spear, Pillar of the Sword.
- Objective #3: Kill Arhalien; Kill 2 Honor-bound Pearhooves.

CHAPTER 9: RACE FOR THE MENHIR

The Ellyrian Reavers have been a thorn in the side of the Dark Elves since first breaching the Unicorn Gate. Nothing has deterred the tenacious defenders of Ellyrion, and despite significant losses, the Reavers still field a powerful force that must be destroyed.

PUBLIC QUESTS

Reaver's End

- Objective #1: Kill 70 Ellyrian Greatriders; Kill 35 Ellyrian Vindicators; Kill 20 Ellyrian Vanquishers.
- Objective #2: Kill 4 Korhandir Elites.
- Objective #3: Kill Lord Itharion Thunderblade; Kill 2 Chosen of Korhandir.

Tor Elyr

- Objective #1: Kill 125 Tor Elyr Inhabitants.
- Objective #2: Protect Dread Sorceress Korthusa.
- Objective #3: Kill Gaevis Goldstride; Protect Sorceress Korthusa.
- Objective #4: Tor Elyr Cleansed.

Whitefire Tor

- Objective #1: Kill 100 House Arkaneth Forces.
- Objective #2: Kill 15 Arkaneth Chillknights; Kill 3 Arkaneth Chillbinders.
- Objective #3: Kill Narraerna Darkmane; Kill 4 Arkaneth Chillmaster; Defend 3 Uthorin Spiritbinders.
- And many more to be discovered!

WARCAMP: NONE

TIER 2

ELLYRION

TO AVELORN

TO AVELORN

LEGEND

RvR Area (Outlined)

Chapter Unlock (Destruction)
8 – Dark Elf Chapter 8
9 – Dark Elf Chapter 9

Chapter Unlock (Order)
8 – High Elf Chapter 8
9 – High Elf Chapter 9

Major Landmarks
1 – Brokenblade
2 – Berhessa
3 – Savage Claw Cavern
4 – Fortress of Korhandir
5 – Tor Elyr

6 – Whitefire Tor
7 – Highvale Cavern
8 – Goldmead
9 – Monument to Nariaelle
10 – Gates of Elthrai
11 – Elyr Caverns
12 – Reaver Spring
13 – Tower of Milunen
14 – Conqueror's Ascent
15 – Starbrook
16 – Windrider Plain
17 – Elyr Gatehouse
18 – Reaver Stables
19 – Bear Caves
20 – Tor Elyr Tower / Manors

Public Quests (Destruction)
1 – Town of Berhessa
2 – Reaver's End
3 – Tor Elyr
4 – Monument of Narialle
5 – Whitefire Tor
6 – Reservation of Honor

Public Quests (Order)
1 – Well Springs
2 – Gate of Elthrai
3 – Ellyrian Stables
4 – Allies of War
5 – Shady Tower
6 – Starbrook Falls

Battle Objectives
1 – Needle of Ellyrion (Healing Boon)
2 – Reaver Stables (Defensive Boon)

Lairs
1 – Stinkfang the Vomitous

1 – Cascades of Thunder

AVELORN

HIGH ELVES

CHAPTERS 10–12

"I have just arrived at the Well of Whispers and heard that the Everqueen has disappeared. Sethrel is calling for volunteers to locate her. She must be found or else Avelorn will be lost. I will, of course, give my life for one as noble as she. I have never known battle, but I will do what needs to be done."

—Theraelle, The Windsinger

CHAPTER 10: GUERILLA TACTICS

While hiding in the forest, Cirribhir kills a lone Uthorin Shade. Then to cause friction between the two houses of the Dark Elves, he removes his arrow and replaces it with a House Uthorin reaper bolt.

PUBLIC QUESTS

Slash and Burn

- Objective #1: Kill 150 Uthorin Forces.
- Objective #2: Protect the Trees from Burning.
- Objective #3: Kill Tethira Ebonsong; Kill Rakthul Swartsword.

CHAPTER 11: CORRUPTION OF THE FOREST

Aeddriel and her troops are trying to contain the disease in the forest and keep it from spreading. The disease is causing creatures to be warped. Aeddriel has sent word to the Everqueen, but has yet to hear back.

PUBLIC QUESTS

The Falls of Renewal

- Objective #1: Kill 100 Spellwrack Horrors; Kill 50 Spellwrack Screamers.
- Objective #2: Destroy the Obelisk.
- Objective #3: Kill Torin the Fatechanger.

CHAPTER 12: KILLING BLOW

Sethrel, a loremaster who was journeying to meet with the Everqueen, finds himself cut off and decides to stay at the Well of Whispers. He finds out that the Everqueen has vanished and that she must be located or else the land of Avelorn has no hope of renewal.

PUBLIC QUESTS

Corruption

- Objective #1: Collect 50 Stone Shards.
- Objective #2: Protect the Shrine of Asuryan for 6 Minutes.
- Objective #3: Kill Goresting Spiteslake; Kill Magnus Magnus; Kill 4 Euphoric Vileshields.
- And many more to be discovered!

WARCAMP: MAIDENGUARD

The Handmaidens of the Everqueen are one of the most elite military forces in Avelorn, and they have established a camp on the outskirts of the open warzone between the High Elves and Dark Elves. They shall launch a full-out attack soon.

DARK ELVES

CHAPTERS 10–12

"I heard there was a change of command, that Illries is to become our new commander. I hope Illries will live up to Kohrith's standards. Illries is definitely devious, but can she lead us through many great battles, I wonder?"

—Simone Gretaious

CHAPTER 10: HOLLOW VICTORY

Kohrith is summoned to see Lord Uthorin himself, and so named Illries as commander of his forces while he is away.

PUBLIC QUESTS

Spirited Resistance

- Objective #1: Kill 100 Spirited Spites; Kill 25 Dryads.
- Objective #2: Kill 10 Ireshade Dryads; Set 10 Trees on Fire.
- Objective #3: Kill Wrathglade Rootwalker.

Wavesinger

- Objective #1: Kill 150 Lothern Sea Guards.
- Objective #2: Secure 9 Bolt Throwers; Gather 150 Reaper Bolts.
- Objective #3: Destroy 400 Wavesingers; Kill Lord Andriel.

CHAPTER 11: POISON

Sarava, a Bride of Khaine who was released by Commander Illries, kills more than a hundred High Elves in the forest of Avelorn.

LEGEND

WARCAMPS:
1 = MAIDENGUARD

1 = ISHA'S FALL

RvR AREA (OUTLINED)

 CHAPTER UNLOCK (DESTRUCTION)
10 – DARK ELF CHAPTER 10
11 – DARK ELF CHAPTER 11
12 – DARK ELF CHAPTER 12

 CHAPTER UNLOCK (ORDER)
10 – HIGH ELF CHAPTER 10
11 – HIGH ELF CHAPTER 11
12 – HIGH ELF CHAPTER 12

 MAJOR LANDMARKS
1 – HIGH ELF HIDEAWAY
2 – HANDMAIDENS APLENTY
3 – HOUSE ARKENETH
4 – JADE WIZARDS
5 – HIGH ELF CAMP
6 – DREADSTAFF'S CAMP
7 – ALTAR OF THE WINDS
8 – ARKENETH IN THE WOOD
9 – UTHORIN IN THE WOOD
10 – BIGHAMMA'S CAMP
11 – CHAOS IN THE PICTURE
12 – EVIL CROP
13 – WAYSTONE
14 – CAVE OF NARIELLE
15 – OAKENSTAFF'S HOUSE
16 – FOREST ALTAR
17 – CHEST OF ORMAGDIN
18 – BEASTMEN
19 – WOOD CHOPPAS
20 – HERALDS OF THE DARK HOST
21 – CAVE OF WHISPERS
22 – NECROMANCER AMBUSH
23 – ANULLI RUINS
24 – BARTHILAS CAMP
25 – EVERCOURT

 PUBLIC QUESTS (DESTRUCTION)
1 – SPIRITED RESISTANCE
2 – WAVESINGER
3 – QUYL-ISHA TEMPLE
4 – EVERSPRING
5 – POOL OF ELTHRAI
6 – DARTIAN FOREST
7 – WATCHTOWER OF AETHWYN
8 – SEA GUARD BEACHHEAD
9 – JADE STAND

 PUBLIC QUESTS (ORDER)
1 – SLASH AND BURN
2 – RITUAL OF CORRUPTION
3 – ROTTEN EMBRACE
4 – FALLS OF RENEWAL
5 – DEATHWIND PASS
6 – SHRIEKING MEADOW
7 – CORRUPTION
8 – WELL OF WHISPERS
9 – STORMRIVER'S END

 BATTLE OBJECTIVES
1 – THE WOOD CHOPPAZ (ARTISAN'S GIFT)
2 – MAIDEN'S LANDING (MERCHANT'S GIFT)

 1 – GHROND'S SACRISTY

  FLIGHT MASTER

Tier 3 — AVELORN

TO ELLYRION

TO ELLYRION

TO SAPHERY

PUBLIC QUESTS

Everspring

- Objective #1: Kill 150 Everguards.
- Objective #2: Light 5 Buildings on Fire.
- Objective #3: Kill Menlari Oceanbreeze; Kill 4 Everguard Wavecrashers.

CHAPTER 12: A QUESTION OF HONOR

Over drinks, Lord Uthorin informs Kohrith that, for peace to be brokered between House Uthorin and House Arkaneth, he must be sacrificed. Kohrith realizes too late that his wine has been poisoned.

PUBLIC QUESTS

Watchtower of Aethwyn

- Objective #1: Gather 75 Shards to Repair the Watchtower.
- Objective #2: Kill 15 Fiendish Spellswords; Kill 15 Fiendish Shieldbreakers.
- Objective #3: Kill Lickwhip Slashgore; Kill Blackclaw Heartrend.
- And many more to be discovered!

WARCAMP: ISHA'S FALL

The Dark Elves have realized that the best way to attack the High Elves is to spread their defenses out. Therefore, they have launched a simultaneous assault on three gates leading to the inner realm from this warcamp.

SAPHERY

HIGH ELVES

CHAPTERS 13–14

"The great dark Raven Horde has come over to Saphery through the passes of Avelorn. The magical heart of the High Elves is in peril. Gathered in the Houses of Learning, we await word from the sages. It is whispered that we may go to the Isle of the Dead to protect the Vortex from the Dark Elves.

—Shendeal of House Thaloden

CHAPTER 13: THORNVALE MANOR

The Dark Elves have focused their forces on the Ithilmar Tower and Thanon Hall in an attempt to weaken the High Elf magic. This must not be allowed.

PUBLIC QUESTS

The Ithilmar Tower

- Objective #1: Kill 150 Raven Cultists.
- Objective #2: Kill 15 Sightless Flamers.
- Objective #3: Kill Harkan the Sightless; Kill 2 Sightless Horrors.

Thanon Hall

- Objective #1: Kill 75 Fogvale Strikers; Kill 75 Fogvale Reapers.
- Objective #2: Protect Galadin Shadowsong.
- Objective #3: Kill Faulgrim Mistblade; Kill 6 Fogvale Assassins.

The Circle of the Winds

- Objective #1: Unlock the 8 Powers of the Wind.
- Objective #2: Prevent the Level of Corruption from reaching 1,000.
- Objective #3: Kill Cerika Blackterror; Kill Serthias Bloodrender; Kill 4 Dread-blight Harridans.

CHAPTER 14: MENUTHII'S BURDEN

The mansion of Vaelynar Sinelian has been overcome by the human necromancers of the Crimson Shroud.

PUBLIC QUESTS

Against All Odds

- Objective #1: Kill 150 Greenskins.
- Objective #2: Destroy 9 Rock Lobbers.
- Objective #3: Kill Frug Ribbreaker; Kill Yukha da 'Uge.

Sweating the Stone

- Objective #1: Kill 150 Ritual Guardians.
- Objective #2: Guard the Menhir Stones.
- Objective #3: Kill Mistress Valira; Kill 6 of Vilira's Channelers.

Hall of the Crimson Shroud

- Objective #1: Kill 100 Shyish Acolytes; Kill 40 Shyish Seers; Kill 10 Shyish Harbingers.
- Objective #2: Kill Orin Blightbinder; Kill Istavahn Bonecrafter; Kill Malina Rathskeller; Kill Barthilas Klienbecker.
- Objective #3: Kill Vedric von Heilbroner; Destroy Stone of Shyish.
- And many more to be discovered!

WARCAMP: NONE

DARK ELVES

CHAPTERS 13–14

"Commander Kohrith's head has been delivered in secret to House Arkaneth, but this hasn't brought about peace between our two houses. We stand on the knife's edge of civil war. Could there be a worse time, on the eve of battle with the High Elf Archmages who guard the White Tower of Hoeth?"

—Naet Iceblood

CHAPTER 13: KNIFE'S EDGE

Seizing Whitemoon Manor will bring powerful relics to the cause, but will it be enough to end the internecine strife between Arkaneth and Uthorin?

PUBLIC QUESTS

Whitemoon Manor

- Objective #1: Kill 80 Whitemoon Apprentices; Kill 60 Whitemoon Scholars; Kill 10 Whitemoon Masters.
- Objective #2: Destroy 4 Wellstones.
- Objective #3: Kill Larotan Stormbreaker; Kill Yrisaea Lifecaller; Kill Alanir Whitemoon.

Trial by Fire

- Objective #1: Kill 50 Scorchgaze Salamanders; Kill 100 Mages.
- Objective #2: Capture 3 Podiums Leading to the Tower.
- Objective #3: Kill Thelafin Blazehand; Kill Lashflare; Kill Flamescale.

Recompense

- Objective #1: Complete the Negotiations.
- Objective #2: Return Captain Syrkin's Corpse; Protect Uthorian Teats.
- Objective #3: Kill 5 Arkaneth Death-crafters; Protect Uthorian Teats.
- Objective #4: Kill Mistress Alliessa; Kill 5 Arkaneth Wrathguards; Protect Uthorian Teats.

CHAPTER 14: TREACHERY

With the houses of the Dark Elves divided, the White Tower of Hoeth remains an elusive objective. A deal must be made as the fight continues.

PUBLIC QUESTS

The White Tower of Hoeth

- Objective #1: Kill 150 Tower Students.
- Objective #2: Kill 4 Keepers of Illusion.
- Objective #3: Kill 3 Loremasters of Hoeth.
- Objective #4: Kill Belannaer.

Ghyran's Embrace

- Objective #1: Kill 100 Jadeleaf Spites; Kill 50 Jadeleaf Dryads.
- Objective #2: Kill 8 Jadehorn Stags.
- Objective #3: Kill 5 Jadetail Griffons.
- Objective #4: Kill Anurion the Green; Kill 3 Jadeleaf Branchwraiths.

House of Cards

- Objective #1: Kill 150 Arkaneth Elves.
- Objective #2: Kill 3 Arkaneth Black Lords.
- Objective #3: Kill Lady Arkaneth; Kill 2 Arkaneth Winglords.
- And many more to be discovered!

WARCAMP: NONE

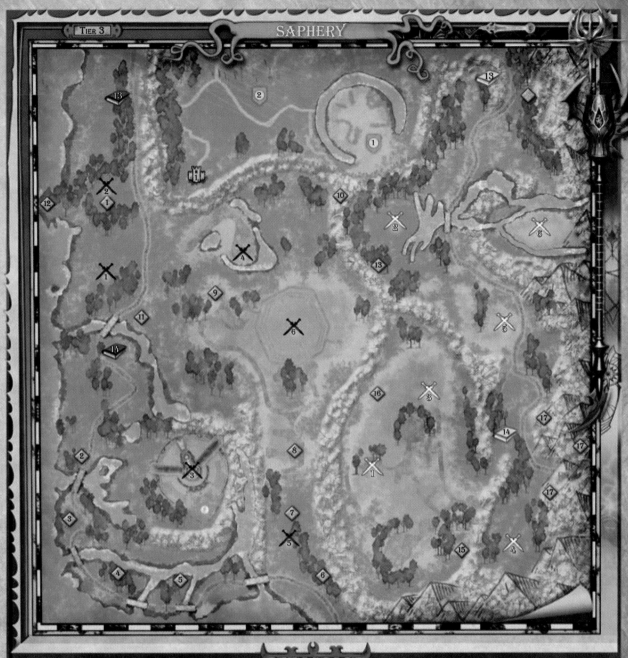

LEGEND

RvR AREA (OUTLINED)

CHAPTER UNLOCK (DESTRUCTION)
13 – DARK ELF CHAPTER 13
14 – DARK ELF CHAPTER 14

CHAPTER UNLOCK (ORDER)
13 – HIGH ELF CHAPTER 13
14 – HIGH ELF CHAPTER 14

MAJOR LANDMARKS
1 – WHITEMOON MANOR
2 – RANSACKED CARAVAN
3 – ARKANETH DEVASTATOR CAMP
4 – DARKSEER'S CAMP
5 – STORMWEAVER'S APPROACH
6 – TURNCOAT'S HIDING PLACE
7 – ARKANETH OFFICER CAMP
8 – STARSIGHT MANSION
9 – MANSION OF EVERMOURN
10 – GRYPHON HATCHERIES
11 – GRYPHON TRAINING CAMP
12 – MAIN PATROLLER CAMP
13 – STORMFIRE'S TOWER
14 – MENHIR STONE
15 – DARK RIDER PATROLLER CAMP

16 – GREENSKIN ENCAMPMENT
17 – MUSHROOMIN' CAVERNS

PUBLIC QUESTS (DESTRUCTION)
1 – RECOMPENSE
2 – WHITEMOON MANOR
3 – WHITE TOWER OF HOETH
4 – TRIAL BY FIRE
5 – HOUSE OF CARDS
6 – GHYRAN'S EMBRACE

PUBLIC QUESTS (ORDER)
1 – AGAINST ALL ODDS
2 – CIRCLE OF THE WINDS
3 – HALL OF THE CRIMSON SHROUD
4 – SWEATING THE STONE
5 – ITHILMAR TOWER
6 – THANON HALL

BATTLE OBJECTIVES
1 – THE SPIRE OF TECLIS
(HEALING BOON)
2 – SARI'DAROIR
(DEFENSIVE BOON)

1 – WELL OF QHAYSH

HIGH ELVES

CHAPTERS 20–22

"Our Dark Kin infest the land like a plague. The carnage and destruction left in their wake sickens me. I swore on my beloved's grave that I would do everything in my power to rid the lands of their filth! Our scouts tell us that the Dark Elves are at the Tower of Ulan Bel. We must re-take the Tower before they destroy it, then we must charge Drake's Rest by way of the Shadowchasm. It is going to be a long night. See you soon, my beloved."

—Yalsea of House Herni

CHAPTER 20: SUBTERFUGE (BEGINS IN DRAGONWAKE)

Onward to Ulan Bel and into the Shadowchasm, the High Elves battle toward Destruction's fortress, the Inevitable City.

PUBLIC QUESTS

Ulan Bel

- Objective 1: Claim 6 Banners
- Objective 2: Kill 4 Uthorin Death Mistresses
- Objective 3: Slay Master Karthorin, Karthorin's Mistress, Karthorin's Champion

Shadowchasm

- Objective 1: Kill 100 Dark Elves, Burn 10 Tents
- Objective 2: Kill 8 Shadowchasm Veilseekers
- Objective 3: Kill Evantir Soulshard

CHAPTER 21: BUYING TIME

It is crucial that the High Elves rest, re-equip, and seek out the training at Prince Endhil's Camp. There will be a great deal of fighting ahead.

PUBLIC QUESTS

The Shrine of the Dragontamer

- Objective 1: Kill 100 Dark Elves
- Objective 2: Secure (3) Caledor's Honor
- Objective 3: Kill Korvus Drakerift, Kill 3 Drakerift Retinue

The Shrine of the Slayer

- Objective 1: Kill 35 Uthorin Shockcaller, Kill 35 Uthorin Stormblade, Kill 35 Uthorin Warbringer
- Objective 2: Protect Lord Serinael Nightspear
- Objective 3: Kill Lorinek Bloodfist, Kill Vathrex
- Objective 4 Kill Lord Merethen Shadowclaw, Kill Norilath. Kill 2 Shadowclaw Terrors

CHAPTER 22: FALL OF TORSETHAI

Finally, this is it, your last push. If you make it, songs will be written of your heroism.

PUBLIC QUESTS

Tor Sethai

- Objective 1: Kill 125 Deathclaw Dark Elves

CALEDOR

- Objective 2: Stop 3 Rituals
- Objective 3: Kill Makal D'rkhen, Kill Vaarghith Sordhan, Kill Illtraneth
- Objective 4: Slay Tarkhan Blackblade
- Objective 5: Slay Beastmaster Rakarth

Pure Power

- Objective 1: Kill 100 Wrathwind Forces
- Objective 2: Rescue Halathan Mournvale
- Objective 3: Kill Cindiriel Rimesong, Kill 2 Fellwind Souldrinker

WARCAMP: NONE

DARK ELVES

CHAPTERS 15–16

"We will take this land just as we did Saphery. The enemy's moral code prevents them from doing what it takes to conquer. Why just yesterday I used one of my fellow Dark Elves as a shield, holding him between me and a half dozen High Elves archers as they let loose their arrows. The sheer look of horror and surprise on their faces gave me the few seconds I needed to kill two of them before I slipped into the chaos of clashing swords."

—Kavel the Cold-Hearted

CHAPTER 15: GROUND ASSAULT

We must first take the tower Aderaal, then to the Vault of the Dragon Princess to break the Will of the Dragon, and hopefully the will of the High Elves. They will soon learn there is nothing they can do to stop us.

PUBLIC QUESTS

The Battle of Aderaal

- Objective 1: Kill 175 Defending Drakeblades
- Objective 2: Kill Sindain Lightwing, Kill Telodil of Caledor, Kill Elerun Leafspinner
- Objective 3: Kill Caerildar the Proud, Slay 2 Sun Dragons

CHAPTER 16: REWARDS OF SERVICE

Today the Dark Elves take the Fortress of Caledor!

PUBLIC QUESTS

Loryndaal

- Objective 1: Kill 100 Drakes
- Objective 2: Destroy 3 Dragon Orbs
- Objective 3: Kill Archmage Arathal

Malyros' Rest

- Objective 1: Kill 40 Drakefall Defenders, Kill 40 Drakefall Wardens, Kill 40 Drakefall Watchers
- Objective 2: Protect 8 Uthorin Drakecaller
- Objective 3: Kill Prince Falanas Drakeblade, Kill Karatrys Flamebreaker, Kill 8 Drakeblade Guardians

WARCAMP: NONE

TIER 4

CALEDOR

LEGEND

WARCAMPS: 1 – Conqueror's Watch   1 – Conqueror's Descent   RvR Area (Outlined)

Chapter Unlock (Destruction)
15 – Dark Elf Chapter 15
16 – Dark Elf Chapter 16

Chapter Unlock (Order)
20 – High Elf Chapter 20
(Chapter Unlock in Dragonwake)
21 – High Elf Chapter 21
22 – High Elf Chapter 22

Major Landmarks
1 – Dragon Shrine
2 – Giant Dragon Statue

Public Quests (Destruction)
1 – Battle of Avethir
2 – The Vault of the Dragon Princes
3 – Kelysian's Landing
4 – Loryndaal
5 – Malyro's Rest
6 – Fortress of Caledor

Public Quests (Order)
1 – Ulan Bel
2 – Shadowchasm
3 – Drakes Rest
4 – Shrine of the Dragontamer
5 – Shrine of Tethlis

6 – Exectuioner's Blade
7 – Tor Sethai
8 – Pure Power
9 – The Might of Ulthuan

Public Quests (Neutral)
1 – Hatred's Way (RvR PQ)
2 – Wrath's Resolve (RvR PQ)

Battle Objectives
1 – Druchii Barracks
2 – Shrine of the Conqueror
3 – Sarathanan Vale
4 – Senlathain's Stand

1 – Hatred's Way
2 – Wrath's Resolve

Flight Master

Portals
1 – Portal to Saphery

DRAGONWAKE

HIGH ELVES

CHAPTERS 18–19

"Dragonwake is a beautiful land, with tall mountain spires and lush valleys. I've always wanted to visit this land, but not under such conditions. The dead Dark Elves litter the land. We have been stacking their bodies as high as we can and covering them in oil, then setting them on fire.

"The night's sky is set ablaze with the Dragon flames atop the Dragonwatch Towers. Each night the sky gets brighter, as more and more Dragons awaken.

"A messenger came to our camp this morning from the Isle of the Dead. The messenger brought news of their success in retaking the Isle. But, she also brought news of the fall of Vaul's Anvil. Scouts were leaving all morning and started returning by early afternoon. As soon as the first scout came back, small detachments started leaving.

"My detachment will be the last to leave. We were the last to make camp this morning. I should be resting but I can't clear my head enough to sit still for a moment, let alone go to sleep."

—Linewair, in a letter to home

CHAPTER 18: DRAGONWAKE

We must rescue the Dragons. The Dark Elves are attacking them, trying to break them. Make sure you re-equip. There will be many Dark Elves to slay.

PUBLIC QUESTS

Dragonwatch

- Objective 1: kill 150 dark elves
- Objective 2: Take and defend the Lunar Braziers
- Objective 3: Kill Commander Lothaik, Kill Spitefire Matriarch

Keeper's Watch

- Objective 1: Release 40 Captured Keepers
- Objective 2: Kill 6 Manticore Riders
- Objective 3: Kill Kruergoth Arios, his Dragon, and Furida Velzus

CHAPTER 19: VAUL'S ANVIL

Vaul's Anvil has fallen into Dark Elf hands. You must take it back. Hundreds stand in your way.

PUBLIC QUESTS

The Cliffs of Vaul

- Objective 1: interrupt Hellebron's rituals
- Objective 2: Destroy the Champions of the Dark Elves
- Objective 3: Kill Lord Vyrran Norinar, Kill Saltharan

Blood Focus

- Objective 1: Free 75 Captured Victims
- Objective 2: Kill Black Heart Bloodhags, Destroy Black Heart Cauldrons
- Objective 3: Kill Velitha the Devoted, Kill 2 Blood Drinker

WARCAMP: DRAKEWARDEN KEEP

After leaving Drakewarden Keep, head east till you get to your first objective, Fireguard Spire. Take Fireguard Spire for a Merchant's Gift. Then continue east till you reach Mournfire's Approach. Take Mournfire's Approach for a Healing Boon. Then go north to Pelgorath's Ember for a Defensive Boon. From there go to Destruction keep, Drakebreakers Scourge. There is one more objective to the far east, but the price will be high to take Malaith's Memory for an Artisan's Gift. Do so at your own discretion.

DARK ELVES

CHAPTERS 18–19

"There is a rumor running through camp that the Sorceresses' wards over the Dragons are awakening. I imagine many will die while attempting to subdue the Dragons before our Beastmasters can bring them under our control. It is only a matter of time before we get the order to move out. I check my gear, sharpen my swords, strap on my scabbards, and make sure of their placement so I can draw my blades unhampered. I check all the straps and buckles of my armor; it is snug. My boots and gloves are well oiled, the leather as supple as my own skin.

"Never before have I fought a Dragon. I pray that the enchantments on my swords and armor are strong enough to withstand the coming flames."

—Weolden the Deadly

CHAPTER 18: DEATH OF DREAMS

The race for the Dragons starts here. You must first take a Sacred Brazier from five score of the guardians.

PUBLIC QUESTS

Keeper's Vigil

- Objective 1: Kill 100 Guardians of Dragonwake
- Objective 2: Captured 8 Dragonheart Watchers
- Objective 3: Kill Terol Swiftstrike, Archmage Lorendiaal and 4 Vigil Master

Dragonwatch Falls

- Objective 1: Kill 150 High Elves
- Objective 2: Take and defend the Lunar Braziers
- Objective 3: Kill Prince Hathiren and 4 Dragonwatch Wardens

CHAPTER 19: FURNACE OF CALADAIN

We must reach Caldadain's Furnace to outfit our Dragons for war. We will have to kill many more High Elves to reach our goal.

PUBLIC QUESTS

The Caladain Steppe

- Objective 1: Kill 100 High Elf Defenders, Command Tent Controlled, Armory Controlled, Stables Controlled
- Objective 2: Kill 6 Caladain Champions
- Objective 3: Kill Tarai Emberstorm, Kill Kidessa Emberstorm, Lauraleth Emberstorm

The Caladain Gate

- Objective 1: Kill 100 Caladain Defenders
- Objective 2: Kill 4 Caladain Griffon Riders, Secure the Landing Area
- Objective 3: Kill the Dragon Rider

WARCAMP: DRAKESLAYER HOLD

You will be entering the battlefield from the east. Malaith's Memory is the closest to your warcamp and it gives an Artisan's Gift. Then head west to Pelgorath's Ember. It gives you a Defensive Boon. And, if you have a strong group, you can take Mournfire's Approach for a Healing Boon. If they put up little to no resistance, you may as well take Fireguard Spire for a Merchant's Gift. You will then be prepared to take Covenant of Flame.

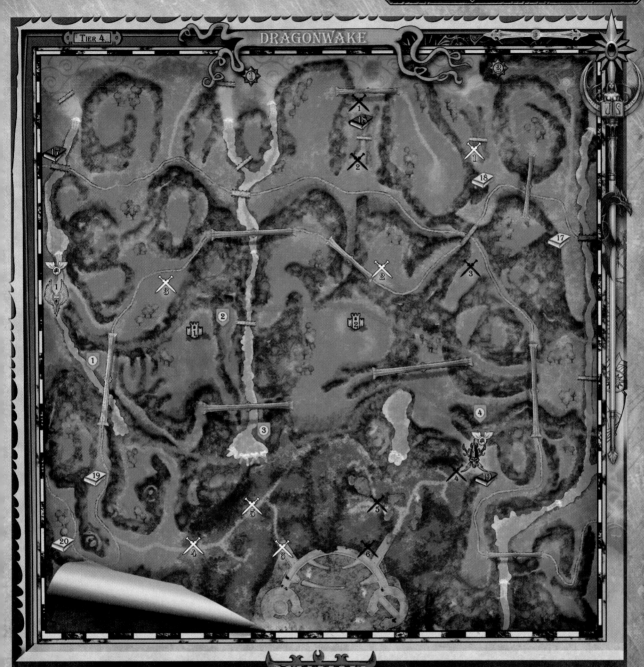

TIER 4   DRAGONWAKE

LEGEND

WARCAMPS: 1 – DRAKEWARDEN KEEP   1 – DRAKESLAYER HOLD

RvR AREA (OUTLINED)

CHAPTER UNLOCK (DESTRUCTION)
17 – DARK ELF CHAPTER 17
18 – DARK ELF CHAPTER 18
19 – DARK ELF CHAPTER 19

CHAPTER UNLOCK (ORDER)
17 – HIGH ELF CHAPTER 17
18 – HIGH ELF CHAPTER 18
19 – HIGH ELF CHAPTER 19
20 – HIGH ELF CHAPTER 20

PUBLIC QUESTS (DESTRUCTION)
1 – KEEPER'S VIGIL
    (STARTS ON BRIDGES)
2 – DRAGONWATCH FALLS
3 – GALIRONS MOUTH
4 – CALADAIN STEPPE
5 – CALADAIN GATE
6 – CALADAIN'S FURNACE

PUBLIC QUESTS (ORDER)
1 – DRAGONWATCH
2 – KEEPER'S WATCH
3 – RESCUE OF AENARES
4 – CLIFFS OF VAUL
5 – BLOOD FOCUS
6 – DOMINION OF KHAINE

BATTLE OBJECTIVES
1 – FIREGUARD SPIRE
2 – MOURNFIRE'S APPROACH
3 – PELGORATH'S EMBER
4 – MILAITH'S MEMORY

1 – COVENANT OF FLAME
2 – DRAKEBREAKER'S SCOURGE

FLIGHT MASTER

PORTALS
1 – TO ISLE OF THE DEAD
2 – TO ISLE OF THE DEAD

EATAINE

HIGH ELVES

CHAPTERS 15–16

"The Dark Elves and their allies have taken the fight to Eataine, striking at the very heart of Ulthuan's strength. It is here that we must push them back or our dark cousins shall tread over our dead bodies on their march to the havens of light."

—Bianthein, Shadow Warrior

CHAPTER 15: EATAINE IN FLAMES

Returning from their defeat in Saphery, the Shining Guard warriors hope to find the reinforcements they needed. Those hopes are soon dashed when they find the heart of Ulthuan's military might already under attack by the dark kin and their allies.

PUBLIC QUESTS

Da Orkwerks

- Objective 1: Free the Captive Artisans, Kill 100 Orcwerks Orcs, Kill 25 Lobba Gits
- Objective 2: Kill 5 Squig Lobbas
- Objective 3: Kill Orcitek Shoddy, Kill 5 Orcwerks Charger

Ceylnath Vineyards

- Objective 1: Kill 50 Gnoblar Ripjaws, Kill 100 Ogre Clawbreakers
- Objective 2: Kill 4 Ogre Hunters
- Objective 3: Kill Folbrak

CHAPTER 16: HOMECOMING

All of Eataine has mustered to push the Dark Elves and those who would fight with them back into the sea. Then we will take the fight to the Isle of the Dead itself.

PUBLIC QUESTS

The Tower of Lysean

- Objective 1: Kill 75 Bloody Sun Greenskins, Kill 50 Bloodsea Corsairs, Kill 50 Bloodsea Reavers
- Objective 2: Kill 20 Bloodsea Deathblades
- Objective 3: Kill 2 War Hydras, Kill 4 Bloodwrath Beastmasters
- Objective 4: Kill Lord Karydrath, Kill 2 Bloodwing Knights, Kill 2 Bloodwing Sorceresses

The Well of Sar-Saroth

- Objective 1: Kill 180 Guardian Spirits
- Objective 2: Destroy Cornerstone of Azyr, Destroy Cornerstone of Ghur, Destroy Cornerstone of Ghyran, Destroy Cornerstone of Shyish
- Objective 3: Defeat Bel-Hathor the Sage

WARCAMP: NONE

DARK ELVES

CHAPTERS 20–22

"The shining towers will blacken. The fields of grass will blow in the wind as ash. The chatter of the village market will turn to tortured screams. And all will be right with the world once again."

—Plaith the Black Hooded

CHAPTER 20: EMERALD STEPPE

We will crush these so-called noble lands of the High Elves and find joy in their sorrow.

PUBLIC QUESTS

Senthoi Pool

- Objective 1: Kill 50 Senthoi Defenders
- Objective 2: Capture the Second Terrace
- Objective 3: Hothenir Dawnedge, Kill 8 Champion Trueblade

The Phoenix Eye

- Objective 1: Claim battlefield locations
- Objective 2: Kill 4 Eversight Windbows
- Objective 3: Slay Faliarin Eversight

CHAPTER 21: BLIND HATRED

We advance on our High Elf kin with cold hearts and blood in our eyes. We will destroy all of them; there will be no quarter.

PUBLIC QUESTS

Blind Justice

- Objective 1: Central Plaza
- Objective 2: Eastern Quarter Secured, Southern Quarter Secured, Western Quarter Secured
- Objective 3: Kill Eltharion the Grim

Spirits of Eataine

- Objective 1: Kill 100 Guardians of Eataine
- Objective 2: Extinguish Biers of the Nobles
- Objective 3: Kill Yrilec the Proud

CHAPTER 22: LAST STAND

The final struggle for Ulthuan is at hand. The last of the Shining Defenders must be crushed and their citadel darkened.

PUBLIC QUESTS

Follow the Light

- Objective 1: Kill 120 High Elf Defenders
- Objective 2: Destroy Hopeless Citizens
- Objective 3: Kill Lord of Truelight and Lady of Truelight

Last Stand

- Objective #1: Kill 100 High Elves.

WARCAMP: NONE

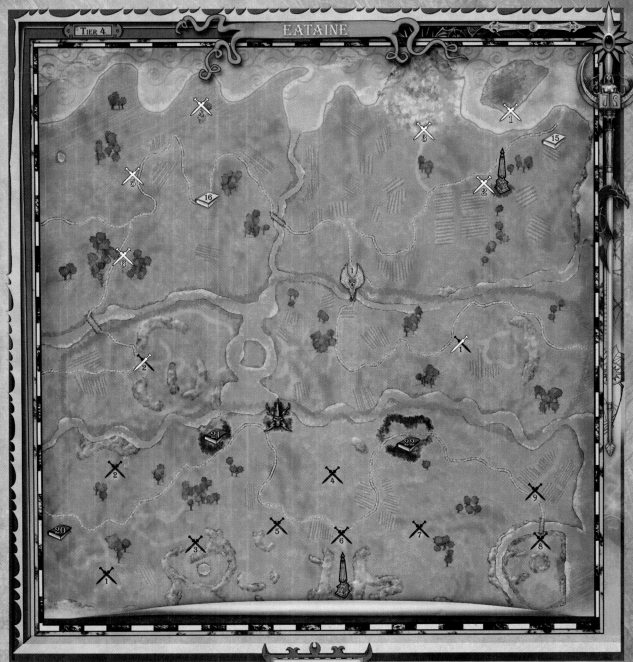

LEGEND

WARCAMPS: 1 – EATAINE MUSTERING   1 – EBONHOLD WATCH   RvR AREA (OUTLINED)

CHAPTER UNLOCK (DESTRUCTION)
20 – Dark Elf Chapter 20
21 – Dark Elf Chapter 21
22 – Dark Elf Chapter 22

CHAPTER UNLOCK (ORDER)
15 – High Elf Chapter 15
16 – High Elf Chapter 16

PUBLIC QUESTS (DESTRUCTION)
1 – Woodsong Manor
2 – The Phoenix Eye
3 – Senthoi Pool
4 – Dawnbreak Manor
5 – Blind Justice
6 – Spirits of Eataine
7 – Last Stand
8 – Glittering Citadel
9 – Follow the Light

PUBLIC QUESTS (ORDER)
1 – Da Orcwerks
2 – Ceylnath Vineyards
3 – Siege of Anyerrial
4 – Tower of Lysean
5 – Well of Sar-Saroth
6 – Neversong

PUBLIC QUESTS (NEUTRAL)
1 – Arbor of Light
2 – Pillars of Rememberance

FELL LANDING

TIER 4

FELL LANDING

TO CALEDOR

LEGEND

RvR Area (Outlined)

Portals
1 – To The Maw
2 – To Butcher's Pass
3 – Unknown

ISLE OF THE DEAD

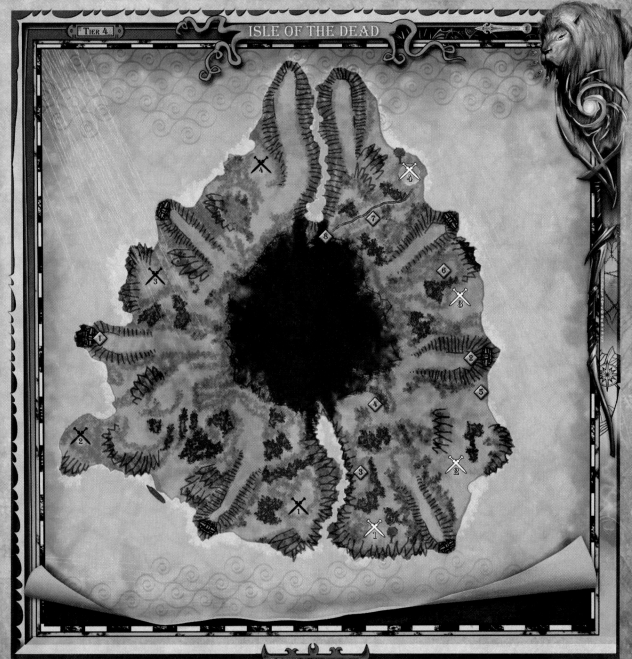

TIER 4

ISLE OF THE DEAD

LEGEND

CHAPTER UNLOCK (DESTRUCTION)
17 – DARK ELF CHAPTER 17
(UNLOCK IN DRAGONWAKE)

CHAPTER UNLOCK (ORDER)
17 – HIGH ELF CHAPTER 17
(UNLOCK IN DRAGONWAKE)

MAJOR LANDMARKS
1 – DARK ELF (ENTRANCE
FROM DRAGONWAKE)
2 – HIGH ELF (ENTRANCE
FROM DRAGONWAKE)
3 – STONE OF TRIALS
4 – SCRYING POOL
5 – SARUTHIL'S STAND
6 – SAVITHA'S STAND
7 – WATCH OF ALTHANIS
8 – CHOSEN PATH

RvR AREA (OUTLINED)

PUBLIC QUESTS (DESTRUCTION)
1 – RITUAL OF LIGHT
2 – RITUAL OF FIRE
3 – RITUAL OF METAL
4 – RITUAL OF SHADOW

PUBLIC QUESTS (ORDER)
1 – RITUAL OF LIFE
2 – RITUAL OF DEATH
3 – RITUAL OF THE HEAVENS
4 – RITUAL OF BEASTS

SHINING WAY

TIER 4   SHINING WAY

TO EATAINE

LEGEND

RvR Area (Outlined)

Portals
1 – To Stonewatch
2 – To Reikland
3 – To Stonewatch

REALM VS. REALM (RVR) COMBAT

Rise an' shine, ladies! Me name is Serg. Welcome to your new warcamp, biscuit-lovers. Get dressed an' outta the wagon, or else I's gonna come back an' plant me boot up your you-know-wheres. It's time to turn you worthless maggots into passable fighters.

Today your trainin' starts. I see some of you is takin' a look around. Maybe your lookin' for the tavern or your motha. Well guesswhat? Neither ain't 'ere! What we do 'ave is a lot of missions, scenarios, an' funerals foryou raw recruits.

We're gonna cover various battle strategies and tips foryour survival. An' we're only gonna cover this once, so listen up! What was that me fatha used to say? "Pain is weakness leavin' the body." You'd best remember that from here on out, recruit.

RVR BATTLEFIELDS

Let's discuss 'ow PvP (player vs. player) works. The whole world is a potential PvP environment. Constant battles exist in every spot of the world. It doesn't mattawhat area. You will have different opportunities in the PvP environment. Killin' an opponent is the basic idea, tho you can do this in many fronts: skirmishes, scenarios, battle-ields, an' campaigns.

The emphasis ain't the typical player vs. player, but realm vs. realm (RvR). What will 'appen out of this is a group effort, massive scale battles, an' lotza winin'. Group effort is fundamental. Granted, the solo effort will 'elp, but only in a small way compared to group efforts.

Sowhat is realm vs. realm? It means that players of Order are locked in a never-endin' battle with the players of Destruction. High Elf, Empire, an' Dwarf players battle hordes of Dark Elves, Chaos, an' greenskins.

SKIRMISHES

A skirmish is another name for open-world PvP. These types of battles are unpredictable 'cos one fight may be one on one, group vs. group, or even three on one. There is no core rules otha than to kill or be killed. The benefits of doin' skirmishes is to gain victory points.

Now that I've mentioned victory points, let's discusswhat that means. Any action a person 'as done in the game usually results in victory points. For example, killin' monsters or players, doin' player quests, or takin' over areas. Once enough victory points 'ave been acquired, the area taken is controlled by the winna.

Always keep moving. Don't give a stealther the opportunity to attack from the back.

SCENARIOS

A scenario is a queued-up battle zone or instance. To join a scenario, you can do two things: Go into a RvR area an' be flagged, then wait for a window to pop up askin' to join, or click on the icon near the map on the player screen. The latter gives a person the ability to do quests while waitin'. Once enough players from both sides 'ave signed up, a window will pop open askin' them if they is ready to join the instance.

There is different types of scenarios. Here are a few game-play types:

- Capture the Flag: Capture the enemy's flag and bring it back to your base.
- Death-Match: Kill the otha side.
- King of the Hill: Strategic areas where one 'as to gain control for a set amount of time.
- War ball: This is similar to capture the flag except there is one item that both teams must grab an' 'old.

Even startin' at Rank 1, scenarios are great to join. What about balance an' goin' against a Rank 10? Well, if your a Rank 1 you advance to about Rank 8, sowhat will 'appen is a new character would 'ave their 'it points increased to that of a Rank 8 an' make the Rank 1 as powerful as a Rank 8.

All scenarios are timed an' come to an end afta 15 or 20 minutes, tho most end sooner if one team gains enough points. All scenarios are score-based up to 500 points. Doin' various things within the scenarios, such as killin' players or possessin' an artifact, will give your realm points. You win if you 'ave the most points at the end of the scenario, or if your team gets to 500 points first. All scenarios 'ave a universal resurrection timer. In otha words, when you die, you may be able to resurrect within a few seconds or you may 'ave to wait a bit (up to 30 seconds). 'Owever, if a buddy resurrects you, you're back in action immediately. Within the scenarios, realms are represented by colors. Red is Destruction. Blue is Order. White is Neutral. All scenarios are bracketed to pit you against players of relatively the same rank. All scenarios 'ave a population cap. For the most part, this ranges from 12-on-12 to 24-on-24.

Strap your marchin' boots on, recruits. We be takin' you on some Empire vs. Chaos scenario runs forthe benefit of your tactics. Let's start wuv the easiest an' work toward the 'ardest:

NORDENWATCH

This is a 12-on-12, Tier 1, Empire vs. Chaos scenario. Anyone between Ranks 1 and 11 can join. There are three control points you must capture. The Fortress, Barracks, an' Lighthouse. The first flag you will capture is the one closest to your spawn point (Barracks forChaos, Lighthouse forOrder). The more people standin' on the flag the fasta you will capture it, an' the fasta the points start rollin' in. The second objective is up to you. You can run straight an' 'ead for the Fortress. Me suggestion is send one or two down the back route, the enemy usually doesn't take this paf 'cos it is long. 'Ave them watch for the enemy to leave the control point an' 'ead up to the Fort, an' then move in to take it while the rest 'ead for the Fort an' capture it. It ain't worth takin' all three flags. Best to try an' 'old the Fort an' one otha control point. So your main force is in one area. The Fort gives the most points, so you wonna 'old it.

TALABEC DAM

This is a 12-on-12, Tier 3, Empire vs. Chaos scenario. Now this, ya Goblin lovers, is a skirmish that takes place in the area of Talabecland near the Talabec River. Three locations are very important 'ere: Town, Bridge, an' Dam. Your first goal would be to gain control of the Bridge, 'coz once you is control of this, a bomb will spawn in the centa of the Town unda the tree. There is two paths toward the Dam where you wonna place the bomb; doesn't matta which you choose. Let one playa grab an' another escort. Don't send everyone; the rest stay behind an' keep control of the spawn point. You do this for a few reasons. One, if the runna is killed an' the bomb not picked up by 'is escort in five seconds, the bomb will respawn in centa of Town. Someone else can grab an' take off toward the Dam. Once you reach the Dam, you place the bomb in the glowin' circle an' move away. Now if the otha side gains control of the bomb, you must keep their runners from reachin' your Bridge an' blowin' it up. Now there is a few ways for smart people to do this. Watch an' see 'ow many go with the runna. If they just a few, send a group afta them an' destroy 'im before he reaches 'is target. If a lot, stay an' gain control of the Bridge an' grab the bomb next time it spawns.

HIGH PASS CEMETERY

High Pass Cemetery is a 12-on-12, Tier 3, Empire vs. Chaos scenario. Anyone Rank 20–31 can take part. There is two capture locations in this scenario: the Crypt an' the Stag. Both sides start behind a closed gate. There are three paths to choose from when the gate opens. One to the left, one to the right, an' one straight ahead. I

straight. An' you must 'old both points to earn points toward the goal of 500. So ownin' one gets you nothin'. There is very little space to move around the tombs. Best to keep the fightin' in the middle of they graveyard where you 'as more maneuverability. Also don't fight on the steps leadin' down afta the gate opens or afta you rez, if the enemy is at the bottem. There are two otha routes that you can take to keep from gettin' camped at your rez point.

Me suggestion would be send one person to the left to take that point, an' one to the right to take that point, an' rest 'ead for middle an' attack all comers to keep them busy. This is by far one of the smallest fronts. I kid you not when I say there ain't much room for you or the enemy to go. So be prepared for full-on combat an' no relief from start to finish.

REIKLAND HILLS

This is a 12-on-12, Tier 4, Empire vs. Chaos scenario. Capture one of three points: Broken Bridge, The Mill, an' The Factory. Unlike otha scenarios up until now, the points you capture are not all up at one time, an' they move randomly. Once it's taken, it disappears afta a short time an' another appears, about 60 seconds later. The centa of the valley is always the first to spawn so get down there as fast as you can when the battle starts. When it disappears, fight your way as fast as you can to capture the next one open. You must move fast an' be very aware of your surroundin' area an' the place of the enemy. There is right no cover. You could leave a scout runnin' around to spot the next spawn an' guide you to it. This is a 'ead-to-'ead clash o'a the spawn points. Don't jump off the broken bridge as you enter. You will take a lot of fall damage or die. Work your way down the mountain an' to the first spawn spot. There is no way back up, once you is down in the skirmish.

BATTLE FOR PRAAG

This is a 18-on-18, Tier 4, Empire vs. Chaos scenario. Unlike most where you get one point for killin' otha players, 'ere you get five points, an' that could mean the difference between winnin' an' losin' at the end. Each side starts out ownin' two flags with one netural one located in the middle. You must 'old the enemy flag for a set time before it is considered captured, so don't run off. Stay an' defend until you control it. The flags fartha back on each realm are the ones that give the most points, but they is also 'ardest to 'old 'coz they is the farthest apart. Would advise 'oldin' yours an' takin' the one in the middle. If the enemy seems weak, then you can make a move for their flag in the back.

There is plenty of places 'ere for casters an' 'ealers to hide, so use them a lot. Remember killin' players 'ere seems to be more important than 'oldin' all the flags, so dowhat ever it takes to lure them out an' kill them.

BATTLEFIELDS

In every tier between racial pairings, there is locations on the map that displays a battlefield icon. The battlefields usually 'ave an objective. For example, an objective could be to defend an area or attack an area. Once the objective is met, victory points are given. This is in close relation to skirmishes 'cos of the open PvP concept, but these are in

Some words of warnin', tho. If you are above a rank limit for a zone, an' you try to go into a battlefield, big red letters will flash warnin' you to turn back or suffa the consequences. Afta the count of 10, if you stay, you are turned into a chicken. That's right, I said a chicken. The spell stays on in the battlefield, an' it lasts a while after you exit. Keeps you power-mongers from beatin' on lesser ranks.

Campaigns

Victory Points

A campaign is a long process that requires everyone's 'elp no mattawhat rank. A key factor in campaigns is victory points. Part of the victory points trickles up to the next tier until eventually it's the last tier. This is 'ow the lowa ranks contribute to the overall scheme of things. What will be seen on the map in each zone is the battlefronts bein' owned by one side. This is displayed with the icon of the winnin' side bein' displayed all over the map. Battlefronts are won by victory points.

Tier 4 is where the final battles happen. Everything is applied like the previous tiers except that there is a neutral area where once it is controlled by the invaders they open new scenarios. These new scenarios give the attackers access to the capital city. At the same time, the defender can push back the invaders and gain control of the neutral zone, which will then allow them to invade their city.

Keep Battle Plans

Keep Basics:

- There is at least one keep per zone, per realm, in all tier pairings except for Tier 1.
- Tier 2 zones have one keep each (two per pairing).
- Tier 4 zones have two keeps each for a total of six keeps (per pairing).

The taking of a keep has three distinct stages:

- Breach the exterior of the keep.
- Breach the keep's inner sanctum.
- Defeat the Keep Lord.

City Sieging

Let's give you an example of city sieging with Altdorf. Afta you win zone control, you can then 'ead to siege the fortress. 'Ere is where it is gonna get very chaotic. Very important you all stay togetha an' close; too easy to be picked off if you're playin' alone. You is to breach the outta walls an' take out the fortress lord to gain access to the city. Now just 'cos you gain entry to the city, does no mean you own it yet. This is when the real fun begins.

You will find a few quest givers inside the city. Get these quest. As you is stormin' the city, these quest tell you to kill civilians, loot, burn buildings, an' encounta boss mobs. As you kill each boss mob, such as the Temple of Sigmar, you will gain access to new instances like the Sigmar Crypts located at the bottom of Temple of Sigmar. I prefer a special group for this—it needs to be done as a raid—but take if possible a tank, healer, mage, an' then fill in the last spots. I do mean real healers, with full healing abilities. The bosses 'ere is 'ard an' it will take all workin' togetha to get them down an' move on.

Also along the way, burn everythin' you can, things like rubbish bins, lampost, an' firebins. There is a possibility of the fire spreadin' if flammable objects is nearby. When you get to the Pavilion area you will need to kill 150 players, burn 50 items, an' control the Battlefield Objectives. NPCs is gonna make this very 'ard on you. You can also break into places like the auction 'ouse an' the tavern, just to raise a little 'ell along your way.

When a city is contested, the battle will be divided into 48-on-48 instances to determine the fate of the campaign. Across all the instances, players will fight in a city-wide Conflict Public Quest, take over battlefield objectives an' participate in city scenarios. All of these actions feed into a pool of victory points, which operates like Zone Control. When the attackers reach 65 percent, they capture the city. Should the defenders reach 65 percent, they will 'ave defended the city successfully.

Siege Weapons

Keeps an' surroundin' areas will have several pre-set locations where siege weapons can be deployed an' used by players. Some siege weapons will simply work by interacting with them for a time to damage pre-determined targets, such as a door. Otha siege weapons, such as the trebuchet, will give players a ground target area effect (GTAE) circle, which they can move to attack specific locations.

There are four types of siege weapons:

- Rams can be used against keep doors or otha pre-selected targets.
- Ballistae can be used against individual players or otha siege weapons.
- Cannons, catapults, and trebuchets can be aimed to fire at a selected location, doing splash damage to players or otha siege weapons.
- Boiling oil can be used to rain down liquid death from keeps and walls.

Siege weapons must be built on siege pads found in the world or on keeps. They can't be used anywhere else, and the number of siege weapons used is limited by the number of pads. Furthermore, siege weapons can't be moved, once placed, although they can be rotated.

Siege weapons don't require a trade skill to build and can be deployed by anyone. They are purchased from warcamps or from an NPC inside the keeps. Once purchased, a siege weapon will take up a single inventory space. These items have no weight, and can be carried and traded by anyone. Players can carry as many siege weapons as they want, as long as they have space in their inventory. When a player deploys a siege weapon, the item will disappear from the player's inventory.

Siege weapons will increase in cost and power based on location/tier purchased. A siege weapon purchased in a higher tier cannot be placed on a lower-tier siege pad. Only one siege weapon can be on a pad at a time. Siege weapons have a life span of 30 minutes and can be destroyed by the enemy before that time.

SIEGE PADS

Siege pads are pre-set locations on which siege weapons can be deployed. They look like large slabs of stone, or engraved pads.

Keeps will 'ave one siege pad per destructible door for placing rams (for the attackers) and several pads for ballistae, cannons/trebuchets, and boiling oil on the bastions (for the defenders). The surrounding area of a keep will have four to eight locations on the frontal arc of the keep for ballista or cannons/trebuchets, and one to three locations per side arc of a keep.

Players have the ability to destroy and repair siege pads. Siege pads can be destroyed by anything, an' a destroyed siege pad cannot be used to deploy siege weapons as the ground is littered with wood planks and metal bits. Siege pads have very few hit points but repair themselves after roughly 3-5 minutes.

RAMS

Rams are large siege engines used to batter down doors. Up to four players can be seated on a ram at time and damage dealt is determined by the number of players present (25 percent damage per person). Rams provide cover from attacks on high, an' player are shielded from 50 percent of all damage that rains down from above.

BALLISTAE

Ballistae are large bolt throwers used to skewer an enemy player or destroy siege weapons. They are mounted on rotatin' platforms on the siege pads to allow for precise aimin', and inflict massive amounts of damage to a single target.

CATAPULTS, CANNONS, TREBUCHETS

Catapults, cannons, and trebuchets destroy whole areas, so you can splash damage to multiple targets. They cannot shoot through solid structures such as buildings, roofs, or otha structures. As such, players inside a keep's gatehouse or inner sanctum are immune to this splash damage.

PUBLIC QUESTS

Public quests (PQs) are generally outside RvR areas an' free from the assaults of enemy players. However, dere are some quests inside RvR area, or neutral public quests, that allow both Order an' Destruction players to participate. Of course, because both sides are eligible, this also means that enemy players may choose to disrupt your attempts to solve the PQ, rather than complete it. You should watch your back more than normal in these PQs, for you 'ave more than just the common foes to worry about.

EPIC QUESTS

You gain control of the city in the same way that you gain zone control. Once eitha side wins, the followin' will 'appen. If the attackin' army gains control of the city, they will 'ave the uppa 'and over the defenders. This will prevent the defenders from re-spawnin' within the city, an' allow the attackers to clear the city streets completely of any impedin' forces. Also, at this time the two epic PQs will open up. If the defenders win, it will work in reverse an' the attackers can't spawn in the city an' the campaign will reset to retakin' the zone.

The two epic PQs is 'ow you unlock the king. Once control of the city is won by the attackin' army, these two PQs will open up. You will still be confronted by defendin' players tryin' to keep you from gainin' access to these PQs to unlock their king. The city scenarios will still be open as well, to allow the defenders a chance to retake their city back more quickly.

BATTLE TO THE KING

This is a 24-man instance. So be geared, 'ave a warband, an' bring your best. You will 'ave to gain control of Tier 4 content. Tho it is a lot of work an' a bit slow, you will do this by winnin' scenarios, claimin' objectives located on your mini-map, an' conquerin' keeps. When all this is done an' your side controls the zone, the gate will lock an' the defenders will be locked out.

DEFENDING

NPCs will 'elp alot when it comes to defendin'. So the defendin' is a lot easier than the takin'. Extinguish fires as you see them. Less things burn, the betta off your side will be. When the enemy rushes through the gates, don't be right up on them. Stand back a bit an' let your ranged attacks 'ave a go at them first. Make sure each group 'as a healer an' they is near their group an' in the back, not in sight where they can be taken out easily.

INFLUENCE

Influence is isolated by chapter. As you progress from location to location, you encounter new chapters that tell you more about the events in the world. Every chapter is full of its own public quests (PQs) an' influence rewards. Influence experience is gained most commonly by participatin' in PQs. As you gain experience, you can claim rewards from that chapter. There is three levels of awards gained from influence: basic, advanced, an' elite. Basic is usually consumables, like potions. Advanced is usually green equipment (less powerful gear), an' elite is usually blue equipment (more powerful gear). You claim your reward by seekin' out the Rally Master. You can always check the rewards of the chapter you're in by clickin' on the Influence Progress bar. It will open up your Tome of Knowledge to the page that details the chapter's story, objectives, an' rewards.

RISKIN' DEATH FOR THE REWARDS

Why would anyone wonna PvP? The only way to get the epic gear in this world is to PvP. Consider personal goals like killin' the most people or gainin' 'igh level realm rank. Most of all, it is fun. Winnin' for the most part gives victory an' Renown points. It's possible to rank up just through PvP action.

Dyin' doesn't result in any major penalties. There is not too many penalties or loss of items or experience. There might be a possibility of a long run back to a battlefield, but it's a minor setback. In a scenario, afta deaf, a person spawns at the beginnin' of the zone, an' there is a waitin' time before that 'appens, which could take up to 30 seconds. Outside of RvR areas, a death spawns you back to the nearest camp. Don't worry 'bout death so long as your 'avin' fun and gainin' ranks.

CAREER CHOICE

The only considerations anyone must take iswhat type of player they imagine themselves. Does breakin' bones with a weapon sound good? Is keepin' your allies from takin' a dirt nap important? Does dealin' a lot damage from afar seem like fun? 'Ere are the careers as they fit with PvP, an' some of their better strategies:

DESTRUCTION CAREERS

BLACK ORC

Black Orcs pride themselves on their excellent battle plans. You start by hittin' somethin', then hittin' it 'arder, and if need be, hit it even 'arder again. Clobber is the start of the plan. Alternately you can use Wot Armor? to start your plan and reduce your target's armor. Trip 'Em Up works well an' deals damage over time while snaring your target. Skull Thumper is the "best plan" and hits 'arder than the previous moves. Shut your Face can silence those pesky wizzies and healers. Use Challenge to taunt opponents so they'll do less damage to anyone but you. Use The Biggest! to 'ave a chance to buff your strength after every hit. Save the Runts will split damage toward your guarded groupmate with yourself, 'elping to keep them alive longer. Where You Going? can root up to four targets 'round you, which can 'elp create some breathing room for your group.

CHOSEN

Cleave is a Chosen's basic attack, and Seeping Wound adds damage over time. Touch of Palsy is a powerful effect that damages your target as long as they are moving. Dizzying Blow will snare your target and if they 'appen to be ailin', their abilities will briefly take longer to refresh. Tooth of Tzeentch deals damage upfront and adds additional damage to the next attack against your target. Use Taunt to reduce the damage your opponent can deal to everyone but yourself. Repel knocks players away from allies you are defending, and Petrify can root them in place an' slow them down. Dreadful Fear is a brief aura that will reduce the auto attack speed of your targeted enemy, and will then radiate an effect that gives everyone in your group a chance to deal extra damage against anyone in your aura.

DISCIPLE OF KHAINE

As a combat healer, you need to personally strike opponents to regain Soul Essence used for healing. Covenants are lastin' auras that provide benefits to you and your group. Using Lacerate on an opponent cripples them with damage over time. 'Coz they are now crippled, Cleave Soul will deal Spirit damage 'stead of normal damage, and Flay will snare your target. If attackin' a caster, use Consume Thought to silence them. Soul Infusion heals over time an' can be quickly applied to anyone in need. Khaine's Embrace can be cast fairly quickly an' will heal everyone in your group. Rend Soul is an offensive ability that will heal allies based on the damage dealt. Terrifying Vision will reduce the damage you take from a single opponent, but will end early if you strike them. When needin' to fall back, use Flee.

MAGUS

Start encounters by placin' your Pink Horror and then cast Mutating Blue Fire to deal a large amount of upfront damage, followed by damage over time. Follow up with Glean Magic to reduce your target's magic resistance. Use Flickering Red Fire while Mutating Blue Fire refreshes. Surge of Insanity is an instant cast and will set back your target's buildin' abilities slightly. Use Theft of Words to briefly silence otha casters. Dissolving Mist deals damage and lowers your target's Toughness, makin' them take more damage. Use Daemon Lash when possible on targets that have closed the gap to you. Tzeentch's Grip can root targets 'round you in place and can give you time to cast longer buildin' spells or to use Flee an' escape entirely.

Use height to your advantage. If there are stairs, go up them and shoot up there. It takes enemies longer to reach you.

MARAUDER

Marauders are all about runnin' up to people and 'acking at them till they stop movin'. A Marauder should always have a mutation on, such as the Gift of Brutality. Use Charge to gain a burst of speed and quickly close the distance with any ranged attacker trying to attack you from afar. Alternately, you can also use Terrible Embrace to drag a victim to you an' your group. Start out by usin' Corruption to lower your opponent's Toughness, and Pulverize to reduce their defenses. Next try stackin' on multiple Rends to get a steady stream of damage. Convulsive Slashing deals a lot of damage over three seconds, afta which it's good to use Flail until Corruption an' Rend need reapplication. For an extra boost of damage, use Ferocious Assault, but try to finish the combat before the negative effect kicks in. If your prey tries to run away, use Debilitate to slow them down.

SHAMAN

Mork wants you to be shootin'. The more you shoot, the more Gork wants you to be healing. Every offensive or healing spell cast will fill your *Waaagh!* pool for the opposite deity. Usin' an ability opposite of what type filled the pool will drain it, which reduces cast times or increases the effectiveness of that spell. Start fights with Brain Bursta, and then quickly toss on Bleed Fer' Me to further damage your target while healing your defensive target. Use 'Ey, Quit Bleeding to keep health topped off and Bigger, Better, an' Greener to restore large amounts. Don' Feel Nuthin can be used as a heal buffer as the recipient will absorb a large amount of damage over 10 seconds. Use You Got Nuthin! on otha casters to shut them down briefly. Continually attackin' will let you instant cast your large heal or instantly rez an ally. If you get in over your 'ead, use Eeeek! an' Flee to try and escape.

SORCERESS

Start encounters with Doombolt and then use Chillwind to add a damage over time effect. Stack three copies of Word of Pain on a target to reduce Willpower and eventually deliver a huge burst of damage. Shadow Spike can add a powerful damage over time to everyone in front of you, diverting healer's attentions from your Word of Pain victim. Usin' Stricken Voices can outright silence the opposing healers, making them unable to react to your incomin' damage spike. Obsessive Focus increases your damage against a single target, perfect for the incomin' Word of Pain. Fire Gloomburst to quickly deal damage and increase your Dark Magic until Word of Pain activates. The higher your Dark Magic, the more damage you can do, but also the more likely you are to damage yourself in the process. With Grip of Fear you can root all those near you, an' get off some damage spells unhindered. If you get overwhelmed, use Flee to escape.

SQUIG HERDER

Summon your trusty horned Squig to bounce 'round an' attack your foes. Use Lots o' Arrers an' Run 'n Shoot to deal the bulk of your damage, usin' Plink to fill in gaps. Poison Arrer is a powerful attack, great for startin' and finishin' a fight. Drop That!! is great against weapon-based classes. Farty Squig can deal a fair amount of damage to everyone near

quickly summon another. You can't shoot at point-blank ranges, so use Cut Ya! to add damage over time and Stabbity to finish off opponents in your face. Use Flee to retreat while your pet attacks your pursuer.

WITCH ELF

With Shadow Prowler you can sneak 'round an' start fights on your own terms. From Prowler you can use openers such as Treacherous Assault to give yourself an edge. Continue with Kiss of Betrayal to increase the amount of damage you do. Follow up with Wracking Pains an' Slice to build up further points for a high damage Puncture finisher. When possible, try to connect with Agonizing Wounds from the rear to reduce armor. If fightin' a caster, use Throat Slitter to silence them. Use Enchanting Beauty to reduce the damage comin' from targets you are not currently attackin'. If there are too many opponents for you to deal with, use Flee to escape.

ZEALOT

Before battle, place marks on both yourself and allies to grant them additional protection an' abilities. Start battles with Scourge an' follow up with Warp Reality once monsters start runnin' toward you. Cast Harbinger of Doom to reduce damage you take once an opponent is attackin' you. With Flash of Chaos an' Veil of Chaos you should be able to heal or prevent a fair bit of damage. If things get too intense, use Flee to retreat from battle. Once safely out of harm's way, you can use Elixir of Dark Blessings to heal a large amount to otha allies or yourself. If they are beyond savin', cast Tzeentch Shall Remake You to bring back your fallen allies. Castin' Mark of Remaking on yourself allows you to self resurrect and 'ave a second chance of savin' your group. Dust of Pandemonium can heal everyone in your group at the same time.

ORDER CAREERS

ARCHMAGE

Archmages rely on all magic in balance. As they cast offensive actions they generate excess energy inside their bodies. The next defensive spell, the Archmage uses this excess energy to help power the spell, making it cast much more quickly. Castin' multiple defensive spells in a row will also generate this extra energy, which will in turn be used for the offensive spells. Archmages function best when alternating between offensive an' defensive actions. When damage is desirable, start with the Law of Conductivity and then Radiant Lance. If the enemies are ignorin' you, Searing Touch will deal large amounts of damage quickly. Pay attention to the 'ealth of your groupmages during combat. When a heal becomes necessary, use Boon of Hysh if you are not currently being attacked. If a faster heal is necessary, Healing Energy will do the job. To combat small persistent damage, cast Lambent Aura. If everyone in your group is damaged, the Blessing of Isha will help heal everyone at once. Cast Prismatic Shield before combat to 'elp increase your groupmates' resistance to magical damage

BRIGHT WIZARD

Due to the volatile nature of the Red Wind of Fire that they manipulate, the Bright Wizard always risks a backlash that could incinerate 'imself as well as his opponent. This building-up is known as combustion, an' the greater the level of combustion a Bright Wizard places into his destructive spells, the more likely they will explode with a critical hit. 'Owever even the most skilled wizard will get burned when playin' with fire, an' pushing the combustion level too high will result in a backlash of magical energy that will damage the wizard 'imself. Begin each fight by throwin' a large Fireball at your enemy. Follow it up with a quick castin' Sear and then an instant Ignite. By this time, Fireball should 'ave inished cooldown, and you can repeat the cycle for anything left alive. When omeone gets close to you, cast Fire Cage on them and fall back to get more distance. In RvR, use Burning Iron to deal damage an' remove valuable action points from the enemy and cast Rain of Fire to deal damage to large groups of enemies. For buffs, make ure to keep Flames of Rhiun and Flame Shield active for yourself and your group. If you are ever desperate for action points, Burnout will provide them at the cost of doin' damage to yourself.

ENGINEER

Wieldin' weapons of the highest craftsmanship, the Engineer brings his own brand of error to the battlefield. Guns an' grenades are his forte, but the true mastery of the Engineer is the gadgets he deploys. Destructive self-powered turrets an' hidden mines help enforce the Engineer's will upon his enemies. Just before a fight, place a turret down and take a few steps away. Enable Slow and Steady for added damage during the pull. Choose your target, and use Focused Fire to start the fight. When the channel ends, use quick Gun Blast. As the target reaches you, fire off Incendiary Rounds. Follow up with Friction Burn and then use Spanner Swipe an' Flashbang Grenade till the target is dead. If your turret ever attracts the attention of a target, step back and return to usin' Gun Blast.

IRONBREAKER

A sturdy tank career, the Ironbreaker is designed to be able to absorb damage while protectin' his groupmates. When the Ironbreaker or his oath friend are attacked, he gains Grudge. Based on this Grudge, he can use powerful attacks an' debuffs to 'elp damage and disable his enemies. Start each fight with a few basic Grudging Blow attacks. Follow those up with a Guarded Attack to increase your armor an' use Binding Grudge to prevent the target from runnin' away. When sufficient Grudge has built up, use Knock Ye Silly to boost your strength an' your oath friend's Willpower. Also use Vengeful Strike for an extremely efficient attack that comes with a little defense boost. If your Oath Friend runs out of action points, trigger Watch an' Learn. Each time you hit someone for the next 15 seconds, you gain more action points! Before the fight, place Oath Friend and Guard on another target who you wish to protect. Rune Priests are a good example.

RUNE PRIEST

Dependin' on his Mastery choices, the Rune Priest can choose from strong single target heals, massive healing over time, or area-effect heals. Supportin' this choice, he gets a number of runic buffs that he can apply to his groupmates. These buffs both increase a stat for the target, as well as give him an ability he can activate every couple of minutes. The Rune Priest must keep a balance between offense and defense. Rune of Restoration is a highly efficient heal, but cannot be used while the Rune Priest is being attacked. While under attack, healing duties should fall to Grungni's Gift. If your entire group is hurt, Blessing of Valaya will help everyone at once. Offensively, things are simple. Start Rune of Immolation burnin' on the target and then blast away with Rune of Striking. If anyone gets close to you, use Rune of Sundering to knock them away. Before combat starts, use one of your Oath Runes on each player in your group, dependin' on their preference.

SHADOW WARRIOR

Scoutin' ahead of the armies of the High Elves, the Shadow Warriors are experts at keepin' distance and usin' their powerful bows. Assumin' they are weak when caught out of position would be a fatal mistake. Shadow Warriors are taught in three different fightin' disciplines: the Path of the Scout, which focuses on long-range attacks, the Path of the Skirmisher, which focuses on short-range but highly mobile attacks, and the Path of the Assault, which teaches highly damaging attacks with a sword. Master Shadow Warriors have learned how to flow from one discipline to another seamlessly, making them one of the most deadly enemies on the battlefield. Focusing on the Path of the Scout, start combat with Festering Arrow. Follow with a Rapid Fire and a Broadhead Arrow. If the enemy 'asn't closed to melee range, repeat the cycle, usin' Eagle Eye instead of Rapid Fire. If he has closed, use Grim Slash to finish him off. For extra bursts of damage, engage the Vengeance of Nagarythe during the combat. If the target begins to cast a spell, fire a Throat Shot to silence him. Before combat, make sure to enable the Scout Stance.

SWORDMASTER

A powerful tank class, the Swordmaster can soak up damage as well as anyone in the world. Usin' the balance system, the Swordmaster has three basic levels of balance. Dependin' on what state of balance he is in, certain abilities are unlocked. Each ability increases the level of balance to the next one in the ladder until the third (or perfect) level is reached, which unlocks the most powerful abilities, and the entire process starts over. Before a fight starts, the Swordmaster should activate Heaven's Blade to enhance his blade with magical power. Startin' a fight, most of the abilities for the Swordmaster are unusable due to a lack of balance. Graceful Strike or Gryphon's Lash will put the Swordmaster into the second stage of balance (improved). He can then use Quick Incision or Eagle's Flight, an attack that will greatly increase his chance to Parry for a short time. These attacks will also move the Swordmaster into the perfect stage of balance. Once 'ere, he can use the powerful Dragon's Talon, which resets the balance level and starts the process over again. If the Swordmaster is fightin' an enemy caster, substitutin' Whispering Wind for Dragon's Talon will silence the enemy for a short time. If a healer or mage is taking frequent damage, Guard can help spread out the damage to the Swordmaster.

WARRIOR PRIEST

Sigmar is a warrior god, and his priests gain divine favor only by fightin' to defend the Empire that he built. The holy symbol of Sigmar is a hammer, and the Warrior Priests 'ave adopted the warhammer as their weapon of choice in honor of their patron. The Righteous Fury of Sigmar fills the Warrior Priest with each swing of their weapon, and this divine power fuels their healing magic. This becomes something of both a freedom and a restriction for the Warrior Priest; 'coz all of his magic is powered by Righteous Fury, he can throw 'imself wholeheartedly into melee combat and then still 'ave resources left to heal with, but at the same time, his healing capabilities become dramatically more limited when there are no enemies in arm's reach. Preceed a battle with Prayer of Absolution. Once in combat, the Warrior Priest can be one of the more challenging classes to play. When attackin' enemies, use Sigmar's Fist to boost your strength, Castigation to lower the target's Initiative, and then Divine Strike and Sigmar's Radiance to deal damage and heal at the same time. If you need to heal large values quickly, use Divine Assault if you are near an enemy to attack them, or Divine Aid if you are not. If you need Righteous Fury to power heals in a hurry, rely on Supplication.

White Lion

Standin' aside his majestic feline companion, the White Lion is a sight to be feared. Wieldin' a mighty great axe, he and his pet are one of the most destructive teams that can be found. White Lions learn three different basic fightin' stances, with each stance offerin' different benefits to 'imself and his pet. Start a fight by usin' Axe Toss to attract the attention of the target. Send in your lion while the target charges. When the target arrives, lead with Coordinated Strike, an attack that both you and your lion use at the same time. Follow up with Pack Assault an' Hack. If you can get behind the target, substitute Sundering Chop for Hack. Repeat this basic cycle. If an enemy is a player, use Charge! to speed across the battlefield an' attack. If you need to bring the enemy to you, tell your lion to Fetch. Outside of combat, engage Trained to Kill to give yourself and your pet important bonuses.

Witch Hunter

The Witch Hunters are deadly fighters who seek out and destroy anything tainted by the touch of Chaos. They lay down accusations at sword point until they're satisfied of their enemy's guilt, and then unleash an execution with the booming voice of their pistol. Their combat abilities are bolstered by a variety of sacred artifacts, such as blessed bullets that add additional effects to their executions, and potent Holy Relics, which can briefly imbue them with great power. Start each fight with Incognito, sneakin' up upon your enemy. When you arrive, launch an opening with Burn Armor, and quickly follow with a Seeker's Blade and then Razor Strikes. Use Absolution when your combo points are full, and repeat the Razor Strike/Absolution chain. If you can get behind your enemy, substitute Torment for Razor Strike an' use Pistol Whip to stun the enemy. Make sure to use Blessed Bullets of Cleansing before combat.

> *Bring potions, potions, and more potions. They can give you the extra edge against an evenly matched opponent.*

Career Match-ups

Tanks

Careers: Black Orc, Chosen, Ironbreaker, Swordmaster

- Strong vs. Melee DPS
- Even vs. Tanks/Melee Healers
- Weak vs. Ranged DPS/Ranged Healers

Melee DPS

Careers: Marauder, White Lion, Witch Elf, Witch Hunter

- Strong vs. Ranged DPS/Ranged Healers
- Even vs. Melee DPS
- Weak vs. Tanks/Melee Healers

Ranged DPS

Careers: Bright Wizard, Engineer, Magus, Shadow Warrior, Sorceress, Squig Herder

- Strong vs. Tanks
- Even vs. Ranged DPS/Ranged Healers
- Weak vs. Melee DPS

Melee Healers

Careers: Disciple of Khaine, Warrior Priest

- Strong vs. Melee DPS
- Even vs. Tanks/Melee Healers
- Weak vs. Ranged DPS

Ranged Healers

Careers: Archmage, Rune Priest, Shaman, Zealot

- Strong vs. Tanks
- Even vs. Ranged DPS/Ranged Healers
- Weak vs. Melee DPS

RENOWN SKILLS

In PvP, experience is given by Renown points. So players will 'ave both a player rank an' a Renown rank. It is said that Renown ranks can go pass Renown rank 100. For player ranks, it can only go up to 40.

Renown is shared between group members. Group members must be nearby an' active in RvR in order to share Renown. For instance, if a group deals 50 percent damage to a target they will split 50 percent of the Renown, while the rest goes to who dealt the rest of the damage. Healers receive Renown for healing from a separate pool. Players who heal in combat receive a little bonus of Renown. This encourages healers to keep healing ratha than try to deal damage.

You can rank up by spendin' time in the RvR area, but it's fasta to pick up regular quests too. Realistically, by doin' PQs an' questin' anyone will level fasta, but a key stat, Renown ranks (RR) will be missin'. With thee Renown you gain, you can increase your stats via the Renown Trainers. Basically, you purchase Renown skills, which can net pure bonuses to stats, or give solo (an' perhaps a group) advantages in RvR itself. Also, there's an option to purchase Champion Equipment, which is fairly powerful equipment that can 'elp in both PvE an' RvR. What is purchased depends on your overall rank an' Renown rank.

Conversely, if you just RvR for ranks, this will be a lot slowa for levelin'. The amount of experience you get from RvRin' is a lot less than simply questin' or playin' out PQs. Also, you will miss out on Tome of Knowledge unlocks an' gear you would get from

Granted Rewards	
Rewards	Rank
RvR Tactic Slot	1
Career Siege Ability	10
RvR Tactic Slot	20
Career Siege Ability	30
+1 Mastery Point	40
Career Siege Ability	45
+1 Mastery Point	50
Rank 4 Morale Ability	55
+1 Mastery Point	60
+ 25 AP	65
+1 Mastery Point	70
+ 50 AP	75
+1 All Mastery Levels	80

Queuin' up for scenarios at all times iswhat I do. Now, if I's in the middle of somethin' or in a PQ, I may decline it, but for the most part I join them as much as possible. The best part is when you're done with the scenario, you appear right back where you were when you joined.

MASTERIES AND TACTICS

You 'ave three paths, each with a theme. Some of your Core abilities "belong" to a path (the Warrior Priest ability Casti- gation belongs in the Wrath Mastery line, for example). Every time you spend a point in a Mastery line, your Core abilities associated with that line get stronga. Higher up the Mastery line are some Tactics, abilities, an' Morales that you can purchase with Mastery points. Your first Tactic, for example, takes three Mastery points to climb up the line, an' then one more to purchase the Tactic itself. Mastery points are gained by gainin' ranks, earnin' Renown, an' from Tome of Knowledge unlocks.

You build sets of Tactics for certain situations. A Warrior Priest, for example, might 'ave a healing set, a soloin' set, an' a PVP set, an' then you make active whicheva set you wonna use. So you're usin' Tactics 'ow they were meant to be.

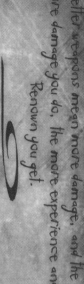

SOLOIN'

I 'ave soloed quite a bit, an' the method that worked best for me is this. It is fairly easy to finish Tier 1 with little to no difficulties in your own racial pairin'. I think all three T1 racial pairings cover Chapters 1–5 of that race's story. In Tier 2 it starts to get to the point that the chapters in one racial pairin' is not enough to get you all the way to Tier 3 (this is with doin' very little RvR in that tier, so if you do a lot of RvR the experience gain there would likely be enough). If you just wonna level as quickly as possible, the fastest way that worked for me startin' in tier was this: If I was startin' Chapter 6 in the Dwarf/greenskin pairin', I would finish all quests/influence in Chapter 6 an' 7, then I would travel over to, say, Empire Tier 2. There I would do Chapters 6, 7, 8, 9, then travel back to Dwarf/greenskin an' do 8, 9, 10, an' 11 there.

The only way to gain experience in PvP fights is to 'elp in a kill or heal your allies. If a ranged attacka, for example, ain't doin' damage, then they're not gainin' any points. Same with a healer. If you ain't healing, you ain't benefitting yourself. Find the battle and do what you do best, and gain some Renown points already.

SKIRMISHES

MELEE STRATEGIES

You need to be close foryour melee attacks to be effective, so close as fast as you can with your target. If he hasn't spotted you right away, charge from his blindside and get off a quick attack from the rear. Deal as much damage as possible in a short amount of time. This will usually send your foe into a retreat. Snare if you can, or slow him down whatever way you can, so your foe doesn't escape your punishing attacks. Against multiple targets, survey the situation to see if you have support or should play defensive, and always, always, use the terrain to your best benefit.

RANGED STRATEGIES

Skirmishes are great for soloin'. A ranged fighter depends on themselves an' no one else. Let's say a ranged attacker is in open country 'unting an Order player. Crossin' the Destruction area an' into the Order area will make it easier to find Order players an' start a skirmish. They will most likely be questin'. There's also a good chance that there could be a whole lot of them, so choose your battles wisely. Also look forstragglers, which is always fun for a ranged attacker to pick off. In me experience, they normally run. The ones that charge me face the same music as the straggler would receive.

HEALER STRATEGIES

Skirmishes will be the easiest place for a soloist to perfect abilities an' tactics. You will make mistakes an' you will lose. Skirmishes is a great place to learn 'ow to battle 'cos you only 'ave yourself to depend on. For instance, you may learn that Marauders will defeat you if you let them get close to you, but if you slow them down an' keep them at a distance they will not be able to match your damage abilities, coupled with your healing.

Skirmishes will likely consist of smaller groups of enemies an' should be easier to manage. You should already 'ave all of your long duration beneficial spells before the battle. Warrior Priests, you should 'ave Sigmar's Grace up. Rune Priests should 'ave Oath Rune of Power up if you are focusin' on damage an' Oath Rune of Iron if you are focusin' on healing output. Archmages 'ave you Prismatic Shield up. If you find your healing cannot keep up with the enemy's ability to dish out damage, then you is probably overmatched. If you can keep up, an' throw in a few offensive spells, you may be able to outlast your opponent, 'specially if your opponent can't heal himself.

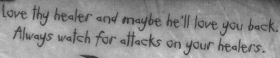

love thy healer and maybe he'll love you back. Always watch for attacks on your healers.

BATTLEFIELDS

MELEE STRATEGIES

Battlefields can be a melee's nightmare. They tend to be a standoff of the two fightings sides. As a tank, you are to go in takin' all chances that the pack will follow, heals will sustain you, an' range attacks will give you support. Othawise you won't last long. What I see a lot of melee attackers do is run in an' try to take down a cloth-wearin' opponent. When your 'ealth drops to 'alf run back to safety an' pray for a heal.

RANGED STRATEGIES

When playin' as a solo ranged attacker in the battlefield areas, stick close to the border of the RvR area for longevity. Creep slowly into the area, always ready to run out. The reason for this is so that if a group chases, there is time to run to safety. There is a great chance of facin' groups goin' solo in a battlefield. Also, there is usually an area where all Destruction is fightin' Order. It's usually 'round the quest objective. Try to find your side. Stayin' with the pack will keep a solo person alive a little longer. Battlefields are usually ranged battles, so ranged attackers will 'ave fun 'ere.

HEALER STRATEGIES

As always 'ave your long duration beneficial spells on. As a solo healer you can contribute to the fight even tho you may not be in a large group. On the offensive side you can 'elp heal the othas tryin' to capture the objectives or let othas keep the guards busy while you try an' capture the objective. Always cast shield spells on yourself or your allies. These spells absorb damage an' also keep actions from bein' interrupted. If you cast a shieldin' spell before tryin' to capture an objective, you will not be interrupted in that action until the enemy breaks through the shield. This may give you the few seconds you need to capture the objective. If you is solo with a small group you could also pull the guards out away from the spire an' shield yourself in combination with healing to give othas time to capture the objective. Keeps aren't always the most important part of a battlefield. Capturin' the otha objectives reduces the amount of guards at the enemy's keep an' gives a safe spot closer to the keep to launch attacks from.

SCENARIOS

MELEE STRATEGIES

Rely on all the tactics you've learned in your RvR experience. Scenarios can range from tight quarters, which is great foryou, and wide open spaces. Learn the scenario, so you'll know when to take chances an' 'ow to surprise the enemy best.

RANGED STRATEGIES

In general, you should 'ave freedom to use your ranged abilities. Most scenarios 'ave several spots to fire at range from, which is great foryou. Learn the scenario, so you'll know where to ambush the enemy or support your side.

HEALER STRATEGIES

If the scenario you join isn't full, you may be stuck in a group by yourself. You need to be able to 'elp the scenario, but also take care of yourself as well. Most of your long duration beneficial spells are limited to groupmates only, so make sure you cast them upon yourself an' then prepare for the scenario to begin. Take a look at the map, an' decide on your plan. If you wonna support the main group then you will need to tag along with them an' either 'elp them take or retain the objectives. Shieldin' spells for the person tryin' to capture an objective, heals for the warriors takin' the brunt of the damage, an', as always, damagin' spells for your enemies.

You can also go off on your own. As a spellcaster, you 'ave the advantage over melee players in that you can start doin' damage to them while they is still far away from you. Therein lies your advantage. Use the terrain an' sneak up on your opponent. Usin' bushes to 'ide yourself, coupled with the ability to attack with spells from long range, is one of the few advantages healers get in player versus player conflict. You may be able to take a sizable chunk of their 'ealth away before they even see you. They might not even see you if you 'ide well enough. This is a great strategy to pick off stragglers from the main group of the enemy.

CAPITAL CITY SIEGES

MELEE STRATEGIES

Solo melee in a capital siege is very tough. Me advice is to stick with the pack an' stay in the front. If you is bein' targeted an' there is no heals comin' your way, start 'eading to the back an' look for a healer. Luckily, melee 'ave enough 'ealth to do this. Otha classes once targeted without a healer are toast. Stay in the center of the scenario an' attack enemies as they tryin' to reach their objectives.

RANGED STRATEGIES

Capital sieges can be amazin' to view for the first time. There is so many things goin' on at once. As a ranged attacker, one has to focus on the surroundings an' know 'ow to 'andle each unique situation. The main thing is to keep your distance in the back. There are a lot of area-effect attacks 'appening, an' a lot of mages tryin' to break down the front. Ranged attackers can't take the damage bein' 'andled in the front as well as tanks, so it's best to stay in the back. I would stay back with the healers. This is 'ow you can 'elp by keepin' anythin' that got through the front off the healers or to keep those pesky assassins off the healers.

HEALER STRATEGIES

A solo healer can contribute to capital city sieges as well. You wonna stay away from the city instances 'cos they is primarily for groups. You can, 'owever, contribute to the capture of the city by defeatin' enemy players within the city an' completin' quests associated with the destruction an' capture of the city. As always, keep your beneficial spells up at all times.

A good strategy when participatin' in a siege as an attacker or defender is to find high ground an' attack enemy players as they come near. This makes it more difficult for the enemy to locate you as well as givin' you extra time to attack them while they figure out a way to get to your location. 'Ide in a buildin' until an enemy is spotted, then pop out an' start your damage. Often times they will 'ave an obstacle to cross, such as steps or a ledge to be able to get close enough to you. This strategy is good against enemies who need to be close to be effective.

GROUPIN'

The best way to gain experience points an' Renown points is to look for an RvR group. A lot of times there are warbands 'cos there is so many people fightin'. A warband is simply a few groups merged into one big one. The max amount of people allowed is 24 per warband. Once you is joined a warband, start 'eading toward the enemy's side. There will be a camp for your side. On the otha side there is a battlefield objective an' then the enemy's camp. Both sides are fightin' for the same objectives.

Renown Rewards: Order Tactics

Tier 1

Orcs Fear Me	Killing Greenskins will reduce the Morale of any opponents nearby at death.	2
Chaos Fears Me	Killing Chaos will reduce the Morale of any opponents nearby at death.	2
Dark Elves Fear Me	Killing Dark Elves will reduce the Morale of any opponents nearby at death.	2

Tier 2 — Requires 20 points spent on Renown Abilities

Refreshing Dominance: Orc	Killing Greenskins will restore a small amount of health.	2
Refreshing Dominance: Chaos	Killing Chaos will restore a small amount of health.	2
Refreshing Dominance: Dark Elf	Killing Dark Elves will restore a small amount of health.	2
Invigorating Victory: Orc	Killing Greenskins will double your AP regen rate 10% of the time.	2
Invigorating Victory: Chaos	Killing Chaos will double your AP regen rate 10% of the time.	2
Invigorating Victory: Dark Elf	Killing Dark Elves will double your AP regen rate 10% of the time.	2

Tier 3 — Requires 40 points spent on Renown Abilities

Greenskin Bane	You inflict 2% more damage against Greenskins in PvP.	2
Chaos Bane	You inflict 2% more damage against Chaos in PvP.	2
Dark Elf Bane	You inflict 2% more damage against Dark Elves in PvP.	2
Dwarven Camaraderie	You receive an additional 5% Morale gain for every Dwarf in your group. This 2-slot Tactic requires RR60.	4
Empire Allegiance	You receive an additional 5% Morale gain for every Empire in your group. This 2-slot Tactic requires RR60.	4
High Elf Lineage	You receive an additional 5% Morale gain for every High Elf in your group. This 2-slot Tactic requires RR60.	4

SKIRMISHES

MELEE STRATEGIES

Stay in the front so that the enemy focuses on you. Keep the fights on the focal points. The whole point of the game is to keep an area controlled by your side.

RANGED STRATEGIES

It's always safer in numbers, as they say. I think it's much better doin' skirmishes in a group. Mainly 'cos a lot of players will be doin' quest alone, which means they will be very vulnerable to your sneak attack. Part of a ranged attacker's job is gonna keep the cloth-wearin' weaklings alive so they can either heal or do damage. Sometimes the 'min' may permit you to do pure damage. It's situational, an' part of the job as a ranged attacker to know when to do what.

HEALER STRATEGIES

A healer is an essential part to any party that will be participatin' in skirmishes. your primary job is to keep yourself an' the rest of the group alive. 'Owever, in a skirmish you can be more of an offensive player. Determin 'ow offensive you can be based on 'ow many opponents you are facin'. If you are facin' a solo player, you can be as offensive as you want 'cos more then likely a solo player will not last very long against an organized group. If the group you are facin' is larger, you will 'ave to balance your heals with the offensive stuff, to make sure no one dies. Remember your primary goal is to keep yourself an' your group alive, so be sure to heal when needed. When you is in doubt about the ability an' size of the force you are facin', just heal an' forgo the offensive spells.

BATTLEFIELDS

MELEE STRATEGIES

If the group is tryin' to get an objective, then more than likely you will 'ave to fight NPCs. Target an NPC an' notify everyone in chat that you are attackin'. If the group is defendin', then allow them to come to you. When they reach the neutral zone, rush in an' attack.

RANGED STRATEGIES

In battlefields, one side is usually defendin' an' the otha side is attackin'. There tends to be a space in between the two. The offensive side tries to creep up slowly an' the defendin' side tries to push them back. A ranged attacker's job is to push the front forward. Do enough damage to a person an' they will back up. Keep doin' this an eventually everyone is backin' up an' your side is pushin' forward. The reverse idea can be used if defendin'.

Save instant cast spells until you need to move. Instant spells can be cast while on the run and usually have a longer recovery time than spells with a cast time.

HEALER STRATEGIES

Healers are arguably the most important part of any successful party on the battlefield. You may not get all the glory, but if your group doesn't 'ave a healer they will not last long against the enemy. Many times the key to defeatin' a well organized group in battle is to take out their healers first.

You must not only keep your group alive while tryin' to capture the objective, but you must also keep yourself alive. your group will not last long without a healer. If one of your party members is gonna try an' capture the objective while the rest of your group fights, cast a shieldin' spell on them. This will give them a few extra seconds on the capture if an enemy decides to start attackin' them 'cos actions will not be interrupted until the shieldin' spell drops.

Renown Rewards: Destruction Tactics

Tier 1	
Dwarfs Fear Me	Killing Dwarfs will reduce the Morale of any opponents nearby at death.
The Empire Fears Me	Killing Empire will reduce the Morale of any opponents nearby at death.
High Elves Fear Me	Killing High Elves will reduce the Morale of any opponents nearby at death.

Tier 2	Requires 20 points spent on Renown Abilities
Refreshing Dominance: Dwarf	Killing Dwarfs will restore a small amount of health.
Refreshing Dominance: Empire	Killing Empire will restore a small amount of health.
Refreshing Dominance: High Elf	Killing High Elves will restore a small amount of health.
Invigorating Victory: Dwarf	Killing Dwarfs will double your AP regen rate 10% of the time.
Invigorating Victory: Empire	Killing Empire will double your AP regen rate 10% of the time.
Invigorating Victory: High Elf	Killing High Elves will double your AP regen rate 10% of the time.

Tier 3	Requires 40 points spent on Renown Abilities
Dwarf Bane	You inflict 2% more damage against Dwarfs in PvP.
Empire Bane	You inflict 2% more damage against Empire in PvP.
High Elf Bane	You inflict 2% more damage against High Elves in PvP.
Orcish Camaraderie	You receive an additional 5% Morale gain for every Greenskin in your group. This 2-slot Tactic requires RR60.
Chaotic Allegiance	You receive an additional 5% Morale gain for every Chaos in your group. This 2-slot Tactic requires RR60.
Dark Elf Lineage	You receive an additional 5% Morale gain for every Dark Elf in your group. This 2-slot Tactic requires RR60.

SCENARIOS

MELEE STRATEGIES

Fight 'round the focal points. The whole point of the scenario is to reach 500 points, so it's pointless to chase otha groups just for points. Remind the group of this fact. People tend to get selfish an' kill everythin' in sight. If the group is defendin', then look for the healer careers an' attack them. If the group is tryin' to take an area, rush in an' attack cloth-types, preferably healers.

RANGED STRATEGIES

Stickin' with your group is key. Dere is a lot of movin' in scenarios 'cos of the design of things. What I do in scenarios as I follow me group is stick to the back. I's even behind the healers an' casters. I assist the melee tank whoever he's attackin'. If an assassin should pop up on one of me cloth-wearin' teammates, then I switch on them an' do what I can to get them off the cloth-wearer.

Bein' way behind everyone also makes you vulnerable to attack, whether it be from an assassin or a group flankin' from behind. Flankin' is very possible in scenarios. It was designed that way. Every ranged attacker has some sort of spell that snares everyone so that they can escape, so be ready to use it. That's why I keep it up an' ready for that purpose alone.

HEALER STRATEGIES

When you first enter the scenario you will be given the choice of which group to join. You wonna join a group that doesn't already 'ave a healer. This will give your entire warband the best chance at success. 'Aving a healer in every group that is participatin' in a scenario is key to survival. When the groups is done bein' formed is a good idea to look at the types of members in your group. If dere is another healer in the group try to divide the memba between yourself an' the otha healer. Another way to do this is to pick a main healer that will stay on the main warrior of the group at all times. This ensures that the healer is entirely focused on healing the person takin' the most damage. the otha healer in the group then tends to everyone else's wounds, includin' the healer assigned to the main warrior. If tha healer falls in battle then the otha must adjust an' pick up the healing for the whole group.

CAPITAL CITY SIEGES

MELEE STRATEGIES

Old the line by preventin' enemies from reachin' objectives. When any cloth opponents get close, take em down.

RANGED STRATEGIES

Regardless if you're defendin' or attackin' the keep, stick with the group, but keep yourself behind everyone. Dere's gonna be a lot 'appening, so stay focused an' attack the tank's target an' keep an eye on your casters to make sure no one is on them.

HEALER STRATEGIES

Da main thing to remember in a siege is that you should nevah evah be on a siege weapon. You are a healer an' healers cannot heal when they is aimin' a cannon. Sure they is cool an' they blow stuff up, but you is a healer an' healers are above petty indulgences like blowin' up a small band of greenskins an' their filthy Squigs.

Durin' sieges, you will be facin' a variety of challenges, from guards to bands roamin' the city. Dere will be battles fought between the main administrators of the city all the way up to the boss. Your job is to keep your group healed no matter what the enemy throws at you. When the enemy drops boilin' oil on your warriors mannin' the ram you must bestow healing energy on them. Keep them alive 'cos they is the only people standin' between you an' 300 pounds of hurt from the next foe chargin' your way.

Renown Rewards: Shared Tactics

Tier 1		
Combat Awareness	5% increased EXP in Realm vs. Realm combat	2
Looter	5% increased gold in Realm vs. Realm combat	2
Tier 2	**Requires 20 points spent on Renown Abilities**	
For Glory!	5% increased Renown in scenarios	2
King of the Hill	5% increased Renown in skirmishes	2
Mission Focused	5% increased Renown in objectives	2
Tier 3	**Requires 40 points spent on Renown Abilities**	
Town Raider	5% increased Renown in cities	2
King Slayer	5% increased damage vs. kings. This 2-slot Tactic requires RR60.	4
Nemesis	Receive 5% less damage from kings. This 2-slot Tactic requires RR60.	4

WILL YOU SURVIVE?

PvP is 'round every corner. Get used to fightin' otha players 'cos the higher you rank up, the more you'll be called upon to 'elp with RvR battles. There is a lot of perks in PvP. You don't 'ave to wait in a queue for otha players. All you 'ave to do is go to an RvR area an' dere is PvP. You can also kill otha players an' still gain experience points. Most of all, your realms stand or fall on PvP play, so get out dere already...yer king needs you!

In a group, healers should be healing at all times, no exceptions.

Renown Rewards: Stats and Bonuses

Name	Description	Cost				
Tier 1 (RR 0-19)						
Might I-V	Increases Strength by 3 per point spent	1	3	6	10	14
Resolve I-V	Increases Willpower by 3 per point spent	1	3	6	10	14
Fortitude I-V	Increases Toughness by 3 per point spent	1	3	6	10	14
Impetus I-V	Increases Initiative by 3 per point spent	1	3	6	10	14
Blade Master I-V	Increases Weapon Skill by 3 per point spent	1	3	6	10	14
Marksmen I-V	Increases Ballistic Skill by 3 per point spent	1	3	6	10	14
Acumen I-V	Increases Intelligence by 3 per point spent	1	3	6	10	14
Unbending Will I-III	Increases Spiritual Resistance by 3% per 5 points spent	5	10	15		
Fireproof I-III	Increases Elemental Resistance by 3% per 5 points spent	5	10	15		
Resilient I-III	Increases Corporeal Resistance by 3% per 5 points spent	5	10	15		
Tier 2 (RR 20-39)	**Requires 20 Points Spent on Renown Abilities**					
Vigor I-V	Increases Wounds by 1.5 per point spent	2	4	6	10	14
Assault I-V	Increases Strength and Weapon Skill by 1.5 per point spent	2	4	6	10	14
Sharp Shooter I-V	Increases Initiative and Ballistic Skill by 1.5 per point spent	2	4	6	10	14
Sage I-V	Increases Intelligence and Willpower by 1.5 per point spent	2	4	6	10	14
Skirmisher I-V	Increases Weapon Skill and Initiative by 1.5 per point spent	2	4	6	10	14
Discipline I-V	Increases Willpower and Initiative by 1.5 per point spent	2	4	6	10	14
Arcane Protection I-III	Increases all Resistances by 1% per 5 points spent	5	10	15		
Reinforcement I-III	Increases Armor by 3% per 5 points spent	5	10	15		
Tier 3 (RR 40-80)	**Requires 40 Points Spent on Renown Abilities**					
Opportunist I-III	Increases Melee Crit Chance by 2% per 5 points spent	5	10	15		
Sure Shot I-III	Increases Ranged Crit Chance by 2% per 5 points spent	5	10	15		
Focused Power I-III	Increases Magic Crit Chance by 2% per 5 points spent	5	10	15		
Spiritual Refinement I-III	Increases Healing Crit Chance by 2% per 5 points spent	5	10	15		
Natural Fighter I-III	Increases Auto Attack Damage by 2% per 5 points spent	5	10	15		
Defender I-III	Increases Block rate by 2% per 5 points spent	5	10	15		
Reflexes I-III	Increases Parry rate by 2% per 5 points spent	5	10	15		
Agility I-III	Increases Dodge rate by 2% per 5 points spent	5	10	15		
Arcane Dismissal I-III	Increases Disrupt rate by 2% per 5 points spent	5	10	15		

GUILDS

Guild Advancement Rewards	
Guild Level	Reward Type
1	A Guild
2	Guild Calendar
3	Taxes and Tithes
4	Guild Vault
5	2 Standard Bearer Titles; Warped/Recruit's Battle Standard, Tactic Slot 1, Tactic Point; Standard Post 1
6	Entry to The Viper's Pit/Sigmar's Hammer; Guild Alliances
7	Guild Store: Crafting Components
8	Guild Auctions
9	Warped/Recruit's Battle Standard Tactic Slot 2
10	Heraldry Reservation; Heraldry Reveal: Base Pattern, Heraldry Reveal: Shape; Heraldry Reveal: Base Color
11	Expanded Guild Vault
12	Standard Ability: Slam
13	Warped/Recruit's Battle Standard Tactic Slot 3
14	Keep Claiming
15	Guild Cloak
16	The Viper's Pit/Sigmar's Hammer Leader's Hall
17	Guild Store: Transit to The Viper's Pit/Sigmar's Hammer
18	2 Standard Bearer Titles; Bloodied/Warrior's Battle Standard; Tactic Slot 1, Tactic Point
19	Standard Post 2
20	Heraldry Reveal: Emblem
21	Guild Store: Upgraded Crafting Components
22	Bloodied/Warrior's Battle Standard Tactic Slot 2
23	Expanded Guild Vault
24	Standard Ability: Rally
25	Reduced Cost Renown Gear
26	Bloodied/Warrior's Battle Standard Tactic Slot 3
27	COMING SOON
28	Guild Store: Upgraded Crafting Components
29	Transit to Gunbad's Entrance
30	Corrupter's/Campaigner's War Standard; Tactic Slot 1, Tactic Point; 2 Standard Bearer Titles
31	Standard Post 3
32	Transit to Bastion Stair's Entrance
33	Expanded Guild Vault
34	Corrupter's/Campaigner's War Standard Tactic Slot 2
35	Transit to Lost Vale's Entrance
36	Standard Post 4
37	Reduced Cost Siege Weapons
38	Corrupter's/Campaigner's War Standard Tactic Slot 3
39	COMING SOON
40	City Heraldry

Your guild banner will fly proudly above the enemy keep. You carry your standard into battle, planting it in the midst of sword and shield to empower your fellow companions with valuable advantages. Friends and allies will be seconds away.

The *WAR* guild system goes above and beyond anything you've seen in MMOs before. If you're new to guilds, then you can expect the communication and friendliness that you get from joining a group of like-minded individuals seeking the same goals in the game. Even if you're an MMO veteran, this guild system has more than a few surprises for you. For those who want to create a guild—and you should if you don't join an existing one—seek out the Guild Registrars found in the capital cities: Altdorf for Order and the Inevitable City for Destruction.

LIVING GUILDS

Call them "living guilds," because they live and breathe just as their members do. A *WAR* guild earns ranks through the actions of its members; whenever a member gains experience or Renown, the guild gains experience. As a guild grows in ranks, up to a 40-rank maximum, it unlocks rewards that benefit the individual guild members and the guild as a whole. You can look forward to extra vault space, special crafting components, additional transportation locations, customized guild standard (banners), Guild Tactics, and more. With a guild tool system that makes recruitment, organization, and announcements easy, you won't feel like leading the guild or participating as a member is a job; you can take all that wasted time you might have in other systems and apply it to what's really important—leveling your guild!

STANDARDS

Once your guild unlocks its standard, you can create heraldry that is completely unique to your guild. Change shape, base color, pattern, pattern color, emblem, and emblem color to give your guild an individual look that will be instantly recognized on the battlefield as you carry your banner into the fray or as it flutters in the breeze above a keep. Two-handed standards are used in battle to grant special Tactics; just plant them in the ground and the ability extends to guild members in its radius. You can pick up your standard and move it to bring the benefit along wherever you go in the fight; just don't let the enemy seize your standard or you'll lose your bonuses (and a little bit of pride). The most powerful of guilds can unlock three standards.

REWARDS

Besides the camaraderie you get from being a guild, you also gain rewards at each rank. At Rank 1, you open a new guild vault to house extra loot, and you gain various other benefits. The rewards are well worth the group effort, so rally those parties together for some public questing, RvR battlegrounds, or dungeon raiding. The "Guild Experience" table shows you how much effort you need to put in to rank up your guild. The "Guild Advancement Rewards" table runs down the payoff for all that hard work. Just remember, you may earn experience for the guild on your own, but it's when you're together as a guild that you'll truly make an impact on the world.

WARHAMMER ONLINE

AGE OF RECKONING

60-DAY PRE-PAID GAME TIME™ CARD

Join thousands of mighty heroes on the battlefields of
Warhammer Online: Age of Reckoning for 60 days of relentless
Realm vs. Realm™ combat without the use of a credit card.
Available at select retailers.

Collect all eight cards
in this limited-run series.

To apply the Pre-Paid Game Time Card to your account, visit:
www.warhammeronline.com/gamecard
and follow the instructions.

www.warhammeronline.com